# PARLIAMENTARY HISTORY: TEXTS & STUDIES
# 17

## 'THE LAST OF THE TORIES'

Bust of the 4th duke of Newcastle, by William Behnes, 1843, white marble (Eton College). Photo © Author.

# 'The Last of the Tories'

Political Selections from the Diaries of the Fourth Duke of Newcastle-under-Lyne, 1839–1850

Edited by

Richard A. Gaunt

*University of Nottingham*

WILEY

for

THE PARLIAMENTARY HISTORY YEARBOOK TRUST

© 2021 The Parliamentary History Yearbook Trust

John Wiley & Sons

*Registered Office*
John Wiley & Sons Ltd, The Atrium, Southern Gate, Chichester, West Sussex, PO19 8SQ, UK

*Editorial Offices*
101 Station Landing, Medford, MA 02155, USA
9600 Garsington Road, Oxford, OX4 2DQ, UK
The Atrium, Southern Gate, Chichester, West Sussex, PO19 8SQ, UK

For details of our global editorial offices, for customer services, and for information about how to apply for permission to reuse the copyright material in this book please see our website at www.wiley.com/wiley-blackwell.

The rights of Richard A. Gaunt to be identified as the editor of the editorial material in this work has been asserted in accordance with the Copyright, Designs and Patents Act 1988.

Wiley also publishes its books in a variety of electronic formats. Some content that appears in print may not be available in electronic books.

*Library of Congress Cataloging-in-Publication data is available for this book*

ISBN 9781119878643

'The Last of the Tories': Political Selections from the Diaries of the Fourth Duke of Newcastle-under-Lyne, 1839–1850 / edited by Richard A. Gaunt
A catalogue record for this title is available from the British Library
Set in 10/12pt Bembo
by Aptara Inc., India
Printed and bound in Singapore
by C.O.S. Printers Pte Ltd
1   2021

# Parliamentary History: Texts & Studies

# CONTENTS

# LIST OF FIGURES AND PLATES

Front cover illustration: Portrait of Henry Pelham-Clinton, K.G., 4th duke of Newcastle, holding a document, in his study, by Henry Nelson O'Neil, 1850, oil on canvas (private collection). The green volume on the table is the duke's diary.
  Photo © Christie's Images/Bridgeman Images.

Facing title page, Plate 1: Bust of the 4th duke of Newcastle, by William Behnes, 1843, white marble (Eton College). Photo © Author.

Table: Correlations for the Newcastle diaries reproduced in this edition, p.38.

# ACKNOWLEDGMENTS

My principal acknowledgment must be to Mark Dorrington, keeper of manuscripts and special collections, University of Nottingham, for permission to reproduce material from the Newcastle of Clumber, Portland of Welbeck, and Denison of Ossington MSS. I am grateful to Karen Robson of the Hartley Library, University of Southampton, for permission to use the Broadlands and Wellington papers. Lord Kenyon kindly allowed me to consult the diaries of the second Baron Kenyon (held privately) and the family papers (now held in Lancashire Record Office). The earl of Mansfield and the duke of Hamilton each allowed me to consult their family's papers at the National Register of Archives (Scotland) in Edinburgh. I acknowledge the earl of Derby, in respect of the papers of the 14th earl of Derby held at Liverpool Record Office, and the Trustees of the Goodwood Estate, for those of the 5th duke of Richmond held at West Sussex Record Office. My thanks are due to the various archivists who have facilitated access to materials in the National Library of Wales, the National Library of Scotland, and the National Records of Scotland. The University of Nottingham enabled me to complete this project through its study leave programme: special thanks are due to the Department of History, School of Humanities, for continuing support. I am particularly grateful to Clyve Jones and Linda Clark as past and current editors of the Texts and Studies series for their generous interest, help and advice in respect of the volume. Linda in particular gave substantial assistance at the production stage and made a significant contribution to the biographical appendix and the index. I am also grateful to Sarah Worrall for her expert copy-editing of the volume. Hannes Kleineke helped with Newcastle's more problematic Latin phrases. For helping with various queries, my thanks to John Hogan, Frances Knight, and Jason McElligott. My debt to John Beckett and to the late Peter Jupp, is ongoing. As ever, my family provided love, support, and encouragement in equal force. So too did Kevin Powell, to whom the book is dedicated with love.

# ABBREVIATIONS

The place of publication is London unless otherwise stated.

| | |
|---|---|
| BL, Add. MSS | British Library, London, Additional Manuscripts. |
| *C.J.* | *The Journals of the House of Commons.* |
| C.P. | Papers of William Henry Clinton (uncatalogued), John Rylands University Library, Manchester. |
| *DL*, III, IV, V | *Benjamin Disraeli: Letters,* vols III–V, ed. J.A.W. Gunn, J.P. Matthews, D.M. Schurman & M.G. Wiebe (Toronto, 1987–93). |
| Dep Hughenden | Disraeli Papers, held at the Bodleian Library, Oxford. |
| D.P. | Derby Papers, held at Liverpool Record Office, 920 DER (14). |
| *EHR* | *English Historical Review.* |
| Gladstone Diaries | *The Gladstone Diaries,* ed. M.R.D. Foot and H.C.G. Matthew (14 vols, Oxford, 1968–94). |
| *HJ* | *Historical Journal.* |
| H.P. | Papers of the duke of Hamilton, N.R.A. (S) 2177. |
| K.D. | Kenyon Diaries. In the possession of Baron Kenyon, Gredington, Whitchurch, Shropshire. |
| K.P. | Kenyon Papers (uncatalogued), held at Lancashire Record Office (accession DDKE 7840). |
| *L.J.* | *The Journals of the House of Lords.* |
| Martineau, *Newcastle* | John Martineau, *The Life of Henry Pelham, Fifth Duke of Newcastle, 1811–1864* (1908). |
| M.P. | Papers of the earl of Mansfield, N.R.A. (S) 776. |
| N.A. | Nottinghamshire Archives. |
| Ne C / Ne 6 | Newcastle of Clumber collection, held at N.U.M.D. |
| N.L.S. | National Library of Scotland. |
| N.L.W. | National Library of Wales. |
| N.R.A.(S) | National Register of Archives (Scotland). |
| N.U.M.D. | Nottingham University Manuscripts Department. |
| *P.M.P. Gladstone* | *The Prime Ministers' Papers Series. W.E. Gladstone,* ed. John Brooke and Mary Sorensen (4 vols, 1971–81). |
| *Protests* | *A Complete Collection of the Protests of the Lords,* ed. J.E. Thorold Rogers (3 vols, Oxford, 1875). |
| Pw | Portland of Welbeck collection, held at N.U.M.D. |

| | |
|---|---|
| QVJ | Queen Victoria's Journals (online edition). http://www.queenvictoriasjournals.org/home.do |
| R.P. | Goodwood (Richmond) Papers, held at West Sussex Record Office. |
| TNA | The National Archives, Kew. |
| *TRHS* | *Transactions of the Royal Historical Society.* |
| *Unhappy Reactionary* | *Unhappy Reactionary: The Diaries of the Fourth Duke of Newcastle-under-Lyne 1822–1850,* ed. R.A. Gaunt (Thoroton Society Record Series, xliii, Nottingham, 2003). |
| *Unrepentant Tory* | *Unrepentant Tory: Political Selections from the Diaries of the Fourth Duke of Newcastle-under-Lyne, 1827–1838,* ed. R.A. Gaunt (Parliamentary History Record Series, 3, Woodbridge, 2006). |
| W.P. | Wellington Papers, held at the University of Southampton. |

# INTRODUCTION

'TIS the last of the Tories
Left, stranded, alone;
All his *quondàm* companions
Converted or gone!
Not one of the right sort,
One True-Blue is nigh,
To cry, "Down with SIR ROBERT!"
Or, "Never say die!"

They have left thee, thou old one,
Too blind e'en for them,
Low Radical notions
All single to stem.
They increase Maynooth grants,
And cut Orangemen dead;
And hear, without passion,
The cry for cheap bread.

SIR ROBERT they follow
Where he leads the way,
To Conservative notions
Fast dropping away.
The old Tory's defunct,
With reluctance you own –
"Though you did", my Lord Duke,
"What you liked with your own".[1]

The 4th duke of Newcastle closed his diary in 1838 with the confident expectation that the Protestant, Protectionist principles which he vouchsafed would soon be in the ascendant, after a decade in which they had been threatened by the 'triumph of reform'.[2] Yet as *Punch* magazine's 'Lament for Newcastle', published at the height of the Maynooth crisis seven

---

[1] *Punch*, viii (1845), 180. The final line is a reference to Newcastle's self-defence after evicting tenants who had voted against his wishes, 'Is it not lawful for me to do what I please with my own?': Hansard, *Lords Debates*, 3rd ser., i, col. 751: 3 Dec. 1830. The phrase is derived from Matthew, 20:15.

[2] *Unrepentant Tory*, ix, 350.

years later, demonstrated, these hopes were to be speedily and spectacularly disappointed. In many respects, the decade after 1839 was to witness more fundamental challenges to the aristocratic, agricultural, and Anglican complexion of the United Kingdom than had been witnessed in the decade preceding it. From 1839 onwards, British domestic politics was dominated by the twin issues of agricultural protection – symbolised most clearly by the fate of the corn laws – and the popular political demand for parliamentary reform represented in Chartism. The deep economic recession of 1837–43 made this situation keen-edged and potentially combustible. At the same time, the challenges to Anglican supremacy represented, in different ways, by the emergence of Daniel O'Connell's campaign for the repeal of the Act of Union in Ireland (1840), the disruption of the Scottish kirk (1843), and the emergence of the Oxford or Tractarian movement in England, led to considerable debate about the nature and strength of the relationship between the established church and the state.

This combination of political, economic, and cultural crises was symbolised, at a personal level, in the person of William Ewart Gladstone, who enjoyed Newcastle's political patronage at Newark at the start of the decade but became progressively less palatable to the duke's political views as the 1840s progressed. Gladstone was led to question long-cherished beliefs and values in the face of changing circumstances, but Newcastle concluded that they made the active assertion, defence, and encouragement of the principles which he had spent his lifetime promoting even more essential. Whilst Gladstone moved beyond the position he had worked out in *The State in its Relations with the Church* (1838), during the Maynooth crisis of 1845, Newcastle defended his own views in print, having been encouraged to believe that his values resonated with a large proportion of the country.[3] Newcastle addressed his countrymen through letters to leading newspapers including *The Standard, The Morning Post,* and *The Times,* which kept his name before the public on issues such as Maynooth and the corn laws. In 1847, he even assumed the role of doughty defender of the aristocracy against what he perceived to be the mockery and disdain of *The Times*. Meanwhile, as the year of revolutions unfolded across the European continent during 1848, Newcastle interpreted events in the light of scriptural prophecy and counselled his erstwhile political leaders to do the same.[4]

The first volume in this edition of Newcastle's diaries, *Unrepentant Tory*, was published in the Parliamentary History Record Series in 2006. The present volume continues the political selections to their close, on 30 May 1850, eight months before Newcastle's death. The entries chart his growing disillusionment with Sir Robert Peel as Conservative Party leader, first in opposition (before 1841) and then in government (from 1841 to 1846). During these years, Newcastle maintained his presence in political life, notably during the debates on economic policy in 1842 and more prominently during 1844–6 in defending the Anglican dioceses of Bangor and St Asaph in Wales, resisting the increased grant to Maynooth college in Ireland, and opposing the repeal of the corn laws. It was Newcastle's actions in facilitating the removal of Gladstone from Newark and the earl of Lincoln (his son and heir) from South Nottinghamshire, during the passage of repeal through the house

[3]John-Paul McCarthy, 'History and Pluralism: Gladstone and the Maynooth Grant Controversy', in *Gladstone and Ireland Politics, Religion and Nationality in the Victorian Age*, ed. D.G. Boyce and Alan O'Day (Houndmills, 2010), 15–40.
[4]See 9 Apr. 1848, Appendix A.

of commons, which symbolised the rupture of the Conservative Party over the issue. However, from Newcastle's perspective, the schism represented a political opportunity. Having encouraged both Lord Stanley and Lord George Bentinck as leaders of the Protectionist (or, as Newcastle preferred to call it, Country) Party, Newcastle went on to support Benjamin Disraeli's elevation to the leadership of the party in the house of commons after Bentinck's death in September 1848. The diaries chart these events in detail, offering a different perspective on the period from that which has traditionally dominated historical accounts of the 'Age of Peel'. It casts fresh light on aspects of mid 19th-century conservatism which have recently begun to attract attention.[5]

The present volume also includes Newcastle's view of events beyond mainland Britain, including its military interventions in India, Afghanistan, China, and the Near East. These were issues which went to the heart of Britain's status as a 'great power', as Newcastle conceived it, and had ramifications in domestic politics. There is less attention to European politics during 1848, though this is because the duke's commentary was almost wholly dependent on the intelligence gleaned from newspapers which was frequently subject to change.[6]

Indeed, a notable feature of the period is the extent to which developments in transport and communications were opening up the world. Following the opening of Euston station, in 1837, Newcastle usually travelled to London by train from Nottingham, commenting on the various methods by which he reached his home in Portman Square. Travel between his principal residence, Clumber, deep in the Nottinghamshire Dukeries, and his Welsh estate at Hafod near Aberystwyth (which he owned until 1846), as well as to other destinations, was undertaken by a combination of coach and train. In 1846, Newcastle also ventured to the continent for a ten-day excursion, his first visit abroad in 30 years. Newcastle took a keen interest in the 'railway mania' of the 1840s, because of possible infringements upon his property by various projected schemes, and as a potentially lucrative source of income.[7]

Newcastle was keenly aware of the increasingly rapid and widespread circulation of newspapers. His appreciation of the rapidity and reach of printed communication, during this period, and his political patronage of favoured newspaper editors (notably Stanley Lees Giffard of *The Standard*), explains the avidity with which he favoured them with his political views. This is the more singular because, as the duke had good reason to appreciate, newspapers were one of the key mechanisms in circulating satire and mockery at his expense. One example is characteristic of their general tone:

In physical conformation the Duke of Newcastle is very tall, very stout, and very unwieldy; with large features strongly marked; a full face inclining to the rotund form; a dark complexion and grey hair. His Grace ... looks rather older than he is. His countenance does not indicate the peculiar qualities of his mind; nor is it one, as a writer

[5] Angus Hawkins, *The Forgotten Prime Minister: The 14th Earl of Derby* (2 vols, Oxford, 2007–8); Geoffrey Hicks, *Peace, War and Party Politics: The Conservatives and Europe, 1846–1859* (Manchester, 2008); Anna Gambles, *Protection and Politics: Conservative Economic Discourse, 1815–1852* (Woodbridge, 1999); John Hogan, 'Protectionists and Peelites: The Conservative Party in the House of Lords 1846 to 1852', *Parliaments, Estates and Representation*, xi (1991), 163–80; Heera Chung, 'From a Protectionist Party to a Church Party, 1846–48: Identity Crisis of the Conservative Party and the Jew Bill of 1847', *Albion*, xxxvi (2004), 256–78.

[6] Geoffrey Hicks, 'Don Pacifico, Democracy, and Danger: The Protectionist Party Critique of British Foreign Policy, 1850–1852', *The International History Review*, xxvi (2004), 515–40.

[7] See 7 Mar. 1846, 18 June 1846, Appendix B.

has observed of the Duke, from which, if you were to apply to it the [physiognomic] principles of [Johann Kaspar] Lavater, you would be able to form any correct notion of his character … as a speaker, [he] is all energy and animation, and nothing but energy and animation.[8]

The diaries offer a painfully honest corrective to the sarcastic barbs produced at Newcastle's expense. As one writer concluded, their 'great importance lies in the valuable extent to which they substantiate and explain his motives and actions as he records the daily happenings and expounds his views or inserts his brief comments. They present a rounder, deeper, fuller picture of the man'.[9] As such, they reveal much about Newcastle's psychology and temperament whilst demonstrating his abiding love for (and interest in) the welfare of his country, his social class, and his children. It is the latter theme which has tended to dominate subsequent accounts of the duke's life, largely through concentrating on his alienation from Lord Lincoln during this period. In 1900, John Martineau, then at work on his biography of the fifth duke, concluded that the relationship between the two men was hallmarked by:

> their high ideals, their family affection, their painful misunderstandings and mistakes; for through all, in both Father and Son, – with a strange family resemblance under widely different circumstances – ran the golden thread of high principle and devotion to duty, ennobling their lives however marred by failure and sorrow.[10]

However, the diaries are at least as revealing in demonstrating the loving relationship which existed between Newcastle and his other children. The persistence with which he sought advantageous employment for his other sons, including his twin sons, Charles and Thomas, and his younger sons, William, Edward, and Robert, are a useful reminder of the dangers of viewing aristocratic families solely through the lens of the heir apparent.[11]

## A Reluctant and Recalcitrant Peelite: Newcastle as Ultra-Tory, 1838–46

Historical understandings of British politics between the 1832 Reform Act and the repeal of the corn laws in 1846 have undergone substantial modification in recent years. The conservative interpretation of the Reform Act's impact has been revised in light of recent accounts, which emphasise its modernising effect on electoral discourse and voting behaviour at constituency level,[12] and on the institutional management of parliament.[13] The Peelite model of politics, with its stress on Peel's successful adaptation and modernisation

---

[8] *The London Journal and Weekly Record of Literature, Science, and Art*, v (1847), 345. The same article contains some tart observations on Newcastle's attitude towards railway speculation.

[9] N.U.M.D., Ne 6 E 4/149/1/11: undated typescript synopsis of the diaries. This may have been drawn up at the time of their deposit at Nottingham (1966).

[10] N.U.M.D., Ne C 13280: John Martineau to Lord Edward Pelham-Clinton, 4 Sept. 1900.

[11] Rory Muir, *Gentlemen of Uncertain Fortune: How Younger Sons Made Their Way in Jane Austen's England* (New Haven, CT, 2019).

[12] J.A. Phillips, *The Great Reform Bill in the Boroughs: English Electoral Behaviour, 1818–1841* (Oxford, 1992); J.A. Phillips and Charles Wetherell, 'The Great Reform Bill of 1832 and the Rise of Partisanship', *Journal of Modern History*, lxiii (1991), 621–46; J.A. Phillips and Charles Wetherell, 'The Great Reform Act of 1832 and the Political Modernization of England', *American Historical Review*, c (1995), 411–36.

[13] Peter Jupp, *The Governing of Britain, 1688–1848: The Executive, Parliament and the People* (2006).

of toryism into a pragmatic, reforming, Conservative Party, and the development of a distinctive two-party system, during this period,[14] has been shown to ignore not only the pressures exerted by different blocs or groups of opinion within those parties, and the distinctive political contribution made by the Whigs (the governing party until 1841),[15] but to underestimate the continuing scope and strength of ultra-toryism within the Conservative Party.[16] The party's 1841 election victory is now seen less as the triumph of Peelite Conservatism of the sort enshrined in the Tamworth Manifesto of 1834 (with its appeal to the new urban, dissenter electorate),[17] than as the confirmation of the party's revived Protestant and Protectionist instincts in its traditional strongholds and on a markedly defensive electoral platform.[18] This makes less surprising the strained relationship between Peel and his followers for much of his 1841–6 ministry,[19] the substantial disaffection evoked by Peel's policies of tariff liberalisation, diminishing agricultural protection and conciliatory overtures towards Irish Catholic sentiment,[20] and the consequent fissure in the party created by Peel's decisions to augment the Catholic training seminary of Maynooth with increased government funds in 1845 and to repeal the corn laws the following year.[21]

A number of historians have also testified to the continuing significance of the house of lords in the British political system during this period, despite the loss of some of its influence over the composition of the house of commons.[22] Despite threats of reform or mass peerage creations, the Lords' inbuilt Conservative majority retained its potential to harass ministerial legislation. Given the rediscovery of the persistent ultra-tory presence among the Conservative peers and the difficulties of synchronising its line of conduct with that of the Conservative Party in the house of commons, a greater appreciation has emerged

[14] Norman Gash, *Reaction and Reconstruction in English Politics, 1832–1852* (Oxford, 1965), ch. 5; D.E.D. Beales, 'Parliamentary Parties and the "Independent" Member, c.1810–60', in *Ideas and Institutions of Victorian Britain*, ed. Robert Robson (1967), 1–19; David Close, 'The Formation of a Two-Party Alignment in the House of Commons between 1832 and 1841', *EHR*, lxxxiv (1969), 257–77.

[15] R.H. Cameron, 'Parties and Policies in Early Victorian Britain: A Suggestion for Revision', *Canadian Journal of History*, xiii (1979), 375–93; I.D.C. Newbould, 'The Emergence of a Two-Party System in England from 1830 to 1841: Roll Call and Reconsideration', *Parliaments, Estates and Representation*, v (1985), 25–31; Newbould, *Whiggery and Reform, 1830–41: The Politics of Government* (Houndmills, 1990).

[16] I.D.C. Newbould, 'Sir Robert Peel and the Conservative Party, 1832–1841: A Study in Failure?', *EHR*, xcviii (1983), 529–57.

[17] Betty Kemp, 'The General Election of 1841', *History*, xxxvii (1952), 146–57; Robert Stewart, 'The Ten Hours and Sugar Crises of 1844: Government and the House of Commons in the Age of Reform', *HJ*, xii (1969), 35.

[18] Edwin Jaggard, 'The 1841 British General Election: A Reconsideration', *Australian Journal of Politics and History*, xxx (1984), 99–114; G.A. Cahill, 'Irish Catholicism and English Toryism', *Review of Politics*, xix (1957), 62–76.

[19] D.R. Fisher, 'The Opposition to Sir Robert Peel in the Conservative Party, 1841–1846', University of Cambridge PhD, 1970; Fisher, 'Peel and the Conservative Party: The Sugar Crisis of 1844 Reconsidered', *HJ*, xviii (1975), 279–302; W.O. Aydelotte, 'The Disintegration of the Conservative Party in the 1840s: A Study of Political Attitudes', in *The Dimension of Quantitative Research in History*, ed. W.O. Aydelotte, A.G. Bogue and Robert Fogel (Princeton, NJ, 1972), 319–46; Aydelotte, 'Voting Patterns in the British House of Commons in the 1840s', *Comparative Studies in Society and History*, v (1963), 134–63.

[20] T.L. Crosby, *Sir Robert Peel's Administration, 1841–1846* (Newton Abbot, 1976); D.A. Kerr, *Peel, Priests and Politics, Sir Robert Peel's Administration and the Roman Catholic Church in Ireland, 1841–1846* (Oxford, 1982).

[21] These events are reviewed in R.A. Gaunt, *Sir Robert Peel. The Life and Legacy* (2010).

[22] Gash, *Reaction and Reconstruction*, ch. 2; David Large, 'The House of Lords and Ireland in the Age of Peel, c.1832–50', in *Peers, Politics, and Power: the House of Lords, 1603–1911*, ed. Clyve Jones and D.L. Jones (1986), 373–405; J.M. Sweeney, 'The House of Lords in British Politics, 1830–1841', University of Oxford DPhil, 1973.

of Wellington's contribution towards the survival and stabilisation of the house of lords.[23] This dimension supplements an appreciation of Peel's strategy of 'governing in opposition' during the 1830s; working to restrain incidents of factious opposition in order to prevent a corresponding reaction on the part of the Whigs' more radical supporters. According to this argument, Peel worked with mainstream Whig opinion, from political necessity as well as in shaping his policy preferences, to effect a *via media* by which to skirt the extremes of ultra-toryism and radicalism. It was only from 1839, at the start of the period covered by this volume, that this policy began to break down.[24]

## (I) *A Watching Brief*

Between 1832 and 1841, the Conservative Party evolved from a minority rump of approximately 150 MPs into a governing party with a majority approaching 80.[25] Yet, during the period of the party's greatest numerical strength, the number of professed Peelites never exceeded one-third of the parliamentary party in the house of commons.[26] At the same time, whilst contemporaries thought the ultra-tories retained the potential to play the game of 1830 over again, by imperilling any Conservative ministry which might offend its leaders, no viable ultra-tory grouping emerged in the house of commons after 1832, in spite of such promising potential recruits as the young William Gladstone.[27]

Why this was the case has principally been explained by reference to the superior leadership exercised by Wellington and Peel, which, it is argued, relegated Newcastle and other 'essentially maverick figures ... to the margins of influence', or by reference to external factors facilitating the absorption of the ultra-tories within the Conservative Party – such as Peel's minority government of December 1834, or the duke of Cumberland's removal from domestic British politics, after his accession as king of Hanover, in June 1837.[28]

In terms of leadership, there was certainly contemporary evidence that the Reform Act had affected a more than temporary disillusionment with politics on the part of the leading

---

[23]R.W. Davis, 'The Duke of Wellington and the Resurgence of the House of Lords', in *Lords of Parliament: Studies, 1714–1914*, ed. R.W. Davis (Stanford, CA, 1995), 97–115; Davis, *A Political History of the House of Lords, 1811–1846: From the Regency to Corn Law Repeal* (Stanford, CA, 2007); F.C. Mather, 'Wellington and Peel: Conservative Statesmen of the 1830s', *Transactions of the Peel Society*, v (1985/6), 7–23; F.C. Mather '"Nestor or Achilles?", The Duke of Wellington in British Politics, 1832–46', in *Wellington: Studies in the Military and Political Career of the First Duke of Wellington*, ed. Norman Gash (Manchester, 1990), 170–95.

[24]I.D.C. Newbould, 'Whiggery and the Dilemma of Reform: Liberals, Radicals and the Melbourne Administration, 1835–9', *Bulletin of the Institute of Historical Research*, liii (1980), 229–41; Newbould, *Whiggery and Reform*, 314–21.

[25]David Close, 'The Rise of the Conservatives in the Age of Reform', *Bulletin of the Institute of Historical Research*, xlv (1972), 89–103.

[26]Gash, *Reaction and Reconstruction*, 148.

[27]N.U.M.D., Pw H 156: Lord George Bentinck to the Duke of Portland, 5 Dec. 1834; Perry Butler, *Gladstone: Church, State and Tractarianism, 1809–1859* (Oxford, 1982), 39.

[28]Bruce Coleman, *Conservatism and the Conservative Party in Nineteenth-Century Britain* (1988), 97; F.D. Munsell, *The Unfortunate Duke: Henry Pelham, Fifth Duke of Newcastle, 1811–1864* (Columbia, MO, 1985), 29, 35; A.S. Turberville, 'The House of Lords and the Reform Act of 1832', *Proceedings of the Leeds Philosophical and Literary Society*, vi (1945), 78; Turberville, *The House of Lords in the Age of Reform, 1784–1837* (1958), 333, 397; D.G.S. Simes, 'The Ultra Tories in British Politics, 1824–1834', University of Oxford DPhil, 1974, ch. 6; Robert Stewart, *The Foundation of the Conservative Party, 1830–1867* (1978), 104; R.W. Davis, 'The Duke of Wellington and the Ultra Peers', in *Wellington Studies III*, ed. C.M. Woolgar (Southampton, 1999), 38, 51.

ultra-tories. Of their traditional leaders, Lord Mansfield declared his intention to retire from political life at the end of 1833 and refused to be nominated for the vacant chancellorship of Oxford University the following year, having convinced himself that Peel and Wellington lacked the capacity or willingness to stem the onward march of religious dissent. Mansfield remained unable to 'perceive the dawn of better days' before his death in 1840.[29] Eldon's death (in 1838) also removed the pole-star by which most ultra-tories had set their course; 'there is nothing like him now in Existence', Newcastle complained. To the last, Eldon remained unreconciled to Peel.[30] Cumberland, who remained the leading ultra-tory, in point of seniority and influence, throughout the period up to 1837, was certainly looked to for leadership. Newcastle claimed that he was the only one of his colleagues, except Lord Winchilsea, who attached 'any value to my opinion'.[31]

Newcastle retained an ambivalent attitude towards political involvement throughout most of the 1830s, with politics and estate business contending for his principal attention. However, his private disgust at 'the polluted atmosphere & pestilent doctrines' of parliament and the 'hateful' nature of politics, following the Reform Act,[32] bore similarities to his attitude after the passage of Catholic emancipation and was not a statement of an intention to retire. Newcastle retained a lingering ambition to be appointed lord lieutenant of Ireland and did not surrender his hopes of political office until after Peel formed his government in 1841. Thereafter, Newcastle had to satisfy himself with the reflected glory attaching to his parliamentary protégés.[33] However, Newcastle had not transferred all his political hopes, or responsibility for managing his remaining electoral influence, to his son and heir, Lord Lincoln, as some contemporaries suggested.[34]

In 1836, the parliamentary sketch-writer, James Grant, described Newcastle as one of the most 'zealous and unremitting' of Conservative peers, when roused; a fact which gave Newcastle much 'greater influence' than his occasional parliamentary utterances 'would lead one to infer'.[35] Some of this 'influence' was undoubtedly the result of Newcastle's continuing status as an electioneer. In 1837, he headed the list of aristocratic contributors to the Conservative Party's election fund; a decade later, he was still being sought out, for electoral assistance, on the party's behalf.[36] Despite the disenfranchisement of Aldborough and Boroughbridge in 1832, Newcastle retained significant electoral advantages – most notably at Newark.[37] The recovery of the borough's Conservative political interests was completed by the re-emergence of the Manners Sutton family in Newark politics during the 1830s and the election of Lord John Manners, for the second seat, at the 1841 general election. Whilst Newcastle's influence in East Retford had increased as a result of the

---

[29]N.R.A.(S), M.P., Box 110, Bundle 10: Political Notes, Sept. 1833, p.66; Box 111, Bundle 2: Notes, Nov. 1833; N.U.M.D., Ne C 5452: Mansfield to Newcastle, 11 July 1837; see 20 Feb. 1840.

[30]*Unrepentant Tory*, 264, 297, 332.

[31]*Unrepentant Tory*, 270–1, 285.

[32]BL, Add. MS 44261, f. 27: Newcastle to Gladstone, 16 Feb. 1833; C.P., Newcastle to Clinton, 24 Mar. 1834.

[33]See 2 Sept. 1841.

[34]N.U.M.D., Pw H 160: Lord George Bentinck to Portland, 26 Feb. 1835.

[35]James Grant, *Random Recollections of the House of Lords* (1836), 95; cf. H.T. Ryall's sympathetic entry on Newcastle in *Portraits of Eminent Conservatives and Statesmen: With Genealogical and Historical Memoirs* (1836).

[36]See 25 July, 17 Aug. 1846, 24 Jan. 1847.

[37]*Unhappy Reactionary*, xxiv.

borough's reformation in 1830, it was not sufficient to ensure the return of his son, Lord Charles Clinton, at the 1835 general election. The difficulties of securing a parliamentary seat for Charles, and his twin brother Thomas, was a recurring source of disappointment for Newcastle throughout the 1840s.[38]

Newcastle defined Conservatism principally in terms of upholding the existing constitutional connection between church and state; in other words, the inheritance of Eldon, to whom Newcastle's *Thoughts in Times Past Tested by Subsequent Events* was dedicated in glowing terms.[39] The duke's devotion to the church/state connection remained paramount throughout these years. Given his hostility to the repeal of the Test and Corporation Acts in 1828,[40] the circumstances surrounding Newcastle's dismissal from the offices of lord lieutenant and *custos rotulorum* of Nottinghamshire in 1839 were unsurprising. Having refused to appoint two nominees (one of them a nonconformist) to the county magistracy, Newcastle embarrassed his party leaders further by engaging in a highly indecorous correspondence with the lord chancellor, Lord Cottenham, on the subject, which ultimately cost him his posts. When the offending correspondence was subsequently published, at Newcastle's request, the matter rebounded to his disadvantage, and he emerged as a bigoted upholder of Anglican political supremacy.[41]

The emergence of the Oxford movement was also a cause of concern to Newcastle. When the post of chancellor of the University became vacant, in 1834, he was mistakenly identified as a potential candidate on their behalf. Nothing could have been further from the truth.[42] Though Newcastle subsequently described Gladstone as a 'Puseyite',[43] he never failed to consider the Oxford movement as dangerous schismatics, whose views threatened the safety of the Anglican church.[44] However, like many ultra-tories, who were regarded as 'illiberal' in religious matters, Newcastle was rather more 'liberal' in matters of social reform. For example, he supported the closer regulation of factory working hours; understandably so, given the long campaign waged on this issue by his former member, Michael Thomas Sadler.[45]

Newcastle's attitude towards Peel's second ministry, during its first three years of existence (1841–4) reflected the opinions which he had formed during the preceding decade. He was personally much closer to Peel than Wellington; a situation which was consolidated during the late 1830s by an exchange of visits between Clumber and Drayton Manor. The duke even raised the prospect of affecting a permanent connection between the two families through marrying his fourth son, Lord William Clinton, to Peel's eldest daughter, Julia. However, politically, Newcastle remained suspicious of Peel's motives and intentions and

---

[38]See 9 May, 7–10, 12 June, 20, 22–3, 25, 29, 31 July 1847.

[39]Fourth duke of Newcastle, *Thoughts in Times Past Tested by Subsequent Events* (1837), iii–vi, xiii, xvi–xvii, lvii; N.U.M.D., Ne C 5434: Eldon to Newcastle, c. 11 Mar. 1837.

[40]*Unrepentant Tory*, 50.

[41]See 29 May, 26 July 1839.

[42]*The Letters and Diaries of John Henry Newman, Volume IV: The Oxford Movement, July 1833 to December 1834*, ed. Ian Ker and Thomas Gornall (Oxford, 1980), 97–100, 114–15; cf. Butler, *Church, State and Tractarianism*, 168.

[43]See 13 July 1842; M.J. Lynch, 'Was Gladstone a Tractarian? W.E. Gladstone and the Oxford Movement, 1833–45', *Journal of Religious History*, vii–viii (1974–5), 364–89.

[44]See 19, 29 Mar., 20 Apr., 25, 29 Nov., 9 Dec. 1841, 23 Jan., 20 Oct. 1842, 24 May, 3–4 June, 14 Sept., 22 Oct., 22 Dec. 1843, 21 Jan., 8, 12 Oct., 2, 20, 27 Dec. 1844, 15, 26 Jan., 17 Feb., 11, 18, 20 Oct., 29 Nov. 1845.

[45]Stewart, 'Ten Hours', 41; Newbould, 'Peel and the Conservative Party', 532–4.

continually encouraged him to abandon his strategy of 'governing in opposition' in favour of a more muscular strategy.

It was not to be expected that Peel's cabinet – which historians have rightly noted was even less ultra-tory in composition than that of 1834–5 – would meet with Newcastle's approval.[46] However, Newcastle refrained from making any recommendations, in the manner of 1828, confining himself to seeking advancement for his younger sons.[47] Yet in spite of a growing closeness between Peel and Lincoln, the latter did not advance quickly through ministerial ranks. The understandable political linkage between the politics of father and son continued to weigh heavily upon the prime minister's calculations. As Peel admitted to the lord lieutenant of Ireland, Lord Heytesbury, in 1845, Newcastle was 'notorious for Ultra-Protestant feelings. He is a Pamphleteer in advocacy of his own views. With great confidence in Lord Lincoln personally, I should fear the impression which his appointment [as chief secretary] would cause would be unfavourable'.[48]

At the same time, Newcastle showed no disposition to concert opposition to the prime minister. When he informed Wellington of his difference with the government, over their bills to reintroduce the income tax and revise a raft of commercial duties, in 1842, Wellington interpreted it as a resumption of the hostilities he had endured at Newcastle's hands during his own ministry. Newcastle took the matter up with Peel, furiously denying the imputation of factionalism which had been levelled at him, and further consolidating the breach in relations with Wellington.[49]

Thereafter, Newcastle pursued a watching brief, unable to make headway with a government which he thought should have looked more favourably upon his views. David Fisher has described the limited extent to which Peel's persistent backbench opponents in the Commons were prepared to go in defying the premier, during the same period. Forcing a change of ministry, or party leadership, was never part of their intentions.[50] It was only when a combination of more favourable circumstances presented themselves, on the Maynooth and corn law issues – by providing a viable alternative leadership to that of Wellington and Peel, on matters which not even their advocacy could make acceptable to the bulk of the party – that ultra-tories like Newcastle could realistically consider mobilising themselves.[51]

## (II) *The Crises of 1845–6*

The links between the ultra-tories of 1828–30 and Peel's opponents during the great political crises of 1845–6 have sometimes been remarked upon, but very rarely explored. Ian

[46]Bruce Coleman, '1841–1846', in *How Tory Governments Fall: The Tory Party in Power since 1783*, ed. Anthony Seldon (1996), 120; see 17 Jan. 1841.

[47]See 28 Sept. 1841.

[48]BL, Add. MS 40479, f. 275: Peel to Heytesbury, 29 Jan. 1845; see 5 Feb. 1845 for Newcastle's (very different) view.

[49]See 14 June 1842.

[50]R.F. Mullen, 'The House of Lords and the Repeal of the Corn Laws', University of Oxford DPhil, 1974, ch. 3; Large, 'House of Lords and Ireland', 390–6; Fisher, 'The Sugar Crisis of 1844', 282, 294–6.

[51]See G.A. Cahill, 'The Protestant Association and the Anti-Maynooth Agitation of 1845', *Catholic Historical Review*, xliii (1957), 273–308; G.I.T. Machin, 'The Maynooth Grant, the Dissenters and Disestablishment, 1845–1847', *EHR*, lxxxii (1967), 61–85; E.R. Norman, 'The Maynooth Question of 1845', *Irish Historical Studies*, xv (1967), 60, 407–37.

Machin concluded that, whilst the anti-Maynooth agitation was more efficient than the analogous anti-Catholic Brunswick campaign of the late 1820s, the likes of Newcastle, Kenyon and Winchilsea 'were now merely auxiliaries in the agitation instead of leading it'.[52] However, there is a danger in overlooking the connections between the two movements in terms of thought, strategy and tactics, as well as personnel. On one level, it was hardly surprising that Newcastle should become a prominent opponent of Peel's policy in 1845–6, given that two more obvious totems of ultra-toryism than Maynooth and the corn laws could hardly have been found. British financial support for the Catholic training seminary of Maynooth had first been instituted by William Pitt in 1795; thereafter it had been a continuing object of anti-Catholic and ultra-tory antagonism. 'We here have the offence upon our heads [Newcastle observed in 1836] of annually contributing to create and foster a body of the lowest and worst priests, and most disloyal subjects that ever betrayed the kind intentions of a benefactor'.[53]

Nor could the prevailing ultra-tory desire for agricultural protection be in any doubt, given the role it had assumed in the Conservative election victory of 1841.[54] During the 1830s, ultra-tories like Newcastle were looked to for encouragement by those seeking an institutional outlet for the support of a Protectionist agricultural policy. In 1836, Newcastle became the inaugural president of the Central Agricultural Association, the first attempt at forming a coherent agricultural pressure group since George Webb Hall's efforts in the 1820s.[55] Despite Newcastle's concern at the intentions of some of its leading participants, which he thought to be 'irrelevant', 'inadmissible' or 'illegal', the Association became the forerunner of the more famous Central Agricultural Protection Society or 'Anti-League'.[56] This was formed in 1844 as a means of counteracting the highly effective propaganda of its principal opponents – the Manchester based Anti-Corn Law League (established in 1838) – which had been touring constituencies in an attempt to generate extra-parliamentary support for their repeal campaign.[57] Newcastle was in contact with the leadership of the 'Anti-League' from the start, and became president of the Nottinghamshire branch during 1845.[58]

However, the Maynooth and repeal crises were principally significant in so far as they witnessed the ejection of the self-identified 'Peelites' from the Conservative Party and offered a corresponding revival in ultra-tory and 'Protectionist' fortunes. Terry Jenkins has argued that, but for the events of 1845–6, the general toleration of the party's backbenchers towards the leadership would have continued.[59] Even after the Maynooth crisis, there was

[52]Machin, 'Maynooth', 62; G.I.T. Machin, *Politics and the Churches in Great Britain, 1832 to 1868* (Oxford, 1977), 170; Mullen, 'House of Lords', 259, 412–14; D.G.S. Simes, 'A Long and Difficult Association: the Ultra Tories and "the Great Apostate"', in *Wellington Studies III*, ed. Woolgar, 81; Stewart, *Foundation*, xii–xiii.

[53]Newcastle, *Thoughts in Times Past*, l; *Unrepentant Tory*, 309.

[54]Jaggard, 'General Election of 1841', 112–14.

[55]*Unrepentant Tory*, 290, 292, 301–3; David Spring and T.L. Crosby, 'George Webb Hall and the Agricultural Association', *Journal of British Studies*, ii (1962), 115–31.

[56]See 13, 23, 25 and 27 Jan. 1844; Mary Lawson-Tancred, 'The Anti-League and the Corn Law Crisis of 1846', *HJ*, iii (1960), 162–83; G.L. Mosse, 'The Anti-League: 1844–1846', *Economic History Review*, xvii (1947), 134–42.

[57]See 15 Feb. 1839, 26 Sept. 1842; cf. H.D. Jordan, 'The Political Methods of the Anti-Corn Law League', *Political Science Quarterly*, xlii (1927), 58–76; John Prest, *Politics in the Age of Cobden* (1977).

[58]N.U.M.D., Ne C 8174: Henry Byron to Newcastle, 6 Jan. 1845; Ne C 7506, 8257: P.R. Falkner to Newcastle, 3 May, 7 June 1845; *The Morning Chronicle*, 15 Aug. 1845.

[59]T.A. Jenkins, *Sir Robert Peel* (1999), 133.

a disposition (in some quarters) to heal divisions. At Newark, Newcastle was informed that 'the great body of the voters would not reject a man for having supported the measure'.[60] By contrast, Newcastle's son, Charles, thought that Peel would have to 'Keep the present Parliament on as long as possible in order to give people time to forget what has happened'.[61]

What made this impossible was the speed with which Peel's conversion to an immediate settlement of the corn laws followed upon Maynooth – an event stimulated by Peel's belief that it was impossible to maintain taxes on foodstuffs after the ravages of the potato blight afflicted Ireland in the autumn of 1845.[62] In these circumstances, the party might have fared better had it gone into opposition, or had the Peelites formed a coalition with the Whigs, as a means of passing repeal, given that all of Peel's cabinet colleagues were originally opposed to his repeal proposals. Newcastle certainly expected this outcome.[63] However, the Whigs' own divisions on the issue, together with Peel's determination to carry the measure, come what may, prevented this from happening and precipitated the final schism within the Conservative Party.[64]

In 1839, Newcastle had been dismayed to hear Peel state a willingness to consider the repeal of the corn laws; a suspicion which had increased after Peel's corn law of 1842 had been announced.[65] D.C. Moore has argued that Peel was attempting to wean farmers off their reliance on protection in favour of more scientific or competitive methods of 'High Farming', during these years. For his part, Newcastle treated such Peelite didacticism with disdain.[66]

Whilst Newcastle retained his own suspicions of Peel, relative to his agricultural and religious policies prior to 1845, Maynooth proved the realisation of his fears. When Peel proposed to triple the annual subsidy to the seminary (from £9,000 to £26,000), making it a permanent charge on the consolidated fund and giving, in addition, a one-off grant of £30,000 towards the college's immediate repair, all the language and passions of 1829 were stirred up once again.[67] Newcastle was far from alone in thinking of Peel as 'Lucifer', 'Cromwell' and 'Judas'.[68] He was vehement in his opposition to the measure in the house of lords; F.C. Mather characterised his attitude as 'explosive' whilst Richard Davis described it as 'certifiably mad'.[69] In striking at the heart of what Conservatism was thought to represent, on the platform it had espoused in 1841, the Maynooth crisis released passions which stimulated a powerful anti-Peelite opposition within the Conservative Party.

[60]N.U.M.D., Ne C 6463: Godfrey Tallents to Newcastle, 23 Dec. 1845.

[61]N.U.M.D., Ne C 5609: Lord Charles Clinton to Newcastle, 25 Apr. 1845.

[62]Norman Gash, *Sir Robert Peel: The Life of Sir Robert Peel after 1830* (1972), chs 15–16.

[63]See 2 Nov., 11, 13–14, 16–17, 20 Dec. 1845.

[64]F.A. Dreyer, 'The Whigs and the Political Crisis of 1845', *EHR*, lxxx (1965), 514–37.

[65]See 19 Jan. 1839, 18–19 Mar. 1842.

[66]See 3, 27 Oct. 1843; D.C. Moore, 'The Corn Laws and High Farming', *Economic History Review*, 2nd ser., xviii (1965), 544–61.

[67]See 5 Apr. 1845; Kerr, *Peel, Priests and Politics*, ch. 6.

[68]See 2 May, 23 Dec. 1845; R.P., 1866, f. 37: Newcastle to Richmond, 25 Dec. 1845; 1692, f. 1794: Newcastle to Richmond, 16 Jan. 1846.

[69]Mather, 'Nestor or Achilles?', 188; Richard Davis, *Wellington, Peel, and the Politics of the 1830s and 1840s* (Southampton, 2002), 17. For contemporary accusations of madness, see 22 Feb. 1846.

This hostility was reinforced, on Newcastle's part, by his perception of the comparative indifference exhibited towards the financial support of the Anglican church. Only months before Peel's proposals for Maynooth were announced, the premier had refused Newcastle's entreaties to apply the financial surplus provided by the income tax to the building of new Anglican churches; 'The difficulty of persuading Parliament to sanction Such an Expenditure Would ... be Extreme', Newcastle was informed.[70] The duke had stressed the need for increased financial support of this nature to Gladstone in the late 1830s and, following his acquisition of Worksop Manor in 1838, both men had discussed the possibility of turning it into a school for the sons of Anglican clergy.[71] The irony of this plan – given that Worksop had been the home of the premier Catholic peer of the realm, the duke of Norfolk – was not lost upon Newcastle.[72]

The similarity of the personnel and issues at stake in the oppositions of 1828–9 and 1845–6 extended to the point of tactics. As with Catholic emancipation, so Peel's opponents on Maynooth and repeal placed their principal trust in a popular appeal to parliament and the crown, through the medium of petitioning and peaceful organisation.[73] The principal import of Newcastle's first 'Public Letter to the People of England', in April 1845, was the exhortation to 'Petition! Petition! Petition!' against the proposed increase to Maynooth. This was a refashioning of Peel's earlier exhortation for Conservatives to 'Register! Register! Register!'.[74] It is sometimes forgotten that much petitioning activity was motivated against liberalising measures, during this period, especially on matters touching religious practice and belief. If Newcastle's achievement is to be measured in the number of anti-Maynooth petitions subsequently presented to parliament, it must be reckoned a success; indeed, the petitioning evidence was even more overwhelming than in 1829.[75] Although there was (as in 1828–9) no disposition to convene a Nottinghamshire county meeting on the issue, Newcastle was assured 'that petitions from individual parishes [were] a more Expressive mode of enforcing their opinions'.[76]

However, as in 1829, the traditional obstacle provided by the crown remained. When Lord Winchilsea presented 'several hundred' addresses to Queen Victoria, in June 1845, he was informed that she was personally favourable towards the measure.[77] The same difficulties were apparent over the repeal of the corn laws. Richmond received even shorter shrift than Winchilsea had done – '3 Seconds' according to Peel – whilst Newcastle noted with disgust that the court kept company with no one but free traders. For their part, Queen Victoria continued to exhibit an interest in Lincoln's political differences with his father,

---

[70]See 18 Jan. 1845. For the wider issues, see Heera Chung, 'The Church Defence Problem in Conservative Politics, 1841–1847', University of Cambridge PhD, 2001.

[71]BL, Add. MS 44261, ff. 70–3, 80–5: Newcastle to Gladstone, 7 Dec. 1838, 11, 26 Feb. 1840.

[72]*Unhappy Reactionary*, 214.

[73]See 18, 23 Apr. 1845, 21 May 1846.

[74]See Appendix A; Henry Miller, 'Petition! Petition!! Petition!!!: Petitioning and the Organization of Public Opinion in Britain, c.1800–1850', in *Organizing Democracy: Reflections on the Rise of Political Organizations in the Nineteenth Century*, ed. Maartje Janse and Henk te Velde (Houndmills, 2017), 43–61.

[75]Machin, 'Maynooth Grant', 64, n. 4; cf. N.U.M.D., Ne C 7499: John Burton to Newcastle, 1 June 1845; Ne C 8241: Thomas Cooper to Newcastle, 19 Apr. 1845.

[76]N.U.M.D., Ne C 8244: Godfrey Tallents to Newcastle, 22 Apr. 1845.

[77]See 20 June 1845.

whilst Prince Albert was to be found denigrating Newcastle for the extent to which he was prepared to press them.[78]

One of the more obvious ways in which Newcastle could oppose Peel was by means of his electoral influence. Before 1845, ultra-tories like Newcastle, who also enjoyed influence in the house of commons, were unable to restrict Peel's freedom of action in the manner of 1829–30. There was no immediate prospect for another, more congenial, political alliance, and no likelihood that Newcastle's MPs could become part of an alternative government or a significant opposition party, as they had done in that period. Nevertheless, the political future of Lincoln and Gladstone was still principally determined by the fact that they owed their seats to Newcastle's electoral influence and support. When both men supported Peel in 1845–6, Newcastle responded in the traditional manner by removing them. This served to keep Newcastle's name, and his electioneering tactics, before the public eye in corresponding measure. At the same time, it raised questions about the extent to which Peel's opponents should engage in electioneering activities, and the degree to which MPs should conform with the known wishes of their electoral patrons or their constituents after changing their minds on great political questions.[79]

The corn law debates have generated a good deal of investigation into this issue; largely from comparing the voting methods of MPs in the divisions on repeal with the socio-economic complexion of their constituencies.[80] But it was events arising from Maynooth that were more telling of ultra-tory attitudes, at least in so far as Newcastle was concerned. Although Gladstone resigned from Peel's cabinet over the Maynooth issue, it had nothing to do with hostility to that measure. His actions at the time raised puzzlement rather than alarm.[81] Newcastle publicly stated that Gladstone's was 'an adverse though not an intelligible course' and regretted that he had not 'been found true to the great cause of Protestantism' – a charge which Gladstone briefly considered rebutting.[82] However, after consulting with Lincoln, he decided not to resign his seat. Nor did Newcastle push him to do so. His first reference to ejecting Gladstone only came after rumours surfaced that he would be rejoining the cabinet – an act which would automatically lead to a by-election.[83]

The same motivations operated with regard to Newcastle's treatment of Lord Lincoln. The *Nottingham Review* thought the most significant aspect of the Maynooth debates was the open manifestation of Lincoln's political differences from his father.[84] Though Newcastle hoped that Lincoln would resist Peel's proposals for the corn laws, his support for repeal

[78]See 10, 23 May, 9 June 1846; N.U.M.D., Ne C 12113: Peel to Lincoln, 11 Feb. 1846; Robert Rhodes James, *Albert, Prince Consort* (1983), 166.

[79]D.G.S. Simes, 'Ultra Tory Organisation and the Catholic Emancipation Crisis of 1828–9', in *Essays Presented to Professor N.C. Phillips*, ed. J.E. Cookson and Marie Peters (Christchurch, N.Z., 1983), 131–61; see 22 Feb. 1846.

[80]W.O. Aydelotte, 'The Country Gentlemen and the Repeal of the Corn Laws', *EHR*, lxxxii (1967), 47–60; George Kitson Clark, 'The Electorate and the Repeal of the Corn Laws', *TRHS*, 5th ser., i (1951), 109–26; Cheryl Schonhardt-Bailey, 'Linking Constituency Interests to Legislative Voting Behaviour: The Role of District Economic and Electoral Composition in the Repeal of the Corn Laws', in *Computing and Parliamentary History: George III to Victoria*, ed. J.A. Phillips (Edinburgh, 1994), 86–118.

[81]N.U.M.D., Ne C 5607: Lord Charles Clinton to Newcastle, 4 Feb. 1845; Ne C 5649: Lord William Clinton to Newcastle, 22 Apr. 1845.

[82]See Appendix A.

[83]See 9 Mar., 4 Apr. 1845.

[84]*Nottingham Review*, 18 Apr. 1845.

had already been made abundantly clear.[85] In these circumstances, it might be argued that Peel was gratuitously provoking his opponents by advancing Gladstone and Lincoln to new cabinet positions in January to February 1846. Under law, such promotions necessitated re-election and, given the delicate state of feeling at Newark, it was unlikely that Gladstone or Lincoln would receive an easy passage at the hands of their constituents.[86] Both men were put in the embarrassing position of receiving deputations from radicals who interpreted their resistance to the duke as revolt against aristocratic privilege.[87] However, it is clear that Peel and Lincoln were intrinsically hostile to those Conservatives, like Lord Ashley, who conscientiously sought a new electoral mandate, given their change of views on the corn laws.[88]

Whatever contests were provoked between Protectionists and Peelites in 1846, resulted either from enforced necessity – such as promotion (Newark, South Nottinghamshire), or death (North Nottinghamshire) – or were the consequence of a voluntary disposition on the part of the MP. It was only once the fact of a contest had occurred that Newcastle intervened. Despite a strong show of support for Gladstone from the local Conservatives, Newcastle facilitated Gladstone's removal from the constituency in January 1846.[89] The following month, he intervened in the South Nottinghamshire by-election, publicly calling on the voters to reject his son. When they did so, through a combination of 'issues and influence', Lincoln exchanged the electoral influence of his father for that of his father-in-law, and sat for Falkirk Burghs, with the benefit of the duke of Hamilton's assistance, until January 1851.[90]

There is a clear line of continuity in Newcastle's thought and action between the events of 1828–9 and those of 1845–6. Whilst John Wolffe thinks it 'surprising' that Newcastle should have supported the conviction that 'MPs should respond to public opinion', during 1845,[91] this was not the immediate product of the Maynooth or corn law crises. Newcastle had evinced a similar attitude when his cousin, William Henry Clinton, felt compelled to retire from Newark in 1829 – as in the case of Gladstone, a retirement which Newcastle did not initiate.[92] In addition, though Newcastle included 'some trite rule[s] to be attended to by Electors in the event of a General Election', when his two public addresses on Maynooth were republished as a tract, this was done on advice, and was not the result of his initiative.[93]

Newcastle's essentially conservative attitude towards electioneering matters was ultimately stronger than his desire to see MPs act in conformity to their constituents' views.

---

[85] See 18, 20, 23 Dec. 1845; *P.M.P. Gladstone*, iii, 13–17.

[86] N.U.M.D., Ne C 11676: Lincoln to Gladstone, 15 Dec. 1845.

[87] N.U.M.D., Ne C 4649, 4651: W. Andrews to Lincoln and reply, 27 June, 8 July 1846; BL, Add. MS 56444, ff. 41–4: W. Andrews to Gladstone, 8 Jan. 1846.

[88] N.U.M.D., Ne C 12226: Lincoln to Ellenborough, 5 Jan. 1847.

[89] J.B. Conacher, 'Mr Gladstone Seeks a Seat', *Canadian Historical Association Report* (1962), 55–7.

[90] See 25 Feb., 5 May 1846, 6 Aug. 1847; J.R. Fisher, 'Issues and Influence: Two By-Elections in South Nottinghamshire in the Mid-Nineteenth Century', *HJ*, xxiv (1981), 155–65; Munsell, *The Unfortunate Duke*, 60–7, 91–2.

[91] John Wolffe, *The Protestant Crusade in Great Britain, 1829–1860* (Oxford, 1991), 298; see 19 Apr. 1845.

[92] Richard A. Gaunt, 'William Henry Clinton and the Perils of the Soldier-Politician', in *Politics and Political Culture in Britain and Ireland, 1750–1850: Essays in Tribute to Peter Jupp*, ed. Allan Blackstock and Eoin Magennis (Belfast, 2007), 176–93.

[93] N.U.M.D., Ne C 8277: James Leith to Newcastle, 28 May 1845.

Although the 'Anti-League' rescinded the rule which had hitherto prevented interference in election contests, Newcastle, for one, was unhappy at giving a free rein to the county Protectionist societies. He urged the society's president, Richmond, to define the circumstances in which the society would intervene in elections, and to ensure that this intervention remained under the control of its central headquarters in London.[94] Similar restraints extended to the practice of buying 40 shilling freeholds, in order to create new voters – a tactic which had been adopted, with some success, by the Anti-Corn Law League.[95] Lord George Bentinck told his father that 'buying freeholds to carry Counties would be perfectly impracticable' and refused to countenance the practice, even when the object in view was his brother's return for North Nottinghamshire.[96]

For all the implications of their language, Peel's opponents in 1845–6 retained the constitutional preconceptions of their ultra-tory forebears. This meant that, ultimately, their opposition was primarily concerned with strength of numbers, and purpose, in parliament. Newcastle did what he could to advance the return of known Protectionists to the house of commons, conscious that their parliamentary weakness in the lower house would imperil the chances of forming a successful opposition.[97] He sent John Stuart, Gladstone's successor at Newark, to see Disraeli as soon as he was elected.[98]

Newcastle's principal concern was not confined to the immediate opposition to repeal, but to securing the foundations of a future third party.[99] During the Maynooth crisis, he informed Giffard that he wished to see 'A clean Sweep … of all existing Statesmen – & their parasites [,] & new men chosen to Parliament Who shall really represent the Noble people of England & act without any Mortal reservation on the pure principle of Political Virtue'. The language, like the project, was remarkably similar to that used by him when discussing earlier ventures.[100]

The chances of success for such an enterprise only began to seem realistic after Lord Stanley refused to remain in Peel's ministry, following the decision to press ahead with repeal. Newcastle realised the importance of obtaining Stanley's support, though he was equally keen to ensure that Richmond – another veteran of the 1830 Country Party – would assume a leading role.[101] Newcastle's brother-in-law, Lord Combermere, even suggested that the party might secure the support of Lord Palmerston – another reminder of previous tactics.[102] However, Stanley remained the principal object of Newcastle's hopes throughout the period. Former political differences were easily smoothed over by the conclusion that he had never 'been in company that suited him'. Yet, despite a personal audience with Stanley, in March 1846, and a long and (as Lord Blake observed) 'platitudinous' letter, two months later, Newcastle failed to elicit a commitment from Stanley concerning his

---

[94]R.P., 1692, f. 1787: Newcastle to Richmond, 4 Jan. 1846.

[95]Prest, *Age of Cobden*, ch. 5.

[96]N.U.M.D., Pw H 201: Bentinck to Portland, 24 Jan. 1846.

[97]See 25 Jan. 1846; R.P., 1692, f. 1798: Newcastle to Richmond, 26 Jan. 1846.

[98]*DL*, IV, 216.

[99]See 22 Feb. 1846.

[100]See 6 May 1843; BL, Add. MS 56368, f. 173: Newcastle to Giffard, 13 May 1845.

[101]See 24, 25 Dec. 1845, 1 Jan. 1846; R.P., 1866, f. 37: Newcastle to Richmond, 25 Dec. 1845.

[102]N.U.M.D., Ne C 5173: Combermere to Newcastle, [n.d.] 1846.

future political course of action. In the meantime, Stanley was the Protectionists' best possible ally, certainly in terms of parliamentary oratory.[103]

If the Protectionists exhibited all the ancestral pedigree of the ultra-tories, then they also inherited their difficulties and dissensions as well. Newcastle – who came to view himself as the *paterfamilias* of the party – complained that his colleagues were like 'a rope of Sand' and were neglecting him.[104] At the level of tactics, he urged the same sort of watching brief on Richmond that he had suggested in 1830.[105] When Richmond informed Newcastle that he wanted the Protectionists to make a stand in the house of lords, at the opening of the 1846 session, Newcastle urged him to give all the appearance of dividing the house (on an amendment to the address) before yielding at the last moment.[106] Similarly, Newcastle was in favour of protracting the repeal debates, in order that it might provide opportunities for Protectionists (in both houses) to speak – an activity with which a good many of their number were unfamiliar.[107] Newcastle thought that the repeal debates had helped to reveal the members of a Protectionist administration, naming Lord Feversham as an example.[108]

However, at the general level of tactics, Newcastle was no more reconciled to the new leadership's strategy than he had been to that of Wellington and Peel. His own preference, during the repeal debates, was for the Protectionists to take 'our ground on general protection not on the Separate & Exclusive ground of protection to agriculture alone'.[109] He privately disagreed with Stanley's tactics – which were to amend the repeal legislation in committee, in the hope of making it objectionable to the house of commons. However, like Lord Kenyon – who advised that 'nothing vexatious … be Done'[110] – he was in no mood to upset the potential benefits accruing from the new party. The Protectionist peers committed themselves wholeheartedly to Stanley, with Newcastle commenting that his colleagues 'were all in friendly humour & determined to be … unanimous'. For this reason, though Newcastle continued to doubt the wisdom of the party's tactics, he refrained from pressing that opposition to the point of an open breach, in order 'not to Split the party'.[111] After the repeal bill passed the house of lords, the Protectionist peers agreed to demonstrate their unity by signing Stanley's protest against the measure.[112] Following a ministerial defeat in the house of commons, Peel resigned as prime minister on 29 June 1846: 'There never was a more awful downfall of any man', Newcastle exclaimed with evident satisfaction.[113]

---

[103]See 13 Jan., 10 Mar., 25 May, 12 June 1846; D.P., 147/14: Newcastle to Stanley, 10 Mar., 5 May 1846; D.P., 176/2, pp. 387–8: Stanley to Newcastle, 11 May 1846; Robert Blake, *The Conservative Party from Peel to Major* (1998), 66–7.

[104]See 8 Feb., 11 Mar. 1846; R.P., 1692, ff. 1811–12: Newcastle to Richmond, 6, 8 Mar. 1846.

[105]*Unrepentant Tory*, 104–5.

[106]N.U.M.D., Ne C 5176: Richmond to Newcastle, 27 Dec. 1845; R.P., 1692, f. 1794: Newcastle to Richmond, 16 Jan. 1846; see 26 Jan. 1846.

[107]R.P., 1692, f. 1823: Newcastle to Richmond, 28 May 1846; see 15 Feb. 1846.

[108]See 25 June 1846; D.P., 147/14: Newcastle to Stanley, 15 Feb. 1847.

[109]See 9 Mar. 1846.

[110]See 6 June 1846; K.D., 2 June 1846.

[111]See 6, 16 June 1846.

[112]See 20 June 1846; *Protests*, iii, 316–20.

[113]See 30 June 1846.

## Apotheosis or Atrophy? Newcastle and the Protectionists, 1846–50

The repeal of the corn laws and the disruption of the Conservative Party, confirmed at the 1847 general election, have cast long shadows over the historiography of the subsequent period, from which historians have only recently begun to emerge. Britain's relative insulation from the continental revolutionary experience of 1848 and its enjoyment of an unprecedented period of economic good health – symbolised in high farming, the Great Exhibition and the new houses of parliament – leant retrospective justification to 'the rightness and inevitability of Peelism' and Peel's actions and methods in 1846.[114] Peel's premature death, after a fall from his horse in 1850, sanctified his name and legacy, gave dignity to the Peelites and fostered their superiority complex.[115] As Michael Bentley notes, Peel's death established 'a reputation for rising above party which the 1850s might have called into question'.[116] For a generation of post-war historians, repeal stood at the gateway of that seamless transition to an 'age of equipoise',[117] in which the confused state of parliamentary parties struck a discordant note with the nation's social stability and political quiescence. For historians, the dilettantes Bentinck and Stanley and the enigmatic Disraeli all seemed more at home on the turf or in aristocratic salons: Norman Gash condemned the Protectionists as 'little more than the agricultural wing of the old Conservative party with a reputation for religious intolerance'.[118] However, in recent years, a greater understanding of the importance of the Protectionists' political[119] and economic[120] arguments has emerged, and an appreciation of both their leadership[121] and cultural roots.[122] As Angus MacIntyre commented, 'by the "liberal Conservative" thesis, protectionism should never have happened'; that it

---

[114] Coleman, '1841–6', p. 469, n. 2; Norman Gash, *The Historical Importance of the Repeal of the Corn Laws* (Tamworth, 1996).

[115] John Morrow, 'The Paradox of Peel as Carlylean Hero', *HJ*, xl (1997), 97–110; Donald Read, *Peel and the Victorians* (Oxford, 1987), chs 6–7; G.R. Searle, *Country before Party: Coalition and the Idea of 'National Government' in Modern Britain, 1885–1987* (1995), ch. 2; Jules Seigel, 'Carlyle and Peel: The Prophet's Search for a Heroic Politician and an Unpublished Fragment', *Victorian Studies*, xxvi (1983), 181–95; J.B. Conacher, 'The Peelites and Peel, 1846–50', *EHR*, lxxiii (1958), 438; E.J. Evans, *The Forging of the Modern State: Early Industrial Britain, 1783–1870* (2nd edn, 1996), 340.

[116] Michael Bentley, *Politics without Democracy, 1815–1914* (2nd edn, 1996), 138.

[117] W.L. Burn, *The Age of Equipoise: A Study of the Mid-Victorian Generation* (1964); George Kitson Clark, *The Making of Victorian England* (1962).

[118] M.S. Smith, *Lord Paramount of the Turf* (1971); Norman Gash, 'Lord George Bentinck and his Sporting World', in his *Pillars of Government and Other Essays on State and Society, c.1770–c.1880* (1986), 162–75; Gash, 'Major William Beresford: Protectionist Chief Whip, 1846–52', *Parliamentary History*, x (1991), 187–8.

[119] Robert Stewart, *The Politics of Protection: Lord Derby and the Protectionist Party, 1841–1852* (Cambridge, 1971); Angus Hawkins, *Parliament, Party and the Art of Politics in Britain, 1855–59* (1987); Angus Hawkins, '"Parliamentary Government" and Victorian Political Parties, c.1830–80', *EHR*, civ (1989), 638–69.

[120] Derek Walker-Smith, *The Protectionist Case in the 1840s* (Oxford, 1933); T.L. Crosby, *English Farmers and the Politics of Protection, 1815–52* (Hassocks, 1977); Anna Gambles, 'Rethinking the Politics of Protection: Conservatism and the Corn Laws, 1830–52', *EHR*, cxiii (1998), 928–52.

[121] Hawkins, *The Forgotten Prime Minister*. Boyd Hilton finds attempts to talk up Derby's role 'unconvincing': 'Disraeli, English Culture, and the Decline of the Industrial Spirit', in *A Union of Multiple Identities. The British Isles, c.1750–c.1850*, ed. Laurence Brockliss and David Eastwood (Manchester, 1997), 58, n. 18.

[122] G.A. Cahill, 'British Nationalism and Nativism, 1829–48: "No Popery" and British Popular Culture', *Journal of Popular Culture*, iii (1969), 480–91; Cahill, 'Some Nineteenth-Century Roots of the Ulster Problem, 1829–48', *Irish University Review*, i (1971), 215–37; Cahill, 'Irish Popery and British Nativism: 1800–48', *Cithara*, xii (1974), 3–18.

did so, was a triumph against the 'form-book of British politics'.[123] Recent writing on the Protectionists suggests they had much to contribute to the key battles fought during Lord John Russell's Whig administration (1846–52); on the degree of state intervention reconcilable with relief measures for Ireland's famine,[124] the fate of the Navigation Laws – the pre-eminent surviving symbol of economic protection, which gave precedence to Britain's merchant shipping fleet in the carriage of goods – and the status of Britain's remaining statutory political exclusions on Catholics and Jews.[125]

It is sometimes argued that Newcastle withdrew from politics in 1846 as a result of having defeated Peel; John Hogan numbered him among the dutiful but generally unenthusiastic drill-squad of 146 Protectionist peers. However, in spite of Newcastle's worsening financial circumstances and his increasing aversion to extended London residence, he remained an important symbol of the continuing appeal and potential political power of protectionism. This was reinforced by his proximity to, and growing appreciation of, the Bentincks and their protégé, Disraeli. The personal and political estrangement between Newcastle and Lincoln – which repeal served to solidify rather than stimulate – was, as contemporaries recognised, one of the more obvious examples of the difficulties standing in the way of Conservative reunion during these years.[126]

## (I) *Conservative Disunion*

The Protectionists had three political options after 1846; they could form a rear-guard ultra-tory style opposition; create a new, non-Peelite, Tory party; or pursue an alliance, either with another conservative group, or with their former Peelite allies. All of these options entailed difficulties of their own kind. In one sense, the prospects for a reunion between the Protectionists and the Peelites was about 'as likely as a coalition between the Methodists and Lucifer', because far more than simple economics divided them. However, about one third of the Peelites returned to the Conservative fold, during the 1847–52 parliament, whilst a further third retained a doubtful allegiance to Peel.[127] The Peelite drift was an understandable consequence of the general apathy exhibited by Peel towards exercising responsibility, leadership, and interest over his followers and a vindication of Stanley's tactics for the Protectionists, at least until the Peelites rebuffed overtures to form a coalition

[123] Angus MacIntyre, 'Lord George Bentinck and the Protectionists: A Lost Cause?', *TRHS*, 5th ser., xxxix (1989), 141–2, 164–5.

[124] D.A. Kerr, "*A Nation of Beggars*"? *Priests, People, and Politics in Famine Ireland, 1846–1852* (Oxford, 1994).

[125] U.R.Q. Henriques, 'The Jewish Emancipation Controversy in Nineteenth-Century Britain', *Past and Present*, xl (1968), 126–46; M.C.N. Salbstein, *The Emancipation of the Jews in Britain: The Question of the Admission of Jews to Parliament 1828–1860* (Rutherford, NJ, 1982); Chung, 'From a Protectionist Party to a Church Party'.

[126] Munsell, *The Unfortunate Duke*, 94; S.P. Karginoff, 'The Protestant Constitutionalists and Ultra-Toryism in Britain, 1792–1846, with Special Reference to Lord Eldon and the Fourth Duke of Newcastle', Murdoch University PhD, 2 vols, 1994, ii, ch. 13; John Hogan, 'Party Management in the House of Lords, 1846–65', *Parliamentary History*, x (1991), 125, 139, calculates that Newcastle attended the Lords on 143 out of a possible 249 days during the period 1846–9.

[127] J.T. Ward, 'Derby and Disraeli', in *The Conservative Leadership 1832–1932*, ed. Donald Southgate (1974), 61; Bentley, *Politics without Democracy*, 131–3; J.B. Conacher, *The Peelites and the Party System 1846–52* (Newton Abbot, 1972), 60–2; Conacher, 'Peel and the Peelites', 448.

ministry in 1851. Until that point, Stanley pursued 'a patient policy that would emphasise non-Conservative differences in a void created by Conservative passivity'.[128]

Avoiding the possibility of Conservative reunion remained a priority for Newcastle, until his death in January 1851. This was unsurprising, given his view that the Peelites were 'tainted' men. Nor was he singular in this opinion. Lord Kenyon inscribed the word 'Sneaks' next to the names of two prominent Peelites (Lincoln and Sidney Herbert) in his diary, whilst Lord Combermere wrote Kenyon an 'enthusiastic' letter attacking Peel's treachery. Not for the first time, Newcastle presented political purity as the sure consequence of political character; a junction with the Peelites, he warned, would 'be a last fatal blow to the consistency & character of public men'. When Newcastle submitted detailed proposals for the composition of a prospective Protectionist ministry in 1847, it consisted of 'a pure Protectionist List … not lingering after former associates & doctrines'. Even Combermere sketched the outlines of an administration which gave more room for an infusion of Peelite talent. Stanley diplomatically side-stepped Newcastle's recommendations by putting the prospects of a Protectionist ministry far into the future.[129]

For men of Newcastle's disposition, everything depended on the attitude of Stanley, Bentinck, and Disraeli, both towards each other and towards their former colleagues. In terms of social status and government experience, Stanley was marked out as the best leader the Protectionists could have. At the same time, he came with a good deal of necessary political baggage, having been complicit in most of the acts of the previous government – Maynooth among them. Whilst Newcastle had long admired Stanley – and considered him to be Wellington's natural successor as leader of the house of lords – he was continually concerned, after Stanley's formal acceptance of the Protectionist leadership, that 'he was too much inclined to join with the Ex Ministers'. Within weeks, Newcastle was advising Stanley against 'all political negociations [*sic*]' of this kind, whilst the following year he promised to speak 'plainly' to Stanley upon the matter; 'this clinging too much to old colleagues whom he has left, & who have left him are his only blots – & Stumbling blocks – these meet him at too many corners, & cramp & impede his operations'.[130]

Newcastle soon perceived that it was the brittle relationship between Stanley and Bentinck, and their differing attitudes towards the future direction of the party, both at the level of policy and in their attitude towards the Peelites, that was the Protectionists' greatest difficulty. Outwardly, both men had much in common. Born within three years of one another into the aristocratic purple, both were primarily men of the track and turf, combining the sort of 'high station and country habits' which most backbench Conservatives found congenial. Both had supported Canning's ministry – a fact which Newcastle regretted – Stanley from devotion to his Whig political mentor, Lord Lansdowne, Bentinck from family loyalty.[131]

---

[128] Angus Hawkins, 'Lord Derby and Victorian Conservatism: A Reappraisal', *Parliamentary History*, vi (1987), 286.

[129] See 25 July 1846, 25 June, 1 July 1848; K.D., 29 Dec. 1845, 31 Dec. 1846; K.P., Box 73: Combermere to Kenyon, 28 Dec. 1845; D.P., 147/14: Newcastle to Stanley, 12, 14, 15 Feb. 1847; D.P., 177/1, pp. 348–9: Stanley to Newcastle, 21 Feb. 1847; N.U.M.D., Ne C 5170: Combermere to Newcastle, 10 Feb. 1847.

[130] See 19 Jan. 1842, 7 Sept. 1844, 15 June 1845, 8, 18 July 1846, 25 Apr. 1847; D.P., 147/14: Newcastle to Stanley, 12 June 1845, 20 July 1846; D.P., 176/2, pp. 195–6: Stanley to Newcastle, 13 June 1845.

[131] Canning was Bentinck's uncle by marriage. See *Unrepentant Tory*, 38.

Yet these factors alone were not enough to guarantee a harmonious working relationship. Bentinck's violent hostility towards Peel had been established in the repeal debates during 1846 and was extended by a public disagreement with Lord Lyndhurst in August 1846. Both served to raise him in Newcastle's eyes, whilst correspondingly weakening the prospects of a quick or harmonious reunion between the two wings of Conservatism. Whilst Norman Gash implied that Newcastle was in some way naive in his assessment of Bentinck's character – because he 'did not race' – Newcastle was not oblivious to Bentinck's habit of injecting some of the rougher aspects of turf politics into those of the house of commons. However, a lack of shared equestrian habits did not affect Newcastle's appreciation of Bentinck, given that he remained Newcastle's 'beau ideal' of an English statesman.[132] Newcastle's political energy was devoted to reconciling the two men for fear that the party would go, by default, to the Peelites. He used a Clumber house-party at the beginning of 1847 to bring them together, in convivial surroundings, in order to concert on policy. However, within weeks, they had exposed their political differences publicly, at a Protectionist dinner under Newcastle's presidency and the duke was forced to play the unusual role of mediator between them.[133]

Further suspicions were created when Lord John Manners retired from Newark in 1847. Newcastle thought it part of a scheme, engineered by the Protectionist chief whip, Major William Beresford, to have Gladstone returned for the borough. He retained his suspicions that Beresford, who was Bentinck's fiercest opponent among the Protectionist leadership, wished to see Gladstone installed as the party's leader. In fact, Manners was making way for his kinsman John Manners Sutton, in deference to the sort of family electoral concerns which still counted for so much in constituencies like Newark.[134]

At the level of parliamentary arithmetic, it was impossible for the Protectionists (whatever Newcastle's contrary expectations) to secure a majority in the 1847–52 parliament without detaching a body of disgruntled ministerial or Peelite opinion. On the occasions where this happened, Newcastle was dismissive of the outcome. His constant refrain to Stanley was 'to resolve to do what is purely right Without any view of catching Peelite or other votes'.[135] The possible augmentation of the Protectionists voting strength seems to have been uppermost in the minds of the party's whippers-in, Beresford, and Lord Eglinton. Newcastle already had suspicions of Beresford's way of thinking whilst Eglinton's readiness to accept the Peelites without Peel was admitted, without demur, to both Newcastle and Lord Lincoln. Moreover, it was Beresford who encouraged the Protectionists to appropriate the title 'Conservative' to themselves during 1848. This has been interpreted as a sensible move 'to recapture the middle name if not as yet the middle ground for the weak and divided Protectionist opposition'. By contrast, Newcastle complained that it was the latest symptom of an attempt to move the Protectionists closer to the Peelites:

[132]See 1, 18 Mar., 21–22, 24 Aug. 1846, 5, 18 Feb. 1847; N.U.M.D., Pw H 212: Bentinck to Portland, 5 Mar. 1846; Pw H 517: Newcastle to Portland, 3 Mar. 1846; Gash, 'Bentinck', 162; Dep Hughenden, 89/2, ff. 216–19: Newcastle to Disraeli, 22 Oct. 1848; D.P. 147/14: Newcastle to Stanley, 12 Feb. 1847.

[133]See 4–11, 23, 24 Jan. 1847; D.P. 147/14: Newcastle to Stanley, 15 Nov., 13 Dec. 1846.

[134]See 25 July 1846, 24 Jan. 1847; *DL*, IV, 259–60, n. 9.

[135]See 15 June, 10, 20 Aug. 1847, 5 July 1848, 31 Jan. 1849.

Protectionists are Conservatives, Peelites are Conservatives, & if Conservatives all, then no difference, & all are Equally Eligible, for whatever purpose. Office, not a Noble Patriotism, or undeviating principle being the Sole object in View.[136]

Newcastle had always shown a disposition to use the term 'Country Party' in preference to that of Protectionist; Beresford's move correspondingly served to entrench that disposition. Wise correspondents seeking Newcastle's aid, such as Disraeli, shrewdly adopted the same terminology in addressing him.[137]

Whilst Bentinck lived, and held the place he did in the hearts of Protectionists like Newcastle, it was unlikely that the political or personal obstacles to reunion would be overcome. Even after Bentinck's resignation of the leadership, at the end of 1847, Newcastle observed 'he is the life & Soul of [the party] … without him it would not have been what it is & deprived of him … it will be nothing'.[138] Bentinck's untimely death the following year was as great a political as a personal blow for Newcastle. Lincoln saw it as the inevitable precursor of 'a great change in the present position of Parties'. Following Bentinck's resignation, Newcastle supported the claims of Lord Granby. Both Bentinck and Stanley were as one in favouring him. Though Granby refused the leadership, at that time, it was his name which resurfaced, as Stanley's preferred option, following Bentinck's death in September 1848.[139]

It was only now that Disraeli began to emerge from the shadows as a potential leader, at least so far as Newcastle was concerned. Before 1848, Newcastle had little knowledge, and made less mention, of Disraeli. If that name meant anything to him before the late 1840s, it was usually in connection with Disraeli's father, Isaac, whose *Curiosities of Literature* he much admired. None of the philippics against Peel during 1846 for which Disraeli is justly famous attracted Newcastle's attention. Thereafter, Disraeli became known to Newcastle only through the agency and society of Bentinck. A growing sign of Newcastle's evident favour towards Disraeli were the gifts of fruit or fowl with which the duke traditionally marked his respect for those in whom he placed political or personal confidence. From Newcastle's point of view, it is clear that Disraeli was marked out as Bentinck's successor – not merely, as he put it to Stanley, as 'the cleverest man that we possess', but because he had been Bentinck's 'Prime Minister … fellow laborer & most confidential friend'. Newcastle had few reservations about Disraeli from a racial point of view (although he referred to the disadvantages provided by his 'Extraction') and whilst considering him rather 'too theatrical', attributed this to his having 'not been hitherto in the best school'. In return, Disraeli expressed his thanks for the 'confidence' which Newcastle had reposed in him 'when Some others were not disposed to Shew it'.[140]

[136] See 1 July 1848; N.U.M.D., Ne C 5615: Lord Charles Clinton to Newcastle, 10 Oct. 1848; Gash, 'Beresford', 188; BL, Add. MS 56368, f. 180: Newcastle to Giffard, 3 July 1848.

[137] See 17 May 1846, 11 June, 17 Nov. 1848, 24. Feb, 3 Mar. 1849, Apr. 1850; BL, Add. MS 56368, ff. 174–5: Newcastle to Giffard, 20 Feb. 1846; R.P., 1692, f. 1806: Newcastle to Richmond, 18 Feb. 1846; D.P., 147/14: Newcastle to Stanley, 7 Jan. 1849; N.U.M.D., Ne C 5477: Disraeli to Newcastle, 16 Oct. 1849; Dep Hughenden, 30/6, f. 85: Newcastle to Disraeli, 21 Oct. 1849.

[138] Macintyre, 'Bentinck', 150; see 14 Feb., 5 Dec. 1847.

[139] See 3, 9, 16, 20 Feb., 22, 25 Sept. 1848; N.U.M.D., Ne C 11694: Lincoln to Gladstone, 4 Oct. 1848; D.P., 177/2, p. 273: Stanley to Newcastle, 8 Feb. 1848.

[140] See 29 Apr. 1844, 24 Jan. 1847, 6 Feb. 1849; Dep Hughenden, 243/2, ff. 170–2: Newcastle to Isaac Disraeli and reply, 15, 18 Jan. 1823; 136/4, f. 146: Thomas Moffatt to Disraeli, enclosing a Black Antigua pine, 15 July

From a strategic point of view, Disraeli was also likely to prove as opposed as Bentinck had been to concerting with the Peelites. Nor were the Peelites minded to look favourably upon a man considered to have hounded Peel from office. As Stanley put it, Disraeli's leadership of the Protectionist MPs 'would be the most powerful repellent we could administer to any repentant or hesitating Peelites'. This, of course, is precisely what Newcastle wanted. Despite Disraeli's early protestation of his unwillingness to accept the duties and responsibilities of leadership, Newcastle needed little encouragement when Disraeli's claims were pressed upon him by Lord Henry Bentinck in November 1848. These were forwarded on the grounds that it would secure the Protectionists 'Existence as a party … upon our maintenance of the purest principles upon which alone we can hope to benefit our Country'. Newcastle's subsequent support for Disraeli owed everything to the ability of Bentinck's advocacy.[141]

Throughout the winter of 1848–9, Bentinck continued to press Newcastle – and other party grandees – to build momentum behind Disraeli, requesting the duke to encourage a number of MPs to attend the crucial party meeting at which the leadership would be decided. At a social gathering of leading Protectionists, during January 1849, Newcastle attempted to canvass Granby's views, given the continuing disposition on Stanley's part to favour a Granby succession. Newcastle found Granby 'too cautious to give me any direct answer', although within days Disraeli was listing him (together with Newcastle) among his leading supporters.[142]

Whilst Stanley disclaimed any part in the outcome of these proceedings – maintaining that the choice of Protectionist leader in the commons lay entirely with the Protectionist MPs there – his own preferences were obviously far from incidental to Disraeli's chances of success. Whilst unwilling to deprive his MPs of their prerogative of choice, Stanley was equally moved by sentiments reflected in Lord Lincoln's sardonic comment that 'The Protectionists elect Leaders but I hope in our Party None will ever attain that eminence who have Not fairly won it for themselves'. Stanley's favourites for the leadership remained unchanged – either Granby or Herries. His reasons were rooted in a perception of the suspicions which existed towards Disraeli among his own colleagues, as much as the possible effects it might engender in the hearts of wavering Peelites. In the absence of unanimity on the subject, the Protectionists were forced back on a politically expedient triumvirate consisting of Granby, Herries, and Disraeli, in February 1849. At least theoretically, this remained in place at the time of Newcastle's death.[143]

(II) *Catholic Relief, Jewish Emancipation*

By definition, the Protectionists were a party brought together by common concern at the thrust of economic, rather than religious, policies. There was an evident contradiction,

---

[140] *(continued)* 1848; 195/4, f. 159: Newcastle to Disraeli, enclosing ducks and pheasants, 13 Feb. 1849; 89/2, f. 216: Newcastle to Disraeli, 22 Oct. 1848; N.U.M.D., Ne C 5474, 5476: Disraeli to Newcastle, 20 July 1848, 23 Feb. 1849; D.P., 147/14: Newcastle to Stanley, 7, 30 Jan. 1849.

[141] See 17 Nov. 1848, 6 Jan. 1849; D.P., 178/1, p. 203: Stanley to R.A. Christopher, 8 Jan. 1849; N.U.M.D., Ne C 5475: Disraeli to Newcastle, 24 Oct. 1848; *DL*, V, 124; Gash, *Reaction and Reconstruction*, 128.

[142] See 9, 20, 24 Jan. 1849; D.P., 178/1, pp. 218–20: Stanley to Newcastle, 14 Jan. 1849; *DL*, V, 130–1.

[143] See 1–3, 5 Feb. 1849; H.P., Bundle 977: Lincoln to Hamilton, 23 Feb. 1848; D.P., 178/1, pp. 193–7: Stanley to Disraeli, 6 Jan. 1849.

therefore, in the fact that, whilst the party's *raison d'etre* after 1846 was defined by its stance on economic questions, its immediate priority was to formulate a response to those concerning religion. Three issues were uppermost. In 1847, William Watson moved a bill to rescind the remaining restrictive statutes, relating to Catholics, contained in the 1559 Act of Supremacy and the 1829 Catholic Relief Act. The following year, the government proposed the establishment of diplomatic relations with the Papacy. Finally, the return of Lionel Rothschild for the City of London, in the 1847 general election, raised, as it had in the case of Catholics 20 years previously, the question of Jewish emancipation.[144]

Newcastle's religious certainties hardened, if anything, with the passing years; indeed, his Protestantism still transcended his protectionism. In 1849, he recorded his 'determination to Save [the farmers] whilst they remained good Subjects & good Christians' and advised Disraeli to advocate a 'line of policy which by being based on our duty to God & man may Enlighten the Nation & induce God's blessing upon us'.[145] Newcastle's first piece of policy advice to Stanley, in 1846, was to support Lord Powis in his efforts to prevent the union of the Anglican sees of Bangor and St Asaph. This was an issue on which Newcastle had interested himself throughout the 1840s, both as a landowner with Welsh estates and from a wish to defend the Anglican church from further assault.[146]

Potential recipients of Newcastle's electoral influence also continued to be recommended principally on the grounds that they were 'neither a Papist nor a Jew'.[147] When Manners announced his retirement from Newark, *The Times* thought it axiomatic that Newcastle had affected this outcome, given Manners' sympathies on the Catholic question. It was a charge which Newcastle felt compelled to repel publicly.[148] Whilst Newcastle admitted his regret at Manners' professed support for Catholicism, the latter was, in other respects, regarded as a champion of orthodox Christianity. Manners was subsequently (though unsuccessfully) brought forward by the Protectionists in opposition to Lionel Rothschild at the by-election created by the defeat of the Jewish Relief Bill in 1849. However, it is clear from the surviving evidence that Manners was an eleventh-hour choice and felt some embarrassment at standing.[149]

Newcastle's own sense of prophetic Christianity was entrenched and, as he saw it, justified by continental events in 1848. The European revolutions of 1848 were interpreted by him as a mechanism of providential justice rather than as a political or social event. He advised both the premier, Russell, and his own party leaders, to refrain from interfering in those events, convinced as he was that they represented the fulfilment of divine retribution. Whilst keen to assure Stanley and Disraeli that he was not a 'fanatic', Newcastle told Stanley that he certainly attributed 'to God, His workings Whether great or Small & in all that is passing'. By extension, he concluded (in common with Gladstone) that the abortive outcome of the Chartist gathering at Kennington Common in April 1848, had 'decided

---

[144]Chung, 'From a Protectionist Party to a Church Party'.

[145]See 8 Mar., 3 Oct. 1849.

[146]See 2 Mar., 23, 25 May 1843, 9, 11, 13, 23–6, 29 June, 1–2, 13 July 1844, 3–4 May 1845, 20 July 1846; D.P., 147/14: Newcastle to Stanley, 20 July 1846. The political significance of the Bangor and St Asaph issue is explored in Davis, *Wellington, Peel*, 13–19.

[147]D.P., 177/2, p. 165: Stanley to Newcastle, 1 Nov. 1847.

[148]Appendix A.

[149]See 30 June, 4 July 1849; *DL*, V, 196, n. 5.

the future fate of England' and was 'indicative of God's will towards us'.[150] This unshakeable belief underpinned Newcastle's hostility to further measures of 'liberalisation' in the sphere of religion, either in conciliating Catholics or Jews – 'I can Never give way on these points – I think them Vital'.[151]

Divergent attitudes on these subjects bedevilled the Protectionist leadership. There were evident differences between the unreconstructed religious prejudice of William Beresford and Stanley and Bentinck, both of whom exhibited 'the innate liberalism on religious matters of … two former Whigs'.[152] Though Stanley had long been admired by Newcastle for his defence of the church/state connection, his emergence as the defender of the Church of Ireland's revenues in the face of Russell's Appropriation schemes, during the 1830s, should not obscure Stanley's corresponding support for the financial endowment of the Irish Catholic church.[153] Bentinck's affinity for the cause of Jewish relief (which ultimately cost him the leadership of the Protectionist party) was stressed by his first biographer, Disraeli, and reflected the latter's own attitude on the question.[154] Consequently, on each of the three major religious issues of the period, Newcastle found himself at variance with his respective party leaders. As he complained, in April 1847, the 'Sore place in our Leaders is, not their unsoundness to the Church, but their liberality [on religion] – this has already made our party very uneasy & cannot fail to prevent Entire confidence'.[155]

Most of Newcastle's efforts after 1846, were directed towards convincing the Protectionist leadership that they should reflect the religious sentiments, as he perceived them, of the majority of the party.[156] He was 'mortified' by Bentinck's conspicuous public support for Watson's Catholic Relief Bill, privately lamenting it to Stanley and unsuccessfully attempting to convince Bentinck, at a two-hour interview, to moderate his views on the question. But Bentinck had long declared his wish to see the Catholics both unfettered and encouraged in their religious practices. Like Canning, before him, Bentinck found his advocacy of Catholic relief a barrier to the whole-hearted support of his followers, and he ultimately resigned the party leadership in December 1847 rather than conciliate them.[157]

The opening of diplomatic relations with the Papacy raised equally strong convictions in Newcastle. In 1841, he had prophesied that the prime minister who attempted to 'try the plan of an interchange of representatives, with a Minister here & a minister at Rome' would be overthrown.[158] The government's proposal to do exactly that, during 1848, came

[150]See 3, 9, 11 Apr. 1848; D.P. 147/14: Newcastle to Stanley, 10, 30 Apr. 1848; Dep Hughenden, 137/3, ff. 136–8: Newcastle to Disraeli, 27 Feb. 1849; 137/3, ff. 127–30: Newcastle to Disraeli, 6 Mar. 1849; TNA, PRO/30/22/7b, ff. 278–81: Newcastle to Russell, 12 Apr. 1848; Roland Quinault, '1848 and Parliamentary Reform', *HJ*, xxxi (1988), 831–51.

[151]D.P., 147/14: Newcastle to Stanley, 5 May 1846, 24 June 1847.

[152]Gash, 'Beresford', 187.

[153]Gash, *Reaction and Reconstruction*, 99–100; Wolffe, *Protestant Crusade*, 238–9.

[154]Benjamin Disraeli, *Lord George Bentinck: A Political Biography*, intro. R.W. Kamphuis Jr. (New Brunswick, NJ, 1998), ch. xxiv; Paul Smith, *Disraeli: A Brief Life* (Cambridge, 1996), 92–105.

[155]See 25 Apr. 1847.

[156]Gash, *Reaction and Reconstruction*, 98–9, 103–5; Wolffe, *Protestant Crusade*, 222–9.

[157]See 1 Mar., 16 Nov. 1847; D.P., 147/14: Newcastle to Stanley, 20 Apr. 1847; N.U.M.D., Pw H 165: Bentinck to Portland, 7 Apr. 1835.

[158]See 23 Dec. 1841.

at just the moment, as Stanley put it, 'when the resignation of Lord George Bentinck on the ground of difference on religious questions seemed likely to place us upon a more unanimous footing'.[159] After Stanley privately indicated his support for the measure, Newcastle concluded that, although 'disagreements & dissentions [*sic*] must break up our party', his opposition to the leadership (whilst 'unpleasant & painful') was necessitated by his belief that 'the Public naturally Expects from us "protection" in Every thing'.[160]

At the same time, though Newcastle implored Russell to reject the Bill, as a means of mitigating God's 'Wrath for our previous national & political Sins', and hoped that, as a result of events in Europe, there was 'probably no Pope to have relations with', Newcastle showed an unusual and, in its own way, significant disposition not to run that opposition to its logical conclusion.[161] Having assumed responsibility for moving the Bill's rejection in the house of lords, he did not proceed to do so. He did this not only from a calculation that he would carry only a dozen or so supporters with him (including the bishops of Winchester and Exeter and the duke of Richmond),[162] but also from a realisation that 'although I myself was not at all Satisfied at giving way – yet I am convinced that this proceeding amongst ourselves will be productive of the best Effects'.[163] Similar considerations meant that Newcastle supported the amendment suggested by his fellow Protectionist, Lord Eglinton, in committee, that no ambassador from Rome should be an ecclesiastic. Although Newcastle thought it 'productive of little or no good', the amendment effectively secured the Bill's defeat, as the Pope refused to accept it.[164]

Newcastle's hostility to the political relief of the Jews, though less apparent than his anti-Catholicism, was nevertheless as enduring. Earlier relief bills had merited his wonder, rather than derision: 'For my part having admitted Papists & Infidels – I can see no objection to the admission of Jews, or Turks or Mahomedans'.[165] The most recent attempt to afford political concessions – Lord Lyndhurst's bill to allow Jews to assume municipal office – had surfaced at the time of Maynooth; a fact which Newcastle thought more than coincidental, and which served to sharpen his hostility on both issues.[166] He grounded this opposition less on anti-Semitic feeling than on grounds of theology and politics.[167] At the level of religion, he attacked the Jews for killing Christ, an act for which they had forfeited 'the favours of their Creator'. This was a position which Newcastle shared in common with many of his countrymen, though not with Peel or Lincoln.[168] During 1848, Newcastle

[159] See 8 Feb. 1848; D.P., 177/2, p. 270: Stanley to Newcastle, 8 Feb. 1848.

[160] See 10, 11 Feb. 1848; BL, Add. MS 56368, ff. 183–4: Newcastle to Giffard, 16 Oct. 1848.

[161] See 20 Aug. 1848; TNA, PRO/30/22/7b, ff. 278–81: Newcastle to Russell, 12 Apr. 1848.

[162] R.P., 1712, f. 1248: Newcastle to Richmond, 9 Feb. 1848; Wolffe, *Protestant Crusade*, 232–5.

[163] See 17 Feb. 1848; K.D., 17 Feb. 1848.

[164] See 18 Feb. 1848; G.I.T. Machin, 'Lord John Russell and the Prelude to The Ecclesiastical Titles Bill, 1846–51', *Journal of Ecclesiastical History*, xxv (1974), 287.

[165] *Unrepentant Tory*, 109, 112, 212, 217, 228, 247.

[166] See Appendix A. On its second and third readings, 51 Conservatives supported the Bill and 22 Conservatives opposed it: Chung, 'From a Protectionist Party to a Church Party', n. 26.

[167] However, Newcastle increasingly referred to Rothschild in dismissive terms as 'the Jew': see 30 June, 3, 4 July 1849.

[168] See 13 Feb. 1848; Newcastle, *Thoughts in Times Past*, xxvii–xxviii; N.U.M.D., Ne C 5472: George Wingfield to Newcastle, 29 May 1837; *Speeches Delivered in the House of Commons by the late Rt Hon Sir Robert Peel* (4 vols, New York, 1972), iv, 744–53; N.U.M.D., Ne C 11693: Lincoln to Gladstone, 23 Sept. 1847.

beseeched Russell to resist conceding relief for fear of provoking divine retribution.[169] At the political level, he attacked concessions on the grounds of principle rather than from a calculation of the likely consequences; 'the sects are too little numerous to do injury – Even in parliament'.[170] However, whilst Newcastle continually proclaimed his personal disposition towards the Jews, this was redolent of his attitude towards Catholics and non-conformists before they had achieved political emancipation in the 1820s; tolerating their religious practices whilst maintaining their exclusion from the enjoyment of political rights.[171] As he put it, after the introduction of the Jewish Relief Bill, 'I own to taking the deepest interest in the Jews – but admission to political power, & legislation on Church matters I would delegate to none but Christians'.[172]

The most dispiriting consequence of Jewish relief remained its potential to expose the public differences between the Protectionists and their leaders on religious subjects. Newcastle noted with regret the ability with which Bentinck had advocated the measure. Lincoln himself commented that only six Protectionist MPs supported the Bill on its first reading, and concluded that the speeches made by Disraeli and Bentinck on this occasion had 'closed their career of Leadership'.[173] Newcastle also remained acutely conscious of the dilemma facing the party, the more so after the Bill passed the house of commons, in February 1848, concluding that the party was 'all to pieces & in a Most Unfortunate way'.[174] However, the likely repercussions of this predicament had already been lessened by Bentinck's resignation of the party leadership. When the Bill was debated by the Lords, in May, Newcastle was gratified to find the Protectionists imbued with 'the very best doctrine, political & religious'; a fact which gave him renewed encouragement as well as ensuring the Bill's rejection.[175] In February 1849, Disraeli, in an effort to convince the party's grandees of his claim on their confidence, told Newcastle that he wished the issue 'were at the bottom of the Red Sea', especially now that Russell had proposed a bill to alter the parliamentary oath as a means of settling the question. But that bill, as Disraeli anticipated, was subsequently rejected by the Lords, and Jewish relief was delayed for another decade.[176]

John Wolffe has argued that the Protectionists' attitude towards religious issues between 1846 and 1850 fell into two halves, pivoting around the death of Lord George Bentinck in September 1848; before then, they served to divide the party from its leaders; after it, Disraeli used issues like Jewish relief tactically to consolidate his claims to the party's leadership. Norman Gash likewise concluded that there was a fundamental difference in outlook between the Protectionist leadership and the backbenchers, the latter coming nearest 'to forming a Protestant party in politics'.[177] Newcastle himself was not insensible of these difficulties or, so far as Bentinck or Stanley was concerned, successful in resolving them. Nor,

---

[169]See 3 Apr. 1848; TNA, PRO/30/22/7b, ff. 278–81: Newcastle to Russell, 12 Apr. 1848; 30/22/7c, f. 10: Newcastle to Russell, 6 May 1848.

[170]See 12 Mar. 1845.

[171]D.P., 147/14: Newcastle to Stanley, 5 May 1846.

[172]See 7, 12 Mar. 1845, 18 Dec. 1847.

[173]See 19, 20 Dec. 1847; N.U.M.D., Ne C 11943: Lincoln to Herbert, 19 Dec. 1847.

[174]See 20 Feb. 1848.

[175]See 25 May 1848.

[176]See 23 Feb., 25, 26 June 1849; N.U.M.D., Ne C 5476: Disraeli to Newcastle, 23 Feb. 1849; K.D., 26 June 1849; Edgar Feuchtwanger, *Disraeli* (2000), 85.

[177]Wolffe, *Protestant Crusade*, 238; Gash, *Reaction and Reconstruction*, 99.

whilst advocating Disraeli's claims to the leadership of the Protectionists in 1849, did he forget the disadvantages provided by Disraeli's vote in favour of Jewish relief.[178] Even whilst Newcastle remained a driving force behind the movement to erect a public memorial to the memory of Bentinck[179] – an enterprise in which he was only modestly encouraged by Disraeli and Stanley – the religious predilections of the fallen leader served to bedevil its achievement in a form that was suitable to Newcastle, for one.[180] In particular, Newcastle hoped that the inscription on the intended statue of Bentinck would stress protection as his leading object. This would have served to smooth down the difficulties which had been created within the Country Party by Bentinck's religious sensibilities.[181]

(III) *Protection and Relief*

Whatever equivocations might have been expected – if not forgiven – in the sphere of religious policy did not extend to the party's economic programme. Protection provided the litmus test for party supporters like Newcastle, who saw it as fundamental to the economic salvation of the aristocracy, in much the same way as opposition to Catholic emancipation had been cherished as vouchsafing the Protestant constitution, and opposition to parliamentary reform the continued political supremacy of the aristocracy.[182] Nor, in the circumstances of the late 1840s, was the advocacy of such a policy necessarily that of an anachronistic or politically moribund minority. The severe banking and financial crisis of 1847, like that of 1825 before it, was attributed to the exigencies of Peel's currency legislation; recently augmented by the tightening of the money supply created by his Bank Charter Act of 1844.[183] The depression in agricultural prices which set in during 1849–50 gave substance to the fears expressed by Peel's opponents in 1846 and suggested that the prospects for the formation of a Protectionist ministry, during a period of corresponding political difficulty for Russell's Whig ministry, were far from fanciful.[184] Outside parliament, pressure was maintained by bodies such as G.F. Young's National Association for the Protection of British Industry and Capital and the Colonial Association, which were dissatisfied with the current state of legislation relating to corn, shipping and banking. Newcastle, who had headed a list of peers in favour of Protection to Native Industry in 1846, was invited to assume a leading role in both organisations.[185] Young's associate, Paul Foskett (described by Disraeli as a 'mad Surrey farmer') sought Newcastle's support for a scheme to petition Queen Victoria to dissolve parliament, in the expectation of electing a Protectionist successor.[186]

[178] D.P., 147/14: Newcastle to Stanley, 7, 30 Jan. 1849.

[179] *Unhappy Reactionary*, 151–7. BL, Add. MS 56368, ff. 181, 185–6: Newcastle to Giffard, 2, 20 Oct. 1848.

[180] N.U.M.D., Ne C 5179: Stanley to Newcastle, 18 Oct. 1848; Ne C 5475: Disraeli to Newcastle, 24 Oct. 1848; Ne C 8777–8: sketches of a proposed memorial; D.P., 178/1, pp. 86–9: Stanley to Charles Newdegate, Stanley to Lord Eglinton, 18 Oct. 1848.

[181] See 9 Apr. 1849; Wolffe, *Protestant Crusade*, 241–2.

[182] Gambles, 'Rethinking the Politics'.

[183] See 8 May, 20 June 1844.

[184] See 11 May, 10 Aug., 9 Sept. 1847.

[185] N.U.M.D., Ne C 6483: H.P. Huntley to Newcastle, 28 Mar. 1849; Ne C 6507/1: G.F. Young to Newcastle, 28 May 1849; Ne C 8765: Henry Heming to Newcastle, 24 Apr. 1850.

[186] N.U.M.D., Ne C 6545: Paul Foskett to Newcastle, 29 Sept. 1849; Robert Blake, *Disraeli* (1966), 291.

However, as in preceding campaigns, Newcastle thought twice about encouraging extra-parliamentary bodies which would, as Stanley put it, in lending discouragement to these initiatives, 'be a sort of "Lion's Mouth" for the reception of all complaints, & the promulgation of all grievances, real and imaginary, against the Queen's Government'.[187] In these circumstances, Newcastle continued to repose his hopes in the undiluted advocacy of his party leaders; 'Protection is most properly decided to be our principle of action', he commented, with evident satisfaction, at the party's formation in June 1846.[188]

The economic issues with which the Protectionists had to contend in Newcastle's lifetime may be roughly divided into three areas; first, those relating to corn, sugar, and the income tax, which might be called the inherited Peelite residue; second, new government initiatives, such as the repeal of the Navigation Acts; and third, the attempt to formulate a Protectionist policy for the future which might prove capable of realisation.

On corn, sugar and the income tax, the party leadership showed itself unwilling to appear reactionary by advocating a simple policy of repealing past legislation. Whilst Stanley proposed a nominal continuation of the duties on corn, during 1848, and even Russell was believed to be toying with this idea, there was no disposition, on anyone's part, to refight the battle of 1846.[189] Newcastle, for one, was dispirited by this early weakening in resolve, and continued to seek salvation 'in a great measure [in restoring] what is lost … by returning to the old System'.[190] In August 1846, he complained that the Protectionist leadership might have spared him 'the trouble of writing my opinion' on the line of conduct to be pursued relative to the sugar duties, then under consideration by the Lords, given that they decided to follow a contrary line and refused to divide upon the question.[191] When the issue resurfaced in 1848, as part of a general ministerial attempt to give relief to the colonies, Newcastle was pleased to find more resolution among the Protectionist ranks.[192] The traditional hostility with which Newcastle viewed the income tax – which Russell proposed to substantially augment and extend in February 1848 – was combined with derision for the justification proffered in the year of revolutions. Newcastle counselled Stanley against sanctioning such an increase from 'any pretended or Silly fear of invasion … or absurd idea of [increasing Britain's] defences'.[193]

However, whatever success the Protectionists had in curtailing the ministry's continuation of Peelite economics usually resulted from temporary coalitions with disaffected ministerial or even Peelite opinion in parliament. This was a necessary practical consequence of adverse parliamentary arithmetic. After the 1847 general election, the Protectionists could only ever muster 227 MPs to the Peelites 91 and the government's 338.[194] Only an exceptional display of resistance from the ministry's usual supporters could advance the Protectionists' cause. Such alliances were not out of the question and helped to decrease the ministry's majority

---

[187] D.P., 178/1, p. 264: Stanley to Newcastle, 4 Apr. 1849.
[188] See 20 June 1846.
[189] See 16 June 1848, 20 Jan. 1849.
[190] See 12 Oct. 1847.
[191] See 5, 8 Aug. 1846.
[192] See 23, 29 June, 9, 12 July 1848.
[193] D.P., 147/14: Newcastle to Stanley, 29 Feb. 1848.
[194] Evans, *Forging of the Modern State*, 404.

on the sugar duties in 1848.[195] Otherwise, it required a particularly strong connection between opposition inside parliament and an equally adverse feeling out-of-doors. Stanley informed Newcastle that the ministry 'would have been infallibly beaten had they not succumbed' to the widespread opposition evoked by Russell's budget, by abandoning their income tax proposals.[196]

The real test of the Protectionists' fidelity to the cause inside parliament – and the strength of their support outside parliament – could only come in opposing new ministerial initiatives. Of these, the one which most clearly raised Newcastle's antagonism was the proposal to repeal the Navigation Acts, which first surfaced in 1848. Newcastle had long been addressed as a 'friend to Navigation', and had taken a keen interest in the hostility evoked by William Huskisson's early attempts at modifying the Acts in the 1820s.[197] At the same time, the evident effect which even the rumours of repeal had on Newcastle's timber sales, given the close correlation between the shipping and timber interests, injected an additional, and very personally felt, economic imperative to his opposition. 'Depression, from Free trade & a Complete panic from the expected repeal of the Navigation laws, Extinguished all notion of purchase, Even at a Gift', Newcastle complained to Disraeli, after a particularly dispiriting timber sale, in February 1849.[198]

The battle over the Navigation Acts afforded the Protectionists additional advantages by provoking the antagonism of a combination of vested interests, each of which were powerful obstacles in their own right. The ministry's proposals raised the opposition of the colonial interest, from the effect that repeal would have on the carriage of their produce; from the shipping interest, because of the threat of competition envisaged by the Acts' sponsors; and, as the commodity most frequently carried, from the timber interest. Evidence of the depth of hostility among the shipowners and sailors was already apparent to Newcastle[199] even before he found Stanley 'all in arms' about the government's plans. Given the facility with which the Whigs and Peelites would ensure the passage of repeal through the Commons, Stanley also declared himself more than ready to lead the assault in the Lords: 'This is a real comfort [Newcastle concluded], for it would be absolute perdition to England if through the infatuated folly & blind vanity of our wretched modern Statesmen Peel & Co other measures were to be adopted, following upon the heels of free trade & other abominations, by which this noble Country would be rendered nerveless & impotent'.[200]

At Bentinck's suggestion, Newcastle composed a letter to Russell, in which he argued, on the grounds of economics and self-defence, that the prime minister should not proceed with a measure which would allow 'a host of foreigners to Swarm along our coasts, carry our goods, & Eat the very bread out of our honest sailors Mouths'. For his pains, he received the curt response from Russell 'that our sailors or our ships [were not] so inferior to those of other nations, as to stand in need of the restrictions which were imposed by

[195] See 1 July 1848.
[196] See 20, 21 Feb., 4, 8, 9 Mar. 1848; D.P., 177/2, p. 319: Stanley to Newcastle, 2 Mar. 1848.
[197] N.U.M.D., Ne C 7061: Samuel Clegg to Newcastle, 29 Aug. 1826; Ne2F/2/1: Newcastle diary, 26 June, 21 Aug., 6 Dec. 1826.
[198] See 26, 27 Feb. 1849; N.U.M.D., Ne C 8381/1: Henry Heming to Newcastle, 27 Feb. 1849; Dep Hughenden, 137/3, f. 131: Newcastle to Disraeli, 6 Mar. 1849.
[199] See 11 Feb. 1848, 23 May 1849.
[200] See 27 May, 11 June 1848.

Cromwell to swamp Dutch competition'.[201] Though Newcastle's letter does not originally seem to have been intended for publication, it was subsequently published in advance of the Bill's reintroduction during the 1849 session, following Russell's abandonment of his earlier proposals. Newcastle hoped that it might 'be of use in causing the people of the interior of England to take more interest in this vital question'.[202] Newcastle himself received a number of proofs that his letter had effected the desired outcome,[203] although scant relief was provided from Nottinghamshire. The secretary of the county's agricultural protection society regretfully informed Newcastle that, whilst 'a very large majority of the respectable Inhabitants in this County would have been anxious to show their conviction of the soundness of protection principles', on this issue, the organisation lacked sufficient funds to circulate a petition to the Lords.[204]

Consequently, opposition to the government's proposals remained primarily in the hands of the Protectionists' parliamentary leaders. It was unfortunate, therefore, that the issue came before the Commons in 1849. By this date, support for the measure had increased among MPs, whilst Bentinck's death, and the institution of the triumvirate leadership correspondingly weakened the Protectionists' standing there. Despite this, Newcastle remained sanguine of their prospects, given the perception that the ministry were divided on the wisdom of pursuing repeal, an external sign of which was Russell's announcement that the measure was to be viewed as a matter of confidence in the ministry.[205] When the Bill reached the house of lords, and Stanley openly announced his unchanged opposition, Newcastle concluded that his leader would 'be as good as his word', and told him that his speech was 'worthy of a Stanley'.[206]

Stanley's leadership in the subsequent debate energised the Protectionists and generated paeans of praise from Newcastle – who commented that his leader's keynote speech 'was as beautiful as anything Ever uttered in the English language' – whilst serving to cut the ministerial majority.[207] Newcastle was less enamoured of Stanley's amendments at the committee stage of the Bill, which he thought unduly founded upon the principle of reciprocity; characteristically, he concluded that Stanley's performance in committee had been 'less great than I Ever heard him'.[208] Everything, therefore, depended on Stanley's strategy and tactics. Newcastle himself had been, for one reason or another, absent from the meetings of the Protectionist peers, when that strategy was discussed.[209] Regardless of the '21 decided Peelites & Wellingtonians' who had opposed the measure in the Lords, the numerical outcome, if slight, lay in the ministry's favour. The Navigation Acts were repealed by law on 12 June 1849.[210]

[201] TNA, PRO/30/22/7c, ff. 34–7: Newcastle to Russell, 24 June 1848; *The Later Correspondence of Lord John Russell, 1840–1878*, ed. G.P. Gooch (2 vols, 1925), i, 189–90.

[202] See 19 July 1848, 28 Jan. 1849.

[203] See 1, 3 Mar. 1849; N.U.M.D., Ne C 6479: Henry Horton Marriott to Newcastle, 28 Feb. 1849; Ne C 6493: Joseph Allen to Newcastle, 2 May 1849.

[204] N.U.M.D., Ne C 6490: J.H. Stenton to Newcastle, 28 Apr. 1849.

[205] See 11, 14–16, 24, 25 Mar., 26 Apr. 1849.

[206] See 30 Apr. 1849; D.P., 147/14: Newcastle to Stanley, 30 Apr. 1849.

[207] See 7, 8 May 1849; K.D., 7, 8 May 1849.

[208] See 21 May 1849.

[209] See 3, 17 May 1849; K.D., 4, 17 May 1849.

[210] See 11 May, 12 June 1849; *Protests*, iii, 362–3; K.D., 12, 14 June 1849.

For the Protectionists to become more than a party of opposition, they needed to formulate the policies of a potential government. Simple hostility to prevailing Peelite and free trade economics might have been satisfying in itself but produced few prospects of wider political success. It needed the formulation of some concrete proposals, reflecting current circumstances, to which the party could be seen to be responding. Newcastle himself was not incapable of finding straws in the wind. He was not averse to seeing the potential economic benefits accruing from events during 1848, maintaining that Britain would step into the void created by an exhausted and self-consumed continent, both in terms of international diplomacy and economic supremacy; 'States Engaged in war & revolution, will Cease to produce, & we may become the Manufacturers & Merchants of the Whole World', he told Russell.[211] Newcastle expressed few sentiments regarding the Protectionists' electoral platform, as set out by Bentinck at the 1847 general election, which included a commitment to the continuation of some form of protection to agriculture, a reconsideration of the Bank Charter Act and a revision of the duties on foreign imports.[212] During that election, Newcastle worked particularly closely with the duke of Portland, in arranging the succession at Retford and Bassetlaw. He also withheld his support from Manners Sutton at Newark, less from any personal hostility to a man who identified himself as 'a Conservative & a Moderate politician', than from a perception that Sutton was not yet 'of Sound & fixed principles' in regard to religion and free trade.[213]

Bentinck's principal concern (in terms of economic and social policy) during his leadership of the Protectionists, related to Ireland – which continued to suffer the effects of famine and distress. Newcastle himself thought that Irish salvation lay in opening up hitherto uncultivated lands and extending the Irish the benefits of the poor law.[214] As far as English farmers were concerned, Newcastle was unwilling to condone the Protectionists' possible advocacy of the repeal of the malt tax, or any scheme of agricultural relief, rather than a specific commitment to protection. Newcastle's greatest fear remained that 'one half of the farmers [would] be irretrievably ruined & [would] pull the landlords down with them, as in Ireland'.[215]

The nature of the malt tax meant it fell primarily on the farmers; indeed, it had been considered one of those 'special burdens' for which the agricultural sector required some form of compensatory relief, such as the corn laws. Previous moves to repeal the tax, led by Lord Chandos (afterwards duke of Buckingham), established the latter's reputation as 'The Farmer's Friend' but met with Newcastle's unfeigned hostility. This emanated from his belief that repealing the tax, which regularly netted some £4–5 million, would create a deficiency that the whole community would have to bear, without affording relief to the farmers.[216]

[211] See 3 Apr. 1848; TNA, PRO/30/22/7b, f. 279: Newcastle to Russell, 12 Apr. 1848.

[212] *The Times*, 27 July 1847; MacIntyre, 'Bentinck', 149–50.

[213] See 29 Apr., 25–29 June 1847.

[214] See 28 Apr., 7, 8 May 1847; MacIntyre, 'Bentinck', 151; D.P., 147/14: Newcastle to Stanley, 2 Mar. 1847; 177/1, pp. 373–5: Stanley to Newcastle, 7 Mar. 1847; Dep Hughenden, 137/3, ff. 133–5: Newcastle to Disraeli, 14 Mar. 1849.

[215] Dep Hughenden, 30/6, f. 87: Newcastle to Disraeli, 21 Oct. 1849.

[216] *Unrepentant Tory*, 264–5; BL, Add. MS 40558, f. 50: Newcastle to Peel, 18 Jan. 1845; Dep Hughenden, 137/3, ff. 122–3, 137–8: Newcastle to Disraeli, 27 Feb., 6 Mar. 1849; David Spring, 'Lord Chandos and the Farmers, 1818–46', *Huntington Library Quarterly*, xxxiii (1969–70), 257–81.

This argument underpinned Newcastle's hostility, whenever rumours surfaced that the Protectionists would adopt the repeal of the malt tax as a matter of policy, in preference to revising or repealing free trade legislation. Newcastle sought Stanley's views on the matter as early as 1846,[217] but the greatest threat came during 1849. The Financial Reform Association – launched from the remnants of the Anti-Corn Law League by Richard Cobden – took up malt tax repeal that year as a means of obtaining the political support of the farmers during a period of depressed agricultural prices and severe distress. Sensing that the initiative might be taken from them, the Protectionist leadership authorised Disraeli to consider methods of equalising the tax burden and mitigating some of the impositions upon landed property.[218]

Newcastle was worried by this move, regarding it as 'a prodigious question – & I hope will be well Weighed & considered before it is announced to the Public'.[219] He subsequently reiterated his arguments in favour of retaining the malt tax to Disraeli, suggesting that the removal or revision of other taxes – such as those relating to hops, windows and inhabited houses – might prove more just and lasting remedies. Moreover, in a remarkably telling passage, Disraeli was encouraged to 'brave the Clamour of the farmers set on by mischievous men':

> The Agricole ... have always been an obtuse, or discontented or perverse race, diffi-
> cult to lead or drive ... They are fine fellows [and] ... the best people we have in the
> Country, but they are gullable [*sic*] & must not be deceived – their alliance is of Supreme
> importance, gain their hearts & Educate their conviction, & I shall not despair of Seeing
> a vast improvement in the Towns.[220]

Newcastle certainly thought this advice had produced its intended effect. Within days of his letter, he was in ecstasies about the speech Disraeli made in proposing his motion for the 'relief of real property'. He thought it was truly 'paternal ... it cares for all, it inculcates goodness, justice & Christianity, & is a model of ... greatness'.[221] Whilst Lord Blake described it as 'one of Disraeli's finer purple passages', the speech was admired by politicians with such divergent views as Russell, Palmerston, Stanley and Peel.[222]

Disraeli remained acutely conscious of the political challenge represented by the Financial Reform Association, complaining to Newcastle that the Protectionists did not comprehend that 'unless the agricultural constituencies are led, they will go, from sheer spite & suffering, to the Radicals'.[223] However, his solutions were not those which, in a matured form, were acceptable either to Stanley, conscious of political realities, or Newcastle, the undying proponent of a policy of pure-protection. As Peel sagely observed, during 1849, 'the Protectionists ... could not conduct the government of this country – that is to

---

[217]See 11 Dec. 1846; D.P., 147/14: Newcastle to Stanley, 13 Dec. 1846.

[218]N.C. Edsall, 'A Failed National Movement: The Parliamentary and Financial Reform Association, 1848–54', *Historical Research*, xlix (1976), 108–31.

[219]See 24 Feb. 1849.

[220]Dep Hughenden, 137/3, ff. 122–7: Newcastle to Disraeli, 6 Mar. 1849.

[221]See 10 Mar. 1849; Dep Hughenden, 137/3, f. 132: Newcastle to Disraeli, 14 Mar. 1849.

[222]Blake, *Disraeli*, 288; *DL*, V, 155, n. 2.

[223]N.U.M.D., Ne C 5477: Disraeli to Newcastle, 16 Oct. 1849.

say – if they adhered to their professed principles, and retained the goodwill of such men as the Duke of Richmond, Lord Winchilsea & the Duke of Newcastle'.[224]

This divergence of opinion was fully revealed during October 1849, when Disraeli sent Newcastle the text of a petition to be considered by the inaugural county meeting of the Buckinghamshire Association for the Relief of Real Property. Whilst the petition did not, as Disraeli put it, 'crudely pray for a return to protection', it suggested a more equitable distribution of local taxation and the establishment of a sinking fund as a means of mitigating the national debt, sustaining the value of landed property, facilitating mortgage rate relief and low-interest loans for farmers. In short, Disraeli argued, it would offer 'a bona fide, though a moderate protection'.[225] Disraeli's clear hope was that Newcastle's support would be forthcoming and that he would respond in kind, by agitating a Nottinghamshire county meeting. Shortly afterwards, *The Buckinghamshire Herald* went so far as to state that Newcastle had this in contemplation; an act for which its editor, George Lathom Browne, was censured by Disraeli: 'People don't like announcements of their intended conduct to appear & first to appear, in strange newspapers'.[226] Newcastle continued to be sought after as a chairman for local agricultural rallies from the time he attended his first agricultural dinner meeting in 1843. As he reluctantly accepted these invitations at the best of times, Disraeli's latest proposals were unlikely to persuade him from his usual inclinations. 'We shall never do any good by temporising', he informed Disraeli in October 1849:

> We are against free trade, we are in favor of Protection – If we are why dissemble in the Slightest degree – let us be rightly & clearly understood … although prudence may require that our views may not be doggedly pressed to an unseasonable time Yet Suppression of our real intentions seems to me to be impolitic, & all diplomacy unsuited to the Case.[227]

Newcastle's hostility was shared by the larger part of the Protectionist party; Disraeli's schemes, as Blake comments, were 'more ingenious than convincing'.[228] The Peelite, Edward Cardwell, stated that Disraeli had been 'loudly disavowed by all his friends. Some in Public, all in Private, discountenance his Schemes & depreciate himself'. This anomalous situation was also apparent to Stanley's son, newly returned to England in March 1850.[229] Disraeli's measures raised opposition in counties where the land tax was at a much lower rate than in Buckinghamshire, which he had extolled as a model for others to follow. This factor certainly underpinned Stanley's hostility towards the proposals. Meanwhile, Disraeli's sinking fund raised the prospect of over-borrowing on the part of farmers, and a corresponding threat that any default in repayment would put them at the mercy of moneylenders, only too keen to deprive them of responsibility for their estates.[230] However, if Disraeli's

---

[224] *The Correspondence of Charles Arbuthnot*, ed. Arthur Aspinall (Camden Society, 3rd ser., lxv, 1941), 252.

[225] N.U.M.D., Ne C 5477: Disraeli to Newcastle, 16 Oct. 1849; *DL*, V, Appendix IV (a) for the petition.

[226] *DL*, V, 240–1.

[227] See 6 Oct. 1843, 12 Apr. 1846; Dep Hughenden, 30/6, ff. 84–9: Newcastle to Disraeli, 21 Oct. 1849.

[228] Blake, *Disraeli*, 290.

[229] N.U.M.D., Ne C 12424: Cardwell to Lincoln, 15 Oct. 1849; *Disraeli, Derby and the Conservative Party: The Political Journals of Lord Stanley, 1849–69*, ed. J.R. Vincent (Hassocks, 1978), 13.

[230] Blake, *Disraeli*, 290; Gash, 'Beresford', 189; Stewart, *Politics of Protection*, 147.

measures of 'relief' proved unworkable, the alternatives proved no more palatable to New-castle. After 1849, Disraeli increasingly looked upon the abolition of the malt tax as the popular rallying policy he had sought. 'It is a pity', Lord Charles Clinton commented to his father, in July 1850, 'that the Party is not Kept in better order than to bring forward things upon which they are sure to split & show their weakness'.[231]

The dilemma between 'protection' and 'relief' lay unresolved until the Conservative Party abandoned its commitment to protection after the 1852 general election. After 1846, the difference of opinion within the party over the extent to which Peelite economics could be unpicked remained a continuous drain on Protectionist time and energies. This situation was exacerbated by a growing Whig-Peelite consensus on the issue and the activities of the Financial Reform Association. The threat of the latter was particularly acute, according to Disraeli, because it represented 'nothing more than … direct taxation, & the confiscation of the aristocracy'.[232]

## Newcastle's Death and Legacy

The final years of a man's life are often interpreted as the appropriate representation of what has gone before. In some cases, the ends of lives are foretold in the passage of preceding events – success or sorrow is crowned, the whole life is summed up with an appropriate climax. If so, then Newcastle's must be regarded as consistent with his previous failures. In his last diary comment on the state of British domestic politics, in April 1850, he was to be found complaining that 'if we, the Country party had had any one who Could have played his Cards well, there would have been an Entire change long ago'.[233] Two months later, he made his last speech in the house of lords, on presenting a petition from South Nottinghamshire seeking agricultural protection. Knowing that he was unlikely to attend ever again, Newcastle took the opportunity of observing that:

> in a very few years England may no longer be able to be recognised as the land of our birth. I need not express to your lordships how deeply this grieves me in prospect, and with what warmth and earnestness I would supplicate you to avert the impending evils and dreaded mischief, if I had the smallest idea that such an effort on my part could avail in the remotest degree.

The speech was printed in *The Standard* (where it was hailed, somewhat optimistically, as Newcastle's restoration to 'health and strength') at the duke's request.[234]

That there was to be no grand apotheosis for Newcastle, in the manner of Welling-ton, is hardly surprising.[235] For him, the rupture of 1846 represented an opportunity to be taken rather than an occasion for regret. Shorn of the Peelite and Wellingtonian influ-ences with which he had been in instinctive disagreement since the early 1830s, the expul-sion of those elements from the Conservative Party in 1846 signified an opportunity for

---

[231] N.U.M.D., Ne C 5624: Lord Charles Clinton to Newcastle, 6 July 1850.

[232] Dep Hughenden, 30/3, ff. 33–7: Disraeli to Newcastle, 16 Oct. 1849.

[233] See Apr. 1850.

[234] *The Standard*, 19 June 1850; BL, Add. MS 56368, f. 187: Newcastle to Giffard, 18 June 1850.

[235] Philip Guedalla, *The Duke* (1931), ch. x; Neville Thompson, *Wellington after Waterloo* (1986), ch. 10.

politics to take the direction he had been campaigning for over the preceding quarter-century. The destruction of Peel was not an end-goal in itself, but a step towards another objective, which Newcastle tried to achieve until his death: an undiluted Protestant and Protectionist party. In January 1849, Newcastle informed Stanley that the party had something distinctive to say, 'upon Corn, Colonies, Navigation laws, Protection, Home Policy, Foreign Policy … [and] the Church Establishment'. At the same time, Newcastle continued to resist what he saw as dangerous 'Symptoms of assimilation', on the part of the Protectionists and Peelites.[236]

Newcastle's own contribution, during these years, is not to be measured in the dwindling number of parliamentary speeches he made during this period; as he was only too keenly aware, his interventions grew more incoherent and disorderly with the passing years.[237] He compensated for this through lobbying, financing, and dining his political colleagues. *The Times,* for one, thought him a peculiar political host for Protectionists to choose to be entertained by:

> Conceive the Dukes of NEWCASTLE and RICHMOND … meeting together in solemn conclave and exchanging the platitudes with which they periodically favour the public by means of the press …We had certainly rather be absent from so dull an assemblage.

However, in spite of potentially promising foundations, Newcastle failed to achieve the aims he set for the post-1846 Protectionist party, in terms of policy and leadership. Divergent views among the leadership, and between them and the majority of the party, on religious issues, or in their varying conceptions of 'protection' and 'relief', or in defining the limits of any possible relationship with the Peelites, remained unbridgeable.[238]

According to Norman Gash, any political party which hoped for success, after 1830, had to take account of the changing nature of English society. For Gash, the Protectionists represented the embodiment of this axiom: 'the Conservative party with most of the brains knocked out'; a party which lacked 'money, men and enthusiasm'; a party which had a 'social rather than a political identity' that was 'too narrow to become the basis of a party of government'. There was certainly no lack of determination to achieve a different outcome; even Peel was to be found looking towards the day when Sir Robert Inglis would lead 'a real old Tory and Church of England, Protectionist, Protestant party; and Lord Stanley acting in concert with him'.[239]

At the time of Newcastle's death, some of the Peelites were returning to the Conservative fold without the party having abandoned its commitment to some form of Protectionist economic policy, whilst Russell, mindful of the strength of an anti-popery feeling to which the Protectionists, in particular, seemed capable of appealing, was about to enter into a sustained anti-popery campaign, related to his Ecclesiastical Titles Bill.[240] It was unlikely

[236] See 22 Mar. 1847; D.P., 147/14: Newcastle to Stanley, 30 Jan. 1849.
[237] BL, Add. MS 56368, f. 184: Newcastle to Giffard, 16 Feb. 1848.
[238] *The Times,* 30 Jan. 1849; see 22 May 1847; K.D., 22 May 1847; D.P., 147/14: Newcastle to Stanley, 19 May 1847; N.U.M.D., Ne C 8318: Lords Malmesbury, Eglinton and Winton to Newcastle, 1 Sept. 1847.
[239] Gash, *Reaction and Reconstruction*, 154; Gash, 'Beresford', 190; Norman Gash, *The Radical Element in the History of the Conservative Party* (1989), 7.
[240] Machin, 'Prelude to the Ecclesiastical Titles Bill', 293–5.

that the hard-core Peelites – Aberdeen, Cardwell, Gladstone, Graham, Herbert and Lincoln – were any more willing to think in terms of Conservative reunion than Newcastle was. Peel remained consistently 'doubtful of the force of Mutual attraction' between them on financial and commercial measures, whilst Lincoln was in no doubt that he was 'one of the four [Peelites] who have all along been placed out of the pale of forgiveness'.[241] As Stanley commented to R.A. Christopher, in 1849, 'as matters at present stand I see no indication of any fusion among the 2 Sections of Conservatives, nor indeed can there well be any till the question of Free Trade is disposed of one way or another'.[242]

In his own lifetime, Newcastle noted (with increasing regret) reports that his son and heir had 'permitted himself to be drawn into the advocacy of principles, the very opposite of all that he formerly professed & in which he was Carefully & anxiously Educated'.[243] Lincoln had even given serious consideration to standing for Manchester, the citadel of free trade politics and economics, in the 1847 general election.[244] Not least of the reasons why Newcastle was so enamoured of Lord George Bentinck was the painful contrast it offered with events close to home. 'I am as proud & as happy as you can be [he told the duke of Portland] to See <u>two</u> of Your Sons Embarked in the Same glorious cause, the principled Salvation of their Country'.[245] Following Peel's death, in July 1850, Henry Bentinck attempted to affect a reconciliation between Newcastle and Lincoln, mindful of the common perception (to some extent shared by Lincoln himself) that he was the Peelites leader-in-waiting. 'I fancied … [the] prospect of an <u>altered Will</u> and an immediate Seat for the County might hasten Lincolns [*sic*] recantation & that the rest of the scattered Sheep would follow in his wake', he informed Disraeli.[246]

Reconciliation between father and son, ultimately, had nothing to do with political ex-culpation on either side. During Newcastle's final illness, his physician, John Dethick, noted that the duke showed conspicuous 'want of feeling towards his family' and took 'a peculiar pleasure in making every body about him (without exception) feel uncomfortable'. He received news of the death of one of his sons, Lord William Clinton, in September 1850, without apparent emotion.[247] However, after Newcastle's death, on 12 January 1851, Lincoln was gratified to report that 'all estrangements were at an end some time before the last scene and that my poor Father died at peace with all his Family & I hope & believe with all the world'.[248] The comment is indicative of Stanley's statement that all his differences with Bentinck had been 'Entirely removed' before his death, and Gladstone's unsubstantiated observation that 'Peel died at peace with all mankind; even with

---

[241] N.U.M.D., Ne C 11995: Peel to Lincoln, 11 Apr. 1847; Ne C 12226: Lincoln to Ellenborough, 5 Jan. 1847.

[242] D.P., 178/1, pp. 201–3: Stanley to Christopher, 8 Jan. 1849.

[243] See 9 May 1847, 24 Jan. 1849; D.P., 147/14: Newcastle to Stanley, 15 Nov. 1846; 177/1, pp. 161–2: Stanley to Newcastle, 17 Nov. 1846.

[244] See 27 Nov., 5 Dec. 1846; N.U.M.D., Ne C 11870, 11872: Lincoln to F.R. Bonham, 29 Nov., 4 Dec. 1846; Ne C 11937: Herbert to Lincoln, 12 Dec. 1846; Ne C 11990–2, Peel to Lincoln, [Nov.–Dec.] 1846; *The Diaries of Absalom Watkin, A Manchester Man, 1787–1861*, ed. Magdalen Goffin (Stroud, 1993), ch. 29.

[245] N.U.M.D., Pw H 517: Newcastle to Portland, 3 Mar. 1846.

[246] N.U.M.D., Ne C 11698: Lincoln to Gladstone, 14 Oct. 1850; Dep Hughenden, 118/3, ff. 146–7: Bentinck to Disraeli, 20 Aug. 1850.

[247] Dethick's account does not reveal any deathbed reconciliation between Newcastle and Lincoln, although it is otherwise candid on Newcastle's 'coolness & indifference' towards his heir: *Unhappy Reactionary*, 283–6.

[248] N.U.M.D., Ne C 11700: Lincoln to Gladstone, 20 Jan. 1851.

Disraeli'.[249] Lincoln's belief was confirmed by Newcastle's last will and testament, in which he declared that he would 'not name anyone but I die forgiving all that has passed'. But perhaps the greatest irony was that, in looking for a model for the duke's funeral, Lincoln fastened upon one which his father had admired for its simple taste and decency: that of Sir Robert Peel.[250]

## The Manuscript

The Newcastle diaries now form accession Ne 2F/1–8 in the University of Nottingham's Manuscripts and Special Collections, having been deposited by the family in 1966. They were first used by John Martineau in his biography of the fifth duke of Newcastle (published in 1908). He described them as 'eight substantial volumes of handwoven paper handsomely bound in green leather, closely written on every page from beginning to end, and, till near the end, with seldom a day without an entry'.[251] During the First World War, they were deposited for safe keeping in a vault at the National Safe Deposit Company, London. Their whereabouts thereafter is unknown. The upheaval associated with the sale and dispersal of Clumber during the 1930s and 1940s must explain the subsequent 'loss' of the diaries.[252] They were not among the principal deposit of family, estate, personal, and political material made to Nottingham University under the terms of the seventh duke's will in 1955, and their whereabouts were still unknown when John Golby, then engaged in researching the duke's life, tried to locate them in October 1960.[253] Since the rediscovery and deposit of the diaries at the University, they have formed part of the Newcastle of Clumber (Ne C) collection. In 1981 they were accepted by the nation in lieu of estate duty and the University was appointed as their custodian. The extinction of the principal family line of the dukes of Newcastle-under-Lyne followed in 1988.[254]

The diaries are contemporaneously bound volumes of unlined paper; they average 290 pages in length.[255] They were subsequently paginated by archivists in pencil. Although the pagination is not indicated in the present edition, the entries reproduced in '*The Last of the Tories*' are easily located in the original manuscript, as this Table makes clear.

[249]D.P., 178/1, pp. 55–6: Stanley to Newcastle, 24 Sept. 1848; *Disraeli's Reminiscences*, ed. H.M. and Marvin Swartz (1975), 33.

[250]TNA, PROB/11/2147: Will of the 4th duke of Newcastle, proved 14 Feb. 1852; N.U.M.D., Ne C 12430: Lincoln to Cardwell, 5 Nov. 1850. For Newcastle's funeral, see *The Illustrated London News*, 25 Jan. 1851, pp. 62–4; *Nottingham Journal*, 24 Jan. 1851.

[251]N.U.M.D., Ne C 13235–6: John Martineau to Lord Edward Pelham-Clinton, 22, 26 Apr. 1897.

[252]N.U.M.D., Ne 6 EC 1/5/1, Correspondence file relating to the National Safe Deposit Company, 1914–18.

[253]*Notes and Queries*, new ser., vii (1960), 396; John Golby, 'A Great Electioneer and His Motives: The Fourth Duke of Newcastle', *HJ*, viii (1965), 201–18. Golby subsequently incorporated research from the diaries in a book for Routledge and Kegan Paul which was never published: N.A., Tallents MS, DD/TL/5/1/2: correspondence between John Golby and Colonel Hugh Tallents, 1969–70.

[254]N.U.M.D., Ne 6 E 4/149/2/14, *Seventh Report of the Keeper of the Manuscripts, October 1965–September 1967*.

[255]The chronological parameters of the diaries are 27 May 1822–4 (251 pages), 1825–7 (273 pages), 1828–12 Mar. 1831 (329 pages), 12 Mar. 1831–4 (335 pages), 1835–8 (285 pages), 1839–42 (288 pages), 1843–6 (287 pages) and 1847–30 May 1850 (275 pages). Each diary has a number of enclosures, consisting of loose papers and newspaper cuttings, sometimes relating to events covered in the diary with which they are stored, sometimes relating to events covered in other diaries.

| Year | Manuscript reference and word count | Sessional dates for the house of lords |
|------|-------------------------------------|----------------------------------------|
| 1839 | Ne 2F/6/1, pp. 1–74 32,000 words | 5 Feb.– 27 Aug. |
| 1840 | Ne 2F/6/1, pp. 75–147 32,000 words | 16 Jan.–11 Aug. |
| 1841 | Ne 2F/6/1, pp.148–213 29,000 words | 26 Jan.– 22 June 19 Aug.– 7 Oct. |
| 1842 | Ne 2F/6/1, pp. 214–88 32,000 words | 3 Feb.–12 Aug. |
| 1843 | Ne 2F/7/1, pp. 1–78 33,000 words | 2 Feb.–23 Aug. |
| 1844 | Ne 2F/7/1, pp. 79–151 32,000 words | 1 Feb.– 5 Sept. |
| 1845 | Ne 2F/7/1, pp. 152–229 34,000 words | 4 Feb.–9 Aug. |
| 1846 | Ne 2F/7/1, pp. 230–87 25,000 words | 22 Jan.–28 Aug. |
| 1847 | Ne 2F/8/1, pp. 1–86 35,000 words | 19 Jan.–23 July |
| 1848 | Ne 2F/8/1, pp. 87–202 44,000 words | 18 Nov. 1847–5 Sept. 1848 |
| 1849 | Ne 2F/8/1, pp. 203–66 25,000 words | 1 Feb.–1 Aug. |
| 1850 | Ne 2F/8/1, pp. 267–75 3,000 words | 31 Jan.–15 Aug. |

Table: Correlations for the Newcastle diaries reproduced in this Edition.

## Editorial Conventions of Transcription

This edition reproduces some 180,000 words of diary text (about half the total for this period) to the same editorial principles as *Unrepentant Tory*. My intention has been to intrude as little as possible into the content and presentation of Newcastle's writing. The duke had his own idiosyncrasies of style and expression as a diarist, but these rarely prevent an understanding of his meaning. As such, there has been little need to make the text more intelligible by correcting significant errors of syntax, dating or repetition. However, the following conventions have been applied:

*New sentences.* I have substituted a colon for a full stop where a new sentence in the original starts in the lower case.

*Contractions.* I have expanded all contractions (other than the ampersand) and normalised superscript. Subsequent additions to diary entries are enclosed within < >.

*Alterations to the MS.* Newcastle's crossing out of erroneous characters, words and sentences has been indicated in footnotes whilst editorial interventions and elaborations are indicated throughout by their enclosure in square brackets. Parentheses represent original inclusions in the text.

*Dates of entries.* The only editorial additions made without square brackets are the dates of diary entries which are standardised throughout to include date, month, and year. New-castle's usual habit was to write the name and date of the month on the first entry for that month and subsequently to use the short form from '2' to '31' (without month) for succeeding days. Similarly, he only usually wrote the year in the first diary entry of the year.

*Extractions.* The symbol […] represents an editorial omission of material.

*Use of [sic].* Newcastle could vary between 'correct' and 'incorrect' spellings reflexively, but many words are consistently styled in a way we would ourselves recognise, such as 'shew', 'favor', ardor' and 'honor'. Similarly, he varied in his spelling of individual names including O'Connel [O'Connell, with or without the apostrophe], Lansdown [Lansdowne] and Russel [Russell]. I have standardised the use of the apostrophe in O'Connell by silently inserting it where necessary. Otherwise, I have left the majority of spellings unaltered and unnoticed, [sic] being used only where the meaning and grammatical sense or the identity of the individual is highly idiosyncratic. I have indicated the correct word where it would otherwise be unclear.

*Punctuation.* I have retained the duke's original punctuation (more often than not the dash rather than the period or comma) throughout. Single and double quotation marks are as used by Newcastle in the MS. Newcastle's use of the apostrophe and of capital letters could be idiosyncratic (he barely used the capital letter A, for example) and I have retained them as in the original. I have also retained Newcastle's italics and the words he underlined or double-underlined for emphasis (rather than to indicate italics) and the symbols / and = that Newcastle seems to have used (on an irregular basis) as alternatives to the usual forms of punctuation for parentheses and periods.

# THE DIARIES

*1 January 1839.* It Seems but the other day Since I began the last book in 1835 = Time passes quickly on and I begin to find that my years yet to come in the common course of Events may not occupy many more books – However here I am at the commencement of a new years [day] having nearly completed my 54th year, Surrounded with immeasurable & great blessings, & I thank God capable of Enjoying them – These periodical anniversaries call for reflection, uniformly the result is, the deepest gratitude to the Giver of all goodness & fixed determination to Endeavour to the best of my ability to merit in Some degree the immense favors bestowed upon me – By God's blessing I will be a firm upholder of his worship & of that Christianity which as I think is most pure in the Protestant faith held by the Church of England – There is an awful struggle before us, Popery is making Every Effort against us & more successfully than could have been Supposed in these times – the contest will be fierce, but the issue is not doubtful – Popery will Eventually fall & at no very distant day – Enlisted on its Side by the Jesuits are Dissent, infidelity, republicanism, anarchy [,] immorality [,] with all the bad passions & all the worst Spirits of the Country – I am persuaded that all we Suffer from is worked & produced through Jesuitical agency, looking to the End, the Establishment of Popery upon the ruins of Protestantism & deeming as they are wont that the means however detestable are Sanctified by the accomplishment of their purpose – This accursed Legion we now have[1] to fight against, opposed to Such an Enemy, it must be Expected that the contest will be one, as for life or death – it will be dinful & terrific, but in the panoply of God's grace we Shall overcome all difficulties & finally vanquish for His glory & our Supreme happiness – This is my view, in this Spirit I arm for the pending contest, & I am assailed by no doubts of the issue – I Expect that this will be a very Eventful year –

*8 January 1839.* Two days ago news arrived from Ireland that Lord Norbury had been shot at in his own garden & was dangerously wounded by slugs – The accounts today announce his death – He has been murdered by Ribbonmen instigated by the Priests – he himself the most inoffensive creature in the world & an Excellent resident Landlord – but he had given some notices of Ejectment which were absolutely necessary & for this he was doomed to pay the forfeit of his life – This is a horrid Event & is only one of many hundreds occurring weekly –

*13 January 1839.* Nothing new today – Tomorrow I must be off in good time as we are going to Drayton Manor on a visit to Sir Robert & Lady Peel[2] –

*15 January 1839.* This is a very nice house & very complete in all its parts – it is not a large house but it is so arranged as to give it a character & an air of consequence – The corridor is remarkably pretty & handsome, so is the library – the drawing room is rather small, but pretty, cheerful & handsomely done up – The dining room is not very large, but of a good Size and decorated – although there may be faults, yet as a whole Exteriorly & interiorly it is a house not of an ordinary Kind – it was built by the present Sir Robert about 4 or 5 years ago –

[1] have precedes this in the original.
[2] Surrey Record Office, Goulburn MSS, 304/A2/13/1/5: Drayton Manor visitors' book lists Newcastle and his four daughters as visitors at this time.

*16 January 1839.* Rode about today & saw the more distant parts as well as the home disposition of the grounds – The place is Entirely new & only lately laid out – but Even now with the trees growing it gives token of what it will be – I do not at all dislike it though many abuse it for the ugliness of the county – I think it gay & by no means uninteresting –

*17 January 1839.* Out Shooting today for the first time, now above two months – Game abounds, I never saw more – We Sometimes have a batch of politics, & I am happy to perceive that my host's Sentiments as far as I have heard them coincide with mine – I think he will do well for the future –

*18 January 1839.* Out Shooting again today, we made great, too great Slaughter – till at last I would not fire at pheasants. News arrived this morning of the death of the Duke of Buckingham rather unexpectedly – & unfortunately they are not prepared in the County with a Successor to Lord Chandos – Here is another Garter & a Lieutenancy to give away – I have had a very Satisfactory conversation with Sir Robert Peel this Evening & I hope that I may have helped to strengthen his ideas upon many points, Especially upon the corn laws & popery –

*19 January 1839.* Left Drayton this morning after having passed a very interesting & agreeable visit – & I think we all parted with Mutual regrets – One thing I lamented namely that last night I thought that Peel was firmly determined to oppose the alteration or repeal of the Corn laws & I was happy in the belief of his general determination & correct views – This morning after breakfast, having read the Times newspaper, he said, "Duke, here is the Times in favor of repeal of the corn laws" & he went on to remark that he Knew the pulse of the Country & would not have made the declaration if he had not considered it to be the Strongest & most popular Side – His decision was Evidently Shaken & his tone much altered – He appears to have contracted a habit of late years of suiting himself to the times, whilst his proper line would be boldly & nobly to lead public opinion – to moralise & reclaim the nation[3] –

*22 January 1839.* It is Said, that the Duke of Cleveland is to have the vacant Garter & Lord Carrington the Lieutenancy of Bucks –

*25 January 1839.* Nothing new today – Except a denial from authority of the rumour of the Queen's marriage with a Coburg Prince –

*26 January 1839.* Lord John Russell in a letter to his Constituents tells them that he Shall be for a low fixed duty on Corn, & would wish to repeal the present law –

*27 January 1839.* No news of political Events from any quarter – it is Evident that Ministers mean to try to Save themselves by a cry against the Corn laws, which will not Succeed & which I trust we shall only attend to by a Steady Support of the law –

---

[3]BL, Add. MS 40426, ff. 78–83: Newcastle to Peel, 23 Jan. 1839, thanking him for his hospitality and attempting to put him right on the corn laws. Newcastle dismissed the article in *The Times* as 'Gross fallacies mischievously advocated'.

*31 January 1839.* The Duchess of Sutherland is dead by which an Enormous accession to her Son's Enormous wealth will arise & make him the richest man in the Country –

*3 February 1839.* I had intended, if able, to have gone to London today to be present to-morrow at the Duke of Wellingtons dinner preceding the opening of the Session[4] – It is very mortifying to be absent, but I am not well Enough to go today & defer my Journey another day, when I shall be better prepared for it –

*5 February 1839.* […] I did not reach London till $\frac{1}{4}$ past 6 – too late for the opening Speeches in the House of Lords – I took Some hasty refreshment & went down to the House – I was in time to hear Lord Brougham Make the best Speech I Ever heard from him – The plot thickens about the Ministers – Their condition is Suitable & that of the most wretched description –

*6 February 1839.* The conviction of those conversant in Such matters is that a dissolution of Parliament is at hand – I myself can See no reason for its [*sic*] but these people Say it is certain – attended an interesting meeting at Lord Roden's, where Mr M'Gee laid before us proofs of a deep conspiracy in Ireland to Supplant Protestantism by Popery & to Effect their object by Every means in the power of man [–] be it the most basely intriguing or the most barbarously ferocious – Lord Lyndhurst was at the meeting & I think will take up the whole business, if he does – he will be successful & the death warrant of the Papists will be Sealed –

*8 February 1839.* But little of more than passing interest – In the House of Lords tonight, there was Some Sparring – & Lord Durham & his Canadian report were again introduced, but nothing done – Lord Glenelg announced that he had resigned his office of Colonial Secretary; he resigned with regret at such a moment but from necessity, as changes had been made in the Cabinet without his Knowledge & Even as we understood in his own office which he could not Submit to –

*12 February 1839.* Nothing of much consequence, we appear to be in a very negative state – action is repressed & quiescence Seems to be the order of the day – Lord Hardwicke had given notice of motion on the State of the navy for this night but he has been requested to withdraw it – & the reason given to me privately is that Sir James Graham did the great mischief to the navy & Peel reduced the force by a thousand men – So that if these facts were publicly discussed the result would be awkward – besides, a great deal has been done Since last year & the navy as compared with this period of last year is in a very much more Efficient State –

*21 February 1839.* The anti corn Law agitators have been Signally defeated in parliament & out of it – in the Lords, the Duke of Wellington has decidedly out argued his opponents – & in the Commons Peel made a Speech of great power & unanswerable argument – The majority against repeal was immense –

---

[4] N.U.M.D., Ne C 5327: Wellington to Newcastle, 15 Jan. 1839, inviting him to attend the session.

*23 February 1839*. […] It has come out by Lord Melbourne's replies to questions of Lord Londonderry that a Spanish chief of the name of Managoni [José Antonio Muñagorri], who has made himself a third party in Spain has now received all our favorable assistance in hope as Lord Melbourne States that the Experiment may be Successful & may be the means of Settling the discords in that distracted Country – This man it Seems, is repudiated by the Queen's & Don Carlos's parties, & how adding a third party of Extermination is to Settle the discord, it is not very Easy to See – It certainly is a new & most remarkable line for any Nation to adopt & certainly most of all for this which should be distinguished for its honor & good faith –

*27 February 1839*. Lord John Russell has again brought forward his Ecclesiastical bill – it was ably opposed by Sir Robert Inglis, but most unfortunately Suffered by Sir R Peel – it is Evident that he was all through his speech labouring & arguing against his Conviction & Consequently propounding fallacies & urging inconsistencies = I would have given much that he had abandoned this line – it is highly prejudicial to himself, to his friends & to the best interests of his Country – Pride & obstinacy Cause him to Support this line because he founded the [Ecclesiastical] Church Commission which has done all the mischief & because he has before followed the Same course, for Expediency – I am convinced & not from conviction & principle –

*2 March 1839*. after various & numerous refusals, Lord Ebrington has at least been induced to accept the Vice Royalty of Ireland & has been made a Peer for that purpose – The matter has been taken up warmly & most properly in the House of Lords – In a debate on the Tithe question Lord Ebrington stated that he thought the Existence of the Church of England in Ireland was an injury & disgrace – & that he could only assent to the compromise because he Expected that when the tithes were in fewer hands that it would Enable them to ["] raise war against Protestantism with greater Energy & Effect" or Something similar to these words but I think Even more Sternly Expressed – It is contended that anyone who has used these words is unfit to govern Ireland & must create dismay amongst the Protestant population – It is really Shocking to reflect that the Government of the Country is constituting itself the worst Enemy of its Church & Every venerable, Sacred & useful Establishment –

*9 March 1839*. I have no letter from Lord John Russell – He has not Written to me for above 10 days[5] notwithstanding that he has received from me Several very important communications, if this culpable neglect continues I go up to London instantly & lay my complaint & the whole state of affairs before the House of Lords –

*12 March 1839*. […] Lord Durham's pacification has been Effected by Lord Normanby [,] the price of the work displacing Lord Glenelg & placing himself in the Cabinet whence he hopes very shortly so to play his game as to be Prime Minister – The whole has been a vile & disgraceful transaction –

---

[5]N.U.M.D., Ne C 5065: Russell to Newcastle, 23 Feb. 1839, concerning Chartist preparations. Newcastle continued the correspondence in successive weeks: TNA, HO/40/47/13: Newcastle to Russell, 2 Mar. 1839; HO/47/40/41, Newcastle to Russell, 5 Mar. 1839; N.U.M.D., Ne C 5070/1–4: Russell to Newcastle, 11 Mar. 1839. See *Unhappy Reactionary*, 109–15.

*13 March 1839.* [...] Our Queen is becoming deplorably unpopular – & her late treatment of Lady Flora Hastings & Miss Davies [Davys], added to the mean reductions in the Royal household, will tell against her poor thing in a Manner unspeakably [t]o her discredit & disadvantage –

*15 March 1839.* a long, mischievous & tedious debate is drawing on in the House of Commons on Mr Villiers' motion to Repeal the Corn laws – It now appears that <u>all</u> the Ministers are to vote with him, but it is Expected that he will notwithstanding be beaten by 80 or 90 – Nobody but an Enemy to good order or a Selfish & Short Sighted manufacturer desires to injure agriculture – it is therefore Scandalous & disgraceful that the ministers Should Support Such a vile party in the State – But they are capable of any thing vile –

*17 March 1839.* Nothing particular today – The corn debate Still continuing in the House of Commons – In the House of Lords it only lasted one night and the abolitionists found few Supporters there – in the Division 24 for 224 against.[6]

*19 March 1839.* Sir Robert Peel made an admirable Speech on the Corn law question – Yesterday being the 5th will probably be the last day of the debate –

*20 March 1839.* The Corn debate is over at last – Division 192 for Mr Villiers' motion [–] 339 against it – Majority 147 [,] which I think is pretty decisive[7] –

*21 March 1839.* The rumour is, & probably well founded, that Lord John Russell will resign & be Succeeded by Lord Morpeth in Office & as Leader in the House of Commons !!!! Speaker abercrombie to be pick [sic] forked into the House of Lords, Spring Rice to fill the Chair [,] or a portion of it – Sir John Hobhouse (Democrat) also to be pitchforked – probably Lord John Russell also – Maccaulay [sic] to be in the Cabinet – most likely many consequent changes – & I think the Substitution, as Premier, of Lord Normanby for Lord Melbourne – If the Country Swallows [this] they will Swallow any thing –

*23 March 1839.* Lord Radnor has carried his motion for a Committee to Enquire into the State of crime in Ireland[8] – The Enquiry will Embrace a wide field & will no doubt bring to light the Popish conspiracy & all its hideous machinations contrived for the overthrow of the Protestant Church & all the Establishments connected with it – The ministers are in dismay & Commotion & it is thought will resign immediately – They wished not to meet the House of Commons yesterday [,] Not one of their Supporters being present [,] but the Conservatives made a house & Lord John Russell gave notice that immediately after Easter he Should move resolutions declaratory of the approbation of Parliament of the Irish administration Since 1835 – thus Setting the two Houses at variance – It is probably a brutum fulmen[9] – The army Estimates & the Mutiny bill which must be passed before Easter are Still to be moved – There is not a measure or point of business of any Kind that

---

[6]The division was 24 (14 present and ten proxies) to 224 (111 present and 113 proxies).

[7]The division was 197 for and 344 against: majority 147.

[8]On a motion to appoint a select committee, on 21 Mar. 1839, by 63 votes to 58: majority five.

[9]'Meaningless thunderbolt'.

is not in arrear, perplexed, puzzled & Embroiled in Such a manner that the public Service is almost at a complete stand still – & in this Condition[10] another Government Will have to undertake the affairs of the State –

*24 March 1839.* Nothing more has transpired respecting the ministerial intentions. Lord John Russell Signified in his petulant Speech that if the House of Commons should approve [,] that the Same system produced heretofore would be continued by Lord Ebrington, if the Government Should be in a minority, others must be found to conduct the affairs of the Country – Lord Melbourne had Said that as long as he had a majority in the House of Commons [,] So long he would continue Minister – acting upon this declaration, it Should be put to the test immediately after Easter –

*28 March 1839.* […] The affair of Lady Flora Hastings is making a great Stir: if it leads to the Expulsion of all the bad & vicious characters from the Court of our young & virgin Queen it will have done good = but the affair is horrible, nothing Ever was more indecent, disgusting & iniquitous – the Slanderers & principal intriguers – Ladies Tavistock & Portman – must be banished from the Court & I Should think from Society & their disgrace must involve that of the Ministers Who have placed Such people about the Court & have given into Such base & infamous plots & proceedings intended [,] it is Said [,] to drive the Duchess of Kent from the Court –

*29 March 1839.* […] Lord John Russell has postponed his motion on Ireland from the 8[th] to the 15[th]. Evidently to give time to O'Connell to raise the people of Ireland which he is about to try to do all over the Island at the same time – What an infamous tricking & traitorous government is the present – It is a real curse on the Country – My astonishment is that it is tolerated from day to day –

*30 March 1839.* O'Connell is doing all in his power to Excite & raise the Irish people – his Speeches & his letters are atrocious – & Ministers wish not only at this but at all other incendiary Mischiefs – This Country is now like a powder magazine, ready to Explode if a spark is applied – The whole world appears to partake of the Same disquietude which disturbs us – portentous doubtless of the coming Events –

*3 April 1839.* a curious scene took place at the Easter Civic dinner – Lord Normanby & a few ministers were there – Sir Robert Peel, Sir Francis Burdett & others = Lord Normanby's health was received with hisses – Peel's with unconstrained applause – In reply to the Lord Mayor's [Sir Chapman Marshall] remarks, he alluded to the Ministerial Measure for depriving the City of the power over its Police[11] [,] hoped that he should be able to preserve their rights & appealed to them whether in future it would not be advisable for the Citizens to look favourably upon those who wished to maintain & uphold other rights & privileges without imputing to them unworthy motives in doing so – When Sir Francis Burdett's health was given, he at once Sallied forth into the field of politics, abused the

---

[10]~~State~~ precedes this in the original.

[11]The Metropolitan Police Act of 1839 enlarged the reach and powers of the original 1829 legislation.

foreign & domestick [*sic*] policy of Ministers & particularly with respect to Ireland – this in the presence of Lord Normanby was so particular that Lord Normanby rose to Signify that [,] if he proceeded, he must beg to reply – The Lord Mayor then very properly Stopped both Speakers – & gave the attorney General [Sir John Campbell] who stated that Ministers had nothing to do with the Police bill & that in legislating he Should do nothing but what met with the approval of Sir Robert Peel – Was there Ever Such a declaration made before – This has been a fine lesson to the citizens & I hope that they will profit by it –

*4 April 1839.* Mail coaches are being discontinued Every where & by railway Substituted for them. The Glasgow & Halifax mails will Cease, the day after tomorrow – I Shall be Surprised if the regularity of the post be not Seriously affected –

*5 April 1839.* The country is in a general state of Combustion – There are Chartist meetings all over the country – These are not numerously attended & are called "failures" – It is a question with me whether this is policy – at the same time there is what is termed a "Split", disagreement, amongst the leaders which is blazoned forth & we are to be led to Suppose that their plots & agitations are at an End. I believe this to be a feint – the Same as I have always believed O'Connell's assumed dislike to the Chartists & Radicals to be – at this proper time he will ally himself with all the discontented & agitators of the land & endeavour to Strike a great blow – This feigned hostility & Separation Enables Each Section to play its part & pursue its course as the public Supposes harmlessly, because small in numbers, divided in intents & thus checking one another – My opinion is that we Shall Soon be undeceived & that we shall see an union of these parties for a grand struggle –

*9 April 1839.* Parliament meets again today – Lord John Russell will be pressed to name the Specific object of his motion on the 15th – it is by many thought that he will be beaten – Lords Normanby & Durham are caballing together & mean to rally the Radicals around them, put themselves at their head & Endeavour to form a radical administration – Lord Normanby has Evidently had an Eye to the Premiership =

*10 April 1839.* Lord John Russell's mountain has brought forth a mouse – He has announced that his motion on the 15th will be "that it is Expedient to[12] persevere in those principles which have guided the Executive government in[13] Ireland of late years, & which have tended to the Effectual administration of the laws, & the general improvement of that part of the United Kingdom" [.] Weak & attenuated as is this "resolution" from that originally menaced it is thought by many that it will not pass the House – for my part, I fear it will – & these vile & wretched men still Continue our rulers –

*14 April 1839.* Sir Robert Peel has announced his amendment which is very warily & adroitly constructed – it is grounded upon the impropriety of meddling with the undoubted right of the House of Lords to Enquire or legislate by original Measures if it thinks fit –

---

[12]~~that~~ precedes this in the original.

[13]~~of~~ precedes this in the original.

*16 April 1839.* Lord Hastings has written & published a very proper letter to Lord Melbourne, complaining that all justice has been refused by the Court in his Sister's / Lady Flora / case, & calling upon Lord Melbourne to advise the Queen to cleanse the Court of the infamous Set which besets & Surrounds it[14] – Lord Melbourne must do Something or the Queen will Soon learn that the public will not tolerate such a State of things – For myself neither I nor my family will go near the Court whilst the miscreants who infect it remain there –

*17 April 1839.* The Debate of the 15th appears in this day's paper – it is adjourned – Lord John opened with a long republican Speech for so it must be characterised which Enforces that the House of Lords Should be the mere Echo of the House of Commons, & that if it asserts its independence that it Should be overcome by a creation of Peers – & such like arguments – Sir Robert Peel followed & then Spring Rice Chancellor of [the] Exchequer – they occupied the Whole Evening – It appears by the accounts in the papers that the people out of doors took an anxious interest in the question –

*18 April 1839.* […] The debate in the House of Commons is again adjourned – no doubt Every Member of the house who has a tongue will think it necessary to Shew that he has one –

*20 April 1839.* […] The Debate Still drawls on – duller than darkness –

*21 April 1839.* The Ministers have triumphed by a miserable majority of 22 [296–318] –

*26 April 1839.* an opinion prevails that the administration is in a very tottering State & cannot last = I Know not what to Say to it – I cannot think that these people will Ever quit office, if they can by any possibility Keep their places – The Queen too Secures to retain them –

*27 April 1839.* The Duke of Wellington was taken ill a few weeks ago & had an apoplectic fit, which I was not aware of untill now – I have expected his failure & I apprehend it Still, he is greatly altered[15] =

*3 May 1839.* […] alexander, the Emperor of Russia's Eldest Son is arrived – we shall have a reign of foreigners for a time, which is always a nuisance –

*4 May 1839.* […] Dined at the Royal academy – The pictures are the best that I have Ever Seen there – There must be some 40 or 50 that would do honor to any Collection – I Sat next to Lord Conyngham = I found that he had that day quitted his appointment of Chamberlain to the Queen – I Could not learn the cause, but I Collected that the attendance was so grievous, that consistently with his duty to his large family – he could

---

[14] The letter, dated 8 Apr. 1839, was published in *The Times*, 16 Apr. 1839.

[15] At the time of the attack (30 Mar. 1839), Richard Cobden thought it likely that 'the Newcastles in the upper house & the Knatchbulls in the Commons [would be] for seizing the reins' if Wellington died: *The Letters of Richard Cobden. Volume I, 1815–1847*, ed. Anthony Howe (Oxford, 2007), 160–1.

not devote so much time to the Queen – Eight More Peers have been Created & More are yet to be Made – Ministers Seem determined to Stop at nothing – We Shall very Soon have to lament disturbance in the Country – The Queen is despised & disliked – the Ministers Execrated & though resistance is not yet made, yet there are limits to oppression & wrong & they will not be much longer tolerated –

*5 May 1839.* Lord John Russell has written a long letter to his Constituents at Stroud – I have not Seen it, but he opposes the ballot & Suffrage & States that the reform bill should be final[16] –

*6 May 1839.* a long letter from the Duke of Wellington this Morning in which he Enters upon the Subject of creating Peers [.][17] He is of opinion that we should not stir in the matter: notice of it according to him would lead to an Encreased creation & the independence of the H. of Lords would be totally annihilated – another batch is to come out immediately & a third is to follow it – This is truly Shameful & heart Sickening, & for this insult & injury we are told that there is no remedy – I cannot believe that taint Submissive –

The Queen was groaned at & insulted when she passed through this [Portman] Square today on horseback = It is most painful to perceive the discredit & disfavor into which She is unhappily fallen –

a Proclamation against the Chartists came out Yesterday – it is a weak & inefficient document. The papers are full of Chartist aggressions & the plot Seems to be thickening Every where – In Wales lives have been lost, & the people at Llanidloes & Newtown Manifest a very turbulent & diabolical Spirit –

It is Expected that in the House of Commons the division Will be ayes 325 – noes 316 – being only 9 majority for the Ministers on the Jamaica question –

Speaker abercrombie has resigned the Chair – in all probability he is to be pickforked [*sic*] into the House of Lords – Something must Come out of the many changes which are occurring & will occur –

*7 May 1839.* The division took place late this morning in the House of Commons on the Jamaica question, numbers ayes 294 noes 289 – Majority 5 – This was unexpected –

In the afternoon [,] never dreaming of any thing less, I was informed that the Ministers were out – I could not at first believe it – but I found afterwards that it was announced in both houses by the respective Ministers – This is indeed a Joyful as it is, by me, an unlooked for Event = It was Said that various people had been Sent for – but no conservative had been Sent for up to a late hour –

*11 May 1839.* […] The post arrived & brought intelligence that Sir Robert Peel who had been charged by the Queen to form a Ministry after having completed his arrangements had been obliged to resign, as the Queen refused to part with her Court ladies, which was required by Sir Robert. This is a dreadful blow – Sir Robert has been caught in his Enemies'

[16]Lord John Russell, *Letter to the Electors of Stroud: On the Principles of the Reform Act* (1839).
[17]W.P., 2/58/130–1: Newcastle to Wellington, 5 May 1839; N.U.M.D., Ne C 5086/1–2: Wellington to Newcastle, 6 May 1839.

trap – he Should have Known better than to insist upon a point which was Sure to meet with resistance on the part of our obstinate, Spoiled & inexperienced young Queen –

*12 May 1839.* My letters inform me that Lord Normanby [,] as I had always Expected he would be, is Prime Minister [–] Lord Durham to go to Ireland as Lord Lieutenant – Such is the report, but I think he will be Home Secretary – in short an Ultra Radical [administration] is to be formed [,] Parliament to be dissolved & Every misery that can arise to a trampled upon & misruled Nation will be our lot – & we deserve it for our sins & for permitting it –

*15 May 1839.* Sir Robert Peel made his Explanation or rather Statement on the 13th: it contained little more than what we already Knew, & detailed the cause of his failure [,] namely that the Queen granted a change of all the Court gentlemen but Would not permit a change of any of the Ladies – Sir Robert Peel did not propose to remove any under the rank of Ladies of the bed Chamber – Lord John Russell Stated that the Queen had reinstated them in office – a Dissolution must follow – Both Sir Robert Peel & Lord John agreed in the Queen's Expression of deep regret at losing her Ministers – The whole has been a vile Juggle –

*16 May 1839.* On the following Evening [,] Lord Melbourne thought fit to make his statement in the House of Lords – he bungled the thing terribly & Seemed to have been over Excited, of Which the Duke of Wellington took advantage by being calm – It Seems Evident that the whole business of resignation was a trap & a gross fraud – It Seems by Lord Melbourne's Statement that he & his Myrmidons are Still the Queens Ministers & likely to remain So –

*17 May 1839.* Every thing is at a stand Still in London – The Queen at the bidding of her rulers has foiled Sir Robert Peel & can look for no other Ministry than Melbourne & Co. but this Co. as the D. of Wellington Says has brought itself & all the affairs of the Country to a "dead lock" & Evidently is unable Either to advance or to recede – They will resort to every Expedient & try Every trick to maintain themselves in office, but the question is, ["] can they go on under any circumstances; will the Country permit them; have they the means of conducting the affairs of the State any longer [?"] – There can be no doubt that the country is thoroughly sick of them, usque ad nauseam,[18] their own friends Even despise them, & they themselves, it is quite clear, have no confidence in themselves – Still they cling to office as a confirmed drunkard adheres to drincking [*sic*] – Parliament is now adjourned for 10 days at a time when the country is distracted from one End to the other, there is no regular government, no information whatever has been given to the public upon this point, & an indirect allusion is all that we have for believing that the Queen has reinstated the incapable in their Offices – Such a State of things will fearfully tend to the Enquiry, whether a female Should fill the Throne of England –

*27 May 1839.* [...] a strange report prevailed today that the Queen had Sent for the Duke of Wellington & that he had already been with Her Majesty twice & was now gone a 3rd

---

[18]'to the point of nausea'.

time in full dress – When I went to the House of Lords – I saw the Duke come in in full uniform with his star on & I soon after went to him & asked him if (as I hoped) he had been with the Queen he answered ["] no – I have been at the Trinity house all the Morning ["] – this Shews how reports are generated on the Slightest possible foundation –

*29 May 1839.* Went to the House of Lords Expecting that Something Might be Said to me about the Lieutenancy [of Nottinghamshire] as a question had been put the night before last in the House of Commons by Mr Baines to Lord John Russell asking him if I meant to lay the correspondence between me & the Chancellor before the House – Lord John replied that unless required by me or Some one authorised to require it by me that he had no intention of doing So – Nothing Said to me[19] – a long debate about Colonel [John] Prince's Execution of Several american borderers & marauders – called brigands[20] – The Duke of Wellington Spoke but Shewed what inroads age was making upon him – he defended Colonel Prince – repeated his objection to the mode in which the war was carried on in Canada – that if a vote did not grant a large army & large fleet that it would be better to abandon the country & that otherwise the whole country [,] the border in particular [,] would be a prey to the greatest horrors –

*30 May 1839.* The Queen has been very ill received at ascott – but Lord Melbourne [was] hooted & groaned at & was very much insulted = Some said, "ah you may be King now but we will not let you remain So long" –

*31 May 1839.* In the debate brought on by Lord Winchilsea's motion [,] Brougham made a most extraordinary & Effective Speech [–] I think it was the finest I Ever heard from him or any one – He laid Every thing bare to the bone, & Exposed all the faults, all the Shifts, all the misdoings of the present Ministers, they writhed under his galling lash [.] I never heard Such a castigation in finer language, it was a brilliant Effort[21] –

*3 June 1839.* It is believed by Some that Lord Melbourne is desirous of letting in to power the Conservatives – & it is said, I believe upon Lord Melbourne's own statement [,] that on the Saturday after Sir Robert Peel's failure the Cabinet council decided that Lord Melbourne should go to the Queen, represent to her their inability to carry on affairs & their recommendation that Peel Should be called in – Lord Melbourne states that [,] at his interview [,] the Queen flew at him in a perfect fury, declared that She never would give way, that she would not give up her ladies, that she would not have Sir Robert Peel & that if Lord Melbourne would not serve her [,] that she must find Some one Else – Upon this it was decided at the Council that they should go on as they were, & that they should Support the Queen's wishes on the ground of honour & feeling, however contrary to the

---

[19]Newcastle was dismissed from the lord lieutenancy of Nottinghamshire on 30 Apr. 1839 over the disputed nomination of two magistrates to the county bench. See *Unhappy Reactionary*, 115–17; QVJ, 30 Apr. 1839.

[20]On 4 Dec. 1838, some 140 supporters of William Lyon Mackenzie crossed the river from Detroit and, after capturing and burning a nearby militia barracks, took possession of Windsor. They were defeated by 130 militia under Prince. Four of the men were summarily executed by his order.

[21]Hansard, *Lords Debates*, 3rd ser., xlvii, cols 1156–91: 31 May 1839.

general interest – This is Lord Melbourne's private Statement, which is base as concerns the Queen, & in my opinion false altogether = I do not believe a word of it –

*4 June 1839.* There is a belief that a dissolution of Parliament is near at hand – why it should be resorted to I cannot imagine [as] the Ministers must lose greatly by it –

*5 June 1839.* […] The debate of last night upon Sir H. Fleetwood's motion for giving [the] county franchise to £10 householders was totally destructive to the ministers & Radicals – Sir Robert Peel played them off to admiration – I am told that his Manner was as Energetic as his language – I now begin to think that the Ministers cannot in any way continue in Office & a dissolution cannot help but must deprive them of all chance of a Majority.

*6 June 1839.* in the Evening to a party at the Duchess of Gloucester's [at Gloucester House] – The Queen &c were there – as there was dancing the Queen of course figured away in Every dance[22] – She was very <u>glum</u>, ungracious & unamicable & must have given more offence than pleasure to the generality of those present – She is proceeding upon a most unfortunate System & will, if she has not already, Estrange the good will & affections of her Subjects – She would appear from her behaviour to be a stranger to all Kindly feelings –

*7 June 1839.* The news of the day is – that at a Cabinet Council Yesterday, it was decided, that the policy of the cabinet Should be to resist the radicals & Encroachments & make a stand upon Lord John Russell's declaration = that they Should Endeavour to carry on the government, & that there Should be no dissolution of Parliament –
Besides this – The Duke of Wellington has been called in to Settle the differences in the Palace – He has at last accomplished, what no other has been able to attain, that the Duchess of Kent Should give up Sir John Conroy who is to go abroad & no more to Shew his presence in the Palace – This may remove Some Cause of bickerings between the Queen & her Mother & may do some good – at all Events a mischievous & vulgar upstart will be put out of the way –

*10 June 1839.* […] went to see the foundation Walls of the new Parliament houses, the wall to the river is built & is a beautiful piece of masonry – The walls are of aberdeen granite –

*13 June 1839.* a Duel took place this morning between Lord Londonderry & Mr [Henry] Grattan – in consequence of the animadversion of the former upon the atrocious speech of the latter who said that if the Conservatives came into power that the Queen's life would not be Safe & that she would be poisoned before 6 weeks had Elapsed after their Entrance to power – Lord Londonderry termed the libeller "base & infamous" [–][23] this

---

[22] The queen found the ball 'dreadfully hot'. Her four dance partners included Augustus, prince of Saxe-Coburg-Gotha: QVJ, 6 June 1839.

[23] The correspondence is published in J.G. Millingen, *The History of Duelling: Including, Narratives of the Most Remarkable Personal Encounters that Have Taken Place from the Earliest Period to the Present Time* (2 vols, 1841), ii, 355–7.

allegation he would not & did not retract – Mr Grattan fired at him [,] Lord Londonderry fired in the air & Mr Grattan became Satisfied with being called base & infamous – These duels are vile transactions – at the Same time it is difficult to Know how to act, to avoid them –

*15 June 1839.* The debate on the Education question commenced last night [.] Lord Stanley in a most able & Excellent Speech moved that the order in Council be rescinded – a manly & Energetic course worthy of him & of the subject – the debate is adjourned, but it is Expected that the government will have a majority[24] – of 12 –

*16 June 1839.* In the East, as I am informed, there is now a prevailing Expectation that a great Conqueror is to appear & that the Iranian nations are to be converted to Christianity – this is to be found in the Koran & I was referred to [George] Sale's Koran to find the passages which foretell this Event[25] –

*18 June 1839.* We were yesterday invited to a Ball at the Palace – but we have been so Slighted & disrespectfully treated (besides the state of the Court) that I would not go – & thus mark my Sense of the treatment[26] –

*19 June 1839.* It is curious to remark the universal disrepute in Which the present Government is held – it is almost universally Execrated & dreaded – go into any shop in this metropolis & you will hear the present Stagnation of trade attributed to the Government [,] the total want of confidence, the apprehension for the future – the tradesmen Say that if the present Government remains in [,] that there will be Such a crash before the winter as never was Known – & that the panic of former years will be nothing to what that of 1839 will be –

*20 June 1839.* The Ministerial majority on the 2nd Jamaica question is 10 – the majority upon the Education Scheme only 5 – & yet they Keep their places & call themselves a government & will commit immeasurable mischief, though they are totally incapable of good –

*21 June 1839.* Lord amherst is about to marry Lady Plymouth, who is the widow of his deceased wife's Son – The late Lady amherst was [the] widow of Lord Plymouth – Lord amherst had many children by the late Lady amherst & Lady Plymouth was always considered & treated in the family as their daughter = The moral feeling ought to act as a prohibition of Such Connexions: they are destructive of Social order & cut up the Established regulations & relations of Society by the roots –

[24] ~~be beaten by 12~~ precedes this in the original.
[25] Newcastle owned the two-volume edition published in 1836: George Sale, *The Koran, Commonly Called the Alcoran of Mohammed, Translated into English Immediately from the Original Arabic; with Explanatory Notes, Taken from the Most Approved Commentators. A New Edition, in Which the Surats, or Verses, Are, for the First Time, Marked*, N.A., DD/271/1, Catalogue of the Library at Clumber, 1865.
[26] QVJ, 17 June 1839.

*22 June 1839*. Lady Flora Hastings has been dying for the last fortnight [,] the world says of a broken heart, if She Should die her death will be attributed to the Queen – & will do her infinite mischief –

*24 June 1839*. an offer has been made to me to purchase Stone from the Steetley quarry for building the Houses of Parliament on terms of permitting the Government to work the quarry themselves, Exclusively [,] & to pay me a Royalty of 3 halfpence & [*sic*] cubic foot[27] –

*26 June 1839*. Dined today at Lord Mansfield's where the Duke & Duchess of Cambridge & Duchess of Gloucester were present – They much disapprove & in a very proper manner of the Queen's conduct – & lament it – The Duchess of Gloucester told me that the Queen Sees nothing of her family & never did – Her aunts are all strangers to her – It is most unfortunate but the Expression of disapprobation is universal –

*28 June 1839*. a meeting this morning at the Duke of Wellington's, to consider what should be done in the House of Lords on the Jamaica Bill – It was finally agreed not to throw out the Bill, but to alter it materially – Counsell is heard at the bar of the House of Lords, this Evening against the bill & on the 1st it is to be read a Second time – The Duke of Wellington also told us that [,] in a few days [,] he will again call us together to consider what will be best to be done by the House of Lords on the Education question. This is a most material Step – one which is looked for & Expected by [the] whole Country –

*30 June 1839*. I have not heard of any thing new today – The Queen is Supposed to be thinking of going to Windsor to avoid being in the Palace at the time of Lady Flora Hastings' death – it is the custom that a dead body Should not remain in the Palace – if Lady Flora's were to be So removed it might Create an outcry or Something worse – The Queen's absence Would obviate all difficulties –

*1 July 1839*. The House of Lords did not divide on the Jamaican bill tonight, Lord Harewood withdrew his amendment = The Duke of Wellington was warm in language & manner – but his reasons for supporting the bill were not Effective – it is a bad business –

*2 July 1839*. a warm debate upon the Jamaica Bill, we divided for Lord Lyndhurst's amendment to leave out the 1st Clause 149 – against 80 = Lord Melbourne committed himself most Extravagantly – he Solemnly declared that if any body or any power failed to do its duty that he would treat that body as he would the assembly of Jamaica – He afterwards Specified that if the Crown failed to do its duty that he would [*sic*] it should be deposed & the like to either body of the legislature or any one in authority –

We met this morning at the Duke of Wellington's when he Communicated the resolutions which are to be moved tomorrow upon Education by the archbishop of Can-

---

[27] N.U.M.D., Ne C 7790: Charles Barry to Newcastle, 22 June 1839. Newcastle was recommended to accept these terms by one of his legal advisors: Ne C 7791: William Eaton Mousley to Newcastle, 27 June 1839.

terbury who is miserable at having to make a Speech upon the occasion of making the Motion –

*5 July 1839*. Long debate in the House of Lords upon the archbishop of Canterbury's motion to address the Queen for permission to debate the Education measure before appropriating the grant of £30000 – We divided proxies included 229 for [–] 118 against – The House was most intolerably hot & made me quite ill –

*6 July 1839.*[28] Lady Flora Hastings died last night – her death will be laid at the Queen's door & will do her much Mischief –

*10 July 1839*. Lady Flora Hastings' remains were removed from Buckingham Palace Early this morning to Embark for Scotland – The opinion of the Medical gentlemen on the post-mortem Examination was that general disease arising from affection of the liver destroyed her – the womb &c was in a healthy & virgin State – Great pains is taking to raise a cry against the Queen –

*11 July 1839.*[29] […] drove down to the House of Lords where we all assembled previously to Going to Buckingham Palace with the address to the Queen – we all went in our Separate carriages So as to form a grave & important procession, which it certainly was, & must have produced a considerable Effect – the day was fine & there was a considerable concourse of people, most of whom cheered us as we passed, whilst Some hissed – we were ushered into the Throne room, where the Lord Chancellor read the resolutions, after which the Queen read her answer – which was certainly most ungracious & improper – It was in Effect, ["] You have no occasion to interfere I shall & will do as I like ["] – I am confident that the answer will give great displeasure throughout the Country – about 100 Peers went up with the address =

In the Evening, though much to my inconvenience [,] I went to the House of Lords, being Summoned on a certain division on the Prisons bill – To our great Surprise [,] instead of dividing [,] the Duke of Wellington Said he not only approved of the bill, but in his opinion it did not go far Enough – There was nothing more to be done than tristé recedare[30] – It is Wretched work thus to be led & thus to be fooled –

*12 July 1839*. The Ministers were Extremely ill received yesterday, they were violently & loudly groaned & hissed as they proceeded to the Palace – But all this is to no purpose, the Queen supports them & they will Keep their places though hated & despised by all – I was told today that the Duchess of Kent has Just appointed two ladies from the wrong

[28] K.D., 6 July 1839, 'Dined Duke of Newcastle'. Also present were the Kinnouls, Lord Falmouth, Sir George Clark, Lady Emily Foley, and Newcastle's children.
[29] *Gladstone Diaries*, ii, 613, 11 July 1839, for a meeting between Gladstone and Newcastle on Newark election affairs.
[30] 'triste recedere' – 'to withdraw with sadness'. A possible source is *Historia Augusta*, a set of late antique biographies of the later Caesars thought to be modelled on Suetonius's *De vita Caesarum*. In chapter 16 of the 'Life of Hadrian', the following appears: 'Et cum ipse auctor esset, ut multi ab eo tristes recederent, dicebat se graviter ferre, si quem tristem videret' – 'And, while it was by his [Hadrian's] own agency that many left him in sorrow, he used to say that it was hard for him to see anyone sad'.

Side of the question – The daughters of Lords Zetland & Suffolk – a sure proof of what her opinions are –

*13 July 1839.* Went to the tilting ground to see the practice for the Tournament which is to be given towards the end of the next month at Eglinton Castle – I never in my life Saw a more ludicrous Exhibition – The Knights for the most part Could neither ride or tilt, tumbled about most ingloriously – after running at the figure on wheels for Sometime, it was announce[d] – that Some of the Knights were to run at Each other – after a time out came Lord Eglinton in gilt armour fully caparisoned – then Lord alford – they rode at Each other for Sometime in the most burlesque manner imaginable – like men in the dark or at blind man's buff – their horses unmanagible [*sic*] & their lances still more so – if their horses jirked [*sic*] them at all their lances broke which was inexpressibly comic, the Knight riding about with his drooping lance the End hanging by a piece of paper – The lances had been Sawed nearly through so that they Should break at a touch – Then Came Mr Gage & Lord Glenlyon – Mr Gage's horse never would Stir, Lord Glenlyon's rushing up at full Speed & meeting nothing, the rider imagining that he had met his antagonist who never appeared – Whips & all sorts of persuasive Stimulants were applied but to no avail – The horse at last severed from the lists & in the Effort to Keep his Seat the lance doubled itself up & completed the Scene amidst the roars of the assembled multitude – The case Seemed to be that the Knights when their visors were down where wholly in the dark & Knew not where they were going: there must have been Some mistake here, for if Knights of old Could See no more than these Knights of mimicry they could not have been very formidable antagonists – after this wretched Exhibition of their prowess, the Eglinton tournament will not Excite any great Expectation & will be at a discount I Should imagine –

*15 July 1839.* all the accounts that I learn from Every one in the inferior & middle classes, as well as my own observation [,] lead me to Know & believe that our domestic Condition now is one of fearful danger – combination dissatisfaction & rebellion are the impulses which prevail among the lower orders – & if time is allowed the conspirators will Eventually deluge the country with blood & devastation –

*16 July 1839.* Riots at Birmingham[31] – expected riots of a Serious nature at Newcastle & Several other places –

*19 July 1839.* The insurrectionary manifestations of the disaffected all over the Country are Every day recorded – impunity invites audacity, & certainly nothing can Exceed the licence of the mob orators & mob writers –

*20 July 1839.* attended a large meeting at the D. of Wellingtons today [–] the theme was Irish Corporations – The Duke's recommendation was to pass the bill which he called a bad bill, but to make certain alterations in Committee. My opinion is that the bill should be rejected, we have Sufficient Evidence of the mischief of the modern & newly fangled

---

[31] N.U.M.D., Ne C 5092: Newcastle has marked a copy of *The Standard* for 17 July 1839 with a speech of Lord Melbourne discussing the Birmingham Riots and the magistracy in the house of lords on 16 July 1839.

Corporations & if proof Were Wanting Birmingham Would now Supply it – if Eternal agitation & popular Election be bad for England [,] what must it be for Ireland, leaving out of consideration the flagitious injustice of the measure, & the certain deliverance of all the towns into the hands of the Papists, the inevitable ruin of Ireland, & the Scandalous Sacrifice of the Protestant cause – The policy of our Leaders is one of lamentable Error –

*21 July 1839.* I have heard today that Lord John Russell has resigned Stating that he can carry on business no longer – There was some vote of the House of Commons last night / Saturday / relative to the poor Law in which the Ministers were in a minority & the resignation is Supposed to be in consequence of this vote[32] – it is added that two Ladies of the Bedchamber Ladies Tavistock & Portman have resigned their situations, I confess to myself that I Entirely doubt this report –

*22 July 1839.* I do not hear that there is any truth in the report of Yesterday – The reports of the Situation of the Country on all Sides is most lamentable = The notion now is to burn & destroy & this is the prevailing threat of the miscreants –

*23 July 1839.* [...] Riots of a serious nature have broken out at Newcastle [–] the authorities have behaved well & for the present perhaps mischief may have been prevented –

The Irish corporations bill was debated last night – I could not have voted for the bill, nor with Lord Roden who was for the Extinction of all corporations[33] – I Could not & would not vote for the Extinction of the old & present Corporations – it would be an act of gross injustice & oppression, & of glaring impolicy – With the recent flagitious conduct of new corporations before our Eyes [,] we may well pause before we give Such pestilences to Ireland –

*25 July 1839.* I went down to the House of Lords meaning to ask Some questions of the Lord Chancellor [Cottenham] respecting Notts Magistrates but I found that it would not be prudent to put them untill I was better prepared[34] = I am Endeavouring to acquire a full Knowledge of Circumstances & if I obtain them I shall tomorrow draw my Shaft – The Chancellor tells me that if I mention the Subject he will read our correspondence to the House = as he held out this threat I was the more sorry to leave the house without doing anything –

---

[32] George Darby's motion enabling guardians to relieve people who had married before the passing of the Poor Law Amendment Act passed by 69–49 votes on 20 July 1839.

[33] The motion to read the Bill a second time passed by 59–8 votes: majority 51.

[34] N.U.M.D., Ne C 5096/2: Notes for a parliamentary speech by Newcastle. 'Since it has pleased the Lord Chancellor to deviate from the System hitherto pursued by his predecessors of being guided in his Nomination of Magistrates by the recommendations of the Lieutenants of Counties, it is Evident that the danger must be great if the appointments now made are not watched with a Lynx-like Vigilance. By taking upon himself to Select & make the appointments – the learned Lord has thrown upon himself the whole weight & responsibility of those appointments. We have seen what deep [,] Nefarious & fearful mischief have arisen from the appointments at Birmingham made for party purposes & which have produced Such deplorable results – My wish is to avert fresh miseries from the County in which I principally reside – I have been informed that appointments in Nottinghamshire since My Dismissal are very questionable'.

*26 July 1839.* Upon Enquiry I found that no appointment of Magistrates had been made Since I left the Office of [Lord] Lieutenant & therefore I had nothing to do but to Explain to the Lord Chancellor how the matter Stood & that as the Supposed Cause of Complaint did not Exist I had no remarks to make – I at the Same time intimated to him that if he desired to read the correspondence to the House, that I had no objection whatever & would give him the opportunity if he wished it – He replied that he Should only have read the correspondence as his vindication[35] – I told him that I had already given directions for publishing the correspondence in the County paper[36] – He assures me that no other appointments had taken place & hoped that I was Satisfied – I replied in the affirmative & here the matter Ended –

*2 August 1839.* It appears that it is from a determination to Stop the Sale of opium that the Chinese Shut up all the English Merchants & put an End to the trade by Seising all the Stock in their warehouses amounting in Value to about £2,000,000 – a most Serious loss to the trade, but I think merited –

*16 August 1839.* The Chartists are meeting in Every direction all over the Kingdom – nothing will stop them but defeat & Slaughter of hundreds of these infatuated & misguided but not less mischievous people –

*29 August 1839.* […] Parliament was prorogued yesterday by the Queen – The Speech is rather a good one – & its contents are favorable – It tells us that the 5 Powers still remain united, that by their means Holland & Belgium have been restored to a friendly state, that by the Same means the affairs of the Levant will be Settled & the integrity of the Ottoman Empire preserved – allusion is made to the Slave trade [,] the fisheries between France & England, Some other minor matters & the internal State of the country –

*31 August 1839.* The army in India has nearly accomplished its objects [.] Shah Soojah has been replaced upon the Throne at Candahar & the army was then to move upon Cabul – It had met with no opposition [.] The climate & length of march had destroyed Some men, but the affgans who were thought to be warlike & courageous have offered no resistance – They are not indisposed towards us, but criticise our proceedings with manly freedom –

*2 September 1839.* The newspapers are full of the Tournament at Eglinton Castle & the dinner of the Cinque Ports people to the Duke of Wellington – The former was marred by torrents of rain which Soused [*sic*] this Seat of folly most unceremoniously – The latter was not Enhanced by the presence of Lord Brougham who was chosen to give the Duke's health in a speech of hyperbolical Eulogy & gross flattery – It is really very distasteful to See this man coddled & petted as if he were the fittest & most valuable friend in the world = I feel Sure that one man, that is Lord Guilford, was absent on that account, who would

---

[35] N.U.M.D., Ne C 5095: Lord Cottenham to Newcastle, 21 July 1839.

[36] N.U.M.D., Ne C 5094: Newcastle to [John Hicklin], editor of the *Nottingham Journal*, 20 July 1839; see Appendix A.

otherwise have been at the Festival – but he is too honest & feels too highly to Countenance what he thinks wrong & inconsistent –

*9 September 1839.*[37] Many changes have Just taken place in the Government – Lord John Russell goes to the Colonies & Lord Normanby takes the Home [Office], where He will Endeavour to do much mischief, Shiel [*sic*], Wyse & O'Ferral, three papists [,] are appointed to Situations in the board of Control, Treasury & admiralty & Baring is made Chancellor of the Exchequer in the room of Spring Rice, pitchforked into the Lords, as Lord Mount Eagle ! Poulett Thompson is transmuted from the board of Trade to Chief government in Canada! a most preposterous & despicable appointment – Sir John Colburn [Colborne] who has done Every thing for Canada is recalled & Sir Richard Jackson, appointed to succeed him as Commander in Chief –

*25 September 1839.* The news from India is not good – There will be Some disaster there, I fear – Our troops are suffering from the greatest privations – Subsistence is most difficult & the Natives are beginning to Shew hostility – affairs look very ill all over the world as well as at home –

O'Connell is said to have had a paralytic Stroke –

*26 September 1839.* Tremendous floods in Scotland – of course destroying & damaging the Crops, as well as houses & bridges – It Seems destined that we shall suffer great misery from a Scarcity of corn bringing with it all the calamities which befall a nation under Such circumstances –

*28 September 1839.* Don Carlos is now Safe in France & a considerable portion of his late army has taken shelter there also – His cause Can Scarcely be upheld now in Spain, although [Ramón] Cabrera & Some others Still hold out & declare that they will not yield =

The affairs of the East are now, & will be, henceforth of the deepest interest – in all probability these affairs which are now assuming Such an active character are to continue so untill the prophecies are fulfilled –

*15 October 1839.* It is Said that Parliament is to be assembled in November to deliberate upon the Queen's marriage to one of the Coburgs – This family is so distasteful to the Country & however good the youth may be the match will not go down & will cause much opposition & general discontent & dissatisfaction –

*16 October 1839.* Foreign affairs remain in the Same unsettled & mysterious state – Russia is intriguing deeply with the Porte & against us – austria is with us alone – France is a traiterous [*sic*] ally, she is pursuing her own Selfish views apart from & in fact against us – No news from asia or its Extraordinary Nation China –

[37] The entry is dated 8 Sept. but is clearly 9 Sept.

*25 October 1839.* The Season is rather productive of deaths. The Duke of Bedford is just dead of apoplexy [–] another Garter to be given away by these miscreants – Several other titled & untitled persons have also dropped off.

*26 October 1839.* Notwithstanding the retirement of Don Carlos, who remains a detener[38] in France, Some of the Carlist leaders Still hold out & refuse to yield, Cabrera is one – in Some engagements lately these people have been Successful against the Queens troops – great cruelties have been Committed on both sides – This [*sic* – these] monsters have no bowels of Compassion or the Commonest feelings of humanity –

   In the East all is pregnant with Events, but as yet but little is Known –

*27 October 1839.* another Duke is dead – The Duke of argyll, died Suddenly in Scotland, also of apoplexy – a place, Lord Steward, about the Court will be vacated –

*31 October 1839.* The movements & assurance of the Papists now very generally attract public attention – The public mind is roused [,] a thing which when no one Else would or did, I attempted [,] but then without much active Effect, although I verily believe that the Seeds were Sown then, which now have taken root & attained a vigorous & rapidly Encreasing growth – This to me is a matter of inward congratulation, for I myself am persuaded of the fact which under God I undertook to Establish –

*2 November 1839.* News arrived from India of a highly favorable nature – our army has continued to advance uninterruptedly – it has taken Caboul & Every other important place but Ghazare held out & shewed a determination to Defend its works – it was attacked, the garrison made a gallant defence, but after battering in breach our Troops Entered & Speedily gained possession of the place, with the loss of only about 100 men – Dort Mahommed Subsequently Endeavoured to make a rally & to attempt annoyance, but his troops became panic stricken & all deserted him but about 300 men – & thus, as it is Said, the War is Ended & we have gained quiet possession of all for which we contended – & have Established more than Ever the Supremacy of our rule by the invincibility of the British arms – I always thought that measures were well taken & that there was a reasonable cause to expect Success – but others Such as the Duke of Wellington & many able Officers thought differently & I therefore considered my opinion as valueless –

*7 November 1839.* Rioting at Newport in Glamorganshire – The Chartists mustered in large numbers = the Soldiers were called out & dispersed them – many of the Chartists were Killed, Some of the Soldiers, the Mayor & others wounded =

*9 November 1839.* The rioters in the South of Wales have not renewed their outrages – but apparently meditate other designs – their leader [John] Frost is apprehended & is to be tried for high Treason –

*10 November 1839.* Nothing of much consequence – It is said that Lord Cooper [Cowper] is to be the Steward of the household – Sir John Campbell Chancellor in Ireland – [Robert]

---

[38] 'à detener' – 'to hold'.

Rolfe a Judge – [Thomas] Wilde Solicitor General & if so he will be opposed & I trust beaten at Newark[39] –

*14 November 1839.* The reception of the Ministers at Guildhall on Lord Mayor's day was So loudly & mercilessly Expressed that it was quite pitiable – Lord Melbourne when his health was given Was hissed & groaned tumultuously & on rising to Speak Was assailed with deafening Sounds of bad omen – He could not obtain a hearing & received an additional proof of public opinion of his deserts –

*17 November 1839.* The bad spirit manifested in Monmouthshire & Glamorgan's [*sic*] has been checked but not allayed = Fresh riots are apprehended & things wear a threatening aspect in that quarter as Elsewhere.

*20 November 1839* […] We arrived at Lichfield on 20th November at $\frac{1}{2}$ past 1 – I there found a letter from Sir Robert Peel[40] telling me that he was obliged the day before yesterday to go to Gapsall [Gopsall] to obey his promise to wait upon Queen adelaide there but that he should be back on tomorrow morning & Entreating that We would go on to Drayton Manor & Stay till his return, this invitation was to [*sic* – so] very Kindly & heartily made in Which Lady Peel Joined that I determined to go to Drayton & here I am in possession of another man's house in his absence but fortunately we found Mr [William] Holmes here who was left under Similar circumstances[41] –

*21 November 1839.* When I came down to breakfast this morning Mr Holmes told me that the Duke of Wellington had had another Seisure & that he had remained Speechless for Some time – also that Summons had been Sent out calling the Privy Council together on the 23rd when the intended marriage of the Queen with Prince albert will be announced to them –
  about 12 Sir Robert [,] Lady & Miss [Julia] Peel returned from Gapsall, he informed me that the Duke of Wellington was not so ill as represented, that it was not paralysis but the Effects of Stomach & indigestion – & that the Duke was much better & about again – The medical men then at Walmer Castle had given him brandy & water & did not bleed him & in short treated the case as one of Exhaustion, for he had had a bad cold & had starved himself for it & feeling himself better on that day had ridden a long way [,] I believe out hunting, & that when he came home he fainted – & on this account the simple remedies brandy[42] & water, feet in hot water & going to bed were applied & had been Successful – The illness of such a man has naturally occasioned an Extreme Sensation –

---

[39]See *Unhappy Reactionary*, 121–2 and Appendix A. The position of Lord Steward went to William Hay, 18th earl of Erroll.

[40]BL, Add. MS, 40427, ff. 235–7: Newcastle to Peel, 17 Nov. 1839. No reply has been traced.

[41]Surrey Record Office, 304/A2/13/1/6: Drayton Manor visitors' book, shows Newcastle and Lord William Clinton were at Drayton Manor from 20 to 23 Nov. and William Holmes was present from 15 to 23 Nov. 1839. See N.U.M.D., Ne C 5695–8: for correspondence between Newcastle and Lady Peel (7 to 22 Dec. 1839) in which Newcastle raised the prospect of a marriage between Lord William Clinton and Miss Julia Peel.

[42]~~applied~~ precedes this in the original.

*22 November 1839.* The accounts from Walmer are by no means favorable. The Duke of Wellington has been blooded & is not easy or better – he continues Weak also or rather loses Strength – which looks ill & my fear is that we shall Soon hear of his death =

a large dinner here today to the Yeomanry who escorted Queen adelaide when she was here, it was a very proper thing to do & the dinner went off very well – Colonel Horne [Thorn] Commanding at Birmingham was here & he Says that chartism is on the advance – & that their designs are of the worst & most diabolical description – Such as their plan for murdering all the policemen whilst they are on their walks – the Same by the centinels – & then for general conflagration, murder, & rebellion –

Sir Robert Peel goes to London tomorrow morning to attend the Council & will afterwards return here – 22 hours will Suffice to accomplish this – a thing perfectly incredible 20 or Even 10 years ago – The meeting of the Privy Council is to announce to it the Queen's intended marriage to Prince albert of Saxe Coburg –

*23 November 1839.* […] I left Drayton Manor for Tamworth where we arrived at 11 o'clock – it is a rail road Station & we Expected to Set out immediately for Derby & Nottingham [.] We did not however Start before 12 o'clock & arrived at Nottingham 10 minutes past 2 – Having things to do at Nottingham we did not leave it till a little after 4 & arrived here, at Clumber, at 7 –

*26 November 1839.* […] Several new Dukes are to be made it is Said. Lansdown [,] Westminster, anglesea & O mercy ! Normanby – !!! then L<u>d</u> auckland an Earl & Sirs [John] Keane & [John] Colburn Peers which they deserve –

The Queen announced her Marriage in a faltering Voice & with an awkwardness which she has not yet Exhibited – it gives no pleasure & created no interest whatever – The Ministers in going to the Palace were hissed & groaned, without mercy – The Duke of Wellington was at the Council to the surprise of Every body –

*27 November 1839.* The Houses of Parliament building Commissioners are at Worksop, also the builders Messrs Grissell & Peto – they are Examining the Steetley quarry, but it is decided that the stone from thence is only to be used in the inside of the building, the Exterior is to be Either of austen or Mansfield stone – the terms which I have offered are £130 rent, if they get more than $\frac{1}{2}$ an acre to pay for it – a lease for 7 years –

*29 November 1839.* Mohammed ali has at length agreed to restore the Turkish fleet – This is a great point gained, it shews that we still possess influence both in Egypt & in Turkey –

*30 November 1839.* The Sultan is giving new laws to his Country, fiscal as well as political & which are intended to render Justice & invest the people with civil rights – they are said to be very well drawn up & well fitted for their purpose –

*1 December 1839.* The Protestant part of the Community is animadverting Severely upon the omission in the Queen's Communication to the Privy Council of her intended marriage, of all Mention of her intended Prince albert of Coburg being a Protestant – it will no doubt occasion a good deal of remark when Parliament meets, which the papers say will be Early in January – though I am inclined to think that it will not be before February –

*8 December 1839.* a fleet is fitting out to reinforce admiral [Thomas] Maitland, & to act against China, to chastise them & redress their ill treatment of our Merchants – The Chinese government was right to prevent the trade in opium but it was not Justified in its treatment of our people –

*12 December 1839.* The Special commission at Monmouth is opened & true bills have been found for High treason against [John] Frost & many others – Parliament is fixed to Meet on the 16th January –

*13 December 1839.* […] The defalcation on the Post office receipts in London, by the new System & rate of postage [,] is on an average £600 a day & has been lately at the rate of £900 a day – The loss by the new system will be prodigious & must be corrected as Soon as Parliament meets –

It is Said & thought that Parliament will be dissolved almost immediately after the meeting – & that a change of Ministers is inevitable –

Lord Palmerston has sent in a String of grievances to the French Government – This is miserable work, he has avoided noticing the Evils as they have arisen, as was his duty – but has delayed it to the last & to a period when he Knows that he is about to quit office – The consequence will be that all the burden of the quarrel or difference will be thrown upon his Successor – This conduct is Eminently worthy of the Shabbies.

*14 December 1839.* I have been told & positively assured that Lord Ludlow, on hearing that the present Duke of Bedford had been left in rather Embarassed [*sic*] circumstances by the manner in which his father had disposed of his property, had informed the Duke that he wished to present him with £100,000 as a free gift to relieve his Embarassments [*sic*] – This is giving with a liberal hand indeed –

It is Said that an Enormous treasure has been recently discovered under one of the Bastions' of Bhurtpoor, [sic – Bhuratpore] & that the army which took the place will receive a large Sum of prize money, it is Supposed that Lord Combermere's Share will amount to not less than £500,000 – if this be true it will be windfall to many, as in Combermere's case, making him one of the Wealthiest men in the Country –

*16 December 1839.* I was informed today of a very curious & interesting fact namely, that the King of Prussia [Frederick William III] had written to the Bishop of London [Charles Blomfield], inviting him over to Prussia & Earnestly Entreating him to Come over to Consecrate Some Bishops for him = The Prussian Church is Presbyterian – The Bishop is considering whether he can & ought to accept the invitation – I hope he will[43] –

*21 December 1839.* The misgovernment & despicable imbecility & dishonesty of the Ministers is now so universally acknowledged & resented,[44] that expressions of dissatisfaction & impeachment issue from all parts of the Empire in language which cannot be misunder-

[43]See N.U.M.D., Ne C 5417: Gladstone to Newcastle, 23 Dec. 1839.

[44]~~slope~~ precedes this in the original.

stood. Their doom I trust is Sealed & I pray for a rule which by Justice & truth Shall restore & Establish this dear Nation on a foundation which no power of man Can Shake –

*22 December 1839.* It is generally understood that the Queen is much in debt – if this be So, it will add greatly to her present general unpopularity as She has £10,000 a year more than the late [King William IV] & his Queen [Adelaide] had [,] So that a grant to pay these debts, will be highly unpalatable to the Nation –

*27 December 1839.* Some apprehension appears to be Entertained that a general rising of the Chartists will be attempted before long – The times are favorable to such an undertaking – great distress prevails Every where – general dissatisfaction, distrust & uneasiness form a distinguishing feature of our present condition –

*31 December 1839.* […] Here Ends a very Eventful year – chequered with good & Evil – immense mischief has been accomplished but then the open demonstration of Everything bad has roused the Nation to a Stronger & better Sense of its duty & now the public mind is So imbued with a right feeling & the Seeds of future good are So well Sown that they must spring up to maturity & bring forth a rich harvest to our great gain & Eventual happiness [.]

*1 January 1840.* Here I am, commencing another page of My Journal for another year – I humbly & heartily return my fervent thanks to almighty God for all his mercies & for all the blessings which he has bountifully bestowed upon me – May I be Enabled to serve Him with the Zeal & faithfulness which is required of me, & may He permit me to Serve my family & my Country with an Efficiency Equal to my ardent aspiration – In this Spirit I begin the year & in the Same may I <u>End it</u> – If I mistake not this will be a year of great & Extraordinary trials & a good conscience & a firm reliance upon God's mercy will be more than Ever requisite to withstand the Eventful occurrences which the period may produce –

*8 January 1840.* The trials at Newport are going on & create great interest through the Country: I shall not be Surprised if all the rebels Escape Without much punishment –

*15 January 1840.* [To London] I reached my house at about 9 = had Some tea & Something to Eat & immediately Went down to the Duke of Wellington's after having dressed, I arrived as the desert [*sic*] was nearly finished [.] Sat about $\frac{1}{4}$ of an hour at table [,] learned what the Duke had Said & we then broke up – There is to be no amendment as it is thought to be unwise to carry an amendment in the Lords where it will not Even be debated in the Commons as they will be Engaged with the notable case of privilege on the Stockdale trial – There Will be nothing therefore for us to do & I shall return to Clumber in two days –

*16 January 1840.* The Queen Went down in person to Open the Parliament, although news of her aunt's death ([Princess Elizabeth] Landgravine of Hesse Homberg) arrived only yes-terday – The Speech States that a marriage With Prince albert of Saxe Coburg is intended & begs that a proper provision may be made for him, then touches Slightly on foreign politics = the war in India, Events in China, Canada &c [,] recommends attention to the Irish Corporations & the prosecution of the Measures recommended by the Ecclesiastical

Commissioners – laments the prevailing distress & Embarassments [*sic*] in trade – States that insubordination has manifested itself by Open Violence & concludes by relying upon the Law & the right Energies of the people to restore & maintain Order –

The Duke of Somerset moved the address [&] Lord Seaford in a good Speech Seconded it – then the Duke of Wellington rose & to my Surprise objected to the omission of the word Protestant in naming the Prince the intended Consort of the Queen – he Concluded by moving as an amendment that the word Protestant Should be inserted before Prince in the address to the Queen – Lord Melbourne objected & declared the insertion of the Word to be Wholly Unnecessary & resisted the amendment – a debate Ensued but finally Lord Melbourne gave in & "Protestant" Prince now stands part of the address – this move was quite unexpected & is a good one, it will give great Satisfaction in the Country =

The Duke of Cambridge though the news of his Sister's death arrived only yesterday, thought fit to Stifle his fraternal feelings & Made a little Speech hoping for the Queen's happiness & laudatory of the young Prince – of Whose good character he bore rather high testimony –

at Sir Robert Peels' this morning it was determined that on Tuesday Week 28th a motion Shall be made expressive of a want of confidence in the Ministers – His language was Warlike & Spirited [–] this will all do & will give great Satisfaction to the Country at large – Who can have confidence in Such Ministers, who can Entertain for them any other feeling than that of infinite Contempt [?] –

*17 January 1840.* It Seems that the Duke of Wellington's amendment of yesterday was not only a surprise to us, but to Every one in the House of Commons. Sir Robert Peel himself Knew nothing of it: So little, that on the fact being reported to him [,] he Sent a friend to the House of Lords to Enquire if it was true – I heard last night that it was Lord Lyndhurst's doing, I happened to meet him today & taxed him With the authorship Which he did not attempt to deny = He Said that he mentioned it to the Duke in the library & that this was the birth, & parentage of the production – It must be owned that it is a very curious circumstance & Shews a want of Concert Which is not very propitious –

*18 January 1840.* The House of Commons is more & more involved in the abyss of privilege in the case of [John Joseph] Stockdale – he was committed to Custody yesterday – On the day after tomorrow the Sheriffs are to be had up to the bar & one does not See where it is [to] stop untill the Judges are Summoned there also – It is thought that the House will be beaten – it will be a miracle if it get out of the scrape with honor –

In the debate on Sir John Buller's motion it is Calculated that at the worst Ministers will only have a Majority of 10 – which on a question of want of confidence will be more than Equal to a defeat –

*26 January 1840.* Lord John Russell has proposed £50000 as the allowance to Prince albert – no alteration to take place if he Survives the Queen – it is a vast deal too much [– £] 20 or 25000 a year Would be more than Sufficient & a jointure of [£] 30, 40, or Even £50000 a year & that only in case he Should have Children by the Queen –

*29 January 1840.* a most unexpected division has taken place in the House of Commons on the debate upon the Provision for Prince albert – Colonel [Charles] Sibthorp moved the Substitution of £30,000 instead of [£] 50,000, & the motion Was carried by a majority [of] 104 [262–158] – Such a result will puzzle our Serpent Ministers very greatly & moreover it will inspire the Queen with Some respect for us, She will begin to discover that we are of Some Consequence & not to be So despised as hitherto we have been. In the House of Lords the Duke of Wellington opposed the Clause in Prince albert's Nationalisation Bill which gives him the precedence of the Blood Royal & places him next to the Sovereign – So intent is the Duke in his opposition to this clause that Peers are called up to London to vote in Committee on the Bill, when it will be Moved to Expunge the clause –

*30 January 1840.* The debate on the 28th, as I am informed, was miserably conducted on our Side, all is very flat & our people not in good Spirits –

*31 January 1840.* Nothing new – The debate was more interesting on the 29th: Sir James Graham, as he always does, made an admirable Speech –

*2 February 1840.* The debate upon Sir John Buller's motion has at last terminated in a declaration by the House of Commons by a majority of 21 that it has confidence in Ministers – an unenviable majority when it is considered how many placemen have voted upon their own competency – the numbers were 308, & 287 – Sir Robert Peel made a noble Speech on the last day = I could only regret that he Said what he did respecting dissenters &[45] Roman Catholics – His Speech was wise as it was noble [,] manly & statesmanlike, & must produce a great Effect –

*5 February 1840.* a debate was Expected in the House of Lords in Committee upon Prince albert's Naturalisation bill – when the Duke of Wellington was to move the Extinction of the clause to give him precedence next to the Queen. Lord Melbourne however gave way & Signified that the clause would be withdrawn = It appeared however in conversation that the Royal prerogative was likely to be Exercised to Effect what would be denied by act of Parliament –

*6 February 1840.* The horrid System & doctrines of Socialism of which Robert Owen is the head has been brought under the notice of the House of Lords by the Bishop of Exeter [Henry Phillpotts] who has most fully exposed the horrors of their doctrine – Their blasphemies & immorality are too villainous to repeat, but yet the Ministers, Melbourne [,] Normanby & Co. – do all in their power to Shield the Wretches who are maintaining & propagating Such Scandalous & horrid doctrines & opinions –

It Seems that the traitor [John] Frost & his companions in iniquity & treason are not to suffer death, their punishment is commuted to transportation for Life, from the beginning the Government designed his Escape & they have Effected it to the debasement of the laws & the Encouragement of all traitors & other miscreants –

---

[45] & precedes this in the original.

*7 February 1840*. There seems to be little doubt that immediately after the Queen's marriage Lords Melbourne & Lansdown will retire & the Government be composed of a more radical or republican Set who are to be against Corn Laws &c & to make universal suffrage, vote by ballot &c government Questions – It is asserted that Lord Brougham is to lead in the House of Lords, Lord Durham to be in the Cabinet – Lord Howick return to it & thus form Such a clique as I trust not Even the patient Endurance of my Countrymen Will tolerate –

*8 February 1840*. Prince albert is arrived – he came from Ostend to Dover in a steamer – where he remained, & was So ill with the passage that he could receive nobody –

*9 February 1840*. Honors are falling thickly upon Prince albert – The Queen has created him Royal Highness – a Field Marshall & a Knight of the Garter – he is also to bear the Royal arms. The Royal nuptials are to take place tomorrow –

*10 February 1840*. This day our Queen Victoria is united to Prince albert of Saxe Coburg – We all drank their health wishing that the Union may be amply productive of good and happiness to the wedded pair & of benefit & prosperity to the Country –

*11 February 1840*. The Nuptials took place yesterday – The Queen & Prince albert afterwards went to Windsor Where they Will for the present reside in privacy – very few attendants are gone with them – The crowd was very great indeed, but unfortunately very little enthusiasm Shewn – the illumination in the Evening was very partial – I Might Say of a Similar nature to the Queen's invitation – only three Conservatives were at the Wedding – The Duke of Wellington, Lord Liverpool & Ld ashley – !!! –

*12 February 1840*. Nothing stirring in the political world – a truce to Strife will be granted for a short Season –

*13 February 1840*. By a letter from Windsor I learn that the Queen's reception there was respectful but by no means enthusiastic – it was the Same in London & Elsewhere = From London to Windsor, the general greeting of the crowd was – ["] God bless the Queen, without her Ministers ["] –
The Duke of Wellington was not invited until Just before the ceremony – The Queen resisted his invitation Saying that ["] she would not have that old Rebel near her ["] – Lord Melbourne answered that she Must & finally he was invited –
The Duchess of Northumberland, formerly the Queen's Governess, was not invited until a few days before the day fixed, So that it was impossible to accomplish the Journey in time to be present – Comment upon these proceedings is unnecessary, I can only hope that they may be amended in future –

*14 February 1840*. News is arrived from China & from India – The Chinese presuming upon their Success made demands which could not be complied with by our Consul Captain [Charles] Elliot – They then threatened to Seise our Ships if we did not comply, they were warned of the consequences if they attempted anything of the Sort but they persisted & actually had the hardihood to Surround two of our Ships of War, Volage 26 guns & Hyacinth 18 – These in self defence were obliged to Open a fire upon the 30 War Junks which Surrounded them & attempted to board – The fire was promptly returned & a regular Engagement Ensued, the result of which was the sinking of five Junks [,] the blowing up of another & the damage of many others & the destruction of from 8 to 900 Chinese – The wish was to Spare these people as much as possible, otherwise the whole of their fleet might have been destroyed – The Chinese fought with much Spirit & determination –

In India a very brilliant thing had been Executed by our troops in the Storming of Kelat which was taken by a very inferior force & the greater part of the garrison of 2000 men including the Chief slain – We also suffered very severely –

The Chinese junks carry from 150 to 180 men – The admiral was very impetuous —

*15 February 1840.* The Duke of Wellington has been Seriously ill again [,] in the Same way as when he was taken ill in the autumn – He is better again –

The Ministers have been beaten on a Motion of Mr [John Charles] Herries who moved for all sorts of Papers relative to the Finances, which were refused by the Government – on the division they were beaten by 10 [182–172] – This will Shew them that they cannot go on as they are & that on Such Questions & many others they cannot rely upon Even a majority of one –

*16 February 1840.* The answer to Enquiries after the Duke of Wellington Were that he was better & had recovered his Speech & that the Doctors did not apprehend any immediate mischief from the attack [.] To me however it is quite Evident that he cannot last long –

The Queen & Co. is returned to London where she will Commence a round of party givings very much to her taste – The honeymoon has not lasted long – Crown heads do not need such trifles I suppose, but my opinion is that a private & sufficiently long seclusion at first is of great value, to cement affections, to settle the parties, to teach them to Know one another & to depend upon Each other –

*17 February 1840.* The Duke of Wellington's attack has been one of a very Serious nature, at one time he was in a Series of convulsions & the Doctors were apprehensive that any one of them might be the last; he is now better, but Keeps his bed – He cannot last long, that to me is Evident, nor do I think that he will be alive at the End of this year – His iron constitution & Gallant Spirit Support him wonderfully – most men would have been destroyed by what he has done –

*19 February 1840.* No very particular occurrence – The same old stale notion seems to be going on at the Palace – The Same familiar dinners & the same riff raff invited to them – a poor look out !!!

*20 February 1840.* With sincere & real regret I have to record the death of Lord Mansfield – He had been Evidently going off for the last Year, the misfortunes in his family Seemed to prey upon him & tended to destroy him – He died at Leamington where he had been Staying for the last month for the restoration of his health – Lord Mansfield was a man of very Superior ability, possibly the ablest man of his day for no one could Say to what Extent he might have proved his powers if circumstances had favoured the Exhibition of his intellect & vast faculty[46] of mind & Speech – He was backward in taking a part unless urged by his conscience to declare his Opinions – Those opinions were of a rare Soundness & integrity for these times, his[47] loss to our party (the <u>real</u> Conservative) Will be irreparable, there is no one Who could think [,] act & reason as he did, with Equal honesty, rectitude, genius & talent – I myself have indeed too great Cause to lament him as a friend, fellow labourer in the Same cause, & a real supporter & a most powerful advocate of the best interests of his blighted Country – There was but one drawback to his being a leading man, Something unfortunate in his manner which was not inviting & pleasing, & frequently approaching to rudeness & sarcasm although it was more in appearance than reality –

*22 February 1840.* a great Protestant meeting which has Just taken place in the Mansion house at Dublin – The Lord Mayor [Sir Nicholas William Brady] in the Chair – Will I trust be attended with very important results – the particular object was to resist the Bill just brought (a 3rd or 4th time) for overthrowing the old corporations & Establishing in their place, others on the new fangled System – It has been my astonishment hitherto that the Country has tolerated & that our leaders have so tamely consented to the overthrow & Spoliation of old cherished rights, privileges & properties – at last those interested & the public have awaked from their trance & the result as I trust & believe will be one of vital importance to Protestant Conservatism – The Speeches at the meeting were brilliant & glowing beyond any I Ever read – Nor did matter or argument lack more than Oratory –

*23 February 1840.* Our people are at last disposed to make war & not to allow these vile ministers any longer to remain in quiet & undisturbed possession of office Suffering them to do what Ever they [please] & commit the greatest Enormities – Since the Commencement of this Session Every opportunity has been sought & seised for Exposing the villainies of our misrulers & of putting them to their wits End to defend themselves = This is the only way to proceed to Establish our claim & to sicken the Wretches of Office – If allowed to remain in tranquillity [,] not only may they remain there for Ever in office, but if by any chance they should be Ejected – they would quickly & Eagerly return[48] to it Knowing that they might make a Sinecure of Office, tolerated amidst Every Species of Enormity & unchided Even for the grossest acts of misgovernment – This change in our tactics will soon cause a most material change in our position –

*27 February 1840.* […] Some very curious treaties & arrangements Seem to have been made by us with Russia & Turkey – our fleet, it is Said, is to be divided into 3: one to occupy the Dardanelles, another to cruise off Syria & a third to take possession of & occupy Candice – this report requires much confirmation –

*28 February 1840.* a letter which I wrote to the Editor of the "Statesman" [and Dublin Christian Record] Irish newspaper, thanking him for sending me his paper & commenting briefly but decidedly upon the Irish Corporations bill, has been published by the Editor, &

[46] powers precedes this in the original.
[47] & precedes this in the original.
[48] to precedes this in the original.

in that Country where the poor people catch at Straws it is creating considerable Sensation – I trust that it may aid in preserving to that Country at least the benefit of their old Corporations[49] –

*29 February 1840*. another victory over the vile Ministers, on Mr [Henry] Liddell's Motion respecting – the Spring Rice Job[50] – The Ministers Suffered amazingly in & by the debate – & were thoroughly Sore & Sensitive to the harassing warfare which is carried on against them – it is the only way of acting, & should have been done long since – The majority against Ministers was 28 [240–212] – and will they resign ? –

*1 March 1840*. My poor Cousin Lincoln Stanhope has died Suddenly: he was 4 or 5 years older than me but we were boys at School together & have always Entertained a very friendly feeling towards Each other = I hope he was prepared for his awful change, but I much fear that he had thought but little upon that momentous Subject –

*3 March 1840*. My little letter to an Editor, not intended for publicity [,] has created a great Sensation – I wish I could Speak, I might then follow up in the house what has been begun out of it = alas I have neither head nor tongue for Speaking —

*5 March 1840*. Lord Westmoreland unfortunately is dead – He, poor man [,] has for Some time been in a state of blindness & imbecility, So that he has been defunct as a member of Society – but he was Lieutenant of Northamptonshire & a Knight [of the] Garter – Which by ill luck Will give to these vile Ministers more patronage –

*7 March 1840*. The Duke of Marlborough is dead – the present Duke Sat for Woodstock – he has offered his Seat to Mr [Frederic] Thessiger who has accepted – This will completely through [*sic*] them out at Newark & will I fear destroy all their Energies –
    at last the privilegemongers, as they are called, in the House of Commons feel it necessary to beat a retreat, & Lord John Russell brings in a bill to authorise by act of Parliament the printing of such papers as the House shall think necessary – This question has lowered all the members, Peel included, very remarkably in the opinion of the public & it will not be an Easy matter, perhaps impossible, to regain their station in public opinion –

*8 March 1840*. Sheriff [William] Evans is released from his confinement by a Vote of the House of Commons but only till the 10th of april – The House of Commons has made a sorry figure & has disgusted & alarmed the generality of the Nation –
    Mr Charles Wood (late Secretary to the admiralty) has Kindly offered to get [my son] Edward afloat & to ensure his promotion, & also to have him placed on Such a Station as he may prefer – This is fortunate – The thing, no doubt, has been planned with Lord Minto, who promised me to do Something for him, & this is the Expedient devised for Effecting what otherwise he does not dare to do –

---

[49] See Appendix A.

[50] A pension of £1,000 p.a. was granted to Sir John Newport for having fulfilled the office of comptroller general of the exchequer (1834–5). Spring Rice succeeded him as comptroller in 1835 and retained the post, with its salary of £2,000, after leaving the cabinet in 1839.

*12 March 1840*. The admiralty has been quick upon dear Edward – His letter offering his Services has been answered by return of post, Signifying that he is appointed a mate to the Cambridge 78. Captain [Edward] Barnard, fitting out at Sheerness[51] – I trust that this promptitude means Something & that dear Edward will be made Lieutenant very shortly & before the Ship goes to Sea –

*14 March 1840*. War is declared with China – Some few Ships are Sending from this country & an armament is fitting out at Calcutta to Send against the Chinese – it is not yet Known what is the plan & point of attack = From 10 to 20 000 men are talked of as the force to be Sent – using the disposable force from Bombay & Madras –

*18 March 1840*. Messrs Grissel & Peto [Thomas Grissell and Morton Peto] have written to Say that it is at last determined to use the Steetley stone for all the inside Work & interior coverts of the houses of Parliament & asking to work the quarries for that purpose at a royalty of 3 halfpence per foot – which is but a poor price –

*20 March 1840*. [...] The Deputation from the Dublin Corporation wrote to me by their Secretary Mr [Thomas James] Quinton informing me that there is to be a meeting at Freemason's Hall [Great Queen Street] on the 26th to discuss the Case of the Irish Corporations' Bill & that <u>they</u> had nominated & were about to advertise me as the Chairman – This is a very Strange proceeding – as a member of the House of Lords I would on no account take a part in proceedings out of doors which were intended to influence the decision of the House – & I have positively declined the honor[52] –

*24 March 1840*. [...] This Evening after dinner a member of the Dublin deputation, Reverend Tresham Gregg – arrived from London – Sent to Explain & to apologise to me for their Extraordinary proceeding in announcing me in the Chair at their meeting on the 26th [.] I told him that the circumstance Was unfortunate for that I Certainly would not attend – but I gave him permission to leave my name in the announcement as a retraction would be very prejudicial – this is the most I could do, & it will probably Subject me to a good deal of animadversion – for which I care little[53] –

*26 March 1840*. Saw Several people this morning – among others [John] Hicklin to whom I gave my letter to publish addressed to the Magistrates respecting the Rural Police which I wish may have its Effect[54] –

---

[51] 'The Cambridge' was launched on 23 June 1815 and had 80 guns.

[52] K.D., 17 Mar. 1840, 'Had with me Lord Mayor of Dublin Dr [T.D.] Gregg &c concerning grand Meeting about Irish Municipal Corporations – Agreed to attend Duke of Newcastle on the occasion'. Newcastle was advertised as chairman in *The Warder and Dublin Weekly Mail*, 21 Mar. 1840.

[53] K.P., Box 71, Kenyon to Lloyd Kenyon, 26 Mar. 1840, 'I am just going to the great Anti Irish Municipal Corporations Meeting at Free Masons Hall. The Duke of Newcastle as usual is Late – won't come till 5 o'Clock to Day. What I undertake I will do as well as I can – Winchilsea I hope will be there & be persuaded to preside'. The meeting went ahead with Winchilsea in the chair: K.D., 26 Mar. 1840; *The Warder and Dublin Weekly Mail*, 28 Mar. 1840.

[54] *Nottingham Journal*, 27 Mar. 1840. See Appendix A.

*27 March 1840*. The Ministers Were beaten tonight upon Lord Stanley's Motion on the Registration for Ireland [250–234, majority 16] –

*28 March 1840*. My morning was occupied by people calling in amongst others the Reverend McGhee [M'Ghee] who is very anxious that an Enquiry Should be made at the bar of the House of Lords into the regular plot (as he affirms & says he can prove) to papalize this Country – he Says that there is a printed document to be Easily produced by which the Pope Makes over England to persons named in the Paper — & various other assertions which he declares he can prove incontestably by Evidence –

*31 March 1840*. There is a Strong rumour of dissolution of Parliament: a motion on affairs of China is to come on next week which Ministers are quaking at – they have given the strictest orders to all their people to be up & present – The motion on repeal of the Corn laws is postponed, it was to have been this Evening & possibly to avoid another defeat: to get rid of all present difficulties & to run the risk of the chapter of accidents, such men as these may recklessly adopt such a measure as the dissolution – but assuredly it will Kill them & they deserve it or any other death –

*1 April 1840*. […] The debate upon the Corn Laws has been adjourned[55] – The debate flat & dull –

*4 April 1840*. The Exaltation of Lady Cecilia Buggins to be Duchess of Inverness has created the most universal & undisguised disgust = The Queen must be miserably without Judgment & a proper Sense of propriety & duty to Elevate Such a Woman under Such circumstances – The Duchess Buggins assumes royalty & actually upon Lady Thomond calling upon her the other day & not finding her at home, she tendered her card to the Servant – but the answer was Her Royal Highness has "a book" which interesting register he produced at the carriage door that Lady Thomond might write down her name "for Her Royal Highness" –
    […] The Corn law debate Ended curiously last night by a Motion for adjourning the debate which was lost by a large majority[56] – Mr [Henry] Warburton then moved ["] that the house do now adjourn ["] which was instantly agreed to & thus the question is disposed of – & the debate at an End –

*5 April 1840*. The Queen believes herself to be pregnant, it is Said, rather Soon to Suspect Such an Event, & is melancholy at it as she Entertains the presentiment that delivery will cause her death – This, if so, is a peculiar weakness, & can only arise from supposing that she will be subjected to the fate of the Princess Charlotte – But she is a Strange, Self willed, unreasonable little personage –

*6 April 1840*. Went to the Levee today [at St James' Palace] – The Queen was not otherwise than gracious, but Said nothing – I made my bow & passed on, making my bow also

---

[55] ~~postponed~~ precedes this in the original.
[56] The Commons divided on the question of adjourning the debate, Ayes 129, Noes 245: majority 116.

to Prince albert who stood [at] Her left hand, He is a well looking young man, good countenance, with dark hair & complexion = Hitherto all agree in speaking well of him –

*7 April 1840.* Called at the admiralty this morning by appointment & had an interview with Lord Minto – my object to obtain promotion to Lieutenant for my Son Edward, who is a mate of 1836. Lord Minto had as good as promised that he would really take an Early opportunity of promoting him.[57] but today when I Saw him he made a Sad face & Said he was in hopes & Expected that Edward had been afloat Since I last Saw [him] & Similar mendacities by way of subterfuge & Excuse – I Could get nothing from the animal, but an assertion that he would be glad of an opportunity to Serve my Son – His last words were – "Well, I will really do what I can for him, I will indeed" – these words from any other mouth might be truth, but [from] this man they Mean nothing [.] I am at a loss how to Serve my dear Son whose situation pains me beyond description –

In the House of Lords a long debate on the Bishop of Exeter's motion for referring certain questions respecting the disposal of the Clergy reserves in Canada by a bill of the Legislature of that Colony – Some noble Lords Such as Haddington [,] Ellenborough & Even Ripon & others took a very Wrong & improper course upon the occasion & Sowed the Seeds of much mischief –

*8 April 1840.* In the House Of Commons last night Sir James Graham brought on his motion relative to China from which So much is Expected, but which I fear will End in Smoke –

*10 April 1840.* The debate on the China question closed last night – Ministers had a majority of only 9 – numbers 271 [against the resolution] & 262 [for it]. I Cannot myself think that Ministers will go out upon it –

*11 April 1840.* Great Expectations were formed of the Event of the division upon the China question – I never Expected any good from it even if the Ministers had been beaten – & So it has proved, there is not the Slightest Symptom of intention to move & the incapable creatures are Contented to Keep their places under any circumstances as long as they can to curse the Country with their galling and intolerable rule –

*12 April 1840.* an order in Council declaring war against China was actually out before the debate, but with their usual dishonesty the Ministers Suppressed it & nothing was Known of it till after the debate –

*13 April 1840.* In the House of Lords tonight we had a motion by Lord Westmeath for a Select committee to enquire into certain circumstances affecting the administration of the Irish poor laws — The Duke of Wellington spoke & Excited my wonder – He appears as you see him Seated to be barely alive, his Eye inanimate, his features inexpressive & his

[57] N.L.S., MS 12048J, 125–6: Minto to Newcastle, 9 Nov. 1839. For Newcastle's continuing efforts to secure his son's promotion, see MS 12048M, 167–8: Minto to Newcastle, 5 Nov. 1840; MS 12048M, 276: Minto to Newcastle, 30 Nov. 1840. See 23 Dec. 1840.

powers Suspended or lost – He rose & it was most painful to see & hear him labouring Slowly on & Endeavouring to convey to the house his View of the case – One could plainly perceive that his mind was aware of the circumstances but that infirmity rendered his faculties Slow & approaching to forgetfulness – yet his Energy of character & strength of mind carried him through, he made good his positions & shewed that he was able to weigh & decide upon the whole question. I was really astonished at the result, it was a wonderful Effort of mind & animal determination –

*14 April 1840.* But little has occurred today of any importance – I presented some petitions in the House of Lords [from Derby, against the Repeal of the Corn Laws] – & the Duke of Wellington roused himself to be very Energetic on the Subject of his remarks of yesterday, again accusing the Ministers of having used him unfairly in Smuggling in a clause in the poor law amendment upon the 3rd reading of the bill when he was absent from the house –

*15 April 1840.* Parliament is adjourned for the Easter holidays – no particular news –

*16 April 1840.* There is a threatening of a rupture with Naples = Our affairs appear to have been conducted in a very improper manner & our Minister Mr [William] Temple, Lord Palmerston's Brother [,] seems to have behaved with a great degree of intemperance & want of Judgement – Our Government Seems determined to involve us in war in Every quarter – & to provide no means to meet hostilities in any quarter –

*25 April 1840.* No news of any consequence – petty Squabbles, Election Committees & Elections are the chief points of interest to others, but very little or none to me –

*27 April 1840.* Went to see the progress made in building the houses of Parliament – the foundation 1 foot above high water mark was completed in a beautiful & honest manner last Summer by the Contractor Mr [Henry and John] Lee – During the Winter the cellars have been built, in my judgment I never Saw work Worse Executed, the Joints Excessively wide, the mortar coarse &c Seemingly bad & the bricks ill Shaped, ill looking & bad quality – If I were a builder or clerk of the works I Should be ashamed of Such Work – & I shall think it my duty to report my opinion to the architect Mr [Charles] Barry –

*1 May 1840.* […] I attended a [dinner] at the Goldsmiths' Hall – It was the first time of my dining there, I was formerly at a Ball given by the Company & like the dinner it was the handsomest & pleasantest thing of the sort that I Ever attended – The Prime Warden is Mr [John Gawler] Bridge of Rundell's house,[58] The Duke of Cambridge & his Son Prince George dined there & Several guests besides the members of the Company. Toasts & speeches after dinner called me forth quite unexpectedly & unwillingly as I was not well or in good nerve – The Goldsmiths are an agreeable [,] intelligent & worthy body of men & it is a pleasure to go among them –

---

[58]Rundell, Bridge & Co., jewellers and goldsmiths.

*2nd May 1840.* This morning a meeting at the Duke of Wellington's[59] – the old Story was played off upon us – of passing the 2nd reading of the Irish Corporations bill & altering it in Committee – all was going on smoothly & they were cutting & carving the thing in their own way & making arrangements for acceding to the Duke of Wellington's proposal, when as nobody Else would I determined to Endeavour to Stem the tide & rouse an opposition to the fatal Course proposed – I asked if any one in the room Could approve of the bill [?] – if a bad bill why allow it to pass another Stage [?] – I Shortly reviewed the present State of Ireland [,] the peculiar unfitness of the present time for passing Such a vitally objectionable bill, with Some other arguments & entreated the Duke to postpone the Consideration of the bill on the 2nd reading upon a plausible pretext – The Duke of Wellington resisted this & amongst other reasons urged that after what has passed it would not be permitted that Ireland Should go without corporations – I replied that Ireland had Corporations & that I did not wish that they should be destroyed in an arbitrary & tyrannical manner, to replace them by newly fangled bodies nominally termed Corporations indeed but being nothing like the old Corporations & calculated to inflict a deadly blow upon Protestantism; to play the game for O'Connell & to overthrow Ireland & the United Kingdom – nothing Could justify our upsetting the present Corporations by our arbitrary will merely because we had the power to do it – I will not detail here what I urged, but the Duke answered that he Could not consent to postponement – What would our friends in the House of Commons Say [?] – how could he & others forfeit their pledge to proceed with the bill [?] – It was notorious that no one approved of the present Corporations – he particularly objected to them on account of their maladministration of their fiscal concerns – another great objection that he had to the existing Corporations was that by the Emancipation act [of 1829] persons of all religions were admissible to offices & yet not a Single Roman Catholic had been admitted into the Dublin Corporation = The Duke Went on in this Strain for Some time = & to opinions So open to refutation I was upon the point of replying went [*sic* – when] Lord Wharncliffe rose & spoke for Some time combating my arguments & recommending that we should follow the Duke's Suggestion & Seeing how little likely I was to do any good by Speaking to persons who were predisposed to adopt any course proposed by the Duke – I Said no more & contented myself with the declaration that I should oppose the 2nd reading & would certainly go with any one who divided the house upon the question –

*4 May 1840.* Our debate on the 2nd reading of the Irish Corporations bill is over. To my infinite Surprise the Duke of Wellington made a Speech of an hour long – beginning So Slowly that One Expected him to Stop at Every instant – however he soon Wound himself up & then spoke with much Energy and Clearness & nearly as he used to speak – Lord Winchilsea Moved that the bill be read in 6 months – I Said a few words towards the End[60] – I had not the Courage to Speak Earlier – & am glad that I did not give a Silent vote – Our minority only numbered 18 – From what I heard Especially from Ld Lyndhurst I am in hopes that the bill will be overthrown in the Committee or rendered So little Suited to their mischievous purposes that the House of Commons will not pass it

---

[59] K.D., 2 May 1840, notes that there were about 70 peers present.

[60] For the reported version, see *The Mirror of Parliament*, ed. J.H. Barrow (2nd ser., iii, 1840), 2735. It is not recorded in Hansard.

when it returns to them – Such a result will be a great blessing – The Duke of Wellington Spoke for an hour – I could not have Supposed it possible for him to Keep for so long upon his legs – I stated that I would not occupy the time of the house[61] [which was] impatient to come to a division, but deeply interested as I was on the Subject I was anxious not to give a silent vote – I would briefly State the two principal points of my objection. First to the principle of the Bill which I considered inadmissable inasmuch as I was of opinion that Parliament had no right to deprive any bodies corporate or other of their rights [,] privileges & possessions, by its Simple pleasure & on the ground of Expediency – delinquency must first be proved, before the Exercise of the most summary punishment – To dispossess the present Corporations of their vested rights & possessions, would be an act of the most flagrant tyranny, injustice and oppression – Parliament was strong, but it Should beware of exercising its powers to crush the weak & oppress the defenceless – The Might of the Strongest was that which was here used against the right of weaker – again I objected because by the Bill all the power Would be transferred from Protestants to Papists & the Corporations of Ireland would become Engines in the hands of the latter for overthrowing the Religion & laws not only of that Country but of Endangering both those interests in the United Kingdom – I should decidedly oppose the 2nd reading & vote with Lord Winchilsea[62] –

*5 May 1840.* It is said that Several of their hitherto Supporters are leaving the Ministerial Side & that Some will actually vote for Lord Stanley's bill tomorrow –

*6 May 1840.* a shocking Event took place last night = Lord William Russell was founded [sic] murdered in his bed – his throat cut & So ferociously that the head was nearly Separated from the body – It appears that the assassin was also a thief – the back door had been broken open, boxes & drawers forced open & valuable articles Selected & taken there from – Little doubt can be Entertained that the Murderer is a discharged servant who was sent away about 3 weeks Since – Lord William was 73 years old – lived in Norfolk Street [–] the only Servants in his house – were one man (a foreigner) & two maids: the discharged Servant was also a foreigner –

*7 May 1840.* The debate upon Lord Stanley's Irish registration bill has been postponed on account of Lord William Russell's horrid murder – The perpetrator of the Horrid deed is not yet discovered –

*8 May 1840.* I do not hear of any news – It is confidently rumoured this afternoon that the man Servant valet to Lord William Russell has confessed that he was the Murderer – If So the premeditated crime & the perpetration under such peculiar circumstances is one of the blackest & most devilish that ever was committed –

---

[61] in that of the house follows this in the original.
[62] The second reading passed by 131 (85 present and 46) votes to 32 (14 present and 18 proxies), a majority of 99; K.D., 4 May 1840. Kenyon surmised that Newcastle might, like him, sign a protest against the measure: K.P., Box 71, Kenyon to Lloyd Kenyon, 5 May 1840. In the event, Newcastle did not.

*11 May 1840.* a meeting took place today at the Carlton [Club] to consider what could be done with the Irish Corporations bill – I was not able to attend by a previous Engagement here at the very hour –

*12 May 1840.* There was a ball yesterday at the Palace, but neither My daughters nor I were invited – [my sons] Charles & Thomas Were invited & went there – The Queen danced with Prince George of Cambridge & the Duke of Roxburghe – It was rather flat and was over Early[63] –

*13 May 1840.* By the factious conduct of the ministerial party in the House of Commons in resisting the motion for issuing a Writ for Ludlow by Endless divisions [,] all business is at a Stand & the House stands adjourned[64] to tomorrow [.] Sir Robert Peel has declared that if this vexatious conduct is persevered in [,] that he will by the Same means Stop the supplies, so that if both sides are obstinate, no public business can proceed & there can be no termination to Such a State of things but dissolution – it is really lamentable to witness the degraded state of this once honored & honorable assembly –

It is thought that a great change has taken place in the Palace = The Queen is represented as being a good deal altered, the people who were the great & Sole favorites are no longer so – Pagets are at a discount – The Queen is doatingly [*sic*] fond of Prince albert & he is considered to be a Sensible, right thinking & worthy Man & it is now thought Evidently leaning to Conservatism – He is working Slowly but as I am informed Effectually – I do not Know him as we are asked to None of the parties – But he stands high for character [,] is very domestic, quiet, civil, obliging, & most anxious to Do Everything that is right –

*14 May 1840.* In the House of Lords we this Evening had a Speech from Sir Charles Wetherell as Council for the Corporation of Dublin. He made a pithy & forcible Speech detecting many fallacies, Errors, & Evils in the Corporation bill which produced their Effect upon the Lords who heard him & upon the Duke of Wellington – in particular – He Spoke for three hours & the hearing of the other Council was postponed to tomorrow –

*15 May 1840.* Mr [Isaac] Butt [,] an Irish barrister of great reputation for his years, being only about 25, was heard at the bar this day following Sir Charles Wetherell – It appeared to me to be the cleverest Speech I Ever heard & I am much mistaken if he will not be the first man of his day – His arguments were irresistible, not amplifying or Exaggerating any thing but strong simple & convincing by their truth – He Completely overturned the Whole Case & made Such an impression as I never before witnessed – The fate of the corporations bill is now Sealed, as it appears to me, Since the first opposition to it was started [,] I have the pleasure to behold, numbers ranging themselves on our Side & coming over to our opinions – The Duke of Wellington is Evidently Conscience Stricken & disinclined to continue any longer in his originally unenlightened course – He now per-

[63]QVJ, 11 May 1840.
[64]~~post~~ precedes this in the original.

ceives all the mischief which the passing of the bill will create & if possible I am Sure he will Stop the bill[65] – I heartily thank God for this –

*16 May 1840.* at a morning Concert of the [Royal] academy pupils, Prince albert was present – I had an opportunity of observing his manners & deportment & all that I Saw pleased me Exceedingly = He is mild [,] modest & civil in his manners & there is a Sense & good feeling about him which naturally induces him to act with peculiar propriety = He is remarkably grave & Sedate with a Strong tinge of melancholy in his appearance, but it is natural not the Effect of being unhappy – His conduct appears to be duly appreciated, he is Evidently a great favorite –

*17 May 1840.* It is Expected that the division on Lord Stanley's bill tomorrow Will be in favor of the bill – & there are those who think that the Ministers will be out by the End of the week = I Know that they are in a very precarious State but their resignation is another thing –

*19 May 1840.* The Debate on Lord Stanley's motion factiously adjourned [.]

*20 May 1840.* This is the third day of the debate having been twice adjourned, with the declaration that they – (O'Connell & his Irish tail [,] in which Ministers Support them) will never allow the bill to pass – to which Sir Robert Peel replies, ["] if you refuse to go on with the bill by obstructive of [*sic* – or] factious divisions, we will do the Same & obstruct any other business that you may bring forward in intervention of the proceeding with Lord Stanley's registration bill ["] –

*21 May 1840.* a Division was Come to at last about 2 o'Clock this morning – it was the largest Ever Known in the house Except upon the occasion of Choosing a Speaker, when Manners Sutton was rejected[66] – the numbers 303 & 306 including tellers making a majority for Lord Stanley's motion to go into Committee of 3. The Conservative party has rallied together admirably & in the most remarkable manner, not one man being unaccounted for & 303 being present in the house – great as this triumph is, it will have little Effect upon the Ministers who are dead to all feeling –

*24 May 1840.* Cambridge & Ludlow Elections have been gained [,] Cockermouth may be in a few days & Radnorshire will follow = this may give us a majority of 5 or 6 in the next division –

*25 May 1840.* The Queen's birth day is celebrated on this day – Went to the Drawing room [at St James' Palace] with two of my Daughters – I never Saw So many people or So few that I Knew – The Queen represents less than Ever – she gives herself no trouble, Speaks to no one, Scarcely looks at people as they pass like flitting shadows. This is very unsatisfactory & is not Commented upon in a very pleasing manner, nor one very favorable to the Monarchy

[65] K.D., 15 May 1840, 'Mr Butt Leaned against Irish Corporations Bill [–] very able Speech – Duke of Wellington resisted further progress'.

[66] See *Unrepentant Tory*, 262–3.

– it is a circumstance deeply to be lamented that Her Majesty Should conduct herself in a manner which must of necessity give Serious dissatisfaction[67] –

*27 May 1840.* a Smart attack made last night in the House of Commons by Mr [Charles Pelham] Villiers who renewed his assault on the Corn Laws = His language was really abominable & unjustifiable – but Some allowance may be made for his Extreme annoyance & irritation that no one of any note would rise to speak & notice his motion – it was treated with contempt & impatience & on a division of a house of little more than 400 [was] lost by a majority of 126[68] – This will settle the Corn law agitation in the House of Commons at last – & out of doors the beneficent prospect of an abundant harvest & prosperity in agriculture will Silence discontent, not felt, but imagined by the Suggestions of hireling miscreants who go about doing the deeds of the Master – The Prince of Darkness –

*29 May 1840.* I hear no news of any consequence, though my time has been past [*sic*] all day with meetings [,] concerts & dinners – There is a concert at the Palace tonight but we of course are not invited – I am in fact better pleased to be away as regards myself but for the Sake of the Sovereign I am Exceedingly Sorry that Such an Exclusion Should Systematically Exist – it is very hurtful to the Cause of monarchy –

*30 May 1840.* […] The Elections in the vacant boroughs are turning out favorably to us – if we gain Cockermouth & Monaghan it will turn out the ministers –

*3 June 1840.* at a Meeting of the Society for Extinguishing the Slave Trade & for promoting civilisation in africa, Prince albert presided for the first time of his being in the Chair = His presence gave very great satisfaction & it is represented that the Prince acquitted himself Extremely well in his new Situation –

*4 June 1840.* The Queen went to Epsom races = It is thought a very Extraordinary thing to have done, as these races have never before been attended by Royalty = to make the thing She is said to have betted freely = her conduct has certainly not produced a favorable impression – These races are of Such a cockney, rabble [,] & gambling character, that hitherto they have been thought of [as] too low & questionable to be honored by the presence of the Sovereign –

*5 June 1840.* accounts are arrived from China – The Chinese Seem determined to take up the war in Earnest & are Encreasing their navy by Every means in their power = They have bought Such large merchant Ships as the proprietors will Sell to them & others they have Seised [*sic*] in Such cases as they have not been willing to sell. This is a singular people – it is curious to speculate what will be the end of all this – My opinion is that this is only a prelude to mighty consequences & that there will be an ultimate conversion to Christianity = Which is Evidently Working its way through out all the World –

[67] QVJ, 25 May 1840.
[68] The Commons divided 177 for and 300 against: majority 123.

*8 June 1840.* The Queen is undoubtedly pregnant & the puzzling question now is – how is a Regency to be Effected [?] – To provide against all contingencies [,] the Ministers must bring this matter forward & they Scarcely Know what to devise So as to accomplish this delicate point in a manner least obnoxious & most likely to be well received – It must be admitted that it is a very difficult matter to handle properly –

*10 June 1840.* The town was in great consternation this afternoon from the Queen having been Shot at – Her Majesty Was driving with Prince albert in a little phaiton [*sic*] up Constitution hill – not very far from Buckingham Palace a man standing upon the foot path, fired two shots from pistols at the Queen as she passed in her carriage – one of the balls lodged in the wall opposite – neither touched the Queen or the carriage – The man was instantly Seised – The Queen passed on & continued her drive = It is not yet Known who the man is & what prompted him to the act – probably he is deranged –

*11 June 1840.* The man Who Shot at the Queen, proves to be a young man of the name of [Edward] Oxford about 20 years of age – There is some mystery about the affair – It Seems as if he was Set on by Somebody – The pistols he Says were given to him – he has been constantly practising Shooting at a mark – He is a native of Birmingham but has been several years in London –

We all went today to write our names down at the Palace & with the Duchess of Kent – addresses were voted in Each house of Parliament [.]

a long debate on Lord Fitzwilliams motion on the Corn Laws = We divided – Lord Melbourne was the only one of the Ministers who voted with us – He also Spoke very Well – Our Majority was very large – there were not Many more than 30 in the minority[69] –

In the Commons the Ministers Were beaten in their attempt to adjourn the debate upon Lord Stanleys bill by 11 = a glorious triumph –

*12 June 1840.* another nights' debate in the House of Lords – we divided twice – first upon the Irish grand Jury Cess bill which was disposed of by Lord Lyndhurst & next upon the Irish Corporations bill which the Duke of Wellington moved to be postponed for a week.[70]

*14 June 1840.* [...] There was a great Meeting of the Ministers' friends at the Foreign Office yesterday & a very stormy Conference – O'Connell was tame, pliant & in Every way accommodating [–] he would Even take the bill or do any thing – Not So the English Members [–] they Spoke very plainly & the Minister Will certainly be left by Some of them – The very meeting Shews the extremity & weakness – It Seems that these are peculiar days for Government business in the House of Commons – the opposition mean to take Monday (tomorrow) which is one of those for debating Lord Stanleys bill & if the Government Submits or is beaten it is of Course all over with it – after complaints of non attendance & an appeal to the patriotism of his supporters [,] Lord John Russell called on his friends to attend in their places & Secure him in a majority —— He then stated that it was his intention to propose a compromise [–] namely to give the Opposition Thursday instead

---

[69] The Contents numbered 42 (34 present and eight proxies) and the Not Contents 194 (127 present and 67 proxies): majority 152.

[70] The first vote was won by 66–96: majority 30, the second by 68–94: majority 26.

of tomorrow – This I understand we shall not agree to & [,] in any case but a rescue by a Miracle [,] I look to the immediate dissolution of the Vilest crew that Ever administered the affairs of this great & much abused country –

*15 June 1840.* With their usual cunning & address the Ministers have again Escaped – When the House met Lord Stanley Moved that the House Should go into Committee upon his bill – Lord John Russell objected & offered any other day in the Week but proposed Thursday which was rejected & Friday is fixed – Lord John afterwards stated that he Should offer no unfair opposition to the Bill & that it should be properly considered in Committee. O'Connell however said that he did [not] consider himself bound by any rules that others might lay down & that he Should consider himself at liberty to oppose a bill so injurious to Ireland in any way that he thought fit – & here the business rests for the present – The Ministers are Evidently beaten, their own friends condemn their conduct & will not support them – One of these things they must do, resign, dissolve, or complete their money votes [,] hazard no more divisions & prorogue as quickly as possible – The latter I fear they will pursue –

*16 June 1840.* If the Ministers are to be believed, their intention is to meet the bill fairly on Friday – they will move an amendment in the first clause [,] if they carry it the bill is destroyed, if they lose it they will resign – Their call upon their followers yesterday was attended to – there were 640 members in the house – but there is So much & great dissatisfaction amongst the ministerial supporters that they cannot be depended Upon for a day = My belief is that the Ministers Will not carry their amendment upon the first Clause of Lord Stanley's bill –

The attempt upon the Queen's life has operated greatly in her favour – Every where she is warmly received – I wish that the whole Event may make a due impression upon her – rouse a Soundly religious feeling within her & Create a paternal feeling towards her Subjects – Which certainly does not at present Exist –

*17 June 1840.* It is reported that Lord Melbourne informed the Queen of the position of his government & told Her that if he Should[71] be beaten on Lord Stanley's bill he must tender his resignation – The Queen received this information very coolly, & did not as heretofore, press him to remain = if this be true, the days of these bad men & Wretched Ministers are numbered, for nothing can Keep them in place but the Countenance of the Sovereign –

*18 June 1840.* We dined yesterday with Sir William Clinton – a family reunion on the occasion of his Second Son Frederick's approaching marriage with Miss Montague 2nd daughter of Lord Montague – an alliance in Every Way Suited to him & one which pleases me very much –

*19 June 1840.* [...] In the House of Lords this Evening we have been deceived into allowing the Irish Corporations bill to go into Committee – I had determined to oppose it, but So

---

[71] ~~was~~ precedes this in the original.

much Was Said against Stirring the question Just now for fear of losing Some votes in the House of Commons tonight [,] as well as not to marr [*sic*] the plan for delaying the progress of the bill in the Expectation of a change of Ministers before the week is out, that many of us remained silent – Lord Lyndhurst gave in his amendments to be printed & considered in Committee & all farther proceeding in the bill was postponed for a Week –

In the House of Commons the grand fight takes place tonight on Lord Stanley's bill in Committee, if the first clause be carried the Ministers must go out – but they Say & declare & it is thought probable that they will have a majority of <u>Six</u> – but that depends upon how Lord Howick & Mr [Charles] Wood vote; if With Lord Stanley the Ministers are beaten. My Notion is that Ministers will be defeated –

*20 June 1840.* I was wrong in my Surmise – The ministerial whip Was too Well applied, they mustered in force & gained a majority last night of 7 – Lord Howick & Mr Wood voted with them – The whole of the Conservative force Voted last night reckoning the pairs – with the Ministers including tellers there were 398 – on our side 391[72] – Lord Stanley very properly announced his determination to go on with his bill – which puzzles & annoys the Ministers for they Know that they cannot Keep their people together & must be frequently beaten –

*21 June 1840.* Courvoisie [Francois Benjamin Courvoisier] has been convicted of the murder of Lord William Russell – Several Singular & providential circumstances led to his conviction – after Sentence was passed, he confessed to the Commission of the crime –

*22 June 1840.* attended a Ball at the Palace – the first that we have been invited to – It was Excessively Crowded – The Queen appeared to be in good humour & pleased – To me, She was Kind & agreeable in her manner, but Said nothing = We merely passed her as at a Drawing room, So that there is no opportunity for Conversation[73] –

*25 June 1840.* I am assured that the Queen is very desirous of a dissolution of parliament & thinks that a very favorable return may be made through Her popularity – Her Majesty forms a very false Estimate of her popularity – It is unfortunately at a very low Ebb –

Regarding Her Majesty's pregnancy [,] Dr [Charles] Locock is the person appointed to attend Her delivery – but hitherto, Strange to Say [,] he has not been allowed to See her & has been obliged to advise solely through Sir James Clark the Queens physician, & it is thought very probable that this System will continue up to the latest[74] time –

*26 June 1840.* The Queen is gone today to a breakfast given by Lord & Lady Ravensworth at Percy's Cross [Fulham] – This is the first Conservatives house that Her Majesty has honored by her presence = Nothing can be more unsatisfactory than Her Majesty's general conduct – it is trivial, partial & wilful – & marked by no trait which is indicative of kind & amicable feeling – This may not be altogether her fault, she is Surrounded by, hemmed in & in the hands of the worst people in the Country & unfortunately She Seems to take pleasure in

---

[72]The vote was 296 for and 289 against: majority seven.
[73]QVJ, 22 June 1840.
[74]~~time~~ precedes this in the original.

Such Company – With all her haughtiness & love of rule, she is not Select in her choice of Company or amusements – She has lately taken to Singing with the professional people at public concerts – both She & Prince albert Sang at the last concert at the Palace & they are to Sing again at a concert at Lady Normanby's in a Short time – This & other things give great disgust & people do not disguise their opinions –

*27 June 1840.* In the House of Commons, they were in Committee last night upon Lord Stanley's bill – Several attempts at division were made, but only one took place & in that the Ministers were beaten by 4 [275–271] – In short it is only upon Extraordinary occasions that Ministers can stand their ground at all & that only by a very few votes – It requires a State of feeling only to be found amongst such people as the present ministers to remain in place – when they Experience how thoroughly they have lost the Support of Parliament & how entirely they are despised & distrusted by the Nation – The Queen, it was confidently told me today [,] is becoming ashamed & uneasy at her Situation –

a very noble action was performed a few days ago by Lord Grimstone, who was riding by the reservoir in Hyde Park, Seeing a crowd he Enquired what it was for & was told that a youth had thrown himself into the water [,] that none of them could Swim or assist him & he had gone to the bottom – Lord Grimstone dismounted, climbed over the iron palisades, threw off his hat & coat & plunged into the water & diving to the bottom brought up the boy – who after Some difficulty in getting him out of the water was Eventually Saved – He proved to be an apprentice who had been ill treated by his Master – Such actions are glorious & deserving of all praise –

*28 June 1840.* Called this morning upon Lord Lyndhurst to Enquire What course he meant to take with regard to the Irish Corporations bill – He tells me that he & the Duke of Wellington are as much opposed to the bill as I am but that they are hampered by the state of the party – as Lord Stanley [&] Sir James Graham when formerly in the Government had assisted in assenting to & bringing in the bill & that with them Peel had also declared in favor of it – that herein laid the difficulty, as they did not wish to disoblige them & yet they Knew that they ought not to allow such a bill to pass into a law – Their object therefore will be to gain time to postpone on Some pretext or other, & to watch the feelings & Sentiments of our three friends as well as of the public = & Lord Lyndhurst assured me that if possible they would arrange for the ultimate loss of the bill = I recommended honesty as the best policy & urged that we Should adopt the Course which became us, namely to do that which is right without reference to the false opinions of others, & to leave the reconcilement of what we do to the better reflection of those who may now disagree with our proceedings = I am most anxious that this bill shall not pass [–] it would Eternally disgrace the House of Lords & destroy the cause of Protestantism whilst it Elevated that of Popery in Ireland –

*29 June 1840.* Had a long conference with Mr Butt in the morning. I wished if there Should be an opportunity to Say Something in the Evening against going into Committee on the Irish Corporations Bill, but when the time came [,] being very far from well & very low, I could not Spur myself into taking any part in the proceedings of the House – I voted upon Lord Lyndhursts' amendment to preserve the rights[75] & I remained without dinner till $\frac{1}{2}$

[75] Lyndhurst's amendment to clause six passed by 60–104: majority 44, with Newcastle in the majority.

10 when I felt too unwell to remain any longer & Went home sick at heart & sick in body = I am told that Lord Stanley is the cause of the whole dilemma in which we are placed – He insists upon our passing the Bill & connects it with his bill for Irish registration = Many [,] very many are Extremely indignant at this conduct of Lord Stanley – if it is pursued it will assuredly break up the party – If he Joins us he should adopt our politics, not we his – The Duke of Wellington, as I am assured, is now decidedly against the bill, & if it depended upon him it would be thrown out of the house =

*1 July 1840.* In the House of Lords last night the Duke of Wellington in a most Statesmanlike Speech opposed the Canada Bill to join the Provinces – His opinion is at variance with that of others, namely Sir Robert Peel [,] Lord Stanley &c who have supported it in the Commons – by the by with the Knowledge that the Duke was opposed to it – & the Duke had the manliness & I say the wisdom to Express the Sentiments & the view of the question which he Entertains –

Mr Butt was with me this morning, they are all So anxious that I should stay to vote on Lord Wynfords' motion to exclude Dublin from the Corporation Bill that I have consented to postpone my Journey untill after Monday 6th [.] I feel very unwell & country air is very necessary for me, but I am bound to render Such Service as I am able on this important occasion –

*2 July 1840.* What is now passing creates much conversation, Speculation &c – It is good that it has broken out now, as a check may be timely given to political trickery & [breaking] of principles, by which the interests of the party are Sacrificed to the loss of character of the individuals who are the chief managers of these odious plots – Lord Stanley & his friends leave Lord Grey's government [,] they soon manifest a disposition to Join us, but they wish to preserve their Consistency – Sir Robert Peel &c Seek their alliance & to obtain it in fact compromise their principles to secure the desired Junction – Hence Sir Roberts too celebrated manifesto to the Tamworth Electors & his policy Ever Since – But Conservatives are censorious of the mischief which attends Such a course, they are beginning to Express a determination to see a different & a better order of things & it will be soon seen that Conservatism in its purity, is Expected, & not a nominal profession which infact differs little from reform & revolution –

We must maintain an adherence to Protestantism, to the old Institutions of the country in Church & State, correcting abuses if necessary but not by upsetting Every thing & depriving us of all that has hitherto made England & Englishmen the Envy & the admiration of the world – If Lord Stanley is to be our ally he must strip off his old political doctrines & prejudices, & Peel if he is to be our prime Minister must represent us in Spirit & in truth or he will not fill that situation – Things must be called by their right names & patriots must be honest & true or they will be viewed as cheats & denied a following –

*3 July 1840.* almost all of a sudden a great disjunction has appeared amongst our party, & without Knowing how or why it has arisen – but good will Eventually come out of it & the chaff will be Sifted from the wheat – people all Seem to be in wonder & amazement –

*5 July 1840.* The Enquiry is ["] what will be done with the Canada bill in the House of Lords ["?] – Lord Hardwicke is resolved to move its rejection & declares that he does so of his own accord Without Communication & unconnected with anyone – We are to divide above 40 tomorrow / they tell me / on[76] Lord Wynfords' motion to Exempt Dublin from the provisions of the Irish Corporations bill –

*6 July 1840.* a long debate on Lord Wynford's motion, & as I was desirous of hearing all that was said on the occasion & had some intention of Saying Something myself I remained without my dinner untill $\frac{1}{2}$ past 11 – When we divided 35 against 72[77] – Nothing Could be More frivolous & vexatious than the pretexts used by the advocates for the bill, they really amounted to nothing & yet for these we were to vote away the rights & privileges of Corporate bodies & Established for the Express purpose of preserving & upholding the Protestant religion in the Country – The Duke of Wellington spoke strongly against the bill & voted for it – He begged of his friends to imitate his bad Example – Lord Lyndhurst left the house & did not Vote – On my return home I found dear Edward here who had Slipped up from Portsmouth for 2 days to see us before leaving England –

*7 July 1840.* Today we had Lord Hardwick's motion that the bill for joining the Canadas should be read in Committee on this day 6 months – Lord Hardwick introduced his motion With an Excellent Speech which from its honest & Earnest tone gained much & warm applause = Lords Melbourne & Normanby Spoke for the bill – The Duke of Wellington spoke most strongly against the bill & represented all the Evils & dangers which Would arise from it – but he concluded with stating that the opinion of the House of Commons was at variance with his & particularly those of the persons with whom he was in the habit of acting on which account he Earnestly Entreated his friends to vote for the bill & against Lord Hardwick's motion – The poor devils who follow him implicilly [*sic*] were, though dreadfully ashamed of themselves, obliged to vote black, white, & what was Still more curious the Duke of Wellington at the head of his followers, was slow in moving towards the bar, I heard Lord Salisbury Say to him, Seeing his consolation, "don't divide go by the Throne". The Duke considered the proposal an instant & turned to go towards the throne whilst he Sent Lord Salisbury to bring back those who had gone below the bar – in the mean time the Duke altered his intention & made up his mind to go below the bar which he proceeded to effect followed by his Satellites – it was indeed a Sorry Sight – & a Contemptible Situation to be placed it [*sic*] – The character & respectability of the Members of the House of Lords ought to be more Considered – [it] should not thus be trifled with, to their degradation & dishonour – We divided only 10 in the house & 107 below the bar[78] –

*10 July 1840.*[79] The Carlists are finally driven out of Spain – Cabrera, Bal Mesada [Captain Juan Martin de Balmaceda] & others with their different troops have passed the frontier & taken refuge in France = at length the horrible Savage & bloody civil war which has raged

[76] tomorrow precedes this in the original.

[77] The vote was 35 for the amendment and 82 against: majority 47.

[78] 'A division is effected in the Lords by the not-contents remaining within the bar, and the contents going below the bar': T. Erskine May, *A Practical Treatise of the Law, Privileges, Proceedings and Usages of Parliament* (3rd edn, 1855), 284.

[79] K.D., 10 July 1840, 'Called [on] Duke of Newcastle'.

for so many Years will be terminated & it is to be hoped that the feelings which should characterise Christianity will again resume their rule –

*19 July 1840.* The Duke of Wellington has again been taken ill in the Same manner as before, but not So Severely as before – The accounts state that he was much better & that he would Soon be well again – I fear that his life is Extremely precarious & that he cannot last long – He will hardly get over the autumn, I think –

*22 July 1840.* The Duke of Wellington is well & about again – The Irish Corporations bill has been postponed by Lord Duncannon but the Duke of Wellington made certain remarks upon the taxing clauses which many hope may ultimately lead to the rejection of the bill – This is almost too great a blessing to befall us –

*25 July 1840.* When the Regency bill was read the other day in the House of Lords [,] the Duke of Sussex thought fit to make a long Speech upon it – criticised & commented upon it & made several objections, plainly shewing that he was not Satisfied & that he was much disappointed that he was not included in the arrangement = The [Lord] Chancellor Said a little in reply, but no one Else Said a word, & the bill passed –

*29 July 1840.* The ecclesiastical revenues bill has Just been read a Second time in the House of Lords after a Strong debate which led to a division – 99 for the bill 48 – against – majority 51[80] – I rejoice that the majority under the circumstances Was So strong – The Bishop of Winchester [Charles Sumner] & Lord Lyttelton spoke, Well against the bill – the latter I rejoice to see taking this line as he is a young man of right mind & ability –

*31 July 1840.* […] Lord Durham is dead [–] he died quite worn out & Exhausted – & only 48 – a clever man with a wretched temper.

*2 August 1840.* The Ecclesiastical duties & revenues bill went into Committee [.] The Bishop of Exeter opposed it in a most powerfully reasoned Speech – The archbishop of Canterbury [William Howley] replied to the Bishop's remarks affecting himself & owned that he was not a Church reformer untill after Sir Robert Peel's speech when the mode of proceeding was suggested to him, which he approved for the Sake of doing something & in which he has subsequently been involved to his own discredit & the great injury of the Church – The Duke of Wellington repeated his opinions of the necessity of doing Something to save the Church & promote religion in the Country, that he always thought that the Church should lead the way in making Sacrifices & farther that it was only when the means of the Church Were Exhausted that the Country & Parliament Should be called upon to do what remained & was then required – This is a lamentable doctrine – So the Church resources are to be run out & the Church beggared before a shilling be voted for the Extension of the Church establishment & promotion of Religion in the Country! –

[80] In the vote on 27 July 1840, there were 99 Contents (67 present and 32 proxies) and 48 Not Contents (34 present and 14 proxies). Newcastle left his proxy with Kenyon: K.P., Box 72, Kenyon to Lloyd Kenyon, 20 July 1840.

*4 August 1840.* [...] Some of the Newspapers & a large portion of the public are Extremely indignant at the passing of the Irish Corporations bill – it is Justly attributed to treachery – Those who have betrayed us are, Sir Robert Peel, who to Keep Lord Stanley consents to advocate & Support his views, the Duke of Wellington & Lord Lindhurst [*sic* – who] in compliance with the requisition of the first, have attempted to blind us first & then have betrayed us = Such Sins will be avenged – / – avenged by God through the agency of man –

*9 August 1840.* [...] a mad & childish attempt has been made by Louis Napoleon who landed with 50 followers from an English Steamer [the Edinburgh], & Endeavoured by stratagem to take possession of Boulogne – They Went up to the Colonne [de Napoleon] & Erected the old Imperial banner on its Summit, they afterwards tried to gain the Soldiers, but met with not the Slightest Encouragement, on the contrary they all turned out against him & attacked him & he was So closely pressed that on his flight he could not regain the steamer Without taking to the Water which he did – the troops fired upon them in the water, several were Killed & Louis nearly drowned – He & his followers were taken & thrown into prison – What will be done with him no one can tell – I think he ought to be tried for the murder of the Soldier whom he Shot –

*10 August 1840.* No particular news today – one is led to believe by the accounts from France that a strong impression was made by Louis Napoleon's mad attempt – it will be well if, now that France is most wild with the prospect of the Shews which will be prevalent when [Napoleon] Bonaparte's bones are brought from St Helena for public interment in France, nothing transpires to raise a flame in favor of the usurper's dynasty to the prejudice of that of Louis Philipe [*sic*] – The thing is possible, out [*sic* – but] still I do not think that it will go far –

*14 August 1840.* Parliament was prorogued on the 11th [.] The speech was worthy of the ministers & of the principles by which they were guided – it Enumerated as benefits some of the very Worst measures which Ever passed a parliament – The Ecclesiastical revenues bill, a most pernicious & fatal bill to the Church – The Irish corporations bill – the Canada bill all fatal measures – This is the worse Session I Ever remember – one more prejudicial & disgraceful to the Conservatives, to their honor, good name & character, it is difficult to conceive & has lowered them in the Estimation of the public 50 per cent – & there is no Saying how much more –

*16 August 1840.* [...] The press & nearly the whole country joins in chorus in Condemnation of the policy & the conduct which the Conservatives have pursued in Parliament this Session – it has been So glaringly delinquent that I am not Surprised at this feeling [,] I am only Surprised that it has not been stronger =

*19 August 1840.* Dr Molesworth Vicar of Rochdale has Communicated to me his wish to found a general measure of the defence of poor Church rates & wishes to consult me upon it & desires to be permitted to call upon me for that purpose –
  The Papists in Ireland are rampant with joy at the prospect of what the new corporations act will do for them: they are doubtless preparing to Eradicate the Protestants wherever

they can find them = & in truth Every thing is done to give them advantage & Protestants discouragement – But the mind of the people is roused & this wretched policy & criminal desertion of our principal men will be rejected & disclaimed & resisted by the Sound Protestant majority of the Nation –

*21 August 1840.* There are Symptoms of war all over the world, but I do not think that there will be any thing Serious in any part – The Ottoman Empire & Constantinople are in a very disturbed & unsettled state […] Russia is Said to be marching a large army into Circassia – if war is waged by any Power it will be by Russia, She is the only Power menacing the Peace of Europe both by political intrigue & force of arms –

*23 August 1840.* The Russians are collecting an army of 200 000 Men on the frontiers of Circassia ostensibly to coerce & Subject that country, but more probably for Some other much more important operations – France is arming, it is Said actively, & now we are beginning to do So – what this means I Know not – but I think it will End in a Junction of the English & French forces against the aggressive Russians –

*1 September 1840.* […] War with France is uppermost in the public mind – The English are quite against it – The French on the contrary Seem in favour of it – but they will be disappointed there will be no war – The war will be with Russia if any & the probability is that We are Manoeuvring in a Sneaking manner, in concert with France [,] to get a large force in the Mediterranean to oppose Russia if She Should make a hostile demonstration with her 200 000 Men –

*2 September 1840.* The Pacha of Egypt, Mahomet ali, [Muhammad Ali Pasha] has openly declared his determination to resist the execution of the Treaty lately Entered into by the 4 Powers[81] = He Signifies that he will not be the aggressor, that he will act upon the defensive, but that he will meet force by force = He has thus Sealed his own death warrant – & it is right that it Should be So – thus fulfilling the prophecy which will Surely be accomplished now as heretofore –

*5 September 1840.* The poor Princess augusta is probably dead [–] she has been ill for some time & the accounts Seem to announce Speedy disolution [*sic*] – She is an Excellent person & Will be greatly lamented by those who Know & are dependent upon her –

   Every device is resorted to in France to Exacerbate the French against England, nevertheless I think the attempt will fail – there will be no war with France –

*9 September 1840.* Wars, tumults, rebellion & anarchy, more or less all over the world – Every Nation appears to be in perplexity – individuals cannot Expect to free from Evils, when Empires are nationally oppressed by them – These may be Signs of the times to those who will understand[82] –

---

[81] The *Convention for the Pacification of the Levant*, signed on 15 July 1840 between the United Kingdom, Austria, Prussia, Russia, and the Ottoman Empire, attempted to resolve the Egyptian crisis.

[82] A much-used phrase in Newcastle's diary, taken from Matthew, 16: 2–3.

*11 September 1840.* Much discussion upon a rumoured coalition between the administration & the Duke of Wellington & Sir Robert Peel – I do not believe a word of it – but if any thing So unnatural Should be perpetrated, it would lead to the utter destruction of the Coalescing parties –

*12 September 1840.* The Paris tumults are apparently quelled – Those at Madrid I cannot understand, but they appear to arise from a state of anarchy & no government – Popery is rearing its head in this Country with all the Effrontery belonging to it – It is well that it Should be So – Nothing Else will lead to its final & not long distant overthrow –

*13 September 1840.* The warlike appearances do not diminish – Yet Still I hope & believe that there will be no war with France – Louis Philippe is stated to have gained his point of fortifying Paris – How Such a project is to be Executed nowadays I cannot Conceive –

*16 September 1840.* Mr [Tresham] Gregg wishes to inform me of the Success of the various meetings formed in various large towns to hear him descant against Popery & urge its Expulsion & the repeal of the unfortunate & criminal bill of 1829 – He tells me that his Success is wonderful & that Every where the demonstration against Popery & for Protestantism is Cheering & decisive – I believe this to be the case, although perhaps the ardent feelings of the Irish gentleman may rather over state the case –

*18 September 1840.* No particular news today – The hostile language of the French press Encreases – the preparations are on a large Scale by land & sea, & pushed with much activity. The fortifications of Paris have commenced — They are to cost by Estimate £4 millions – but more probably it is thought, the double of that Sum – We are actively commissioning Ships & Several Ships of first class are ordered to sea as soon as they can be made ready –

*19 September 1840.* The French Minister is making great diplomatic exertions at Constantinople, & is opposing himself Singly to all the allied powers – It is difficult to conceive what object France can have in view in taking this part –

an affair of great injustice is now before the public – a Captain [John] Reynolds of the 11th Lancers, appears to have been most tyrannically & unjustly treated by his Commanding officer Lord Cardigan – appeals are made to the Commander in Chief [Lord Hill] but he sides Entirely with Lord Cardigan & denies all Enquiry & will not listen to the Statements & representations of Captain Reynolds – the affair will make much noise & will do much injury to those who have treated Captain Reynolds with So much injustice & harshness — We are arriving at those days where Might beats right, & force is Superior to Justice[83] –

*20 September 1840.* If the accounts are to be credited there are strong Symptoms of giving way on the part of ali Pacha, & I hope & Expect that we Shall Shortly learn that he has

[83]The incident arose when Reynolds ordered a bottle of Moselle wine at a formal mess dinner for a visitor, which was served in a black bottle. Cardigan thought that this was an act of disobedience, having banned the serving of porter, which also came in black bottles. Reynolds was arrested and subsequently reprimanded by Lord Hill.

complied with the terms of the allied powers that all prospects of war on that account have terminated – From What may be collected from the departments it appears that the French Nation is as averse to war as England is –

*26 September 1840.* Lord & Lady Powis & their daughters left us this morning, they Were delighted With this place – & we are most Sorry to have lost their agreeable Society –

*27 September 1840.* The Princess augusta is gone, She died on the 23rd [.] She was an Excellent person & of the good old Stock – Old Lady Dysart is dead at the age of 95 –

*30 September 1840.* There is a rumour of Mehemet ali having given in, by Consenting to all that the 4 powers require of him –

*5 October 1840.* News is arrived of the destruction of Beyrout [*sic*] after a bombardment of 9 days, – other places Will no doubt Share the Same fate – what the consequences will be it is difficult to foretell – but still I cannot think it possible that France will go to war to Support by her Single Exertion a rebel & cesesser [*sic*] upon the throne –

about a fortnight or three weeks ago there was a fire at Devonport where three ships were destroyed & other damage to a great amount in the dock yard – the undoubted work of an incendiary – Now there has been the Same thing at Sheerness, Ships of the line burned &c & as at Plymouth faggots trains &c found Shewing it to be the work of an incendiary – yet notwithstanding all this no guard or watch is Set to preserve our navy & dock yards from destruction – It is Suspected that the work is perpetrated by Some foreigners or persons Employed by a foreign power –

*6 October 1840.* The King of Holland [William I] has abdicated the Throne in favor of his Son [William II] & has retired into private life, intending to marry a Papist Lady of his Court [Henrietta d'Oultremont] which marriage has been much opposed by his family & people –

Farther accounts from the Mediterranean – with details of the destruction of Beyrout, & blockade of alexandria – also from China – Some Skirmishes between our Ships & Junks in Which the crews of the Junks appear to have behaved uncommonly well – & our own brave fellows most admirably – From India the accounts state that we may have Enough to do to Keep our ground & nothing but our military Skill & Consummate Conduct Secure us in our frontiers –

There is a great contest for the Lord Mayoralty & the Strongest Exertions Making to Keep out the Wretch Alderman [James] Harmer – the vile Editor of the Execrable Weekly Despatch –

*9 October 1840.* The war party in France is becoming very noisy & forward [–] the Minister [Adolphe] Thiers threatens to resign if war be not made, to which the King is disinclined – it is Said however that he has been obliged to give in to the war cry & yield his opinions & wishes for present – I doubt not that he will temporise & Eventually avert a war which he must See Would be ruinous to France –

*10 October 1840.* Prince Louis Bonaparte has been condemned by the Peers to imprisonment for life in a French fortress – a very lenient verdict for such an offender – He will
soon be loose again Somehow or other, I doubt not =

*13 October 1840.* The Revenue accounts shew a very large deficiency on the year as compared with the past deficient year – namely of £676000 on the present year – mismanage-
ment & want of Confidence, not a want of means, are the Sole Cause of the deficiency –
    The Marquis of Camden is dead – another Garter to be given away by the vile creatures
now in Office – The Lieutenancy of Kent falls also to their gift –

*15 October 1840.* No news from abroad of much importance – The French Government
has <u>authorised</u> the singing of the revolutionary Marsellaise [La Marseillaise] hymn = it has
already Effected great mischief by Exciting that Excitable people – the national guard is
assuming an authoritative tone & risings are Expected & have arisen in various parts –
Much Judicial & retributive punishment is yet reserved for France –

*25 October 1840.* The news from France is Excellent today – Thiers has resigned – Louis
Philippe objected to the Speech which created a decided difference between him & his
Minister of which he was but too happy to avail himself – & Thiers & his whole cabinet were dismissed [...] the King has acted in usual manner – bold, able, prudent &
decisive – I Sincerely wish him Success, he deserves it for his wisdom & patriotism –
His life was again attempted only a few days ago, by one of the war madmen, & yet in
the face of this danger the King fearlessly takes a Step which he Knows to be right at
the risk of his life & Even, in the Opinion of Some but not in mine, of his Throne –
If he is Successful the idea of war is at an End – indeed, the great point of objection
to Thiers' Speech was the insertion in it of a call upon the Nation, for 150 000 more
Troops –

*26 October 1840.* Lord Holland died rather Suddenly on the 22nd [.] He died of gout in
the stomach – he had long been a great Cripple from gout – He is no loss in any sense
– He has always been a bad liver, thoroughly unprincipled in Every respect & I presume,
like his wife, a professed atheist = He was Chancellor of the Duchy of Lancaster & of the
Cabinet – He has been latterly at the head of a party in the Cabinet consisting of Lord
Lansdown & Some others who have opposed Lord Palmerston's foreign policy – His death
may therefore Cause Some difference in the ministerial measures –

*27 October 1840.* The news from France is uncertain – at home a Coalition is still talked of
& believed – but the idea is so monstrous that I cannot Entertain it for a moment –

*2 November 1840.* The new Rural police system is becoming very unpopular [,] in many
Counties they have rejected it [,] as in Derbyshire, Somerset &c [,] in others it has only been
adopted partially; & lately in Leicestershire the encrease of force, which was called for, has
been refused – I trust that a very short time, Especially when it touches their pockets, will
bring Englishmen to reason, & induce them with one accord to Extinguish a System So
utterly inconsistent with Every principle of their former cherished & valued Constitution –

*5 November 1840*. Today the French Chambers meet − It will be a curious & interesting point to learn the result & whether the new Ministry will Stand or fall = Lord John Russell is about to reunite himself to a daughter of Minto, he is 50 & She 25 −

*6 November 1840*. In France the new Ministry is Every day gaining ground in public opinion & is Expected to have a majority of 30 in the Chambers − The war frenzy, which prevailed Chiefly at Paris is fast declining, & peace will be maintained − The press is to be controlled & revolutionary Meetings, Songs & writings to be repressed −

*7 November 1840*. The King's Speech made on the 5th in Paris is arrived by Express is [*sic* − it was] published & was in my hands this morning before 12 o'clock − This would Seem Wonderful Some years ago but now in these days of Steam it Seems nothing −

*12 November 1840*. News from the East − Our armies are exposed to great trials [,] difficulties & Some loss − The native Chiefs are now roused to make opposition & to Endeavour to recover what they have lost. Kelat has been retaken & other places garrisoned by English troops have been attempted & were in danger of falling − In China our fleet had arrived & operations were about to Commence −

*14 November 1840*. The Death of Lord Camden caused a Vacancy of Chancellor of University of Cambridge − The Duke of Northumberland High Steward was Elected Chancellor − a Strong contest has Just been concluded for the High Stewardship − Lord Lyndhurst has been Elected by a majority over Lord Lyttelton of 485 − Lord Lyttelton polled 486 votes − being a very young Man & urged on by too much Self Sufficiency, this contest has done him harm = however [,] defeat will be a lesson to him & teach him to Know himself −

*22 November 1840*. The news has arrived today, very unexpectedly, of the Queen's accouchement − She has been delivered of a Princess no doubt greatly to the disappointment of all − Very great & uniform mystery & secrecy has been observed throughout & nobody Knew what was going on −

*24 November 1840*. The Queen & infant Princess are going on prosperously − Her Majesty is so Strong & hardy that She makes nothing of this matter −
   The French Ministry is going on well − it will probably prove to be the best that France has had Since the accession of Louis Philippe −

*28 November 1840*. The accounts of the attack & capture of acre are arrived: it Seems to have been a most gallant & very brilliant affair conducted & led by Sir Robert Stoppard [Stopford] in person − The loss on the Side of the unfortunate Egyptians was very great indeed a whole batalion [*sic*] of 1500 was blown up together − the carnage dreadful − Large Stores of Every Kind, 300 pieces of ordnance, & a considerable treasure fell into our hands […] Our loss has been Small − I fancy that I perceive a Specially overruling Providence in all that transpires, Especially in this peculiar quarter −

*29 November 1840*. General [William Henry] Harrison has been elected President of the United States by a very large majority = He is Elected for 4 years from March next, when

President [Martin] Van Buren will go out of office – Harrison is brought in by the Democratic & anti English party, & it is Supposed that he will obstruct the boundary question as much as possible & maintain Even by force of arms the right to the territory which they have Endeavoured to filch from us & assert to belong to the district of Maine – The Election of this Man Will assuredly bring about a crisis in american affairs. The beaten (& the best) party will not tamely Submit, & in all probability civil war & Eventual breaking up of the Union will be the consequence = We here see the blessings of the ballot & universal Suffrage – It is Stated that for the last 9 months the whole Union has been a continued Scene of strife, bribery, corruption & intimidation far belong [*sic* – beyond] any thing Ever Known before – 5000 are Said to have been driven about from place to place at the Service of the highest bidder – Sometimes acting on one Side [,] Sometimes on the other –

*3 December 1840.* Nothing new from abroad – at home the Queen & Princess are doing marvellously well, not a minutes illness from the moment of birth –

*4 December 1840.* The youth John [Edward] Jones who about 2 years ago obtained admission to the Palace, has again intruded himself & was found concealed under a Sofa in the Queens Sitting room = how he got there does not appear or why = it appears in this day's paper –

*5 December 1840.* The name of the young vagabond who was found in the Queen's dressing room is a Edmund [Edward] Jones = He appears to have no other motive for his conduct, but that of making himself notorious – The best punishment for him & Similar characters would be a Sound Scourging which Should not be Soon forgotten –

   Lord Palmerston does not scruple to publish that Lord Holland invariably reported all that passed in the cabinet to Mr Edward Ellice who regularly transmitted the whole information to Monsieur Thiers – Such infamous rascality I hardly Ever heard of but these men are capable of any thing base, villainous & detestable – For Lord Holland I always entertained a great aversion [–] atheists[84] & free thinker, could only be Worthless –

*6 December 1840.* The Ships under the command of the Duc de Joinville which Went out to St Helena to bring back [Napoleon] Bonaparte's remains – are returned with their precious freight — The last French papers announce their arrival at Cherbourg – The foolish pageant will now commence & Serve to distract the attention of our giddy neighbours for a short time –

*7 December 1840.* By the failure of Messrs Wrights Bank – [Henrietta Street] Covent Garden, many will be serious losers – I am assured that the Duke of Norfolk will lose at least £ 70 000 –

*9 December 1840.* accounts arrived of our Successes & prowess all over the World – in Egypt – India & China – In the first Commander [Charles] Napier has managed his affairs So well that he has obliged the Pacha to give in on Every point & Submit to his terms – He Evacuates Syria, gives up the Turkish fleet & consents to the whole of his Syrian army

[84]& precedes this in the original.

being conveyed by our fleet to alexandria – The Pacha is to retain the hereditary Pachalic of Egypt – & thus the war is Ended – triumphantly & beneficially as regards ourselves –

In India with Small & very inadequate means We have Managed to Keep our ground & gain Successes over the Enemy. Successes not lightly Won for Dost Mahomed [Dost Mohammad Khan] fought valiantly & rallied & returned twice or thrice to the charge, before he would own our Superiority by flight –

In China we have taken possession of the island of Chusan & in all probability have pushed our Successful operations up the country, which Evidently begins to tremble & crouch to our Superiority in, Science & arms – The thunder of our guns & the daring approach of our forces have for the first time Extracted from the Chinese authorities an acknowledgement of our Equality, & communications of a very Civil nature have been made to us by Some of the Chinese authorities –

*13 December 1840.* It is considered by good judges that we require an addition of at least 20000 men to our infantry to do Even the peace duties in Great Britain & Her dependencies –

Symptoms of a revival of prosperity to our trade & Commerce are thought to be perceptible & [a] better State of things is anticipated by the Ensuing Spring = The depression upon almost Every branch has for Some time been most deplorable – a great many failures are now occurring in various quarters –

*14 December 1840.* […] I hear no news here Except that Lord Palmerston has disagreed with the Cabinet & has threatened to resign: the fact, I suspect, is that his Lordship is looking to a Change & as usual wishes to be on the winning Side –

*20 December 1840.* The Pageant of the interment of [Napoleon] Bonaparte's remains has passed off without any disturbance of the peace – The populace Exhibited no revolutionary or bad feeling – on the contrary they merely gazed in wonder & amusement at the gaudy Shew & Shewed the greatest good humour towards the English & all others collected upon the occasion – The revolutionary party is miserably low, & the government gaining ground daily –

*23 December 1840.* an extensive promotion in the Syrian fleet has been made – 41 mates have been made Lieutenants, but my dearest Edward has the mortification not to be included = His cause has hitherto been very unlucky – Lord Mintos Son [Charles Gilbert John Brydone Elliot] who is a Commander & had a Small ship off acre will be made Post = He is two years Junior to Edward & passed full two years after his passing – & yet he is now many years before him & in an Enviable position in the Service – This is too bad[85] –

*29 December 1840.* It now appears that Captain Napier was no[t] authorised to negociate with the Pacha & Sir Robert Stoppard has refused to ratify his treaty – He has himself negociated with the Pacha & has gained his compliance with all his terms – The Turkish

---

[85] Elliot entered the navy on 6 May 1832. He was promoted to lieutenant on 27 June 1838 and commanding officer of the sloop 'Hazard' on 16 July 1840. He was involved in the bombardment of Acre (Nov. 1840) and was subsequently promoted to captain on 16 Aug. 1841.

fleet is to be immediately restored, Syria [,] Candia &c Evacuated – Sir Robert Stoppard Engaging for the 4 powers that the deposition of ali by the Porte Shall not be Enforced – but it is understood that his retention of the Pachalic Shall be restricted by many necessary Conditions [.]

*31 December 1840.* With this day we conclude the old year – If I could I would observe the rule de mortuis nil nisi bonum[86] – but Justice requires that it Should not acquire a false reputation – many bad things have been done & [especially so] far as acts of parliament go, & continued dismemberment of the old constitution, with as much transformation of our institutions & all that which forms character, as the space of time will admit of, the greatest injury has been done to the State – / To counterbalance this in Some measure, the public mind is very considerably ameliorated, & though our So called leaders have Shamefully misbehaved themselves & have Served to mislead public opinion, yet thank God the good Sense of the nation views matters in a truer light than they have done & is steadily advancing towards the attainment of that goal which [,] if one reached by a nation [,] must Secure for it lasting & most Extraordinary blessings – as for myself & what concerns my family I have nothing to complain of & much, very much for which to be most thankful & humbly grateful, Prosperous I have not been, neither I or mine, but in that I may See the goodness of God who will not permit the vanities of this World to dazzle & Seduce by the bright illusion of Success, or the giddy allurement of too much worldly Enjoyment —

*1 January 1841.* [...] I commence this year with a full determination to do my best to deserve, as much as I am able, the blessings So graciously Shewn to me – But little is within my ability, but that little I must make available to the Extent of that ability – I fancy that I see indications of amazing Events which probably may be largely developped [*sic*] Even in the present year –

*8 January 1841.* accounts are arrived from China & the East Indies – Our vigorous & bold operations have quite over awed the Emperor of China – admiral [Charles] Elliot had gone up to Pekin [*sic*], had been received by the Emperor, who declared his friendly intentions, that all which had been done amiss had been by mistake & that he was willing to make any reparation – He agreed to pay 2,000,000 to reimburse our Merchants for the loss of the opium which had been Seised, & as Governor Linn [Lin Zexu] had been the Executive aggressor in seising the Merchanise & ill treating the British, all which he declared he had done without orders, he signified his wish to deliver poor Linn up to us that we might do as we pleased by him – Thus is this affair terminated – & most advantageously & fortunately for us –

In India Dost Mahomud has been beaten & has Entirely submitted & resigned Every thing to us, So that we have now full possession of all the Country from the ganges to the Indus & to the Persian frontier. Such Success is quite miraculous – I mean this in its literal Sense – Providence has given us what without Such aid could not have been atchieved [*sic*] –

---

[86] 'Of the dead, [say] nothing but good'.

*17 January 1841.* Now that the time approaches for a change of administration, Seeing that the present miserable crew can only Exist by toleration & contrivance – The public mind is Every where & upon Every occasion very unequivocally Expressed respecting any administration which may Succeed the present, coming in under Conservative Colours. The press & public meetings have Expressed their opinion very generally that the old Story will not do – the doubtful men, the old hacks in office will not be endured = men of worth, of Sound principles, & tried friends to Church & State will be the only men who will find favour – no compromising, no temporising, no Equivocation will be permitted, & if Sir Robert Peel composed his ministry of Such ingredients, he will most assuredly fail in the most signal manner – I rejoice with Exceeding Joy to witness Such an Existing growing temper of the national mind, it is that alone which can, & by God's help it will [,] Save us Eventually from the pernicious State into which the nation has been cast. This is the frame of mind which I have long been wishing & looking for & thank God, it is at last arriving in full force – & a very remarkable Sign it is –

*20 January 1841.* Captain Reynolds of the 11th Hussars of black bottle celebrity tendered his resignation at the Horse Guards on the ground of not being able to live in the regiment with Lord Cardigan – Lord Hill begged that he would revoke his intention & much negociation took place on the Subject – the result was that [,] as the price of his staying in the regiment, 6 months leave was to be granted to him, which had been refused by Lord Cardigan: he was to be allowed to pass 2 years at the Senior department of Sandhurst College, & never again under any pretence to be required to serve under Lord Cardigan – These terms most strange to say were granted – & thus an inferior officer has actually dictated to the authorities at the Horse Guards.

*25 January 1841.* Ld abingdon aged 57 is to be married to Lady Frederika Ker aged 24 –

*27 January 1841.* The Session opened yesterday with a Speech from the Throne of very peculiar brevity & meagreness – The debate upon it has not reached us, but I think that Some Strong remarks will be made upon the omissions [.]

*28 January 1841.* The debates on the Speech in both houses are as flat [,] meagre & un-interesting as the Speech itself – The members & the public Seem to take no interest in the proceedings in Parliament – & the former are flying back from London as fast as con-veyances can transport – I never remember such a dead feeling before – To what can it be attributed? The irresponsive conduct of our Leaders – The Duke of Buckingham Was So angry at the Duke of Wellington's Speech, that he would not dine with him afterwards —

*3 February 1841.* [...] The rumours respecting Mehemet ali are incorrect – all is now settled – The Sultan has consented to grant to him the Pachalic hereditarily – & ali has Surrendered the Turkish fleet, which is to sail immediately for Constantinople, under the command of admiral [Baldwin Wake] Walker = ali has certainly behaved in the noblest manner – & barring his cruelty & oppression is deserving of the rule which is granted to him –

*4 February 1841.* Canterbury & Walsall elections are both gained & two Conservatives Seated instead of two ministerialists – the former by a large majority 173 the latter by

38[87] – This gain to our Side, I believe, makes the numbers Even in the House of Commons – arrangements have been made for the trial of Lord Cardigan on the 14th [.] He is to take his trial at the bar of the House –

*5 February 1841*. Sensible of their weakness [,] the ministers yielded to Lord Stanley & actually voted for his motion although O'Connell divided the house upon it –

*6 February 1841*. Little interesting in Parliament [,] nothing doing in the House of Lords: in the Commons [,] Lord Morpeth brought in his Irish registration bill, which is almost a new reform bill & gives votes to men rated at £5 instead of £10 – which [is] thought to be highly objectionable by Lord Stanley –

*7 February 1841*. The Duke of Wellington has been attacked by another of his Seizures [–] he was taken ill in the house of Lords & nearly fell down from giddiness in the head & other unpleasant Symptoms – He was immediately taken home, where his medical men quickly attended him & he is said to be nearly well again – This is quite Evident – He is no longer fit for public business, & if he continues to attend in the House of Lords it will kill him –

*9 February 1841*. The Duke of Wellington is Said to be better – he has had a very bad attack, & his attendance to public business Seems to me utterly ought [*sic* – out] of the question, Even if he lives, which I think is Very doubtful –

*10 February 1841*. The Duke of Wellington is recovered & it is Said will resume his usual avications [*sic*] – So much the worse for he is totally unfit for public business & must do harm to himself & others – I was told confidentially that the doctors are of opinion that his affection is a paralysis of the brain –

Monmouthshire is won from the government party – Mr Tracey [W.H. Tracy] has resigned & Mr Octavius Morgan Comes in –

*11 February 1841*. By dint of audacious & unblushing bribery & use of the Queen's name, the ministerial candidate Lord Listowel has triumphed at St albans – The Conservative Candidate however, Mr Benjamin Bond Cabbell [,] has wisely abstained from any act of the Kind & will certainly come in on petition[88] –

*12 February 1841*. […] The Duke of Wellington was invited to act as Sponsor for the Duke of Saxe Gotha, Prince albert's father, & was Sufficiently well to attend the Christening of the Princess Royal in the capacity –

[87] At Canterbury, the Conservative George Symthe beat the Whig John Wright Henniker Wilson by 772 votes to 628: majority 144. At Walsall, the Conservative John Neilson Gladstone beat the radical John Benjamin Smith by 362 votes to 335: majority 27.

[88] The Whig William Hare, 2nd earl of Listowel, beat the Conservative Benjamin Bond Cabbell by 252–205 votes: majority 47.

*13 February 1841.* The support of Lord John Russell's bill for renewal of the present Poor Law bill with many bad additions, by Conservative Members [,] has given great umbrage – I greatly fear that for this county [Henry Gally] Knight has Endangered his Seat by a strong Speech in favor of the present law & amended bill –

*16 February 1841.* a Dissolution of Parliament, to take place before Easter, is talked of as a nearly certain Event –

*17 February 1841.* The trial of Lord Cardigan for fighting a duel with Captain [Harvey] Tuckett, commenced yesterday in the House of Lords [.] It Commenced with much ceremony, & the arrangements must have incurred an Expence Which the nature of the affair is not worth – a Duel is a most Condemnable transaction, but Viewed as it is by Society in general it Seems out of place to try Such a Case in State in the House of Lords[89] =

*18 February 1841.* The trial has terminated rather abruptly by the acquittal of Lord Cardigan, by a flaw in the indictment & failure in proving the identity of Captain Tuckett – It is perhaps well that it has Ended thus – but it reflects little credit on the law or Lawyers, for no one can doubt that it is all a preconcerted Juggle – The country has been put to a very unnecessary Expence for a few hours of State deception –

*19 February 1841.* Political Events crawl on most languidly – Much feeling is created in the country by Lord John Russell's new poor law bill [.] Knights' Speech upon it has done him irreparable harm in the County & I greatly fear that his seat is Seriously Endangered by it –

*21 February 1841.* But little transpires, apparently all is quiescent in public affairs, but in fact I believe the very reverse to be the case – I believe that there never was a period When greater changes were working – I am convinced that an immense deal of Secret & underhand work is going on which few dream of –

*22 February 1841.* Wynyard, Lord Londonderry's fine house, has been consumed by fire – Such is the report, I trust that it may be greatly Exaggerated – Lord & Lady Londonderry are abroad[90] –

*24 February 1841.* Lord Stanley opposed Lord Morpeth's bill in a very long & according to report a remarkably fine Speech – The Ministerial bill will be carried they Say by 8, but we think by not More than 5 –

*27 February 1841.* The debate is over & the division come to – after stirring Every thing – [Thomas] Wilde brought out of his bed, Sir [Edward Thomas] Trowbridge [Troubridge]

[89] The duel, which took place on Wimbledon Common, arose from Tuckett's account of the 'black bottle' affair in the *Morning Chronicle*. Cardigan was tried for injuring Tuckett.

[90] 'Except the loss of relatives or any principal functions of mind or body, no calamity can Equal destruction by fire': BL, Add. MS, 40429, f. 124: Newcastle to Peel, 23 Feb. 1841; N.U.M.D., Ne C 6137/1–2: Peel to Newcastle, 28 Feb. 1841. Wynyard was subsequently rebuilt.

voting with his daughter dead in his house two days before – the majority in favor of Ministers was 5 [299–294] = if Mr [Henry Negus] Burroughes whose daughter is dying, Granville Vernon who is abroad [,] & Colonel [William Edward] Powell who did not choose to attend [,] had been in the house – the Majority on this to them vital question would have been 2 – In committee they are Sure to be beaten –

*3 March 1841.* Lord John Russell has again given us the Slip – notwithstanding his pledge to go on with the bill, he now announces that he wants farther information & that he will postpone the future consideration of the bill untill after the Easter recess, by Which time the information will be obtained – if anything could Sink a set of men lower than they are, this would do it –

*4 March 1841.* It appears to me very likely that a Dissolution of parliament may be resorted to before or immediately after Easter –

*5 March 1841.* […] The grand Jury has found a true bill against Mr Mccleod [Alexander McLeod] for murder in the affair of the Caroline, & he was to take his trial at the end of this month. The americans Seem bent upon a hostile bearing towards England, & if Mccleod be condemned of course a war must Ensue.[91]

*6 March 1841.* In the debate upon the Bishop of Exeter's notice relative to the presentation of a petition from certain inhabitants of Canada complaining of the illegal incorporation of the Roman Catholic Seminary of St Sulpice, the Duke of Wellington Spoke out boldly & Significantly, & went So far as to call upon the public to interfere to prevent a violation of the principles of the Reformation – as he termed it – The Duke charges the Governor General Lord Sydenham with this illegal & unconstitutional act –

*9 March 1841.* The american Congress appointed a Committee to investigate & report upon the Case of Mr Mccleod – The deliberate report of the Committee is that Mr Mccleod is guilty of murder & Should Stand his trial – Thus in the most scandalous manner prejudging the Case – a warm debate took place upon the adoption & reception of the report & it was Strenuously [opposed] by Mr [John Quincy] adams late President of the United States [.] However after much Exciting language against England, the report was received & thus the matter stands, if Mccleod is tried & condemned War is inevitable – & adams & other rational men agree that america is in Every respect utterly unprepared for war –

*11 March 1841.* […] The Eastern affair is again opened, by the terms sent to the Pacha by the Porte / The latter requires that no member of the Pacha's family Shall Succeed to the Pachalik, but under the approval of the Sultan, his army shall never Exceed 20 000 men, he shall [appoint] no officers above the rank of captain which shall be nominated by the Sultan, his fleet is to be reduced & he is to build no More ships of the line – In Short by these & other Stringent provisions, Such as the Supervision of their proper Execution by

---

[91] McLeod, a Canadian, boasted that he had been involved in the sinking of an American steamboat which had been supplying the Canadian rebels with arms. Three years after the sinking took place (29 Dec. 1837), he was arrested by the Americans and charged with the murder of a sailor killed in the attack.

Turkish inspectors, the power of the Pacha is reduced to a mere Shadow, of which he is of Course perfectly aware & refuses to ratify the treaty in such terms. The whole is in Entire contravention of the terms guaranteed by England & of which we are bound by Every tie of honor & state of policy to require & obtain the fulfilment [–] & who is it that, alone, has done all this in opposition to Every thing honest & in defiance of our Solemn national Engagements? It is Lord Ponsonby our ambassador at Constantinople !!! & yet this man is permitted to remain in his situation to sully the national honor & marr all the political operations of the Government by which he is Employed. The whole System & discipline of this Wretched & vile Government is unexampled & monstrous –

*13 March 1841.* […] The Bishop of Exeter's motion to address the Queen to withhold her assent to the ordinance for incorporating the Popish Seminary of St Sulpice in Canada was to have come on on the 12th & great preparations were making on both Sides – The Duke of Wellington wished it to be generally Known that he cordially Supported the Bishop, but that Lord Ellenborough would take the opposite Side & would go with the Government – I wish he were there altogether – Under the pretext of requiring more information, the Bishop has been prevailed on to postpone his motion for a few days – doubtless that the faithless & rascally Government may resort to & practise some trick to out manoeuvre & dishonestly to carry their point –

*14 March 1841.* Questions have been asked & observations made by Sir Robert Peel & Lord Francis Egerton, respecting the Hatti Scheuff [Hatti-Sherif] of the Sultan to the Pacha – Lord Palmerston admits that the terms, as reported [,] have been offered, but that he Knows nothing officially – He hobbled out of the business very lamely – In my observations the other day I did not remark that the Turkish fleet had been given up by the Pacha & was actually in the port of Constantinople, this was on the faith of the Convention & yet [,] after that, the terms were offered by the Sultan which I have already named –

*17 March 1841.* The Bishop of Exeter has made his motion, but alas, for the honour of man & what is due, from a high character, the Duke of Wellington has deserted one may Say betrayed him – after the strong & decisive language used by the Duke on a former occasion [,] one would have little thought that he would thus deceive others & blast himself – But he has done it, & nothing can be Said in Extenuation, but that he is in his dotage – He gives as his reason that there Were Existing precedents of which [he] was not before aware & that he must have forgotten them as he himself must have been a party to them = To what are We fated? doubtless to much suffering from which we can not now see a prospect of relief – The Duke of Wellington has done more mischief to his country than all his brilliant victories can redeem – alas! That one Should have to avow this! –

*18 March 1841.* […] The Examination of Mr [William] Stanley, Secretary to the Poor Law Commission in Ireland [,] took place in the House when he was pretty well sifted by Some of the Lords especially Lord Glengall, who caused him scarcely to Know whether he Stood on his head or his heels – I never read of Such an Exhibition – it Seems distinctly proved not only that the poor law authorities have neglected their duty, but that they have prostituted their power to political purposes, & most iniquitously falsified the returns called for & made to the House of Lords – The business is only Just begun, it will probably End in a Severe reprimand, probably a new modelling if not a breaking up of the board of Commissioners – The trickery & dishonesty of the proceedings Must destroy whatever little confidence may have previously Existed –

*19 March 1841.* The authorities in Oxford have taken up the matter of the Oxford tracts publication, by [Edward Bouverie] Pusey, [John Henry] Newman &c & have determined to Separate their opinions from those of the University: a great deal of discussion, correspondence & argument is going on between the parties & I hope that it will Eventually purge the University of these Erroneous & pernicious doctrines which have arisen among a few Weak, vain [,] but well-meaning men –

*20 March 1841.* The Duke of Wellington's conduct on the Bishop of Exeter's motion has occasioned strong animadversion & deep disappointment. It is most unfortunate but the Conduct of our leaders disheartens our party & shakes all Confidence in the Country generally – we are in a pitiful plight Just now –

*21 March 1841.* Many of the advocates of the new Poor law are beginning to alter their tone & to Shrink from their advocacy in consequence of the loud expression of public opinion – Sir Robert Peel is one of these – The figure which the Poor Law Officers make before the House of Lords will not Encrease the public respect for them.

*26 March 1841.* The inaugural address of the new [American] President [William Henry] Harrison appears in this day's papers, it is long & wordy & full of analytical remarks, but it is altogether in a good though republican Spirit – Public opinion appears to have bettered in favor of England & I think that we Shall have no war – In France the apprehension is at an End, she has at last acceded to the treaty, & has joined the 4 Powers –

*29 March 1841.* It is asserted that the archbishop of Canterbury has at length found it necessary to interfere, & authoritatively to interdict the publication of the Oxford Tracts by Messrs Pusey, Newman & Co. = If what is Said of them be true there is little difference between them & Popery – They have done infinite mischief already –

*2 April 1841.* The accounts from america are pacific – it Seems to be certain that all differences will now be amicably adjusted – The Same course has been followed by France, who has now Joined the alliance upon certain Stipulated terms – the Main points being – that the Pachalic Shall be hereditary in Mehemet ali's family, & that the Dardanelles Shall be Shut to all Ships of War & open to all Merchant Ships – The Effect of these pacific arrangements is a rapid rise of the funds [–] 3 per Cent Consols being nearly 90 –

*4 April 1841.* after a very long investigation in the Ecclesiastical Court at York [,] the Dean of York ([Sir William] Cockburn) has been "deposed & deprived of all his Offices & Emoluments as Dean of York" – This is a strong & universal measure, but not more So than Cockburn's conduct deserves – nothing can have been Worse in Every respect = dishonest, unclerical, & contumacious [,] he has disgraced the office & drawn down upon himself this well merited punishment[92] –

*6 April 1841.* The latest news from america is not So favourable – The state of new York Seems determined to Keep & try Mcleod, the President is doing all he can to induce them to abandon it & to accommodate the matter –

*8 April 1841.* Whatever may be done to gratify the animosity & bad feeling of Some of the States of america, it is very Sure that the Confederation will not join in a war with England: first, the States generally are against it, next their Means are absolutely wanting, their finances being in the very lowest State – then their utterly unprotected frontier by Sea & by land – their Entire inefficiency for want of preparation of any sort, without army, navy or Stores – & lastly with an outraged Slave population of above 2 millions ready to turn against an oppressive population of 13 millions – already variously divided against itself –

*9 April 1841.* Good news by Express from China – Our differences are all accommodated with the Celestial Empire & war has ceased upon terms honorable & advantageous to us – The island of Hong Kong is yielded to us – 6 millions of dollars to be paid as an indemnity – Trade to be renewed on a footing of Entire Equality – & Every thing that was to be [is] restored to its former footing – There may be other Stipulations – but this news has come Express from Malta & is not given in detail, merely a brief Statement of leading facts – Thus again we are returned to peaceable relations with the rest of the world – [to] ourselves the glory & may it please God that we may prove ourselves worthy of this high destiny & distinction –

*11 April 1841.* The accounts from the East, from India & China [,] appear in detail – The poor Chinese have felt the power of our arms & have learned to fear it — The poor devils must be brave & fight away in a desultory manner as long as they [are] able, but Seem to have no more idea of discipline or European warfare than the men in the moon – Our affairs in that quarter have been committed to [Charles] Elliots & that is Enough to Stamp its character of inefficiency & nothingness = In India, we are going on well & almost miraculously overcoming Every thing & carrying all before us – Prudence is not forgotten, though heroism & Consummate ability direct our arms & Councils – I mean in what relates to local negociations or management –

*20 April 1841.* a change of ministers in Turkey & a promise immediately to adjust the differences in the way of giving those terms to the Pacha of Egypt which were guaranteed by England & the other powers.

The Bishop of Oxford [Richard Bagot] has forbidden the publication of the Oxford tracts –

*22 April 1841.* Commander [Charles] Napier is returned to England – he appears to do as he pleases any where & on all occasions – immediately on leaving his Ship he proceeded

---

[92] Cockburn was found guilty of simony but later acquitted on appeal to the court of queen's bench.

to Liverpool where they have trumped up a Sort of triumphal reception for him, given him a dinner where there was very little to Eat & bespattered him with praise, to which he replied in terms Sufficiently Egotistical of himself & vituperative of others, proving himself a worthy member of the tribe to Which he belongs –

*24 April 1841.* Lord Morpeth has announced that he Shall move & [*sic* – an] alteration in the qualification on his Irish registration & that he will Substitute £8 for £5 – O'Connell Sneered & Several of his friends are Said to have divided – Evidently he will lose by his concession –

*25 April 1841.* The Same languor & indifference which characterised the proceedings of Parliament from its opening to the Easter Recess, to Judge by what has already appeared [,] Seem likely to prevail throughout this Session – The fact is that our leaders have strangely mismanaged Every thing, they are not in favor & no one feels impelled with ardor to Serve men, who Serve the cause So ill – It is a sad misfortune – nor does a remedy present itself – There is alas no choice, but to Endure what cannot be cured[93] –

*27 April 1841.* The newspapers have brought good news this morning – a meeting has been holden at Sir Robert Peel's when he declared to the members present that it was his intention to oppose Lord Morpeth's registration bill in toto, not on this clause or on that, not in detail, but on the broad principle of it's [*sic*] badness, & on those grounds, he would propose to reject the bill in plain terms – This is the true & proper way of acting & if this mode is persevered in Peel will not want for Zealous Supporters[94] –

[My son] William arrived this Evening from Nottingham & he tells me that the news had arrived of the total defeat of the Ministerial bill – & now what will these miserables do they must resign –

*28 April 1841.* I learn today that the majority against ministers was no less than 21 [270–291]. The accounts Say that there was great commotion [.] Lords Melbourne & John Russell had had audiences of the Queen followed by a Cabinet Meeting & various other indications of tribulations – most people think that they will dissolve the Parliament instantly –

*29 April 1841.* No farther information as to what Ministers mean to do – Many think that they will yield to the disgrace & quietly submit to Lord Howick's amendments & thus contrive to Keep their places – the miserables will do any thing that is unworthy & tricking, or if pushed to an Extremity they are very likely to dissolve parliament merely to do as much Spiteful mischief as possible –

*30 April 1841.* The lately Elected President of the american States, General [William Henry] Harrison was very ill when the last accounts from america arrived, by those Just received he is dead – He has survived his honors only a few, about 30, days – it is Said that the excitement & fatigue of his election, brought on the disease which destroyed him – he is

[93]'What cannot be cured must be endured': Robert Burton, *The Anatomy of Melancholy* (1621).

[94]Newcastle wrote to Peel endorsing this line of proceeding: N.U.M.D., Ne C 5287: Peel to Newcastle, 29 Apr. 1841.

Succeeded by the Vice President, John Tyler; the law provides that in the Event of the death of a President, the Vice President Shall Succeed, as of Course – Tyler is represented in the american accounts of him to be a man of great ability & high character, & if they may be believed, a most Extraordinary man, of great energy & 55 years old – We Shall Soon Know what are his real qualities –

*2 May 1841.* [...] On the main clause of Lord Morpeth's Irish Electors bill – the Ministers were beaten by a majority of 11 [289–300] – Lord John Russell then announced to the house that he gave up the bill –

*3 May 1841.* Every body thought that Ministers must resign but instead of that the Chancellor of the Exchequer [Sir Francis Baring] comes down to the house [,] opens his budget & Signifies that the colonial trade is to be thrown open, the sugar duties reduced, that on timber the Same, the corn laws to be abolished & in lieu a fixed duty, making it a matter of taxation to produce a revenue of 400 000 – There never was any thing so basely & recklessly Wicked as the design of the whole proceeding = benefit to the Country is not thought [of,] what will gain or Secure place to themselves is the only consideration never mind at what risks or at what cost – but the Villainy will bend upon themselves = all are disgusted & in dismay[95] – Even their own friends are leaving them – In a few days we Shall See the Event –

*5 May 1841.* News from the East by overland dispatches – It is not good, we have Experienced Some defeats & lost many officers. The Chinese are procrastinating & it is thought making war–like preparations – & it is Supposed that we shall have to renew hostilities –

*6 May 1841.* In the House of Commons little doing – tomorrow will be the push When Lord Sandon will move the rejection of the ministerial Scheme for the Sugar duties –

*7 May 1841.* Lincoln went to London today to be present & vote at the debate tonight – all the colonial people & Slave Emancipators are up in arms, as well they may be when Slave made sugar is to be reduced 100 per Cent & our own free Sugar is Still to be left burdened with heavy duties –
[...] In all our Encounters with the Chinese it is admitted that they have universally conducted themselves with gallantry & courage –

*8 May 1841.* Tomorrow morning will convey the news of last nights' debate – no doubt there will be a large majority against Ministers – What they will do afterwards is not So Sure – It is thought that a large majority must prevent dissolution, if So, there will be no choice, but to resign —

*9 May 1841.* The ministers have contrived by trick & Expedient to put off the Evil hour – By a very unprecedented & unfair manoeuvre [.] Lord John Russell opened the debate in a very long Speech discussing the whole financial Scheme of the Ministers taking it

---

[95] See N.U.M.D., Ne C 5577: Lincoln to Newcastle, 1 May 1841.

Entirely out of the hands of the Chancellor of the Exchequer & rendering it difficult for Lord Sandon to treat his limited view of the Subject Which was confined to the Sugar question alone – This is quite a characteristic trick of a most dishonest & petty fagging Set of men – Of course there was much speaking & the next day being Saturday the debate was postponed to Monday – it is Expected to last until Tuesday or rather perhaps till Wednesday Morning, when the fate of this Vile Set may possibly be determined – The Ministers themselves have given it out that if they are beaten they will resign – But no credit whatever is to be given to a Syllable that they may utter –

*13 May 1841.* […] The Debate Still adjourned – The Ministers are at their wits End – The Queen Sent for Lord Spencer to Consult him – his opinion was that Ministers must resign & could not dissolve – There are Several points [,] removal of Sugar duties & financial grants [,] Which must be Settled before dissolution, & altogether under Such a recourse impracticable – which is most fortunate –

*14 May 1841.* The debate still adjourned to the wonder of Every one for there is nothing to say upon Such a Worn out Subject, & it is Evident that Ministers only seek to gain time & trust to the Chapter of accidents –

*16 May 1841.* The debate has been again adjourned – it began on Friday Week – Saturday & Sunday being [out] – by adjourning on Friday last to Monday next, tomorrow, they again have the benefit of two more days' respite, it is Expected that they Must Certainly divide tomorrow, Ministers will probably be beaten by 40 or 50 & on Friday they will resign – this is the bill of fare – The Queen has at length made up her mind to part with these vile Servants = I am told that the Duke of Cambridge has communicated this information – & I was also informed that at the Ball at Buckingham Palace on [the] 14th the Queen was markedly civil to Sir Robert Peel –

*18 May 1841.* We have accounts this afternoon from London by which it appears that [,] after all, & in spite of an understood agreement between the leaders, the debate, last night Monday, has again been postponed – Sir Edward Knatchbull moved the adjournment on Friday last & no doubt he opened the debate yesterday & was the only Speaker on our Side – for it Seems that there Were 12 Speakers on the ministerial Side & only 1 on ours – I have Several times Said that this was the only way to deal with the affair [–] let them Speak & make fools of themselves as much as they please but let us not follow their example – I am glad that this plan has been adopted – The Ministerial breath must be soon Exhausted [.] Lord John Russell must Speak at last & then Peel will answer him & the debate will close = It Seems to Exceed all former absurdities, that a House of Commons Should be Engaged in 8 or 9 nights of Successive debate to the neglect of every other matter, on the question of an amendment, that foreign Sugar Shall not be admitted at a reduced duty – But so it is – & Men Such as the contemptible ministers now in Office have accomplished[96] this Extraordinary feat = During this time however constant squabbles & discussions are going on in the Cabinet. Lord Melbourne is for giving up quietly – but Lord Clarendon are [*sic*]

[96] done it precedes this in the original.

for dissolution & Staying in – It is Said that Lord Spencer Was actually present, I cannot believe it, at a Cabinet council & advised against dissolution & for resignation – Lord Grey is understood to have given the Same advice – Tomorrow or at all Events on the following day we Shall learn the upshot of all these deep intrigues & pitiful manoeuvrings = With Such people it is impossible to guess what will be done –

*19 May 1841.* The debate is at last Ended – The Times newspaper of this morning received at Nottingham this afternoon, gives the intelligence that on a division this morning there was a majority against ministers of 36 [319–283,] a larger majority than they looked for, but not quite so large as we Expected – However it is an immense majority under the Circumstances, & many of them will Still continue to vote with us – What will be done is Still unknown – My idea is that they will hold on – Perhaps Lord Melbourne may feel that he must go out, but Lord Clarendon & the violent men, will mistake their position So much as to think that they can by Effrontery carry on the government – all will depend upon the Queen, if She abets them they may yet for a time continue to hold office –
    There were only 17 Speakers – Sir Edward Knatchbull who was by right in possession of the house waived his claim [.] Mr [Charles] Wynn said that it was useless to detain the house as there was nothing to Say – Mr [George] Smythe made a Short Speech & then 12 ministerialists in Succession had the hardihood to address the house – an exhibition Which I will venture to assert never before was made [.] These vile men are now begrimed with dirt & low indeed in the Estimation[97] of their Countrymen – No men Ever were regarded with So great Contempt & disdain.

*20 May 1841.* Nothing new today – no house in the Commons –

*21 May 1841.* To the surprise of many, but not to mine – The Ministers have determined not to quit their Stations. Lord John Russell announced last night that the Chancellor of the Exchequer would bring forward the annual Sugar bill on Monday next / 24 / & he Lord John will move the repeal of the Corn Law on 4th June. This is Setting parliament & public opinion at defiance with a Vengeance – They will be beaten of Course on the Corn question & they mean to dissolve upon the Expected but not yet Effected anti corn law Cry – Nothing can be more Wicked & infamous than all this – but they Seem bent upon their own & their Country's destruction if they Can Effect [it] – I trust in God that they will be grievously dissapointed [*sic*] in their Expectation of raising commotion, & that an impeachment of the Whole Miscreant Set will assuredly attend Such Villainy –

*22 May 1841.* Parliament is adjourned to Monday = no news from London – all remains without any alteration since yesterday –

*25 May 1841.* Lincoln writes to me that Sir Robert Peel gave notice in the House of Commons last night Monday that he would move on Thursday "that Her Majesty's Ministers being unable to carry those measures which they Consider Essential for the public welfare are unworthy of the confidence of the House & that their retaining Office under Such

[97] ~~contempt~~ precedes this in the original.

circumstances is at variance with the Spirit of the Constitution" [.] This will do – & I have little doubt that it will be carried – Then what will Ministers do [?] Will they resign or dissolve [?] – The latter I believe they Cannot do now as the duties are not renewed & no Supplies voted –

*26 May 1841.* The miscreant Ministers are as Slippery as Eels [–] no one can hold them – Sir Robert Peels' notice of motion is for tomorrow / Thursday / & Lord John Russell has announced that on Friday he Shall move that the house on its rising shall adjourn to Tuesday – So that they will not Suffer the debate to close on Friday, they will gain the Subsequent days & from Tuesday will probably continue from night to night to adjourn the debate so as to prolong it to Such a period as may best Suit their iniquitous purpose –

*27 May 1841.* a good deal of Sparring & warm discussion in both houses – I wish I were in London now [–] it must be a Very interesting time –

*29 May 1841.* […] Sir Robert Peels' Speech on making his motion the night before last, was an admirable one, Eminently Well calculated to Effect his purpose – No one however can pretend to anticipate what the Ministers Will decide upon Eventually doing; Lord Worsley I am Sorry to observe has announced his intention of Supporting the Ministers whose measures he reprobated the other day & from whom he declared at Lincoln that he had withdrawn his Support –

*30 May 1841.* The Debate is of course adjourned – in the Course of the debate the Speakers connected with the government make no scent [*sic* – secret] of their intention to dissolve – they Say that they May have lost the confidence of Parliament [,] of the house Chosen for them, a house reformed according to their Contrivance & invention = but yet they Say ["] though we have lost the confidence of this Parliament yet we are Sure that in an appeal to the people we shall retrieve our fallen fortune ["] – Vain hope, dishonest, lying assertion ! They Know well Enough that there is no chance for them – but if they can Effect Some mischief, their vile hearts will by So much be gladdened –

*5 June 1841.* The debate on Sir Robert Peels' motion of want of Confidence in Ministers still continues, it is Expected to conclude last night, that is this morning –

*6 June 1841.* The Debate is over – a majority of 1 – for Peel's motion [–] numbers 312 & 311 – Lord John Russell Said that he would announce his intention on Monday – Peels' reply Was Excellent, also Lord Stanleys Speech – Lord John it must be admitted Spoke well & cleverly & made a very good fight, as indeed he always does – In his Speech he openly declared that he had advised the Queen to dissolve the Parliament & Stated pretty clearly that Her Majesty Would Support them to the last –

*8 June 1841.* It was thought that the Ministerial plan Would be to propose last night to raise supplies for Six Month's Which if agreed to by the Conservative party – Parliament Would be immediately dissolved – I can hardly think that we should be able to consent to such an arrangement. Lord Melbourne is understood to be in favor of resignation Without dissolution – The cabinet is full of divisions –

*13 June 1841.* So regardless of all decency are the Ministers that they have appointed Mr [Edward] Stanley [,] Secretary of the Treasury & Whipper in, to be Governor of Madras !!!

*14 June 1841.* It is not Known on what day parliament will be dissolved: the System & pleasure of the miscreants in power Seems to be to Keep all in hot water & painful uncertainty –

*15 June 1841.* Nothing new – The coming Elections Engross universal attention – it is Said by Some that[98] there will be in the new parliament a Conservative Majority of 80 –

*17 June 1841.* The vile Ministers are making changes in their cabinet & other Offices, as if they were in full assurance of remaining & as if nothing had happened – Some of the Changes are of the most objectionable description –

*22 June 1841.* Today Parliament is to be dissolved by the Queen in person, an ungracious act which usually is personally avoided by the Sovereign = The Elections, are going on Extraordinarily Well Every where –

*24 June 1841.* all is bustle & activity now – Candidates are all crowding into the Country & the Strife is begun –

*27 June 1841.* […] Lincoln goes tomorrow as he Wishes to be in London to give his vote for Westminster: Captain [Henry John] Rous [,] brother of Lord Stradbrooke, opposes the Sitting Members Delacy Evans & [John Temple] Leader –

*30 June 1841.* as yet few Elections are Known – We have the report that 3 Conservatives & alderman Wood are returned for the City & that Lord John Russell is rejected – he came only 5th [.] Lincoln is won & Several other places, but Several are also lost which were reckoned upon –

*1 July 1841.* It now unfortunately turns out that Lord John Russell is returned [–] he was 4th on the list = Joy has been turned into sorrow at this & how it could have happened is hardly Known[99] – The Elections are chequered with good & bad fortune & lead one to Suppose that our majority Will be between 30 & 50 –

*2 July 1841.* Nothing very material has occurred = of the Elections hitherto reported – 224 members are returned & the Conservative gain out of that number is 10 –

*3 July 1841.* The contest for the mastery, as yet, is much less in our favor than I had assumed it to be – Of the Members for boroughs already Elected there are 146 Conservative & 145 Ministerial – a wonderfully close race, & what it [*sic* – is] also remarkable, the votes polled

---

[98] that precedes this in the original.
[99] John Masterman (Conservative) polled 6,339, Matthew Wood (Whig) 6,315, George Lyall (Conservative) 6,290, and Lord John Russell 6,221.

are nearly Equal on both Sides & the Successful Candidate is rarely the Winner by more than a very few Votes [.]

*4 July 1841.* The returns from the Boroughs today are adverse – The Counties begin next week, when we may Expect better fortune –

*8 July 1841.* I learn today that [the] Cardigan Election has not been Successful [.] Mr [John Scandrett] Harford has not turned out Mr Price [Pryse Pryse] who had a majority over him of 19 Votes[100] – I am very Sorry for this – we tried hard for & were very near Winning it –

*9 July 1841.* [...] The West Riding [of] Yorkshire is won by a large majority – Messrs Wortley & Beckett Denison have beaten Lords Milton & Morpeth – the numbers for the 4 – Wortley 12,740 – Denison 12,374 – Milton 11,639 – Morpeth 11,583 – Lord Morpeth is Secretary for Ireland & a Cabinet Minister – So, that this is a great triumph.[101] Mr [Edward] Stanley another Minister is beaten in Cheshire – & O'Connell will be beaten in Dublin – The Elections have turned out so well that there will be a majority of more than 50 –

*10 July 1841.* [...] Contrary to Expectation [,] Lord Worsley has been reelected for North Lincolnshire [–] he is 1000 ahead of [Robert] Christopher & very much more of [those] Cast – although differing in politics I am not Sorry for his Success[102] –

*13 July 1841.* The Elections by this days report are Most favourable – Lord Howick has been beaten in Northumberland – O'Connell & his colleague in Dublin & Several other places won from the Ministerials[103] – we shall probably have a majority of little less, possibly more than 80 – which is really almost incredible —

*18 July 1841.* I have been truly grieved to learn today the Sudden death of Lord Feversham – I have Every reason to be gratefully thankful to him – he was Ever a Kind & Warm friend to me, perhaps the Kindest I had; I have Every reason to lament his death –

*29 July 1841.* The Queen is gone to Woburn where there were gay doings – Her Majesty has lately been to Panshanger & Brockett [*sic*] Hall = She is I believe going to visit Some other places –
 The Duke of Wellington has already issued his Circulars for attendance, on the opening of Parliament on the 19th next –

[100]The result was 305–285: majority 20.

[101]John Stuart-Wortley (Conservative) polled 13,165, Edmund Beckett-Denison (Conservative) 12,780, Lord Milton (Whig) 12,080, and Lord Morpeth (Whig) 12,031.

[102]Lord Worsley polled 5,401 against the Conservative Robert Christopher on 4,522: majority 879.

[103]In North Northumberland, the Conservatives Charles Bennet (1,216) and Addison Cresswell (1,163) pushed Grey (1,101) into third place. In Dublin City, the Conservatives John Beattie West (3,860) and Edward Grogan (3,839) beat O'Connell (3,692) and Robert Hutton (3,662).

*30 July 1841.* The Elections being over, a temporary tranquillity Seems to prevail, Soon to be broken when Parliament meets on the 19th [.] The Struggle will then be fierce without Example, or I am much mistaken –

*3 August 1841.* The Reports of the State of trade are deplorable – & those who warn the public are preparing men's minds for the disasters Which may presently Ensue = at Manchester there are 800 hand loom Weavers out of Work –

accounts from China Just received State that[104] Commodore Sir Gordon Bremer had Sailed for Canton with a reinforcement of troops & fresh instructions & that Most active operations Were[105] to commence immediately & Every Effort made to compel the Emperor to yield to our terms =

*5 August 1841.* There is a report that Parliament will not be assembled, for despatch of business [,] before the middle of September: if So, the breach of faith on the part of the Ministers is truly monstrous, & Joined to their previous conduct will merit if it be possible impeachment – If it be practicable to prolong their own stay & to Keep out their opponents, by any means or profligate or base trick [,] these Ministers, Will be Sure to practice it –

*6 August 1841.* […] It is understood that it is the intention of Sir Robert Peel not to oppose the Election of the present Ministerial Speaker Shaw Lefevre – This decision is unwise, it is unusual when a party is strong Enough to do otherwise & is a Confession of Weakness or inability – it makes a bad Start – There are certain advisers, who are not fit to be advisers, who are assuming the right & qualification to advise & will assuredly do much mischief by their Meddling & busy Self Sufficiency =

*7 August 1841.* admiral Sir Robert Stoppard has been most Warmly & generously received by the public Since his arrival in England: he is now at Portsmouth undergoing a Series of dinners given in his honor, & at these he has acquitted himself Exceedingly well – it is quite clear that to him we are Mainly indebted for the glorious issue which attended our arms & negociations in Syria –

*10 August 1841.* The newspapers announce that it is intended not to oppose the reelection of the late Speaker (Lefevre) – it will be a rather curious result that a party with a triumphant Majority of 80 Should not Elect a Speaker from its own ranks –

*18 August 1841.* […] Corn is rising in Various parts of the continent, the Same in England – the State of the weather is Supposed to have injured the crops – It will be a very distressing case for most Countries Where insurrectionary movements are also Shewing themselves –

*20 August 1841.* Parliament met yesterday – Mr Lefevre was reelected Speaker proposed by Lord Worsley & Seconded by Mr [Edward] Buller = The Queen is not to

---

[104]that precedes this in the original.
[105]~~may~~ precedes this in the original.

open it in person – the Ministerial papers Say, to mark her disapprobation of the new Parliament –

*21 August 1841*. The ministers made a wretched figure at the opening [–] their benches Were most wretchedly Empty owing to the many of their Members who have not been reelected – They must feel their degradation for they are despised by all & hissed by the rabble as they walk along the Streets – I may add that they richly deserve all the Contempt, scorn & detestation which are heaped upon them by the public in general –

*22 August 1841*. The public is now Speculating upon the possibility, perhaps the probability, of the present Ministers Continuing in their places not withstanding the large majority against them = This Experimental trick has already occurred to me & I think it not unlikely to be resorted to by the vile people in Office = If it is [,] I trust that impeachment & the halter will be their ultimate reward –

*25 August 1841*. [...] Parliament has opened with a Speech by Commission from the Throne & [,] as was expected, including in a very marked Manner all the topics So objectionable in the ministerial budget of the last Parliament [.] This is not only an insult to the Country but a Shameful abuse of the Queen's name, & a Most cowardly & base leaning upon Her influence & authority, & involving Her in all the disgrace & odium Which has attended & will attend the Measures of her Ministers.

The debates Could not reach us, but it is stated that Sir Robert Peel meant to meet the ministerial abomination by declaring that Parliament [,] whilst it deplores the Wretched Condition into Which the Country has been brought, yet firmly but respectfully declines to discuss questions proposed by the advice of Ministers Who do not possess the confidence of the Parliament or the Country – This must throw them & [,] I Suspect, is not the result which these Wretched & vile men looked for – an amendment is to be moved & Seconded by Mr Wortley & Lord Bruce – No Conservative will Speak but Sir Robert Peel who will Say as much as he thinks necessary & the debate or rather the Speechifying will be left Entirely to the discarded crew – who will be mad with Shame & Vexation –

*26 August 1841*. In the House of Lords the debate is over: on the address the Ministers of course Were beaten by a large majority & the amendment carried against them.[106] In the Commons the old farce of adjourning the debate was continued – the Supporters of folly & misrule had it all to themselves & I trust that no one but Sir Robert Peel will Speak on our Side & then the Ministers will find their impudence & folly properly met by the Contempt & disdain of those who matter –

*27 August 1841*. The debate Still continues in the Commons; that is [,] all the speaking is on one Side, I am rejoiced to perceive that this mode of treating the matter is rigidly adhered to – it must produce its due Effect –

[106]The vote was 96 Content against 168 (155 present and 13 proxies) Not Content: majority 72.

*28 August 1841.* again the debate is adjourned – It is to be hoped that this most inconvenient & Senseless System will be discontinued =

*29 August 1841.* The Debate is over: after 4 days one Sided discussion the result is a majority of 91 against Ministers in a house of 634 Members present [269–360] – & yet notwithstanding this nothing has been done by the Ministers towards resignation, no audiences of the Queen, no Cabinet Councils = but on the other hand a cool insinuation that they mean to remain in their places & Conduct the public affairs = This State of things is wholly unprecedented, what will be the issue cannot be guessed, but it cannot last long for they must call upon parliament for Supplies, & I presume that, of Course, these will be refused to Such an administration – & then it is impossible (one Should think) that they can longer Entrench themselves in their offices –

*31 August 1841.* at last the vilest of all concievable [*sic*] administrations is no more – Lord Melbourne in one house & Lord John Russell in the other announced yesterday that they had resigned their offices & that they only held office untill their Successors were appointed – What a real blessing that the Country is no longer to be Cursed With Such mischievous incapables –

Sir Robert Peel had been Sent for by the Queen & had gone to Windsor, but nothing was Known of the Composition of the new administration – indeed it was well understood that Sir Robert Peel had Studiously avoided Even Speaking to his friends upon the Subject, So that there Should be no opening for remarks of any Kind –

*1 September 1841.* Nothing is yet Known of the appointments in the new administration – The names of Several who have been With Sir Robert Peel are mentioned, but the offices are not named – it is Said that the offices are already filled & the ministry formed –

*2 September 1841.* The names of the Members of the new administration are now Known –

| | |
|---|---|
| Sir Robert Peel – 1st Lord Treasury | Lord Haddington 1st Lord [of the] admiralty |
| Duke of Wellington a Seat in Cabinet | Lord Wharncliffe – President [of the] Council |
| Lord Lyndhurst [Lord] Chancellor | Lord Ripon – President board of Trade |
| Lord Stanley – [Secretary] Colonies | Lord Ellenborough President [board of] Control |
| Ld aberdeen Foreign [Secretary] | Sir Edward Knatchbull Paymaster [General] |
| Sir James Graham Home Secretary | Sir Henry Hardinge Secretary at War |
| Goulburn Chancellor [of the] Exchequer | Lord De Grey Lord Lieutenant of Ireland |
| Duke of Buckingham [Lord] Privy Seal | Lord Elliot [Chief] Secretary [of Ireland] – |

besides many other minor appointments – I confess that I should have liked to have gone to Ireland – & I am Convinced that I Could do good there – but I ask not, Merit not, & no one (perhaps I am not fit) will drag Me[107] from obscurity –

---

[107] me precedes this in the original.

*3 September 1841.* The formation of the administration Continues & I hope that it act[s] for the good of the Country – The Ministers were to kiss hands yesterday –

*4 September 1841.* No other news than the resignation of the Seals of office by the Old & the gift of them by the Queen to the new Ministers =

*5 September 1841.* It is Said that Prince albert has Communicated to his household that those who Compose it, must be of the Same politics as the Queen's Minister = The Queen at the audience given to all the new ministers, Seemed to be unhappy, but behaved herself with Entire propriety & is Said to have done nothing of which Sir Robert Peel has any reason whatever to Complain –

*7 September 1841.* Parliament met again yesterday, of Course no business was done & it will be forthwith adjourned to about the 20th –

*8 September 1841.* But little news, the Ministerial appointments are Still proceeding = Peel appears to be following the precedent of Lord Melbourne, & is appointing to all the Court offices, women as well as Men – This is not right –

*9 September 1841.* No very particular news this day – Parliament is adjourned to the 17th –

*10 September 1841.* There is little doing just now – but the reformers are Evidently preparing for battle & will Enter upon it with great virulence & activity as I think –

*11 September 1841.* The appointments are now almost all made, including those about the Court. The Lord Chamberlain's office after Several refusals is to be filled by Lord De La Warr [–] The Duke of Rutland declined it. The Duchess of Buccleuch after Considerable negociations [*sic*] & various reports, is to be Mistress of the robes –

*14 September 1841.* all Seems to be going on So quietly, that there is nothing to record. Sir Robert Peel is to be reelected without going to Tamworth. The exministerial party is doing its utmost to Excite the public mind but the party is too despicably low to be heeded or Sympathised with – Their time may Come & their past misdeeds forgotten, as their aptitude & readiness for mischief Shall become more required –

*16 September 1841.* The newspapers are principally occupied with the very long & faultily odious Speeches, of the Various Members Who from having accepted offices have had to appeal of the Constituencies –

*17 September 1841.* Parliament met again yesterday – Sir Robert Peel very Wisely & very properly, in My opinion, Simply Stated to the House the different points of business which it was absolutely necessary to carry through the House during the fortnight that Parliament would be Kept together – He abstained from all general declarations, or Exposition of policy, which has been So inconveniently adopted of late years by any incoming administration – By pursuing this System he will Keep his Supporters & disarm his opponents – It is most unstatesmanlike as well as imprudent to announce the intentive [*sic* – intentions] &

bind oneself down to do So & So – thus Exposing yourself to failure & to the attacks of opponents & the cavils or criticisms of party Supporters[108] –

In america the President, Tiler [*sic*], has Singly put his veto upon the Bank measure passed by both Houses of Congress – The Bill is thus quashed & it is not a little singular that a Democratic Constitution Should give Such an immense power to the Executive Individual.

*18 September 1841.* My concerns of Every description Seem to be blackened & blighted by reverses & failures too constantly repeated not to be discerned as something not altogether in the Common Course of things – it is Cruelly disheartening, mortification & disaster break down the toughest Spirits – & Embitter the Joys of life – Sometimes I feel as if I Could hardly Stand against the accumulated annoyances, but God is infinitely Kind to me & Enables me to Support myself under these trials in a manner which frequently astonishes me, & calls forth my deepest gratitude – I console myself with the hope & trust that dabit Deus his quoque finem[109] & that when I may better deserve it more prosperous days may Shine upon me –

*19 September 1841.* The Skirmishing in the House of Commons has begun – Lord John Russell attacked Sir Robert Peel, but could get nothing out of him – but a very able Speech –

*23 September 1841.* The Parliamentary proceedings are Smoothly Sliding Without the Slightest impediment [–] the government is all powerful at present –

*28 September 1841.* Wrote to Lord aberdeen today[110] to try if he will do any thing for [my son] William – Peel was testy & refused to concern himself at all for him – neither Kindly nor altogether Courteously – but Such is the man – & one cannot wash a blackymoor white[111] –

*1 October 1841.* Lord aberdeen's answer is arrived, obliging but not very Encouraging – he Says that if he should be able to do any thing for William, it can only be as an unpaid attache to Some Mission – & for this he Suspects that I may think him too old.[112] It will certainly be very irksome but I shall advise William to put up with it – the impossibility of obtaining any thing under the Exclusion Ministry has aged him for apprenticeships, but he must undergo it, as Such is the case –

[108]BL, Add. MS 40486, f. 66: Newcastle to Peel, 8 Aug. 1841, advising him not to bind himself with a public declaration of intentions: 'if you were to make a public announcement of your political plans & principles, a great Variety of opinion Would prevail in the discussion of them, & division Would Commence at the outset of your administration'.

[109]'God will put an end to these troubles as well' – Virgil, *The Aeneid*.

[110]BL, Add. MS 43237, ff. 378–80: Newcastle to Aberdeen, 28 Sept. 1841. Newcastle observed that he had not asked for patronage from Melbourne's government because 'No application from me Would have been attended With the Slightest Chance of Success'.

[111]BL, Add. MS 40488, ff. 230–2: Newcastle to Peel, 11 Sept. 1841; ff. 234–5: Peel to Newcastle, 16 Sept. 1841; ff. 237–8: Newcastle to Peel, 21 Sept. 1841.

[112]BL, Add. MS 43237, f. 392: Aberdeen to Newcastle, 30 Sept. 1841.

*6 October 1841.* Parliament will be prorogued in a few days – the business, what little there was, is nearly all completed –

*7 October 1841.* accounts are arrived by Express from Marseilles that Canton has again been taken by the British Troops & also the island of Hong Kong – no particulars –

*8 October 1841.* Parliament was prorogued yesterday –
Despatches are arrived from China. £6 millions of dollars are to be paid by Canton, & it Seems to be the intention to go all along the Coast to levy contributions from the different towns on the Coast = In fact a [buccaneering] Expedition –

*9 October 1841.* It appears that the notorious Captain [Charles] Elliot, Who has bungled [,] thwarted & injured Either by imbecility or fraud Every Chinese affair, has done the Same in this last business & Stopped the forces in their cause of glory & usefulness Just at the critical moment when their [*sic* – they were] about to reap the fruits of their Exertions by triumphant victory, which Would produce the greatest moral Effect upon the people –

*10 October 1841.* Lord Dinorbies [Dinorbens] house, Kinmel in North Wales [,] has been burnt down, the house is nearly destroyed, but the books, pictures plate & Effects Were Saved –

*15 October 1841.* […] Lord Ellenborough is to go out Governor General to India, an Enormous appointment for him – Lord Fitzgerald / Vesey / Commonly Known as greasy, is to Succeed him at the Board of Control –

*16 October 1841.* Very little passing in the world that I Know of = a pamphlet of Lord alvanley Seems to occasion Some talk – it is upon the State of Ireland & what ought to be done – he criticises passed acts & policy, & Suggests Some measures & Schemes for the ameliorating of her condition – but one chief Scheme is the payment of the priests, & that will never do[113] –

*17 October 1841.* McLeod's trial is coming on & the New Yorkers are clamorous for his Conviction & Execution – indeed it is believed that if he should be acquitted that they will murder him [–] & I believe it – nothing can be more ruffianly, bloody & lawless than the american democrats & [they] are Equal to any act of enormity or crime – It is Confidently Stated by the last packet that the States of New York & Maine &c on the borders, are collecting men & arms to attack the Canadian frontier & that in Canada there are many prepared to Join them & again to hoist the Standard of insurrection & rebellion [.] Our troubles are not over in that quarter –

*20 October 1841.* an English Protestant Bishop is to be Sent to Jerusalem & a protestant Christian Church Established there

---

[113]Lord Alvanley, *The State of Ireland Considered, and Measures Proposed for Restoring Tranquillity to that Country* (1841).

accounts from america are daily Expected, the result of the trial of Mccleod will be the point of interest – & it very probably will decide the question of war, or peace With america, not but that my own opinion is that the Union will not Support the Sanguinary & execrable views of the northern States –

*21 October 1841*. […] By the Caledonia We have the latest news = McLeods trial was postponed to the 4th October & it now appears that the accounts of the popular ferment about it was Exaggerated, as at Utica [,] Where the trial is to take place, there was no more appearance of any Extraordinary movement than on the occasion of the usual assize proceedings –

*23 October 1841*. The Queen Came to London from Windsor a few days ago, preparatory to her "accouchement", this is now Expected to occur on any day, & Expresses are Kept ready to Send to all the Ministers &c the moment that Her Majesty is taken unwell –

*26 October 1841*. The trial of Mcleod has begun, but when the accounts came away it was Expected to last many days –

*27 October 1841*. Edward has received his Commission [as Lieutenant] & on applying for Service has been appointed to the Harlequin 16 gun Sloop – Commander [George Fowler] Hastings – She is destined for China. I wish She Were a larger Vessel[114] – Edward seems to like his destination –

*28 October 1841*. The Exchequer bill fraud Seems now to be the object of public attention – It appears that bills, copies of Each other, are in circulation, in Some instances that have been discovered as many as three copies – The defaulter is Mr [Edward Beaumont] Smith [,] Chief Clerk in the Controller of the Exchequer's Office – He has confessed Every thing – but he States that he cannot give the amount of forgery, as he Kept no account or record of the issues – It is understood that the amount may be from £150 – to 200,000 – Lord Monteagle is Controller & receives a Salary of £2000 – for this he does not Even condescend to Sign his name but has delegated this duty to Mr Smith, who has been Still farther assisted by two more Clerks' – Had Lord Monteagle done his duty & signed the Bills himself there would have been no fraud – Such was [the] System of those lately in office – & I feel assured that in Every office of the State, the Same Criminal neglect of duty will have prevailed –

*30 October 1841*. The population census, Just made up & published [,] gives an amount to Great Britain & Ireland of 27,000,000 Souls – an Enormous population for the Extent of Country –

*31 October 1841*. […] News is arrived of the acquittal of McCleod in a manner truly Creditable to himself, to the Judge & Jurors & american Counsel – It is a most Valuable issue,

---

[114]The 'Harlequin' (1836) was part of the racer class of ships built for the royal navy during the 1830s. It had a length of 100 feet 6 inches (30.6 m) at the gundeck and 78 feet 10 inches (24 m) at the keel. It had a crew of 120 officers and ratings.

for independent of its Justice, it must produce a good feeling between the two Countries which must be of infinite national benefit to america –

*1 November 1841.* We have passed the day in talking over all matters in any way relating to Edward's Service & long absence from home – it is a long time to look forward to & makes one melancholy to think that when we part tomorrow morning it may be never to meet again –

*2 November 1841.* My very dear Edward came Early this morning to take leave of me = dear & noble fellow ! he was deeply affected at parting from us all with So many chances against our being altogether reunited – It is indeed a painful necessity for a parent to part from his children, the more Especially when he feels Every day how Entirely they may Compose the full Measure of his happiness or misery – May God Spare his Valuable life to be an ornament & benefit to humanity –

a dreadful fire has Consumed the greater part of the Tower of London = The armoury with 200,000 stand of arms, all the ancient armour &c & numerous Effects have been destroyed – The loss to the Nation is Estimated at <u>one Million</u> [pounds] – Tomorrow I Shall hope to learn that the destruction may not have been So great as at first reported –

*3 November 1841.* The fire is the prolific topic for the newspapers = There is a detailed Story given respecting a light Seen in the Boyers' [Bowyer] Tower, Which looks very like incendiarism – an investigation is set on foot –

*4 November 1841.* [My son] William has been appointed an attaché to the Embassy at Vienna[115] – Sir Robert Gordon takes him as a confidential man & of the Same politics, the other attachés being appointed by the late vile ministers – Diplomacy is by no means a favorite profession With me [.] I have a very bad opinion of it, & always dread its consequences upon individuals [,] but there was nothing Else for William to do, & he has rather a leaning to it –

*6 November 1841.* News arrived from China & India = The Plenipotentiary & admiral – Sir Henry Pottinger & Sir William Parker, arrived at Canton on the 9th [of] august = The vigour & plain dealing of their proceedings had already produced a Wonderful Effect upon the Chinese & given hopes & confidence to our Merchants – a large float of 9 Sail of Men of war & Steamers & transports were to sail instantly for the North – 7 Sail Were to remain at Canton – Large bribes had been offered to Sir Henry Pottinger by the Chinese – but of Course refused – Query – had Captain Elliot received bribes? –

*7 November 1841.* My dear [son] Charles is bent upon not being idle = He Seeks Service, he tried to be appointed one of Lord Ellenboroughs' aides De Camp but he applied too late & failed – Lord Ellenborough recommended him to apply to Lord Saltoun who is offered the Second in Command in China – he is Extremely desirous of attaining this staff appointment & has asked me to write to Lord Saltoun an old friend of mine – which I

[115]BL, Add. MS 43238, f. 124: Aberdeen to Newcastle, 2 Nov. 1841.

have done, although I have a very great dread of China & the East = Charles has already committed or I Should demur about Writing –

*10 November 1841.* The Queen was Safely delivered of a Prince [Albert Edward] at 11 o'clock yesterday morning – She & the infant are perfectly well –

*14 November 1841.* Charles tried to be appointed Aide.De Camp to Lord Ellenborough but was too late in his application. Lord Ellenborough was very Kind to him & promised to do what he could for him = He advised him to apply to be on Lord Saltoun's Staff who is going out Second in command to China = I wrote to Lord Saltoun for him but he cannot take Charles as he has but one Aide De Camp & had appointed his nephew = Charles is anxious to be Employed more actively but I am Scarcely Sorry that he does not go to a climate so ill suited to Europeans –

*16 November 1841.* The Queen Dowager [Adelaide] is rather better, if She is strong Enough to bear up against the disease she may throw it off & partially recover, but this is Scarcely to be Expected & the fear is that if She Cannot Continue to Expectorate freely that She will be Suffocated – Her patience & resignation is Most Exemplary.

*17 November 1841.* The accounts of Queen adelaide continue better – She Sleeps & is more Easy, but the disease remains the Same[116] –

*21 November 1841.* Whether from accident or design incendiarism has greatly Encreased lately, murders, Suicides & Sudden deaths – a grand [*sic* – hand] grenade was thrown into the Horse Guards the day before yesterday, & another also into the Barracks at Charing Cross Each Exploded with a loud report, but fortunately did not [do any] injury to the Sentries or the buildings –

*22 November 1841.* This is my last day with my dear [son] William – Tomorrow morning he leaves me for London from whence he will go almost immediately to Enter upon his new career & Join Sir Robert Gordon at Vienna – Diplomacy is not a profession that I by any means admire – a foreign residence never improves an Englishman, foreign morality & habits are So unsuited & contrary to ours, that it is a fearful thing to launch a person into Such a Vortex of corruption – I have given him & fortified him by all necessary advice & I trust & believe that he will profit by it –

*24 November 1841.* a Commission for Enquiring into the best mode of promoting the fine arts in the United Kingdom has Just been appointed – It is to my view a Strange medley of names for a very Strange purpose – There are 23 names 11 being opponents & reformers & some I Should think Knowing as much of fine art as they Know of what is passing in the Moon – 2 are Roman Catholics – 2, I believe, atheists, 2 of doubtful politics & Several of the remainder little qualified to Effect much good on Such an Enquiry – This is one of Sir Robert Peel's trumpery Vanities, he wishes to set up for a Macaenas,[117] but in this he

---

[116] Queen Adelaide survived but drew up directions for her funeral at this time.

[117] Gaius Cilnius Maecenas (68–8 BC) was a generous patron of literature and art.

has mistaken his powers, he has little Knowledge of & no real feeling for art = it is not in his nature, he therefore wishes to affect it, & thence this immortal Commission –

*25 November 1841.* a fierce controversy is on the point of arising between the Weak & Silly Schismatics followers of Dr Pusey, calling themselves "anglicans" & the regular Churchmen of Oxford – I trust that victory will not be for a moment doubtful – but the Puseyites [,] Strange to relate, have made many proselytes & rapid strides – one, [Richard Waldo] Sibthorp, has Just been converted to Popery[118] & it is Confidently asserted that at least 10 other Oxford clergymen, anglicans, are ready to Embrace it – Such an Event is truly incredible in this age – but it is an age of wonder, & what is most improbable is the Surest to happen[119] –

*26 November 1841.* The foolish title which was given in the gazette to the promotion of arts Commission has been cancelled & the following Substituted in its place – certainly an improvement though Still a Silly one for a vapouring object – "The Queen has been pleased to appoint (here follow the names) Her Majesty's Commissioners for the purpose of inquiring whether advantage might not be taken of the rebuilding of the houses of parliament for promoting & Encouraging the fine arts"[120] –

I learnt with deep regret this morning that Lord Harewood is dead – My account States that he fell off his horse on his return from hunting – He was one of those men who rarely appear & who where Existing command universal respect & Esteem = He possessed a clear & shrewd understanding [,] Expressed himself Calmly, distinctly & Well – was always listened to with attention & considered in his way as an oracle = He was a Country gentleman if Such a phrase may be used = possessed great influence & was most deservedly looked up to & will be deeply lamented as a great private & public loss = He was a fine, remarkable looking man, hearty untill latterly & 74 or 5 year of age –

*30 November 1841.* The clergyman who Signed himself academicus, & stated that there [were] 10 other clergymen ready to Embrace popery & to propagate it, was called upon by Mr Fabre [Frederick William Faber] & others to give his name – this he has done in a long letter of great interest published in last nights' Standard – He signs himself – "Golightly" [Charles Pourtales Golightly] a resident at Oxford & an M.A. of 11 years Standing – He brings forward Some astonishing facts & shews but too clearly the rotten State of a portion of the members (So called) of our Church = However all this is most providential, must demand & receive Explanation, & lead to that Consummation So devoutly to be wished –

*1 December 1841.* The Duke of Wellington has refused in the most determined manner to receive the Deputation from Paisley – In this he has acted properly, but he has not managed it prudently. Distress is now made the popular handle for assault of public characters &

---

[118]Sibthorp was a fellow of Magdalen college.

[119]N.A., DD/TL/2/1/65: Newcastle to Godfrey Tallents, 25 Nov. 1841, enquiring whether a local choral society 'has any thing to do with that lamentable schism', Puseyism, in which case 'I Shall beg at once to have nothing Whatever to do with it'.

[120]*The London Gazette*, 23 Nov. 1841, supplement.

assuredly these men will Visit the result upon the Duke in the bitterest manner – In his answers to the deputation he Styles himself <u>Field Marshall</u> the Duke of Wellington & declares that he holds no political office under the Crown, & on that account declines Seeing these people –

*2 December 1841.* The americans from the Main [*sic*] State are Encroaching upon the disputed ground in a most unwarrantable manner, making settlements, culling & carrying away the finest timber, cutting canals of Communication & Exercising Every right of ownership, without any molestation from us – What are we about? Since 1839, when the main people began to Encroach upon the boundary, they have pushed themselves forward & Established themselves 70 miles up the Country = It is much to [be] feared that with the determined disposition now Shewn & the preparations making that a conflict must & ought to be the consequence, for Such outrages upon what may be & is claimed to be our territory cannot be permitted –

O'Connell is swaggering away, & ruling the roost most gloriously, as Lord Mayor of Dublin – but the rent of the repeal association is falling off & there is a very great Split among the rascals = O'Connell & his Satellites have quarrelled with Lord Shrewsbury & the English Roman Catholics & are abusing them in the Coarsest & Most opprobrius [*sic*] language = "When rogues fall out then &c &c"[121] –

*4 December 1841.* There is Some notion of a disagreement amongst Ministers on the Corn Laws – I think it not unlikely – Sir Robert Peel, is not, I fear, Steady upon this point – indeed I have my fears, that of several others we Shall find him disposed to innovation – Vanity will be his ruin – He wishes to be a Solon[122] & a Macaenas, as well as a Demosthene & Cicero[123] =

Queen adelaide is very much better & is Expected to recover, it will be a wonderful recovery, if it should be one –

*8 December 1841.* The State of Missisipi [*sic*] has come to a resolution to repudiate its debts, which are chiefly for money advanced from England to the United States Bank & other commercial concerns – the loss to England will be very disastrous, for it is Expected that the other States will immediately follow the Example of this unprincipled State – it is Said that nothing can equal the state of ruin & degradation of Character which prevails throughout america –

*9 December 1841.* The Puseyite followers, have many of them made an open profession of Popery a Reverend [*sic*] has Written a Very Clever letter upon the Subject which is likely to produce much Effect with a Certain class = The delusion is truly lamentable & Cannot fail to produce infinite mischief – This is probably the deceptive Effort which is to be made previously to the final overthrow of Popery – To real & Sincere Protestants

---

[121]'When thieves fall out, honest men come by their own', from John Heywood, *Dialogue of Proverbs* (1546). Subsequently adapted as 'When rogues fall out, truth is revealed, and honest men get justice'.

[122]Solon (640–560 BC) was an Athenian statesman, legislator, and poet.

[123]Demosthenes (384–322 BC) was a Greek statesman and orator of ancient Athens. Marcus Tullius Cicero (106–43 BC) was a Roman statesman, lawyer, and philosopher.

it must be a cause of alarm & cannot be mistaken as a warning & Sign for great Counter Exertion –

*10 December 1841.* It is rumoured that the young Prince is to be called albert Edward – I hope not = The thing though trifling in itself, would be neither popular or politic – The name of Victoria has always been a drawback upon the Queen's popularity, & the Same Will attend that of albert –

*14 December 1841.* When I went to Coutts' [Bank] today I there learnt to my great regret how much Lord Strangford was implicated in the Exchequer bill fraud as far as he was concerned in the loan to Mr [William] Morgan of £40,000 on deposit of exchequer bills to that amount – 39 out of the 40 proved to be forged bills –

*18 December 1841.* […] The only Event is the death of Lord Westmorland & the vacancy of a Garter & Lieutenancy of Northamptonshire – The Minister will be much puzzled in the disposal of both –

*22 December 1841.* […] The death of Lord Westmorland Will remove Lord Burghersh from Berlin – it is yet uncertain who will Succeed him there – probably Lord Heytesbury –

*23 December 1841.* The Pope's Secretary of State [Luigi Lambruschini] is Just arrived in England – Such an appearance is quite new & must Excite Surprise – if it be intended to try the plan of an interchange of representatives, with a Nuncio here & a minister at Rome, that will not do, the plan will fail = & the prime minister who places the Scheme will be overthrown –

*1 January 1842.* This year that I am Entering upon is the 57th that I have Seen – Here I am, thankfully Enjoying the State of health & life to which it has pleased God to call me – My family is now all grown up – My last [child] Robert attained his majority a few months ago – they are all well & Sound in mind & body […] my pecuniary Embarassments [*sic*] still Continue & cause me much anxiety, but in a Short time I hope to Effect a change & to Commence Surmounting my difficulties = I am not dismayed or cast down, though grievously annoyed, My confidence is in the Great Disposer of Events & my own determined Exertions –

I have been shocked to learn the sudden death of my poor friend Lord Falmouth – he died suddenly in his bed by the Side of Lady Falmouth – Supposed of a disease of the heart –

*8 January 1842.* a China mail is arrived, & despatches from our Commanders there – Sir Hugh Gough, admiral Sir William Parker & Sir Henry Pottinger – The Expedition has taken amoy, with no difficulty & no loss of life – There was a great deal of firing on both Sides for two hours but with little loss Even to the Chinese = Troops were landed Who Soon carried the fortress which the Chinese thought impregnable & which in other hands would be nearly So –

In India, our difficulties are coming upon us – Under a bad & stupid commander our troops have been cruelly mauled in attempting Some almost impregnable passes, but for accident the whole force might have been lost –

*11 January 1842.* [...] Nothing of much consequence has occurred today [.] Lord ashburton, has [been] appointed to negociate & Settle american differences = he goes to america almost immediately –

*18 January 1842.* News from america – Sir Charles Bagot is arrived in Canada. The american treasury is described as being bankrupt – the demands upon it urgent & not a dollar to pay with [–] they Know not what to do – Surely the country cannot long continue in such a state – it must break up the Union & destroy all government –

*19 January 1842.* The laying of the first stone of the new Royal Exchange Was the occasion of grand doings in the City – Prince albert laid the Stone & afterwards dined with the Lord Mayor [Sir John Pirie] – at this dinner Lord Stanley made a speech (which I have Extracted & laid in here) which I think is the neatest & best Speech of its kind that I Ever read –

*23 January 1842.* Dr [Ashurst] Gilbert, Principal of Brasen Nose [*sic*], is to be the new Bishop of Chichester = This appointment is in Every respect most Creditable to the [Prime Minister] Sir Robert Peel – It Shews his direct preference of the Sound orthodox clergy – for Dr Gilbert has been a foremost & upright opposer of the Pusey doctrines – He is also an able & rightly minded man, & moreover was a chief mover of that body Which rejected Sir Robert Peel when he offered himself for reelection [as MP for the University of Oxford in 1829] = This then is magnanimity as well as wisdom –

The contest for the poetry professorship at Oxford is over, Mr [Isaac] Williams has retired & Mr Gurbett [James Garbett] will be Elected – The two Committees Compared notes when it appeared that Mr Garbett had a large majority, but Mr Williams had above 600 votes – Too many to be the advocates & Supporters of a mischievous delusion[124] –

*14 January 1842.* Nothing new today – I have received an invitation to the Christening [of the Prince of Wales at Windsor] on the 25th [–] in Such weather & under present circumstances it is a great nuisance –

*25 January 1842.* [At Windsor Castle for the christening] Ceremonials of the day have gone off remarkably Well – The King of Prussia [Frederick William IV] is a stout, fresh coloured, good humoured looking man, plain, hearty & Kind in his humour & as I am told a great favorite in his own Country – [...] Potsdam is a most magnificent Palace, with all its appendages on the grandest Scale – Windsor Castle is nothing to it I am told – The picture gallery alone is so Superb, as to make the founder's name illustrious, Even if the great Frederick had not been otherwise Known –

The Eton boys Shewed warm feeling & as much honor as they Could testify to the King when he passed through: the King was much pleased with their ardor =

[124] Garbett succeeded with 921 votes to 623: majority 298.

The whole proceedings at the Castle were well done, & the dinner in St George's hall was very fine = There was among other things an immense punch bowl in the evening Several times filled With mulled claret, in all a hayshead of Claret Was <u>cleared</u> by the Company & Some other able assistants – 300 people were said to have Slept in the Castle & 600 to have been fed –

The Queen has not quite recovered her Confinement but is well, the infant appeared to be very fine & healthy –

*26 January 1842.* Breakfasted with all the Company at the Castle & returned to London by rail road at about 1 o'clock[125] –

*30 January 1842.* The King of Prussia is inspecting our various Establishments: he is to dine with the Duke of Wellington & the Duke of Sutherland & in the course of a few days returns to his own Country –

*1 February 1842.* […] The Duke of Cleveland is dead, we gain a Conservative Duke in his Son –

*2 February 1842.* The Duke of Buckingham has resigned his office of Privy Seal – but retires with one of the Garters – it is supposed that a difference about the new Ministerial corn law alterations is the cause of his retirement – whatever it is it will prove a great Embarrassment to the Government measure & not improbably may cause its failure –

*3 February 1842.* […] The Duke of <u>Buccleugh</u> [Buccleuch] has been appointed the Duke of Buckingham's Successor to the Office of Privy Seal – how he should have been Selected for a Seat in the Cabinet, is what I cannot conceive – any body may now aspire to that honor –

*4 February 1842.* Parliament was opened yesterday by the Queen in person, With very great State – The King of Prussia also attended & went in State in the Queen's carriages – all were most loudly greeted & well received – The Speech is altogether a good one – though Some points are objectionable to my view. Sir Robert Peel does not throw off auspiciously – in my opinion. The Duke of Buckingham resigning his post on account of differences on the Corn question, & Ld ashley publicly Stating that Sir Robert Peel will not agree to his proposals for better regulating of factories – these two popular questions will have to be fought by Sir Robert Peel who places himself on the wrong side in both cases = then he gives notice the first thing, in breathless haste, that on Wednesday he Shall move for a Committee of the whole house to Consider the Corn Laws with a view to an alteration & amendment of the Same = When it is recollected that on this very point the last ministers were turned out of Office, by being out voted in the House of Commons, it certainly appears to be most Strange & inconsistent in the extreme for Peel now to propose an alteration of those laws which he before Supported, & originally helped to frame, & by which Support he carried a majority with him & overthrew the Ministry – I think he will fail, and I must own he deserves it − The thinking part of the Nation will be Staggered at the inconsistency & will With hold its confidence, which was not & has not been very firmly entertained − It is <u>most</u> unfortunate −

*5 February 1842.* The King of Prussia was to Embark & leave England yesterday for his own dominions bequeathing a good name as the Sure result of conduct Such [as] his has been Since he first came into this Country − His behaviour has been perfect & Estimable in Every relation = & I must add very different from that of the crowned heads who have before Visited England − it has commanded & gained universal respect & Esteem =

*6 February 1842.* Nothing very particular − Some bills have already been brought in, & ministers appear active, & I hope the Session will be shortened −

*8 February 1842.* Very disastrous news is arrived from India − The affghans have risen; have surprised & killed a vast number of our Officers & men & there is Every probability that many more will be Sacrificed − our troops have behaved in the most heroic manner, but treachery, numbers & no inconsiderable Skill & bravery have prevailed over them − the natives got possession of the passes & without Extraordinary Exertion & great loss we can neither go to the succour of [the] distressed corps nor retreat when absolutely necessary − Sir Alexander Burnes & 8 officers were killed at once in the rising at Caboul − He is an officer of uncommon merit & accomplishments & is an Extreme loss −

In China we are all Successful, but it is to be feared that the time is gone by when our Success will avail any thing −

*9 February 1842.* Military Men of Experience Seem to be of the opinion that the downfall of our Indian Empire has commenced & that neither by holding our false position, nor by retreat & concentrating within our proper boundary the Indus [,] Can we restore our fallen fortunes = I would yet hope that if we prudently retire behind the Indus & maintain ourselves on that line for Some time with discrimination & Success that our disasters will be forgotten & our rule of opinion & acknowledged Superiority be restored. It is Evident however that all now depends upon prudence & good government [−] a false step must be our ruin −

*10 February 1842.* Nothing new Except the beginning of Sir Robert Peels' Speech on the Corn law, but it goes no farther than the preliminary observations on trade & commerce −

*11 February 1842.* Sir Robert Peel's project turns out to be that 20s Shall be the maximum duty paid when the average price of corn is 50s a quarter − at the Same point according to the present Scale a duty of 36s 8d is paid − this is a wide difference, & I much doubt if on consideration it will be considered satisfactory, by the agricultural body − the basis of the old law was a protecting price of about 86s, of the present 70 to 72s − if the farmer can on the average realise 56s per quarter for his wheat corn [,] he & his landlord may be Well Satisfied − On Barley − the maximum duty is to be 11s when the average price is 25s − & On Oats − a maximum duty of 8s when the average price is 18s [.][126]

---

[126] See N.U.M.D., Ne C 5880: Lincoln to Newcastle, 10 Feb. 1842, for commentary.

*13 February 1842.* I am told that the corn growers generally are Satisfied With Sir Robert Peel's Scheme & Scale of prices – at the Same [time] there are many conflicting opinions – & I Suspect that in Parliament it will be much combated –

*18 February 1842.* Lord John Russell's motion for Substituting a fixed duty for the graduated Scale has been negatived by a Majority of 128[127] = The largest majority for many years –

*21 February 1842.* I was informed yesterday of the dangerous illness of my Excellent friend Lord Winchilsea, he was reported to be so ill that his Son had been sent for – I most Sincerely hope that nothing may happen to deprive us of so good a man –

*23 February 1842.* The corn debate Still drawls on in the Commons – they are now on Mr Villier's motion to abolish all corn duties –

*25 February 1842.* […] There has been a meeting in Buckinghamshire of the agriculturists at Which the Duke of Buckingham was present, & at the dinner in the chair – He made a Speech Explanatory of his view of the corn question & appeared to lament that he differed So much from many of his friends – He remained of the Same opinion which [he] had always maintained, there was no reason for altering them & he regretted that others had thought fit to change theirs – However he Should always under any circumstances remain their firm friend whether under the Same cheering influence as heretofore or under a less Encouraging incentive – The Duke very properly Said nothing about his resignation of office – Strong resolutions were said to have been passed at the meeting – and they were Justifiable though certainly the Event is most unfortunate, considering the Course which has been taken, unnecessarily as I think by the administration –

*26 February 1842.* Mr Villiers motion to abolish the corn laws has been negatived by an immense majority of 303 [90–393] –
    Lord Winchilsea is much better, & I trust likely to regain his former health – He is very weak – a relapse might be fatal & is most to be apprehended –

*27 February 1842.* The House of Commons divided on Sir Robert Peel's corn Scheme – the majority in favour of it amounted to 202 [306–104] = a very great number of the opposition Kept away, which accounts for So large an amount. In the Committee I shall not be Surprised if the Scale is much altered & made more nearly to approach Mr Christopher's Scheme –

*28 February 1842.* I learn today with infinite pleasure that Lord Winchilsea is so much better as to dine down stairs & Lady Winchilsea writes that he Seems quite well again though Still very weak = His Son's miserable Conduct & his undutiful & unnatural behaviour to his Father has been a chief cause of His illness. Lady Winchilsea Says, she is Sure it will Shorten his days –

[127] The vote was 349–226: majority 123.

*1 March 1842*. France demurs to accede to the treaty already Signed by Russia, austria, Prussia & England for the abolition of the Slave traffic, & granting the right of Search mutually – america also resists the treaty – France does this With a Very bad Spirit towards England which is Exhibited on all occasions which present any thing like a pretext for this mean, Jealous & rankling manifestation of hatred =

*2 March 1842*. News from India dated Calcutta January 11 — arrived at Suez February 11 & Shipped from alexandria on the 14th. The advices are not pleasant – The division of the army at Cabul is in a pitiable condition – Some accounts State that they have only a few days provision – others that Since defeating the Enemy they have obtained an abundant Supply – I fear the fact is that they are almost without provision & more in danger of starvation than the Sword of the enemy = though he is numerous [,] watchful & daring – it is feared that Every man will be lost – no reinforcements can reach them on account of the deep Snow & Severe winter, which is Expected to last till april – a dreadful prospect for these poor fellows =

*3 March 1842*. Lord Hertford is dead – another Garter vacant – He has been for some time a martyr to the gout & latterly in a wretched State [–] he has been a complete Sensualist, & might justly Expect the consequences – He must die very immensely rich = His Sons were born abroad & are certainly not his, for they were born after he ceased to live with his wife & she was living With Some Frenchman, Jesuit, Sebastiani [Horace François Bastien Sébastiani de La Porta], or some one of that stamp =

*6 March 1842*. In parliament all Seems to be courtesy & agreement = The opposition are pursuing quite a new course – and seem to have taken the Conservatives in opposition for their model –

*8 March 1842*. Very little going on – Every thing is particularly still & flat – Very little or no Elasticity is manifested in great or little affairs – a considerable portion of criticism is arising upon Sir Robert Peel's government, I fear he will Soon be a good deal vexed, & I fear too not altogether without reason –

*9 March 1842*. The last accounts from India confirm the death of Sir alexander Burnes, he was murdered by affghans who feigned to have business with him – Sir William Macnaghten our Envoy has been murdered in the Same manner, & General [William] Elphinstone has died of gout – our affairs in that quarter (Cabul) are in a wretched plight –

*10 March 1842*. The accounts from India appear more in detail today – fears are Entertained that the whole of the corps consisting of between 5 & 6000 men, at Cabul has been destroyed in an attempt to make a retreat[128] –

*11 March 1842*. The Ministerial corn bill has passed the 2nd reading in one night's debate, by a majority of 108 [284–176] – Tonight Sir Robert Peel will announce his financial

---

[128]Elphinstone negotiated an agreement with Wazir Akbar Khan, to evacuate Kabul and fall back to Jalalabad, 90 miles away; the force was attacked as it began its retreat. Some 4,500 troops and 12,000 civilians died.

statement — I much fear that he will rest upon an Income tax for his means – if he does, he commits an Egregious fault for which he & we Shall Suffer –

It is Said that a Garter has been offered to & refused by Lord Melbourne – This is liberality with a Vengeance.

*12 March 1842.* One can think of nothing but the horrors of the wholesale butchery & villainous treason by which so many of our unhappy Soldiers have been Sacrificed in India – authentic accounts are not yet arrived – but there can be no doubt of the horrible fact of the immolation of thousands of gallant Creatures [,] Victims of a miserable & Short sighted ambition.

*13 March 1842.* Sir Robert Peel has made his Statement, which occupied 3 hours & $\frac{1}{2}$, & is Said to have[129] been a most able and remarkable Statement, & by all accounts to have given the utmost universal Satisfaction – all this is most Singular & inexplicable – He removes the advantages, needlessly as I think, [performed] by the present corn laws, from the landed interest, and they are contented & Satisfied – He lays a tax upon Income [–] the most odious & inquisitorial tax in the whole range of finance & Every body pretends to be in raptures = There is Something very Strange, probably very wrong in all this – but if people like it – Certainly it must be Submitted by the few who not only dread but hate it – 3 per Cent is to be laid on income [–] those of £150 [and below] are to be Exempted & farms under £300 a year are to be exempt – all income [whether] landed, funded [,] Homes, railroads, trades, professions, all to be taxed [–] altogether he computes that the new taxes will give £4,380,000 – which Sum is to provide for the deficit of the i.e. £2,370,000, & taxes remitted £1,210,000 – & to leave a balance of £520,000 – to meet Casualties – I have not yet read the Speech & will postpone my opinion Untill I have So done –

*15 March 1842.* The Public, or the newspapers for it, affects to be in Extacies [*sic*] at Peel's income tax & financial measure – I admit the ability of the Statement & of all the arrangement – but in itself the income tax is a bad & odious one & I do not like it – I opposed Lord Liverpool when he wanted to continue it [in 1816], & all beat him[130] – Possibly there may be no tax which can Effect what the income tax can do – it is a most convenient tax, for the Minister, but a most dangerous one for the Public – a few week's acquaintance Will turn this greeting into wonder that its demerits Were not at once perceived – The new Corn bill will lower the price of corn & price of labour – The income tax Will deduct a Sensible amount from the nominal income, already overburdened with charges = & thus deprived of any Superfluity, the poor & working Classes, will also feel the diminution of Expenditure in purchase & Employment –

*17 March 1842.* In a debate upon matters relating to the Church of Scotland [,] Sir James Graham Signified that it was the determination of the Government not to legislate, but to

---

[129]have precedes this in the original.

[130]Newcastle composed an eight-page paper on the subject, possibly for publication: N.U.M.D., Ne C 5252: 'Observation on continuing the income tax at the present time', 6 Feb. 1816. For his more positive view of the tax, see C.P., Newcastle to Henry Clinton, 19 Feb. 1816.

abide by the law & to Enforce [it] most rigidly & impartially – this is quite right, it will Soon produce a proper & beneficial Effect, after a little fruitless struggling –

The Duke of Norfolk is dead, which vacates another Garter [–] there are now four to be disposed of –

*18 March 1842.* There appears to be a growing apprehension that the new corn law, will lower the price of corn & the value of land – the income tax will come most unfairly & injuriously upon the depressed landholders[131] –

*19 March 1842.* What I anticipated is now proving to be the case = Objections to the Income tax are springing up in Every quarter – It will prove to be a great stumbling block – & so I fear will the new Corn law – The acclamation is fast Subsiding – people were caught by the glare of the Eloquence & the lucidity of the statement, but they now begin to look upon facts as "stubborn things"[132] – The line adopted by the Government on the Poor Law, has given much displeasure, many friends openly opposed the Government & Sir Robert Peel was Evidently alarmed – It will do good & may check his self sufficiency which was becoming much too rampant –

*20 March 1842.* The battle goes on rather fiercely in & out of the house against Peel's measures & opinion on Corn, finance & poor law but he fights stoutly & I must Say most ably – at the Same time I think him much in the wrong – He propounds measures which are most distasteful, injurious & obnoxious & then if any resistance or dissatisfaction is Expressed – he Says, ["] oh very well – I think this right it is for you to Judge whether You will adopt my measures or those of the noble Lord – (Russell) take which you please but it decides the fate of the Government ["] – This is not fair & honorable to us – it is bullying & ungrateful & leaves us no choice but Hobson's – that or none[133] – The System pushed to this extreme will not do –

*22 March 1842.* a dreadful & deplorable Event is announced today – Lord Munster has committed Suicide by Shooting himself with a pistol – no reason is at present assigned for this commission of this wretched act – the only circumstance mentioned is that he had been in low Spirits for Some weeks –

*25 March 1842.* The opposition are foiling Sir Robert Peel by moving adjournments, they forced him to give up the other night, but he declared his determination to take the Sense of the house on his measure before Easter – however the opposition has again obliged him to postpone the discussion & the intervention of the Easter recess, postpones all farther discussion to the 4th of april to which day the house is adjourned –

---

[131] For its effect on Newcastle, see N.U.M.D., Pw H 174/1: Lord George Bentinck to Portland, 16 Mar. 1842.

[132] 'Facts are stubborn things; and whatever may be our wishes, our inclinations, or the dictates of our passion, they cannot alter the state of facts and evidence', according to President John Adams of the United States of America.

[133] The phrase 'Hobson's choice' is said to have originated with Thomas Hobson (1544–1631), a livery stable owner, who offered customers the choice of either taking the horse in his stall nearest to the door or taking none.

*27 March 1842.* It seems that Lord Hertford left £280,000, his Villa & all its Effects to the Countess Fichi [Zichy-Ferraris] – £25,000 & all his wines Valued at £10,000 = to Mr [John Wilson] Croker – & to Lady Strachan's <u>maid</u> £12,000 a year in landed property & £100,000 in money! – with numerous & immense legacies, to foreigners & others – The present Lord Hertford (who is not the[134] late Lord's Son) & cannot be as he was born abroad after Lady Hertford left him & was living with General [Jean-Andoche] Junot will Succeed to about £100,000 a year, which must be unencumbered –

*30 March 1842.* It is now stated that the former representations of the provisions of Lord Hertfords' will are not correct – & that the accounts are amazingly Exaggerated –

*2 April 1842.* There is a report that Lord Ripon is about to resign, the reason assigned, that he does not like to permit a public statement to be made that a revenue will be derived from the duty on corn –

*3 April 1842.* People have had more time to think & consider & they now begin to find out that Peel's Schemes are fallacies in many respects & if carried will be highly injurious – The farmers are beginning to be frightened & are becoming very discontented – Stock has fallen very much, So has corn, So is wood – with diminished means & Encreased imposts on land, the consequences must be fatal – It Seems to be a persuasion that Peels' "political Economical" measures were quite uncalled for & totally unexpected Even by the manufacturers & those who hoped to benefit by low prices – – To my comprehension nothing can be more clear, than, that if you deprive the more wealthy of their wealth, you deprive them of the means of Employing the poor & giving Encouragement, by purchase & otherwise, to trade & manufactures – as to calling a rent roll "income" it is nonsense – from the produce of one Estate by rent &ca, Which at the Same time, as most properties are, may be unfortunately burdened with mortgages, how <u>very</u> little comes to the proprietor in the Shape of income – The imposition of Such a tax is as imprudent as it is unjust –

*5 April 1842.* […] an Indian Mail, Just arrived, confirms all the dreadful rumours previously circulated = 10,000 persons [,] troops & camp followers [,] have been Slaughtered & only 3 or 4 have Escaped = The whole Event Seems to have been brought about (Judiciously I would almost Say) by the blindness, infatuation & utter imbecility of all those Engaged – The details are not yet given =

*6 April 1842.* From [Charles Rudolph Trefusis] Lord Clinton, who is his brother in law, I have Just heard of the death of the good old <u>honest</u> Lord Rolle – He had arrived at a great age, but his strength of body & activity of mind Sustained him in a vigor which few possess at 86 –

*9 April 1842.* I find people Extremely angry with Peel & greatly nettled at his Self-ish & overbearing behaviour – They dislike the measures, but yield most unwill-

---

[134]~~his~~ precedes this in the original.

ingly from a desire to avoid falling again into the hands of the dishonest & worthless incapables –

*11 April 1842.* I never Knew anything greater than the dissatisfaction at Peels measures – they appear to me to meet with no advocates in any quarter – high or low – & I am astonished at his perseverance in measures So obnoxious & So distasteful to Every one – The carrying of those measures will be the ruin of the party & of the country –

*12 April 1842.* From a foolish partiality Sir Robert Peel was very nearly in a minority last night on Mr Thomas Duncombe's motion that the order Should be rescinded which forbid the reception of petitions pending a proposed tax – Peel's majority was 1 [221–222] – whether that Member will Still Exclude petitions remains to be Seen, [but] it is thought that the rule will be dropped –

*13 April 1842.* We are in a curious & certainly not Satisfactory State [–] great disagreement amongst ourselves – reasonable dissatisfaction with our rulers & distrust of them – The result a thorough stagnation of Everything – are they signs of the times? "on the Earth distress of nations with perplexity"[135] –

*14 April 1842.* I sat for my bust yesterday to Mr [William] Behnes – it is for Eton College – This artist has been Selected by the Eton authorities who have asked me to Sit – I should not have Selected him, he is stiff [,] graceless & unmeaning, & I am Sure will never make a good work –

*15 April 1842.* The Queen had her first Ball tonight, we were there, I never Saw So full an assembly – it was also very brilliant & went off remarkably well[136] –

*17 April 1842.* [...] Tomorrow the House of Lords commences the consideration of the measures which have passed the Commons – We begin with the Corn Laws –

*18 April 1842.* We had the debate on the new corn bill tonight = It Was curious to observe the utter apathy not to say disgust which pervaded most of the peers upon the question & it Seems to accompany all the ministerial measures – by the time I went away, a very great number had left the house & I dare say that my Example may induce others to do the same – if I had voted at all I must have Voted with Lord Stanhope[137] – & I was unwilling to vote against the government if I could avoid it –

---

[135]'And there shall be signs in the sun, and in the moon, and in the stars; and upon the earth distress of nations, with perplexity; the sea and the waves roaring; men's hearts failing them for fear and for looking after those things that are coming on the earth: for the powers of heaven shall be shaken': Luke, 21: 25.

[136]QVJ, 15 April 1842.

[137]On the question 'that the word "now" stand part of the question', peers voted Contents 119 and Not Contents 17: majority 102. Stanhope was in the minority.

*19 April 1842.* In committee this night Lord Melbourne moved that it Would be desirable to substitute a fixed duty for the graduated scale – this was outvoted by a large Majority of which I was one[138] – I did not get home till between 2 & 3 [a.m.] –

*21 April 1842.* as far as I can Judge, all may be Said to be averse to the new Ministerial measures, feeling persuaded, as I am also, that the most disastrous & ruinous Effects must be apprehended from them – & yet, these are doggedly persisted in – I cannot Comprehend what is meant by adopting Such a line of conduct –

*24 April 1842.* The fancy ball about to [be] given by the Queen, is all the talk of the town – all who I have seen condemn the folly, which has not Even the merit of being original = as it is borrowed from what was done lately at the French court – The Queen & Prince albert are to be [Queen] Philippa & [King] Edward III – & the Court all in costume of the Officers of that day – Others will represent other Courts of other times – My Sons have been invited to be in the Duchess of Cambridge's Set, but they have, I think wisely, very respectfully declined –

*25 April 1842.* […] In the Evening attended a Ball at the Palace[139] –

*26 April 1842.* My bust in model is nearly completed: it is a Very Excellent work & does great honor to the artist Behnes –
   a fete at Holderness house to celebrate the coming of age of the Eldest Son of Lord & Lady Londonderry – a Serious accident had nearly occurred = the gallery is lighted by lanterns in the roof – people were on the leads looking through the windows upon the company below – Some of the panes of glass were Suddenly broken & fell plentiously [*sic*] & with a great crash among the people below – 2 ladies were a little Scratched but no more mischief done – it might have been very Serious –

*27 April 1842.* Mr Behnes has completed my bust in the clay today = I never Saw a nearer representation of nature[140] –

*28 April 1842.* attended the Queen's Drawing room [at St James' Palace] today with two of my daughters – Her Majesty looked tired [,] Serious & bored[141] –

*29 April 1842.* […] In the House of Lords we had Some Sparring this Evening, but no business –

*2–3 May 1842.* Nothing very worthy of note – balls & late hours are not very favorable to doing anything in the day – my journal falls a sacrifice too to the unnerving business –

---

[138]Contents 71 (49 present and 22 proxies) and Not Contents 207 (117 present and 90 proxies): majority 136.
[139]QVJ, 25 Apr. 1842.
   [140]'It has been pronounced by the best judges not only a perfect likeness but as a work of Art equal to any of my best productions': N.U.M.D., Ne C 7357: William Behnes to Newcastle, 26 June 1843. See Plate 1.
   [141]The event lasted from 2 to 4 p.m.: QVJ, 28 Apr. 1842.

*4 May 1842.* News from India & China – our prospects are brighter – Lord Ellenborough had arrived at Calcutta – Saving what was reported in the last accounts, no fresh disasters have occurred – […] in some places particularly at Jellalabad, the affghans have been taught a lesson Which has checked their cause & presumption – a very large force is collecting under General [George] Pollock –

In China little has been done – The forces are concentrating to make a leading attack upon Pekin –

*6 May 1842.* Heard from [my son] Edward from the Cape – by this time he is with the China Squadron Sailing for the North of China & at the End of this month operation[s] will be commenced against Pekin[g] – Lord Fitzgerald told me that there is much defection among the affghans & that at Jellalabad ackbar Khan [Akbar Khan] was wounded & it was thought to have been done by one of his own Sirdahs –

*9 May 1842.* The Town is mad about the coming "fancy ball", as it is called, at the Court – We are not invited, & I am truly glad of it, for if I had been invited I Should not have gone, I am too much out of patience & disgusted With the whole thing – The Queen & Court are in my humble opinion making great fools of themselves, by so degrading themselves into mere mummers, & I am very Sure that the affair will be productive of very great public mischief –

*11 May 1842.* The mode in which committees are chosen for trying Election petitions is so monstrously bad that the cry against them is universal = Justice or Common fairness is utterly out of the question – & its Effect is of the most demoralising nature – it must instantly be altered – it is one of Peel's schemes, & a Complete failure, as I fear many others will prove to be –

*12 May 1842.* On a motion of Lord Lansdowne on the injustice & impropriety of making foreigners pay income tax on the stock which they hold in the English funds, I took the opportunity of Stating how much I disapproved of the Ministerial measure of the Income tax as well as the tariff & other measures on the free trade principle.[142] I believe noble Lords on all sides of the house were not a little Surprised & if I Judged rightly those on the Ministerial bench were very much annoyed – I was Sincerely Sorry for it on Every account, but my Sense of duty & my conscience would not allow me to be Silent –

*13 May 1842.* The puppet Shew at the Palace is the talk of the town today as it has been for the last fortnight = The Queen's dress Seems not to have been admired – Prince alberts' Very much[143] – Parliament adjourned this afternoon for a week –

---

[142] Hansard, *Lords Debates*, 3rd ser., lxiii, 468: 12 May 1842.

[143] This was the first of the *bal costumés* held by Queen Victoria, each highlighting a different period of costume. The first event, on 12 May 1842, represented dress from the 14th century with Albert and Victoria dressed as Edward III and Queen Philippa: QVJ, 12 May 1842. See below, 10 June 1845.

*16 May 1842.* Nothing very particular today – The Ministerial announcement of the intended course as to the poor law is likely to create Serious dissatisfaction –

*19 May 1842.* Today, I Know not why, the Queen's Birth day is Kept – I dined at Sir Robert Peel's, a large dinner, & afterwards went With my Daughters to a terrible Squeeze at the Duke of Wellington's – Though we tried hard we could not get away out of the heat & noise untill 3 o'clock [in the morning] –

*20 May 1842.* In the House of Lords the case of the Marquis of Townsends' bill came before the house in the Shape of a Petition presented by Lord Sydney, from Lord Charles Townsend brother of the Marquis & claiming to be his heir, on the ground that the children of his Wife were illegitimate – The Eldest of these children [John Townshend] calls himself Earl of Leicester & now sits in the House of Commons as a Peer's Son & designated by that title – it is a case of most Extraordinary & barefaced impudence – their legitimacy being utterly impossible & openly known to be So –

*24 May 1842.* In the House of Commons last night there was a division upon Mr [William] Miles's motion respecting the new Tariff — The division was apparently a small one, but large when considered that above a 100 of Some of the most respectable men among the Conservatives voted against the ministerial measures[144] – on the other hand the Minister was Supported by the opposition who with a very few Exceptions voted with him = This Support of itself convinces me that the Minister Must be wrong – I want no better proof – But the fact is that Peel is playing with the opposition & by this means is carrying measures in accordance With their views, which we Shall hereafter rue in Sack cloth & ashes[145] – The Stanley alliance is the ruin of our party [–] Lord Stanley associates Entirely with his former friends – When Ever he gives dinners, it is invariably to all the chief Members of the opposition – This is an indecency to Say the least of it –

*26 May 1842.* There was a little life in the House of Lords tonight – Some sparring & smartness, but no question of importance – The [Lord] Chancellor Spoke particularly well on the Copy right bill –

*30 May 1842.* at a ball at Lady Sondes' I was informed of the Queen having been Shot at in the afternoon – I was as much Surprised at the Event as that I had not heard of it before – It Seems that on the previous day Prince albert or Some other person had remarked a man with a pistol in his hand which he pointed at the Queen – additional information was gained on this point & it was a [matter] of debate Whether the Queen Should go out or not – The Queen was asked if She would go out & she replied in the affirmative but She took the Kind precaution of not requiring any Lady to go with her – Prince albert accompanied her [–] on their return home close by the palace a man fired off a pistol as Some Say [–]

---

[144] The committee divided on the question that the words proposed by Mr Miles, to take the duty on livestock by weight, be added. It was defeated by 113 votes to 380: majority 267.

[145] Sackcloth was worn as mourning by the Israelites and was a sign of submission (1 Kings 20: 31–32) or of grief and self-humiliation (2 Kings 19:1); it was often associated with ashes (Daniel, 9: 3).

others that it flashed in the pan [–] However the man was Seised, & on the matter being made Known to the houses of Parliament both houses immediately adjourned –

*31 May 1842.* The man who Shot at the Queen yesterday proves to be a cabinet maker of the name of [John] Francis [,] not above 20 years old, respectably connected & well brought up, but latterly having led an irregular life – from what we hear [,] it does not appear that this man is concerned in any plot, it is merely a Solitary emanation from his irregularity – both Houses [of Parliament] have voted an address to the Queen & it is to be carried up tomorrow – all the town has been Enquiring at the Palace today –

*1 June 1842.* a Levee today [at St James' Palace] which was most numerously attended – I went & made my bow, but finding that the going up with the address afterwards would be nothing but a bustle I retired to my carriage & gladly returned home – it was desperately hot in the rooms & the Queen, poor thing, Seemed to be oppressed & excessively fatigued[146] –

*2 June 1842.* In the House of Lords Lord Kinnaird made a very foolish motion for a committee to Enquire into the cause of the present distress = He treated the Subject very improperly & alluded to Every thing most calculated to Excite the people to resent their Suffering – The Duke of Wellington replied in a very odd Speech, not as I thought very happy or prudent [,] the Duke of Richmond made a Short, but I thought one of the best speeches I Ever heard from him, or indeed from any one – Statements were made that thousands in the manufacturing towns were living upon 8d a week =

*5 June 1842.* [...] With the operation of Peel's financial measures, ruin of the most formidable [nature] must, as I apprehend, be the inevitable result.

*10 June 1842.* Went to the House of Lords this Evening with the intention of opposing the Income tax bill – I found that the House was up & the discussion on the 2nd reading postponed to Tuesday 14th [–] this is inconvenient to me as I proposed to leave for Wales on that day – I have previously written to the Duke of Wellington informing him of my intention to vote against the bill[147] –

*11 June 1842.* [...] a proclamation has just been issued against light Sovereigns which [is] most unfortunately timed as it creates great vexation, inconvenience & loss – it has done much mischief by appearing at a time when trade & traffic are So much & Seriously crippled.[148]

*14 June 1842.* [...] I received a most improper letter from the Duke of Wellington in answer to mine from Clumber, apprising him that I should vote against the Income tax bill – I

[146] QVJ, 1 June 1842.
[147] BL, Add. MS 40510, ff. 88–9: Newcastle to Wellington, 8 June 1842. This was forwarded to Peel: 40510, f. 86: 10 June 1842.
[148] *London Gazette*, 7 June 1842. The proclamation proscribed gold sovereigns of less weight than five pennyweights two grains and a half, and gold half sovereigns of less weight than two penny-weights thirteen grains and one eighth.

would not reply to this letter, but send it to Sir Robert Peel from whom I have received in return a most Satisfactory letter[149] –

*16 June 1842*. The accounts from the manufacturing districts are this day very bad – The distress & destitution of the labouring classes is daily becoming more urgent, it will Shortly be awful – & the language used by the Government & its measures will tend greatly to Encrease the distress & exacerbate the misery –

*17 June 1842*. […] I attended the debate on the 3rd reading of the Income tax in the House of Lords – it has been a long business & any thing but Satisfactory – Those on our Side made but a bad figure, they have a rotten cause to defend – Lord Lansdown made the best Speech I Ever heard him Make – We divided upon his amendment – & then upon the adjournment of the debate[150]– at this point I thought I might Save myself trouble if I said a few words & announced my intention of Voting against the bill[151] – & now I have done upon this business, for my friends on the opposite Side have Shewn themselves So factious that I Shall not attend on the next occasion & thus avoid uniting with them.

*18 June 1842*. Francis who Shot at the Queen has been found guilty & condemned to be Executed – It is a very proper issue –

*20 June 1842*. Nothing very remarkable – my mind is too fully Employed upon matters of extraordinary importance to me [and] my family [–] Concerns which cause me almost overwhelming anxiety – my financial difficulties which require my most Energetic attention – & public affairs in which I am almost pledged to take a part, but which to do properly is almost beyond my reach although I have this Evening made notes of a Speech which I might make tomorrow, if I had more Confidence in myself & which would represent my view of the whole Subject in a manner which might not be discreditable to me or useless to the public – I have So little inducement to take Such a Step that I hardly think I shall think it worth my while to attempt any thing =

*21 June 1842*. Farther reflection has Suggested to me the fruitlessness of troubling myself to take part in a discussion on which the greatest Eloquence Even would avail nothing – I

---

[149] BL, Add. MS 40510, ff. 90–1: Wellington to Newcastle, 10 June 1842; ff. 92–3: Newcastle to Peel, 13 June 1842; f. 94: Peel to Newcastle, 14 June 1842. Wellington told Newcastle, 'I Sincerely Wish that an Administration May be formed Whose Measures May be approved of and Supported by Your Grace and Your Grace's Friends'. Newcastle defended himself against this charge, telling Peel, 'I have No "friends" that I Know of, I have Studiously avoided canvassing the opinion of any Member of the House of Lords, nor do I Know of one single Vote to be given against the Income tax Except that of Lord Stanhope'. Peel closed the matter by recognising that Newcastle's opposition was 'a Conscientious one, [and] is not intended to Embarrass – and it does not abate my Esteem & regard for you'.

[150] The vote on the question 'that the words proposed to be left out stand part of the question' was Contents 112, Not Contents 52: majority 60. The vote on the question 'that the debate be adjourned till next Tuesday; was Contents 55 (40 present plus 15 proxies), Not Contents 186 (95 present plus 91 proxies): majority 131. A further vote on the same question resulted in Contents 36 (25 present plus 11 proxies), Not Contents 159 (77 present plus 82 proxies): majority 123.

[151] Hansard, *Lords Debates*, 3rd ser., lxiv, 88: 17 June 1842.

determined therefore not to attend the House. I am not quite Satisfied with my decision, but upon the Whole I believe that I have Judged rightly in adopting this Course[152] –

*24 June 1842*. I determined to write a long letter to [Lord] Lincoln recommending the course which I advise him to pursue – I shall be Very glad if he decides to adopt my Suggestions – I am persuaded that it will be beneficial to him privately & publicly – The Worst of it is that the office & politics of the party So Entirely Engross his thoughts that he hardly allows himself to think upon any other Subject –

*30 June 1842*. I read today a Speech made by Sir Robert Inglis on the occasion of Mr Roebuck's motion that Mr [John] Walter should be ordered to attend the Committee of which [he] is the unfit Chairman[153] – which delighted me beyond all Expression – I would rather have made that Speech than all that have distinguished Peel in this Session [–] the latter are devoid of all but ability, ingenuity & Eloquence – the former replete with Every high & noble Sentiment & the most lofty & admirable defence of the inherent constitutional rights of Englishmen. It must produce great & lasting Effect throughout the Country –

*1 July 1842*. The fight in the House of Commons against arbitrary Encroachment is determinedly & ably carried on – a Major [William] Beresford has Shewn himself a Spirited & clever defender of British rights – in all their Wrong doings Peel & his followers are found mixed up – He has hardly done a right thing Since he came into office –

*2 July 1842*. The Indian mail is arrived, Earlier than usual – By what has already transpired, it appears that In Affghanistan our Troops have been Entirely Successful, ackbar Khan [Wazir Akbar Khan] has[154] sent Captain McKenzie [Colin MacKenzie] to offer to give up the prisoners but upon what terms is not Known. General Elphinstone is dead –

In China – the Chinese have been the assailants on Some of our posts but have been repulsed with loss – It Shews however that the Chinese will not submit tamely & that they are no longer afraid of meeting us – & may give us much trouble – The particulars will probably appear tomorrow, when one may be able to judge better of the nature of their proceedings –

*3 July 1842*. The discussions in the House of Commons are assuming a new Character – Peoples eyes & mouths are opening & they are beginning to say now, what should have uttered long ago – Mr [John] attwood has attacked Peel's new Errors, Very openly [,] very Strongly, very truly & very ably – Peel is highly incensed at it, replied with his usual ability, but failed in his arguments, as I think – I am quite Sure from what he let fall, that he has the intention at no distant day, of abolishing the Corn laws – He Seems to be bent upon trying the most Startling & fearful Experiments –

---

[152] The third reading of the Property Tax Bill passed the Lords by a vote of 99–28: majority 71.

[153] In a debate on the Select Committee on Election Proceedings relating to the Nottingham election of 1841: Hansard, *Commons Debates*, 3rd ser., lxiv, cols 702–19: 28 June 1842.

[154] has precedes this in the original.

*4 July 1842*. Being Monday there is no London post today – but news has arrived this afternoon that the Queen was again Shot at yesterday – I Know no more at present = The other man's, Francis' Sentence had just been commuted to transportation for life & to hard labour in the most penal parts of the Colony[155] = This is the 3rd time that the Queen has been shot at – What can be the Cause of this [?] =

*5 July 1842*. The name of the man who Shot at the Queen is [John William] Bean [–] he is only 18 or 19 years old – a small deformed creature, & a bad character – He is a Jeweller out of work – The pistol Snapped when he attempted to fire it = he was immediately Seized, but escaped with the loss of his pistol, which was examined & found only to be loaded with paper hardly rammed down – it is most singular that these wretches should Seem only to wish to make themselves notorious without doing any bodily harm to the Queen = it will be very difficult to know what to do with this fellow – a Sound daily flogging for some weeks, would do him & others a great deal of good, & would Suit the cases better than any thing, Sending them afterwards to a penal Colony –

The accounts from India are published – General Sale nearly destroyed the force which attacked him under ackbar Khan = all our military operations had been Completely Successful –

*6 July 1842*. Colonel Dundas Son of Lord Melville, has been dismissed from his aide de campcy [*sic*] to the Queen & command of his regiment for Some expressions used by him disrespectful to the Queen = I do not Know what Were the words or their meaning – So that I cannot Judge of the Severity of the Sentence –

*7 July 1842*. The report of the quarter's revenue is upon the whole not bad = there is an Encrease of £200 000 as compared with the Same quarter of last year = a scarcity of coin Especially Silver is very much complained of –

*8 July 1842*. In parliament there is little to give Satisfaction = The ministerial measures are bad [,] perhaps ruinous, & the language on both Sides is Such as to be unfit for gentlemen to use – It Seems to be a most black guard & disorderly house – Lord Stanley appears to have made a very impudent Speech last night –

*9 July 1842*. I learn from London that Peel & his government are becoming very unpopular = Certainly he has done his best to render himself So, & it will be strange if he does not Eminently Succeed –

*10 July 1842*. The radicals & opposition in Parliament are becoming very factious & are obstructing the Supplies as much as they can: Peel will not have Easy work of it, & it is Entirely his own fault, he has made friends of none & his acts have been those of a fanatic –

*13 July 1842*. Miss [Helen] Gladstone, daughter of Mr [John] Gladstone of Liverpool & Sister of William Gladstone M.P. for Newark & Vice President [of the] board of Trade

---

[155]On 8 July 1842, he was sent to Norfolk Island, 800 miles east of Australia.

– has renounced her protestant faith & has become a convert to Popery = She is now Serving her novitiate in a Nunnery – It is very deplorable that Such things Should happen in England = Many ascribe it to the Brother's Puseyite writings & opinions –

*14 July 1842.* Sir Robert Peel has brought in a bill by which that class of miscreant who wishes to make himself notorious by snapping a pistol at the Queen – Shall be transported for 7 years – or imprisoned for 3 [–] & be publicly or privately whipped thrice – This Sort of delinquency is to be tried in the ordinary way & treated as a high misdeameaner [*sic*] = The transportation for 7 years is too little unless it is intended to send them to the hulks for that period –

*15 July 1842.* [Elizabeth Armistead] The widow of Charles Fox the celebrated parliamentary opponent of Pitt is Just dead at the great age of 96[156] –
    The accounts from the manufacturing districts represent their state as growing worse – The Effect of the new measures must greatly tend to Encrease them –

*16 July 1842.* a Deplorable accident has deprived the Duke of Orleans of life [...] the horses in his carriage ran away & he most imprudently plunged out of the carriage & was greatly hurt So much So that he only lived a few hours [...] The Duke was 32 – He is represented as much beloved & a great loss to the French Nation & to Europe in general – He was handsome & Engaging in manners – The whole family is unpretending & gentlemanlike – The King is in his 69th year – but hearty & well = a minority might Cause the most lamentable disasters to France & to Europe. I most particularly lament this Sad Event – The Orleans family is noted for its domestic virtues, of which the King & Queen are the mainspring & Example –

*17 July 1842.* The papers are full of accounts of the melancholy death of the Duke of Orleans – It is most universally & unfeignedly regretted, he Seems to have been generally beloved & to have been the hope of France & of his family – not that others of his family are not Equal to him – but that he as heir to the throne was considered competent to fulfill the duties With ability & propriety –

*19 July 1842.* The newspapers & other publications are now beginning to make Very Strong Commentaries upon Sir Robert Peel's conduct of the government – I rejoice at this because I do think it too bad, that he Should have So utterly deceived the Conservatives as in Every instance to adopt the Measures & policy of the former administration, which was to be the most incapable of any Ever Known in this Country – & I should add as dishonest & Shabby as it was incapable –

*22 July 1842.* The Government has thought it prudent to give way on the Poor law bill – having carried the first clause for the continuance of the Commissioners for 5 years & of Some other points of the same nature – the law is to remain as it is untill the next Session when a bill is to be brought in which is to Settle the question as far as the government

---

[156]She was 92 at her death.

is concerned – It is wonderful how much ground Peel & through him the Conservative party have lost & deservedly, by what has been done during this Session – I predict a not very long rule to Sir Robert.

*23 July 1842*. The tumultuous meetings at various places have been quieted by [the] military = To my view there is no prospect of any real relief from the prevailing general distress in all manufacturing districts & which in Some measure affects Even the agricultural parishes – I apprehend that before long the Starving part of the population will take the law into their own hands –

*24 July 1842*. I am informed that Sir Robert Peel begins to flag & to Shew that work has made a considerable impression upon him – It is only now that he is beginning to feel the nature of his situation – He must now perceive that a man however powerful through circumstances & highly gifted in talent & ability, must lose his friends & the consideration of his party if he chooses to act in defiance of all precedent & in opposition to the principles & opinions of his natural but disregarded Supporters = When he beholds the ruin that he is bringing upon his Country = his feelings & reflections will not be Enviable –

*30 July 1842*. Peel gave way the other day about the poor law & having carried the clauses for continuing[157] the Commission for 5 years he postpones the rest of the bill to the next Session –

*2 August 1842*. […] I went the Uttoxeter & Stafford road in order to See Shugborough [,] Lord Litchfield's [*sic*], where Every thing in the house is selling off by [George Henry] Robins – I Expected to be much gratified by seeing a very fine & Superior place — The Entrance to the grounds is through a river of Some width & though in this peculiarly dry time the river was low yet the water nearly came into my carriage – when I arrived at the house I found it Situated almost in a marsh & a very poor house of Stone – the interior is comfortable but not grand & the rooms very low – The books I believe are pretty good [–] the first days Sale was over yesterday, the books Sold ill – indeed there was very little company – The furniture [,] ornaments &c were of a very moderate description […] a few good pictures – a Vandervelt,[158] a great beauty I should much have desired to have it – but I am nearly as poor as Lord Litchfield – I did not stay long, as there was little to attract attention –

*12 August 1842*. […] Lincoln tells me that Peel made a magnificent Speech in answer to Lord Palmerston's motion on the Events of the Session –

*13 August 1842*. Parliament was prorogued yesterday – It is believed that we are negociating for the retreat of our army to the East Side of the Indus – This is what I have desired from the beginning & I am convinced that it is the only wise & politic course to take –

---

[157] ~~the~~ precedes this in the original.

[158] Willem van de Velde, 'The Calm, with men of war at anchor', was purchased at the sale by Henry Farrer on 10 Aug. 1842.

There is a fearful disposition to organised meeting all over the Country – Manchester appears to be very nearly in the hands of the mob & it Serves these Vile millowners right, who with one Exception only I believe have been all active anti Corn law men – Singularly Enough the men have used this as an argument against them –

*14 August 1842.* Vast assemblages of unemployed workmen continues in various parts but principally at Manchester & Glasgow = at Manchester it is Extraordinary to observe the forbearance of the mob – but little injury or spoliation of property has hitherto been Effected – They took possession of the rail roads & had them Completely in their power = they stopped the trains & in one instance threw Some Stones at an arriving train – but they have meritoriously forborn [*sic*] to injure the rails – a remarkable feature of the present proceedings.

*16 August 1842.* The accounts from the disturbed districts are very unpleasant indeed – The disturbance is Encreasing greatly & a great deal of determined audacity is manifested: at Preston the Soldiers were obliged to fire upon the mob & many were Killed & wounded = my fear is that the [distressed] people will not be Easily intimidated – Even though a military force be brought against them – Troops are Sending towards Manchester from all quarters & Some from Ireland, which appears dangerous = Two brigades of horse artillery are gone from Woolwich = as the troops passed through the Streets of London & at the Station, they were very much insulted by the attendant mob [–] groans, hisses & yellings assailed them very abundantly. This is all very Serious – there is another lamentable feature in derision & abuse of the Church to which much of the present Suffering is imputed – how it is impossible to conceive – but it pleases the multitude to make the assertion –

*17 August 1842.* The accounts from the Manufacturing districts do not record any instances of violence – The agitation seems to Extend & may be Expected to show itself more or less in most manufacturing places = The colliers appear to be the most determined – but when they are tried they may not prove to be more daring than the rest –
　　The Duke of Wellington is gazetted Commander in Chief [of the army]: this I think is done to avoid placing Lord Combermere & other claimants in the Office = perhaps to feed his Graces vanity & caprice & prejudice[159] –

*18 August 1842.* The contagion is spreading, all of the working classes are meeting & turning out in all the manufacturing towns & districts & they appear to be well organised & very determined – They Say that they will never return to work untill they have obtained the peoples' charter –

*19 August 1842.* […] Things in the riotous districts remain much the Same. The great Error appears to me to be – to have permitted these men to parade the Country, doing as they pleased – & above all Suffering large meetings to take place where the multitude was Exposed to hear atrocious & Seditious Speeches from the Chartist demagogues –

---

[159] *The London Gazette*, 16 Aug. 1842. Newcastle had solicited the position for Lord Combermere: BL, Add. MS 40499, ff. 115–16: Newcastle to Peel, 7 Jan. 1842; f. 117: Peel, to Newcastle, 11 Jan. 1842.

*20 August 1842.* I hardly Know what to make of the accounts of the rioters in the disturbed districts – but upon the whole I am inclined to think that the heat of the thing is Subsiding & that the people are beginning to tire of active Exertions in a business likely to be So profitless – In Staffordshire lawless bands have proceeded in Various directions Visiting gentlemen's houses & burning Some – They threaten to Serve Trentham the Duke of Sutherlands house in this manner – My family is rather anxious for Clumber – I apprehend nothing[160] –

*23 August 1842.* The accounts of the disturbances are not improved. I can Scarcely make out what is likely to be the issue –

*24 August 1842.* The disturbances appear to be gradually Subsiding /– The Queen has not given up her intention to Visit Scotland –

*29 August 1842.* Nothing very particular – The Queen & Prince albert Embarked from Woolwich today for Scotland =
    The disturbances are subsiding but the people Still continue out of work & in Some places are Very Sulky –

*30 August 1842.* The disturbances are Supposed to be nearly Extinguished – it is thought that the actors have been So punished that they will have learnt Such a lesson as Will prevent any recurrence to Such proceedings in future — I wish it may be So but if there Should be the Slightest grounds for discontent I Entertain a full Expectation that they will break out again & more formidably than hitherto –

*3 September 1842.* The news from India is dreadful & heart rending – Surrounded by Enemies, the almost impregnable passes Stockaded & defended in front & rear & Every difficulty being in the way of the advance or retreat of any of the corps, no additional Embarrassment Seemed to be required to favour the Enemy = However, it is not So = The Simoom, the heat, the privations & hardships Which they have undergone, have decimated our troops – & sickness is destroying the army rapidly – it is disheartened at the inaction & cast down by Suffering, it is disorganised, discontented & mutinous. My apprehension is & has been that we Shall fail & Signally So — Every thing Seems to Concur, to Make What is passing in that quarter appear to be the fulfilment of Prophecy & that in fact the affghans are the most powerful remnant of the ten Tribes,[161] who will crush the northern army & Eventually walk triumphantly into Jerusalem lead by that omnipotent arm of God in fulfilment of his Promise – a few Month's With [*sic* – Will] develop this – I have no doubt of it, & am prepared to see the work miraculously accomplished –

*4 September 1842.* The despatches & accounts from India are published & prove that the telegraphic account was a Shameful Exaggeration = Though not particularly favorable the

---

[160] For earlier reports that Clumber was under threat from Chartists, see *DL*, III, 148–9.

[161] Ten of the 12 tribes of Israel were said to have been deported from the kingdom of Israel after its conquest by the Neo-Assyrian empire around 722 BC. The ten tribes were those of Reuben, Simeon, Dan, Naphtali, Gad, Asher, Issachar, Zebulun, Manasseh, and Ephraim.

accounts are by no means discouraging, nor have any fresh disasters occurred Except that the Bala Hisla [Bala Hisar fort] has been taken −

*6 September 1842.* The papers are full of accounts of the Queen's visit to Scotland. all is rejoicing, but Still Some things have not turned out So well as might have been. Her Majesty Should consider how much trifles tell on Such an occasion −

*8 September 1842.* The accounts of the State of the country are by no means Satisfactory to me = Some of the men have returned to their Work [,] others still remain out & are pillaging & marauding about the Country & constantly attempting to control the others & make them leave work = There have been Several collisions between the two parties − In a Short time this State of things will grow into a very unpleasant & dangerous disease[162] −

*9 September 1842.* No news of much consequence = The Queen is giving much pleasure to her Scotch Subjects & is very warmly received −

*10 September 1842.* The death of the King of Hanover was reported yesterday but there was Some doubt of the truth of the report. Today it is stated not to be true as to the death, but that he is dangerously ill at Dusseldorf where he was officiating for the King of Prussia who is too ill to attend himself at the great reviews of upwards of 60000 men Who are now assembled there = The King of Hanover is & always has been greatly disliked, but I think he will be a loss as his political views are good & he possesses Very considerable influence in the German Especially Prussian Courts −

*11 September 1842.* The King of Hanover is very ill, & Supposed dangerously. He was married it Seems by the accounts not long ago to a widow of Some Counsellor & his Son is to be married in the Spring of next year =

*15 September 1842.* The american boundary affair has been Settled & has been finally ratified by the american Government in Congress − Lord ashburton is returning home − I fear that it will be found that we have conceded nearly Every thing − tomorrow the terms will appear in print.

*16 September 1842.* The particulars of the Treaty have appeared: without knowing more of the case in detail it is impossible to form a Judgment upon the merits or demerits of the treaty − This good must result from it − a cause of complaint & dispute which has long Existed is now removed. The americans have shewn great good will towards us [&] to our Envoy & they do not Consider any advantages that they have gained in the light of a triumph[163] −

---

[162] ~~decease~~ precedes this in the original.

[163] The treaty (9 Aug. 1842), established the border between Lake Superior and the Lake of the Woods, originally defined in the Treaty of Paris in 1783; reaffirmed the location of the border (at the 49th parallel) in the westward frontier up to the Rocky Mountains; defined seven crimes subject to extradition; called for an end to the slave trade on the high seas; and agreed that the two parties would share use of the Great Lakes.

*17 September 1842.* The Queen has left Scotland & returns to London by Sea – We Shall be henceforth relieved from the Wretched stuff & nonsense Written from Scotland =

*18 September 1842.* The Queen has completed her sea voyage & landed at Woolwich, no doubt very glad to be back again & out of the Ship – She again Suffered from Sea Sickness –
   The weavers still remain unemployed – sulky, mischievous & discontented – harassing the military & only acting when the Soldiers are absent –

*24 September 1842.* We hear but little now of "turnouts" but all the discontent remains & it is very probable that the Workmen though returning to work for a while only contemplate an outbreak upon an amended plan –

*25 September 1842.* a Very Serious fire at Liverpool (supposed to be incendiary) which has caused a very considerable loss of life & property. the fire has been principally of warehouses & Cotton to a large amount –

*27 September 1842.* Nothing passing that I Know of beyond the ordinary notice of affairs – Except that Lord Wellesley is dead = He was perhaps the cleverest & most accomplished man in the Country take him for all in all = If his Character had been Equal to his powers & ability he would have been at the head of all things –

*28 September 1842.* Lord Wilton is Sent out with the garter to the King of Saxony [King Frederick Augustus II] – a most unworthy representative of our Queen – His character & conduct Command no Esteem here & will not Exalt the English name abroad – He is a toady of the Duke of Wellington, his only claim to distinction –
   Wheat has fallen here to 48s the Quarter [,] a ruinous price, but one which, it is thought, which will continue for some time –

*29 September 1842.* The weavers in Scotland particularly at Glasgow have turned out & have created a great Sensation – Farming produce live & dead are decreasing greatly in Value – Sheep 6s a head [,] black cattle 2 to £3 per head – The result of all this will be lowering of wages & lowering of rents & there will follow a change in Every relation, in fact a revolution with its attendant misery & anarchy –

*2 October 1842.* Several of the leading Chartists, 10 in number, have been arrested & are to take their trials for Seditious if not treasonable acts of delinquency – If one may Judge by what is going on [,] the Government Seems to be aware of Some plot of an Extensive & dangerous nature –

*3 October 1842.* a very growing alarm is taking hold of the public mind. a letter from Wales tells me that the panic there is great indeed – my tenants are many of them giving me notice to quit owing to the alarm which is felt & the impossibility to turn any thing into money – Here it is beginning to be the Same thing – Droves of animals come to market but go away unsold – Such was the Case at the great Barnett [*sic*] fair when thousands went away unsold & unsought for [.]

The Same will Speedily be the Case with the produce of the Earth & Peel's nostrums will glare with rueful[164] delusion & blast with ruin & dismay the finest Country upon the globe –

*4 October 1842.* Discontent & dismay Seem to Encrease Every day – nor is it to be wondered at – all the newspapers & other publications having had Experience of the mischiefs which were sure to attend all the late measures of the Government are now obliged to record in their Several publications the deplorable Effects which are rapidly Exhibiting themselves of declining prosperity & approaching ruin = The Events are Wonderful & questionless are Signs of the times & in fulfilment of Prophecy –

*6 October 1842.* The Ottoman power is fast waning – revolt, apathy, treachery, incapacity all tend Silently to Extinguish a Power of which it is foretold that it shall so decay = "wear out"[165] is the expression in our translation = austria appears to be called forward by a tacit & general consent to take a prominent part in deciding the differences & placing herself more in a position to be the ruling influence over Turkey than any other – Should this preference be acted upon, prophecy Will be Still farther fulfilled, & the expected crisis be more evidently manifested as very near at hand –

*8 October 1842.* The Indian mail is arrived – The accounts from the armies in the North announce that they are on the move [.] General [William] Nott is ordered from Candahar or Cabul & Generals [Robert] Sale & Pollock from Jellalabad to the Same point – nothing more is Known – There appears to be a want of unity & a disjunction not very favorable to success – In China delay & inactivity seems to be the order of the day – a place had been attacked by our troops, why, does not yet appear & there We Sustained a greater loss than has yet been Experienced – the Chinese are improving in the art of war Especially in gunnery & are disposed to resist & fight bravely – I fear that our time is passed & that what could have been Easily accomplished two years ago, will now be impossible – Disease both in India & China was taking off a good many – May God protect my dear [son] Edward –

*9 October 1842.* Lord Wellesley has been buried in Eton College Chapel: he is considered to have been one of the most distinguished Men & scholars that Eton Ever produced –
The trial of many more Engaged in the late conspiracy & disturbances is now going on under Special commissions one at Chester, another at Liverpool –

*12 October 1842.* Not much Stirring in the way of news = Very few people in London – but in Every street & by Every public house there are Knots of vagabonds collected who appear to be talking Something over, but whether it [is] what they shall next have to drink, what pocket they Shall pick, what throat they Shall cut, or what villainous project general, individual or political they Shall next Execute [,] I cannot pretend to divine –

*13 October 1842.* I hear of nothing of any particular consequence today = dissatisfaction arising from failure & ill Conceived Measures is becoming very apparent – things are going

[164]~~the~~ precedes this in the original.
[165]Daniel, 7:25.

backward & will be Still Worse before long – the accounts from Manchester, Paisley &c are very unpleasant, but to me not by any means unexpected – I have foreseen that it will be So – & the State of the manufacturing people will be most deplorable & alarming in the winter.

*14 October 1842.* What I but too much apprehended, has with too much probability taken place – I fear that my dearest Son Edward has fallen a Sacrifice to the climate = Lincoln came to London yesterday & called here in the afternoon but I was out = This morning he called again & told me that it had been Stated in the Hampshire Telegraph = that the Harlequin & Some other Ships had arrived at Hong Kong on the 29 May & that Lord Edward Clinton of the Dido had died of fever – The letter was dated 2nd June – There is an inaccuracy as to the Ship – Lincoln has made Enquiries Every where at all the Offices – admiralty, foreign, colonial offices, India House &c & they Know nothing of it neither have [they] heard any thing through any private channel = Lincoln has written to the Editor of the Hampshire telegraph & his answer will arrive tomorrow – unless this information be to be relied upon we can Expect no other untill the next mail – it is a wretched state of anxiety and uncertainty – For my part I Entertain no hope of being reprieved – I have fully Expected to be apprised of this Calamity & I was hardly Surprised when Lincoln communicated it this morning – I will wait for the Editor's answer tomorrow[166] –

*17 October 1842.* […] we have learnt today that Lieutenant [Henry Gage] Morris of the Harlequin has written to his brother giving a full account of our dearly loved Edward's death & many details which are intended for us, God almighty has dealt most mercifully with us in allowing this awful calamity to be broken to us So gradually & above all by thus so Soon dispelling that agony of Suspense [*sic*] to which we thought we were doomed for the next three weeks – to the arrival of the Mail =

*20 October 1842.* The charges of the various Bishops to their Dioceses are published & much commented upon – It is lamentable to observe the Schism which appears to Exist among them & the Clergy of the Church –

*25 October 1842.* If the accounts from Paris are to be credited the distress there is Even greater than in London – Shops are closing in numbers & failures of all Kinds taking place – It may be difficult to Know to what cause to attribute this – I myself consider it to be one of the Signs of the times – "on the Earth distress of nature with perplexity"[167] –

Sir Charles Bagots' Extraordinary proceedings as Governor of Canada call for Serious comment – That any man having the power Shall Systematically put down the English, & loyal party [,] & in its stead to place in Office & high position men who are Known to be traitors & disaffected in Every way to British rule & who have actually been proscribed by other Governors & rewards offered for their apprehension, appears to me to be an

---

[166] *The Hampshire Telegraph*, 10 Oct. 1842.
[167] Luke, 21: 25–26.

infatuation, or madness, or weakness, or culpable impolicy, which nothing can Excuse & which must soon call forth the universal censure of the British Empire[168] –

*28 October 1842.* […] The Encrease & Extent of commercial distress in France is like a visitation – & I have no doubt is so = We Shall be plagued for our sins. "With divers [*sic*] Kinds of diseases & Various Kinds of death" "men's hearts failing them for fear, looking[169] for those things which are coming upon the Earth"[170] [.]

*30 October 1842.* Though the Surface appears quiet yet in Every part of the world work is going on which must very Shortly cause Events of the greatest magnitude – In Canada Sir Charles Bagot's measures must beget results of no indifferent nature – it is not a Small matter to disgust friends by Elevating Enemies – This has been done by favoring & promoting to places of trust & to the highest offices in the Colony the French party & Selecting for Chief Officers men who have actually been persecuted & for whom rewards have been offered – This may lose us the Colony & it may involve us in War with america – In Europe Some political measures of the first magnitude are on foot – Russia has Established her interest in Servia & the Turkish affairs are pretty much in her hands – austria does not subscribe to this neither does Prussia & it is Said, that these two States are forming an union & alliance to resist Russia, the more Especially as this latter is Setting herself up as the rallying point & defender of the whole Slavonic race – On the other hand the Germans are Endeavouring & rather Successfully I believe, to raise a national feeling in Germany & to rally the Germans as a nation under one head. France Seems disposed to ally itself with Russia – in this case, we shall be allied with the Germans, & if it comes to a conflict, as it probably will, the Struggle & contest will be tremendous – It will involve Still more Extensively the mighty contest of Nations – & the Slain may probably require 7 months for their burial in the valley of Hamon Gage.[171]

*1 November 1842.* The State of this country & of the Empire at this time is calculated to cause the greatest anxiety – The uneasiness [,] instability & want of confidence Exceeds any thing in the Memory of man – Here in England trade & commerce is completely at a stand – If any thing is brought to market, there are no bidders [,] no Enquiries after whatever the article may be; nothing is to be turned into money & Sources of revenue appear to be drying up – The public mind is in a very feverish & vastly unpleasant condition [.] I never remember any thing like it, & what makes it the more lamentable is that no prospect of amendment presents itself – The present prospect is from bad to worse –

*8 November 1842.* The armies began to move in march on Cabool […] They are marching as lightly as possible, & with few followers – Evidently intending to act with rapidity &

---

[168]Bagot appointed a new executive council which was not built along party lines. Many critics complained that it was comprised of radicals and former rebels who wished to sever the British connection.

[169]~~for~~ precedes this in the original.

[170]Luke, 21: 26–8.

[171]'It will come to pass in that day that I will give Gog a burial place there in Israel, the valley of those who pass by east of the sea; and it will obstruct travellers, because there they will bury Gog and all his multitude. Therefore, they will call it the Valley of Hamon Gog. For seven months the house of Israel will be burying them, in order to cleanse the land': Ezekiel, 39: 11–12.

decision – it is thought by some that the operations are undertaken too late in the season – This Seems not to be unlikely – but much depends upon what they have to do – Fire & destruction, mark their way too much to please me [,] burning villages & towns, & destroying the vineyards & Mulberry trees much because the natives Set much Store by them – There is great disease & loss of life in all quarters – in short it appears as if we had Every difficulty & danger to contend against – &, <u>for what</u>? To prosecute [an] unjust & infamous War, & to Endeavour to shew that we have the power to vanquish our foes & to lay waste their Country –

*9 November 1842.* By private correspondence from India, it is stated that the unfortunate prisoners male & female, have been removed from Cabool to many miles off to Some places in the Mountains near to the Hindoo Koosh – So that there is no chance of getting possession of them by our march upon Cabool – The move, Especially at this late Season, appears to be an inanity – We shall be fighting with the air, & no object can be obtained but that of adding to our bad fame as destroyers – By it We risk the loss or bad treatment of the unfortunate prisoners – It is a Sad business ! – & as strange as it is Sad – Nott marches upon Cabool from Kandahar with part of his Corps, & detaches the remaining part under General England immediately to the South to Quettah – Pollock does the Same from Jellalabad – We will Suppose that they meet at Cabool – they Shall occupy it – What then [?] – the Enemy will not meet them in a general Engagement = they will have nothing to do. the intention appears to be to quit the Country, & we will Suppose the best & being able to do nothing, the army will retire from Caboul, (as it is said) by Jellalabad, through the horrid passes & fortresses to Peshawar – if it pleases God that this may be done, it will be well – but I greatly fear some miserable reverse – I fear that Some how or other that army will be Entangled & that Eventually Scarcely a man of them will repass the Indus. The plan seems unintelligible & useless = I can understand, but I would not have recommended, that Nott's Corps Should march upon Caboul – by way of bravado, occupy it for a few days & then pass on to join the corps under Pollock at Jellalabad, which corps, as retreat is intended, would retire as the other advanced – & Even this no one will deny will be a most dangerous & difficult operation: the forward movement therefore of Pollock, When very shortly he must have <u>to retrace his steps</u>, is to me quite inexplicable – Unless there be Some plan of proclaiming Dost Mahommed [Dost Mohammad Khan] or any Chief agreeable to the affghans when we arrive at Cabool I can see no use in the movement – it is worse than useless – but if we finish the war by doing the thing handsomely [by] placing a popular Chief on the throne we may yet retire with honour & advantage. If this is not intended – then I Say Nott ought to have returned his whole Corps by Quettah & to have crossed the Indus by the Southernmost & Easiest pass, Entering the Scinde Country in force, over awing & Settling <u>them</u> & finally making Such arrangements as Shall Secure to us the frontier & navigation of the Indus – Pollock of Course would withdraw from Jellalabad to Peshawar or attack – & there await Events – This would terminate this hitherto disastrous & fatal business almost gloriously because we Should be in a position to do any thing we pleased on the Eastern Side of our boundary, the Indus – We might be magnaminous or[172]

---

[172] ~~of~~ precedes this in the original.

repressive, Kind or severe, as might be necessary, always I trust being <u>Just</u> & <u>merciful</u> which Should be the foundation & ground work of all our rule –

*12 November 1842.* The long Expected but Still much dreaded letters are at last arrived. Captain [George Fowler] Hastings had Written on the 1st [of] June from Hong Kong, but most unaccountably it has only now reached us – In addition to his own Short but feeling account, he Sends the Surgeon's report of my Ever dear Edward's illness by which it appears that he breathed his last on the 12th May – & his Earthly remains were afterwards committed to the deep – all bear testimony to the universal love & affection which he had Secured to himself – & also to his high conduct as an Officer[173] –

*14 November 1842.* Many compliments & laudatory reflections are bestowed by the press upon what took place at the Lord Mayor's feast a few days ago = The Lord Mayor [John Humphry] is a Radical MP & [,] on giving Sir Robert Peel & Her Majesty's Ministers [,] he highly Welcomed them & Expressed his belief that they were well fitted to serve the country in the best manner = Sir Robert Peel returned the compliment, Said he Knew no party & would always do that which he thought best for the Country – one of the objects of their policy was "to Encourage the demand for labour & to Extend the commercial prosperity of the Country" & he does this by letting in foreign produce & by Crippling all the resources of the Country = Various compliments were bandied between Lords Stanley, John Russell & others – it is plain that the Evident object is to rule unrestrained & without an opposition – I am confident that [he] will continue to introduce measures more & more injurious to all interests of the Country, which will involve us in ruin –

*18 November 1842.* […] German accounts State that Prince Metternich is in a very declining State of health & much apprehension is Entertained for his recovery – His death will cause a blank & probably a change of affairs – He is looked up to as the first man in Europe —

*20 November 1842.* a Stir in Earnest is, I hope, making in favor of Church Extension, as it is called – that is to Encrease the accomodation [*sic*] & furnish as many churches as the present deficiency, as compared with the population requires – The only way of acquiring this inestimable advantage will be by compelling the Minister to bring forward & complete the Measure – By no other means will this be obtained – if obtained with proper Endowment & a well regulated, properly disciplined clergy = the value of a blessing So Efficient will be inestimable, & would render England the happiest & most Enviable country, that imagination can figure to itself –

*21 November 1842.* Sir William Clinton writes that he has been appointed Lieutenant Governor of Chelsea in the room of Sir [George Townshend] Walker deceased = It is no compliment, in my opinion, to be named to an inferior post when a man has Just claims to the

---

[173]Lord Edward Pelham-Clinton died on the 'Harlequin' on 12 May 1842 and his body was committed to the deep off the Gulf of Siam. There is a memorial to him in Hong Kong Cemetery. The following year, Newcastle corresponded with Lord Haddington at the admiralty about the efficacy of Dr Stanbury's fever drops as a treatment for sailors: N.U.M.D., Ne C 5174–5: Haddington to Newcastle, 17 June, 9 July 1843, enclosing advice received from Sir William Burnett, physician general to the navy.

very highest, this is the case with Sir William, his Services, his Experience, his thorough Knowledge of his profession, his standing in the army, in Society, & in the high Estimation of Every one who values intrinsic Worth, make him Eligible to the Command in Chief or any principal situation – If I am not much mistaken, what is meant is this – ["] You Sir William are one of those now named to be Commander in Chief – but I, Duke of Wellington do not acknowledge this, I wish to let you Know that you are only fit to be Lieutenant Governor of Chelsea, take that & be Satisfied, more you shall not have ["] –

*22 November 1842.* [...] an Express from Paris brings the intelligence, that news had arrived at alexandria that peace had been concluded with China on the terms of a Sum paid by China of 21,000,000 of dollars – the island of Hong Kong ceded to us in perpetuity – The tribute to be paid in three years, Cheusan [Chusan] & some other islands to be retained by us untill the treaty is fully accomplished.

*23 November 1842.* The newspaper today is Extraordinarily interesting – It brings intelligence from India as well as from China – Generals Nott & Pollock had Joined at Cabool which had been Entered by our troops – General Nott had had Some hard fighting near Ghuznea, & General Pollock in the passes were [*sic*] he drove the Enemy in the most gallant & masterly manner from their strongest holds terminating with a battle with Some 16000 of the affghans in which, as Nott on the other Side, was completely victorious, putting them to flight & taking Every thing from them = We had recovered many of the prisoners, male [,] female & children, at Cabool & it was confidently Expected that in a few days the remainder would be liberated = Thus far, as was to be Expected, all is well – if we now retreat, it will still be well – but if we remain in the country victory will be turned into disaster.

The news from China is confirmed & the despatches arrived [–] our Success is most Complete & the Chinese thoroughly Subdued – we shall now do what we like with them & the opening for our Commerce, at this period of ruin & depression; is one of the greatest God Sends that Ever befell a Nation at its most critical crisis = it will restore & revivify our trade & commerce as if by magic –

*24 November 1842.* Farther advices from India by which we receive the truly gratifying intelligence, that all the prisoners are now recovered – Sir Robert Sale was charged with the pleasing task of marching forward to meet & Escort them & to welcome his nobly merited Wife [Florentia] – It is now given out that the War is Concluded – I hope it is but I shall not consider our armies in Safety untill they are again on the left bank of the Indus = What an Event to befall any Minister Especially When his own acts have not Caused it – The arrangements had all been made by Lord auckland before he left India, & to Speak the truth these advantages are only the fruits of those preparations, Wonderfully Executed it must be Ever remembered by General Pollock – By the termination of the Wars in India & China Simultaneously we are placed in a dazzling position, & one of immeasurable advantage, if the most is made of it –

*28 November 1842.* I have been reading many of the despatches from China Which are Exceedingly voluminous & Just published = I never rose from the reading of anything with greater pleasure. I never before Knew any thing of the Commander in Chief of the

Expedition – Sir Hugh Gough – but he appears to me to be an Officer of first rate talent & Very Superior merit – His views, plans & operations Seem to be most admirable & only equalled in merit by the manner in which they were Effected – The discipline of the army must have been more perfect than Ever was Known – for it is Stated that not a Single case of plunder or drunkenness was Committed – a fact hitherto quite unexampled – but which Joined with our humanity & good faith has already raised the British name in China – So as to inspire the utmost respect & confidence = In the Words of Sir Hugh Gough So admirably conceived & Expressed, "The happy result (peace) has under Divine Providence been Effected by the irresistible power of Her Majesty's arms by land & Sea, & I trust its desirability will in no Small degree be insured, not alone by the manifestation which has been made of that power, but by the high respect Entertained by a conquered foe, for our forbearance, our Justice & our humanity" –

*29 November 1842.* affghanistan is Evacuated & our Troops are to be Withdrawn to the other Side of the Indus – This is announced in a very clever & very able paper of the Governor General Lord Ellenborough – it is a very important Event = The Governor General disclaims any interference in affghan affairs [–] he leaves it to them (if they can) to chose [*sic*] their own Sovereign – The whole measure is wise & With the Exception of the too vain–glorious flourish of marching upon Caboul & planting the English flag there = we get out of the Scrape with honor & dignity –

*2 December 1842.* It is a great puzzle for a Minister who has to reward merit, such as has been gained by the various officers in Command in India & China = Peerages are really out of the question, & other distinctions are variously objectionable = but Combermere, who is now here, has Suggested a mode of rewarding military & naval Services which appears to me not only unobjectionable but Excellent = namely to give officers a Step in rank = by this means officers would be rewarded professionally & in the manner most grateful & appropriate to an honorable mind = I shall Suggest this Expedient to Sir Robert Peel –

*4 December 1842.* an Express mail is arrived at Suez from China & brings the account of the Emperor of China's approval of the treaty but he will not ratify untill it has been previously Signed by the Queen of England – One half of the first installment [*sic*] has already been paid –

*6 December 1842.* The Indian Mail is arrived bringing continued good accounts from India & China = The whole Short campaign in India has been one of the finest things Ever Executed – No man before him Ever displayed more consummate skill, Judgement, valour & Every highest military quality more preeminently than General Pollock – His marches through the mountains Surpass in Scientific military glory any thing Ever attempted & Executed by man & hitherto Considered to be utterly impossible for human accomplishment – Every officer concerned with him, Generals Nott [,] Sale & [John] McCaskill all have done their duty most admirably & have terminated a most unpromising project with a brilliancy & Effect; productive of the most beneficial & overpowering consequences to British interests in India – Captain [Bulstrode] Bygrave the last prisoner had returned to the Camp by permission of ackbar Khan who Seems to be a noble Savage – We have recovered all the prisoners – retaken & destroyed Every Strong place – beaten our opponents in the field & in the fortress, thoroughly outwitted them [–] cunning & wily as they are [–] & shewn them that we are an even match for them in Every way – The army was to retire by the northern route to Peshawar – it[174] may yet have to Encounter difficulties incidental to the Country & I shall anxiously look for an account of its arrival in safety on the left bank of the Indus –

*7 December 1842.* Nothing can Exceed the Jealousy of foreign Nations, Especially France, at the brilliant & Extraordinary Success of England all over the world – if they can find the Means, which is the only hindrance, they will assuredly go to war with us = & if they do, having our hands clear, we Shall Serve them; as others have been Served –

*8 December 1842.* a good deal of dissatisfaction is Expressed at the niggardly manner in which our brave officers have been rewarded, in comparison with all former precedents – The Duke of Wellington & Sir Robert Peel are too Jealous to lavish favors upon any, or bestow praise upon any but themselves & their opponents – Their friends have no Chance –

*17 December 1842.* Some people who I have Seen Seem to be of the opinion that the ruin of the country is fixed & that Sir Robert Peel must go forward with the Measures which he has Commenced & that the result must be the near Extinction of duties, a declaration of National bankruptcy & the reduction of the interest of the national debt to at least one half = If our Prime [Minister] Should So Continue & advance in Error, unquestionably ruin Will Ensue – but I Say return while there is time to old principles, & by that means Save the Country.

*18 December 1842.* a long service in Quebec Chapel [Portman Square] today & a good though rather startling Sermon from Mr [Alfred] Williams[175] = He attempted to account for natural deformities & imperfections as the works of God – & Seemed to lean to a hypothesis that that Same agent to whom the power of making is delegated but who is as it Were a mere automaton is the power to whom is to be attributed whatever may be imperfect – I cannot conceive a more Visionary & useless theory = Especially when causes may be assigned for many of the imperfections which are to be found Some times hereditary Some times from Casual causes which perhaps if minutely Examined into might be traced to its real Source –

Had a long conference with Lord abinger about my proceedings in my affairs, he could not afford me all the information I required nor indeed So much as I gave him credit for possessing, but still I derived a good deal of benefit from his remarks & opinions – He told me that he had made half a million in his profession.

*27 December 1842.* an Extensive Bank in Yorkshire & a very large Corn dealer at Wakefield have failed [,] the latter for [£] 500000, which are Expected to cause very Extensive misfortune – Trade Every where Continues in a very low & depressed state – at Liverpool

---

[174]~~yet~~ precedes this in the original.

[175]The service was in aid of funds for the Royal Dispensary for Diseases of the Ear, which was established in 1816: *Morning Post*, 19 Dec. 1842. Newcastle was a subscriber to the three volumes of Williams' *Sermons* (1836–43): N.A., DD/271/1.

there has been another conflagration, the third very great fire within this year = The losses very great –

*28 December 1842.* The Message of the President of america has reached us – it is as usual very long winded, but not much in it – Except the open acknowledgment that the Republic is Bankrupt, & that Every Nation of the world Especially England refuses to negociate Even what he calls a very Small loan – Here is a fine lesson for republican pride, made Still more repulsive by treachery, fraud & systematic dishonesty –

*31 December 1842* […] We have here arrived at the termination of one of the most Eventful years in the history of this Country & of the World – But if this year, which is only preparatory [,] be Eventful, what may not the Coming Year be [?] –

*4 January 1843.* I see that Lady Codrington has died Suddenly – She has been ill for some time – She was my first cousin – a very amiable & Excellent creature –

*7 January 1843.* The Statement of the quarter's revenue is bad – a deficiency of nearly a million on the quarter, & the Same amount on the whole year as compared with the last. The Income tax is [as] yet very partially collected, when the whole is paid it will more than cover all deficiency – If Corn, tariff &c had been left as they Were & no Income tax [,] I Suspect that there would have been a Surplus instead of a deficiency – Especially if an additional duty had been put upon tobacco –

*10 January 1843.* The Indian Mail brings accounts of the arrival of our army on the Indus – The Second division of the army under General McCaskill was attacked in the passes & lost many men & a great deal of baggage – it is Said that this was owing to neglect of occupying the heights previously to Entering the defiles [–] it is Strange that the Eminent practical Example of General Pollock's operations, had not established as a rule the adoption of an Essential precaution, which has acted in a manner as a master Key to these murderous & all but impassable passes –

*14 January 1843.* […] I am informed by Some of the intelligent & respectable tradesmen here, that trade & commerce never was Known at this time of year to be in So deplorable a Condition – they Say that it is truly Wretched = I much apprehend Some terrible catastrophe if Sir Robert Peel does not alter his Views & measures –

*15 January 1843.* Bread has become much cheaper Even here in London – the price of the quatern loaf is now 7d [–] a few months ago it was $9\frac{1}{2}$ d [–] the average price of wheat in Mark lane is not more than 50s [,] of Great Britain 47s 4d, a ruinous price & [one which] must destroy the landed interest if it continues –

*16 January 1843.* Perplexity, uncertainty & want of confidence, Seem to depress & Confound almost Every one who thinks at all: from all I can learn, I am fearful that there is too much reason to dread the measures which will be proposed & [,] if proposed, carried in the approaching Session of Parliament [.]

*17 January 1843.* Ministers &c are now all collecting here, preparing for the approaching opening of the Session – I cannot learn that any one Knows what is to be done –

*18 January 1843.* I went today to look in at the national gallery, which Certainly is a very poor thing – I have not Seen it for a long while – Some works by [Francesco] Francia pleased me more than any in the room – Our own inimitable [David] Wilkie Shines conspicuously amongst the old masters & Exceed any in design & nature, nor are his pictures behind them in Expression or colouring –

*19 January 1843.* People are coming into London preparatory to the approaching Session – they Seem full of Enquiry, but at fault for information – no one Knows any thing –

*21 January 1843.* a dreadful Event occurred yesterday Evening [.] Mr Edward Drummond Private Secretary to Sir Robert Peel was Shot by a man of the name of [Daniel] Mc-Naughton – The wretch came close up to him & fired into his body = he fired two shots in quick Succession [–] one took Effect the other missed – the ball Entered the left Side above the hip [,] traversed the back without hurting the Spine & lodged on the right side of the belly very near the Surface [,] So near that a Slight puncture of the lancet let it out – Mr Drummond is doing Well today, but he is of a full habit of body & it is not impossible that inflammation may Ensue – The man has been Examined, but will say nothing [–] he is a native of & has lately come from Glasgow – & there can be little doubt that the motive is political & that his intended victim was Sir Robert Peel, for whom he mistook Mr Drummond & having Seen him go in & out of the Treasury presumed that he was Sir Robert: the man had been lingering about the neighbourhood of Whitehall for nearly a fortnight passed [*sic*] & had been remarked by the Police –

*22 January 1843.* […] We Called to enquire after Mr Drummond – the doctors thought Very ill of him yesterday, but he had a good night & is better today – nothing has yet been elicited about the assassin [–] Enquiry is making about him at Glasgow & Paisley –

*26 January 1843.* […] Poor Mr Drummond is dead of the wound given him by the wretch McNaughton – it Ended in Mortification & he died yesterday morning – Sir Robert Peel is much affected at the Event – Poor man his turn may come when he little thinks of it, & I think nothing more likely than that he may fall by the hand of an assassin –

*27 January 1843.* […] Dismay & deep regret prevails Every Where at the shocking result of Successful assassination in the case of poor Mr Drummond who was universally liked.

*29 January 1843.* It comes out in Evidence, that upon one of the Policemen Enquiring of McNaughton whether he Knew who he had Shot – he answered – "Why it is Sir Robert Peel is it not?" McNaughton did not deny this Statement – the inference therefore is conclusive – Sir Robert will require all his fortitude to meet the opening of the Session, he is not engaged in a good Cause & he must Know that many good men have left him.

*31 January 1843.* Sir Robert Peel is by no means in an Enviable Situation – He is feeling Excessively the death of Mr Drummond, he Knows that he is himself the mark for an assassin

& what is most distressing is that Lady Peel is in a wretched State from apprehension & anxiety & is So unwell as to make Sir Robert very uneasy – & in this State he has to meet Parliament & to wrangle with litigious disputants – It will require more than ordinary Energy of mind, to bear up against & overcome these oppressive circumstances, with the Knowledge at the Same time that he does not stand well with the Country & with his hitherto Supporters –

*3 February 1843.* The Session of Parliament opened yesterday = The Queens speech was delivered by Commission – The topics are rather numerous [–] the settlement of the boundary question in america, the termination of the wars in China & afghanistan – a treaty of commerce with Russia, which is new to me, & of which they speak in high terms – Mediation between Persia & the Ottoman Porte. The Settlement of Syria – The Queens loyal reception in Scotland – these are the bright points = The others are, the general distress, the defalcation of the revenue – but a confident hope is Expressed that, the new trade with China & the new treaty with Russia, assisted by some arrangements connected with our domestic policy which are hinted at, but not named, will tend to relieve the one & to revive & Encrease the other – The Speech is markedly guarded as to any Measures to be adopted or proposed during the Session, & in this I think the Minister has deviated wisely from the practice [followed] of late years –

*4 February 1843.* The debates upon the address of course occupy the columns of the papers – In the House of Lords the Old Duke of Wellington was remarkable for his energetic, Sensitive & petulant but keen defense [*sic*] of Some Government measures, Especially the wars, & of the Governor General of India [Lord Ellenborough] of whom he Said, that there was not a halt or a march wrong or out of turn – This is rather too much of the partizan – In the House of Commons Sir Robert Peel Spoke Early & not long – Evidently desiring to avoid answering unpleasant remarks which were sure to be made by the opposite side = How Ever questions were put to him about his future intentions, Especially & pointedly on Corn & commerce – His reply was that neither on one or the other should he propose any Essential alteration this Session – he on the contrary Should oppose any, he did not approve of yearly alterations, but he gave his hearers to understand, that in the next year, or when he had a fit opportunity, that he Should not abstain in the Same manner, but should proceed with what he had begun, & that as his sentiments of the last Session were unchanged So all his future measures would be based upon the Same views & principles, & Would[176] be but a continuation of what he had only commenced – This information will occasion prodigious mischief: it will Keep Every interest in The Empire in a feverish alarm, anxiety & uncertainty, & will penalise & fetter all Exertion, & Speculation, in trade, commerce & agriculture, domestic & foreign – it is a death blow to the revival of trade & prosperity of the country in general.

*8 February 1843.* […] Sir Christopher Bethell Codrington is dead – Lady Codrington my first cousin died Suddenly about a month or 6 weeks ago & now her husband has died after a very short illness –

---

[176]~~his meas~~ precedes this in the original.

*12 February 1843*. In Parliament, the chief point of attack is Lord Ellenborough's proclamation about the Sandal wood gates removed by our retiring army when we raised the
fortification of ghatznee [Ghazni] Which had been taken from Somnauth [Somnath]
800 years ago by Sultan Mahmoud [Mahmud] & were Erected in the Sultan's tomb at
Ghatznee – In reply to Mr [Robert] Vernon Smith, Sir Robert Peel made the most
prudent, the ablest & cleverest Speech in reply &, as far as he could, vindication of
Lord Ellenborough that Ever was made, certainly the most So that Ever came under my
observation —

*18 February 1843*. [...] The debate upon Lord Howick's motion dawdles on [–] on the new
House of Commons system – which must disgust the house as well as the Nation –

*21 February 1843*. It is difficult to fix on any one topic to tell of – So much is happening,
so much is jumbled together, confusion, disquietude, discontent, distress & great personal &
general misery, but Still but little reference to the great Causer of all Events – & untill that
disposition be prevalent we may not hope that the plague Will be staid – on the contrary
we must Expect that confusion will be worse confounded –

*22 February 1843*. Nothing new. Parliament was engaged in voting thanks to the Governor
General & the army in India for their brilliant Services in affghanistan –

*25 February 1843*. Mr [John] Walter brought forward his motion to amend or alter the new
poor Law – it was lost in not a full house by a majority of 56[177] – by so many being absent
it appears as if many were in favor of the motion who feared to commit themselves – The
Ministers adopted a very bad tone in defence of a bad law (a reform law) & will have done
harm by Such unmeasured defence – indeed Sir James Graham absolutely asserted that this
law had Elevated the character of the poor = & taxed Walter with popularity hunting – a
very unwarrantable accusation in my opinion – There were 188 Members present in the
House.

*26 February 1843*. In moving the navy Estimates, a reduction of £450,000, is announced,
& a dimunition [*sic*] in the force of 4000 men – It is reported that the Income tax will be
found to produce [£] 6,500,000 – but competent Judges believe that it will rather be from
8 to 10 Millions –

*2 March 1843*. Saw many people on business & in the Evening dined at the Welsh dinner at
the Freemason tavern [on Great Queen Street] – a Very good & numerous meeting [,] Mr
Frankland Lewis in the chair: the Charity [is] in a very flourishing Condition = all went
off Exceedingly well[178] – a very Strong feeling was Expressed respecting the union of the

---

[177]The vote was lost by 58 votes to 126: majority 68.

[178]The meeting of the Honourable and Loyal Society of Ancient Britons, which operated charity schools, is
reported in *The Morning Post*, 3 Mar. 1843.

Sees of Bangor & St asaph – I do not think it can be done – if it be it will create immense & universal dissatisfaction[179] –

*4 March 1843.* The Crown Prince [George] of Hanover was married to the Princess Mary [Marie] of Saxe altenburg on the 18th February –

*5 March 1843.* McNaughten the murderer of Mr Drummond has been <u>acquitted</u> !!! on the ground of insanity – a wretched & most unfortunate decision – & as unjust as it is unwise – The probability is that now Every fanatic will think that he may do Such things with impunity – We are altogether wrong in our views of right & wrong –

*6 March 1843.* Chief Justice Tindall tried the case of McNaughten: after having heard the Evidence of the medical men, the mad doctors, he took upon himself to stop the trial & directed the Jury to acquit the prisoner upon the ground of insanity = The Verdict & the instruction give universal dissatisfaction – & well they may – this construction of law unsettles all preconceived notions of right & destroys all confidence in law as a check & protection – no man's life is safe – & as has been very justly observed [,] if mad doctors were pressed for an opinion upon the case of any one referred to them – there is not a man in the Empire who they would pronounce to be perfectly Sane – that is to have no "monomania" [,] the term adopted [for] delusion, Eccentricity or Something of the Sort, which Should impare [sic] his Sanity – The doctrine is most dangerous, & [in] this case the Mad doctors have charged the Jury & directed the Verdict[180] –

*8 March 1843.* The assassination mania is proceeding to gain ground & to be produced & advanced by the Encouragement which it has received – I fear that the instances will be numerous & multiplied – The Chancellor of the Exchequer [Goulburn] has been threatened by a man of the name of [John] Dillon –

*15 March 1843.* Nothing very interesting going on: in Parliament, an abundance of Spun out long Speeches but not much in them. The fashion is an odious one – the best Speech too much lengthened seldom fails to tire, but an indifferent one of length is past Endurance – Fame, & not public utility [,] is the object of the speaker, & this is the basis of long Speeches –

*16 March 1843.* Long debates in both Houses of Parliament upon the state of the landed interest, but principally on the old corn Subject – The movers in both houses Lord Mounteagle in one & Mr [Henry] Ward in the other were well beaten – The [Anti] Corn law

[179]In 1836, legislation was passed on the advice of the Ecclesiastical Commission to unite the two Welsh dioceses of Bangor and St Asaph in order to endow a new diocese for Manchester. This had still not been achieved by the 1840s and opposition to the measure began to grow.

[180]The ruling stated that 'to establish a defence on the ground of insanity, it must be clearly proved that at the time of committing the act the party accused was labouring under such a defect of reason, from disease of the mind, as not to know the nature and quality of the act he was doing, or as not to know that what he was doing was wrong'.

league was Severely handled by Mr George Bankes & others, & not Very pleasant reflections made upon Ministers for tolerating the League.

*18 March 1843.* […] In parliament / [House of] Commons / Speeches & opinions on the dangerous Subject of privilege – dangerous, because the doctrines maintained are of that arbitrary & tyrannical character to which many leading & influential members of that assembly have shewn themselves to be much too prone –

*19 March 1843.* […] Sir Hugh Gough has been appointed Commander in Chief in India – a most fit appointment –

*22 March 1843.* I am told that Every thing in London is miserably flat = meat is decreasing in price & all articles lowering – The funds however are at 96. – But it is reported that there will be a still greater falling off in this quarter's revenue than in the last – When will our Senators learn wisdom & rely upon Common Sense, instead of empty Concerts [?].

*23 March 1843.* The papers are occupied with Speeches of hours long of Lord Palmerston, Peel, Macaulay [,] with an adjourned debate after all in the question of the Washington treaty as to the boundary between Canada & america – These intermenable [*sic*] speeches & interminable debates, are really an intolerable nuisance, & as to wading through the prosy Stuff of which generally they are composed [it] is quite impossible. I have determined to be in ignorance, & when I see a long speech I invariably shun it –

*24 March 1843.* Southey the Poet [Laureate] is dead, he has for the last few years been in a state of Encreasing imbecility, & of late perfectly unconscious of what was passing around him –

*29 March 1843.* Nothing very worthy of remark = Squabbles in Parliament about the Supplies – but no harm done –

*1 April 1843.* The report of Parliamentary proceedings which I read yesterday was only the brief Early report of the Same afternoon – on reading the debate in full, I have the pleasure of observing that my letter (doubtless) has had the Effect of giving a new tone & view – & instead of final Exactments & arbitrary stretches of power, & partial injustice – all is smoothness, generosity & Kindness – one Striving with another to do tardy Justice to the unseated member [Walter] & to grant a better name & character to Nottingham Town[181] –

*5 April 1843.* The over land Indian mail is arrived – as I expected, the war in India is not over, General Napier has had a hard Contest with the Beloochies [Al Balushi/Balooshi] who were in great force & fought desperately for 3 hours – their loss was very great [&] So was ours – from two to three hundred men & 10 officers – We Shall not have the details before tomorrow or the next day –

---

[181] The debate concerned a new election writ for Nottingham. Newcastle's letter was referenced in the debate by Thomas Duncombe: Hansard, *Commons Debates*, 3rd ser., lxviii, 155–83: 30 Mar. 1843. See Appendix A.

*6 April 1843.* The accounts have not yet come out [,] but it is Said that the state of this Quarter's revenue is more favorable –

*8 April 1843.* It appears by the dispatches that the Beloochees under the ameers were 22 000 strong, whilst the force under Sir Charles Napier was only 2800 = The Beloochees fought desperately & frequently rushed in Sword in hand upon the British, but the valour & discipline of our Troops withstood all their Efforts & they were, Eventually, Signally overthrown –

*11 April 1843.* a large meeting at ailesbury, has declared against the late Corn law & Tariff, & resolved to petition parliament against them as they are bringing ruin upon the farming & labouring Classes –

*12 April 1843.* an awful & very remarkable instance of Sudden death occurred in the case of Lord Hopetown – When the House of Lords broke up [,] he went to the stand & ordered a hack cabriolet & ordered the man to drive him to Stevens's Hotel [18 New Bond Street] – which he did, & on arriving there, [he] opened the door but did not get off his box – finding that his passenger did not get out, he left his box & went to the door & pulled the gentleman by the leg thinking to awaken him but he did not move, & finding it in vain – he rang the Hotel bell which was answered by the porter, who thought that Lord Hopetown must be very ill & sent for his Servant, who when he came felt for his pulse & found none – he then Sent for a Doctor, but it was ascertained that he was perfectly dead – Lord Hopetown was not 40 – Lady Hopetown is miserably ill at Brighton, they have one Son [–] a puney, sickly boy – Sudden deaths & all sorts of accidents & afflictions are very numerous –

*14 April 1843.* […] The accounts from different places State that trade is reviving, though very gradually – It is to be Expected that this must be the case to a certain very limited Extent – that is to the Supply of what is really wanted = I do not think that it will go much farther than this – but I wish I may be mistaken.

*16 April 1843.* The Duke of Sussex is very ill – it is Supposed that he is not likely to recover – His decease will not be a loss to many = I fear that I am uncharitable Enough to attribute to him no one good quality – I will not go so far as to pronounce that he possesses Every bad one[182] –

*19 April 1843.* There really is Scarcely anything to notice. Parliament is in Easter recess, & there is a truce to idle prating, for the Speeches for the most part are little Else –

*20 April 1843.* O'Connell has not attended to his parliamentary duties lately, not this Session – & by all accounts is wholly wrapped up in his repeal agitation, in which it is said he has

---

[182] These feelings were reciprocated. Newstead Abbey MSS, 1991–2146, duke of Sussex to Thomas Wildman, 18 July 1842: 'I believe [Newcastle] to be an uneducated, ignorant being, crammed with a great deal of bigotry as well as possessing a great want of judgment and sense, yet I have always heard of him as a kind, good natured creature'.

made very formidable progress — It is difficult to foresee the whole Extent of the Mischief which may arise from this — It is inexplicable why the Government tamely permits this agitation, why the anti corn law league, & why Chartism, Except that Sir Robert Peel wishes to be thought liberal or is afraid to take upon himself the responsibility of crushing these hotbeds of Rebellion –

*22 April 1843.* The Duke of Sussex is no more – He died yesterday, at a little after 12 o'clock =

*23 April 1843.* [Lord] Lincoln was called to London yesterday on account of the death of the Duke of Sussex – he was obliged to leave his family at a moment & unfortunately his Eldest boy Just becoming Very unwell = no man with a family should be in office, Especially when Situated as poor Lincoln is = a man's family calls for & requires a man's almost undivided attention, to do his duty by them properly –

*26 April 1843.* The Queen has been brought to bed of a Princess [Alice] – both are doing well –

*27 April 1843.* […] It is said that trade is reviving Every where, & that at Manchester, though the wages are very low, there have not been so many mills at work for the last 5 years – I wish that this information may be true –

*28 April 1843.* The Duke of Sussex has desired that he may be buried in the public Cemetary [sic] at Kensal Green = Where he will be by the side of [Richard] Carlisle [Carlile] the atheist & others of his Stamp not uncongenial to him in life, & so in death, = The funeral is to be public, & the Duke of Cambridge Chief mourner [–] it will be a very awkward & anomalous business –

*29 April 1843.* I am informed that much uneasiness is beginning to be felt, by the Government, about Ireland – The orange party have joined the Repealers under O'Connell & have almost all of them become subscribers to the Rent – it is said that[183] above £500 a week is now collected, to affect repeal – Sir Robert Peel's conduct has disgusted the Protestants, as much as it has ruined & alienated the agricultural & trading interests = They can sell nothing & turn nothing into money – discontent & want of confidence are working fearful havoc in the feelings of those who might be fast friends – It is the Same here, & unless there is a change of Measures, Every individual in the Country must become bankrupt =

*30 April 1843.* a great division of opinion upon the Ministerial Ecclesiastical Courts bill has been manifested, nearly 80 Conservatives have voted against it[184] – Sir Robert Peel appears to fail in the merit & value of all his Measures = He is becoming a most unpopular & distrusted Minister – & is raising a storm which will burst upon him before long –

---

[183] that precedes this in the original.
[184] The vote was 186–104: majority 82.

*1 May 1843.* The population of Ireland by the Censuses of 1821 – 1831 – & 1841 – Were as under –

In 1821 – it was – 6,801,827 – Thus shewing that the increase
    1831 – " " – 7,767,461 – between 1821 – & 1831 – Was, 965,574 –
    1841 – " " – 8,175,278 – = 1831– & 1841 – 407,872 –

The decrease in the rate of Encrease is Extraordinary, & Shews that Something has decidedly checked the progress of population in Ireland –

*2 May 1843.* It is quite melancholy to hear the Same account from Every one of the dullness of trade & little doing in Every business be it what it may – it is also very admirable to observe the patience & fortitude with which nearly all Endure the grievous mortification, & great Suffering which Such a State of things must of necessity bring upon them. To Sir Robert Peel & his measures they are mainly indebted for what afflicts them, & I greatly fear that they have by no means Seen the Worst –

*3 May 1843.* a debate in the House of Commons upon the Education in Factories bill, in which Some ministerial alterations have been made to please the Dissenters, but which, as it deserves, will fail –

*5 May 1843.* The Duke of Sussex was buried yesterday at Kensall Green cemetery, where it was his royal pleasure to be placed in search of Vulgar popularity after death, as during life =

*6 May 1843.* I am told that Extreme dissatisfaction prevails at the present & future prospect of affairs as now conducted by Sir Robert Peel – People See the revenue falling off & their own means rapidly decreasing & they begin to perceive that free [trade] principles & an income tax are not the most prospering measures that can be adopted, & they are determined to take the matter up & to oppose Peel & his measures unless he will[185] plainly make his Election to be a Conservative instead of what he really is. People talk of forming a third party that may be relied upon, to the Exclusion of the reformers, Should Peel be overthrown –

*7 May 1843.* Sir Robert Peel announced his plan of Church Extension – it consists in this; he will borrow 600,000 £ from the Queen anne's Bounty fund to be replaced hereafter by the Ecclesiastical Commissioners, & from this he will pay £30,000 a year to additional clergymen to be planted in populous districts, very frequently & preferably where there are no Churches to Serve – this is the amount of his measure – It is a mean & tinkering Scheme & I must confess in the true Spirit of Peel –

*9 May 1843.* The Government is Surrounding itself with all Kinds of difficulties & Embarrasments, [*sic*] & all of its own making – Ireland is assuming a most unpleasant appearance,

---

[185]will precedes this in the original.

& all arising from a neutral & temporising policy, displeasing all & giving confidence to none but the mischievous – The rent collected last week for the repeal rebellion was £700 – a formidable Sum in aid of mischief – In England the farmers have at last discovered & felt the injury done to them & meetings are holding in different places, where the cry is to displace Peel – With all his ability [,] he appears to have no notion of doing anything but what is adverse to the good of his country – & yet perhaps, Strange as it may appear, he may be persuaded that he is acting rightly – if this is so – his Error is <u>Judicial</u> –

*12 May 1843.* a very Extraordinary letter from Mr Fox Lane [Sackville Lane-Fox] to O'Connell, appears today in the Standard – He announces that he means to open the Roman Catholic Emancipation question again, & if he does, & does it well Soberly, soundly & rationally, he will Cause a feeling of no ordinary degree = It may be productive of immense consequences =

Lord Fitzgerald is dead after an illness of only a few days = He was President of the Board of Control & a Cabinet minister – a clever man & a very good Speaker, the best among the Ministers in the House of Lords –

*13 May 1843.* People seem to be dying off fast. Two Generals with regiments are dead – Lord Forbes & Sir Hilgrove Turner – The weather is Extremely Variable & trying for old & young –

*15 May 1843.* I have read Sir Robert Peel's speech in the debate on the Corn Laws – & I have no hesitation in pronouncing as my conviction, that he means to abolish the corn laws & all duties which can be called protective – He is a direct free-trader – he will perpetuate the income tax & raise it to any point he pleases, So as to produce whatever may be required for purposes of revenue = What his notion can be I am at a loss to conceive = but whatever it is mistaken grossly mistaken – he must be [–] & the assassin of his Country he most assuredly is both in Church & State –

*17 May 1843.* a Storm is brewing Every where against Sir Robert Peel & I must own that he fully deserves it = He proves himself to be a very dangerous man in power –

*19 May 1843.* a reverend gentleman, Mr [William O'] Higgins, calling himself Bishop of Ardagh [,] has distinguished himself very much at a Meeting at Mullingar at which another Bishop [Edward Adderly Stopford, Bishop of Meath] was in the chair & O'Connell the <u>great</u> guest, the day being <u>Sunday</u> [14 May] = His <u>Lordship</u> as he is styled distinguished himself by the violence & audacity of his speech, I must also add by its ability = He asserted formally that all the Roman Catholic Bishops & priesthood were Repealers & that they were determined to carry repeal & die in the cause, if necessary = = He gloried in being of <u>low</u> extraction & thanked God that he owed nothing to any aristocrat living, except the unutterable contempt which he bore to the whole class – The language used at these meetings is of the most seditious nature & [,] as far as <u>Expression</u> goes, those Concerned declare that they will have self government – Popery Seems determined to try to obtain the mastery [–] if persevered in a struggle must Ensue, for surely <u>Now</u> Peel & the government must Strike or they are lost =

*21 May 1843.* a fierce debate is not unlikely to result from Lord Stanleys bill for permitting the importation of Canada flour at a very low duty, nearly nominal at the rate of 1s a quarter for Wheat = It is a Shameful & glaring injustice to the English farmers, & one which I trust they will resent with becoming Spirit & Knowledge of their interests – The debate has been adjourned to Monday 22[nd] – & Saturday & Sunday will have intervened for consideration – So that I hope the friends of agriculture may come down in force & declare their dissent from So ruinous a Measure – The Ministers Seem to be bent upon the utter ruin of the Country –

*22 May 1843.* [My son] Robert arrived this afternoon […] He tells us that they are all in dismay about the probable result of the ministerial measure – & that Sir Robert Peels majority will be very greatly diminished by driving so many of his hitherto Supporters to vote against him – I wish he were beaten it would Serve him very right, & if he were no longer at the head of affairs the Country would not lose by it –

*23 May 1843.* Tonight Lord Powis brings on the 2nd reading of his bill for Saving the Bishoprics of Bangor & St asaph from the destructive & revolutionary grasp of Parliament & its agents the Ecclesiastical Commission[186] – I am very Exceedingly anxious about the result & have written to him Entreating him not to give way but to push the House to a division, if he is opposed, let who will ask him to abandon his most meritorious task[187] – It is in fact a point of inestimable importance – if he Succeeds it may check the downward & Sweeping cause of Parliament & the [Ecclesiastical] Commission, if he fail, a division will Shew who are real & Who the pretended friends to the Church, & will raise a voice which Sir Robert & Co. will not be pleased to hear –

*24 May 1843.* The debate on the Canada corn bill is terminated, & very unexpectedly I believe in a large majority in favor of the bill – a majority of 188 [344–156] – I am very sorry for this – Peels' most mischievous Career ought to be Checked – & a measure So injurious to British agriculture, passing at Such a time [,] will necessarily create much bad feeling –
    It is confidently asserted that Dr Pusey had made an open public profession of Popery – by as much as I can understand from the pulpit in Christ Church Cathedral [Oxford] – If this be So, it must bring this Schismatic faction to a point –

*25 May 1843.* Lord Powis raised a debate by his motion on the 23rd & gave the Duke of Wellington an opportunity of Saying Some very improper & impolitic things – but he did not persevere in his object & withdrew the motion – I very much regret it, he ought to have pushed it to a division – The weak archbishop of Canterbury [William Howley] opposed the motion, the Bishop ([Edward] Denison) of Salisbury Supported it in a very right & Very able Speech –

---

[186] 'A Bill for Preventing the Union of the Sees of St Asaph and Bangor', *Sessional Papers of the House of Lords*, 1843 (114), iii, 335 (16 May 1843); 1844 (109), v, 619 (20 May 1844); 1845 (99), v, 481.
[187] N.L.W., MC2/84: Newcastle to Powis, 18 May 1843. Newcastle informed Powis that he had sent his proxy to Lord Kenyon and criticised Peel's measures for tending to 'weaken, lower, & ruin the high interests of Church & State'.

*26 May 1843*. a very unpleasant manifestation of Spirit has Shewn itself at Manchester = a party of the 13th regiment were drinking in a beer Shop & quarelled [*sic*] – two of them left the house & prepared to fight in the Streets – Some police interfered, when the Soldiers fell on them & were joined by the mob – The police was reinforced, & so were the Soldiers & the mob = there was a Severe affray which lasted for Some time = the mob & the Soldiers acting together against the police – They attacked the police Station, several hundreds of the Soldiers, Combining With Some thousands of the mob in the affray = Two companies of the 18th were ordered out to assist the police against their Comrades = whilst marching there Some of the Soldiers cried out within hearing of their Officers that the Police were "damned Scoundrels & had not had half Enough of it" = The mob was Eventually dispersed & many prisoners taken – but order is not restored – This state of things had been going on for some days – The town is in a state of great uneasiness & [,] owing to a revulsion of trade, there is a large "turn out" parading about the Streets. The affair is a very unpleasant one & has not Ended yet – it shews that the soldiers are disorderly & disposed to be good friends with the mob, & not a cheering Symptom at a time when their Services may be much required both here & in Ireland –

The Kirk of Scotland is finally Split – The non interventionists With the Moderator at their head & 400 clergy – left the General assembly after making a public protest = They have Separated for Ever from the Established Kirk, & have Set up for themselves under the Title of "The General assembly of the Free Presbytery Church" – Dr [Thomas] Chalmers is chosen their Moderator – & thus is the Conflict begun – where it will End no one can tell –

*27 May 1843*. a Mr [William] Christie moved in the House of Commons, that Oaths & Subscriptions Should be abolished at the Universities, & that Dissenters of all descriptions should be admitted there – Liberalism had made so much progress that the motion was not Scouted – Goulburn, Chancellor of [the] Exchequer opposed it but not stoutly – & Lord Stanley actually approved of it, but gave Some finely spun reasons why he could not vote for it – Sir Robert Peel took no part in the debate, nor did he Seem to have interested himself about it for the motion was defeated by a majority of 75 in a house of about 275[188] – & yet on the Canada Corn question Every Vote could be raked up & forced down to the house – but on a free thinking motion no Exertion need be used to quash the abomination – Thus it is – & Surely these are Signs of the times –

*28 May 1843*. Several Magistrates in Ireland have been dismissed for attending repeal meetings – Lord Ffrench, Daniel O'Connell & others[189] – The Lord Chancellor [of Ireland, Sir Edward Sugden] struck their names out of the Commission – Questions have been asked about the matter in the houses of Parliament & to a question put by Some one [William Smith O'Brien] to Sir James Graham Whether if any Magistrate attended a Repeal meeting his name would be stricken out of the Commission – he replied, that, it certainly Would = all this is acting properly, & what Should be done – the fault is Ever having permitted the sedition to have proceeded so far –

[188] The motion was lost by 105–175 votes: majority 70.
[189] Sir Michael Dillon was also dismissed.

*30 May 1843.* Great Efforts Seem to be making Every where to raise the standard of rebellion, assertedly, not to use force but argument – but nevertheless as great Efforts are also making to gain over the Soldiers & to detach them from their duty – I think it is to be feared that they may be in Some respects too Successful – The language used is highly Seditious – & Yet it passes unpunished –

*31 May 1843.* a great number of arms & troops are Sending over to Ireland, we must not be too Sure that nothing Shall happen here –

*1 June 1843.* There appears to be more animation & contentious Spirit in Parliament than I have Known for a long time – The opposition fancy that it is a time for them to do Something & accordingly very troublesome they are, whilst Peel from having disgusted & injured his friends, & having disappointed all the best part of the Nation, is but very feebly & very unwillingly Supported –

*2 June 1843.* all over the country, an uneasiness is manifested & a disposition to riot & outrage – The workmen are "turning out" again – & Serious affrays between the Soldiers & inhabitants in Several places – In Wales a Set of people calling themselves Rebecca & her daughters have been allowed to proceed with their outrages with so much impunity that now their force is becoming formidable & creates much tremor where their outrages are committed – In Ireland, we Must presume that the government Expects nothing less than civil war as troops are hurrying over, & all Kinds of Stores, Engineers & artillery to Survey [,] repair & Strengthen the forts, & to defend them, & Ships of war to guard the coasts = Can all this danger have come upon the Government unawares, or has it permitted rebellion to organise itself to Such a fearful extent unmolested & unnoticed, So that it should ripen to full maturity before striking [?] – in Either case it is not defensible in my opinion, for who can foresee what oceans of blood may be Shed before the rebellion be crushed [?] – In short we are in a fearful State & the government by no means fulfills our Expectations –

*3 June 1843.* The Vice Chancellor of Oxford [Philip Wynter] & 5 others are engaged in Consideration of Dr Pusey's sermon – the investigation is not public – but it is said to be decided that there is no question as to the popish tendency of the doctrine, the only doubt is respecting the Consequences, in the shape of penalty –

*4 June 1843.* The penalty inflicted by the Vice Chancellor & 5 Doctors is very lenient indeed – Dr Pusey is suspended from preaching in Oxford for two years – Dr Pusey has Entered a protesting letter against the Judgment –
  The King of Hanover is come over – he arrived on Friday Evening (2nd) the day of the Royal christening, His Majesty was Godfather to the infant Princess & was Expected to be present but it seems that the Court had not the Courtesy to wait for him & the Christening was hurried through without him – The Princess is Strangely named alice Maude Mary –

*7 June 1843.* […] The King of Hanover is[190] quite a lion now, all London is calling upon him –

---

[190]a crossed out but an illegible word precedes this in the original.

*8 June 1843.* […] another battle has been fought in Scinde with a great disparity of force by Sir Charles Napier – This will clear the Country & give it Entirely ours = Sir Charles is a very clever Officer & has managed his affairs admirably – Lord Ellenborough's views & his Execution of them appear to me to be what they Should be – He takes the Indus for the boundary of our Eastern Empire & means to improve & perfect all within it – The advantage of a free navigation of the Indus, will, in my opinion, be incalculable – No doubt, Lord Ellenborough will by canal or otherwise improve the navigation from the sea up the flat country & the river will then be Sufficiently Serviceable for Steam passage –

*9 June 1843.* The most active preparations continue to be made in Ireland – <u>why</u> at this very particular moment & all of a sudden all people Seem puzzled to conceive – In Ireland itself the proceedings are a good deal derided –

an affair between the police & the mob in which the former fired upon the Mob & Killed & wounded many is very awkward & there seemed to be no provocation for Such an Extreme act – The Soldiers too are behaving ill & fighting amongst themselves –

*10 June 1843.* a Canada mail Just arrived brings news of Sir Charles Bagot's death – poor man, the termination of his career has not added to his peace or reputation –

*11 June 1843.* The King of Hanover took the oaths & his Seat in the House of Lords on Friday last, as Duke of Cumberland, & I dare [say] he felt proud & pleased to find himself again Seated amongst British Senators –

The division & Contentious Spirit now prevalent Exceeds any thing that I have Ever witnessed – The Conduct of the Government most materially aids this –

*15 June 1843.* It is thought that the King of Hanover means to remain here, what his object is, whether private or political nobody Seems to Know = By the Court he has hitherto been treated very Cavalierly – He dines with the Queen today, the first civility – Prince albert & the Queen are going [on] So well that I Sincerely hope he will do nothing to shake or weaken the happy union & good intelligence between them – Their conduct in a conjugal point of view, is a fit & rare Example to the whole Country –

*16 June 1843.* O'Connell's Speeches at Kilkenny & Mallow [on 8 and 11 June] have been more audacious & more open than hitherto he has thought fit to Express himself – In my opinion nothing can be more Seditious, & rebellious than his language, & if it be not noticed unquestionably treason is licensed & law is a nullity –

*18 June 1843.* It is hardly credible how much Sir Robert Peel has lost in fame, favor & confidence – he never was a popular man, now people begin to perceive that he is not the man that the Country wants – & it So happens, that Every Scheme & Measure of his has not only signally failed, but has been positively injurious – His desertion of Protestantism as the basis of Church & State government, has called down a Curse upon his head by Which the Country Suffers –

*19 June 1843.* The high road to confusion Seems to be crowded & crowding & yet the Government sits still – but the consequence will be, & indeed is – that people will not tamely submit to be sacrificed, & will take the law into their own hands if the government Supinely withholds its assertion of it =

*21 June 1843.* […] I Saw the King of Hanover this Evening at Sir Robert Peel's – He is looking Even older & more infirm than I was taught to Expect – He was very hearty & Kind & asked me to Come & See him =

*22 June 1843.* […] In Wales, the people calling themselves Rebeccaites have mustered in large numbers, &, as in Ireland, have made a demonstration of physical force in Carmarthen – they proceeded to destroy the Union workhouse & Were So Engaged when the military came up – they made little or no resistance – a great many were Secured & the Workhouse Saved from destruction – however Subsequently they went in force & destroyed & burnt the turnpike gate – & then dispersed – it is not Known what has become of them – they [are] Supposed to be Keeping together as they have not returned to their homes –

*25 June 1843.* Very great uneasiness is felt at the State of the Country generally – of Course as regard Ireland particularly, but it seems more to be Suspected that the people in the North of England are too particularly Connected with the rebels in Ireland – this confirms my View – & that before the termination of the year, we Shall witness fearful doings – In Ireland the farmers are refusing to pay rent – on the principle of what they call "fixity of tenure" – I think it Will be much the Same in Wales – & possibly not unfrequently in Some parts of England –

*27 June 1843.* The offer of prizes for the best Cartoons has produced 140 – drawings – I went today to see the Exhibition of them in Westminster hall – I was surprised to See Such productions which are certainly honorable to British art – Especially when it is considered that none but unknown & young artists Ever offer themselves as Competitors on Such occasions – The drawing is generally good & correct & the design & composition far beyond what Could have been Expected –

*28 June 1843.* all has been motion this afternoon as the Princess augusta of Cambridge was this Evening married to the Duke of Mecklenberg [in] the City at 8 o'clock. Some 500 people were invited, we not among the number – I saw the Princess in the morning driving through Berkley Square & looking as unconcerned as if nothing were going to happen –

*29 June 1843.* The Queen held her first Drawing room today – I understand that it was Very full –

  The insurrection or rebellion or riot in Wales – by Whatever name it may be called is gaining ground formidably – Since the affair at Carmarthen – they have mustered in force in the neighbourhood of Newcastle Emlyn – & took possession of the town [,] burnt down the Workhouse [,] destroyed the gates &c – The Dragoons were sent against them – the rebels met them on the bridge & overthrew them – unhorsed them [,] took their arms from them & threw the men into the river – one man was drowned – the others So Seriously injured that none are fit for Service. This is a most Serious affair – it bears a worse character than any that I have Ever Known –

*30 June 1843*. The account of the Skirmish on the bridge turns out to be a hoax = it appeared in the Standard but is contradicted today –

*6 July 1843*. It turns out that the account of the overthrow of the Dragoons on Newcastle Emlyn bridge, was utterly false & merely a hoaxing fabrication –

*9 July 1843*. The Revenue shews a deficiency, which would be Very great but for the income tax, which Exceeds the Estimate – It is to be hoped that from henceforth the receipts which have been So cruelly crippled will gradually encrease & with it the Revenue in spite of the blind quackery of the Tariff – for trade is beginning to revive, & appears to be Effecting this in a manner at once prudent & Effectual – The only sure way of proceeding to obtain a Steady & wholesome state of trade is not to over produce –

*10 July 1843*. […] In Ireland rebellion is ripening fast, thanks to the liberal & infatuated permission of our Government – it is thought, that many weeks cannot Elapse Without an outbreak –

*12 July 1843*. The Ministry is losing ground Every day by its Vacillation, & fearful concessions to the Enemies of the State & of all order = The conduct of the Minister is inconceivable = He Seems determined to destroy all confidence in himself,[191] to apply no remedy to Crying & pressing Evils & dangers, & to cut away from under us all which can tend to be a Support of the Super structure – We must go to pieces if Something reparatory be not resorted to quickly & resolutely –

*13 July 1843*. The interminable debates continue in the House of Commons night after night on the Same Subjects to the Exclusion of all necessary business – If the Government has finished its business why not prorogue the Parliament, if not why not advance the business quickly & then close the doors [?] – but why the Government Should Suffer idle talking to obstruct all public business & trifle with their constituents & make themselves worse than ridiculous is what I cannot understand, neither can I guess at the possible advantage of Such a System –

*15 July 1843*. at last a division has taken place in the House of Commons on Mr [William] O'Brien's motion [on the Arms (Ireland) Bill] – Sir Robert Peel proves himself More & more unequal to the task which he has in hand – The Secret is that he has done that which is right, & he dares not to act with the Spirit & Energy Which befit the present times – Every day makes a hole in his reputation, & diminishes the confidence which alone can Enable him to carry on the government =

*17 July 1843*. [At Hafod] Several turnpike gates in this County / Cardigan / have been attacked & destroyed at Lampeter, at Tregannon about 10 miles from here & in other places

---

[191] These last four words appear in the original as 'in himself all confidence' and above them the numbers '3 4 1 2' indicating the order in which they should be read.

– notice has been given by the Rebecca people that they will immediately destroy the gates near aberystwyth –

*18 July 1843.* a large meeting has been holden at Paris, of literateurs [,] Editors of newspapers, Deputes &c, where it was determined to open a Subscription in favor of O'Connell & Ireland = & that when a large Sum of money was raised Monsieur Dupere Rollin [Ledru-Rollin] was to go to Dublin & pay over the amount to O'Connell – The Meeting appears to have been in Earnest & it resolved to give Every Sort of assistance [,] men & arms if required, to Enable O'Connell to triumph over his Oppressors = This certainly is a very awkward feature = a very large Sum will no doubt be raised from France, Italy & Roman Catholic States – which will swell the rebel resources to a large amount = Sir Robert Peel will now begin to perceive that his policy is positively criminal & that nothing can Excuse Such an Experiment being tried upon National affairs –

*19 July 1843.* No change in public affairs – rebellion proceeds undisturbedly, & Sir Robert Peel declares in the House of Commons that he can advance none of the public measures because of the obstruction which he meets with from the opposition who will make long Speeches, & adjourn the house from night to night – What a miserable confession / Why does he not prevent it – & why has he permitted rebellion to attain Such a height & Strength [?] – but now that all the world admits that O'Connels' acts & words are traiterous – Why does he not immediately Strike at The Traitor? I am lost in wonder at the influence which can be guiding Such a man as Sir Robert Peel –

*21 July 1843.* […] Lincoln writes that he has been to Bristol with Prince albert to see the launch of the immense Steam Ship named Great Britain – he Says that it is 100 ft longer that [*sic* – than] the largest Man of war in the Service, that it was a beautiful Sight, the Prince Enthusiastically received, & perhaps 200,000 people present[192] –

*23 July 1843.* Peel is proposing to close the Session, & has given notice that he means to abandon most of the bills which he brought in at the beginning of the Session = I do not regret the abandonment of any bill that he has introduced – all have been most objectionable, Some positively bad = He has given almost universal dissatisfaction – & I cannot think that he will long remain Minister = Those who relied upon him most, if they will own it, have been disappointed, he has proved himself to be thoroughly unequal to his task – He has not a great mind, & is neither calculated to lead a party or to be the guiding Minister of this great Country –

*26 July 1843.* Ministers are giving way to please their opponents [,] spoiling still more their poor measures, & Complimenting in a Servile & miserable manner those against whom, for what they have done & will do, they ought to wage a sturdy warfare – It will not do, the policy neither can or Should answer, & must terminate in disgrace – In the mean time rebellion is ripening rapidly all over the Queen's dominions, & the consequences, will too soon sadly force themselves upon our notice –

---

[192]N.U.M.D., Ne C 5579: Lincoln to Newcastle, 20 July 1843.

Here in Wales, the Rebeccaites are pursuing their course untill Just now without interruption = Within these few days, private information has been received & Several men taken after a resolute & bloody resistance – It is Said that their Leader, Rebecca, is Known – & that he proves to be a Cauas Wilson, a London attorney, of great notoriety – 7 feet high in Stature –

*28 July 1843*. a Vacancy for Durham was occasioned by Lord Dungannon [Arthur Hill-Trevor] being unseated on petition – it Seems that Mr Powis [Thomas Purvis] Was brought forward on the Conservative interest, but Would not consent to be Lord Londonderrys nominee – Lord Londonderry then went against him & gave his Support to Mr [John] Bright, Quaker & anti Corn law leaguer – & he is come in ! Truly, this good Lord Londonderry is most unintelligible[193] –

*31 July 1843*. In his speech in reply to Lord John Russell, Sir Robert Peel States from a document which he held in his hand, that the trade With america, that is the Exports from England [,] have fallen off for many successive years Since 1836 – in that year the Exports amounted to [£] 12,500,000, & in 1842/3 they were only [£] 3,500,000 – On this occasion when he had to defend his conduct of the Session, he made but a Sorry reply – his defence was mostly apologetical, by no means happy in manner or matter, to me apparently the worst Speech I have Known from him, poor in Spirit, & Evidently proceeding from a crest fallen man –

*1 August 1843*. The Duke of Wellington Valiantly opposed himself to the prayer of a petition from Lord Oranmore, presented & urged by Lord Fortescue [,] that the Irish priests Should be payed out of the Revenues of the Church = For so much we thank him – it is good –

*2 August 1843*. The Duke of Dorset [Charles Sackville-Germain] is dead, & a Garter vacant – The title is now Extinct – & it is remarkable, that only two relations are left of this family – a Sister of the late Duke & his niece [Caroline] the daughter of his late Brother [George] married to Mr Stafford [William Stopford] –

*4 August 1843*. Mr [Henry] Wards motion for the overthrow of the Irish Church has been abandoned –

*6 August 1843*. affairs in & out of Parliament remain much as they Were [,] an Encreasing dissatisfaction & uneasiness, & I must own not without a cause, for it must be acknowledged that Peel has disappointed all but the disaffected who are delighted to profit by the aid which he affords them.

*13 August 1843*. The Queen has been unexpectedly civil to [my sons] Charles & Thomas, they were asked to dine at [Windsor] Castle & in the Evening there was dancing – Her

[193]John Bright beat Thomas Purvis (Conservative) by 488–410 votes: majority 78.

Majesty danced with Thomas, & they tell me that She was very pleasant & made the Evening very agreeable[194] –

*15 August 1843.* […] as the vextous [*sic*] proceedings of the Rebeccaites continue, a party of Dragoons, probably a troop, is to be Stationed at aberayvon [Aberavon] in the County – I am informed that they have never before had any military in this County –

*18 August 1843.* The arms bill has passed at last – & the Government brings in another bill, for incorporating the pensioners, if necessary, clothing them in a plain dress, paying them Extra & putting them under the Mutiny act –

*23 August 1843.* By a report which has been given in, So Say the Papers, there are 10698 parishes in England & Wales, & it is believed upwards of 12000 Churches –

*25 August 1843.* Parliament was prorogued by the Queen in person yesterday [.] The Speech contained very little – alluded to Some bills passed during this miserable Session = then to the disturbances in Wales & lastly to those in Ireland, Expressing a determination to maintain inviolate the Union &c –

*28 August 1843.* [At Dolgellau, I saw] my old acquaintance Lord auckland Who I had not Seen for years – He came to ask us to go into his room whilst our's was preparing, telling my Daughters that they would find his two Sisters [Emily & Fanny] there – We went & Sat with them for about half an hour & then went to our own room, where we were very glad to have Some dinner = Neither Lord auckland or his Sisters are much altered by their residence in India –

*5 September 1843.* […] The Queen has landed at Trefort [Treport] in France & has been received with Every attention by the King of France –

*6 September 1843.* I Saw a letter from Ireland today which speaks of the <u>coming crisis</u> as of a thing inevitable – & that the Queen's Speech has displeased the rebels very much, & that there is no relaxation in the Spirit by which they have bound themselves to O'Connel & to repeal –

*12 September 1843.* The Queen has returned to Brighton from her French Expedition & in a few days She is to repeat the Same by going to Ostend,[195] to See [Leopold I] the King of [the] Belgians –

*13 September 1843.* […] There are Various opinions as to the value, of the crops – Some Say that the Ears are deficient, others that it will not Yield well, but many think as I do that it will be above an average crop – No one can adequately Estimate the great & infinite

---

[194] N.U.M.D., Ne C 5590: Lord Charles Pelham-Clinton to Newcastle, 8 Aug. 1843.
[195] antwerp precedes this in the original.

benefit to the Country which a good & plentiful harvest will confer = & we cannot be too thankful for Such an inestimable blessing –

*14 September 1843.* another of the Oxford men [William Lockhart] has become a convert to Popery! it is miraculous how this heresy, as we must call it, in our Church is gaining ground – it is Said that a very great many others have done likewise but that the facts have been Smothered, by the recommendation of the <u>Record</u> – who asserts that if nothing is said & no noise Made about it, the accession to the popish ranks will be very great indeed – There cannot be a stronger sign of the near fulfilment of Prophecy –

*15 September 1843.* The Queen has landed at Ostend & taken up her residence in a house provided for her there –

*17 September 1843.* […] The accounts from Spain represent the Country to be in a State of chaos – It is utterly impossible to make out the Various parties now contending for mastery – Here in this country, if more care be not taken [,] We Shall Soon be in a State not very unlike that of Spain – The Scum in the fermentation is getting uppermost, & at present they are doing this almost with impunity –

*22 September 1843.* The Queen is returned to England from Belgium & is gone to Windsor –

    all accounts from manufacturing districts represent them as in an improving State – The press Sedulously advises caution not to overproduce – if the Manufacturers Will adhere to this, all will be well, & they may have a regular, steady & fairly remunerative trade – but if Encouragement creates greediness, & a wild Endeavour to make hay whilst the Sun Shines, thinking only of the present & not of the future day, worse distress than Ever will Ensue & a dreadful period will Ensue –

*26 September 1843.* […] almost the only newspaper that supports Sir Robert Peel is the Standard & perhaps the Morning Herald may generally be added – The conservative press is otherwise unfavorable to the Peel policy & measures – but a new auxiliary has arisen in the Morning Chronicle, which is rather ominous & forebodes no good – Certainly its support will not Strengthen the Premier –

*30 September 1843.* The patience & Endurance of the most degraded people may be strained too far, & Such has been the case in Greece – There misrule was personified, & [if] Ever a people were Justified in resisting lawful authority it was there where Otho the Bavarian was seated on a throne, for which by habits, by prejudices & by nature, he was & is utterly unfit – He was placed there by European agreement when Extremely young, of a bad stock, & incapable of improvement – if he was bad at first [,] he has become Worse Since, & has proved that nature forbad him to assimilate, in any one thing or feeling, with the Greeks – The result is a revolution which has been perfectly Effected in a few hours – The Bavarians are Expelled & the natives have forced a Constitution upon their puppet King Otho which he has not dared to refuse –

*2 October 1843*. The Greek revolution has been Effected in a manner the most creditable to themselves – with temper, firmness, good sense, & humanity – The leaders of the movement never attempted to terrify by cruelty & violence, & when the King consented to what was required [,] the army retired to their homes, & the populace also, with the utmost order, good temper & moderation [.]

*3 October 1843*. Sir Robert Peel's Speech at the Lichfield agricultural Meeting has been the Subject of much remark – Sir Robert is not a very Knowing agriculturist, & is not practically acquainted with the cultivation of the Soil, with stock, &c &c What he Knows he has gained as a lawyer, by his brief – & yet he unwisely Sat up for a Speaker at the dinner & made as I think a very foolish Speech & Evidently Spoke of things that he did not understand. The Speech was Shallow, Speculative, falsely theoretical & gave no information, for he had none to give – Ne Sutor ultra recpidam[196] would have been wisely observed by him – He advised farmers to travel, Said he would give leases to his tenants, if they asked for them, but he was Sure that they would not ask – favored the allotment System, (in this he was right) & Expressed his opinion that a flourishing state of agriculture was beneficial to the Strength & glory of England – of this there can be no doubt – it may be called a truism!

*5 October 1843*. […] Disturbances have arisen in Scotland by the non interventionists, Especially in Rossshire where the people have behaved with much roughness & an approach to brutality[197] – & as I think Symptomatic of a popular outbreak before long – The Peel Government will teach the whole Empire to rebel –

*7 October 1843*. a few days ago there was the largest Sale of cotton in one day Ever Known at Liverpool – this of course denotes demand & a stir in our manufactories – indeed the fact of revival of trade is announced from all quarters, whether it will continue is another question – if pursued with moderation I have no doubt that a very fair trade will be maintained – but this is So uncertain that[198] it can hardly be reckoned upon – for where money is to be had there is sure to be too many competitors for it –

The landed interest is now in a fair State – want of confidence is the Worst Enemy, but prices are tolerable & are remunerating – wheat about 56s a quarter & Stock fetching a fair price – But, there are many boils & blanes – In Ireland, Wales, & Scotland [,] proceedings of a most dangerous Character, defy the Government & threaten the future peace & Security of the country – for this we have to thank Sir Robert Peel & Co. – but mainly I really believe Sir James Graham & Lord Stanley – The proceedings in these three parts of the Empire have attained an alarming height, & are still Encreasing in power & prevalence.

*8 October 1843*. The Steamer which was to have brought the now due Indian Mail has left alexandria without it & brings over the crewe & passengers of the Mammon & also

---

[196] 'Sutor, ne ultra crepidam' – 'Shoemaker not beyond the shoe', a phrase used to warn against speaking beyond your expertise, first recorded by Pliny the Elder (c. 23–79 AD).

[197] The Resolis Riot took place on 1 Oct. 1843.

[198] that precedes this in the original.

Colonel [George] Malcolm who is returned with the Treaty with China ratified[199] – So that this great point is happily Effected, & a very great atchievement [*sic*] it is, one of infinite importance in Every point of view, religious, moral & political – Now that this treaty is Effected, it is to be hoped that a considerably Encreased business in trade will be the consequence –

*10 October 1843.* at last the Government is beginning to awake: a Proclamation has been suddenly made at Dublin = The Grand meeting which was to eclipse all others was to take place in Dublin on last Sunday (8th) [.] The Lord Lieutenant [de Grey] & Chancellor [Sugden] Were in England, but they were Suddenly hurried off to Dublin: the Privy Council met & on the afternoon of Saturday [7th] the Proclamation was issued warning people not to Meet on the next day [at Clontarf] & calling upon all persons to assist in Suppressing & dispersing Such meeting if it should take place – rather Short notice & rather Sudden determination – but the conduct of Government has been & is unaccountable – The Proclamation is a good & proper one but it ought to have been issued six or Eight months ago when Sedition had not become a habit & a System – O'Connell immediately called a meeting & issued a counter proclamation Signed by himself – Stopping the meeting & making Some reflections on the conduct of Ministers – He Sent Expresses Every Where to keep the people at home & prevent their appearance in Dublin on the following day – The Government is now fairly committed & it must act – better late than never but late indeed it is – no doubt this decision has been accelerated by the accumulating disorders in the Country – in Wales, in Scotland & now in England – for Encouraged by what has been tolerated Elsewhere, the Chartists & the anti Corn Law League, is again agitating most formidably – It is Said that the organisation of the League, is the most Complete & formidable that was Ever designed & Executed – So that the Government may well wish to cope with the different bands Separately & not when in Conjunction too formidable for Even a Strong government to contend with –

*11 October 1843.* By the accounts from Ireland – it appears, that not–withstanding all O'Connel's diligence, a vast number of people came on Sunday 8th from all parts & in complete ignorance of any hindrance to the meeting = a great array of Troops & artillery was paraded, & Every outward Shew of precaution taken – but nothing whatever occurred [–] both people & Soldiers, were peaceable, quiet & orderly – & the people returned quietly to their houses as obediently as well Educated Children – This may appear well – & it is good that these men are under Such control that they forbear from riot & drunkenness in which they heretofore So freely indulged – but in reality it displays a discipline & a moral hold over them which is truly formidable – The drama is begun how will it End [?] – The Government must proceed [–] if it halts now, it is lost –

*12 October 1843.* One now looks to Irish news, from the peculiar picture of affairs there, with Extreme curiosity & interest – The meeting, first, of the Repealers, took place on Monday, & there followed the dinner at which O'Connell made long speeches – Though he launched out into violent invective against individuals & ridiculed & condemned the

---

[199] The Treaty of Nanking (Nanjing) was ratified on 29 Aug. 1842.

Proclamation, & told his hearers that they must & Should yet have repeal, yet he contrived with consummate address to observe the utmost prudence – He announced that he meant in the course of a few days to have meetings in Every parish of the Island to petition the Queen to dismiss the Ministers –

*13 October 1843.* Owing to the bad & boisterous weather there is no news from Ireland – It is rather comical to observe the tone of the ministerial toadies who lauded to the Skies the "do nothing" System of Ministers, & repeated almost daily their refutations of others' charges, by apostrophising on the deluge of blood which would have resulted from doing at first, what has been done now – But this is the age of lying, Selfishness & inconsistency –

*16 October 1843.* O'Connel & Some of his associates have been arrested – there has been nothing new but the Government thinks that there is a Sufficient case against him to warrant Such a proceeding – this has been my opinion for the last 6 or 8 months – no post today. I learn this from a private Source – & Know no more.

*17 October 1843.* […] O'Connell has been arrested most courteously, & in a merely pro forma manner [,] as he & the others are admitted to bail – & to take their trial at the next term – John O'Connell his son, [Thomas] Steele, Dr [John] Gray & Some others of not inferior note, are his companions in bail & for trial[200] –

*18 October 1843.* all apparently quiet & Submissive in Ireland – In my opinion this is the most formidable Symptom of disease. The Submission is Systematic & no doubt the result of policy – but, if I am not greatly mistaken [,] there is a wide confederacy & a deep plot – & a sympathy combining under one System & Subjecting to one rule, a League over the Whole of the Empire = In Separate parts there are Separate grievances complained of which are made to appear the ostensible causes for agitation, but which in fact are purely political & treasonable = Thus in Ireland, "the Repeal of the Union" [,] in Wales, "tolls, tithes, rates, poor Law, rents &ca" – in Scotland, "The Church question – non intrusion, & Secession" – & in England the most organised of all, "The anti corn law League, & Chartism" [.] I Entertain no doubt whatever that the whole is Set going & fomented & devised by Jesuits, & that many months Will not Elapse before we witness Such a Combined Explosion of the whole, as will Shake the whole frame of Government –

*19 October 1843.* Troops are Still going over to Ireland – Should any thing happen in England, there will be little but the yeomanry to act with – O'Connell continues to play the yielding game, which he will do to gain time to throw his opponents off their guard, but when it Suits his purpose & he sees the proper time he will resume his bluster & bullying & perhaps something more –

*20 October 1843.* […] the Scotch are returning rapidly to their former State of religious disorganisation = The Village Church is deserted by all but the minister & his family –

---

[200]Those arrested on 14 Oct. 1843 were Daniel O'Connell, John O'Connell, Thomas Steele, Charles Gavan Duffy, Peter James Tyrrell, and John Gray.

Whilst the Seceders gather in multitudes on the hills to hear the Free Churchmen preach – at the present moment this must lead to mischief of a Serious Kind –

*21 October 1843.* The accounts from Ireland & in England are not to my mind Satisfactory – as I Expected, the Chartists & Leaguers, are Stirring – [Joseph] Sturge of Manchester, is gone over to Ireland to concert measures with O'Connell – & I have little doubt that they will Endeavour to Effect a diversion in favour of the Repealers – already some very Strong language has been used & I fully Expect that in a very short time they will be in full activity & movement –

*22 October 1843.* In the contest for the City representation – Mr [James] Pattison anti corn law Leaguer has beaten Mr [Thomas] Baring the ministerial candidate – it is a great triumph for the Leaguers[201] –

another clergyman at Oxford, & a confidential assistant to Dr Pusey the Hebrew professor, [Charles Seager] has Embraced Popery – numbers that one Knows of have done the Same. It is a fearful failing in the present day –

O'Connell intends to prosecute Mr Hughes the Government informant for perjury — He will infallibly out wit his opponents, who Evidently are afraid of him & what they are now doing = though it is right –

*24 October 1843.* a Mail from India is at last arrived – little news, all was apparently quiet – In Scinde Sir Charles Napier retained the country in Subjection = Lord Ellenborough had Established himself at Bunackpore [Barrackpore] – Two armies of observation under Sir Hugh Gough & Sir [William] Nott were formed = Old Dost Mahommed [Dost Mohammad Khan] was ruling Caboul with his usual Energy – but Candahar was much disturbed – Upon the whole we may be well Satisfied with the present State of our Eastern affairs –

*25 October 1843.* In Ireland those who are opposed to O'Connell & his proceedings are beginning to Speak out fiercely – Why did they not do this before? Why have they only taken Courage when O'Connell is in bonds? Although it may be against the greatest wretch that Ever lived, I cannot bear to See him attacked when he is down & only When he is down = O'Connell merits to be hanged, but it is cowardly to set at him when his hands are tied –

*27 October 1843.* Sir Robert Peels' Speech in the Chair of the agricultural dinner at Tamworth, is the topic of discussion – I do not like it – much is foolish, Some injurious & very little practically good – whilst I think that it discloses Some very bad future designs – I shall Keep the speech by me, & watch him closely[202] –

*28 October 1843.* There is a report in Ireland, currently believed [,] that the Government means to abandon the Prosecutions !!! Such a thing is incredible –

---

[201] Pattison polled 6,532 against the Conservative Thomas Baring on 6,367: majority 165.

[202] The speech, on 24 Oct., was published in *The British Farmer's Magazine*, new ser., vii (1843), 479–94.

*29 October 1843.* The victory of the "Leaguers" in London by the Election of Patteson [*sic*] has very much Elated them & depressed well disposed people = a vacancy for Salisbury has Just occurred & the Leaguers have announced that they will fill it up with a man of their own, in the place of the late Conservative Member Mr Wadham Windham [Wyndham] – at Kendal they mean to do the Same[203] –

*31 October 1843.* The Queen has returned from her visit to Cambridge –
The Special Commission in Wales is proceeding With the trials – one man [John Hughes] has been convicted –
O'Connell persists in holding his arbitration Courts, & has opened them in due form – & has had large Repeal meetings in the new Hall, called "Conciliation Hall" =

*1 November 1843.* The Special Commission in Wales is closed – & the prisoners were all convicted though Some were very Slightly punished – [John] Hughes, the Rebecca [,] was Sentenced to transportation for life, but commuted afterwards for 20 years – others are transported for 7 years – all went off quietly but what Effect punishment will have upon the Welsh remains to be Seen –

*2 November 1843.* By a new plan O'Connell now carries on his debates in "Conciliation Hall" with closed doors – persons are now refused admittance on paying at the door as formerly – what he means by this it is difficult to understand –

*6 November 1843.* […] Judge [Charles] Burton's charge to the Jury in the Court of Queen's Bench Dublin has Just appeared = In my opinion it is a lame affair, & conveys to my mind the notion, that it is intended to allow O'Connell & Co. to Escape =

*7 November 1843.* Every [thing] Seems preparing both at home & abroad for that State of disunion & contest which is predicted in "the latter days"[204] [–] that time may be at hand & its Sure harbinger is Even now present & proceeding –
The Grand Jury in Dublin have not yet returned the Bill – no Easy matter indeed considering that it is 39 yards long of close printing = Surely there must necessarily be flaws in an indictment of Such Extraordinary length –

*9 November 1843.* Still the Dublin grand Jury is in deliberation – & it is not Known whether it will return a true Bill or not – The attorney General [Thomas Cusack] Smith, has Shewn his cleverness & determination & promises to be a match for those with whom he has to deal – The Judges appear to be twaddlers.

*10 November 1843.* The Grand Jury have at last found a true Bill against O'Connell & others – & the attorney General has given notice that he means to file another bill of

[203] For Salisbury, see 25 Nov. 1843. At Kendal, the radical Henry Warburton triumphed over the Conservative George William Pierrepont Bentinck by 182–119: majority 63.
[204] The return of Israel according to prophecy: 'Afterward shall the children of Israel return, and seek the Lord their God, and David their king; and shall fear the Lord and his goodness in the latter days', Hosea, 3: 5.

Indictment against 4 of the Same gang on other Counts = So that he appears to be in good Earnest –

*12 November 1843*. The new bills announced by the attorney General are against O'Connell & 3 others for attending illegal meetings – this is to try the legality or illegality of the Repeal association – Surely a very clumsy mode of proceeding – Why not consult the Crown lawyers & abide by their decisions [?] – if they declare the meetings to be illegal, the Government Should Stop them & allow no one to attend –

*14 November 1843*. Luton [Hoo], Lord Bute's, has been in great part consumed by fire – most of the fine things there have been Saved, the books, MSS, &c from the Splendid library, also the pictures [,] plate, furniture [,] ornaments &c &c – Some of the pictures were, among them two by Sir Joshua Reynolds – the Effects Saved were through the admirable presence of mind & intrepidity of the House Keeper [Mrs Partridge] –

720 of the inhabitants of Reading have memorialised the Commissioners of the Treasury to use Conciliatory means & not to Employ the military for the Suppression of the disaffection & outrages in Ireland & Wales – Of course the memorial will be listened to –

*17 November 1843*. an attempt has been made by O'Connell's Counsell [James Whiteside] to quash the indictment, by a plea of the witnesses not having properly Sworn – whatever other result may attend this plea, it causes delay & very great delay = The attorney General has strenuously opposed the plea on good grounds, as I think, & being overruled, he put in a demener [demeanour], which was also overruled, by the Bench – He is in an awkward Situation –

*18 November 1843*. O'Connell has outmanoeuvred his prosecutors – by trick & cajolery he has succeeded – the stupidity & Something Else of the Judges has given him the Superiority over the attorney General – his plea has been accepted & the attorney Generals demener to it refused & now the hearing will probably not come on before February – people in general lament this [–] I think it fortunate, for it openly declared that the legality or illegality of agitation for repeal is to depend upon the issue of the trial – consequently if acquitted & I am confident that no Jury will dare to convict, the agitation of repeal, with all its concomitant Enormities, will be legalised, & then there Would be indeed "the devil to pay"[205] = The trial I consider at an End, & I deem it best that it Should be So – if I had to act, I should take the opinion of the law Officers, without doubt they would decidedly pronounce the manner in which O'Connell agitates for Repeal illegal & treasonable – in that case, I would permit no meetings or assemblages whatever, if attempted I Would disperse them, & capture & try the ringleaders, but these I would clap into prison, & not allow them to go at large, of course they Should be tried, if convicted all would be well, but if acquitted upon one charge, I would then arraign them on another & So tire out or crush these abominable & most mischievous Villains –

*19 November 1843*. a good deal of alarm & distrust is arising from the Encreased & Encreasing power of the anti Corn Law league & the recent Sayings & hints of Sir Robert Peel

---

[205] Attributed to Thomas Brown, *Letters from the Dead to the Living* (1707).

– my opinion is that this alarm is by no means destitute of foundation & that Sir Robert meditates as regards Land & the Church Some measures which will Startle people when they [are] laid before them – Sir Robert was not quiescent in the last Session for nothing = He was quiet then to strike hereafter – & the blow will be against the Church & State, although with Every profession of loving & upholding Each of them –

*21 November 1843.* The Duc & Duchesse de Nemours are now over here Visiting the Queen – about a fortnight or three weeks ago, the Duc de Bordeaux came to England & first went to Scotland where he visited about & has latterly been Staying for some time at alton Towers, Lord Shrewsbury's, where a number of people & Roman Catholics have been collected to meet him = a house has now been Engaged for him in London for three months certain – The appearance in England at the same time of these two personages gives rise to many Enquiries & much conversation – but far more in France where the newspapers are filled with conjecture & political discussions – The Duc de Bordeaux is not acknowledged here & is treated as a private gentleman & not invited to the Court – a Strange distinction, when Such a man as [Baldomero] Espartero has been received not only by the Queen but by the public authorities with almost royal honors & respect –

*22 November 1843.* The Queen is preparing to jaunt again & proposes on the 28th to go to Drayton, Sir Robert Peel's, the Queen Dowager will also be there – Her Majesty remains there two days & then goes to Chatsworth, & from thence to Belvoir Castle – She then returns to Windsor, I believe –

*24 November 1843.* No very particular news = The League is making Every Exertion to carry the Election at Salisbury & will probably succeed –

*25 November 1843.* The Salisbury Election is over – The Leaguers are beaten after a very Severe contest & Mr [John] Campbell is Elected[206] =

*26 November 1843.* The proceedings against O'Connell are Virtually Stayed: his trial is postponed to the 15th January next – which is as much as to postpone it ad Grecas Calendas[207] – This is a most disgraceful issue to the Government but under the circumstances I am Sure that it is the best thing that can happen –

*27 November 1843.* The Queen commences her visitations today – She goes first to Drayton Manor & remains there for two days = It is a bad time of the year for Such Excursions, places do not look at their best & if the weather Should prove unpropitious [,] people will be puzzled to Know what to do with Her Majesty & her appendages –

*28 November 1843.* There appears to be nothing of moment any where, Events in plenty but little more than a continuance of what has been, in Ireland there is no change, in the

[206] The Conservative Campbell triumphed over the Whig Edward Pleydell-Bouverie by 317–270 votes: majority 47.

[207] The phrase 'ad Grecas Calendas' was attributed to Caesar Augustus. The calends were specific days of the Roman calendar, not the Greek, so the 'Greek Calends' would never occur.

Country generally I do not think there is reason to hope that Either tranquility or prosperity are before us –

*5 December 1843*. News from India, the principal is that the horrid Murders of those in & about the throne of whoever rules in the Punjaub, are continued – Such revolting doings must be Stopped by us, & no doubt Lord Ellenborough will interfere – From China & the rest of India there is little of interest = In Cabool all is confusion & anarchy – ackbar Khan [Wazir Akbar Khan] is now opposed to his father [Dost Mohammad Khan] – & the affghans are Stirring to get possession of Peshawar –

*8 December 1843*. The Queen returned to Windsor yesterday, no doubt infinitely pleased as she has reason to be with her Visits [.] The weather has been beautifully fair & fine – & She has been Entertained in a manner Equalling any thing that Windsor Castle itself has Ever produced – The reception & Entertainments at Chatsworth & Belvoir must have been Splendid & magnificent – at Chatsworth the Scenes must have been Some of Enchantment – & Superb almost beyond description –

The Standard announces, as if from authority [,] that Sir Robert Peel, will certainly resist any alteration in the present Corn laws, during the next Session. This is good hearing – & I must own quite contrary to my formed opinion of what he will do –

*9 December 1843*. In his Speech at Kilkenny, at the dinner given to Mr O'brien, O'Connell States that the Government had Endeavoured to compromise the matter with him, to buy him up – but he declared that he was above corruption in the great cause of Repeal, that nothing, no bribe, no threat, could induce him to desert the cause of his Country, & that he had rather rot in a dungeon, than be a traitor to the great cause in which he was Engaged = If this be true, it is indeed a Strange piece of underhand work, & only redounds to the credit of O'Connell –

*10 December 1843*. Lord Spencer (the farmer's friend) has declared himself in a speech at Northampton against the Corn laws, for repeal & a free trade !!! Mr [Pierce] Butler an Irish repealer & a dismissed magistrate, has been elected M.P. for Kilkenny County [unopposed] Mr Timothy O'Brien, a Repealer [,] was proposed by O'Connell, as Mayor of Dublin & has been Elected – a bad list this –

*11 December 1843*.[208] The last of the Windsors is dead. The Earldom of Plymouth is Extinct[209] –

*14 December 1843*. Incendiary fires are commencing again in some parts of the country chiefly in the Southern counties – it causes a good deal of uneasiness, & the people are thought by Some to be in a State ripe for mischief =

---

[208]For a false report of Newcastle's impending marriage, spread by Baron Philipp von Neumann, see N.U.M.D., Pw H 176/1: Lord George Bentinck to Portland, 11 Dec. 1843.

[209]On the death of Henry Windsor, 8th earl of Plymouth.

*15 December 1843.* Parliament is prorogued to the 1st of February, then to meet for the despatch of business – This meeting a fortnight Earlier than usual, is, I presume, to accomodate [*sic*] our little Queen, who will wish, as Early as possible, in the next year to commence her Excursions by Sea and land, visiting Prussia, &c &c & we Know not what other Countries = This is the mania now –

*16 December 1843.* The 13th regiment of foot vacant by the death of General [Edward] Morrison has been given to Sir Robert Sale, who commanded the regiment in India & So gloriously defended himself at Jellalabad – He is a brevet Colonel only of 1838 – & low down on the list – So that not only is this a high compliment, but also an unprecedented preferment in these days – Promotion in rank would have been a better reward, I think –

*21 December 1843.* Lord Lynedock [Lynedoch] is dead after a short illness – He was of a great age & remarkable for being the oldest man Existing in his class of life – He was in his 94th year – He was a General in the army & a distinguished Officer, & possessed his faculties to the last – His Energy & physical powers were very great, & untill quite lately he rode & walked about & Even went out Shooting this Season, so much less did age affect him than most other people, by very many years younger –

*22 December 1843.* Mr [John Henry] Newman, confederate with Dr Pusey, has openly declared in favor of Communion with Rome, of celibacy, of monachism, & one may say of nearly if not all, the Errors of Popery = These things all add to the Signs of the times, & look like what is to appear in the latter days –

*26 December 1843.* There is no news in the papers, & nothing at home = The incendiary fires continue – The labouring & manufacturing people are shewing signs of discontent & uneasiness, which before long may assume a more Serious aspect –

*28 December 1843.* Incendiarism is Encreasing very much, the distress is great amongst the laboring poor in the Southern Counties, but the real reason of these fires in my opinion is political, it was so many years ago [during the Swing Riots of 1830] – a device as I then thought to work out the then Ministry[210] – Lord Grey came in & the fires Soon ceased – The Same game is being played now, & if they can turn out the present men & get in others, the fires will again cease – I Should pay no other attention to them, than Endeavour to get hold of the Culprits, & these I would punish in the Severest Manner that the law permits –

*31 December 1843.* The language used by the Leaguers openly at their meetings is most atrocious, & how it is permitted, is to me, like most acts of the present Government, truly a wonder – They Speak of Shooting Sir Robert Peel, or aversion to a Royal family, with as much tranquillity as they Would talk of abolishing the Corn Laws – a Government must not Expect to be Supported or respected which permits Such atrocities & Such usurped power – – and now we have arrived at the end of a most Eventful Year = a year marked,

[210]See *Unrepentant Tory*, 126–7.

politically, very peculiarly by a new System as applied to Governors & governed – The former permitting the latter to carry their Schemes to the most Extreme lengths – witness, the Repeal agitations in Ireland, the Systematic riots & outrages in Wales, & worst of all the anti corn law League in England = a fatal opposition to good government has taken root, & we Shall Soon reap its fruits & dire Effects – Nothing can be less cheering than our prospects at home – disaster & confusion appear to be on the ascendant – & one hears & Knows of nothing which is likely to lead to an amendment –

*4 January 1844.* The new plan of Government adopted by the late Governor of Canada Sir Charles Bagot, has not answered – it was Sure to fail as it gave the power & authority to the democratic & French party – Sir Charles Metcalfe Soon Saw that it would not do, & has proceeded to put things upon a different footing, dismissed the chief Officers & has taken a different line – but he is of course in hot water for a time – Prudence & firmness may help him out of the awkward position in which he is placed by the liberal views of his predecessors – but in Such a country it must be a doubtful question –

*5 January 1844.* The new Constitution in Greece is hitherto working well [.] There is a prudence, a moderation & a patriotism prevalent, which, if continued, must place Greece in a very desirable position. Unlike all other revolutions, Except our own [in 1688], this in Greece has been bloodless, calm & unattended with feuds & animosities. The assemblies are about to sit, & the choice of President, & other officers, as well as ministers, has been most Judicious & wise – a people acting thus deserves Success and prosperity –

*12 January 1844.* There is much curiosity in the following occurrence – admiral Sir Charles Nugent, Senior officer of the British navy [,] is Just dead, at the head of the Generals of the British army is General Sir George Nugent, a remarkable circumstance of itself, but it appears that these two Veteran Officers were[211] Brothers, & more over were Twins –

*13 January 1844.* In Several Counties, meetings of the Farmers are taking place for protection of their interests – Essex took the lead in good Earnest & others are following the Example – Much ability & determination have been shewn by the farmers, & I think that Sir Robert Peel will be obliged to alter his tone & intentions – if he does not, I think that his official career will not be of long duration = That he Should have permitted the [Anti–Corn Law] League to Exist So long unmolested, is of itself alone, a disgraceful blot among many of his administration –

*14 January 1844.* The horrible worship at Juggernaut, is about to be discountenanced by us, as long ago it ought to have been – £6000 – a year has hitherto been paid to Support this dreadful worship – it is from henceforth to be discontinued, & the worshippers & votaries will themselves have to defray the Expences attendant upon this most Extraordinary Pagan idolatry[212] –

[211]were are in the original with the word were underneath.
[212]Juggernaut was worshipped at the city of Puri in India.

*19 January 1844.* O'Connell's trial is at last Commenced – The attorney General has made his opening Speech, which is of Extraordinary length, & is Said to be good –

*20 January 1844.* In Canada a Strong majority has proved the feeling of the assembly in favor & Support of the Lapontaine [Louis–Hippolyte Lafontaine] ministry – But the Governor Sir Charles Metcalfe Seems disposed to stick to his purpose, & in consequence the English party was rallying Strongly round him – This is the way to act to deserve & Ensure Strenuous Support –

*24 January 1844.* Sir Francis Burdett is dead – a few days ago Lady Burdett died after a long illness & is yet unburied – Sir Francis is a historical character & needs no comment from me = Since he became conservative he has been of much use to the cause = his place cannot be filled by any living man, & he will be much missed –

*25 January 1844.* The Irish trials continue through all Sorts of interruptions, tricks & chicaneries = I do not expect that they will Ever be fairly terminated =
    The newspapers State that the "League" is much discomfited by the firm & determined front Shewn by the farmers – the Struggle may be a desperate one but the Leaguers will be beaten –

*27 January 1844.* The tone of the Farmers, at their meetings which are becoming universal, is very clearly & ably announced, & will prove decisive of the course which the Minister must now take, if he means to remain in office – it is most fortunate that they have been roused to this demonstration.

*31 January 1844.* Lady Hastings (who is a very queer woman) has requested that one of the hands of the late Marquis may be cut off & given to her – which she will have pickled & preserved & will Keep as a memorial of him – a person observed that it would have been well if She had valued it as much when her husband was alive –

*2 February 1844.* [...] Parliament opened yesterday – The Queen's Speech is as negative as any thing I Ever read – The tone about Ireland is decisive, all Else is words which may be interpreted in any way that may please the imaginations of twenty people – In Ireland things are done unknown to other climes – The conduct of the pending Trials has been a curiosity in Such proceedings from the commencement = & now the Court has been interrupted by Mr [Gerald] Fitzgibbon Stating to it, that he had Just received a note from the attorney General [Thomas Cusack Smith] to challenge & call him to account for what he had Said of him in the course of his address to the Court in the performance of his duty as an advocate for the Traversers – The attorney General is of Course bitterly condemned by many – by others defended, & by these it is Said that the language was So offensive & intolerable that he could not Submit to it, & that a regular plot & plan were made to set at him & run him down & Endeavour to entrap him into doing as he did. There is no other way in Ireland, it Seems, by which a gentleman can defend himself against the foul & disgraceful language of a coarse & Slanderous opponent – The Court never interfered & allowed the man to proceed although he was uttering insult upon insult – The Government has made a wretched mess of the affair from beginning & I fear it will be the Same to the End[213] –

*3 February 1844*. The debate upon the address is chiefly remarkable by the Extraordinary diversity of opinion of the opposition [.] Lord John Russell was almost a Supporter of Peel – & Peel has, by his pride & obstinacy [,] done much harm, by declaring that he will not be fettered by any declaration that under no circumstances will he alter the Corn Laws, & that he will not be driven into Saying so to please any party whatever – The case is that he is fencing, & will not make honesty his best policy –

*5 February 1844*. The Duke of Saxe Cobourg Gotha, Father of Prince albert, is dead: he died quite Suddenly, about an hour after he was first seised – of Something Spasmodic, it is understood –

[…] From returns that have been made, it appears that about £53,000,000 are now invested in railroads – & more are at this time projected than in any former year =

*6 February 1844*. Lord Spencer's Speech[214] at Northampton declaring his approval of & adherence to "the League", has been the fortunate cause of the universal movement amongst the Farmers = Lord Spencer has been formally Called upon by Some of the leading agricultural associations to resign his Post as President of the Royal agricultural Society of England which his Lordship has very clumsily declined to do – This is again fortunate, as it will break up this great but very ill constituted Society – The Society was already declining & had fallen Very much into the hands of one party – The Reformers –

*7 February 1844*. The Irish Trials are at last drawing to a close – O'Connell has made his [case] in his own defence – instead of lasting for 3 days as was Supposed – it was only for a few hours – Of all the advocates who have addressed the Court, O'Connell appears to me to be the worst Speaker – The Speech is a bad one, ill argued, ill constructed, ill Expressed – vulgar & Suited more to a mob than a court of Justice – in fact – it is Evident that the whole speech is meant for out of doors – & principally to discredit the Jury & to raise a national cry against them – No doubt that the speech suits O'Connell's purpose, both present & future, but as a production of a great lawyer or a great man, Every one must consider it poor and unworthy[215] =

*9 February 1844*. The Roman Catholics pretend to be Excessively offended at the Exclusion of all Roman Catholics from the Jury list in Ireland – amongst others the English Romans have taken the matter up & have had a Meeting [at the Freemasons' Tavern with] Lord[216] Camoys in the Chair – The language was of the most Violent & improper description – Espousing the cause of O'Connell – giving hearty cheers for him – & voting a resolution that the Exclusion of the names from the Jury list was an insult to the whole body, for

---

[213] For these events, see Henry Shaw, *Shaw's Authenticated Report of the Irish State Trials* (1844), 342–74.

[214] ~~letter~~ precedes this in the original.

[215] *Shaw's Authenticated Report*, 466–516.

[216] A crossed out but indecipherable word precedes this in the original.

which they would require ample Satisfaction – it is Evident that they determined to [assert] themselves – & it is well that it Should be So –

*10 February 1844*. The proceedings in Parliament are more marked by active Skirmishing than anything Else – Except a motion by Lord ashley on the conquest of Scindh [*sic* – Scinde], on which it is Said he made an Excellent & able Speech, but was Evidently quite wrong in the line he took –

*11 February 1844*. Lord Carlisle is very ill, & is Expected to die – Lord Morpeth Was Just making preparations for coming into parliament by the resignation of his brother [Edward Howard] for Morpeth – but all this is stopt [*sic*] & he most probably will Soon be a distinguished Member of the other house – This, Lord Grey's & Lord Derby's fragil[e] state of health, will in all probability take their 3 Sons, all conspicuous men, into the House of Lords.

*13 February 1844*. at last the Irish Trials are brought to a close – The Jury after long consultation, Several hours [,] came into Court at past 11 at night, of last Saturday (10th) & delivered their Verdict, which was read by the Clerk of the Court – Their were 11 Counts – To the two first & many others there was "no finding" = on others a Verdict of guilty = on 5 Counts guilty = on the 6 others, no finding & Could not agree – The Jury were returned to reconsider their Verdict – but as it was so late & the Jury not agreed, it was at last resolved that the Court should adjourn to Monday morning when the Jury was to give in their Verdict – It seems that a Verdict cannot be received in Court after 12 o'clock on Saturday night – However the Verdict may be considered as against the Prisoners.

*14 February 1844*. after much difficulty, the revised Verdict has been given in & O'Connell is found Guilty on all Eleven Counts – when this was done the Court quietly Separated & was adjourned to the next Term – the 15th of april – Judgment therefore is Suspended – & may or may not be passed on that day, but not before that time – So that this Traitor is at large & wholly unpunished untill [*sic*] that time arrives When it is Even thought that he will not Even be imprisoned but only fined a heavy fine – if this be So – there may as well be no laws, no Judges, no Juries – the Guilty & the innocent, the good & the vile, are to be regarded alike, with this disadvantage that a bonus is given to the Wicked[217] –

a long debate on vote of thanks to Sir Charles Napier & the army in Scinde – the vote was opposed & a division of 9 against it of which Lord Howick was one[218] – Sir Robert Peel made a very long Speech in introducing the Vote & dwelt in the strongest manner on the merits of Sir Charles Napier: they unquestionably are not undeserved, & no man living, could have done better as a man & a Soldier [,] but some of the praise was Evidently fulsome, & it is Easy to perceive why it was laid on with So lavish a tongue = Sir Charles is of adverse politics, & liberality requires that [,] where a political opponent is concerned, upon him caresses & Every tribute of praise [,] renown & unqualified approbation is profusely Showered Whilst upon a friend, the greater his merits the less is he regarded – Such was the

---

[217] *Shaw's Authenticated Report*, 663–78.
[218] The vote was 164–9: majority 155.

case the other day with the Irish attorney General Smith – when he was attacked nothing could be more feeble & insidious than the defence –

*15 February 1844.* Lord John Russell has made his motion upon Ireland in a long Speech – answered in another long speech by Sir James Graham [.] Lord Normanby has done the Same in the House of Lords, & in both houses the debates have been adjourned – It is Evident why [–] in the House of Commons O'Connell is to be present – He has Suddenly given it out in orders at Dublin that he shall go over to England for a few days & Speak on the question of Lord John Russell's motion – Who Ever heard of greater assurance & brazen impudence [?] – a convicted Traitor, awaiting Judgment, dares to appear in Parliament & take an open part in its proceedings – My opinion is that it would be an indelible degradation to the Government, to the House of Commons, to the laws & people of England, if this pestilent fellow be allowed to Enter, to sit in & address the House – It ought not to be permitted – & there is an End to all Justice, all decency [,] if Such a breach of all propriety be of an instant allowed – We Shall See how they will act – my fear & my belief is that no notice will be taken of Such a flagrant insult –

*16 February 1844.* It is Stated in the Standard that whilst Mr [David] Ross was Speaking O'Connell Entered the House of Commons [,] on which there was the greatest uproar, but it was late & there was no time to report more as the paper Was Just going to press –

*17 February 1844.* Nothing in the Shape of remark or objection to his Entrance transpired respecting O'Connell's presence in the house. It Seems to me to be a most mistaken view of Such a case –

Lord Sidmouth is dead = he has for many years past lived in retirement – but Such men as he are Much Wanted now – He was one of our English Worthies & Statesmen & men of his stamp are unfortunately Extinct – He was one of the most instructive men I Ever Was in Company [with] – a man of irreproachable Character – intelligent, firm, Kind, decisive – certainly a great & good man – His Memoirs, if they Should Ever be published, will be preeminently Curious & interesting[219] = In years past I had Seen much of Lord Sidmouth & I should be ungrateful, if I did not retain a high Esteem & regard for him –

*18 February 1844.* Lord Stanley is said to have made the best Speech he Ever Spoke on the never Ending debate upon Lord John Russells motion on Irish affairs – I have not read it yet – tomorrow I shall Endeavour to accomplish what is a real undertaking [–] to wade through a speech of hours long – Seldom giving any thing new, & pompously recapitulating what Every body has Known for months past –

*19 February 1844.* The Duke of Wellington was reported to have been again Seised with one of those attacks to which he was subject – He has thought fit to address the following letter which does not appear to me to Substantiate the assertions made in it = it is one of the curious productions to which His Grace has been Very prone, of late – "London 16 February 1844. Field Marshall the Duke of Wellington presents his compliments to the

[219] George Pellew, *The Life and Correspondence of the Rt. Hon. Henry Addington, First Viscount Sidmouth* (3 vols, 1847).

Editor of the Times newspaper – It will Save the Duke Some trouble if the Editor will be So Kind as to announce that there is not one word of truth in a paragraph of the Times news paper of the 16th instant headed 'the Duke of Wellington'. The Duke has not been better in health for the last twenty years than at present. He was not on horseback on Wednesday – He went to & returned from the Horse Guards on foot through the Streets, followed by his groom with his horse, which was not mounted on that day" – The writing [of] this letter & its contents, Speak for themselves !!!

*21 February 1844.* The Wearisome & tedious Irish debate still drawls on & is again adjourned – John O'Connell Spoke as a convicted conspirator in the last night & in language which of itself he Should be tried for – but it was quietly permitted by the house – & the disgrace & indignity of being invaded by convicted Members Seems to be quite unfelt & disregarded –

*23 February 1844.* […] The Irish debate Still lingers on in the House of Commons [.] The Irish attorney General Smith – made his Speech last night [–] the only one of the night – it is Said to have been one of the most clear, convincing, well-ordered & Eloquent Speeches Ever made – & commanded universal applause – This is the man So traduced, by his (Even official) friends – another night will probably close the debate, which will then have[220] lasted Either 8 or 9 days –

*24 February 1844.* The eternal debate is again adjourned – & as attorney General [Frederick] Pollock was Speaking yesterday when the post came away – & as O'Connell, Sir Robert Peel & Lord John Russell in reply will have to Speak, the probability is that it will go into a tenth night !!!!! – Speaking & adjourned debates is become quite a disease – O'Connell attended the weekly [Anti–Corn Law] League meeting at Covent Garden Theatre & was received with the most rapturous & boisterous applause of men & women – not as avowedly Stated in his Character of a Leaguer – but a convicted & glorious Traitor –

*25 February 1844.* at last this Irish debate is over – it closed on the 9th instead of the 10th night of it, as I yesterday thought probable – Sir Robert Peel made a very long but not in my opinion a good Sort of Speech – however it was not Satisfactory to my Views of what Should be – & as relates to the Roman Catholics any thing but what is Satisfactory to a Steady & thinking Church Protestant – I think the Speech will do him much harm in many ways – with all his caution & wariness & trick of debate, I think the Speech was injudicious & disingenuous – The majority on division in a very full house was 99 [225–324][221] –

*1 March 1844.* […] I dined with the Welsh men being St David's day, at the Fremason's [sic] tavern, Sir John Walsh in the Chair – & a Very good chairman – I had to Speak, & Endeavoured to deliver an Epitome of my views for the advancement of the arts, agriculture, manufactures, Commerce & religion in Wales – all which was received with great attention, favor & approbation – The whole went off well & pleasantly[222] =

---

[220] of precedes this in the original.

[221] For commentary, see N.U.M.D., Ne C 5905: Lincoln to Newcastle, 24 Feb. 1844.

[222] The meeting of the Honourable and Loyal Society of Ancient Britons was reported in *The North Wales Chronicle*, 5 Mar. 1844.

*4 March 1844.* […] The Queen is Expected to be in her bed about the beginning of July –

*6 March 1844.* The Express from Paris brings the telegraphic account from Marseilles of the overland Indian mail, that there has been a great battle at Gwalior, that we have taken the Strong fortress by Storm, that we lost 1000 men & our opponents 6000 –

*10 March 1844.* The speech of the Chancellor of the Exchequer [Goulburn] on proposing to the House the reduction of interest on the $3\frac{1}{2}$ per Ct Stock, one $\frac{1}{2}$ per Cent, is in my opinion a perfect Specimen of the useful & real English mode of Speaking – & it would be well if the honorable House would follow his Example – not a word too much or too little – clearness of Statement, high principle, a manly, honest & truly British tone pervaded the whole – The $3\frac{1}{2}$ per Cent Stock amounts to [£] 250,000,000 – He proposes to reduce the interest on this Stock $\frac{1}{4}$ per Cent for the next ten years – then again another $\frac{1}{4}$ per Cent So that the interest on that Stock Shall be 3 per Cent & this rate of interest he guarantees for 20 years afterwards = I do not see why he should not have made the first period 5 years only – but the view & arrangement is admirable, honest & considerate. He then makes a very valuable & important arrangement by which the quarters' payments shall be Equalised Which will be productive of the greatest convenience & advantage = The measure is altogether good & is highly approved of – The Saving to the public in interest – will be between [£] 6 & 700,000 annually for 10 years & double that Sum hereafter – Equal to the liquidation of [£] 50,000,000 of debt –

*11 March 1844.* The Indian accounts are very full – There were two hard days fighting between our troops & the natives of Gwalior – The ominous part of the affair is that the forces on Each Side were nearly Even, one circumstance which has rarely, if Ever, happened before – Our army under the Commander in Chief [,] Sir Hugh Gough, a first rate officer – Consisted of 14000 infantry [,] about 300 cavalry & 50 guns = The Enemy from 14 to 15000 infantry – 3000 cavalry & 100 guns – Lord Ellenborough, Lady Gough & daughter [Frances] were present & as it were in the action – Surely a Singular act of amateurship for the ladies – who were frequently in danger – & I Should Suspect that his Excellency the Governor General must have been rather "de trop"[223] or, anglice, in the way – The natives fought with the utmost obstinacy, Spirit & determination, when firing ceased it came to a hand to hand fight & they were only over come when British Strength & valour was found to be Superior to their own = One may Exclaim with Just pride ["] who are Equal to Englishmen ["] ? –

*14 March 1844.* a great dinner given to O'Connell at Covent Garden theatre by the foul Spirits of the Country [on the 12th]. Mr Thomas Duncombe in the Chair – Lord Shrewsbury & many M.Ps present & about 1000 diners – besides company in the boxes = O'Connell buttered the Englishmen whom he had hitherto abused, told them they were born to be United & denounced the late trials, the Judge [Edward Pennefather], the attorney General [Cusack Smith,] the Jury, the Government – & represented that he had been illegally convicted of no crime – & went as near to the wind as he dared – but carefully ab-

---

[223] Unwelcome.

stained from using any openly Seditious & inflammatory language – He is gaining ground among the worthless & revolutionary English – & hopes to create a protective party in England –

*16 March 1844.* In a communication from Hong Kong it is stated – that in the island there is a handsome Roman Catholic Chapel built of Stone – also Stone chapels of Baptists, Methodists & Several other dissenting Societies & Even a neat Mahometan Mosque – but the Church of England place of worship is merely a matted tent, too cold for people to enter at the time of year (December) when the letter was written – This really [is] Shameful & most inexcusable – it appears that where all other things were well considered & provided for, no thought or provision whatever was bestowed upon the Established religion of the Colonials.

*19 March 1844.* O'Connell has transferred the agitation from Ireland to England. He is quite a lion here now — feted & caressed, he is not as a malefactor, but a triumphant hero – and yet all this is quietly endured by the government =

*20 March 1844.* a Serious Shake to the Peel Ministry took place last night in the house of Commons – when it was outvoted in two divisions on Lord ashley's amendment for Substituting, in the Factory bill, a restriction of 10 instead of 12 hours a day as the Maximum of labor in factories[224] – It is unaccountable to observe the obstinacy & infatuation with which Ministers Seem determined to brake [*sic*] their heads against this wall – but so it is with them – a good measure & Especially if it is one favored or proposed by Conservatives is Sure to be opposed but this cannot last long – Conservatives are tired of it, all good & reasonable men are tired of it, the Country is tired of it. Peel, never popular, is mistrusted & is losing ground daily – a great crisis is drawing near [,] unquestionably matured by the Course which he has taken Since he has been minister, & which day by day is destroying the country –

Great alarm is felt here at the Strike of the Colliers in Staffordshire & Some other places – it is asserted confidently that there is a most dangerous & formidable Combination among them, for mischief, & that an universal Strike & turnout is arranged for the 25th to take place Simultaneously from one End of the Kingdom to the other = if So, the consequences will be awfully Serious – for these men are described to be very violent now, why I Know not, & their determination will not be behind their violence –

*21 March 1844.* […] Lord Lonsdale too is dead – at 86 – His Successor will not be a Substitute for his father – He was a Knight [of the] Garter & I observe that I shall now be the Second [in seniority –] the Duke of Rutland being the first –

*22 March 1844.* Much dissatisfaction is felt at the results of the Ministerial policy & measures of 1842 – They have unquestionably failed – founded on free trade principles the results are now proved & felt to be injurious to British interests – whether it be by lowering of import duties or removal of restrictions – Trade & commerce is very much revived & reviving at

---

[224] The government lost two votes on 18 Mar. 1844; the first by 170–179: majority 9, the second by 161–153: majority 8.

the present time, but that must be very much ascribed to the abject depression Which prevailed for a long previous period, & which penalised Every thing, & caused the outrages amongst the workmen which annihilated all manufacture & of course reduced all stocks in hand to Scarcely a Sufficient Supply – Foreign as well as domestic Stock being almost Exhausted, orders to Supply wants & deficiencies have flowed in & have put all hands in motion though at low wages & Small profits – I have been told that orders are to such an Extent that with the fullest Exertion they can Scarcely be completed by the autumn, when fresh orders will arrive – This certainly is a good lookout for the present, but will it last under the present system, & when, by the Extraordinary favor & Encouragement which has been Shewn to the foreign manufacturer & trader, the results of foreign industry & Exertion, a very great part of it carried on by British Skill capital & labor, begins to come into full play & operation [?]

*23 March 1844.* It is a fact, founded upon official documents, that the declared value, which is the real value, of the cotton manufactured goods Exported from this Country in the year 1815, was 19,045,820 £ & in 1841 it had Sunk to 16,225,536 £, being less by 2,820,264 £. The Encrease of quantity in the interval was from 21,480,792 £ – to 58,816,522 £ [–] that is to Say, that if the Same prices had been obtained in 1841 [,] the quantity Exported in 1841 as in 1815, the return would have been nearly 59 millions instead of a little above 16 millions – If the return of last year were furnished it would Shew a very large encrease in quantity over 1841, & a still more outstanding depreciation in Value – From this it is clear that Encreased quantities, So far from Encreasing Exchangeable Value, decrease it – how therefore can there be a question about restricting the hours of labour, when it is clear that the labourers cannot possibly have any other means of protection [?] –

*24 March 1844.* The debate in Committee of the Factory bill is over, with a most remarkable result – The government proposal of restriction to 12 hours was lost by 5 – Lord ashley's for 10 hours was lost by 7[225] – this was the very Same proposal[226] which was carried by 9 in the Same House of Commons a few nights ago!!! – What is now to be done [?] – Lord ashley has acted nobly, Sir James Graham & ministers doggedly & meanly – they will assuredly Suffer for it –

*26 March 1844.* Sir James Graham announced to the House last night that it was the intention of the Government to Stand upon 12 hours as the utmost limit of labour in factories – Lord ashley Said he was determined to oppose it as long as he lived & that he had no doubt of carrying 10 hours Either now or in a Very Short time hence – & So he will, to the disgrace of the Government with its obstinate & perverse doggedness –
[…] The East India Directors have determined to Encrease the number of their regimental Officers = a most important Step for Securing discipline & Saving of life – The want of officers has been too lamentably felt in all our late Stupendous operations –

---

[225] On the motion that the blank be filled up with the word twelve the vote was 186–183: majority 3. On the motion that the blank be filled up with the word ten, the vote was 181–188: majority 7.

[226] ~~decision of the~~ precedes this in the original.

*27 March 1844.* The debate on the Factory bill is postponed from the Monday to Friday, when Some conclusion is to be arrived at by the Ministers whether they will alter their opinion & concede 10 hours, or stand upon their 12 hours & if outvoted throw up the bill =

*28 March 1844.* Sir G. [*sic* – James] Graham has moved to <u>with</u>draw his bill – & to bring in a new one on Friday – if he is wise he will insert <u>10</u> hours – It is really Surprising how much a by no means popular Ministry has lost in <u>public</u> opinion in the last fortnight – it has been fatal to it – Peel will not Stand but Graham is a bug bear =

*29 March 1844.* The arrangement now Settled is that Sir James Graham withdraws his present bill & brings in a new one this day which is to be a mere nothing, only regulating Some minor points – & Lord ashley is to bring in a Substantive bill of his own to restrict the hours of labour to 10 hours = it is questionable Whether he loses or gains by this – he avoids opposing a Government measure – but probably he may have several With him, who would not Support him, if in opposition to a great measure – these Squeamish gentlemen are wretched creatures, & deserve the contempt which is felt for them –

 We are beginning to feel Seriously the Effect of the Strike among the colliers – The Stocks are very low & in a short time coals will be So Scarce as to be hardly obtainable at any price – I have only 3 weeks consumption on hand, & must husband my Stock very rigidly – The Effects of this Strike if persisted in will be very Serious – now that Every thing goes by Steam – railways, Steam Vessels, factories &c &c will all be Stopt [*sic*] – The Colliers have the public at their Mercy & in the present State of the laws there is no help for it – it is an all important question –

*31 March 1844.* Prince albert is gone to Germany – it is Said that he goes on a visit of condolence to his Saxe Gotha family – this may or may not be the reason – I Suspect that he is gone to look after Some money – This is the first time that he has absented himself for 12 hours from the Queen's side [–] now that he has broken the Spell – I trust that it will not lead to too frequent repetition – The Queen loves him most affectionately & devotedly, & I must devoutly hope that he may never give her cause for uneasiness or Ever disturb an union which has hitherto been So perfect & so Exemplary –

*4 April 1844.* […] Lord abinger was taken Suddenly ill after leaving the Court & reaching his lodgings at Bury [St Edmunds]. He had performed his Judicial duties with his usual activity & Energy throughout a hard day, & on reaching home was taken ill – an apoplectic Seisure is Supposed to be his illness – he is quite insensible & has never Spoken –

*7 April 1844.* […] Lord Eglintoun [Eglinton] has Just Sold his Estate at Eaglesham for £217000 to a Mr Gilmore [Allan and James Gilmour] the rental of which is nearly £10000 a year – Gambling, the Tournament [,] open house, & a host of other Expenditures have forced this Sale, as I presume – it is stated to be one of the finest Estates in the West of Scotland – it must be a capital investment = yielding $4\frac{1}{2}$ per Cent –

*10 April 1844.* Our interference at Constantinople with regard to Christians has at last been completely Successful & henceforth Converts to Christianity will not be persecuted

& Executed by the Turks = It has been a very hard fought business – The Porte was determinedly obstinate –

*14 April 1844.* Lord abingers death will occasion much difficulty. Sir Frederick Pollock is a valuable attorney General & his loss cannot be Supplied Even by Sir William Follitt who is in a wretched state of heath – He probably will not live many months, & after him there happens to be nobody of Eminence – Mr Fitzroy Kelly is Expected to be Solicitor General but there are woeful flaws in his character – then there is Mr [Frederick] Thessiger [Thesiger] & the Scene closes – he is nothing remarkable – & the falling off will be great indeed –

*16 April 1844.* another agitation is to be added to those already Existing & in force – a Society for the protection of the Church – So We have, the great Repeal agitation in Ireland = The anti corn law League here – opposed to which is the agricultural protection Society organised on the League plan – The Factory agitation = We may add though not much noticed at present the Chartist faction – & now the Church protection which may be very Extensive – This is a formidable state of things – & all arising from Peel's Supineness & mischievous or mistaken & blind policy – The Repeal agitation is an old Story, but it was allowed to attain its Enormous Strength by Peel. The League Existed when he came into power but he allowed it to domineer & act as it pleased, & he Even adopted its maxims & paid Court to it, So that the farmers to defend themselves were obliged to adopt unconstitutional & very objectionable & dangerous measures – Peel has Shewn his disposition to countenance & Even support the Papists frequently in opposition to Protestants – & this forces the necessity on the part of Churchmen to unite & agitate for the defence & maintenance of their Church – The Country must Shortly be convulsed by Such agitations & the government will be, as it now is, insulted & despised: an Extraordinary obstinacy induces Peel to resist the 10 hours clause in the Factory bill, & the result will be his Expulsion.

*17 April 1844.* It is positively Stated & appears to be Credited that Sir Robert Peel had by letter directed the Lord Lieutenant of Ireland [Earl de Grey] to promote or appoint no clergymen who was opposed to the National system of Education – This put the Clergy & their friends in a boil = & a Strong ferment arose – The Bishops thought it most prudent to question Sir Robert in private rather than in Parliament [.] Sir Robert then avowed that Such a letter had been privately & confidentially written to the Lord Lieutenant but Since unfortunately it had been divulged & as it was So vehemently objected to, he Should not abide it, & Should leave the clergy to act as they pleased = If this be true – it is indeed a base & disgraceful proceeding –

*20 April 1844.* The trial of O'Connel & others came on again yesterday – when the scoundrel put in his writ of Error, which will impede the proceedings for many weeks, & probably over this Term – thus delaying the Judgement – It is really shameful that this "protestant fellow" should be allowed to Set all law & custom at defiance, & rule Every thing as he pleases – It is a mockery of Justice to act in Such a manner –

*21 April 1844.* Some compromise appears to be going on between the Government & Lord ashley on the 10 hours clause – I much regret this on all accounts – he will be out manoeuvred & Sacrificed & the Government [,] if it attains its End, will gain it by crooked policy & disreputable intrigue –

*24 April 1844.* a terrible <u>Kick up</u> in the House of Commons – Mr [William] Ferrand was called upon by Mr [John] Roebuck to say whether he had uttered the speeches which were attributed to him & in Some of Which he had charged Sir James Graham & Mr [James Weir] Hogg with foul practices for particular purposes – Mr Ferrand acknowledged that he had made Such assertions – he was then called upon to Substantiate his charges – & tomorrow he is to do this – The house was a bear garden, & a disgrace to the Commons of England[227] –

*25 April 1844.* Mr Ferrand began a Speech, and all was breathless Expectation = but he was soon assailed by the Same vollies of abuse, noise & <u>mobbing</u>, which was Exhibited Yesterday – He renewed his declaration that he abided by the reports of his Speeches in "the Times", & what he had acknowledged yesterday – he added that he plainly perceived that he was not to Expect Justice from the House of Commons as the party & unfair demonstration of yesterday was again Exhibited against him – he took up his hat, bowed to the Speaker & left the house – His motive for this is unknown = a discussion Ensued & on Friday, tomorrow, Mr Ferrand is to be called upon to Substantiate his Charges –

*27 April 1844.* Mr Ferrand appeared in his place yesterday, as ordered, & being called upon made his Speech – But it was not [what] the Honorable Members required & Expected – He merely repeated that what was reported in the Times newspaper was Substantially what he had Said, but that he would not Submit to be Judged by the House of Commons: it was not a court of honor or Justice & he appealed from the people of England against Such an assumption of power by the House – He was ready to meet any charges any where Else – He has thus out manoeuvred the usurping & honorable house – Sir Robert Peel then proposed a resolution that [,] as Mr Ferrand had failed to Substantiate his charges, against Sir James Graham & Mr Hogg – therefore these two Gentlemen were declared guiltless of the accusation brought against them by Mr Ferrand – here Ended the brutum fulmen[228] – Peel did not dare to go any farther, & though at first there was a great deal of bullying about Expelling Mr Ferrand it was then thought [to] be highly advisable to Say nothing about Such a penalty for his Sin =

*28 April 1844.* Lord Ellenborough is recalled by the Board of Directors from the Governor Generalship of India – this information has broken upon us like a thunderbolt, it was totally unexpected. The Government disclaims any Concurrence in the measure & declares that it is Solely the act of the Direction [*sic* – Directors] – How Ever I have no doubt whatever that it has been managed by the Crafty Sir Robert = The Directors no doubt Know that it will not be disagreeable to him, & therefore they have presumed to venture upon a Step at once

---

[227] Ferrand attacked their conduct regarding the Nottingham election petition; Hogg was chairman of the committee that heard the election petition in 1843.

[228] 'empty threat' or 'meaningless thunderbolt'.

unusual & improper – The Charter gives them the power but it has not been Exercised for a century, & it is impossible to Suppose but that if Sir Robert took up Lord Ellenborough's Cause, that the Directors would as soon think of Journeying to the Moon, as of recalling the Governor General – No one Knows why the recall is made –

*29 April 1844.* I should have mentioned that in the debate on Mr Ferrands business on the 26th Mr [Benjamin] D'Israeli made one of the cleverest Speeches in mitigation of Mr Ferrand's delinquency, that Ever was made – Mr [George] Smythe, Lord Strangfords Son [,] also made a Speech of very remarkable cleverness & talent –

*5 May 1844.* I have been informed by this post that Sir Henry Hardinge has been appointed Lord Ellenborough's Successor & is to be both Governor General & Commander in Chief in India –

*7 May 1844.* It Seems to have been determined that the King of France is <u>not</u> to pay a return visit to our Queen this year, but the rumour is prevalent that the Emperor of Russia [Nicholas I] will do So – my advice would be that he Should remain at home [–] he will do no good here –

*8 May 1844.* In bringing forward his project for the renewal of the Bank [of England] Charter, Sir Robert Peel took an Extensive view of the whole Subject, & announced his plan – it appears to be a Sequel of his former too renowned currency bill [of 1819]. He aims at limiting the issues & thereby Seeks to Enhance Still more the value of money, & to depress the value of all that which money helps to produce = It is to be apprehended that this Scheme will be productive of fearful consequences – & it Seems to me that [,] in common Justice & honesty, he must also take another huge Step – & proceed to an Equitable adjustment of the public debt – reducing the original contracts from the Value of the former times to that of the present day – as Effected mainly by Sir Robert himself – This question of currency, is another occasion upon which he was opposed to & differed from his Father – & as it seems to me, for that Very reason [,] he follows up his former opinions with a pertinacity & obstinate pride – little to his Credit –

*9 May 1844.* The Irish Trials are postponed ! & will not Come on again for hearing untill the next term – This is really farcical, contemptible & intolerable –

*11 May 1844.* Sir augustus D'Este, as he is called – Son of the late Duke of Sussex, has applied to Succeed to the Dukedom of his late Father – the matter is before the House of Lords, & has been referred to a Committee on privileges, which is now Sitting –

*12 May 1844.* Lord ashley moved his clause in amendment upon the factory bill in Committee – in a Very Eloquent, feeling & highly toned Speech which made a great impression, it was opposed by Sir James Graham in a harsh and Very antagonist[ic] Speech, & it is greatly Evident from what has come to light that Government has been Working hard by threats & cajolery to gain over & influence many who before voted with Lord ashley & many who from the awkwardness of there [sic] position did not vote at all – but as Lord ashley observed this does not much Signify "for Such a candle has been lighted as will not be

Extinguished untill the good has been accomplished".[229] The Ministers in all their acts appear to be cutting their own throats & ruining Every interest of the Country –

*14 May 1844.* Lord ashley has moved his clause to the Factory bill in a most Eloquent & able Speech & in that noble & lofty & feeling tone which so well becomes one in his situation – He proposes to limit the hours of working to 11 hours a day untill 1847 – when 10 hours is to become the limit – This alteration of his original time is unfortunate, & the waiting untill 1847 for the beneficial period, are both mistaken views & arrangements – but the Subtle & all compelling Control of the government which has been indefatigably at Work will beat him.

*15 May 1844.* after a long debate upon the factory bill & a (parturieunt montes)[230] speech of Sir Robert Peel – threatening all Sorts of things & foretelling all Evil to the State, if Eleven hours Should be decided upon instead of 12 – the mouse was born in the Shape of a division in favour of 12 hours – For Lord ashley's clause 159 – for Ministerial clause of 12 hours = 297 [majority: 138] – after the declaration of the division, the mill owners & others in the house – hooted Lord ashley – The Minister & the House of Commons is ruined – Peels' conduct Seals his fate –

*16 May 1844.* The Effect of the Ministerial Exercise of authority & cajolery is quite Extraordinary – not one single Journal applaudes [*sic*] Sir Robert Peel & his tricks & his Joseph Surface[231] plausibility – it will not do he is found out – it is all over with him, he can never recover the Shock which his character has received & he richly deserves all the punishment & disgrace which may arise from his unworthy proceedings – Every print [,] Every person appears to be against him – & there were any one nearly approaching to his power of Speech – His power Would cease tomorrow – But – it So pleases God that there is no one – & as a Just punishment for our Sins, the nation must be scourged by Peel untill it returns to better ways, repents in sackcloth & ashes, & God in his mercy may permit a release from the Scourge, & place us under the rule of a greater & better Minister –

*17 May 1844.*[232] The Jews are beginning to separate among themselves: at Francfort [Frankfurt] there has arisen a complete Schism – two thirds of the numerous Jews at that place leave there [*sic*] old persuasion – The new party call themselves "Reformers" – refuse circumcision, & deny the Messiah – These are among the very many Signs of the times Which in the plainest manner indicate the approaching wonderful Events which are to astound the unconscious World –

---

[229] The phrase was that of Hugh Latimer to his friend Nicholas Ridley, as they were about to be burned as heretics for their teachings and beliefs outside Balliol college, Oxford, on 16 Oct. 1555.

[230] *parturiunt montes, nascetur ridiculus mus*: a quotation from Horace's *Odes*, translated as 'the mountains are in labour, (and) an absurd mouse will be born'.

[231] A selfish, greedy hypocrite and liar in Richard Brinsley Sheridan's *The School for Scandal* (1777).

[232] N.L.W., MC2/200, Newcastle to Powis, 17 May 1844: 'let no consideration induce you not to press your just & Sacred cause to a division, if necessary … Peel would cajole anyone and oblige those who act with him to do the same – he does not mind who he drags through the mud if he may only carry his points – right or wrong'.

*18 May 1844.* There does not Seem to be one dissentient Voice among the impartial people of England respecting Peels' pig headed obstinacy on the Factory bill, but Especially of his unwarrantable treatment of the House of Commons. These worthy gentlemen are threatened with his resignation [,] but above all with a dissolution, & presto they turn on their heels, & would stand on their heads, or any thing to avoid such direful consequences − This will never be forgotten & history will record this among the worst acts of a false & Self willed Minister −

*19 May 1844.* Sir Thomas Fremantle has been appointed Minister at War, & Mr [Charles] Hope whose qualifications are yet to be Known is placed in his late honorable position, of whipper in to the House of Commons & a Secretary of the Treasury[233] −

*21 May 1844.* Some Welcome rain today − if We have Enough of it, it Will be Essentially beneficial = What with Peel's measures & the Season, if the latter mends no more than the former will [,] We Shall be in a Woeful plight indeed − but God is good & he may yet take compassion upon us − if times[234] Should again prove adverse I Shall be almost ruined =

*23 May 1844.* There have been many singular instances of late, of married people dying within a Week of Each other: another occurred a few days ago − Sir John Lowther died, about 5 days since, Lady Elizabeth his wife followed him a Very few days afterwards − Sudden deaths are innumerable − & murders & horrid deeds are recorded Every day − verily Society is disjointed & disorganised & all nature convulsed −

*26 May 1844.* The Irish Judges have declared that they refuse to grant a new trial to O'Connell & others =

*1 June 1844.* at last the Eternal & nauseating Irish Trials are over − after a really disgraceful Exhibition of 6 Months − a new trial has been refused, & an arrest of Judgment denied [.] The Sentence has been passed − & what is it − O'Connell the ring leader & arch rebel − is to be imprisoned for 12 months & to pay a fine of £2000 − & afterwards to give Surety for his conduct for 7 years himself in £5000 & two Sureties in 2500£ Each − The Judges gave him the choice of his prison, a thing unheard of I presume − & the rebel Chose the Penitentiary [Richmond Bridewell in Dublin] − where I believe he has fitted up snug rooms for himself − The other rogues are to be imprisoned for 9 months [−] pay £50 − & give Sureties for their good behaviour for 7 years − There was a great deal of Curiosity & interest − & most indecent cheering & applause of O'Connell in Court, but no other popular manifestation in his favor −

*2 June 1844.* The Emperor of Russia has suddenly made his appearance in this country = no idea of his arrival was Entertained & the greatest bustle prevails to prepare for his reception − He was expected to have arrived at Woolwich, as soon as the news was published of his intention − what has caused this sudden irruption, I cannot divine = The King of Saxony

---

[233] The position of parliamentary secretary to the treasury went to John Young.

[234] ~~them~~ precedes this in the original.

[Frederick Augustus II] is already here – he arrived a few days ago – The King of France's visit is talked of for the autumn –

*4 June 1844.* The Emperor of Russia arrived on the 1st at 10 o'clock at night – He is come, quite in private & apparently on the Spur of the moment: he has taken all by surprise – passing hastily through Berlin & the Hague & only staying a few hours at Each – Curiosity cannot be his object – he has been here before – He remains at the Russian ambassador's home [Philipp von Brunnow] & has intimated to Prince albert that he will remain there for Some days – & for the present will not accept appartments [*sic*] in the Palace – Prince albert took Sir Robert Peel to the Emperor the day after his arrival – & the Emperor called upon Sir Robert on the following day making a very hurried visit of about $\frac{1}{4}$ of an hour –

*7 June 1844.* The Savage races of albania, Bosnia, Syria &c are making an Exterminating war upon the native Christians – Nothing can Exceed their lawless barbarity, & the horrors of their ungovernable Excesses – they search for & violate the women & youths, murder the men & plunder their property – their object seems to be Extermination.

*9 June 1844.* I am much pressed & wished to be present on Lord Powis's motion for the 2nd reading of his Bangor & St asaph [Bill] – I have been ill & deaf from a prevalent disease here – if I am better So as to hear a debate I will go – the Subject is one of vital importance – it is on the 11th [.][235]

*11 June 1844.* I abandon my Journey to London, with much regret. I do not feel myself in Sufficiently good heart to undertake So long a Journey for one debate[236] –

*13 June 1844.* Contrary to Expectation Lord Powis carried his bill through the 2nd reading by a majority of 12 [–] on division Contents 49: not contents 37 [majority 12]. The Duke of Wellington Spoke against the bill urging the poorest arguments or rather no arguments at all & moved to read the bill in 6 months [.] It is a very gratifying reflection, to think that the House of Lords has done its duty So manfully & rightly –

*16 June 1844.* My letters from London bring me the unexpected announcement that the Ministers are out[237] [.] They were outvoted on Mr Philip Miles's amendment on the Sugar duties which he carried by 20 [221–241] in a very full house – The fact is that Sir Robert Peel's measures are So Entirely Contrary to rational opinion & the public feeling that people are tired of being rough ridden & cajoled & hence the Various votes in Each house – &

---

[235] N.L.W., MC2/209: Newcastle to Powis, 7 June 1844. Newcastle informed Powis that he had sent his proxy for use by Powis, Combermere, or Kenyon, and attacked the Ecclesiastical Commission 'as a national nuisance, which has been & can only be productive of grievous injury to the Church & State. What has been gained by the suppression of Bishoprics in Ireland or in England? Depend upon it nothing but loss – &, what must be thought in High Heaven of our proceedings here below, when on the altar of a worthless, Senseless, and wicked Expediency, we Sacrifice Even the cause of religion itself'.

[236] N.L.W., MC2/216: Newcastle to Powis, 11 June 1844. Newcastle regretted his absence but 'might have been led into attacking [ministers] in no measured terms not only for their opposition to your bill, but for their other manifold & great delinquencies – most Especially for their Unitarian bill – a mortal blow to the Church not only nationally … but morally … I cannot Express to you how I lament it all'.

[237] N.U.M.D., Ne C 5906: Lincoln to Newcastle, 15 June 1844. He dated this letter 7 p.m.

more Singular Votings may be anticipated – My notion is that Peel does all this purposely to separate from his usual Supporters & gain the alliance of Lord John Russell & his party, & thus, as possibly he may think, form a coalition which Shall be invincible. I am quite Sure that he has been at this for Some time –

*19 June 1844.* The Sugar bill went into committee on the 17[th] & Sir Robert Peel then took occasion to State his Views & intentions – he retracted nothing & required the house to rescind their Vote of the 14th & this they did in obedience to his command by a majority of 22 [233–255] thus a Second time Sealing their disgrace & Peel's ruin – but this State of things cannot last = The clouds are gathering all around & will break before long –

*20 June 1844.* Sir Robert Peel's manner, mode, conduct & language have given very great offence & must make many Exceedingly inveterate against him – The farmers are Stirring again, having acquired a notion of the thing of which certain of them Seem quite willing to avail themselves as before the meeting began in Essex – & thus have petitioned against Sir Robert Peel's Bank Charter bill, as certain to produce the most baneful injury to agricultural interests, by restriction of currency & consequent depreciation of Every thing – of labour, produce & profits – The mode is unconstitutional, but Peel conjured up the hydra & he must & ought & I hope will Suffer by it –

*23 June 1844.* I have prepared to go to London tomorrow to be present at the debate on the Welsh Bishopricks bill – which I consider to be of the greatest importance or I would not go, Just now –

*24 June 1844.* I left Clumber at 5 o'clock this morning, & arrived at the Nottingham Station a few minutes after the 7 o'clock train had started – I went to the Inn, Shaved & had Some breakfast & left by the 8.20 [a.m.] train & arrived in Portman Square at $\frac{1}{4}$ past 3 – wrote some letters, dressed, Eat a mutton chop & went down to the House of Lords – to my infinite disappointment – the opposition to the bill is reserved for the third reading & it is to be defeated on[238] the grounds of not having obtained the Queen's consent to the bill – The Scheme is Shameful & rascally –

*25 June 1844.* What I learned yesterday merely opened a new view of Ministerial opposition to good measures, & gave me a fuller insight into their trickery & unworthy conduct. I endeavoured to dive into the whole mystery & investigate the pros & cons to my new view of the particular case before us – Lord Powis's bill – I determined to ask Some questions tonight of the Duke of Wellington which Should force him into divulging the truth = Having made notes of my questions & replies, & having formed an opinion in my own room – I went out to ascertain if I was right, & in Some instances I found that I was wrong to a certain degree from not having Known all that had occurred. I went to Lord Powiss [*sic*] & talked over the whole matter with him for a long time – I told him my views & my proposals & he approved – but he did not like to come to any conclusion untill he had had a meeting with the usual persons with whom he had hitherto advised – I wish him to force

---

[238]by precedes this in the original.

from the Duke of Wellington a distinct declaration whether the Queen will or will not give her consent to the debating & passing of the bill in the House of Lords – If he will not declare then I advise that the 3rd reading Shall be postponed as it will be a Solemn mockery to debate it under Such uncertainty – in case of denial then I advise to abandon the bill – but to throw all the odium & responsibility upon the Ministers, & to warn them of the odium which they will So unwarrantably cast upon the Queen's reputation as Defender of the faith […] & then I wish, or offer to do it myself, Lord Powis to announce that he is determined not to abandon his object, but will try all lawful means for its Success – & as one of them he will move on Monday instead of the 3rd reading of his bill, that the House do address the Queen to leave the two Welsh Sees in their present State & immediately to institute or initiate a Bishop of Manchester – I have passed all my morning in doing what I can to infuse Spirit & firmness & resolution to do what ought to be done – & I trust & believe that I have not been un–Successful – I then went to my own private businesses & returned home more dead than alive – I was most dreadfully tired yesterday & Shall not recover for Some days –

*26 June 1844.* Mr Staveley [William Owen Stanley] asked Sir Robert Peel in the House of Commons last night Whether it was his intention to Oppose the Lord Powis's bill when it came into the Commons & whether the Queens consent would be given to the debating of the bill – Sir Robert answered that he Should certainly oppose the bill – as to the Queen's consent, it was a nice point & required consideration it would be referred to the Speaker, if he decided that it was necessary then he, Sir Robert, Should think it his duty to advise the Queen not to give her assent – !!! So now we have it out – My neighbour Lord Kenyon is an Early Man [.] I went to him as Soon as I had made this discovery – & I requested him most Earnestly to See Lord Powis & urge him to strike the iron whilst hot – to require the Same declaration from the Duke of Wellington & then to proceed as I wrote yesterday – & that I would return & be present to assist to the best of my power – I then got into my carriage & left by the 11 o'clock train & arrived here [at] Clumber a little before 8 [p.m.] – found all well –

*29 June 1844.* I learn from London that it is decided to divide on the 3rd reading of Lord Powis's bill – of course we shall be thrown over if we have a majority by the Duke of Wellington putting in the Queen's veto to the question ["] that the bill do pass ["] – I do not approve of the proceeding for we shall appear like fools when thus thrown over – & I do not think that we shall stand So well as if we threw all the odium of refusal upon the Minister – besides we are not so sure of a majority –

*1 July 1844.* Slept at Nottingham last night & was at the Station before 7 [a.m.] – but as they were preparing to put my carriage on, I was informed that it could not go by that train being a mail train – I consequently Went by the $8\frac{1}{4}$ train & arrived in London at 3[p.m.]: had Some dinner & went down to the house [of Lords] = I Saw Lord Powis there & he to my Surprise informed me that the Duke of Wellington did not mean to oppose the 3rd reading, & Would Suffer it to pass – after Some discussion the Duke of Wellington rose & in a very lame manner – announced that he had not Even then the Queen's consent to the discussion of the bill – he Supposed therefore that the bill would pass as it had been before approved of by their Lordships – but he cautioned the Bishops against voting for a bill in Such a manner as it would be Establishing a dangerous precedent for them – depriving them of the protection of the Crown & Exposing them to be dealt with here after according to the temper of parliament – after a good deal of discussion Lord Mounteagle moved that the bill be read in 6 months – this it was Sought to avoid, but before the question putting – the Lord Chancellor [Lyndhurst] came forward & Said that he was placed in a very awkward position & that under the circumstances he thought that it would be proper to appoint a committee to Search for precedents – arguments were raised upon this & much Said by various peers – & then Lord Canterbury [,] to favor the Ministers, moved an adjournment of the house – all this was too much to bear [.] I could not Sit Silent & I rose & told them that the whole was an unworthy manoeuvre,[239] to get rid of the bill [and] calculated to make the House appear ridiculous – that it was trifling to pretend that there was any more difficulty in putting the question on the 3rd reading, than on the 2nd or any other proceeding [*sic* – preceding] Stage – I asked why that they had not Searched for precedents before, they had had time Enough – & if the Queen's consent were necessary why it had not been given or denied properly & without reserve [?] – as they were Searching for precedents I recommended them Searching to discover whether they had not been acting illegally in creating the (Ecclesiastical) Commission & despoiling, changing & mutilating the temporalities without the leave of the Church = Parliament could not act thus, it was illegal[240] – Lord Powis finally rose & Expressed his opinion that under present circumstances it would be best to postpone the farther consideration of the bill, untill the report of the committee were received – The motion for adjournment was put & I am Sure Would have been lost, but our people chose to give way & thus the matter has Ended – Disgracefully to the Ministers [,] unfortunately for the Queen, & degradingly for the House of Lords – I am disgusted with them all – they have no constancy, firmness or principle, they act for Shew, that is[241] the only impulse – but the day of retribution will come, when they will [be] called to a Severe account – I can plainly perceive that it is utterly useless to go against the current – I have given myself much useless trouble which is Entirely thrown away – & by what I have done tonight, I have not been Successful in gaining converts to my plain Sense view of Such Matters – I withdraw & shall not trouble them again untill I perceive a more favorable opportunity for taking a public part =

*2 July 1844.* Those who wish to have me with them are in a fidget, they perceived that I was not pleased with the progress of Events yesterday & they apprehended that I might have no more to do with them – that in fact was my intention – but Lord Kenyon came as moderator this morning & begged me to go with him to Lord Powis & talk the matter over with him Which I did to my great inconvenience as I go away tomorrow & have much to do = The Committee met today and the farther consideration of the 3rd reading is postponed to the 8th: precedents were of course found for obtaining the Sovereign's assent to the discussion of measures affecting the regal privilege but no instance was found of

[239] The phrase 'unworthy manoeuvre' was picked up by *The Times* in an editorial comment on 2 July 1844.
[240] Newcastle's speech was noticed by *The Times*, 2 July 1844, but not reported. It was not heard by reporters amidst the noise in the Lords.
[241] it precedes this in the original.

denial of assent – I shall not attend future debates [,] it is useless & nothing will be done, but by the will of the Duke of Wellington –

*7 July 1844.* Nothing particular – The Ministers have been well Jostled in the House of Commons where Peel in particular behaved very ill upon the Poor Law discussion & Lord John Manners took him up well & Spiritedly = He was Eventually forced to do what was right – as he was a Short time Since to declare himself in favour of protection to agriculture – These are lessons which will do him good to [a] certain degree & to that Extent may Keep him in order = He learns that he is not to be Dictator – But this is a miserable manner of conducting the affairs of the Country –

*12 July 1844.* The Government has given way & has granted a Secret Committee in both houses to investigate the case of opening letters in the Post Office by the Secretary of State [James Graham] – I am convinced that this concession is wrong – at first ministers, tried to crush the question with a high hand but they Subsequently lowered their tone & Sir Robert Peel went so far as to Say that he yielded to Enquiry in consequence of the public Excitement which had been created, which rendered Enquiry necessary = this is Establishing a very dangerous precedent in these lucklist [*sic* – luckless] times[242] –

*13 July 1844.* Lord Powis has abandoned his bill & has withdrawn his motion to read the bill a third time – I think it right to withdraw the bill under the abominable circumstances which attend it = but the abandonment ought to have been accompanied by the severest Strictures & remonstrances & appeals – & a declaration that he would adopt Every mode to Effect his great object, & he ought immediately to have moved the House to address the Queen to permit the parliamentary discussion of the bill – This is a crest fallen termination –

*20 July 1844.* [...] They are hurrying over the business in a most indecent manner having Wasted the last 6 months in doing next to nothing, but mischief –

*24 July 1844.* Bills of the most exceptionable nature are being hurried through the House of Commons as if they had been postponed to this period in order that they might be almost Smuggled through the house without notice or debate = in the House of Commons Peel moved a grant of £8000 to finish the Nelson Monument, although he will not move for a Shilling for the Church – In the House of Lords the Chancellor is handing bills through which are quite abominable, one brought in by Lord Beaumont for removing Every Species of remaining disability to Roman Catholics has passed through Committee – If the bill passes – Popery Will display itself openly over the face of the Country, & outrage the Protestant feeling, whilst doubtless it will gain many converts by its Shew & Specious pretensions – I deeply lament that I have not been able to live in London this Season, that I might have Watched these proceedings & Spoken my Mind about them –

*1 August 1844.* To my view of the matter all is going politically wrong with us as far as the Government is concerned, their measures are really abominable, & not only do the

---

[242]The scandal arose when it was revealed that the British government, at the behest of the Austrian government, had opened letters sent to the Italian nationalist Giuseppe Mazzini, who was then resident in London.

principals do wrong themselves, but they patronise & adopt it in others – Lord Beaumont brings in a bill to relieve Roman Catholics from Every remnant of check & control – & the power of the [Lord] Chancellor is Exercised in its favour & Straight away the bill passed = opposed in report by the Bishop of London [Charles James Blomfield] but nothing more, & he did not divide the House – all sorts of measures are now passing through both Houses of Parliament [when] there are not 20 members in attendance & bills pass that no one Knows any thing of – this is truly shameful –

*5 August 1844.* I wrote to [my son] William yesterday – to tell him that I had applied to Lord aberdeen to advance him but without much prospect of Success – Lord a's answer is obliging & civil which is more than Some are – but he holds out no promise of any immediate promotion[243] –

*7 August 1844.* The Queen was yesterday morning delivered of a Prince [Alfred] – Both are as well as possible, & Her Majesty is So well that the Physicians do not mean to publish any bulletins –

*11 August 1844.* The Session of Parliament is now over = by adjournment [.] The House of Lords to the 2nd September [,] the Commons to the 5th September [.] This unusual termination is for the purpose of receiving the opinion of the Judges on the law case referred to them of O'Connell's writ of Error – as to whether the trial was or was not fairly & legally conducted – Mr [Richard Lalor] Shiel in his last Speech has the impudent Effrontery to call the Jury (because Protestant) a Sectarian Jury – In my opinion these fellows ought not to be permitted to hold Such language – I Should like to see them taught to think & Speak with decency & decorum, & not to be permitted to insult at their pleasure, the Established Religion of the Country –

*12 August 1844.* Joseph Bonaparte [,] formerly King of Spain, is dead – His Brother Louis, once King of Holland [,] is now the head of that family & his Son [Louis] is now a prisoner at Havre – for Endeavouring to incite a rebellion in France –

*14 August 1844.* The King of Prussia [Frederick William IV] has issued a very amiable & paternal letter to his Subjects, thanking them for the Kind interest taken in his personal Safety, by his Escape from the assassin's attempt who fired two pistols at him & which Struck him on the breast but did not wound him – His Brother & heir [William], arrived in England today On a Visit – The King of France is Expected about the middle of September –

*24 August 1844.* It now appears that Mehommet ali [Muhammad Ali] is mad – at alexandria he Shut himself up & would not allow any one to come near him – he then Suddenly Started off for Cairo, & from thence declared that he would have no more to do with Egyptian affairs, & after that Suddenly went off to Mecca where he intends to reside – on his way he borrowed a very large Sum of money from an unfortunate Bey, who will never See his money again, & it is thought that the Exhausted State of his finances, is a cause

[243]BL, Add. MS 43243, ff. 114–15: Newcastle to Aberdeen, 31 July 1844; f. 120: Aberdeen to Newcastle, 3 Aug. 1844.

of his aberration = but persons who Saw him above two Years ago, declare that his mind was Evidently unsettled then – & there was sufficient cause for it in the then State of his political affairs – It is Said that his Son Ibrahim will not take the government upon himself & the Turkish Court dreads a fearful revolution in Egypt, Syria &c –

*25 August 1844.* By this days post we learn that the Viceroy of Egypt Mehemmet ali has changed his mind – he now renounces abdication, & has consented to give up his pilgrimage to Mecca – he was Expected in alexandria, the day after these accounts came away =

*3 September 1844.* The Judges have given their opinion upon O'Connells writ of Error – There is a difference of opinion among them upon Some clauses & other matters, but it does not [matter –] they all agree that it was a fair trial & the decision Just & right – & that the Sentence of the Court below (the Irish) Should be affirmed = Some remarks Were made by the Lord Chancellor [Lyndhurst] & other law Lords in the House[244] & the Consideration of the Judges opinion postponed to the 5th –

*6 September 1844.* It turns out that after debate the House of Lords has upset the Judges' opinion & has determined that the Judgment of the Irish Judges shall be reversed [.] Here is a pretty business – & how was it done – The Lord Chancellor [Lyndhurst] made a long Speech agreeing with the Irish Judges – Lord Brougham followed in the Same Strain [–] Lords Denman, Cottenham, Campbell were the other way [,] a division followed & numbers were Even – The Lord Chancellor alluded to the Embarassment [*sic*] of his Situation – & called for another division With the Same result = He then proposed a third division, & Lord Wharncliffe rose & Stated that "lay Lords Knew nothing of the matter & proposed that all lay lords should abstain from Voting & leave the house". There were not a dozen lords in the house – & he Knew, for he could see, that there were not five law lords in the house, 2 of whom were for & 3 against[245] affirming the decree of the Irish Court – This most impudent & unaccountable proposal, was adopted: the lay Lords left the house, & the majority of the 3 adverse law lords of course decided the question & O'Connell is now at large & to be liberated forthwith.

It is impossible to conceive a proceeding more fraught with Evil & mischief – both to the House of Lords & the Cause of public Justice – but upon the heads of the doers be all the responsibility & I Sincerely hope the Exclusive punishment = I am convinced that this Was a preconcerted trick – If the Government had chosen to Support the Judges & their own Irish attorney General [Thomas Cusack Smith] – of course nothing could have been Easier & more Sensible than to have required a Sufficient number of Lords to attend in their places, but no Such thing [,] they place themselves by trick & Collusion in a Situation to be out voted – & the result was certain & could not be mistaken –

*7 September 1844.* Parliament was prorogued on the 5th [–] a new writ was previously moved for Lord Stanley who has accepted the Chiltern hundreds & is to be called up to

---

[244] of House precedes this in the original.
[245] against precedes this in the original.

the House of Lords – & be the leader instead of the Duke of Wellington [who is] utterly unfit for the business –

*8 September 1844.* Condemnation of the late proceedings appears to be universal – Lord Wharncliffe meets with no Supporters in his unprecedented & most unconstitutional Suggestion to the lay Peers – all the Evil consequences which may & probably must arise from it, will overwhelm the Ministry – O'Connell may prosecute for false imprisonment & I do not Know what Else – & more over he may now agitate with impunity –

The news was received in Dublin with the Wildest & most heartfelt demonstrations of Joy, & preparations Were instantly Set on foot for a triumphal procession on the liberation of "The Liberator" –

*9 September 1844.* The Prince [William] of Prussia is returned to his own Country. The infant Prince was christened on the 7th alfred Ernest albert = The Queen & Prince albert are going to Scotland – They are to occupy Blair Castle in great privacy – The Prince will Shoot & the Queen ruralise in the beautiful country around the Castle –

*10 September 1844.* With his liberty O'Connell has resumed all his former habits & practices, & Something more – He talks most arrogantly & promises repeal – his language at any other time would be considered flagrantly Seditious but now it is all right & permissable – but a Crisis must arrive Shortly – & the day of reckoning will be awful –

Miss [Eliza] Peel is Said to be very ill So much So that Sir Robert Peel left the Queen at Woolwich Just as She Was about to Embark, & went off immediately to Drayton Manor –

*1 October 1844.* nothing very new – O'Connell is resuming his full Swing in Ireland –

*2 October 1844.* The Duke of Grafton is Just dead – He was 85 –

The Queen in her Steamer passed this place [Bridlington] today at 12 o'clock on her return from Scotland – She was accompanied by 4 other Steamers – there were many Ships in this bay at the time, & the scene was remarkable for animation & interest –

*8 October 1844.* The principal topic for public attention[246] is the Election of Vice Chancellor of Oxford which [is] made of importance by [the] Church party – Dr [Benjamin Parsons] Symonds of Wadham is the man proposed by the Church party – & he is opposed by the whole body of the Puseyites – but I trust & So must Every friend of the pure Church, that these last cannot be Successful.

*9 October 1844.* The King of France arrived at Portsmouth yesterday morning & Soon after left for Windsor[247] – He [is] described as being loaded with presents & determined to outdo the magnificence of the Emperor of Russia – a fine thing for the Court retainers –

*11 October 1844.* The papers are full of the King of France's Visit – today a Chapter of the Garter is to be holden – if I had been there I Should have had to introduce His Majesty as

[246]for public attention precedes this in the original.
[247]~~London~~ precedes this in the original.

one of two Senior Knights – I Excused myself alledging [*sic*], which is the case, that I am not well –

a report of the Quarter's revenue Just published, Shews[248] a considerable Encrease, as it is Said but the accounts were so lately received that they could not be printed in the newspaper of this Evening –

*12 October 1844.* […] Dr Symonds was Elected Vice Chancellor for Oxford by an almost unanimous majority – the opposition was factious & disgraceful & must damage their bad cause –

*14 October 1844.* Lord Ellenborough is arrived at Portsmouth from India –

*15 October 1844.* The King of France is returned to France – He has conducted himself admirably here – & gained great Esteem – The Queen & Prince albert go with him to Portsmouth, go half way over the Channel in company, & then go to the Isle of Wight to pass a Short time –

*16 October 1844.* Lord Ellenborough has been created an Earl: rather a curious termination of his Eastern career, after having been So unceremoniously Expelled from his Government –

*17 October 1844.* The King of France was unable to Sail from Portsmouth on account of the boisterous weather: he waited for Several hours & then left for Dover meaning to go over to Calais – Which he accomplished the next day & has arrived Safely in France –

*24 October 1844.* […] The Queen is returned to Windsor – Her Majesty Seems much inclined to be restless & locomotive –

*29 October 1844.* The Papers are filled with accounts of the Queen's procession into the City [of London] to open the Royal Exchange – it was Supposed to have gone off well & to have produced a very good Effect —

*6 November 1844.* It is considered to be very probable, indeed almost inevitable that Otho King of Greece will be deposed, his conduct is So foolish & tyrannical, absolute perhaps – that when he again Endeavours to resume his absolutism, the patriotic party will quietly & immediately depose him = a fate Which he Justly merits, & I hope that the Greeks will choose their own Sovereign & make the crown hereditary –

*8 November 1844.* I received a few lines from [my son] William yesterday informing me that there was a vacancy at Vienna & wishing me to write to Lord aberdeen for the appointment – I have done So this day in urgent terms – but I Shall be most agreeably Surprised if my anticipation of unsuccess Should prove groundless[249] –

---

[248]~~States~~ precedes this in the original.
[249]BL, Add. MS 43243, ff. 288–9: Newcastle to Aberdeen, 8 Nov. 1844.

*9 November 1844.* Changes in the Cabinet are talked of in the resignations of Lords Ripon & Haddington – but no difference will be made as Some of the lower ones will be Elevated in higher posts –

*16 November 1844.* The Queen has returned to Windsor from Burley [Burleigh] – Her Majesty has adopted a curious fashion of turning her host out of his[250] house & occupying it herself – Lord & Lady Exeter & family went to Stamford whilst the Queen was at Burley – rather an odd mode of paying a Visit –

*23 November 1844.* I have been invited to Windsor Castle to attend the Chapter of the Garter on 12th of next Month – but I Shall Excuse myself =

*26 November 1844.* News is arrived from america – The Elections for President are sufficiently closed to make it certain that a Mr [James] Polk is the President Elect, beating Mr [Henry] Clay [,] the best man in the Republic = a first rate Orator & man of ability – Polk is a perfectly unknown & untried man & is brought in by […] the Extreme republicans – it will create great Confusion – The accounts State that nothing could Exceed the infamy of the Elections, on both Sides – bribery, intimidation & false personation to a degree perfectly incredible –

In Canada the Elections are Said to be going Well, a decided majority for the Conservatives = the first time that it has been so – We may therefore hope that a new Era of prosperity may Commence in the train of the new Councels [*sic*][251] –

*30 November 1844.* The Effects of the late measures are now beginning to be Sensibly felt – The importation of cattle, and other animals [,] is greatly Encreased – above 70 head of live fat cattle were imported into Hull from Holstein last week & were all Sold in Rotherham market to the great disgust & injury of the farmers – who loudly Complain – By the Batavier Steamer above 60 head of fat live cattle were imported into London the day before yesterday, besides quantities of Sheep & pigs – & many thousands of poultry, fowls, geese, turkies [*sic*] &c & loads of fruit, vegetables & potatoes – & this is done Every Week now – In fact the foreigner is Straining Every nerve to Supply our markets with Every thing from his Soil – If this is not political folly & suicide of the most insane description, common sense must decide – This I Know full well, that the nation will not long Endure it – if it did it would deserve to be ruined = Our Eyes are practically opening to the gross fallacy & hideous political quackery of the tariff, admission of Corn, timber & other free trade iniquities –

*1 December 1844.* […] The Princess Sophia of Gloucester is dead – She is Stated to have been about 72 years old – Her death was unexpected from any previous illness which threatened life –

*2 December 1844.* a most Serious hubbub is arising on Church matters – The Bishop of Exeters <u>indefinite</u> but attempted decision upon the case of one of his Puseyite Clergyman

[250]~~the~~ precedes this in the original.
[251] The Canadian Tories returned 41 seats against the Canadian Liberals with 40 seats and two independents.

[Reverend James Shore] has Caused alarm for the present & forethought for the future. The Clergy will now have to take up the matter & in conjunction with the laity to require the Bishops to reconsider the rubric & to Enforce uniformity, Something like this must be done or Endless Confusion & mischief Will Ensue[252] =

*3 December 1844.* The Ottoman Porte is wretchedly distracted in its Councils [–] it wishes to please all & is obliged to yield alternately to Every power – The hostility to Christians is very great & [,] Whenever & wherever the deed can be done, a Christian is Sacrificed to a Mogulman's hate –

*5 December 1844.* If the accounts in the papers are to be believed [,] a general strike of the Colliers is recommencing – If they are bent upon mischief, or rather if the political demagogues & leaguers are Seeking to make a bad use of these deluded men, this certainly is the time & Season for accomplishing their purpose = That it is their intention I have no doubt, & if it is their will, they may now find the way of creating the greatest confusion.

*9 December 1844.* The full rigor of winter prevails – Every thing is bound up & dead – With So little rain & moisture as we have had for nearly the whole year, it will be wonderful how things can Exist, & yet they look unusually well = There are many people out of Employment – this Severe Weather will be dreadful to them = provisions are cheap, if they can buy them – Wheat from 40 to 42s a quarter – meat under 6d a pound –

*10 December 1844.* Lord Limerick is dead at 87. His medical man, Mr [Martin] Tupper of London, the Eminent apothecary, who had attended upon him for 40 years, went to give his attendance as usual – on the day after Lord Limerick's death Mr Tupper was found dead in his bed at Lord Limerick's in [South Hill Park] Berkshire –

*11 December 1844.* Wrote to [my son] William today to tell him that my application to Lord aberdeen in his favor had been unsuccessful[253] –

*19 December 1844.* a list of Commissioners, has appeared in the Gazette,[254] of Charitable bequests &c in Ireland – in which [,] with the archbishop of armagh [John George de la Poer Beresford] at the head of the Commission [,] there are more Romanists than protestants & Several Roman Catholic archbishops & Bishops So Styled among the number [–] this is the first time that Such personages having been publicly acknowledged as most reverend & right reverend – The augury is by no means good or Satisfactory –

*20 December 1844.* The Bishop of Exeter & his writings & proceedings, occupies the public press & attention – His proceedings are causing very great confusion & doing inconceivable mischief –

---

[252]Shore was imprisoned for attempting to secede from the Church of England and officiate in his own chapel as a nonconformist minister.

[253]BL, Add. MS 43243, f. 289: Aberdeen to Newcastle, 16 [*sic*] Nov. 1844; N.U.M.D., Ne C 5647: Lord William Pelham-Clinton to Newcastle, 4 Jan. 1845.

[254]*The London Gazette*, 20 Dec. 1844.

*27 December 1844* [...] The Bishops of Worcester [Henry Pepys] & Salisbury [Edward Denison] have put forth Charges entirely opposed to the Bishop of Exeters views – & the Bishop of Exeter in a letter published & in yesterday's papers – wherein he abandons his position, gives up the Surplice, & in fact, though he does it in his own clever & dignified manner, Sounds a retreat[255] –

*31 December 1844.* The newspapers announce that the Queen is again in <u>that interesting State</u> which will deprive her of the pleasure of her Yacht excursions in July & august next –

*4 January 1845.* News is arrived, from India, China &c – It has been well remarked that the Speed & facility of Communication is now So improved as to be a thing to wonder at – The King of France's Speech was <u>published</u> in London & in circulation <u>within 16 hours</u> after it was made to the Chambres – a feat that would have considered utterly impossible Even 5 years ago – The Indian mail has been brought from India & its details of very great length indeed, printed & published & circulated <u>within one Short month</u> – It is next to incredible =

In China trade is Encreasing & things going on well [–] the Chinese are fast losing their repugnance to intercourse with strangers – Commerce is flourishing & as it is Said the State of the Country very Satisfactory in India – we are proceeding peaceably & cultivating the arts & improvements of peace = The Marhattas however of the South & mountainous Countries, not very far from Bombay [,] have risen & become insurgent & are giving trouble & have caused some loss of life – Education it is Said, is attended to & is making progress – & a great canal of 275 miles long, called the Dovab Canal [Upper Bari Doab Canal] is to be made at an Expence of a $\frac{1}{4}$ of a million Sterling Which will be of incalculable benefit & advantage to the Country – affghanistan is Said to be Settled down in quiet under the rule of Dost Mahomed, a fact of vast importance to us & to them =

*5 January 1845.* To the regret of all who value distinguished merit, Sir William Nott, So celebrated in the unfortunate affghanistan War, is dead – He died on the 1st of January – to the great grief of the Welsh who idolised their hero – To shew their respect & regard the town of Carmarthen & neighbourhood intend to give him a public funeral – General Nott died at Carmarthen – he had an Estate near to it [Job's Well] where he Was building a residence – The State of his health had precluded his reception of the public honors which had been Shewn to the other distinguished officers who had Come over from India about the Same time –

*7 January 1845.* The quarter's Statement of the revenue Shews an Encrease on the quarter of nearly £500 000 = & on the year of £1,163,600 as compared with the preceding year[256] –

Sir Charles Metcalfe, Governor of Canada, is Said to be dying – The fatality of Canadian Governors is most Extraordinary – one after the other die in a very Short time after they become Established there =

---

[255] The letter was dated 23 Dec. 1844: *The British Magazine and Monthly Register of Religious and Ecclesiastical Information, Parochial History, and Documents Respecting the State of the Poor, Progress of Education, &c*, xxvii (1845), 68–9. Also see N.U.M.D., Ne2F/7/8: diary enclosure, 'Anglicanus' to the lord bishop of Worcester, 27 Dec. 1844.

[256] N.U.M.D., Ne2F/7/15: diary enclosure, state of the revenue from *The Morning Post*, 6 Jan. 1845.

*8 January 1845.* The Queen &c is going to the Duke of Buckingham's at Stowe, & not long after She will visit the Duke of Wellington at his very miserable residence [Stratfield Saye] –

*9 January 1845.* Received an answer from Sir Robert Peel to my letter written about ten days ago – in which he concurs in the principle of my Scheme for relieving properties in open & mineral counties, as in Wales – from the injurious pressure of the Crown rights, but very properly objects to my financial calculations – I having <u>merely</u> given millions instead of thousands by an Error of Calculation which fairly Shewed me to be a bungler in that art – If my Scheme can be So arranged as to make it worth while for properties to clear their lands from Crown rights & change them into a moderate rent to the Crown – a great & Essential good may be effected – & a very handsome revenue obtained for the Crown = The measure might be made very popular[257] –

*10 January 1845.* Murders are raging in Ireland Just now – it may be Said to be very prevalent Every where = So is Suicide, So is Sudden death –

*11 January 1845.* The Queen has Settled £1000 – a year upon Sir augustus D'Este that being the income which he lost by the Duke of Sussex's death. What an income for the Duke of Sussex to have bestowed upon his Son & [,] if given at all by the Queen, how much too little for her to settle – & the poor man is really in want –

*13 January 1845.* The accounts from all quarters are of the most flattering description – Revenue Encreased, trade flourishing, people Employed, distress diminished – Universal peace = Such is Stated to be our condition at the opening [of the] year – The statement may be rather overwrought but still it is not very far from the truth = and yet confidence is wanting – there are doubts on mens mind, there are apprehensions for the future, & many think present prospects deceitful – In these apprehensions, I must own, I participate – & am prone to think that appearances may be delusive, & the calm deceitful –

*14 January 1845.* The news of the day is. The Grand duchess of Mecklenberg Steling [the] Duke of Cambridge's daughter = was brought to bed of a Son who died immediately – the Duchess is doing well –
   The Irish archbishops & Bishops have put forth a Strong & Stirring manifesto against the present State education system in Ireland: it is an admirable document & must claim attention –

*15 January 1845.* after having Set his whole Diocese by the Ears, & done all possible mischief by a display of his authority in favour of Puseyism – he Suddenly has abandoned his position, in deference as he / the Bishop of Exeter / Says to the archbishop of Canterbury's letter, & now recommends his clergy to return to & proceed in the usual course of

---

[257] BL, Add. MS 40556, ff. 352–5: Newcastle to Peel, 30 Dec. 1844; 40481, ff. 307–8: Peel to Newcastle, 8 Jan. 1845; 40481, ff. 309–11: Newcastle to Peel, 10 Jan. 1845. For a parallel (and uncomplimentary) correspondence between Peel and Lincoln, see 40481, f. 305: Peel to Lincoln, 11 Jan. 1845; 40481, ff. 312–13: Lincoln to Peel, 12 Jan. 1845.

teaching & administration of prayer &c hitherto used by the Church of England[258] – The archbishop's letter is a poor milk & Water, balancing & neither one thing or the other piece of Composition = & will Evidently End in <u>dividing</u> the differences – in the most approved fashion of modern tactics & morality = & religion & politics & government –

*16 January 1845.* The Morning Herald tells us that Sir Charles Metcalfe is to be a Peer – if So – he is the first peer created by Sir Robert Peel = & why this peculiar choice is made, is not very intelligible = Sir Charles has done well [,] I believe, at all Events he has always done his best – but no Signal Services have been rendered & Even if they had why add to the overloaded peerage = & make that the only recompense or reward for doing duty well [?] –

*18 January 1845.*[259] […] Sir Charles Metcalfe is gazetted as a Peer by the title of Baron Metcalfe – Mr [John Harvey] astell tells me that he is not married & is afflicted with a cancerous complaint which must very shortly destroy him – another Peer is to be created = Sir Nicolas Tyndall is to be titled [.][260]

*19 January 1845.* Some changes are to take place in the Government offices. Lord Ellenborough is to be 1st Lord of the admiralty – & Lord Haddington, much to the regret of the navy I believe, goes to the Board of Control – Which Lord Ripon resigns, & retires altogether – he is in declining health –

*20 January 1845.* The Queen's Visit being over – The Duke of Buckinghams' great ambition – The Duke Shuts up Stowe, & is to live at Wootton [Wotton House] upon £10,000 a year = He is now done up – Since his father's death he is Said to have laid out £75,000 on Stowe, fitting & furnishing &c –

There is a report that the Queen is to Send a Message to Parliament Soon after the Meeting begging that the title of King may be given to Prince albert – I trust that there is [no] foundation for this report – it would be very distasteful, & I trust would be Stoutly opposed –

---

[258] *The Ecclesiastical Gazette, or, Monthly Register of the Affairs of the Church of England*, vii–viii (1845), 149 reproduces the bishop of Exeter's letter, dated 8 Jan. 1845.

[259] BL, Add. MS 40558, ff. 49–50: Newcastle to Peel, 18 Jan. 1845. The letter was finished on 20 Jan. 1845. It contained Newcastle's recommendations for applying surplus revenue; either by committing £1m for church building, or by remitting impositions such as the window tax, the legacy duty, stamp duties on deeds of transfer of property, auction duty, the duty on post horses and hack chaises: 'You cannot Spare the Malt tax, & in my humble Judgment its abolition would but little benefit the Farmers'. In his reply, Peel rejected a grant for church building: 'The difficulty of persuading Parliament to sanction Such an Expenditure Would at any time be Extreme – and it Certainly is not diminished by the Contentions and Divisions Which are So fatally disturbing the Peace of the Church and Exercising Such an injurious influence on Society', 40558, ff. 51–2: Peel to Newcastle, 22 Jan. 1845. Newcastle acknowledged Peel's letter and gave fuller details of his church building scheme in a letter which Peel did not acknowledge: 40558, ff. 55–9: Newcastle to Peel, 24 Jan. 1845. Lincoln, having seen this correspondence, sarcastically recommended that his father be made chancellor of the exchequer – 'I am afraid the Financier had an eye to his own interest when he pressed the repeal of the stamp duties on <u>deeds of transfer of property</u> and of the <u>Auction–duty</u>. He has at any rate <u>benefitted</u> the <u>State</u> by his contributions to a larger amount than Most Men on these two heads': 40558, ff. 53–4: Lincoln to Peel, 23 Jan. 1845.

[260] *The London Gazette*, 17 Jan. 1845.

*21 January 1845.* The Queen is gone to Strathfield Saye to pay a visit to the Duke of Wellington – his Brother Lord Mornington is dangerously ill & may die at any hour –

Lord St Germans is dead at an advanced age – this will take Lord Eliot away from the Secretary's post in Ireland – What will or can they give him here [?] –

*22 January 1845.* In the absence of any thing more Entertaining the newspapers are full of the Queen's Visit =

*24 January 1845.* among the many who are dying [,] Lord Mornington is one – he fortunately has Survived during the Queens Visit to the Duke of Wellington – The iron Duke has taken care not to <u>rain</u> himself in preparation for the Queen = In this I must own he is right –

*25 January 1845.* a Judge, [John] Gurney, has resigned – & a good many law changes will be consequent upon this resignation –

*26 January 1845.* Religious differences are our leading bane just now – & they are as rank as ever – Still the Surplice party is obliged to Succumb to the popular opinion, by no means Equivocally demonstrated – & in this instance it is in Some degree fortunate, though in others liable to danger, that public opinion Should check very mischievous & pestilent innovations – The Bishop of Exeter has withdrawn from the contest & his clergy are retiring in like manner = but too much after the Parthian method[261] –

*1 February 1845.* Nothing new respecting the appointments, or any Confirmation of them[262] – So that I trust that as regards Lincoln it may be untrue = it would really be too Shocking for him, as my Son who have Ever Supported the Protestant Established Church of this Country, to Sit cuckoo like in Mr Gladstones' [Cabinet] Seat to espouse a cause which he feels the absolute necessity of abandoning, as one which no Christian & Churchman can assent to – Lincolns Career of undutifulness & office worship, Endeavouring to gain as much as he can of the world at the risk of losing his Soul is a wretched contemplation = He was once every thing that I could wish, my hope & my pride = His marriage with that vile woman his Wife [Lady Susan Hamilton] has been his ruin, & disregarding all my Counsels & throwing himself into unworthy hands has lost him = He is now a bad Son, & Exposes himself to all the ruin which attended absalom[263] or any other faithless & undutiful Son – God grant him a speedy view of his grievous Error, & Endue [*sic* – imbue] him with humble mindedness & contrition –

[261] The Parthian shot was feigning retreat to draw the enemy out, then turning and shooting at them when exposed.

[262] Gladstone informed Newcastle of his resignation from the government on 30 Jan. 1845 over the Maynooth Grant; Lincoln was rumoured as his successor. In the subsequent correspondence, Newcastle took the opportunity of expressing his disagreement with government policy: *Unhappy Reactionary*, 135–6; *Letters on Church and Religion of William Ewart Gladstone*, ed. D.C. Lathbury (2 vols, 1910), i, 168; BL, Add. MS 44261, ff. 96–9: Newcastle to Gladstone, 3 Feb. 1845; N.U.M.D., Ne C 11781: Gladstone to Newcastle, 5 Feb. 1845.

[263] Absalom was the third son of David, king of Israel. He was a great favourite of his father, but the pair were estranged. Absalom's fate was used to warn against false ambition, vainglory, and unfilial conduct.

*2 February 1845.* no more account of the changes – Parliament opens on the 4th & arrangements must be difficult & inconvenient – Office [concerns] have long beset & Enthralled
poor Lincoln & have Systematically stolen him away from me, his natural Chief, Earliest
& Surest friend & best adviser – but that Would not Suit their purposes – I do not Suit
them –

*4 February 1845.* […] I am still in hopes that Lincoln has not taken a Seat in the Cabinet
– it would be ruinous to him – I wish from my Soul that he had more independent & a
higher mind – but he is too much like an office clerk, & has all the pedantry of a mere
official drudge – He Sees nothing beyond Office & gaining a majority, never mind how –
in the House of Commons = If we [*sic* – he] could & would take a high line I Should be
proud of him = as he is he annoyes [*sic*] me beyond measure – to See him the tool of Such
fellows as he assorts with vexes me to the Soul –

*5 February 1845.* The Queen opened the Parliament yesterday in person. The [Speech] has
arrived – it is as usual a meagre production – but there [are] Some objectionable things in
it. Some of it is really twaddle – The debates will be given tomorrow –
    I observe by the lists of those attending the Cabinet Counsels that Lincoln is really put
into the Cabinet [as First Commissioner of Woods and Forests] – as he has no Experience, & has done nothing to distinguish himself above others & can be little beneficial
in council [,] Such an Elevation is as useless as it is uncalled for – this I must in candour
State –

*6 February 1845.* The debates on the 4th were carried to considerable length – much was
Said by Several respecting the distress among the tenant farmers & laborers – & a determination Expressed that the Government Should be made to attend to their interests
– much was also Said about the intended advancement of the Roman Catholic Church
& its votaries – Sir Robert Peels' language was strong & determined & most authoritative, as if he Knew that he could not only call but make, black, white – but this ground
will be disputed & by God's blessing, he may be made to rue his misdeeds – I think him
Scheming [,] plausible & dishonest – I may do him injustice, but my belief is that I am not
wrong – the Sequel will Show[264] =

*7 February 1845.* Scarcely any thing or rather nothing worthy of record – as concerns
myself, it Seems that all I undertake fails & that I am doomed to disappointment, whilst
others Succeed without any difficulty & almost as a matter of Course – This is all very
afflicting & very trying, but my unshaken trust is in God, & He has good reasons for what
is done – Possibly my turn may Come Some day, & if not here perhaps hereafter I may hear
the blessed words – ["] Well done thou tolerably good but faithful Servant Enter thou into
the Joys of thy Lord ["][265] –

---

[264] Newcastle had engaged in another attempt to advance his private concerns with Peel, who gave them short
shrift: BL, Add. MS 40558, ff. 402–5: Newcastle to Peel, 30 Jan. 1845; 40558, f. 406: Peel to Newcastle, 1 Feb. 1845.
    [265] From the parable of the talents: Matthew, 25: 23.

*12 February 1845*. The Opposition is Endeavouring to flag up Something which Shall discomfit or rather discomfort the Ministers – but all these gentlemen are So little respected or looked up to, that nobody heeds or attends to them –

*14 February 1845*. […] By the accounts issued from the national Debt office, which have just appeared – the results of the operations upon the Debt from 1822 to 1844 – Show the total annual interest Saved during that period amounts to 3,051,600 £ – also accounts of unredeemed public debt from 1817 to 1844 & the amount of unfunded debt in Exchequer bills – from which it appears that in 1817 the capital of the unredeemed funded debt was 1,796,200,191 £ & the annual Charge 29,842,814 £ – while in 1844 the former was 772,169,092 £ – & the latter 28,516,882 £ – The amount of capital in Exchequer bills in 1817 was 44,650,300 £ & the interest 2,173,927 £ – while in 1844 they were respectively 18,407,300 £ – & 594,851 £ –

*16 February 1845*. In his financial Speech Sir Robert Peel States that on the 5th of april he will have a Surplus of [£] 5,000,000 – He proposes to Encrease the navy by 4000 men & putting more Ships in commission, & making new Steam docks – & an Encreased Estimate for the Ordnance to repair & improve our defences – Some duties he reduces – on Sugar, 1,300,000 on Export [–] Coal 118,000 – Other duties he proposes Entirely to remit – So that no duty will in future be paid. on Staves 320,000 – Cotton wool 680,000 – auction duty 300,000 – Glass 640,000 [–] being a total reduction of £3,358,000 – besides the Extinction of I think 430 articles of import included in the last tariff – He proposes to continue the Income tax for 3 years longer – These are the main features of the Speech = nothing Said about the appropriation of Some of the Surplus to the building of[266] Churches – an act which would bring a Sure & plenteous blessing with it to the nation – nor any intimation or Expression in favor of benefitting & promoting the culture of the Soil = The first a blasting omission – the second an ungrateful & most impolitic neglect & which will Ere long recoil upon the Minister –

*17 February 1845*. Mr [William George] Ward has been condemned by Oxford Convocation, & has been deprived of his degrees &c [–] in Short is Expelled from the University & the Church – as he most richly deserves –
 The Stone altar case has been decided also = & has been adjudged to be unlawful – & is to be removed = in consequence the Camden[267] Society who were the perpetrators of the deed, is[268] about to dissolve itself – The meddling mischief of its members has been offensive & Culpable – These restless innovators are the pest of these times[269] –

*19 February 1845*. Peel's financial & other measures, & railroads [,] Engross the public attention – Many praise, very many dare not complain of the all powerful Minister = I told

[266]~~which~~ precedes this in the original.
[267]~~[Camden] Club~~ precedes this in the original.
[268]~~are~~ precedes this in the original.
[269]The Camden Society installed a stone altar and credence table in the Round Church, Cambridge, which was condemned as popish. The vicar, Richard Faulkner, brought a case against them in the court of arches. The judgment (delivered on 31 Jan. 1845) ordered that the altar be removed and replaced by a wooden table. The society was dissolved and was replaced by the Ecclesiological Society in 1846.

him that during this Parliament he may do any thing[270] – In my opinion his policy is based upon the most unsound & mischievous fallacy – above all he deserts Religion & the Land – an ingratitude which must at Some time cause his downfall – In the mean time he is omnipotent & overbearing =

*20 February 1845.* The Marquis of Westminster died on the 17th at his grand place Eaton hall – he was 78 = & I believe had had very little previous illness – when I last Saw him, he appeared to be active & hearty = His wealth, must be immense –

*21 February 1845.* Little going on but parliament work – There, that is the Commons – Sir Robert Peel is transcendent – He rules the roost most Supremely & carries all before him – He makes black white, turns Every thing inside out, wills & it is done, transforms supposed impossibilities into Simple realities & in short pro hac vice[271] is omnipotent – His power is most wonderfully Encreased & yet he is distrusted & unpopular [–] his whole system is one of bold & daring Experiment the very opposite of Every thing that has preceded it – & may be Justly considered most fearful – Paradoxes Sometimes prevail, but if they fail – how dreadful & anarchical will be the State of the Country – & yet Strange to Say there is not a man capable or bold or honest Enough to oppose him = There is Something beyond human ken in all this – & when one contemplates the Extent to which a powerful & dangerous man may carry his mischievous & revolutionary doings, it makes one Shut one's Eyes & Shudder as if on the brink of a precipice –

*22 February 1845.* The Debates in the House of Commons are Very warm – The Ministerial side assume a very high tone, & the opposition are greatly nettled & very personal & aspreous [*sic* – asperous] – The Session is likely to be a very violent one –

*25 February 1845.* […] The Duke of Hamilton must be in Extasies [*sic*] of delight & pride – The <u>Grand</u> Duchess Stephanie of Baden is arrived [&]was received by His Grace & Lord Douglas & Escorted to Portman Square where this great personage is to be the Duke's guest – & all England will Know it for it is published in full length in the papers – !!!

*28 February 1845.* […] a pompous & minute account of the State reception to the Queen of the Duchess Stephanie of Baden – altogether a very mockly royal & farcical affair – She proceeded <u>in State</u> in <u>two</u> of the <u>Duke of Hamilton's</u> carriages to Buckingham Palace where She was received by Sundry Officers & conducted to the Queen – there was afterwards a grand banquet – in honor of Stephanie –

*2 March 1845.* Little passing of much interest – a contention going on in the House of Commons whether Sir James Graham – Secretary of State, Shall be allowed to open letters in the Post office <u>or not</u> – as he pleases – & give no account of his proceedings – The Ministerial bottle holders & parasites uphold the practice & defend Sir James & do themselves

---

[270]BL, Add. MS 40558, f. 57: Newcastle to Peel, 24 Jan. 1845. See above, 18 Jan. 1845.

[271]For or on this occasion only.

no honor – the practice is an odious & intolerable one & ought to be defined & restricted with great precision –

*7 March 1845.* Sir Robert Peel announces his intention of moving to remove Jewish disabilities & to allow them to Sit in Corporations !!! what next I should like to Know [?] – of Course that they should sit in Parliament [–] as I often Said, this Man in his plenitude of power & absolutism will be the Ruiner of his Country – no one can feel better disposed towards the Jews, than I am – but I should consider it to be an insult to God & my Country to Confer upon them political power – & Simply, because they are not Christians –

*8 March 1845.* Mr [William] Williams as appears by report in the papers – had a motion on the books for the 6th to enquire into the nature of the transaction by which a sale had been made to me by the Crown amounting to between 10 & 1100 £. For Some [unaccountable] reason this Williams was not in the House & Mr Joe [Joseph] Hume took up his friends motion & moved for the production of papers which he named – Lincoln then made a Statement of the transaction which was plain & true, & of Course carried conviction with it – but in his anxiety to clear & Vindicate himself, he forgot me – & though he has made it appear that he acted with Stern honesty – yet he left it open for public Speculation & doubt whether I had not Endeavoured to gain what ought not to be granted to me – I must therefore write a public letter of Explanation – Since I have no communication Whatever with him – for he has communicated nothing to me Even upon this subject which So intimately concerns & must So deeply interest me – But alas so it is ![272] –

*9 March 1845.* It is Evident that in the midst of the most unexampled Success Sir Robert Peel & others are conducting themselves so imprudently by their arrogance & growing self confidence that a feeling Very unfavorable & consequent resistance is arising –

*10 March 1845.* There is a report that there are to be more changes in the Ministry – Mr [Henry] Goulburn is said to be about to resign upon religious grounds, why I cannot justly perceive, for He voted with Peel for Roman Catholic Emancipation [in 1829] & What is now to be done, though heinous & guilty [,] is a flea bite in Comparison to that measure of natural iniquity – Others are Said to be about to resign on the Same grounds –

*12 March 1845.* The Lord Chancellor [Lyndhurst] has dared to bring in a bill for the removal of Jewish disabilities – & their Lordship's will Submit to & pass it, as will the Commons where Peel proposes it to them [.] It is truly lamentable to See how things go on, if we were a Heathenwise Nation, we might take the Same course – No one can be better disposed towards the Jews than I am, but as I have before written I should consider it a Sin to give a Jew political power in a Christian country & Especially in one were [*sic*] a representative System prevails – The State plea of an anomaly is the Excuse. The Quakers [,] Nemarians

---

[272] The motion was for 'Copies of all Surveys and Valuations of 7,438 acres, 36 roods of land belonging to the Crown, adjoining to the Duke of Newcastle's Hafod Estate, in Cardiganshire, which has been sold to his Grace by private contract for £1,049 15s. 9d., by Her Majesty's Commissioners of Woods, Forests, and Land Revenues': Hansard, *Commons Debates*, 3rd ser., lxxviii, cols 398–407, 432–40, 6–7 Mar. 1845; see *The Times*, 8 Mar. 1845, for a letter from Newcastle's estate agents, Daniel Smith and Son, defending his conduct.

& others are not bebarred [*sic* – debarred] from political power – why should the Jews [?] – I would answer, ["] do not remedy one Evil by creating another – deprive the Quakers &c of a power which they cannot Exercise with advantage to the State ["] = it is the principle that I Contend for the sects are too little numerous to do injury – Even in parliament –

*26 March 1845.* a letter which I wrote after having reads Messrs Hume & Williams' motion, & remarks & insinuations about the Hafod purchase of the Crown, has appeared in the Standard newspaper, but much after the proper time – the delay has arisen from the liberty which I gave him to the Editor [Stanley Lees Giffard] who I Know, to publish or Suppress, to curtail or alter or correct, as he thought best: at first he thought it would be unnecessary to print the letter – He Subsequently Shewed the letter to a friend & he advised him to publish it = it was then Sent to me in a printed form, I corrected the press, & altered a good deal – & finally in that Shape it appeared in last night's Standard – with reasons in the leading article for not having published Sooner – the date being the 12th of this month[273] –

*27 March 1845.* The appearance of my letter, has caused many well-wishers to write to me[274] – nothing can be more Satisfactory & truly gratifying than these letters – their tone is precisely that which if I could have devised it I Should have of all things desired –

*28 March 1845.* […] I continue to receive numerous most truly gratifying letters from perfect Strangers, but Evidently good & true men – It is Every thing to me = I shall Keep these documents amongst my most precious archives – I would not change my situation for any other in the Kingdom –

*29 March 1845.* It gives me the truest gratification to perceive that the general opinion is in favor of the views which I take: it Evidently is not worn out, but only repressed by the newly fangled doctrines which have been promulgated, by most public men of the latter, Especially of the present day.

*30 March 1845.* I continue to receive letters & papers from Various quarters[275] –

*3 April 1845.* Railroads occupy public attention almost Exclusively but another Subject has arisen of deep interest – The Ministerial intention to Encrease the grant to Maynooth – Sir Robert Peel brings it on this night in the House of Commons – Petitioning in all quarters is most general, & public feeling is deeply Excited =

*5 April 1845.* Sir Robert Peel has brought forward his popish Scheme as regards Maynooth – & [*sic*] Endowment of £27000 a year Settled [–] an Enlargement of their power of tenure of lands to £3000 a year – an incorporation of the College – & an additional grant for the

[273]See Appendix A. *The Standard*, 25 Mar. 1845; N.U.M.D., Ne C 8212/1: Giffard to Newcastle, 27 Mar. 1845. For its publication, see Ne C 7463, 8216: James Leith to Newcastle, 24, 28 Mar. 1845.

[274]N.U.M.D., Ne C 8211: William Henderson to Newcastle, 26 Mar. 1845; Ne C 8594/1–2: Daniel Smith and Son to Newcastle, 31 Mar. 1845.

[275]N.U.M.D., Ne C 8228: N.R. Macdonald to Newcastle, 3 Apr. 1845; Ne C 8232: J. West to Newcastle, 8 Apr. 1845.

year of £30000 = This will do, I presume [,] & Show our Premier in his true colours – but will the Nation Endure it? I think not – Their feelings are too Strongly Excited to permit a relapse & at present they are quite up in arms[276] –

*7 April 1845.* […] we ourselves are not unlikely to be involved in war – The american presumption & attempts to Swindle us out of the Oragon [*sic*] Country has wrung from Sir Robert Peel & Lord aberdeen expressions of a very warlike & determined character –

*13 April 1845.* […] I did not open my post bag untill Very late – its contents were Such as to rouse & invite me to immediate action, & I wrote a hurried & possibly not Sufficiently considered address to "My Countrymen" on the present state of affairs Especially as regards the Encouragement of Popery – which I sent off without Copying, to be inserted in all the papers in order that it may be Speedily & generally circulated throughout the Kingdom – I wish it may produce the effect which is intended[277] –

*15 April 1845.* […] I have been much hurt to learn the death of [the] Marquis of Down-shire who when riding over part of his Estates in Wicklow accompanied by his Son Lord Edwin & his Steward, suddenly fell off his horse, <u>dead</u> – He was deservedly, Exceedingly [,] Esteemed & respected, & in these times, Such a man can be ill Spared in Ireland where he has always manfully & prudently taken the proper course –

*16 April 1845.* an address which I wrote to the people of England on the 13th has been inserted in all the papers = my object is to rouse them to a sense of their situation, & to induce them with as much unanimity as can be obtained to apply an instant & Effective remedy to Peel's unparalleld [*sic*] & most perfidious aggressions – I Should not have at-tempted this had I not been led into it by the fact made Known to me So very generally lately, that amongst the commonalty of England at all Events, I possess a host of friends & supporters, who Esteem me & have long valued & admired my Exertions & faithfulness in Every right cause – these are their general Expressions – I Shall now prove their Sincerity, for I make, I am aware, a very unusual call upon them to adopt a very unusual course – by God's blessing & aid I hope to Succeed in my daring attempt –

*17 April 1845.* To my shame & unspeakable regret Lincoln has made a Speech upon the Maynooth measure throwing himself headlong into it, identifying himself with all its Evils & great Evil doer, & Kicking over Every principle on which he has been educated & to which I believed him to be firmly attached – but this follows from being connected with bad men & deserting the Councils & his allegiance to his Parent & best friend – I am grievously & deeply hurt at this – His Speech has done him no credit in any point of view – it was wholly unnecessary & might have been well Spared – for it was a mere

---

[276] For local opposition at Newark, see *Unhappy Reactionary*, 136; N.U.M.D., Ne C 9258: T.F.A. Burnaby to Lord Lincoln, 2 Apr. 1845; Ne C 9266: anti–Maynooth petition signed by 48 constituents from Bingham, Nottinghamshire; Ne C 8244: Godfrey Tallents to Newcastle, 22 Apr.1845; Hansard, *Commons Debates*, 3rd ser., lxxix, col. 522: 11 Apr. 1845.

[277] See Appendix A. N.U.M.D., Ne C 8235/1: draft address, dated 13 Apr. 1845; Ne C 6453: James Leith to Newcastle, 15 Apr. 1845.

repetition of what had been much better Stated by others, Weak, poor & unargumentative & Shewing no high range of view = as a Speech Even it has greatly disappointed me, no originality, no point, no Elevated Expression, or noble or generous warmth of feeling – With a very Strong memory & now too much confidence, he thinks length of Speech of more consequence than matter, & a repetition of trite Statements a fit Substitute for Eloquence – like most converts he is unusually Strenuous in asserting his adhesion to Peels' measures & his conviction of the Superexcellence of this one in particular – He never gave a more unhesitating Vote in his life –

*18 April 1845*. I receive many letters respecting my address[278] – I am at present doubtful how it will answer – at all Events the Struggle will be very Severe – I Shall write one more letter Embracing all that I think, fit to advance, & then Stop – more may cloy & become Stale – all that I desire to do is to call forth Such an Expression of public feeling & opinion as really Exist – not to create Either – one is lasting & Valuable – the other only of temporary consideration, which would Evaporate when the 9 days wonder is over –

*19 April 1845*. The plot thickens very fast, opinions & the holders of those opinions are becoming very warm & very Earnest indeed – the country is roused, a Serious Contest must arise, & between the Parliament & the People – The Question then arises ["] what is to be done [?"] I say, ["] Simply this – Let the people resolutely require their Representatives to Support their opinions & wishes, if they will not, then require them to resign ["] – but this most probably none will do – So that as long as this Parliament lasts a majority will be devoted to Peel – The People however must be firm & must protest over & over again with unflinching determination & then as Lord Manvers Says in his quaint way — ["] The firm of Bobby Peel & Co. which is fast breaking up, will Stop payment & be completely dissolved ["] – Then will come the immense Solution – Parliament will be dissolved & if the people of England will act Soundly, deliberately & with undeviating discrimination & Sufficiency of unanimity to Secure a desired result – we may hope for Such a Parliament as never was Known [,] aiding & approved of by the Nation, & irresistible only if representing & Enforcing that alone which is right & nationally beneficial – This is almost an Utopian idea, but if we are fit for it, by God's help it may be accomplished – Weak & feeble in intellectual Strength & wholly unversed as I am in matters of this Kind, & extraordinary as it may be in Every point of view, I cannot conceal from myself that if any one can be instrumental in accomplishing this end, I am probably the only man in the Country in a position to bring it about – I write this in the privacy of my Chamber & before the God who, for his wise purposes [,] may be conducting Such a frail & inefficient mortal as I know myself to be to perform deeds far beyond my presumed & Estimated Strength – The Single accident of my letter to the Standard may be the foundation of Events of a magnitude now quite uncontemplated by human Ken – Oh, that I had my Son with me & not against me in

[278] For reactions, see N.U.M.D., Ne C 6455: [n.d.] April 1845, George Purdy to Newcastle; Ne C 8236: 'A Churchman' to Newcastle, 16 Apr. 1845; Ne C 8240: W. Hastings Kelk to Newcastle, 19 Apr. 1845; Ne C 8247: John West Giles to Newcastle, 23 Apr. 1845.

the fulfillment of all that may be good, great, glorious [,] generous, Elevated & Christianlike !![279]

*20 April 1845*. after 6 nights animated discussion [,] the debate upon the Maynooth grant & Endowment is terminated − for the bill 2nd reading 323 [,] against it 176 [,] majority 147. It is a bad & grievous thing to witness − but punishment will fall upon the evil doers − Sir Robert Peel made a most weadling [*sic*], artful, Jesuitical Speech [,] able of course but replete with fallacies & dangerous doctrines − The debate has been most remarkable for the extraordinary Spirit, ability & Earnestness with which it has been Sustained on Each night of the discussion =

*21 April 1845*. No post from London today − I have received Several letters from the country, all hearty, approving & ready to lend Every aid in their power − one begs to be allowed to print & publish my letter for general circulation − On no former occasion have I Ever Known Such real interest & settled dislike to a measure as has been & still is manifested on this occasion − If men's minds are ripe or ripening, we may hope to accomplish great things =

*22 April 1845*. […] I have another address to the Nation nearly ready but I wish to reflect well before I issue this last address[280] =

*23 April 1845*. among the Schemes & proposals subjected to my Consideration &[281] approval one today from a Mr David Russell of York, Strikes me as Excellent & had never occurred to me − it is that Cities & Towns Should Send up Deputies with addresses to the Throne & to wait upon & present them to the Queen in person = It Seems to me that this must have its Effect − it must influence the Queen, & it will Shew the Minister that the Nation is against him & that it will not be trifled with − Peel is incurable & this is the only way to deal with him − as long as this parliament lasts & he remains in Office −

*24 April 1845*. I am very hardly worked Just now & have the greatest difficulty in Keeping pace with my Encreased correspondence & attending to my 2nd address which requires deep reflection & consideration − of course it will be critised [*sic* − criticised] by all, & I must be cautious to do no harm, if I do no good − I have not [been] able to answer of [*sic* − or] acknowledge a tithe of my correspondence −

*25 April 1845*. I sat up nearly all night that is to 6 this morning to finish my address − I shall now consider it well & Seriously − & probably make any alterations, additions & omissions − I do not altogether like it − I must be reconciled to it, before issuing it from the public press −

[279] Newcastle was supported by two of his other sons: N.U.M.D., Ne C 5609/1−2: Lord Charles Clinton to Newcastle, 25 Apr. 1845; Ne C 5649: Lord William Clinton to Newcastle, 22 Apr. 1845.

[280] The letter was written on the recommendation of Giffard, who had written to Newcastle on 18 Apr. 1845. See Appendix A.

[281] & precedes this in the original.

*27 April 1845.* Sir Robert Peel's Speech on Mr [Henry] Ward's motion [on Maynooth], is really, in my opinion, contemptible, it is absolutely & utterly unworthy of a Protestant Prime Minister & below his reputed & acknowledged talent as a debater –

*28 April 1845.* The ferment throughout the country is going on & Encreasing rather than diminishing – Today there is to be a meeting at York to consider whether they Shall Send two deputies with an address to the Queen & they mean to invite all other Cities & Towns in the United Kingdom to do the Same –

I Shall consider well, tomorrow, whether it may not be a fit time now to issue my Second address –

*29 April 1845.* Lord Castlereagh who never resides in Ireland & has nothing to live upon his allowance from his Father, has been appointed [Lord] Lieutenant of County Down in the room of Lord Downshire deceased – a most barefaced reward for voting with, & lauding to the Skies [,] Sir Robert Peel – & for risking his Seat in Parliament in a vile Cause – this is indeed political morality: but Sir Robert reckons that it will produce its Effect & make martyrdom a profitable rage [–] accordingly we find Lord Norreys devoting himself to the good cause & a candidate for martyrdom, in hopes of getting Something by it[282] –

*30 April 1845* […] Sir Robert Peel's Speech on Mr [Charles] Law's motion that the Endowment of Maynooth Shall not be taken from the Consolidated fund, was most Extraordinary, he really appears to be demented = glories in being opposed to the public opinion, & avows that whether in or out of office, he will never ceases [*sic*] to do Every thing in his power for the Roman Catholics – if this does not ruin him & his friends with the English people, I Know not what will – & this is the poor Queen's adviser[283] –

*2 May 1845.* Every day adds to the unpopularity of Sir Robert Peel – no one Ever more deserved a fall, like Lucifer's, never to rise again [,] than this perfidious man – I wish it may be soon at hand [.] The Queen & the nation have need to fear whilst we are in his power & Subject to his dark & pernicious intrigues –

*3 May 1845.* The debate on Lord Powis' motion to save the Sees of Bangor & St asaph came[284] on last night, it will probably be carried [,] as no doubt some arrangement has been made between Lord Powis & the Government[285] –

*4 May 1845.* Contrary to Expectation Lord Powis's motion was violently opposed by the Government & lost by a majority of 32 – numbers including proxies for 97 – against

[282] N.U.M.D., Ne C 5610: Lord Charles Clinton to Newcastle, 3 May 1845.

[283] At a meeting of the central anti–Maynooth committee on 30 Apr. 1845, Rev. H.L. Adams declared that he was seeing Newcastle, Lincoln, and Gladstone the following day: A.S. Thelwall, *Proceedings of the Anti–Maynooth Conference of 1845: With an Historical Introduction, and an Appendix* (1845), 68. Gladstone met a deputation from Newark on 1 May and discussed his position with Lincoln afterwards: *Gladstone Diaries*, iii, 451–2; *P.M.P. Gladstone*, ii, 277.

[284] came**s** in the original.

[285] N.U.M.D., Ne C 8243: Earl Powis to Newcastle, 22 Apr. 1845, enclosing a proxy which was subsequently entered in support of the Bill.

129[286] – I deeply regret this result = The Duke of Wellington Spoke in the most positive & unfeeling (iron) manner – Lord Stanley appears to have Spoken very well, with good feeling, & plenty of argument, but in my opinion from quite wrong conclusions & most decisively against any concession whatever – So that we have nothing to expect in the way of yielding –

*8 May 1845.* The Duke of Wellington has long been anxious for an heir to his honors & fame = His Eldest Son Lord Douro has been married Several years but has no children which has been a great disappointment to the Duke of Wellington [–] he induced his other Son Lord Charles to marry last year, & now he is made happy in being a grandfather to a grandson [Arthur Wellesley] – The birth took place the day before yesterday –

*10 May 1845.* No news of any consequence = Parliament is adjourned for the Whitsun holidays –

*11 May 1845.* Mr [Joseph] Hume has given notice of a call of the house for the 22nd with the intention of forcing O'Connell & the Irish Members to attend = who declare that they will not – & if the Sergeant at arms [Major-General Sir William Gosset] goes over to arrest them that they will Set him & his authority at defiance – but they will come over & will demand a hearing at the bar of the house for infringement upon the liberty of the Subject – it is thought that Peel will try to Stifle this motion from fear of collision with the Irish members. This is very likely, & would not be unworthy of the Jesuitical Peel[287] –

*13 May 1845.* I have such an infinity of writing & So much to do that I find myself very much behind hand in my work – & I may be obliged to go to London on the 19th [.]

*14 May 1845.* Busy writing letters in answer to the very many which are in arrear – afterwards took my 2nd address in hand & have been occupied till last [*sic* – late] at night revising correcting & adding to it – went to bed, late & not very well –

*15 May 1845.* Finding that there remained more to do at my address than I Expected [,] occupied the whole of the day & very hard too, with an unwilling mind & an aching head – at last I believed that I had got it all pretty well together & as well as I could make it, & sent it off late in the Evening, for London – perhaps it <u>may</u> but I fear it will not, be published on the morning of the 17[th]. I shall now be anxious to see it out – as the debate on the 3rd reading Maynooth bill, comes on on the 19th [.]

*16 May 1845.* I feel much relieved & more at liberty by having Sent off My address – but I am a good deal subdued by my Exertions [.] I was quite ill yesterday Evening – with a splitting head ache [–] a good night's rest has nearly restored me, with the addition of a good nosebleeding – my letters all continue to be most Satisfactory – & Some of them convey curious accounts of the State of the Country – My position Enables me, & I believe that

[286] The Contents were 97 (63 present and 34 proxies) against 129 (71 present and 58 proxies): majority 32.
[287] There was no House on the 22 May 1845 and Hume dropped his motion the next day.

I shall be the chief instrument in upsetting Sir Robert Peel & his government & possibly
of effecting the Subsequent regeneration of the Nation – it will be a glorious work, if God
Should give me grace & aid to Effect it –

*18 May 1845.* I have heard today from London that [James] Leith, after copying off my
address [,] had Shewn it, as I desired, to a qualified critic [George Croly], & very able man,
himself, a writer – & his opinion is, that it wants no alteration, & that it is in Every respect
calculated to Effect the purpose intended = the only alterations which he has made, being
to Erase Some portions wherein I have "Stated my pretensions too[288] lowly" [–] I am sorry
that he has done this, as what I wrote could only be felt by myself, & as a truth teller it
became me, although others might be good Enough to Estimate me more than I value
myself[289] –

*19 May 1845.* This day the 3rd reading of the Maynooth bill comes on in the House of
Commons – no doubt there will be a cloud of petitions from all parts of the country [–]
probably Such universal petitioning was never Known before – Peel I hope will perish [–]
he richly deserves any punishment –

*20 May 1845.* My public letter was published yesterday in the newspapers but unfortunately
full of blunders, omissions & mistakes – I am told that it was talked of & Considered all over
London & had made a considerable impression, & that it was thought to be not unlikely to
cause Some influence over the debate of last night – 3rd reading Maynooth bill in House
of Commons – So far so good – I have reason to be thankful for my Success = & to thank
God for permitting it = which would not be, if it were wrong[290] –

*21 May 1845.* The maynooth debate on the 3rd reading came on the 19th in the House
of Commons [–] Mr [George] Bankes spoke well & made the best & bold[est] Speech –
The house adjourned Early, a little before 12 – The Queen had a great Ball that night – &
many of the M.P.s no doubt attended it –

*22 May 1845.* The debate again adjourned = none of the Ministers Spoke on Either night
– Either Small or great = a great compliment to the Country & their Commons friends –

*23 May 1845.* The debate in the House of Commons is over – they divided between 2 &
3: yesterday morning – for the Maynooth bill 317 [,] against 184 [,] majority 133 – For
this majority Peel is indebted to his opponents – at least half his numbers, must have been

[288]in precedes this in the original.

[289]Croly is identified as the 'qualified critic' in N.U.M.D., Ne C 8280: James Leith to Newcastle, 'Saturday'
[17 May 1845]. Croly had earlier described Newcastle as 'a man who hates forcing or being forced forward' and
as 'a thoroughly honest man [who] may live to be a great shelter to the right cause in the day of trial': William
Ross Thompson, 'The Letters of George Croly to William Blackwood and his Sons', Texas Technological College
PhD, 2 vols, 1957, i, 145, 170. Also see Croly's 'Observations on the Duke of Newcastle's Letter [to Lord Kenyon]',
*Blackwood's Edinburgh Magazine*, xxv (1829), 67–71.

[290]For the publication's history, see: N.U.M.D., Ne C 8267–8, 8271, 8274, 8277: James Leith to Newcastle, 16,
19, 20, 24, 28 May 1845.

from the opposite Side of the house[291] – The only Ministers who spoke were Sir James Graham, & Sir Robert Peel = the chief argument of the first, that theology Should never be mixed up with politics or legislation = by the last – that the violent & Extraordinary opposition of the nation, only strengthened him in his greater determination to carry the bill – a Constitutional & worthy remark, truly, for a Prime Minister of England = & for which I trust that they will treat him, as he well deserves –

*25 May 1845.* […] as might be Expected, my last letter is being attacked in the newspapers = I am quite aware that there are many points of attack for an ill natured & ill conditioned writer or Speaker – but they cannot defeat what is advanced although they may quiz & Satirise – at this I oftener laugh, than feel hurt or offended – I am told by numbers that, it is very much liked & has made [a] great impression – people wish to have it published as a tract in a cheap form[292] –

*26 May 1845.* The second reading of the Maynooth bill [in the House of Lords] is fixed for the 2nd [of] June – I Shall have to go up for it = My present intention is to interrupt the debate by Stopping the Minister Soon after he has opened, by rising to order & Enquiring whether the Queen's Special permission has been obtained to debate the question[293] – if the reply may be in the affirmative, then I Shall Say that it cannot be done as it will be contrary to the coronation oath, act of Settlement &c – move that the debate be forthwith adjourned, having previously moved an address to the Queen praying Her Majesty to Consider what She is about & to retract Her consent – if it should be answered that they have not the Queen's consent, then I Shall move that the discussion be dropt [*sic*] & all farther proceedings in the bill Stayed – I shall be firm & Endeavour to fight my way through, this to me, very novel proceeding – & if I can I shall impart my Scheme to nobody, as Surprise will be Every thing – besides, it will be very amusing to play off upon the ministers their own trick upon the Bangor & St asaph bill last year – If I am foiled & overruled upon all these points, I shall then threaten a pro munire,[294] & this I think they will not be able to withstand, unless there may be objections with which I am not acquainted but if the act Still Exists = this measure comes clearly Within the act = I fear that I shall make but a lame figure in the business – but at all Events it will raise a debate & cause reflection, & I am sanguine Enough to think that it may be Successful –

*27 May 1845.* But little news besides gossip in the newspapers – Peel is losing more & more Every day = No minister Ever declined So fast – & no one Ever more rightly deserved a fall – I learn from London that about 57 Peers will be the amount of our minority – a gentleman has written to me to propose the Establishment of a Club on Sound Church &

---

[291] 169 Whig MPs and 148 Conservative MPs voted for the Bill.

[292] See *The Times*, 20 May 1845, for editorial comment.

[293] Hansard, *Lords Debates*, 3rd ser., lxxx, col. 1161: 2 June 1845, for Newcastle's intervention; N.U.M.D., Ne C 5688: Lord Robert Clinton to Newcastle, 5 June 1845.

[294] The Statute of Praemunire (16 Ric. II, c. 5), enacted in 1392, was intended to limit the powers of the papacy in England, by making it illegal to appeal an English court case to the pope if the crown objected, or for anyone to act in a way that recognised papal authority over the authority of the crown. It was not repealed until the 20th century.

State principles – & no doubt that it will be the best means of forming & maintaining a Sound party –

*28 May 1845.* Nothing new – all Seems to be peace & quietness at present, & no doubt Ministers think that they have overcome all their difficulties & Silenced all opponents –

*1 June 1845.* I am told today that we Shall have above 50 with us on a division – I am a good deal tired down & hope that I Shall be in better condition for the fight tomorrow – I have not yet prepared my notes, & finished my readings &c So that I shall be in considerable dread of unfitness –

*2 June 1845.*[295] Prepared myself as well as I could for taking a part in the debate of this night – The Duke of Wellington opened the debate in a Speech that Kept him upon his legs for full an hour – a specious, fallacious Speech – & well calculated to mislead – Several Spoke, the debat[e] adjourned at between 1 & 2 in the Morning[296] –

*3 June 1845.* The debate protracted to nearly 2 o'clock & again adjourned –

*4 June 1845.* after a long & animated debate we came to a division about 4 in the morning – our numbers on division were for Lord Roden's amendment – 59 against it [&] 155 [for it] – majority 96 – for the 2nd reading present 144 proxies 82 [ = ] 226 against it – present 55 proxies 14 [ = ] 69 – majority 157 – The debates on Each night were Kept up with very great Spirit – & very good Speaking – 4 Bishops voted for the bill[297] – It is a Sad result & the country will view it will [*sic* – with] great displeasure –

*5 June 1845.* What I wrote for yesterday Should have been dated as this day for it was between 4 & 5 this morning that the division took place[298] – I have in the course of the day been doing a great deal of my own private business, which I have completed & Shall be ready to start tomorrow on my return to Clumber –

[295] N.U.M.D., Ne C 7499: John Burton to Newcastle, 1 June 1845, requesting Newcastle present an anti-Maynooth petition, which he did this day.

[296] According to report, 'When Brougham [tonight] attacked the Duke of Newcastle for interrupting the Duke of Wellington in his speech on the Maynooth Bill, Lord Lyndhurst tugged Brougham familiarly by the skirt of the coat, observing, "Newcastle is warm; he is flaring up: don't add fuel to the fire". "I can't help it", replied Brougham. "My dear fellow", continued Lyndhurst, "adding fuel to the fire is in this case literally taking coals to Newcastle". The joke was too powerful for Brougham to resist; so he laughed, and sat down': *Punch*, viii (1845), 262.

[297] The bishops of Durham (Edward Maltby), Norwich (Edward Stanley), St David's (Connop Thirlwall), Worcester (Henry Pepys), and Chichester (Ashurst Gilbert), voted in favour.

[298] K.D., 5 June 1845, 'Divided 4 [in the] Morning 69 to 226 [on] 2nd Reading Maynooth Bill [–] In Minority [–] Sad fall of the House of Lords [–] Able Speech of Lord Stanley [on the] wrong side [–] Signed Lord Farnham's Protest – Duke of Newcastle brought me home'.

*10 June 1845.* The newspapers are Still full of the Queen's foolish ball costume which has made So much talk for Some time & which took place on the 6th & happily now is no more[299] –

*14 June 1845.* busily preparing for going on the 16th [to London –] making notes for my Speech as I pack up my papers & see any thing that requires comment or observation –

*15 June 1845.* I had written to Lord Stanley begging that if possible the debate on the 3rd reading might be put off for a day as it would be very inconvenient to me, not being well &c but I received for answer that the Duke of Wellington would admit of no delay = I therefore at great discomfort & inconvenience to myself proceed on my way to London this Evening [.][300]

*16 June 1845.* Left Nottingham at $8\frac{1}{4}$ by railway – all Seemed to be delay on the road as I was anxious to be Early in London – The train ought to have arrived at $2\frac{1}{2}$ but it was nearly an hour after its time, so that it was nearly 4 o'clock before I arrived in Portman Square – very tired, very hot, with a bad head ache & quite put out, I had to, dress, shave, dine & collect & read my papers before going to the House of Lords = I did not Enter the House till past 6 – & found Lord Campbell Speaking, who opened the debate & had been Speaking for Some time – I made two unsuccessful attempts before I could gain a hearing = So that altogether I was pretty well tired – Fatigued, heated & annoyed with a Splitting head ache, I gave myself some credit for courage in rising (very little prepared) to speak on Such an occasion, I believe that I was some time upon my legs, often losing myself but Still persevering [during] my consiousness [*sic* – consciousness] & I <u>must</u> say that the House was very Kind & attentive to me – I of course made a very bad Speech but Still I got out a great deal of what I wished to say, but omitted much that I would have Said – However I rattled the Ministers well & I believe put in Some unpleasant blows – I was most rejoiced when I thought I could conclude my Speech & never Sat down With greater satisfaction, for I was quite ill & my head burning – for the rest of the Evening I was nearly & often quite asleep – I had not had above 5 or 6 hours sleep for several nights – I deeply regret to think that this wretched bill is now passed – I did not reach home till nearly 3 o'clock[301] –

*18 June 1845.* Waterloo day – the Iron Duke had his usual dinner & I almost think it will be his last = as a Soldier he has done us good service, as a polititian [*sic*] irreparable injury – Whenever he goes he will be no loss to the Nation.

---

[299]See above, 12 May 1842. The ball was held on 6 June 1845 and attendees wore dress from the period 1740–50. See QVJ, 6 June 1845. Newcastle's son declined to go 'as I cannot afford to pay forty pounds for three or four hours torture': Ne C 5611: Lord Charles Clinton to Newcastle, 14 May 1845.

[300]D.P., 147/14: Newcastle to Stanley, 12 June 1845; N.U.M.D., Ne C 5177/1–2: Stanley to Newcastle, 13 June 1845.

[301]Hansard, *Lords Debates*, 3rd ser., lxxxi, cols 564–72: 16 June 1845; K.D., 16 June 1845, 'Maynooth Bill 3rd Reading [–] in Minority 50 to [181] – Good speech Bishop Llandaff [Edward Copleston] & Winchilsea [–] Duke of Newcastle brought me home $\frac{1}{2}$ past 1'. The vote was 181 for (104 present plus 77 proxies) and 50 against (34 present plus 16 proxies): majority 131.

*19 June 1845*. at the House of Lords presenting Some petitions &c[302] —

*20 June 1845*. a few days ago Lord Winchilsea had an audience of the Queen to present to Her Several hundred addresses [.] Her Majesty received him very Kindly, & he took the opportunity of laying his view of the case before Her — he told me that he spoke to Her Majesty for above 10 minutes — & made many Subsequent remarks — The Queen told him that She must not differ from her Ministers — but she added ["] besides that I am individually in favor of the Bill ["] — on this Lord Winchilsea made his bow & retired — Prince albert was in the room —

*23 June 1845*. Engaged from 11 to 4 on a railway Committee in the House of Lords — not a very pleasant occupation & withall Very tiring in this hot weather & not being well[303]

*24 June 1845*. as yesterday Engaged from 11 to 4 in the Committee room, & obliged immediately to go home & read & answer my letters &c — afterwards too happy to get a little air & Exercise — I think that we are doing Some good in our Committee — We have detected Error & gross misconstruction so as to Endanger the public safety in an unwarrantable manner — we resume tomorrow —

*25 June 1845*. We have been released from our Committee today about 2 o'clock — we divided upon the preamble & were beaten, that is, Lord Southampton & I were in the minority — as we considered that the public Safety in the construction of this railway, Edinburgh & Hawick, is to be perilously disregarded & hazarded, whilst the paramount consideration to the projectors is cheapness —

*26 June 1845*. I Know of no particular news Exclusive of gossip — It is Said that at the Review in the Park the day after tomorrow, the Queen means of [*sic* — to] appear on horseback = In imitation of Queen Elizabeth[304] I Suppose —

*27 June 1845*. at a musical party at Mrs R. Cavendish's I saw & Was introduced to Mohan Sal [Lal] — the man by whose care & Exertions the prisoners taken in the disastrous business of the retreat from Cabool, were well treated & preserved. To him I believe they were chiefly if not Entirely indebted for their safety = He has been rewarded by a pension [of] £1000 a year = He is a mild, pleasant & most intelligent man, with polished manners, good address & Speaks English perfectly — There [are] two or three of these Easterns going about now in Society, & one Cannot but feel a deep interest in their welfare — They must be a most interesting people, Judging by the Specimen one Sees here — Mohan Sal is a native of Cashmire [Kashmir], & told me that the Climate of Cashmire & of England are quite similar —

---

[302] From Nottingham, and two other places, against the Maynooth grant.

[303] In addition to Newcastle, the committee comprised Lords Sydney (chairman), Foley, Calthorpe and Southampton. The evidence taken (23–25 June 1845) is summarised in *The Railway Chronicle: Joint–Stock Companies Journal*, i (1845), 757.

[304] In her speech to the troops at Tilbury in Essex in Aug. 1588.

*28 June 1845.* [Leopold] The King of the Belgians is come over & there was to have been a review for him in Hyde Park today but on account of the bad weather it has been postponed to the day after tomorrow –

*30 June 1845.* The attorney General, Sir William Follett, is dead, he died the day before yesterday – He had been in a very declining state of health for the last two years, & had Scarcely been able to do any business Since his appointment – In acquirements as a Lawyer, a Speaker & authority he was a very Eminent man, & perhaps there is no one who can fill his place = I am told that he was not a man of general & Extensive information – Mr Fitzroy Kelly will most probably be made Solicitor General & Sir [Frederick] Thessiger be promoted to attorney General –

The State of Ireland is Said to be dreadful at this time – People are leaving the country as fast as they can afraid for their lives – Lady Scarbrough told me today that two gentlemen clergyman connected With her by marriage, Reverends Mark Beresford & L'Estrange, feel it to be necessary to leave their livings with their families, although anxious & Excellent Clergymen [,] & that all others who can afford it propose to do the Same – Murder is So common & the Murderer So protected, that the life of no one is Safe – if the destruction of any one is doomed, a Stranger from a distance is hired for a few Shillings, he does the deed & instantly decamps & his detection & arrest rendered impossible by the invariable protection afforded in Every case by the bystanders or neighbouring peasantry & all this goes on without any apparent interference on the part of the Government –

*14 July 1845.* In the House of Lords this Evening, the privilege case of Baker & Harlow superceded all other business[305] – the law lords were amusing the House with long Speeches & Lord Brougham appeared to be more mad […] than usual – actually declaring that if any one called him to account for what he had said in his place in the House of Lords &[306] were to bring an action against him in a Court of Law that he Should appear to it, & would think it a proper proceeding – Nothing is too preposterous or too mischievous for this man to Say – He & most law lords are a great nuisance in the House –

*15 July 1845.* The Queen & Prince albert – Dowager Queen & other Royalties [–] are gone to Portsmouth to visit the Exercising Squadron before it Sails on the cruise – The Queen is to accompany it for some distance, She will be out two days – at the End of the Week She goes to the Isle of Wight for a fortnight & [–] when Parliament rises – She will go to Germany = People think unfavorably of Such restlessness = It is Said that Her Majesty desired that many bills Should be postponed, in order that she might not be detained in London = Some have been postponed in consequence but She is not pleased that any have been retained – Her Majesty is said to be a little hasty, Sometimes throwing her Slippers

[305] The case concerned Thomas Baker of Hammersmith, formerly superintendent of C division, Metropolitan Police, who was required to give evidence before the Lords Select Committee on the Game Laws. John Harlow of 9 Leicester Square commenced an action for damages against Baker as a result of the evidence given on the occasion. Harlow was found guilty of a breach of privilege and taken into custody but was released after expressing contrition and agreeing to withdraw the petition.

[306] that precedes this in the original.

at her attendants, Sometimes boxing the Ears of her Maid of honour, & often is guilty of these little indiscretions –

*19 July 1845.* It is Said that the Queen goes the day after tomorrow to the Isle of Wight & from thence direct to Germany, leaving Parliament & the Country to do without her, & most improvidently to teach them that She[307] can be Spared – If She goes during the Sitting of Parliament [,] Lords Justices must be appointed, & if She Stays longer than a month a Regency must be appointed –

*20 July 1845.* Earl Grey is dead – he had for a long time been in very declining health – he was 82 – He had been one of the most distinguished men of His day – When he was first minister, he had past his miridian [*sic* – meridian] & felt that he was not what he had been used to be = a little before he became prime Minister [in 1830], I remember his Saying in the House of Lords – non Sum qualis Eram, non Eadem Et artus non mons[308] – He will not be missed, as he had totally retired from public life when he went out of office = Though a man of high mind, still he was guilty of having done a great deal of mischief – under[309] his auspices the Reform bill passed & many other dangerous measures –

*21 July 1845.* Lord Canterbury [,] notorious for a long time Speaker of the House of Commons as Manners Sutton, died this day Suddenly, he came up from his place near Exeter [Rockbeare House], & was found in the rail road carriage, at a Station near London in a fit = he remained in a state of insensibility untill the time of his death this day at about 2 o'clock –
    a long debate in the House of Lords upon the Irish Universities bill – There were only 2 Bishops present – & the House Miserably thin = Lord Carnarvon moved the postponement of the bill but we did not divide as we should only have numbered 5 or 6 – a wretched reflection – under the circumstances I thought it best to say a few words of disapprobation & repudiation of the whole bill in Every point of view, religious & political[310] – We are fast Sealing our doom, & most assuredly we shall Suffer for our heinous wickedness –

*23 July 1845.* Sudden or very rapid deaths have been Extraordinarily frequent among parliament men within a week – 4 Peers – Lords Denman – Grey – Canterbury, & yesterday Lord Bateman – also 2 M.P.s Mr [Edward] Clive & Mr [Alexander] Murray [of Broughton] – The weather is certainly very disposing to illness & Sudden affections, Such as fits, apoplexy &c –

*31 July 1845.* The King of Holland [William II] is now on a visit to this Country but why he is here it is difficult to guess – as soon as it was Expected that he would arrive [,] the Queen hurried off to the Isle of Wight, & got out of his way as Effectively as She Could – & all are condemning her bad manners & want of common courtesy – The King of

[307] ~~they~~ precedes this in the original.
[308] 'I am no longer what I was', from Horace, *Odes*, iv, 1.
[309] ~~he was~~ precedes this in the original.
[310] Hansard, *Lords Debates*, 3rd ser., lxxxii, col. 790: 21 July 1845.

Holland has been dubbed a Field Marshall in our Service, by way of recompense = The Solitary notice of or compliment to him that has been deemed worth Shewing to him [.]

*2 August 1845.* […] Heavy Storms of rain today, there are fears for the harvest, & the price of bread has risen here & in London –

*7 August 1845.* It is Settled that Parliament is to be prorogued by the Queen in person on Saturday 9th & thus will terminate one of the vilest Sessions on record –

*8 August 1845.* The Queen is by way of affecting great locomotion – She is to leave the Isle of Wight tomorrow morning – when She arrives in London [,] She is to go to the House of Lords to prorogue the Parliament & then immediately afterwards goes to Woolwich where She Embarks to proceed to antwerp – The day after tomorrow is Sunday – & if Her Majesty had a proper adviser about her, She would be advised to hold the Sunday in greater reverence – Her whole proceedings, are very Strongly animadverted upon =

*9 August 1845.* In the House of Lords Some conversation took place about the Sovereign going abroad = Lord Campbell asked the question & Enquired whether any provision was to be made to Supply the place of the Queen during her absence in Germany, by the appointment of Lords Justices, or any other Contrivance – The Lord Chancellor Lyndhurst answered, that Ministers intended to do nothing, & thought nothing necessary, that in the present state of things & with the facility of Communication that the Sovereign might leave the country whenever She pleased without the Slightest inconvenience = So – now it is laid down that [,] in fact, the presence of a Sovereign is not necessary [,] he or she may bear the title & dignity, but the regal presence for the Execution of any business, is found to be now a days altogether unnecessary – In Such times as these such a discovery may lead to very puzzling & Very unpleasant consequences – The Nation generally is by no means pleased & satisfied by what the Queen is doing –

*10 August 1845.* Parliament was prorogued yesterday – The Queen afterwards Embarked at Woolwich & was to reach the mouth of the river – where the [Royal] Yacht[311] anchors for the night = This morning, Sunday, she sails or steams for antwerp where they will arrive late in the afternoon – the Queen will not land & Sleeps on board the Yacht tonight – Tomorrow She will begin her Journey – one it must be observed very distasteful to her Subjects – The Speech contains nothing, & is a poorer concern than usual – it is however bordering upon insulting when it notices Several of the acts of the Session –

*12 August 1845.* Ireland is rekindling into a ferment – The Protestants are determining [not] to be repressed, despised & injured any longer – a Spirit is flying through the Country, caused greatly by the discharge of Mr [James] Watson from the Magistracy because he attended an Orange meeting on King William's day – this has roused them all & they are determined to Shew themselves & to meet Every where for a Similar celebration – They are right too – let them only act properly & they will be calling into action the only thing that can Save

---

[311] Yatcht in the original.

their lives & properties – Peel will soon learn the Effect of his vile policy – on him will rest all the blame of what may follow[312] –

*15 August 1845.* Great Protestant meetings in Ireland – & a resolution to reconstruct Orangeism – Execrations of Peel – & well they may Execrate him – he drives them to this confederation to Save their lives & their properties – Ireland is in a dreadful state & must be a prey to[313] Excitement of the fiercest nature – England & Scotland I firmly believe, are not far behind – What lurks Secretly is not so turbulently Expressed, but the leaven is there, & the result of deep craft & stratagem will one day bust [*sic* – burst] forth into high fermentation Should an occasion present itself – Peel Knows now what he is about, he is trying to upset Every thing to serve his own purposes – but he sees not that although he may Sow the Seeds of democracy & revolution – he will not reap the harvest = I am convinced that he is Enclosing the Queen in a net, & Encouraging her to do what will risk her Throne – His aim is also to upset the nobility, the Church, Every person of merit & distinction, whether colleagues or supporters, he will Sooner or later Sacrifice them, & turn them lose [*sic* – loose] & bankrupt in character & reputation – & then he is infatuated Enough to think that he will rule Supreme.

*16 August 1845.* Several Elections are going on at this time & almost all terminate in favor of the Conservatives – at Sunderland Mr [George] Hudson has come in instead [*sic* – in place] of Lord Howick[314] –

*18 August 1845.* The newspapers are filled with accounts of our Queen's reception in Germany – & the musical festival at Bonn to the memory of [Ludwig van] Beethoven – the great Composer, who was a native of the Town –

*20 August 1845.* The annexation of Texas to the american Union, now an old Story of a fortnight, has created in that quarter & Every where Else the greatest indignation at the utter faithlessness, & political infamy of the United States – it is however their road to ruin, the Union must break up before long – it is now So Extensive, So Weak & So disunited, that it must be destroyed by its own weight –

*22 August 1845.* although Ireland is in a ferment, & a vast deal of mischief going on in that Island – yet for the present it is Smouldering, & tranquillity apparently prevails –

*24 August 1845.* In Germany but Especially in Saxony,[315] a very great Stir is making towards a reformation = a man of the name of Rouge [Johannes Ronge] formerly a popish priest, is the modern [Martin] Luther, & his followers are now becoming very numerous & are asserting their power – at Leipsig [Leipzig] Serious disturbances have taken place, directed

---

[312]C.P., Newcastle to W.H. Clinton, 12 Aug. 1845: 'Ireland – thanks to Peel – is in a dreadful State – & the harvest prospects are So bad that it is difficult to foresee what may be the Result of a bad harvest With the Miserable state of the landed interest'.

[313]of precedes this in the original.

[314]Hudson polled 627 votes to Thomas Perronet Thompson's 498: majority 129.

[315]Germany precedes this in the original.

against Prince John of Saxony who is Strongly opposed to the modern reformers – the troops by his command fired upon the people & Killed many = They are highly Exasperated – & it is thought that Several of these incidents will result in very Serious consequences – The Queen is not gone into Saxony at a very pleasant period –

*26 August 1845*. Protestant meetings going on vigorously in Ireland – an immense meeting at Lisburn of 40,000 people at which Lord Downshire presided, & which terminated peaceably & properly – The Spirit is strongly aroused & it is most right that it should be so – it is [the] only thing to save themselves from being trampled upon & annihilated –

*31 August 1845*. The Guardians of the poor of Marylebone have refused to obey the order of the Poor Law Commissioners, to Establish asylums for the houseless poor in their parish = Commissions are now named to Such an Extreme, & Commissioners interpose so unconstitutionally & so arbitrarily with all local affairs, that the interference is intolerable & must & will be resisted =

*5 September 1845*. So much determined opposition has been shewn to comply with the mandates of the Poor Law Commissioners to form District asylums for the poor – that the order has been rescinded – This is right – Such mandates are So Subversive of all local & parochial rights, privileges, & Even Existence, that it is the duty of Parishes to resist Such orders – although they may be according to act of Parliament –

*6 September 1845*. The Times newspaper is Extremely Shocked & angry that our Queen Should have been present at a batter Slaughter of deer at Saxe Gotha, witnessing it for two hours, seated in "an Easy chair", seated in a luxurious building, with music playing, whilst the butchery in the Enclosure was going on – There is too much truth in the remarks, the revolting Sight ought not to have been witnessed by our Queen –

*7 September 1845*. The Queen was to anchor yesterday Evening off the mouth of the Scheldt & there remain this day, being Sunday: tomorrow She will reach the Isle of Wight [,] remain on board the Yacht all night, & go to Osborne house the following day – Her German Excursion has given any thing but Satisfaction to her Subjects =

*9 September 1845*. abdul Meschid [Abdulmejid I] Sultan of Turkey, is coming out as an important character – he is very young & hitherto has been given up to the Excesses of his Hareem & Every Eastern luxury – He has now, of his own accord, apparently, but as I suspect by the advice & direction of our ambassador Sir Stratford Canning, taken upon himself to direct the affairs of his Empire = he has dismissed his Ministers & chosen others & Shews a determination to act vigorously, wisely, & in conformity to the usages of other nations = instead of drowning or Strangling his Ex Officials, he pensions them off & Still Shews them attention & Kindness – all these things are very remarkable in Eastern governments, & testify the Surprising change which is gradually taking place among them.

*10 September 1845*. To the astonishment of all we hear that Our Queen has suddenly gone to visit the King of France. She was received in all due form by the King & family at Treport [Tréport], who conducted her to the Chateau D'Eu [Château d'Eu] = this news is very displeasing – & the more so as the Prince de Joinville not many days ago came freely to sound & survey the coast about Brighton & inspected the pier there – & this after the pamphlets which he has written, So hostile to England & her navy[316] – it is considered as a great insult – The Queen is going the way to hurt herself Considerably in the Estimation of her Subjects –

*11 September 1845.* The Queen is returned to the Isle of Wight. She made the passage yesterday morning direct from Treport in $8\frac{1}{2}$ hours – She Stayed two days with the King of France at Eu – apologies for having done what She has done are insinuated in the papers, & the pretence is, that it was all a Sudden thought – but we Know here that it was no Such thing, but a Settled plan – a pilot for the Line was taken from hence by Captain [Frederick] Bullock in the Porcupine when he went to await the Queen's arrival at antwerp –

*12 September 1845.* Lord Winchilsea has resigned his commissions as Justice of the Peace & Deputy Lieutenant in Several counties in which he has property – Kent [,] Lincoln & Northampton I think = his reason is that as Mr [James] Watson has been arbitrarily dismissed in Ireland that he disdains to hold these offices in England from sympathy in Mr Watson's wrongs, & as he tells me to be free as air to Engage in whatever he may be called upon to do for his oppressed brethren in Ireland – I have the highest Esteem for Lord Winchilsea but I much regret that he has taken this Step, it is quite wrong & mistaken – he ought to remain to do what good he can in his capacity as a Magistrate, in which he is quite Superior –

*3 October 1845.* […] Lord Spencer & Lord Ely, are dead within a few days of one another = both after very short illness –

*7 October 1845.* The Queen is reported to be in a family way –
a combined French & English attack by ships, of a fortress in the Island of Madagascar is an unfortunate affair – it ought never to have been engaged in & failed[317] –

*10 October 1845.* The accounts from India indicate the intention of the Governor General [Henry Hardinge] to follow in the steps of his predecessors & by force of arms to put down the anarchy in the Punjaub [Punjab] & to annex it to our territories in India, & this is right if we are to maintain the possession in India –

*11 October 1845.* Mr [John Henry] Newman has at last declared himself – He has resigned his Canonry, & has openly avowed his apostacy, & is now a declared member of the Church of Rome – one man, a pupil of his, a Mr [Ambrose] St John is gone with him, but it is Expected that many more will follow – it is a dreadful & most deplorable infatuation –

[316] Francois Ferdinand Philippe Louis Marie d'Orléans, Prince de Joinville, 'Note sur l'état des forces navales de la France', *Revue des Deux Mondes*, 15 May 1844, 708–46, was reprinted in a pamphlet in several editions.

[317] On 15 June 1845, three men-of-war (two French and one British) attacked the fort and town of Tamatave to show displeasure at the Hova authority's laws and treatment of their European subjects.

The reports of the quarter's revenue is that there is a considerable deficiency – on the year, as compared with the last of upwards of [£] 800,000 – The accounts were to be published today –

*18 October 1845.* Mr Newman, the apostate, has at length openly renounced the Church of England & Protestantism & has been formally received into the Church of Rome, Several people mostly clergymen have gone with him, & it is Expected that many more will follow – Dr [Edward] Pusey is wary & hangs back, but professes Popish tenets more avowedly than Ever, if he does not go of his own accord he will [be] turned out of the Church, as it seems to be impossible that he Should be allowed to remain in it –

*20 October 1845.* They are in as great alarm in Ireland, as they are at Oxford, where the utmost consternation prevails on account of the late miserable conversions – Ireland is represented to be in dismay at the alarming failure of the potatoe [*sic*] crops – The most lamentable results are anticipated, as potatoes are the staple food of the Irish –

*22 October 1845.* Lord ashley has written a letter to his Constituents of Dorset informing them, that he does not attend to their dissatisfaction with him, that he shall not alter his Course — that the corn laws are Sure to be abolished – that there will be fearful commercial distress, that neither Lord John Russell on one Side or Peel on the other care a farthing about it, & will leave the country in an hour of especial difficulty without a refuge or resource[318] – Here is a pleasant picture if his Lordship be right, as I think he is –

*23 October 1845.* No very particular occurrence, although very many things of deep interest are in progress – Lord Roden has issued a long letter, full of able Statements & Excellent remarks shewing the danger to the State & to Protestantism of the prevailing Ministerial measures & the perverted notions of a numerous class among us –

*27 October 1845.* The potatoes in these parts [of Shropshire and Cheshire] are badly affected, but by no means useless – from Italy to England the disease is alike & great distress on that account, anticipated.

*2 November 1845.* It appears that there is an intention on the part of Sir Robert Peel to admit foreign Corn at a duty of only 4s per Quarter, the papers State that a Cabinet Council has been holden & that nothing is at present to be done = the notion was that an order in Council would immediately be issued to admit foreign corn on these terms – I presume that there must have been a majority in the Cabinet against the Scheme – & it is asserted positively that a Junction is Settled between Peel & Lord John Russell & I believe that it is not only desired by Peel but that it will be Effected –

*5 November 1845.* […] I had much Conversation with the very intelligent & remarkably civil & civilised people of Manchester, & found that all were free traders, So bent are they upon throwing open the Corn trade that they are willing to Sacrifice all protective duties

---

[318]See Edwin Hodder, *The Life and Work of the Seventh Earl of Shaftesbury, K.G.* (1886), ii, 118–20.

upon their own productions = I was told that at least 9 out of 10 in Manchester are free traders – I could not be convinced that Such opinions are not a fallacy & delusion –

*7 November 1845*. Lord Montague is dead – I have not heard what he leaves to Colonel & Mrs Frederick Clinton –

*9 November 1845*. Lord Stewart de Rothsay is dead – his title is Extinct – he had only two daughters Lady Canning & Lady Waterford –
    Lady adela Villiers has disappeared – She left her father, Lord Jerseys, house at Brighton before dinner & has not been heard of Since – She is only 17 – but a most forward young lady – & probably brim full of romance – it is thought that She is gone off with Some tall gentleman who is reported to have been seen with a young lady of her description at the railway Station – Lady Jersey & her other daughter were on a Visit at arundel Castle –

*11 November 1845*. The talk of the day is the elopement of Lady adela Villiers [–] it is supposed that She is gone away with some man but nobody Knows or Suspects who – She left her Fathers house at Brighton with a Small bundle & has not Since been Seen –

*12 November 1845*. It is now ascertained that Lady adela Villiers went off with a Captain Ibbotson [Charles Parke Ibbetson], they proceeded to Gretna green & were married there = Lady Jersey is furious & Lord Jersey Cut to the quick. Lady adela was his favorite daughter & left with him [,] as he is unwell, to be his companion –

*23 November 1845*. a List of new railway Speculations appears in the Times & is a most curious document, by it, it appears that there are Somewhere about 800 new Schemes which are to come before Parliament this next Session = Some most decisive measures must absolutely be taken by the Government to stop this desperate State of things – dangerous, dishonest, pestilent & ruinous –

*27 November 1845*. [My] Poor [son] Thomas tells me that he has Suffered Considerably in his railway Speculations – I am truly Sorry for it but Such misfortunes all Speculators must be liable to – The ruin which will Shortly Ensue from railway Speculations will be tremendous – it must come [,] nothing can prevent it – the madness of Speculators must be Suicidal, & will cause & accomplish the catastrophe –

*28 November 1845*. We hear a good deal about a defensive arming in this country, fortifications to be made & troops to be raised – a complete system of military organisation Established – but who the enemy is, & why it Should be So peculiarly necessary now [,] one is at a loss to guess Even, certainly not to discover – my belief is that if it is against any body, it is against ourselves – the pretext is a foreign Enemy, & the pretext covers the Sneaking preparation against ourselves – The militias are to be called out in Some new fangled way So as to be recruiting Serjeants to the regular army –

*29 November 1845*. Many more [converts] to Popery from among the beneficed Clergy, & a vast many more are on the point of leaving the Church – it is a melancholy & shocking

Exhibition & is now becoming quite a rage – a great many women & ladies are turning Papists –

*30 November 1845.* I am glad to See that Major [Godfrey Charles] Mundy, Eldest Son of General [Godfrey Basil] Mundy is made Lieutenant Colonel & appointed Deputy adjutant General in New South Wales – he is a very deserving Officer –

*4 December 1845.* 788 lines of railways have been given into the Board of Trade to be brought in as bills & considered in the coming Session of Parliament – besides the impossibility of the thing – the fact of So many wild & costly projects is of itself Sufficient to put a Speedy Stop to the Speculation – these projects must absorb more than the capital of the country = & the Evils [*sic*] Effects will Soon be too Sensibly felt in the falling off of trade & the revenue of the Country [.]

*5 December 1845.* The Times announces that the differences in the Cabinet are Settled – how it comes to Know this, if true, may puzzle a good guesser, but it farther States that Parliament will be called together Early in January & that a Consideration of the Corn Laws will be recommended in the Royal Speech & will be brought forward in the two Houses by the Duke of Wellington & Sir Robert Peel – if this be So – no one can foretell the Extent of the Ensuing mischief –

*6 December 1845.* The Standard contradicts the Statement of the Times & brands it as an infamous forgery & falsehood –

*7 December 1845.* The Times maintains its statement & asserts its truth, whilst the Standard adheres to its denial as if from authority – which it probably is –

*9 December 1845.* The americans appear to be bent upon war – although they must Know that no country is more unfit for it – War must inevitably break up the Union, & rise up one or more ambitious men who will aim at Kingly power over them –

*10 December 1845.* The Squabble between the Times & the Standard Still continues whether the Ministers are or are not agreed to give up the Corn Laws –

*11 December 1845.* at last the cat is out of the bag – a letter from London informs me that "Ministers have resigned" – & that the Queen is Said to have Sent for Lord John Russel – if this be true, then I fore see, what has long been my Conviction, that there will be a coalition between Peel & Russel – & I most Sincerely hope that it may take place, as then Peel will be Shewn in his true colours – as the primest hypocrite & most Shameless political traitor that Ever was – I have little doubt that all this has been Schemed between Lord John & Sir Robert & that the former will have been Sent to by the Queen, if So, at the Suggestion – of Sir Robert – The newspapers do not Contain the news – & I Know no details –

*12 December 1845.* Nothing more today, than that Lord John Russell is gone to the Queen – Tomorrow possibly Some secrets may be made public.

*13 December 1845.* Lord John Russell had not returned to London – but it was understood that he had been charged by the Queen to form an administration & that he had undertaken it – as I Surmised it Seems that Peel has had Secret communications with Lord John a full week ago. Peel wrote to him at Edinburgh to apprise him of what Was happening in the Cabinet, & probably, on that account he instantly published his letter to the London constituency declaring his new view of abolishing Corn laws & adherence to the [Anti–Corn Law] League,[319] Lord Morpeth did the Same – Peel then advised him Secretly to draw near to London, & he did So, Peel advised the Queen to send for Lord John & She did So = first waiting at Osborne house in the Isle of Wight to meet him, but as he did not arrive within the time, Peel returned to London but there he Saw Lord John privately before he went to the Queen & if this is not a vile conspiracy against the Queen & the Nation I Know not what is – Peel with [*sic* – will] side with Lord John most probably, I think, he will coalesce with him & complete his treasons, & like Judas hang himself.[320] This will be a fit termination of the Jesuitical career of the greatest political Scoundrel that Ever Existed –

*14 December 1845.* But little intelligence about the formation of a new Ministry – One of pure Russellites it is idle & farcical to think of, it could not Stand one week or one day in Parliament & a coalition with Peel will be so infamous that public opinion will Scout it down before parliament assembles – The Extracted account from the Times is I am Convinced a true Statement of facts – & I Set it down as historical truth –

*16 December 1845.*[321] Lord John Russell does not appear to get on with his administration. He & Lord Landsdown are Said to have gone to Windsor, but Lord Lansdown some say is against repeal of the Corn Laws & upon the whole it is thought that Lord John will not be able to get together a ministry of his old friends = then – probably will follow the Junction with Peel, & upon that assuredly the Execration of the Country –

*17 December 1845.* It is Said that Lord John finds some difficulty in forming an administration = The total repeal of the Corn laws are not palatable to all his friends & they do not choose to act in common with Cobden – Lord Lansdown is one of these – Lord John may probably fail – but there is said to be another Contrivance on foot by which a Sort of intermediate, or half & half ministry [,] shall be formed by which Such a man as Lord Lansdown shall be at the head [,] & others from both sides of the house of Similar principles, Shall be brought together & called an administration – in it will not be, Either Russell or Peel – When these Knaves have pioneered the way, Supported by Russell & Peel – then these latter will be called upon to Join & thus openly Effect a Coalition – it is a very Cunning scheme in all its ramifications, & Especially as it may regard a general Election –

[319]Russell's 'Edinburgh Letter', 22 Nov. 1845, in Spencer Walpole, *The Life of Lord John Russell* (1889), i, 406–9.
[320]Matthew, 27: 1–10.
[321]*Memoirs and Correspondence of Field Marshal Viscount Combermere, GCB from his Family Papers*, ed. Viscountess Combermere and Captain W.W. Knollys (2 vols, 1866), ii, 267, for a letter from Newcastle to Combermere of 16 Dec. 1845, announcing Wellington's resignation as commander in chief. Newcastle thought that this was 'really wrong; he was bound to retain it till things were settled' but urged Combermere to solicit the position.

*18 December 1845.* Still nothing done – but Lord John Russell's letter to the Queen was Sent on Tuesday 16th Stating what he could or could not do = the probability is that he cannot form a Ministry on the Extreme principles which[322] he has avowed & that Lord Lansdown or someone of that Cast will be Commissioned to form one of moderate odds & Ends – that is, of men of no Character, & on whom no reliance can be placed – In reference to the rupture of Peel's ministry – I have been told that Lincoln was among the dissenters – a circumstance which rejoices me Exceedingly –

*20 December 1845.* Ld aberdeen is Supposed to have betrayed the Secret history of the Cabinet Squabbles to the american Minister [Louis McLane] – a pretty Set they Seem to be = Peel has made them all Knaves[323] –
    It is thought that Lord John Russell will now complete his Ministry & that it will receive the Support of the Peel party – likely Enough = Lincoln I now find to my Sorrow – & deep displeasure, is with Peel in all his vortex of abominations =

*21 December 1845.* Lord John Russell's difficulties have been insuperable, he himself & his party have acted with infinitely higher honor than Peel's gang = Lord John communicated to Peel that unless he would Support him he must fail. Peel was to[o] wary to promise this – & Lord John gave in – the principal cause of breaking up his Embryo was that Lord Grey refused to Sit in the Same cabinet with Lord Palmerston as foreign minister —

*22 December 1845.* The farce proceeds & <u>Sir Robert Peel</u> has gone to Windsor <u>to obey the Queen's commands</u> – what a Sickening prospect to think of being again Subjected to the villainy of Peel's Jesuitical rule = he has of course Engaged to reform a Ministry of his lackies & victims –

*23 December 1845.* The members of Peel's Ministry are not Known but a list is given in which Lord Brougham !!!!! appears in[324] the place of Lord Wharncliffe who died a few days ago – & was previously President of the Council – It is stated also that Lincoln is moved to the Board of Control, of which he Knows as much as of the mountains in the Moon – but he must be rewarded for his <u>faithful</u> Services to his wretched Judas – the idea of all this, & that Lincoln of whom I once thought So highly & So proudly Should be Steeped in all the wickedness & unworthiness of passing Events under Peel, Shoots into my heart, grieves & wounds me beyond all power of description –

*24 December 1845.* Today I have a letter from Mr Gladstone, who tells me that he has accepted the office of Secretary of State for the Colonies & War = he Enquires whether I will again bring him in for Newark = I have replied – ["] Certainly not ["] – If [my son] Charles will Consent to stand & will engage to cooperate with me, & not with Peel – I

---

[322] whiche in the original.
[323] This was widely rumoured to be the source of *The Times*' intelligence: N.U.M.D., Pw H 188/1: Lord George Bentinck to Portland, 17 Dec. 1845.
[324] in precedes this in the original.

shall put him in Gladstone's vacancy[325] – I have in my answer to Gladstone made Some most Severe Strictures on Peel[326] – Tomorrow we Shall have the mortification of Seeing all the appointments –

Lord Stanley has left Peel, & accepts no place – I trust that he will be in opposition, & then we may make a good & spirited fight against Peels' revolutionary atrocities –

*25 December 1845.* […] I had a letter from the Duke of Richmond today, & I am in much hopes from the sort of hints which it contains that not only will he be a strong opponent but that Lord Stanley may Join or assist us – I have written to the Duke to urge him to Lead a third party which with Lord Stanley may be very formidable[327] –

Peel has reformed his ministry & he & all of them are gone into the Country – all the Same people have returned to their Same offices, So that all this farcical puther has been for nothing, & that Peel in his waywardness Knew =

Lord Stanley is the only one who leaves him, & the President of the Council not yet appointed – I feel pretty Sure that is offered to Lord Brougham but he is in the South of France – I am very glad to find that Lincoln has not Changed office – it will also make his reelection unnecessary[328] –

*27 December 1845.* Parliament is prorogued to the 22nd January, then to meet for despatch of business – & a pretty time we Shall have of it Seeing the State into which the Country is plunged. Peel has a grievous load[329] of political Sin to answer for, & private worth & good character, will assuredly not be allowed to be a make weight against the Seduction & inducement to public misdoing which he So Extensively holds out to the Community, & practices upon his wretched dupes & followers –

*31 December 1845.* […] I am here arrived at the End of another year = I have nothing to regret it for but that I am So much older – as far as my family is concerned, I am only more & more wretched in that particular – Lincoln is utterly Strange to me [–] I have had no communciation with him for a year & a half – & he is I fear my bitter Enemy = Charles thinks it better to lean to Lincoln than to me & is polite but no more = Robert

[325] On Newcastle's protracted attempt to persuade his son Charles to stand for Newark: N.A., DD/TL/2/1/84: Newcastle to Godfrey Tallents, 26 Dec. 1845; DD/TL/2/1/85: Newcastle to Tallents, 28 Dec. 1845; DD/TL/2/1/86: Lincoln to Tallents, 29 Dec. 1845; N.U.M.D., Ne C 12157/3/1–2: Lincoln to Peel, 26 Dec. 1845; Ne C 7887: Tallents to Newcastle, 27 Dec. 1845; Ne C 11679/1–2: Lincoln to Gladstone, 27 Dec. 1845; Ne C 4576–7: Tallents to Lincoln, 28, 29 Dec. 1845; Ne C 7890: Tallents to Newcastle, 29 Dec. 1845; Ne C 12218/1–2: Tallents to Lincoln, 1 Jan. 1846. Charles followed Lincoln's advice throughout this period.

[326] BL, Add. MS 44261, ff. 101–2: Gladstone to Newcastle, 22 Dec. 1845; ff. 103–4, Newcastle to Gladstone, 24 Dec. 1845.

[327] Newcastle attacked Peel as 'the vilest … man that ever was, except Oliver Cromwell' and asked Richmond to help persuade Charles to stand for Newark. In his reply, Richmond offered to help: R.P., 1866, f. 37: Newcastle to Richmond, 25 Dec. 1845; N.U.M.D., Ne C 5176: Richmond to Newcastle, 27 Dec. 1845.

[328] N.U.M.D., Pw H 192/1–3: Lord George Bentinck to Portland, 28 Dec. 1845: 'The Duke of Newcastle turns Gladstone out of Newark, this will be a pretty Strong hint to Lord Lincoln & I Can not but think the prospect of half his Cabinet Ministers losing their Seats would have a very beneficial effect upon Sir Robert Peel'. See below, 9 Feb. 1846.

[329] ~~weight~~ precedes this in the original.

has deserted me without a pang, & gone over to the Same quarter – William is away, poor Thomas I believe is the best effected to me –

*1 January 1846.* With the utmost gratitude to God for the blessings which He permits me to Enjoy I again begin a new year – I begin under no very favorable auspices, having great things to do, & being deserted by my children whom I had trained up to be in a position to render me their useful assistance in my age & in time of difficulty = I may call however but no answer is made, & in place of repaying me for my devotion to them, they fly from me, & offer Shuffling Excuses for doing So – In this instance I write of Charles, others have cut all communication with me, Lincoln Setting the wicked example – May God forgive him & them – though he may punish, to check them – & it would be a mercy that this Should happen to them in good time[330] […] In politics I see little to cheer me, Strong but perfidious & treacherous Ministers, a temporising people, a female Sovereign [,] trade falling off, distress in prospect, discontent & approaching revolution glimmering on the horizon – I think & hope that we are in a way of forming a strong third party, but this will depend upon circumstances & very much if not Entirely upon what part Lord Stanley may take –

*2 January 1846.* The newspapers record the Sudden death of Lord Portarlington two days ago [and] that of Colonel [John] Gurwood who committed Suicide [–] these Events are happening perpetually, & are among the Signs of the times =

*3 January 1846.* another sudden death is announced – Lord Portarlington went from his drawing [room] apparently in perfect health into the adjoining room, his dressing room – a Sort of gurgling noise was heard from thence Soon after, & on Entering the room he was found to be dead –

*10 January 1846.* Poor Frederic[k] Mundy is dead – he died Suddenly at his living of Winston [Durham] on the 2nd [.] He had been for Several years in a very precarious state of health from paralysis & latterly he has been So afflicted that life must have been a misery to him. his brother the General [Godfrey Basil Mundy] is gone to look after his affairs – I fear that there will be much to do,

*11 January 1846.* […] a Chapter of the Garter has been summoned for the 19th at Windsor Castle – I have been invited to dine & sleep there, if it Should be convenient to me to attend – I have written to Excuse myself – I fear however that I must dislodge myself to [be] present at the opening of the Session on the 22nd –

*13 January 1846.* In a letter from the Duke of Richmond he hopes & Seems rather to Expect that Lord Stanley may head a country party[331] [–] if he Should & manfully Espouses right

---

[330] Newcastle told his land agent, 'I am in direct hostility to Peel's Knavery and most dangerous & jesuitical policy – he would deceive the Devil if he be not too wily [*sic*] even for such a Man': N.U.M.D., Ne C 4578: Edward Wollett Wilmot to Lincoln, 2 Jan. 1846; Ne C 4579/1–2: Godfrey Tallents to Lincoln, 2 Jan. 1846.

[331] R.P., 1692, f. 1787: Newcastle to Richmond, 4 Jan. 1846, suggesting that a central committee issue election funds to county protection societies; f. 1794: Newcastle to Richmond, 16 Jan. 1846, suggesting Richmond propose an amendment but not put it to a division.

principles it will be very Strong – My Expectation is that he will Shine in that capacity & display his qualities, if he really has them, in a very different light from which they have Ever yet appeared – He has never yet been in company that Suited him –

*15 January 1846*. Some doubts have been Expressed to me of Mr [John] Stuart's political views & opinions [.] I have written to him to ascertain what are the facts of the case & whether he is a free Man or an Expectant of office under Peel – If he does not satisfy me, I Shall Endeavour to get in Sir Charles Wetherell in his place – he would be invaluable in the House of Commons Just now, & would smash Peel to atoms by his clever home truths announced in the most ludicrous & tucking manner[332] –

*19 January 1846*. […] Busy all day getting ready & preparing for going to London on the 22nd for the meeting of Parliament [–] an Eventful occasion! – I was invited to attend the Chapter of the Garter holden today at Windsor Castle & to dine & Sleep there – but I have respectfully made my Excuses –

*22 January 1846*. Left Nottingham this morning by the 10 o'clock train Expecting to be in London at $\frac{1}{4}$ to 3 [–] but the train was so long & heavy that it was delayed above two hours – it was 5.20 [p.m.] before I reached Portman Square – as I was obliged to dress & eat a little dinner, I was too late to hear all the most interesting part of the discussion in the House [of Lords] – but the scene was very Extraordinary at the Excitement, Evidently great – it is Easy to See that Ministers will lose a vast many of their present followers & Supporters if they pursue the mad course which Peel has chalked out – The Duke of Beaufort, Lord Salisbury, [Lord] Malmesbury & others declared that they Should go against their friends in office, The Duke of Richmond put the question to the Duke of Wellington why he had resigned & resumed office. The Duke Sheltered himself under privilege & Said that he could not divulge the Secrets of the Cabinet without the Queens permission – we are to have the disclosure on Monday 26th – I was told in the House that Peel was Speaking long & openly & declaring that he had abandoned his former notions of protection[333] &c [.] People are disgusted & alarmed, & I consider the Peel dynasty as defunct – he is a lost man =

*23 January 1846*. The declarations of Sir Robert Peel & the course of outrageous desertion of all his former professed maxims of government have so astounded all people that they Seem to be paralised [*sic*] ostupuere omnes[334] [*sic*] they Know not what to think, what to do, or which way or to whom to turn – & yet they talk & think of this alone – tomorrow probably they will [be] more awake from their trance & be more disposed to action – the only thing to be done at this time –

---

[332]Stuart was recommended as a suitable successor for Gladstone at Newark and was subsequently returned, to Newcastle's satisfaction: N.U.M.D., Ne C 6466: William Henderson to Godfrey Tallents, 5 Jan. 1846; N.A., DD/TL/2/1/89: Newcastle to Tallents, [30] Jan. 1846; *Unhappy Reactionary*, 136–40.

[333]~~free trad~~ precedes this in the original.

[334]'obstupuere omnes' – 'all listened in amazement and did not approve of such things', from the tale of Philemon and Baucis in Ovid's *Metamorphoses*.

© *The Parliamentary History Yearbook Trust 2021*

*24 January 1846.* Nothing very material has transpired today – it is understood that Peel's notable plan is to leave Corn with a mere <u>protective</u> duty of 6s per quarter to diminish annually 2s So that in three years there will be no duty: it can only be in mockery & Scorn that he does this – the duty as <u>protection</u> would be worse than useless – Very many resignations of minor office men & people about the Court are Spoken of – Peel no doubt is pretty Confident that he will carry his measure or he would not act as he does –

*25 January 1846.* I find that Lord Stanley will not head a party now not from any indifference but because there is no one to do the work in the House of Commons – I have always foreseen this difficulty & stated it in my public letters – but still with good courage I think the thing may be done [.] I would turn out Peel, if I could, & then get over the Session & dissolve Parliament – The business then would be to discover & bring forward capable men & the country might be Saved – Fear[335] is the worst Enemy that we have to contend against = Yorkshire is to be contested[336] & when Peel brings forward his measure, it is to be met in the first instance with asking for time that the country may Consider the proposal – 3 weeks are to be asked for & if opposed a division taken – The worst feature next to fear, is that there is no Concert [–] our new party ought to get together & be prepared for any thing but this is not done for want of leaders – our position is Singularly unfortunate, but by no means a lost case if cleverly & manfully met –

*26 January 1846.* The Duke of Richmond made his Enquiries in the House of Lords this Evening & the Duke of Wellington made his <u>Explanation</u> & reply – & a lamer, less satisfactory & more miserable performance, has rarely been Exhibited – he clearly proved that he has acted in a manner to disgrace any man who pretends to be a Statesman –

The Duke of Richmond asked me to attend a meeting the day after tomorrow, but as I had made Every arrangement for going tomorrow, I begged that he would Excuse me, although I declined with much regret[337] –

*29 January 1846.* Sir Robert Peel has opened his Pandora's box – if the country can survive through Such trials as he is about to attempt to impose upon us, it will be the greatest miracle that Ever was Exhibited to a wondering & indignant people – The manufacturing as well as the agricultural community are now <u>in for it</u>, & great as their Elasticity is, I cannot conceive that the issue to them can be any thing Else than total ruin –

*31 January 1846.* Parties are now in the most singular state that Ever was Known – & all have been So unsettled & unhinged by the late Ministerial delinquency & defiance of all honor & Justice, that individuals Know not how to act, the uncertainty however is working well, & Secessions from the Peel ranks are multiplying Every day –

---

[335] ~~the F~~ precedes this in the original.
[336] N.U.M.D., Pw H 201/1: Lord George Bentinck to Portland, 24 Jan. 1846.
[337] R.P., 1692, f. 1798: Newcastle to Richmond, 26 Jan. 1846, regretting his absence from the meeting.

*1 February 1846.* I learn today that Lord Jocelyn resigns his Seat for [King's] Lynn & Lord ashley for Dorsetshire − a vast many more resignations will follow − I have very Strong hopes that our minority of 50 will be turned into a good majority −

*2 February 1846.* Captain [Arthur] Duncombe tells me that he means to resign his appointment of Groom in Waiting [to Prince Albert] =

*3 February 1846.* It is curious, that at Tamworth, where Peel has ruled Supreme for many years, Ever Since he retreated from Oxford [,] a large meeting of principally farmers has been holden, at which their neighbour Sir Robert has been very freely spoken of & a Strong manifestation made, which may Endanger his Seat for the borough − at all Events he will hear many very home truths at a future Election − Since I have had a remembrance of any thing, I have never Known Such public alarm, Excitement & general & active movement − It Surely must & I hope will crush Peel for Ever − He Justly merits the contempt & hatred of his Countrymen [.]

*4 February 1846.* The attempt to raise an opposition to Lord Morpeth in the West Riding has failed as Mr [George] Fox Lane retires = his medical [advisers] have Stated that his health is not Equal to the Exertion −

*6 February 1846.* Peel is resorting to Every Species of trick to Support himself [−] the tenders of resignations are So numerous that he has now refused to accept them & will not allow the [election] writs to be moved for −

*7 February 1846.* accounts are received by the overland despatches from India that a great battle has taken place which lasted 3 days & 3 nights without intermission & they were Still fighting when the accounts came away − The British were Said to have the advantage & had taken 65 cannons − Very great Slaughter on both Sides − we Shall not hear untill the next mail what Shall have been the issue of this Sanguinary & hard fought battle − The Seiks [*sic* − Sikhs] invaded our territory & crossed the Sutlege [Sutlej River] with 50,000 men [−] they had not retreated when the accounts came away − Sir Henry Hardinge (Governor General) commanded the Centre, the Commander in Chief Sir Hugh Gough the right, & General [John Hunter] Littler the left −

*8 February 1846.* I very much fear from what I learn that Peel will carry his point − Those who are opposed to him are a rope of Sand − nothing is done in concert & things are allowed[338] to take their chance − For instance, the Duke of Richmond who promised when I left London to write to me & acquaint me of all that was done & doing, has never written to me = if there is no concert, success cannot be Expected = It is most lamentable & What is going on grieves me to my Soul −

*9 February 1846.* To my infinite Surprise I have learnt this day that Lincoln has accepted the appointment of [Chief] Secretary to Ireland [,] vacates his Seat, & will be at Newark

---

[338]and precedes this in the original.

this Evening – there never was any thing So ill advised, & as I am driven to do So – I Shall oppose him with all my means – Mr [Thomas] Hildyard comes forward to oppose him [.][339]

*13 February 1846.* […] I learn from London that Since our friends have acquitted themselves So Well in the House of Commons & Especially Since Mr [Augustus Stafford] O brien's brilliant & able Speech, that the Country party has risen So much in public Estimation, that Peels' Majority is dwindling Every day, & from 130, or 40, of 10 days ago it is now reduced to 50 & Still diminishing & I fully Expect will Eventually turn into a majority [*sic* – minority] – Peel has taught the House of Commons to discover that they will be able to do much better without him[340] –

*14 February 1846.* [My son] Charles returned to London today – I have at last brought him to change his mind about Parliament & I hope now to See him Seriously turn his mind to Mental improvement beyond the barrack yard, & to see him acquit himself respectably as a useful M.P.[341]

In consequence of what has passed between us [,] the Duke of Portland has written to Lord Henry Bentinck & he will now be a Candidate to fill the Vacant Seat for North Nottinghamshire – Nothing can be better than this[342] =

*15 February 1846.* I am informed that the debate is likely to be protracted through the whole of the next week, this will be very much to our advantage – it will bring out our Speakers & Enable us to use many votes from the places where vacancies have[343] [been] caused by resignations – Several more are Just added – & there are 2 resignations of office of Lords of admiralty & some in the Queens' household – Lincoln's Election is I believe going much against him – & altogether our good fight in a great cause is prospering –

*18 February 1846.* I hear nothing of much consequence today as touching politics – but I have received the afflicting intelligence of my dear & valued friend & cousin's death Sir William Clinton – We all most deeply lament his loss, he was the best of men, & truly a distinguished ornament of our family – no family could boast of two better & more distinguished men & Officers than he & his late brother Sir Henry –

*19 February 1846.* I have Sent a Short address to be published about Lincolns Election & I hope it may do good, opposing free trade & other bad notions, lamenting Lincoln's espousal

---

[339] In Peel's view, 'There was a certain risk in hazarding Lord Lincoln's seat, still the possibility of his carrying it against the Duke of Newcastle, would be such a triumph, that it was well worth risking a failure. I approved this': QVJ, 5 Feb. 1846.

[340] See N.U.M.D., Pw H 203/1: Lord George Bentinck to Portland, 11 Feb. 1846.

[341] Later in the year, Newcastle considered bringing him in for Newark, in the place of John Stuart: NA, DD/TL/2/1/90: Newcastle to Godfrey Tallents, 27 June 1846; see below 26 July 1846.

[342] The vacancy resulted from the death of Henry Gally Knight. N.U.M.D., Pw H 516: Newcastle to Portland, 13 Feb. 1846; Pw H 206: Lord George Bentinck to Portland, 14 Feb. 1846; *Unhappy Reactionary*, 140–4.

[343] have precedes this in the original.

of them, deeming him thoroughly beaten, & Suggesting to him to resign – This Will be a Service to him & to the Country[344] =

*20 February 1846.* I received a copy of my address today which has been Circulated by this time all over the Country –

*22 February 1846.* My letter has made a great sensation. The London papers have taken it up & in a manner that I least Expected – The Times Even Sides with me & condemns my Son = This being the case, I trust that Sooner or later my poor Son may See the Extreme folly of his ways, & that his conscience may Smite him for his heinous Sin towards his Parent – The remarks which are made upon him & the mortification which he is likely to Suffer may I trust teach him humility also – a virtue of which he Stands much in need[345] =

My labours to form a party are I trust Succeeding, if formed I pray that it may be an honest one in or out of office – In the latter case I shall form no part of it as I should decline office of any Kind = I have no ambition but to benefit my Country & if I can See others doing this I Shall be Supremely happy[346] –

*23 February 1846.* No London accounts, as there is no post – a letter received yesterday mentions the Expectation that the debate will be Kept up all this week, as So many members Seemed anxious to Speak, whenever one Sat down there [were] 10 or 20 rising together – although the debate has lasted a fortnight only 3 ministers have hitherto Spoken –

*26 February 1846.* […] The debate in the House of Commons may perhaps continue to next week [,] although it is thought that there may be a division tomorrow =

*27 February 1846.* The accounts of the battle [of Mudkinear] near Ferosepoor [Ferozeshah] have arrived – nothing in the history of our Indian Warfare has been more desperate – the Slaughter has been immense Especially of officers, who no doubt were under the necessity of putting themselves unusually forward to Encourage their men to the hand to hand fight – The celebrated generals [Robert] Sale & [John] McCaskill, & Major Broadfoot a most distinguished & useful Company's officer Were Killed & though we claim victory & have taken most of the Sihks Cannons – yet before we can overcome Such an Enemy it is pretty Evident that we must Engage in Many more desperate Struggles – To me it appears that the Governor General Sir Henry Hardinge who has acted in a military capacity & the Commander in Chief [Sir Hugh Gough], are one of [*sic* – or] the other, or both highly culpable – They Seem to have made no preparation against the formidable invasion of the

---

[344]See Appendix A. Also see Hansard, *Commons Debates*, 3rd ser., lxxxiii, cols 1167–81: 19 Feb. 1846, for a discussion on John Collett's motion condemning the interference of peers in elections; N.U.M.D., Ne C 11974/3: Peel to [unknown], [19] Feb. 1846.

[345]On 20 Feb. 1846, Lord Ashley wrote in his diary, 'We could wish the Duke of Newcastle was avowedly mad, and then we should have him shut up, and prevented from writing such letters as that touching his Son & the contest for [South] Nottinghamshire – Was the like ever seen before? A father publicly writing and canvassing against his Son! and using, moreover, such language as, were it to proceed from any other, would involve the necessity of a personal account among Gentlemen of the "Code of Honour"': Southampton University Library, SHA/PD/4, f. 70. For satirical comment, see *Punch*, x (1846), 112.

[346]R.P., 1692, f. 1806: Newcastle to Richmond, 18 Feb. 1846; BL, Add. MS 56368, ff. 174–5: Newcastle to Giffard, 20 Feb. 1846.

Sikhs, the divisions of the army Scattered & lying wide & when they had to get together it was necessary that the main part of the army Should make pound marches of 50, 40, 30 miles a day for 3 or 4 Consequitive [*sic*] days before they could be Embodied [–] Without water, or Supplies of any Sort [,] Exposed to the greatest fatigues & hardships, & brought into the field for action broken down with fatigue & privation. Where was their information or foresight? how could[347] from 40 to 80,000 men [,] as Some Say, cross a river in Such force, with a prodigious train of heavy artillery baggage & attendants, Enter a Country & remain there for Some days & not be Seen or heard of? & how could it be permitted, that the Sikhs Should be able to collect Such a force in their own country, & that we Should not receive the intelligence of it which the commonest tyro would have deemed it necessary to obtain, & consequently counteract, or make the fullest preparations to meet? This part of the business is culpable in the Extreme, but when we come to the fight nothing is provided, of artillery nothing but a few light field guns, & a very small Supply of powder – So Small that the guns were Soon Silent & the men worn down with fatigue & want of food were compelled as the only Expedient to Save ourselves from annihilation, to attack with the bayonet & rush into the very mouths of the heavy guns of the Enemy = no troops, no officers on the face of the Earth but our own would have been found to perform Such Extraordinary feats of valour & hardihood – what I blame is the want of Knowledge & fore thought Which Should thus try men So heedlessly & culpably risk Such a noble army = & yet no doubt all Sorts of honors will be heaped upon the Chiefs = Who are brave Enough I admit, but utterly unfit to command armies – Sir Henry Hardinge never Commanded more than a regiment: how could he be fit to Command in Chief, Especially when he had holden none but civil appointments for the last 30 years [?] –

I was told today that an arrangement is to be made to bring Lincoln in for Wilton. Lord Somerton is to resign his Seat, & Mr Sidney Herbert will have Lincoln returned for his close borough of Wilton – I am truly Sorry for this – not only will Lincoln's health not be fit for the undertaking, but he will now go to Ireland, deriving no benefit from reflexion upon his late folly & total loss of principle, no Check will be put to his down ward & guilty cause [*sic* – course] & he will be made the tool & victim of the crafty & villainous Peel to disgrace himself & ruin his country – I will not attempt to describe all I feel on this Subject – I could not if I would –

*1 March 1846.* The Debate is over – the House divided yesterday morning at 3 o'clock – & I am Sorry to write a larger majority against us than I had Expected – the numbers were – against Mr [William] Miles's amendment – 337 – for it 240 – Majority – 97 – Lord George Bentinck Spoke last & Surprised the House & the public by making one of the most Effective & brilliant Speeches Ever made – overthrowing all Peel's arguments & applying himself thoroughly to the details as well as to general Subject: it was a masterly Speech – but unfortunately ill heard & ill attended to – for Evidently a certain Set was determined to annoy him & Stifle his arguments by noise So that the reporters Should not hear him = the house besides was impatient after So long a debate & at the late hour of

---

[347] how could precedes this in the original.

the night to go to a division – It is much to be lamented that he did not Speak Earlier –
but he has proved that he is Equal to anything that can be required of him[348] –

*2 March 1846.* Sir Thomas White called here Just now – & tells me that he arrived in
London about $10\frac{1}{2}$ on the 28th [–] on reaching Lincolns house he learnt that he was
dining with the apostate Peel – but on Sending to him he soon came to them – he declared
that what had been done[349] was not his doing – told them that he should not appear & that
he Knew nothing about the matter – but he would not Sign any paper declining to Stand
– & thus the matter Stands [,] the polling begins tomorrow, & I do not see how it can be
Stopped [,] Even if the Man gives in, as I believe he wishes to do now – finding that he is
in a very foolish scrape –

*7 March 1846.* The Duke of Richmond wrote to me, & I yesterday received his letter
inviting me to a meeting of Peers at his house on the 9th to Consider & determine how
we may best act in concert with our friends in the House of Commons – I could not go
today being totally unprepared – tomorrow is Sunday, & on Monday I could depend upon
no train to take me to London in Sufficient time for the meeting – I have asked the Duke
to postpone the meeting to the 10th & I will be there[350] –

*8 March 1846.* My anticipation of the State & position of our armies in India are confirmed
by the news just arrived – There is a probability of inlestine [*sic* – intestine] disunion among
the Sikhs themselves, if they hang together, our army will not find it an Easy matter to
conquer & take possession of & hold the Punjaub – & yet this they must do, if we are
to retain our rule over India from the Indus to the Ganges – I go to London tomorrow
morning –

*9 March 1846.* Left Clumber this morning at 7 [a.m.] & Nottingham by the 10 [a.m.] train
& arrived at the Euston Station $\frac{1}{4}$ to 4 [p.m.] – The meeting at the Duke of Richmond's
was for 3 o'clock [.] I immediately took a hackney cab & drove to the Duke of Richmond's
[Portland Place, Marylebone], where I found the meeting Still in discussion – which lasted
for about $\frac{1}{2}$ or $\frac{3}{4}$ of an hour after my arrival – as far as I could make out, for I was so tired
& confused from the noise & whirling of the railway, the question had been whether the
course to be taken Should be on the introduction of the bill to the House of Lords, to
refuse to receive it Singly as apart from the whole Scheme of abolition of protection, & to
reject the partial bill, by Voting that we will wait untill the Entire measure be brought in
before discussion – The other plan & as I understood, according to Lord Stanleys opinion,

[348]Newcastle recommended that the speech be published: N.U.M.D., Pw H 517: Newcastle to Portland, 3 Mar. 1846; Pw H 212: Lord George Bentinck to Portland, 5 Mar. 1846: 'The Duke of Newcastle has written to me what he told you & wants me to correct my Speech that he May bind it up in gold & red Morocco to place in his library'. It was subsequently published in *The Morning Post*, 23 Mar. 1846; Pw H 215: Bentinck to Portland, 24 Mar. 1846.

[349]Having been defeated in his re-election for South Nottinghamshire on 25 Feb. 1846, Lincoln's name was put forward in the contest for North Nottinghamshire which Lord Henry Bentinck went on to win: *Unhappy Reactionary*, 143–4.

[350]R.P., 1692, ff. 1811–12: Newcastle to Richmond, 6, 8 Mar. 1846. Newcastle noted that three trains ran from Nottingham to London Euston, at 7 a.m., 8.30 a.m. (arriving at 2.45 p.m.), and 10 (arriving at 3.15 p.m.).

was to let the first reading pass & take the vote on the second reading – I confess that as far as I at present understand the question, I incline to the first proposal, as being plain, direct, intelligible = & taking up our ground on general protection not on the Separate & Exclusive ground of protection to agriculture alone = a Committee was formed to regulate proceedings, & two Peers elected / Lords Malmesbury & Eglinton – Who are young & zealous & who are to act as a Sort of whippers in of the party = & whose immediate particular duty will be to ascertain the intentions of all Peers & to Know who we may really depend upon – Thank God, our party is now formed & will have a fair Start, & by His blessing may be instrumental in Saving Our Whole Country from ruin & degradation – The party will be [the] Strongest that has Existed Since the time of [the Younger] Pitt, & what is of the utmost importance in perfect sympathy with the nation – barring a few who have been the authors of all this vile treachery — Specially, the otherwise much to be respected men of Manchester, but more tomorrow when my head & body are fresher. It is confidently Stated that we Shall throw out the bill – Ministers I am told only hope to win it [in] the House of Lords by 5 = but this Even Several peers told me today, is a mistake – & as far as I have been Enabled to form a Judgment, & I rejoice to think So, is quite wrong: this however in the course of a week or ten days will be pretty accurately authenticated –

*10 March 1846.* I saw Lord Stanley today & had a long conversation with him on the present & future State of affairs – he Spoke of Every thing with great moderation, but Expressed himself decisively respecting protection = he will lead us when the proper time arrives but does not think it advantageous that he should do so immediately – he told me that the Duke of Wellington is infact against the measure & will be glad to see it lost – if it should be carried through both houses, he feels assured that the Whigs will not stand by Peel but will immediately cast him off, & that Peel will retire into private life — the Duke of Wellington also merely retaining, which he will do doubtless as long as he lives, the post of Commander in Chief – Lord Stanley I fear has rather too much hankering after Some of his late colleagues, & in my opinion it would Entirely damage a new administration to have anything to do with them – The best informed Even does not Know on which side will be the majority in our house – but it Seems certain that on whichever side it is declared, it will Either way be very Small.[351]

*11 March 1846.* very busy today with various people offering Suggestions & communicating & receiving information respecting our present & future proceedings – I find Lord George Bentinck a most useful, able, willing & intelligent public man. I told him that I proposed once more to address myself in print to my Countrymen & the farmers in particular – & he quite approved of the plan[352] – I did not shew him the address which I wrote last night, but I did Shew it afterwards to Mr [C.E.] Michele, [Editor] of the Morning Post who told me that he liked it much, called it a "beautiful letter" as it appealed from the heart to the heart, & he was Sure would produce the best Effects – It will come out the day after tomorrow =

[351] D.P., 147/14: Newcastle to Stanley, 10 Mar. 1846, requesting an interview 'as regards our present & future prospects'.

[352] N.U.M.D., Pw H 213: Lord George Bentinck to Portland, 10 Mar. 1846.

*12 March 1846.* […] Finished touching up & completing my letter & Sent it to the Editor –

*13 March 1846.* My letter appears in the Morning Post this morning = I am annoyed to see that it has been altered by the Editors, which is very improper & injures my meaning in Some degree[353] –

*15 March 1846.* Our friends in the Commons are going on famously – They are to Keep Peels' vile measure in jeopardy there, so that we shall not have it [in the House of Lords] untill after Easter – which is the right way of proceeding –

*17 March 1846.* The Same beautiful weather continues and all idea of famine or deficiency has Entirely vanished = The price of potatoes, is Even rather lower than last year, notwithstanding all the outcry upon the Subject –

*18 March 1846.* Our party is fighting valiantly & skilfully in the House of Commons. Lord George Bentinck taking the lead with Extraordinary ability for such a new performer – Peel finds his progress impeded by postponements & other obstructions –

*19 March 1846.* It is rumoured in London that there is disastrous news from India, by private advices – I fully Expect Such intelligence from the miserable manner in which our political & military matters have been conducted = The rumours mention that Sir Henry Hardinge has been Killed, & three officers of rank tried for cowardice & many other things – The Duke of Wellington is reported of [*sic* – to] be aware of the Events but has not revealed them.

*21 March 1846.* The Indian Mail is anxiously Expected but not arrived –
    Lord Stanley on presenting Some petitions in the House of Lords against the Ministerial Measures, declared his belief as well as hope that the bill would not pass the House of Lords = This was dextrously & well done = it was what we wanted –

*25 March 1846.* I learn that Peel's revolutionary bill is to be Kept in the Commons, & will be allowed to proceed no further than the 2nd reading before Easter – & that it will probably not be brought into our House much if any before May – Corn was selling today at Worksop from 58 to 62s –

*27 March 1846.* It is said that the Duke of Portland has Signified that he will Subscribe £25000 to the funds of any Society the object of Which Shall be to put down the anti Corn law League –

*28 March 1846.* There has been Some little awkwardness in the House of Commons about Some bargain attempted to be made by Mr [John] Young of the Treasury & Lord George Bentinck, that the latter Should let the Irish coercion bill pass provided that the government

---

[353]Thereby disappointing his expectations – 'It would be useless to Send you a Manuscript copy of the Letter as no doubt it will be pretty accurately printed in the Morning Post': BL, Add. MS 56368, ff. 176–7: Newcastle to Giffard, 12 Mar. 1846. See Appendix A.

Should agree to let the third reading of the new corn bill Stand over untill after Easter – If Lord George gave Encouragement or Even Countenance to any Such proposal Even for a moment he acted very unwarrantably & I am willing to hope that he did no Such thing –

*29 March 1846.* Mr [John] Stuart made his first Speech the night before last [as MP for Newark] & acquitted himself Extremely well – I feel pretty Confident that he will suit the House of Commons –

*31 March 1846.* Sir Robert Peel Evidently feels & Shews that he feels that he is gone, he loses consideration Every day & can never regain his Station =

*1 April 1846.* […] The Indian Mail is arrived – but instead of being disastrous the news [of the Battle of Aliwal] is most glorious – Sir Henry Smith made the first impression by beating the Siks [*sic*] with his little army, defeating them thoroughly, taking their artillery, camp, baggage [,] in Short Every thing & driving them head over heels across the river – The Siks however behaved heroically well – This being done it was necessary to make preparations for a grand advance of the Whole army – When all was ready they did advance & there followed Some fighting of the deadliest Kind, the result was that after a Series of actions the Siks' army Was Knocked to pieces & completely defeated = they then began to treat – & Sir Henry Hardinge's terms were Submissive, asking pardon, disbanding of the remnant of the Siks army, payment by them of the Expences of the war, their conquered country to be restored to them & the young Mararajish [*sic*] to be Secured on his throne = This is our magnanimity, I hope it is good policy – Our Generals have retrieved they [*sic* – their] military character – Sir Henry Smith appears to be the best & most accomplished Soldier & Commander among them – but Sir Hugh Gough has behaved admirably well, & so has the Governor general [Hardinge] — The two last are to be made Peers[354] –

*4 April 1846.* The thanks of both Houses of Parliament have been most Warmly voted to the Commander in Chief in India [Sir Hugh Gough] & the officers under his command & the whole army – never were thanks more thoroughly & Justly Earned than on this occasion – what the Troops have done is almost passing believe [*sic* – belief] – it is wonderful –

*9 April 1846.* By the official accounts of the Revenue it appears that there is a deficiency of [£] two[355] millions & $\frac{1}{2}$ on the year & Sundry most Extraordinary & inexplicable Juggling's played with the figures [,] Especially as regards the amounts of Customs & Excise for the last year –

*10 April 1846.* So much to remark upon that I hardly Know what to note – but it mostly relates to Peel's miserable political Conduct –

*11 April 1846.* The Holidays for the House of Commons are to be very restricted – the House is adjourned to the 17[th] – The House of Lords to the 21st –

---

[354] N.U.M.D., Ne C 5172: Combermere to Newcastle, 1 Apr. [1846].

[355] 2 precedes this in the original.

*21 April 1846.* In the House of Commons they can make no progress. The Lords met on the 17th & did nothing – The adjourned debates on the Irish coercion bill & the Corn bill were fixed for yesterday but no one attended [–] the house was counted & only 38 Members present. Sir Robert Peel was not in the house – Evidently a Contrived failure –

*22 April 1846.* The House of Lords met yesterday – Lord Brougham remarked upon the defection of business in the House of Commons –

*23 April 1846.* The Subject of railways Seems to be that which now <u>most</u> occupies the public attention = Legislative care is come too late [–] one half of the Country is already cruelly injured or ruined by them –

*28 April 1846.* It is Stated in the Warden ['Dublin Warder'], that Lincoln has left Dublin to try if he can get in for the Falkirk district of burghs, in which Hamilton is included, in the room of Mr [William] Baird a Conservative who has retired[356] –

*29 April 1846.* It is actually true that Lincoln is canvassing the Falkirk burgs [sic –] there is a long account of it in the papers today – a more offensive reception of a Candidate never was given to any one – I am astonished that any man of common Spirit & high feeling could for a moment Submit to Such indignity – but alas, he Seems to be lost to generous & noble feelings, & thinks of nothing but place & power, & cares not what he does or what he loses provided that he may obtain & maintain that paramount object –

*30 April 1846.* In[357] the Standard of today – an account from Falkirk appears & Lincoln is obstinately continuing his Efforts as heretofore in Notts' & has been & is pursuing the identical tactics that he pursued here – taking them by Surprise, useing [sic] trick & artifice wholly unworthy of him, talking of walking in the Constitution, but dealing underhandedly with a man who Sells to him as far as he is able his seat & his Constituents – & then makes the Egregious mistake that by harrangues of hours long he can Effect that which has an opposite Effect by wearying & creating distaste at Egotism – These Falkirk burgs are the most radical in Scotland, & whilst Lincoln is thus giving Severe pain to his family & friends, & losing character & consequence, he is utterly unmindful of his wife & family from whom he has been absent for many weeks – Lady Lincoln has been obliged to go to Brighton for the benefit of her health & as I learn today is very ill there – How little could I have guessed Even that Lincoln Could ever be brought to act thus!

*2 May 1846.* The nomination at Falkirk has taken place – Lincoln & Mr [John] Wilson were proposed – & both addressed the Electors – Lincoln very Coldly & unfavorably received – on a shew of hands not more than a dozen were held up for Lincoln but a poll was

[356] Lincoln's return had been in contemplation for some weeks: N.U.M.D., Ne C 4638: John Young to Lincoln, 26 Mar. 1846; Pw L 53: Henry Burgess to Lord George Bentinck, 25 Apr. 1846; H.P., Bundle 902, Lincoln to the duke of Hamilton, 29 Mar. 1846; Hamilton to Lincoln, 31 Mar. 1846.

[357] ~~By~~ precedes this in the original.

demanded for him – what folly & bad feeling to persist under Such circumstances, & to incur Such unnecessary Expence & Expose himself to ludicrous failure –

*3 May 1846.* The Irish coercion bill has at last passed the first reading. Peel has fixed the 25th to read it a 2nd time = This pressing bill!! How thoroughly this man is fallen & lost owing to his own baseness.

*5 May 1846.* To my infinite Surprise Lincoln has Succeeded & has the honor to have been Elected a representative for the radical Falkirk burghs – his majority Was only 11 [506–495] – I am Sorry that he is now Enabled to Expose his infirmities & absurdities in Parliament which (as he has now by practice become an adept in the true Peel phraseology & most approved mode, of Calling black white, & pretending to be candid & honest When he Knows that he is nothing of the Sort) no doubt he will be too happy to retail & Enunciate from the Ministerial bench, ore rotundo[358] – Peel Entrapping him all the while, which he in his vanity does not perceive –

*8 May 1846.* Here in Protestant England, Especially in Parliament the[359] highest praise is bestowed upon Jesuits & papists – Whilst in France & Elsewhere, the very reverse is the case – & the French Chambres are now so outrageous against the Jesuits that they are nearly unmanageable – We are grievously & most lamentably in a deadly Error –

*9 May 1846.* The vile Corn bill will be out of the Commons, Early in the next week, it is thought = it will be debated in our house on the 21st [–] I too much fear it will not be defeated in the Lords[360] –

*10 May 1846.* at the Queen's party the other day, it has been remarked that there were Scarcely any invited but Free Traders –

*15 May 1846.* I learn today from [my son] Charles that Lincoln has the gout in his feet & heart as I read his writing – I trust that this is not the case – but when I was able to Communicate with him I always told him that office & his mode of living Would destroy his health, & that his duty to his family demanded that he Should take proper care of his health – alas he poor fellow, sets himself against any advice of mine – & he will not only in this but in other things woefully Suffer for the disregard – & pay a heavy penalty [.]

[358]With full or round mouth.

[359]the precedes this in the original.

[360]Newcastle wrote to Stanley ahead of this, offering his support and outlining his political creed: 'On all questions of Reform, I have always been a most decided opponent, & mainly because I am a Stupid matter of fact man, & adhere to practice, attaching little or no value to theory … I can Know nothing of the Dissenter, I tolerate him, but I Cannot legislate for him'; D.P., 147/14: Newcastle to Stanley, 5 May 1846; 176/2, f. 387: Stanley to Newcastle, 11 May 1846.

I have found it to be utterly impossible to complete my business so as to leave tomorrow[361] –

*16 May 1846.* […] Lincoln I trust must be better, as I See his name as answering a question in the House of Commons –

*17 May 1846.* […] The Corn importation debate finished yesterday morning: the majority 98 [327–229] – one more than on the 1st division [.] The Country party has made an immortal Struggle –

*21 May 1846.* [London] Dined this Evening at Lord Combermere's [–] a large party – The farmer's from all parts of England had a Meeting today at Willis's rooms [King Street, St James's] – The meeting was So numerous that one or Even two rooms would not hold them – It was therefore divided & the Duke of Richmond took the chair in the upper room, the Duke of Buckingham in the lower – It went off admirably & people told me who were there that they & others were perfectly astonished at the ability displayed by the farmers, who were made the Speakers upon the occasion – They passed resolutions of a nature to Stimulate the Energies of the House of Lords –

*22 May 1846.* […] Lincoln I understand is Very ill with gout all over him & as it is Called in his Chest – most dangerous I should fear, Especially when according to all accounts he takes no care of himself & has nobody with him who has any influence over him to induce him to do So – it is a wretched business altogether, & I cannot go near him.
Went for a Short time to the House of Lords this Evening –

*23 May 1846.* I was told the other day by Lord Salisbury that the Single reason for the Duke of Wellington adopting the new notion of free trade & free trade in Corn, to which he was previously adverse, was a letter from the Queen begging of him to alter his determination, to give in to Peel's new views & to resume his Seat in the Cabinet or, he would break of [*sic* – up] the administration, which would throw her into difficulties. The Duke immediately complied & now risks the ruin of his Queen & his Country –

*25 May 1846.* The Queen was Safely delivered of a Daughter [Helena] this morning –
Our debate on the Corn importation bill commenced this Evening. Lord Ripon opened the debate in a wretched Speech = at 9 [p.m.] Lord Stanley rose & Spoke for above 3 hours – it was without Exception the best, the most Efficient & most perfect Speech I Ever heard in my life – The manner, the matter, the high tone, without bombast, bluster or insolence, the all Comprehensiveness, for it Exhausted the Whole Subject, but above all the truthfulness, noble views, of all that is Exalted & imitable for a Nation Stamped it as a performance of boundless utility, & inestimable worth – – I do believe that a better & more brilliant Speech never [before] was made – it was incomparable – The Duke of Richmond in moving the opposition to the bill, made a remarkably good speech – the debate will probably last many nights –

---

[361]Newcastle was not present when 47 peers met on 16 May 1846: K.D., 16 May 1846.

*26 May 1846.* The debate went off very well in our favor, we are gaining ground on the majority it is Said −

*27 May 1846.* Holiday today for our comfort − Derby day − Tomorrow We Sit again, but it is not unlikely that we Shall again adjourn & if So We Shall not Conclude till after the Whitsun holidays −

*28–29 May 1846.* after a very long debate begun at 5 o'clock yesterday we divided at 5 [a.m.] this morning − majority for the Vile Corn importation bill, 47[362] − Lord Dalhousie Spoke well on the Ministerial Side − he is a young man of Superior faculties[363] −

*30 May 1846.* Not recovered the fatigues of the Killingly hot house & long night's debates − but better this Evening − The Duke of Wellingtons Speech was really quite abominable = poor man he is in his dotage, but presumes to speak with as much authority & pretension as if he was in his prime − His language however must be noticed when we meet again on the 4th [of] June −

*2 June 1846.* I Saw in the Standard newspaper this Evening that [my son] William has been appointed first attache at Constantinople [.] I can hardly believe it, I have heard nothing of it −

*3 June 1846.* I wrote this morning to Clinton Dawkins who is Secretary to Lord aberdeen & he confirms what I had Seen in the Standard & William is now actually received into the profession & is the first of the Several attaches at the Porte − it is a very desirable appointment I am told [−] Sir Stratford Canning being our best diplomatist & Constantinople being now the best position for diplomacy −

*4 June 1846.* The Customs duties was debated today − Lord Dalhousie[364] opened & Duke of Richmond moved reading the bill in 6 months − the debate was not long though Several Speakers [−] we did not divide −

   I took an opportunity of meeting Ld aberdeen & thanked him very much for his Kindness to William − with which he Seemed very much gratified − He told me With Sincerity that William had acquitted himself with great credit hitherto, that he was very much disposed to work & that he was highly deserving of Encouragement − William gets £300 a year by this appointment −

*5 June 1846.* an unexpected debate & division arose this Evening on Lord Ripon bringing forward − Lords Hardinge's & Gough's annuity bills − The original intention was to vote £2000 a year to Lord Hardinge, to sustain his tille [*sic* − title] &c − but the East India Company voted him £2000 for life & then the Government thought fit to reduce the

---

[362] The vote on the second reading was 211 for (138 present and 73 proxies) and 164 against (126 present and 38 proxies): majority 47.

[363] R.P., 1692, f. 1823: Newcastle to Richmond, 28 May 1846, seeking an extended debate in order to give 'a fair chance to Every Speaker whether debutant or old Stager'.

[364] ~~Ripon~~ precedes this in the original.

parliamentary grant to £1000 a year during life = this was thought to be So niggardly & unjust that it was opposed – we divided – & the Ministers were beaten by 18 [*sic* 26–38] –

*6 June 1846.* Today we had a meeting of Protectionist peers to Consider what amendments Should be proposed in the Committee on the Corn bill – The meeting was a large one & a good deal Said [–] Lord Stanley made a good Speech & in a most pleasant way – but Still I did not concur with him – The object is to alter the bill in Committee So that it Shall be rejected by the Commons – It is proposed first to move that the protective Clauses of the present bill Shall be Continued untill 1849 – but Substituting 10s as the lowest duty to be paid – if this be lost then another amendment will be proposed Embracing a fixed duty = & it is said to be probable that one or other of these amendments will be carried. Now my view is first, that it is very unlikely that we Shall in any way gain a majority, if so, then that we Shall have Shifted & quitted our Strong ground, that our consistency will be gone & that we may Consequently lose public confidence, Sooner Should We continue to maintain the law of 1842 – & take advantage of the Duke of Wellingtons hint – & if we can alter the new bill & restore the old one in a new Parliament – I was listened to with Kindness & attention, but the original proposals were adhered to & the course to be pursued will be on the 11th to resist going into Committee & to debate it on that & the following day [,] being Friday, when we Should not divide but go into Committee pro forma & take the debate in Committee on the Monday following to last for Several days – We were all in friendly humour & determined to be & were unanimous & the meeting [went] off vastly well – although to my mind grounded on what I think to be a false & baseless foundation –

*8 June 1846.* Ibrahim Pacha [Pasha] arrived today in London, he is lodged at Mivarts Hotel[365] – He will miss Some of his Eastern Cooling luxuries, Such as fountains, baths &c –

To Judge from the present aspect of things, Ministers Will be out in a few days – a meeting was holden at Lord John Russells on Saturday last (6th June) when it was determined that he & his party Should oppose the Irish Coercion bill – this must be fatal to Peel – for I trust that we Shall look on & Suffer him to die by the assassin hands of his new allies –

*9 June 1846.* attended a Committee at the House of Lords [–] the Harwich branch to the Eastern – it came to us from the House of Commons but we turned it out – the House of Commons was 5 days over it, we were four hours & I believe did the business Effectually –

This is Kept as the Queen's birthday, among the illuminations one of the most conspicuous was V.R. a wheat sheaf & the motto ["] Free trade ["] =

*10 June 1846.* It is fully Expected that on division, on the Irish coercion bill [,] Peel will be in a minority, & in that case of course he must resign – His ministry is virtually Extinct already –

*11 June 1846.* […] Our debate in Committee on the Corn bill Commenced tonight – Lord Stanhope opened with an Excellent Speech & moved that the bill be read in 6 months –

---

[365] It was known as Mivart's Hotel until it was sold and renamed Claridge's Hotel in 1854.

Lord Wicklow made a very Clever Speech on this night [–] We adjourned to tomorrow – Ibrahim Pacha & his attendants were in the house = unfortunately it was very dull & much pantomime whilst he remained, which was for several hours –

*12 June 1846.* There was some good speaking tonight, but by far the best Speech from Lord Stanley – we did not divide but went into Committee pro forma, the debate to be taken on Monday, 15[th] –

*13 June 1846.* Exceedingly hot all the morning & almost impossible to move & take Exercise – dined with Lord Eglinton where we had a large party dinner – it was very pleasant & animated – & we discussed many things to much advantage –

*15 June 1846.* In an atmosphere in the House of Lords of about 80 [degrees] I Should think [,] we went into Committee on the adjourned Corn debate [,] it was animated & Sharp, Duke of Buckingham moved to leave out the duration of the duty Clause – our matters Were mismanaged & we divided unexpectedly at an Early hour, about 11[p.m.], when Several of our people were absent. I had intended to Speak & many others would have done So if required, but we were not looked after & the division came upon us quite by Surprise – Our numbers were for the amendment 103, against 136 [majority 33] = Our conquerors had the bad taste to cheer, a thing I never Knew done before –

*16 June 1846.* Lord Wicklow moved an amendment in Committee this night – for a fixed duty of 5s [–] a most nonsensical & improper amendment Certainly & contrary to my Views but Still I divided with him upon it not to Split the party – a long & animated debate – I rose to Speak & was on my legs & actually began, but it was wished that I Should give way to a new member – I did not try again – we divided 107, & 140 [majority 33] – dreadfully hot & painful to Sit in the house –

*17 June 1846.* This fortunately is a holiday for us – the intense heat quite destroys one, & takes away all power or Energy – dined at [Lord] Combermere's [–] a large political party –

*18 June 1846.* Fagging all day about railway business in which I am too Effectually foiled – Waterloo day & no house for us – went to a ball with my daughters = real Suffering from the Extraordinary heat – we shall have Some terrible disease I fear = in consequence of it –

*19 June 1846.* In the House of Lords tonight the Duke of Richmond Withdrew his motion – the bill passed Committee & Report[s] on Monday [the] 22nd –

*20 June 1846.* We had a large meeting of Protectionist Peers today to agree upon our future course – Protection is most properly decided to be our principle of action – in this Spirit after we lose our Corn protection, we are to oppose the Customs tariff bill & contend against any farther diminution of duties = We are to have Several divisions in the next week, & Lord Stanley has prepared a most able protest on the Corn bill Which we are all to Sign –

*22 June 1846.* Renewed debate in Committee, – & a good deal of Sharp work – two divisions, one on Lord asburtons [*sic*] resolution on which we considerably Encreased our minority & another on hearing Counsel for the Silk weavers, when we had a Majority of 1 in the house, which was by proxies turned into a minority of 4 – if Ever it is moved to abolish proxies I shall vote for the abolition[366] – about 10 o'clock a welcomed [*sic*] storm of thunder [,] most vivid lightning & heavy rain came on, more to the Satisfaction of all present than the stewing debate –

*23 June 1846.* Resumed debate on report & two very near divisions[367] –

*24 June 1846.* I have a great deal to do & much trouble about railways – with various Success – no house today –

*25 June 1846.* The Corn importation bill passed the 3rd reading this Evening[368] – a more Execrable measure or one more villainously carried by Every trick [,] artifice, treachery & dishonesty never passed the House, & we Shall rue the day when this Pandora's box was opened. Lord Feversham made an Excellent Speech, & Lord Gage one of a very Superior nature = which had been most carefully written & Studied, & was Excessively well Spoken with all accuracy of diction & Emphasis & inflexion of voice – The Speech might have been $\frac{1}{2}$ an hour or $\frac{3}{4}$ long – Evidently Every word gotten by heart & finished up with peculiar care – a wonderful Exploit of memory –

*26 June 1846.* I was Examined in Committee room D as witness on the Sheffield & Lincolnshire & Midland & Grimsby railways. I gave such Evidence in conjunction with others that I think the former bill must be lost[369] –

Last[370] night a division took place in the Commons on the Coercion bill & Peel was beaten by a majority of 72[371] = This has thrown him into Confusion & he is at his Wiles again, they have been for Some days pompously announcing that they were packing up & clearing their houses – giving offices &c – but I think it a mere ruse & that Peel will stick [.]

*27 June 1846.* Nothing more is Known = Peel was to go to the Queen in the Isle of Wight today – Her Majesty is to come to London on Monday 29[th] – & I am convinced that a Juggling plan will be devised to Keep Peel in –

*29 June 1846.* Engaged all day on a Committee – at the Sitting of the House – Duke of Wellington announced that the Ministry had resigned but would carry on the Government

---

[366]Lord Ashburton's resolution was defeated by 47–70: majority 23; on the silk weavers, the vote was 74 for (43 present and 31 proxies) and 78 against (42 present and 36 proxies): majority four.

[367]The votes were 33–50: majority 17, and 50–75: majority 25.

[368]*Protests*, iii, 316–20.

[369]According to newspaper report, Lord Somers was in the chair: *Sun*, 27 June 1846.

[370]This precedes this in the original.

[371]The vote was 219–292: majority 73; N.U.M.D., Ne2F1/15: diary enclosure, analysis of the division on The Protection of Life (Ireland) Bill, 1846.

untill a new one was formed – this looks suspicious – He Said too that the Queen had Sent to the only alternative Lord John Russell – Ld. aberdeen announced that the Oregon question was terminated & that our terms had been agreed to by a majority of 38 to 12 in the Senate – This is very good news –

Lord John Russell is in very low Spirits it is Said, his brother [Lord George Russell] is dying, & he Excused himself from attending immediately to the Queen's commands – Queer Enough –

*30 June 1846.* Lord John Russell is gone to the Queen in the Isle of Wight, this day – he takes with him, a list of persons who are to form his ministry – Many I am told are very angry & much disappointed – among these [is] Lord Clanricarde who is to be postmaster with a Seat in the Cabinet –

Peel's high Eulogy of [Richard] Cobden last night has Caused universal disgust & Seals his ruin & disgrace as a public & private man – There never was a more awful downfall of any man –

*1 July 1846.* again attending the Committee – 3rd day – being very far from well & Should be very glad to lay by = I do not hear of any hindrance to the formation of the new Government [.]

*2 July 1846.* 4th day of Committee [–] quite tired of it & ill – The Queen has not yet come to London nor is it Sure when She will come – The Duke of Wellington is to remain Commander in Chief – but he declares that he shall abjure political life – it is time that he Should do so, & I trust that he will adhere to his declaration – Sir Robert Peel & family are gone into the Country –

*3 July 1846.*[372] We finished our Committee on the Gorbals gravitation Water Works today a little before 4 – with great gratification to ourselves that we were at length quit of it[373] – It is understood that, Lord John Russell applied to Peel for permission to invite 5 of his late Cabinet to Join him, to which Peel replied that he had no objection individually but that he would not advise these persons to accept the invitation, as it would look like tenacity of Office. How like this meanly minded man. Lord John afterwards asked the Duke of Wellington if he would Sanction his applying to 3 members of the late Cabinet to Which he replied ["] none whatever ["], & at Lord John's request Wrote to these three [,] Lincoln, Sidney Herbert & Lord Dalhousie: fortunately for these individuals, they declined[374] = this is report – but believed to be true – a good many Peers in the House this Evening but no business done, no Ex or other Ministers present –

*4 July 1846.* Of course one hears a great deal during a day passed among people who are sure to discuss passing Events = I dined out & afterwards went to Lord Salisbury's

[372]K.D., 3 July 1846. Kenyon called on Newcastle, among other peers.

[373]The final act (1846) allowed the Gorbals gravitation water company to build works and earth dams to supply water to the population of Glasgow living south of the river Clyde.

[374]N.U.M.D., Ne C 12157/20–1: Peel to Lincoln, 2, 3 July 1846; Ne C 12232: Jonathan Thompson to Lincoln, 5 July 1846.

party but nothing more than generalities were given – Lord John Russell has formed his administration & new [election writs] are moved for those who have to Vacate their Seats – Lord John has issued his address to his London Constituents – on Monday, day after tomorrow, the Lord Chancellor [Lord Cottenham] takes possession of the Seals & the late Ministers will at a Privy Councill [*sic*] resign their offices = The Queen is in London.

*6 July 1846.* I have had a great fuss all this day about railways in which I am interested Especially Sheffield & Lincolnshire, & went down to the house [of Lords] to oppose the 3rd reading but it did not come on –

The Ministers were in their places but we were in large force expecting something – Lord Lansdowne however Solicited an adjournment of all proceedings for a week or ten days which was agreed to –

*7 July 1846.* In the House of Lords tonight – On Lord Vyvian moving the 3rd reading of the Sheffield & Lincolnshire bill, I told the house that I greatly objected to the bill & moved that the debate upon it be adjourned to Thursday week the 16th as public business was postponed to that time on account of the position of the new Government: we had a Sharpish fight, but Brougham Stood my friend & Supporter, two of the Ministers also backed me & I finally carried my point – I believe for the first time in my life[375] –

*8 July 1846.* This afternoon we went[376] a large party consisting of about 100 lords & commons to dine at Greenwich [–] we went & returned by Steamer – Lord Stanley in an Excellent Speech accepted the Leadership & Shewed us how we ought to act – all went off remarkably well – there was no fault but its length – we did not break up till near 1 o'clock & I did not get home before 2 [a.m.][377] –

*16 July 1846.* Full of business again today – principally on my railway matters = which Kept me to so late an hour that I could not go to the House of Lords –

*17 July 1846.* Much Engaged this morning & in [the] afternoon attended in my place in the House of Lords to oppose the 3rd reading of the Sheffield & Lincolnshire bill – I had to make a longer Speech than I am want to address to their Lordships, & got through it rather better than usual – I was not without Expectation of Success, but I Soon found that the House was not in my favour – I made the best fight I could, & did not give way untill I had placed my motion in the Lord Chancellor's hands, but as I perceived that it was Evidently useless to divide, I withdrew my motion –

*18 July 1846.* Dined at the Duke of Richmond's – a man dinner – a very pleasant party & an abundance of political talk – free, intellectual & highly Satisfactory – Lord Stanley was

[375] Newcastle's agent advised him that he would not get £350 per acre from the Sheffield and Lincolnshire company for the land they required from him: N.U.M.D., Ne C 7917: Edward Woollett Wilmot to Newcastle, 4 July 1846.

[376] had precedes this in the original.

[377] *Nottingham Journal*, 17 July 1846, reported the attendance of 40 peers and 60 MPs at the Trafalgar Tavern, Greenwich. Newcastle was among the peers who addressed the meeting.

there, & we had a great deal of discourse upon present & future matters, & I am rejoiced to find that we agree in views, I was much afraid that he was too much inclined to Join with the Ex Ministers, but I find that they are only Exceptions & not Exceptionable – & upon all other points we agree most cordially – in Short I believe that we are all as nearly of one mind as can well be Expected of Such a large body – We are going on well – However it is very much Expected that a dissolution will take place Very Shortly = & it is Said that it will be caused by the result of the debate on the Sugar duties –

*19 July 1846.* Nothing very particular – a long conference with Mr Stuart Satisfactory & useful, as all are with him[378] –

    Sir Robert Peel cut his foot by treading on a basin & breaking it [–] I Suppose when washing his foot – he was laid up by the accident[379] & the Joke [is] "that he had cut another of his Supporters" –

*20 July 1846.* Engaged with one person or another during the whole day – had then to write letters[380] – a rapid dinner & then to the House of Lords – Lord Powis moved[381] the 2nd reading of his Bangor & St asaph bill in a long speech = we divided a little after 10 [p.m.] = as far as I could catch the numbers they were 37 & 26[382] – However we had a good majority & Lord Lansdown then very handsomely announced that he Should give no further opposition to the bill through the House of Lords. I rejoice at this result. Peel's Government did not & would not have acted thus –

*25 July 1846.* […] Major [William] Beresford came to me today to tell me that Lord John Manners had Suddenly written to his Constituents at Newark to inform them that he intended to resign his Seat & that he had reasons for doing this instantly – To one who Sets Such a Store by a Seat in Parliament as Lord John does – it is Evident what is at work – I at once told Major Beresford that I Saw through the Scheme & that the intention was to let in Gladstone, with whom & others I believe the Protectionists are negociating to gain what is not worth having, the Slippery Support of tainted men = it is a false move & will be the ruin of the party, if it should cause a doubt of our Sincerity & good faith = In this instance I can See clearly that I was played upon today & that the good Major was Skirmishing & reconnaeturing [*sic*] –

*26 July 1846.* a long conference with Mr Stuart today – I told him many things & believe him to be a man of Strict prudence & honor & integrity –

---

[378]Newcastle told Stuart about the possibility of replacing him at Newark with Lord Charles Clinton. However, 'the result of this was, no apparent willingness now to lose him … I had no wish to gratify With regard to my Son … that I on my part had no wish for a change & that I Should continue my Support to him': N.A., DD/TL/2/1/91, Newcastle to Godfrey Tallents, 19 July 1846.

[379]~~addis~~ precedes this in the original.

[380]For example, to Stanley, hoping that he would support Powis: D.P., 147/14: Newcastle to Stanley, 20 July 1846.

[381]~~brought~~ precedes this in the original.

[382]K.D., 20 July 1846, 'Carried it by his blessing 38 to 28'; 24 July 1846, 'Lord Bexley voted with us this year for Welsh Bishops [–] Had Proxies been called [I] believe we should have had 88 to 52'.

*28 July 1846.* [...] By a letter from Lord John Manners written from Hagley, I learn that he does not mean to offer himself for Newark at a General Election – I am farther informed that Lord Granby is to Succeed his Uncle Lord Charles [Manners] for Leicestershire & Lord John to take Lord Granby's place at Stanford [*sic* – Stamford] – [Manners] Sutton of Kelham to offer himself for Newark[383] –

*29 July 1846.* The division on the Sugar duties upon which Lord John Russell <u>declared</u> that he would Stand or fall was <u>265</u> for <u>135</u> against – <u>majority 130</u> – I am much Surprised at the Smallness of the minority & the largeness of the Majority – but I never thought with others that the Minister Would be beaten – the question of dissolution is now Settled – The Minister will go on quietly to the End of the Session, & meet Parliament probably in February next – when if he proceeds moderately & wisely he will not be meddled with, but if he attempts bad measures [,] he will meet with the most determined opposition – Lord George Bentinck – made an admirable, I am informed a great Speech on this occasion – I deeply regret that the measure is carried – Peel made a miserable figure – it will be curious to See who he carried with him to reinforce the Ministerial ranks –

*30 July 1846.* The West Indian proprietors, at a large meeting [,] have declared that the measure now adopted is So ruinous to their interests that it is their determination to cultivate their Estates no longer = Lincoln I grieve to see Voted in Peels' train –

*2 August 1846.* Sir George Murray, is dead – a most distinguished Military Officer – & a very clever & accomplished man. The labor & confinement consequent upon Editing the Duke of Marlborough despatches &c no doubt destroyed him[384] –

*4 August 1846.* Dwarkenant Tagore [Dwarkanath Tagore] the celebrated Hindoo [Hindu] – So remarkable for his Enlightened goodness, usefulness & wealth – died the day before yesterday – He will be a very great loss to his own country – I am very sorry for his death having Seen him often, & having Known him a little – He died of a liver Complaint –

*5 August 1846.* I had a letter today inviting me to a Meeting of Peers at Lord Stanley's, to consider whether it will be advisable to divide in the House of Lords on the Sugar Duties question, & requesting me to write my opinion upon it, if, I cannot be present – I have returned my opinion in writing, & advising to divide for reasons which I have given –

*7 August 1846.* The Duke of Wellington attended Sir George Murray's funeral – it was on the day of the terrible storm – Sir George was always of the most Essential use to him, & many thought that he was a Superior General to the Duke – with the army he was a much greater favourite than the Duke – who was infinitely indebted to him for his masterly arrangements –

---

[383]Manners Sutton came forward under Lord Lincoln's urging: N.U.M.D., Ne C 12224/1: J.H. Manners Sutton to Lincoln, 2 Aug. 1846; Ne C 11687: Lincoln to Gladstone, 10 Aug. 1846.

[384]*The Letters and Dispatches of John Churchill, First Duke of Marlborough, from 1702 to 1712*, ed. Sir George Murray (5 vols, 1845).

*8 August 1846.* I learn that it is not intended to divide on the Sugar duties in the House of Lords – they might have spared me the trouble of writing my opinion, I thought so when I wrote – but still I would not withhold it = They are decidedly wrong –

*12 August 1846.* a remarkable instance of a turn in public opinion has taken place at the St albans Election – Lord Listourel [Listowel] Vacated his seat by acceptance of a Situation about the Court – Lord of the bedchamber – I believe – On the day of nomination he was opposed by Mr Benjamin Band Cabbell – who had been beaten by the Same Lord Listourel – in two preceeding [*sic*] Contests. To the Surprise of all he is now returned by a large Majority, 115 out of about 400 Votes polled [264–149]. I think this will check all idea of a dissolution –

*16 August 1846.* The Ministers are trying to carry & Even originate measures of very Considerable importance at the fag End of the Session when there are not Sufficient Members in town to make a house – In a great measure they have been checked by the firmness of a remaining few =

*17 August 1846.* It is asserted that an immediate Dissolution of parliament may be Expected – a letter from Messrs Beresford & Newdigate [Charles Newdegate] announces this & Solicits contributions to a Protectionist fund for the purpose of Supporting the Candidates in this interest – This Event is a great disappointment to us, as we were making preparations for a foreign tour, on which we intended to Start on tomorrow fortnight – I fear that we have great troubles before us = The potato crops are Said to be failing worse than last year [,] trade is beginning to decline, doubt prevails in all minds, & Should distress add to the perplexity,[385] we may Expect most disastrous times.

*19 August 1846.* The Deaths of two persons very Eminent in their lines are announced in the papers of this day. Sir Charles Wetherell & Baron Dedel [Salomon Baron Dedel] = Sir Charles, was a matchless man as an advocate [,] whatever line he took up, & his principles were fixed & unmoveable by any consideration – He died from being thrown from the carriage in which he was travelling, which occasioned concussion of the brain & he was never conscious, afterwards – he was 76 – Baron Dedel was Minister of the Netherlands – he was brought up a[t] Eton – & altogether an Englishman in appearance, manner & habit – He was universally Esteemed, most popular, – a clever & very able man –

*20 August 1846.* Changes are taking place in our foreign Embassies – Lord Ponsonby is appointed to Vienna to replace Sir Robert Gordon – Lord Normanby to Paris to replace Lord Cowley – it is feared that Sir Stratford Canning will not go back to Constantinople & that Lord Howard de Walden will be appointed to succeed him: a Sorry Successor indeed =

---

[385]'And there shall be signs in the sun, and in the moon, and in the stars; and upon the earth distress of nations, with perplexity': Luke, 21: 25.

*21 August 1846.* Lord Lyndhurst has Essayed to give Lord George Bentinck he a Roland for his Oliver[386] – however inculpatory Lord George might have been, he was not Scurrilous – This the Ex Chancellor has been, Every Expression & Epithet which can be used to underrate & vilify another[387] has been used by Lord Lyndhurst to crush Lord George – but it will not do – he has not only mistaken his man, but he has also mistaken the public Estimate of Lord Lyndhurst's character, & besides this – he has not Exculpated himself but has distinctly Shewn that the grounds of Lord George's accusations were all correct – & the gravest part of the charge was fully admitted by Lord Lyndhurst & he added that the blot had never been hit before – but now it would be remedied by the new [Patent Commission] bill passing threw [*sic*] the House –

*22 August 1846.* Lord George Bentinck has made a rejoinder to Lord Lyndhurst [–] no ways abased by Lord Lyndhurst's concentration of Vehement Elocution – & Shewing him Still more & more & others with him – I was Sure that Lord George was not the man to give way or to faint under the burden laid upon him = he has vanquished all hitherto & he will remain master of the field –

*24 August 1846.* No particular news – Lord Lyndhurst has made a counter Statement to Explain away Lord George Bentincks last Stinging Statement – The old intriguer, deaf & well versed as he is, was not Successful, he was not prepared for meeting a plain statement – & has Signally failed –

*25 August 1846.* It is now thought – that Parliament will not be dissolved this year – the issue of the St Albans' Election has opened the Ministerial Eyes to the probable results –

*26 August 1846.* Parliament is now to be prorogued in a few days – This has been a most Extraordinary Session – few on record more so – a great Extent of mischief has been done [–] more folly shewn – more public characters blemished & blasted – more trifling – less public gain, or more public loss, I never remember = The most business has been done by the Russell ministry – but at haphazard & almost in the dark, but being at the End of the Session there is no one to stop them – we are now in a woeful plight, & I apprehend coming disasters of a momentous nature –

  In addition to the complaint among the potatos [*sic*], the turnips are Supposed to have a disease, but both are atmospheric only = the turnips are mildewed [&] Eaten through (the leaves) by insects, & caterpillars are Eating the green leaf to the fibres – they tell me here that the Cuckoos are of the greatest use in Eating these caterpillars.

*29 August 1846.* The accounts from all parts of the Country are very distressing – what with the effects of free trade, want of confidence, Social dislocation, distrust of public men, & the general distress which is but too probable, our prospects for the future, are very gloomy indeed – We must place no confidence in Princes [,] nor in any child of man, but alone in

---

[386] An allusion to the stories of Roland and Oliver, legendary knights of equal might. Bentinck accused Lyndhurst of being involved in 'a nefarious job' regarding the justiceship of Bombay. The dispute led to a series of assaults and counter-assaults in succeeding days.

[387] a precedes this in the original.

Him who Can Save as well as punish[388] – We merit castigation & we Shall have it with a fearful Severity, I fear = I pray God to Spare us, & in His mercy to purify & make us to be more worthy, of his Mercy –

*3 September–25 October 1846.* for the Hiatus See My foreign Journal [.][389]

*26 October 1846.* [Having just returned from my overseas trip to the continent] I yesterday thought it my duty to see Lord Palmerston & to communicate to him not only what I had heard & Seen abroad, but also the conclusions which were the result of my attentive observations[390] – I remained with him for a long time & he Seemed to be very Much obliged to me for the information Which I gave him & which he told me was in many respects new to him – He gave me the history of the French marriage business & placed me au fait on a point upon which as regards the personages & parts I was previously very ignorant – He told me that Louis Philippe had behaved Exceedingly ill & Knavishly & that he had Even broken his promise to our Queen made at Eu – which was that he would not attempt to marry his Son [Antoine Duke of] (montpensier) [*sic*] until the Queen of Spain [Isabella II] had been married & had had children – His Majesty is a very Clever & able man, but he is Said to be as finished a rogue & as Supreme a rascal, as can be produced – I offered My remedy under the present circumstances, namely to come to a Convention with the French King, in which all Europe Shall concur & be parties – that by no possible means Shall the Crowns of France & Spain be united; nor Shall any treaty offensive & defensive be concluded & publicly acknowledged between these two powers, unless with the universal Consent of the other powers of Europe – Many other Subjects of Conversation were discussed between us which nunc prescribere longum est & I have not time for it.[391]

*10 November 1846.* Parliament has been prorogued to January 12[th] & Lord John Russell has refused to open the ports – in both instances he has acted most properly, wisely & firmly –

*26 November 1846.* In India disturbance is again the order of the [day and the] promised tranquillity which it was announced with much pomposity had been Secured by Sir Henry, now Lord Hardinge, for his great deeds [,] is not secured at all – as might have been foreseen by any calm & Sober thinker –

The famine panic is Subsiding Very much, it has been greatly Exaggerated –

a Commission is to be Established to manage the affairs of the Duchy of Lancaster – a most farcical Job – Lincoln is to be one of the Commissioners – What he or any of them

---

[388] 'Put not your trust in princes, in mortal man, who cannot save': Psalm, 146: 3.

[389] This volume has never been traced.

[390] N.U.M.D., Ne C 5180: Palmerston to Newcastle, 25 Oct. 1846, agreeing to meet. See below, 25 Oct. 1847.

[391] 'which it would be tedious to set out now'.

are to do, nobody can guess – There was <u>nothing</u> to do before, what there can be for 5 Commissioners to do can only be a division of nothing[392] –

*27 November 1846.* There is a talk of Lincoln's Standing for <u>Manchester.</u> I trust that there is no truth in the report, he has injured himself & me, & given me Sufficient annoyance without adding this degradation of himself to his other misdemeanors [*sic*] – He Seems to have lost all proper Sense of Self respect & to be reckless of what he does, provided that he may be at liberty to gratify his ambition & his vanity in pursuing a political phantom[393] –

*3 December 1846.* I am afraid that there is no doubt that Lincoln is trying to be called forward for Manchester –

*4 December 1846.* Trade is much depressed, the factories are, many of them, working only Short time =

*5 December 1846.* There is no longer any doubt that Lincoln is to be put up at Manchester, but he will be opposed by Quaker Bright who is a fitter man to represent Such a place as Manchester[394] –

*8 December 1846.* Lord Pollington announces that he Shall give up the representation of Pontefract. His father [the Earl of Mexborough] is quite a bankrupt –

*9 December 1846.* the most Extraordinary & Sudden rise has & is taking place in the price of Cotton at Liverpool, it has already risen 50 per Cent & upwards – The manufacturers are in dismay –

*10 December 1846.* Cattle, Sheep & corn & other provisions are being Exported from France for England – the people have violently & tumultuously opposed this & have not permitted the Embarkation – This will be the case to a very awkward Extent, if the foreign governments Sanction the Exportation of food –

*11 December 1846.* a movement is now making with Some activity to Effect the abolition of the Malt Tax, & it is said that the Protectionists are to take up the Cause – I should greatly lament this, as we cannot afford to lose the tax which yields above 4 millions = & the farmer would hardly, if at all, be benefitted by the abolition.

*15 December 1846.* It is now found that the americans will Extinguish our Cotton trade – they possess the raw material & they now manufacture to a large Extent & already Jostle us very inconveniently even in India, China & other places – their goods are much cheaper

---

[392]On the commission, see D.P., 147/14: Newcastle to Stanley, 15 Nov., 13 Dec. 1846; 177/1, f. 161: Stanley to Newcastle, 17 Nov. 1846. Stanley believed that the commission arose from 'complaints made by the Queen & Prince Albert of the small amount of revenue which comes from the Duchy into the Privy Purse'.

[393]N.U.M.D., Ne C 11870, 11872: Lincoln to Bonham, 29 Nov., 4 Dec. 1846.

[394]For an assessment of Lincoln's chances (from Peel's relations in Manchester), see N.U.M.D., Ne C 11990, 11992: Peel to Lincoln, [Dec.] 1846. In the event, John Bright and Thomas Milner Gibson were returned unopposed.

than ours & quite as good – our future is not promising – thanks to Sir Robert Peel and his villainous measures –

*16 December 1846.* Sir Charles Morgan is dead at a good old age 82 or more – but he was hale & active & well & Went off at a very short notice from cold – His Son [Charles Morgan] who married Miss [Rosamund] Mundy comes into an income of above £40,000 –

*20 December 1846.* Sunday – after going to Church we took a long walk to lionise the town – we passed the Duke of Wellingtons Statue on our way to the Houses of Parliament = it is a very poor work of art, & certainly most inappropriately placed where it now is, over the archway in Piccadilly opposite to the Duke's [Apsley] house = it is now to be permanently placed on a pedestal facing the Horse guards on the Parade – preparations are making for altering the Queen's [Buckingham] Palace – it will be improved by what is to be done to it, but it is a miserable affair & never can look well – & as to dignity & fitness it is a disgrace as the residence of a Sovereign of this Country –

*22 December 1846.* It is now fixed that, Parliament Shall meet on the 19th [of] January for despatch of business, a very inconvenient time & an unnecessary deviation from the usual time of meeting in February –

*27 December 1846.* The Reverend Hugh Stowell who is a distinguished Clergyman at Manchester, has put the question distinctly to Lincoln whether he will grant or favor any farther concessions to Roman Catholics: Lincoln has Evaded the question, in the true Peel fashion, & answered that he is not yet the declared Candidate for Manchester – How lamentably unlike this is to Lincoln of Some years ago, or I must Say what would be Expected from my Son – but his delight seems to me to be to run Counter to me [,] his family & his ancestors in Every thing –

*28 December 1846.* In Turkey & at Constantinople reforms are going on as Else where, at Rome they have a reforming Pope [Pius IX] & at Constantinople, the Seat of the other Heresy [,] they have a new Minister of Religion, Just appointed [,] who is a reformer, & one, if not the best informed & most learned man in the Empire = It is most curious to watch these contemporaneous changes –

*31 December 1846.* News from India – Nothing very particular had taken place since the last accounts = But it is Evident that Events of magnitude are in preparation =
　　The american Presidents' [James Polk] Message is arrived [–] it is described as being on the whole favorable to us –

*1 January 1847.* […] In the past year my trials have been great, my dissappointments [*sic*] great, my family disquieted & not alleviated. The Social & political appearance of all around one More & more threatening & unfavorable – We must be prepared for coming trials of the most formidable description, but with a firm reliance upon the all gracious Hand which has so often afforded Succour & protection [,] we Shall be Enabled to combat, possibly to overcome [,] the appalling difficulties, Sorrows or dangers which may assail us –

*3 January 1847.* News from India, the disturbances in Cashmire [*sic*] have been put down & our troops have returned to Lahore = but it is vain to think that our tenure of India will be any longer peaceable, it is Evident that the Excellence of our rule & the force of our arms will alone maintain us in the government & possession of that Vast territory –

*4 January 1847.* Charles arrived this Evening = to our great pleasure – he comes to assist me in doing the honours to a very large party assembling this week – Lord Stanley & a great many others[395] =

*5 January 1847.* The conversions to Popery Especially among the Clergy are proceeding to a fearful, lamentable & remarkable degree [.] It appears to me to mark the period in which we live, & to announce the Spurious Success of Popery which is to precede its final fall –

I am now fitting up my library – I have had the things here for Some years – but left them remaining in their boxes, untill more prosperous times might Enable me to open the doors of my house – it & the other arrangements in my house will be finished tomorrow, & on the 7th it will be opened for the first time in honor of a Company which I trust may never disgrace it – for England requires better & a different Sort of men from those which we have had of late years –

*6 January 1847.* Busily Employed fitting up my house for the very large party which we are Expecting – My library is to be opened in its best garb on the occasion – it certainly looks very beautiful & very magnificent –

*7 January 1847.* My preparations are Scarcely completed & some of my guests are come today =

*8 January 1847.* This has been a very fagging day – People many coming from very far did not arrive untill nearly 8 [p.m. –] Lord & Lady Stanley did not arrive untill that time – Some Even later: it must have been 9 o'clock – before we Could Sit down to dinner – We Sat down 26, altogether –

*9 January 1847.* Today we went out Shooting & on the Manor hills, we were 10 guns, but we had not very great luck with the pheasants = We Killed 119 pheasants – hares & rabbits, no wood cocks – fortunately no accident occurred [.]

*10 January 1847.* Sunday – my pew has hardly, if Ever, been So full as it was this morning – afterwards walked about to See the place –

*11 January 1847.* Lord & Lady Stanley & many others left us this morning. I hope that this "gathering" will have been attended with a good & useful result – Our two leaders met here without have [*sic* – having] previously concerted their plans together –

[395] For the invitation, see D.P., 147/14: Newcastle to Stanley, 15 Nov., 13 Dec. 1846; 177/1, f. 161: Stanley to Newcastle, 17 Nov. 1846.

*14 January 1847.* The last remnant of our party, Lord & Lady Sondes left us this morning, & we went to Newark in the Evening to attend the Ball –

*15 January 1847.* Returned home today – not well & very much Starved with the cold – What must the poor people feel with deficient clothing & Empty Stomachs – We are to Encreas[e] Wages to 13[s] 6[d] a week =

*19 January 1847.* The Session for 1847 was opened today by one of the very poorest Speeches from the Throne that I Ever heard. The topics were meagre, ill & unmeaningly Expressed & almost puerile – Lord Stanley made a wise & masterly Speech, noble & gentleman like, thoroughly becoming his position, one which must do much good through the Country & must raise him high in the Esteem & confidence of the Country[396] – There was rather a large attendance of Peers – but amongst the public [,] to Judge by the numbers within & without the House, very little interest in what was going on appeared to prevail –

*20 January 1847.* I heard that there was much discussion as to who Should first address the House of Commons last night which would thus constitute the first Speaker [as] the opposition Leader – whether [it] Should be Lord George Bentinck or Sir Robert Peel: the point was agreed to be referred to the Speaker [Charles Shaw-Lefevre], & as Eventually Lord George took his place exactly opposite to the Treasury bench, Sir Robert Peel not being then in the House, & that he afterwards addressed the house before Peel & in the character of opposition Leader, I presume that the point is now Settled & that Lord George & his friends are now Established as the regular opposition –

*21 January 1847.* The distress & deficiency of food & dearness of provisions is greater in France than here, & the great Expenditure of money on railways & other public works, have greatly affected the Bank of France [–] it is in great difficulties at this moment – The Bank of England has wisely & generously come to the aid of that of France & by its timely aid may Save it from ruin – However it will affect the money market here & has already Encreased the value of money – There can be no question that we are all in a most ticklish position, & that the most prudent forethought will be required to ward off or mitigate the impending difficulties –

*23 January 1847.* Much Employed all the morning – in the Evening dined at the Carlton Club – a large dinner of Protectionists – between 60 & 70 – I went as I heard that Lord Stanley was to be in the Chair – but to my very great annoyance, on my Entering the room, they came to me and Said that they were at great loss for a Chairman & wished me to preside – I replied "that I had been informed that Lord Stanley was to be in the Chair", but, I was told that it had been altered & that others had refused it & that it was universally wished that I would take it, I pleaded Suddenness, unfitness, distaste & all Sorts of things, but finding that it would inconvenience, I Consented & did the best I Could to play my part, Which was well & very Kindly received & appeared to give much Satisfaction, after the Queen's I gave Lord Stanley's health: he replied in a long & Explicit Speech, & laid down

---

[396] D.P., 147/14: Newcastle to Stanley, 17 Jan. 1847, regretting his inability to be present for the start of the session.

rules of action & proceedings in Opposition. In doing this, he made Strong Strictures upon Various opinions & Conduct & language which Lord George Bentinck took to himself, for on my giving his health next, he after thanking me for my affectionate Expressions towards him which Could only arise from my having Known him from his youth upwards, he proceeded with great warmth & Extraordinary Energy to observe upon Lord Stanleys remarks, complained of his treatment & defended his own views of policy [–] in Short there was Evidently a Complete breach between them – Lord Stanley replied but in Some things I thought he rather made the matter worse. Both are warm & generous spirits, & will not readily conceal what they feel – Lord Stanley from drill & habits of office has more artificiality about him than Lord George who is really unsophisticated, & certainly is a noble fellow – I have been Excessively annoyed that these Scenes [,] which threw a damp over all & destroyed the Meeting, Should have happened under my presidency – I tried for the rest of the Evening to accomodate [*sic*] matters, but in vain –[397]

*24 January 1847.* Sunday – but after Church I have been occupied all day in Endeavouring to reconcile the two Leaders So that no interruption to their combined action, Should destroy our valuable Party – I first Saw Lord George Bentinck & afterwards Lord Stanley = Lord George is So hurt, & justly [,] that Even I could scarcely make an impression upon him – he told me Every thing in the honesty of his heart & I must fairly Confess that Lord Stanley has not used him well: it is Lord George Who has done Every thing & who has by his Spirit & abilities given that consistency to our Party which I am perfectly persuaded no other man could have done – because no one thinks & acts as he does – Mr [Benjamin] D'Israeli was present during my long interview with Lord George –

The fact is, that Lord Stanley clings to his former associates, & as Lord George has no liking for them & has been unrestrained in his language towards them by which they have been Crushed & he himself Elevated by their Exposure & fall – So he is now an obstacle – & the object I can clearly perceive, is to drop him as Leader in the House of Commons, & as I now do not doubt, to place Gladstone of all the people in the world, in his Stead – This I put together from what Major Beresford mentioned last night, that if Lord George was obstinate, they could Easily get another leader = & on my remarking that no one Could Supply the place of Lord George he Said – ["] the man I mean is a man of great ability, a good Speaker, has been a Cabinet Minister but has not a Seat in Parliament, we must have a Seat for him ["], & he looked at me as if he waited for me to Say, ["] can I be of use in procuring him one [?"] – but he did not mention his name = & I did not identify the man until this morning – now all this I utterly abhor – it is crooked, mean, ungrateful & foolish in the Extreme – Such proceedings can never lead to good –

I went to Lord Stanley and when with him I told him my mind freely – he with his usual adroitness Excused himself for what he had done yesterday – & Said, ["] you heard what I Said & you Knew that I had not planned any lecture, strictures or animadversions on Lord George's conduct & language & policy – as you Know much of it arose out[398] of the conversation I had with the Duke of Buckingham across you ["] – &, much of this – but I told him – ["] ah, but Lord George Says differently, he Knows & tells me, that you

---

[397] See Gladstone's comments on the dispute in *Gladstone to his Wife*, ed. A. Tilney Bassett (1936), 71.
[398] ~~from~~ precedes this in the original.

have Said the Same things to him over & over again, & as he Expressed himself you have Said the Same, fifty times before Lady Stanley – but he cared nothing for what you Said to him in private, however unpleasing it might be, but to be lectured & criminated & abused at the head of his regiment So publickly [*sic*] he could not Stand or tolerate, & he answered you with indignant resentment, defending his own Views, & repelling what he Considered to be your scorn ["] – Lord Stanley perceived that he was discovered & ceased to defend himself – after a long conversation Embracing a wide party View & the foolishness of acting in this manner, he told me – ["] well I am truly Sorry for what has passed I fear George Bentinck will not Easily forgive me, but I will take the Earliest opportunity of proving to him by word & deed, that I value his cooperation & friendship & shall make it Known to him in a Substantial manner ["] – I agreed with Lord Stanley & afterwards with Lord George that all allusions or Explanations Should be avoided, & that they Should Strive to meet as usual, & let their acts Shew that their union was restored – after Seeing Mr Stuart & reporting to him alone most of what had occurred – I went home, as it was very late – & after dining wrote a long letter to Lord George, as it was too late & I too tired to Call upon him this night – & tomorrow I return to Clumber –

*5 February 1847.* Last night Lord George Bentinck brought in his [Railways (Ireland)] Bill & Explained its intentions & provisions to the House of Commons: it appears that he introduced it in a Speech of very great ability which called forth the Just admiration of the whole house – it is Extraordinary how this hidden treasure, now that it has been discovered, Shews itself forth to the wonder of his admiring Countrymen – & yet with all this he himself remains the Same – without vanity, conceit or presumption – Such instances are rare indeed! The intention of the bill is by affording Government assistance to railways in Ireland, to give Employment to the people, to better the permanent condition of the people & country & to place it in a rank with the rest of the Empire, at the Same time that industry & good habits are promoted in Ireland – The Effect of Lord George's Exertions is wonderful – it is the theme of universal praise, Even by those opposed to him – but Lord John Russell, Said that as he preferred his own measures, he Should not adopt the bill, & Should Stop it by interposing the Royal prerogative on the next discussion of the bill –

*12 February 1847.* The 2nd reading of Lord George Bentinck's bill was to come on last night & it was understood not only that Lord John Russell would oppose it but that if he were beaten upon it that he was resolved to resign – Why, I am at a loss to conceive, for Every body admits that it is a good bill – I do not think it likely that the bill will be carried – but the division will be fatal to the Ministry & will beget Strife with us, & that Strife will Elucidate the state of parties, & Shew persons & things in their true colours – a very short period may Elapse before Lord Stanley may be called upon to form an administration[399] – & then I pray that Magna Veritas prevaleat[400] =

[399] Newcastle wrote three letters to Stanley, detailing the programme of an incoming Protectionist government and suggesting cabinet offices: D.P., 147/14: Newcastle to Stanley, 12, 14, 15 Feb. 1847. Also see N.U.M.D., Ne C 5170: Lord Combermere to Newcastle, 10 Feb. 1847. Stanley did not think a call to office likely '& I need not therefore examine very closely the Programme contained in your last 2 letters': D.P., 177/1, p. 348: Stanley to Newcastle, 21 Feb. 1847.

[400] 'magna est veritas et praevalebit' – 'truth is mighty and will prevail'.

I received news today of the death of the Duke of Northumberland – No particulars, but it must have been Sudden – He was a very old friend & Schoolfellow of mine, we were in the Same form at Eton, & born in the Same year within a month or two of Each other – Gout in the Stomach, I Suspect, has taken him off –

*13 February 1847.* The debate on Lord George Bentinck's bill, owing to the lateness of the hour [,] did not come on the 11th, but was postponed to the following day – Lord John Russell declared his intention to oppose it –

*14 February 1847.* The debate on Lord George's bill is adjourned to Monday 15th tomorrow = amongst others [Henry] Goulburn Spoke against it = So Peel will Side with the Ministers – Mr Stuart my member for Newark made an Excellent Speech which has gained him much consideration. Lord George wrote to tell me of this, & at the Same time gave me the satisfactory & most agreeable information that he and Lord Stanley had quite made it up – they have agreed "that Lord Stanley Should Show more dash, whilst he Lord George Should Shew less daring"[401] –

*15 February 1847.* […] The Duke of Northumberland was found dead in his bed – with no appearance of death – & as if in a quiet Sleep =

*16 February 1847.* Mr Robert Peel Eldest Son of Sir Robert, has been appointed Charge d'affaires at Berne – This with the State in which Switzerland now is, is too bad – Mr Peel has been only two years or So, Supposed to be in the profession, but always flying about never at the Embassy doing & learning business – Very wild [,] rather mad, a spendthrift, gambler & roue – & certainly unfit to be placed in charge any where – but he is Sir Robert's Son & therefore placed over the heads of all others. So with William [Peel] another Son in the Navy – He has barely served his time through all ranks – but is now a Commander & was made in June of last year – Whilst others with Equal claims[402] are toiling with doubtful Success – & Subjected to disheartening disappointments –

*17 February 1847.* O'Connell is unwell, & unable to attend Parliament [–] he is Said to be declining in health & going off – His occupation's gone, his day gone by –

*18 February 1847.* Lord Manvers has lost his Sister Lady Frances Stevens [Stephens], she is another amongst the multiplied number of Sudden deaths – She went off, as in a Sleep, & they Scarcely Knew that she was dead –
    after a debate of three nights Lord George Bentincks' bill has been lost by a majority of 322 to 113[403] – Sir Robert Peel made a long & verbose Speech against the bill, quiet but insidious – Lord George immediately rose & replied to him in a very long [,] spirited & able reply – truly Surprising as coming from a man wholly inexperienced in debate, with

---

[401] Untraced.

[402] i.e., Newcastle's sons Lord William Clinton (serving in the diplomatic corps), and his late son Lord Edward Clinton (who served in the navy).

[403] The vote was 118–332: majority 214.

the Exception of his participation in[404] it towards the End of last Session – He appeared to me to upset most of the arguments of his opponents & triumphantly to vindicate his own course & opinions =

*19 February 1847.* Lord Elgin after a tedious voyage is arrived at Baten & the next day left for Montreal – to assume his Government –

[The University of] Cambridge is now very busy to provide herself with a Chancellor in the room of the Duke of Northumberland – Having received Encouragement Lord Powis had declared himself a Candidate, but Since that Prince albert has been put up – & no doubt that this illustrious but useless monopoliser of all honors will be the Successful Candidate – Lord Powis Could be of use, he was at the University & Either in or out of Parliament he would be able & willing to defend their privileges now So often attacked – But what can Prince albert do [?] = nothing = but dress himself out Very prettily in the Chancellor's robes –

*20 February 1847.* Lord George Bentinck is much grieved & disappointed at the behaviour of our people – he Says that they behaved Scandalously – & So they did [–] nearly one half Must have deserted him –

The factory bill – to restrict work to 10 hours, was carried on the 2nd reading in a Small house – I forget the numbers but they [were] something like 186 & 99 – clear majority 87[405] –

*23 February 1847.* a Scheme[406] of Military Colonisation is to be adopted as an Experiment & if found to answer to be Established as a System, which is to work in this way – after 15 year's service and[407] good character, a Soldier is to be Entitled to 1 or 2 acres of land in New Zealand – a cottage provided for him, passage paid out & adequate wages guaranteed to him —— He is to wear an outpensioner's uniform & be liable to serve whenever called upon – after 7 years residence he will be Entitled to the fee sample of the house & land – The plan appears to me to be a very good one, but may perhaps be amended with advantage –

*24 February 1847.* The Duke of Northumberland is to be buried in Westminster abbey – it appears that there is a family Vault in the abbey –

*25 February 1847.* The Chancellor of [the] Exchequer [Charles Wood] has opened his Budget – He will want 10 millions for Ireland & will raise it by loan on the Surplus of the revenue which he anticipates: no new taxes for this year = The Sum is Enormous & the propriety of the Expenditure more than doubtful in my opinion –

*26 February 1847.* I am informed that [my son] Robert is gone to Ireland = His business, to deliver out provisions to the poor & necessitous from Monsieur [Alexis] Soyer's [soup] Kitchens – I am told that he himself has offered to do this without pay – What his object

---

[404] in precedes this in the original.

[405] The vote in question was 195–87: majority 108.

[406] ~~System~~ precedes this in the original.

[407] ~~a Soldier~~ precedes this in the original.

can be in making the offer & placing himself in Such a Situation We cannot imagine – at present I Know no more than this –

*27 February 1847.* […] a most unseemly contest for the Chancellorship vacant by the death of the Duke of Northumberland is now going on at Cambridge between Prince albert & Lord Powis – The latter had been invited to offer himself, had accepted & declared himself – when Some people in the University put up Prince albert & addressed the Prince on the occasion, but he declined the honour as it was [not] <u>unanimously</u> tendered – However the sycophantic Cantabs would not be satisfied & are determined to Elect Prince albert, believing as they Say that he Secretly wishes it – I wish he may be beaten as he deserves [it], for not putting his veto upon such improper proceedings – but after two days polling it appears that the Prince is ahead 65 at 5 o'clock – the numbers being for him 828 – for Lord Powis 763 =

*28 February 1847.* The Prince albert has triumphed – he has beaten Lord Powis by 112[408] – which is his triumphant majority: after all it is <u>really</u> a degradation to one in his position to fill the office of Chancellor –

*1 March 1847.* I have forgotten to notice the passing of Mr [William] Watson's bill through its second reading on the 24th last by a majority of 3 [102–99] – This bill is to abolish all remaining penal statutes which affect the Roman Catholics – it is mischievous, improvident & wrong in Every point of view to allow this bill to proceed [–] it ought to have been stopped by Every [friend] of his Religion & his Country – & yet most unwisely & inexcusably Lord George Bentinck voted for it; & Seemed to think that he acted liberally & richly by So doing – Not above 3 or 4 of his party went with him, but voted against the bill = & feel greatly displeased with him & immensely mortified[409] –

*4 March 1847.* […] When the Cambridge Deputation waited upon Prince albert he coolly told them that it gave him the utmost pleasure to have been Selected to fill the high Office of Chancellor of an University So ancient & So distinguished as Cambridge – The meanness is provoking & Sadly unworthy – First he declines of [*sic* – if] the opinion in his favor be not unanimous, & then allows a contest with one of the Queen's Subjects, & when after a Severe Contest he gains a Majority of only 112 – – he unblushingly hugs himself at attaining an honor which is incompatible with his peculiar Situation & shows how greedily a Coburg can grasp at any thing however Small or however great –

*5 March 1847.* an opposition was again made to the Factories bill in which Sirs [Robert] Peel & [James] Graham & others of that Clique Joined, but they were beaten by a Majority of 100 & the bill now goes into Committee[410] – I think this is the only instance in which

---

[408] The final vote was 954–837: majority 117.

[409] D.P., 147/14: Newcastle to Stanley, 2 March 1847; 177/1, p. 373: Stanley to Newcastle, 7 Mar. 1847, discussing the state of cultivation in Ireland.

[410] The vote was 190–100: majority 90.

labor Should be interfered with – but in this case it is as necessary & advantageous to the masters as to the work people – men women & children –

*6 March 1847.* I am given to understand that the result of a careful report of above 150 of the most Eminent agriculturists all over the Kingdom, States that there is not So much as an average Stock of Corn on hand & in Stack yards as is usual at this time of the year – & that of barley in many cases there is not Sufficient Seed left to Sow the ground for this year's Crop = Upon a good harvest, under God, Every thing will depend –

*17 March 1847.* The open Sale of arms on market days & in the Streets & market places in Ireland by public auctions is become So flagrant that Various places in Ireland have petioned [*sic*] Parliament against it – Guns are Sold at 2[s] 6d a piece – this Seems incredible – the fellows who Sell them recommend them as being fit to bring down an agent at 150 yards = & these are the people that we are about to Spend 10 millions upon –

*20 March 1847.* On the 24th it is appointed that the nation shall hold a general fast & humiliation = I think & hope that it will be generally & piously observed, & it is to be hoped that the Eyes & the hearts of the nation may be opened, that we may repent of our Sins & Supplicate for a deliverance from our afflictions, & that those intended, if we repent not, may be averted from us[411] = The French are laughing at our humiliation & make a Jest of it – May they do likewise –

*22 March 1847.* Not much going on in Parliament [–] what is doing, very little to my Satisfaction – I much fear that Symptoms of assimilation are beginning to manifest themselves & that the country is not yet to be liberated from unprincipled men –

*23 March 1847.* Practical people tell me that the corn is looking well Every where – prices are falling – no doubt owing as well to the immense importation of food into the Country, as to the promise of the Crops –

*24 March 1847.* Today the Fast was observed here with great reverence & a general participation, I never Saw So full a congregation in my Chapel – there must have been 100 people present –

*25 March 1847.* above 708,000 – people are now Employed by the relief Committee in Ireland – the Expence for the month of February nearly [£] one million [pounds], for labour only on public works – wretchedly Executed & of little use or Value – !

*30 March 1847.* austria is quarelling [*sic*] Seriously with the Pope = the former wishes to encrease her power in Italy, this Pope is a strong & perhaps an ambitious man, & maintains the rule in his own Country, (well, if he do not try to rule in others!) – Something Seems to be going on in that quarter, which may generate a new order of things very different to His Holiness's intentions, for he is a reformer – & reform & popery will not walk well

---

[411] See Psalm, 107.

together – Popery to be popery must be always the Same – if it change it will be Something Else, & its infallibility will cease & be no more –

*1 April 1847.* The Duke of Bedford has been invested with the Garter vacant by the death of the Duke of Northumberland –

*5 April 1847.* […] Immediately on the adjourment [*sic*] for the Easter holidays the workmen proceeded to break up our temporary House of Lords [in the Painted Chamber], & on meeting on the 15th our Sittings will in future be holden in what is said to be our Splendid new room –

*8 April 1847.* […] Mr Stuart who came here from London yesterday, thinks it most probable that Parliament will be dissolved in July –

*15 April 1847.* I rejoice inexpressibly to see that a division has been taken in the House of Commons, & that Mr Watson's, what he calls Roman Catholic relief bill has been thrown out on going into Committee by a majority of 39, the numbers being for the amendment – 158 [–] against 119 – – This is creditable to the Commons & I trust will lead to good[412] –

*17 April 1847.* The Lords met in their new room on the 15th [.] I have heard no very minute description of it, but it is Said to be very large, too large probably as Peers cannot hear one another across the table, & almost overpoweringly gorgeous – if this be so, it is ridiculous –

*23 April 1847.* Left Nottingham this morning by [the] $10\frac{1}{2}$ train, arrived safely in London $\frac{1}{4}$ past 4, & found myself again with my Daughters in Portman Square – Dressed [&] had our dinner immediately & before six o'clock I was in the House of Lords: heard all the debate Except Lord Clarendon's Speech which was very ably opposed by the Duke of Montrose who moved that the bill [–] Customs bill – Should be referred to a Committee – we divided about 9 o'clock, on our Side 48 – Ministers 57 [majority 9] – but in this number a large portion of Peelites. This is Lord Stanley's first division & it will improve – I am certain that we could beat both Ministers & Peelites if proper pains were taken –

*24 April 1847.* […] Combermere tells me that Lord Stanley asked him this morning to move an amendment upon the Government bill for altering the State of the army, a most perilous measure [.] It comes on on Monday 26[th] – a very Short notice – Combermere is not a practised Speaker, he never Speaks but there is no man in the army who is more capable of Speaking practically on this question En gros Et En detail[413] – & I Shall be most anxious on Every account that he shall make a good figure as well as a Strong impression

---

[412]D.P., 14/147: Newcastle to Stanley, 20 Apr. 1847, expressing his relief at the Bill's defeat, regretting differences with Lord George Bentinck over the measure, and commenting on the remaining business of the session, including the Tenants Rights Bill.

[413]Wholesale and in detail.

– Lord Stanley is acting most wisely & handsomely in pulling people of his party forward – My belief is that on the 26th we shall divide very Strongly [.]

*25 April 1847*. I have had confirmed today what I much feared, i.e. that the Sore place in our Leaders is, not their unsoundness to the Church, but their <u>liberality</u> towards the Roman Catholics – this has already made our party very uneasy [,] cannot fail to prevent Entire Confidence, & on the hustings will assuredly operate very Seriously to our disadvantage [.] I have already opened ground against Lord Stanley[414] & if I have the opportunities, I Shall certainly Speak plainly to him upon this most vital point – this & Clinging to[o] much to old colleagues whom he has left, & who have left him are his only blots – & Stumbling blocks = these meet him at too many Corners, & cramp & impede his operations & marr [sic] the triumph of the ablest & greatest man we have –

The Country is in a really piteous plight – in the midst of Storm & tempest & danger of being cast upon Sunken rocks, we may be Said to be at Sea without rudder or Compass[415] – It must Soon be made manifest to all that man is incompetent to Extricate us from our dangers & difficulties, & that God alone Can Save us –

*26 April 1847*. Debate on the army Enlistment bill – Lord Grey opened in a very long Speech touching upon the whole State of the army & Some very mischievous & perilous observations on the Same – Then Lord Combermere rose to move his amendment & got through his work very well & far better than I Expected = for he hates Speaking & never speaks in the House of Lords. His Speech was full of matter & practical remarks that were most valuable. I heard the whole Speech but unfortunately the Reporters did not & consequently the Speech has been lost to the public, which is much to be lamented – The Duke of Wellington was sitting on the cross benches at first & he directed his address to him & towards the reporters, but the Duke changed to the Wool sack at the table to hear better when Combermere turned towards him – [so] was no more heard by the Reporters = The Duke of Wellington is really opposed to the bill it is said but was mean Enough to talk nonsense in favor of it & on division Voted for it = Lord Stanley made a brilliant & admirable Speech, not long but Equal to if not surpassing any thing I Ever heard from him. We divided & the numbers were for the bill [108] against it [94] majority 14. The Peelites Except Lord Winchester voted with the Ministers[416] –

*28 April 1847*. a meeting at Lord Stanley's to consider the Irish poor law relief bill – this is a very important Measure & will Effect an almost total change in the Social State of the Country by means of the delicate mode of managing landed property – Many Irish land lords were present & displayed an admirable feeling – It was decided not to oppose the bill, but to try for Several alterations in Committee –

[414]See above, 15 Apr. 1847.
[415]See Acts, 27: 17–20.
[416]The vote was: Contents, 64 present and 44 proxies, total 108, and Not Content, 53 present and 41 proxies, total 94: majority 14.

*29 April 1847.* [...] Much Engaged all day about petition to Parliament & proceedings therein to control the Sheffield & Lincolnshire railway companies, who are unaccommodating [,] tricking & Stinging to the lowest degree = I fear I Shall not beat them[417] –

*30 April 1847.* My railway matter in one way or another Engrosses nearly all my time[418] –

*1 May 1847.* Lord Cowley is dead – His Son is now at Constantinople – Charge d'affaires = in Sir Stratford Canning's absence [he] is managing all the business of the Embassy, & as William tells me in a manner not to make Sir Stratford's absence a loss, although he is acknowledged to be our best diplomatist.

*3 May 1847.* Today I have had Such long conferences relating to the railway affair that I have [been] hindered from doing much Else – I went down to the house of Lords but the particular business [of the] army Enlistment bill in Committee was put off on account of the Duke of Wellington's absence on account of his brothers death –

*5 May 1847.* My railway matter is concluded today, I with draw my petition, & I am led to Expect that I may now obtain good instead of bad terms[419] –

*6 May 1847.* The last accounts by the India Mail inform us that the death of ackbar [Akbar] Khan was Supposed to have been occasioned by poison administered at the instigation of his father Dost Mahomed [Mohammad] = He was certainly a man of great qualities, but where his bad passions were concerned a fiend as his father must be –

*7 May 1847.* I did not attend the debate on the Irish poor law last night being unwell [.] I went to the House Early & obtained a pair for this night & tomorrow – There were two divisions one on Lord Monteagle's proposal to make the law temporary – nothing can be more objectionable to my view of Such things – a trial for one year can be no trial at all, & is worse than useless – however it was Carried by 13 [63–50]. Lord Stanleys proposal to give the appointment of relieving officers to the poor law Commissioners Was rejected by 6 [59–53] – the committee was postponed to this night – I wish that Lord Stanley may tonight carry his amendment that the rates Shall be paid by the occupiers of land, as in England, & hereafter it may be Expected that the Social condition of Ireland may be Essentially Changed & be more assimilated to that of England – I am told today, that if

---

[417] *C.J.*, cii (1847), 434: 'A Petition of the Most noble Henry Pelham Duke of Newcastle, praying that he may be heard, by his counsel or agent, against certain parts of the Manchester and Lincoln Union Railway (Deviation) Bill, was presented, and read. Ordered, That the said Petition be referred to the Committee on the Bill; and the Petitioner heard, by his counsel or agent, upon his Petition, if he think fit; and counsel heard, in favour of the Bill, against the said Petition'. The petition was presented by Richard Spooner: *Globe*, 29 Apr. 1847.

[418] *Sun*, 29 Apr. 1847 reported the cross-examination of Mr Paget in committee on the Eastern Counties Railway (Spalding to Newark) Bill, on behalf of Newcastle. The duke had petitioned against the Bill (15 Apr. 1847), which proposed to extend the line across the River Trent above Newark: *C.J.*, cii (1847), 351.

[419] A similar process had occurred the year before: *C.J.*, ci (1846–7), 1059, 1087.

the Ministers are beaten tonight, that they are determined to dissolve on Monday – this I Should think is a mere threat a la Peel –

*8 May 1847.* The Irish poor bill continued in debate in Committee on the various Clauses all last night untill 12 [midnight] & adjourned to Monday next = The Ministers were beaten on two important points & are Evidently much disconcerted – on one clause they were beaten by 19 [54–73] – I hope that the bill will not be crippled So that it must be thrown up – for Such a bill perfected would be Every thing to Ireland – in the End a blessing & resuscitation –

Provisions are Still rising in price – Wheat rose 5s in price in the last week in Mark Lane & the present price is 85s the quarter, the highest price for full 30 years[420] – & yet the importation has been great indeed, & last year's crop was considered to be a fair average & although I myself always thought it was a deficient crop Wherever I Saw corn growing –

*9 May 1847.* There is now a Serious talk of dissolution of Parliament [,] may be in a month, at most 6 weeks – & Every body is busy finding Such places as they can get hold of – I wish to get [my son] Charles in, & I believe he will have to offer himself for Weymouth –

I believe that there is now Scarcely a doubt that many of the Servile adherents to Peel, Lincoln I fear among the number, will wish upon their fate & Join the Reformers, by coalescing with the Ministers, & will be placed in office for their renewed apostasy – I write this with Shame & grief – it will be the ruin of the receivers & received – It must ruin Lord John Russells party & the whole will fall together, despised & spurned by the Country – it will be then & only then that our party will rise –

*10 May 1847.* again in Committee on the Irish poor law tonight, Lord Stanley proposed his great amendment in a very able Speech & there was a long discussion – finally we found, that So many were leaving us, that we Should have been in a minority of less than 30 – having above 3 to 1 against, & it was thought most prudent to decline a division – Our party behaved very ill – & Lord Stanley must have felt very uncomfortable – but we must Struggle on, adhering to what we conceive to be right & await better times – They may Come when we least Expect them [.]

*11 May 1847.* Nothing very particular – I learn from the Country that wheat was Selling at Worksop & Retford as high as 93s a quarter – but the late rains have greatly improved the appearance of the corn & it is Expected that present prices will decline – The money distress in manufacturing places is Stated to be most Serious – discounts unprecedently [*sic*] high. Some have been done at 17 $\frac{1}{2}$ per Cent [.]

*12–14 May 1847.* On this Evening [14th] we went to a Ball at [Buckingham] Palace – On going up to the Queen to my Surprise I found Her Majesty quite gracious in appearance. She Said nothing but by her manner & countenance Expressed more than words would do

---

[420] N.U.M.D., Ne2F/8/18: diary enclosure, pencil notes in Newcastle's hand, including '8 May [1847] Wheat 85/- a quarter. Highest for 30 years, on 11th 93/- per Quarter'. See below, 11 May 1847.

– For Some years Her Majesty has been pleased to be absolutely rude & uncivil to me & my Daughters – an Excellent assembly & very pleasant[421] –

Since the opening of the Session: It is affirmed that no measures have been taken by Ministers without previous Consultation with Sir Robert Peel = & he has been quiet & approving – Ministers have now ventured to act for themselves [&] have proposed a loan of £600,000 for Irish railways – Peel is [in] wrath at this rebellion & opposes as violently as he is able – He is in a contemptible position[422] –

*22 May 1847.* Thinking that our people were too little sheppaded [*sic* – shepherded] I determined to lead the way & give a Collecting dinner this day to Lords & Commons to the number of about 30 [–] all went off very well & Seemed to give much satisfaction to all present – I must fairly avow that I never Saw any thing handsomer & better done – I took great pains to make it So, as it was the first political dinner I Ever gave[423] –

*24 May 1847.* The Duke of Buckingham is Said to be in great difficulties – Stowe to be Sold & all sorts of things – I believe that he is in a very bad plight, but not So bad as report gives out – Such matters are always Exaggerated –

[…] Daniel O'Connell died at Genoa on the 15th last – Peace be to[424] him – his power had waned & he will neither be missed nor regretted –

*29 May 1847.* The new Pope Pius professes to be a great Reformer & liberal – he has already acted upon his maxims & has done many popular things & is about to give a free constitution of Government to his people – He is very popular with the people –

Our Finances at home are said to be in a very awkward State = The Bank is placed in a situation of much difficulty & embarrassment – The monetary difficulties under which we are now Suffering, are Said to be caused Exclusively by Peels' banking bill [of 1844] acted upon by the Exchanges being against us – It will I hope End in revoking or remodelling this ill adapted & bad ruinous measure =

*6 June 1847.* for several days after the 12th last I was unable to attend to my Journal – once in arrear I had not time to recall & record what had passed & the arrears have gone on untill this day – Many interesting circumstances have been forgotten & not noted – a very material cause for dissatisfaction & Enquiry has arisen within these few days – namely an armed interference in the affairs of Portugal by England, Spain, France & austria – It appears to me to be a most unwarrantable act – & Ministers will be called to account for it.

---

[421] There were about 1,200 people present: QVJ, 14 May 1847.

[422] Newcastle kept up his diary intermittently during this period. On 18 May, he was in the Lords for the committee stage of the Army Service Bill. He was in the minority on the division (38–30: majority eight); K.D., 18 May 1847, 'Brought Duke of Newcastle & Lord Combermere [home] from House of Lords'.

[423] D.P., 147/14: Newcastle to Stanley, 19 May 1847; K.D., 22 May 1847, 'Dined Duke of Newcastle Grand – Duke of Richmond, Lords Mansfield [,] Stradbrooke [,] Sheffield [,] Combermere [,] Southampton [,] Ashburton [,] George Bentinck [,] Stanley [&] Colchester'.

[424] too in the original.

It is Said to be a Scheme of Prince alberts' to Support his Cousin [Ferdinand II] in Portugal married to the Queen [Maria II][425] –

Lincoln brought on a motion about colonisation for Ireland a few days ago – it created very little interest [,] only between 40 & 50 Members present, & I understand was a very dull & flat affair – Lincoln held forth with pertinacity for nearly two hours, reading quantities of papers & Spinning out one of [his] tiresome Sort of Speeches which pass for meritorious but which are as useless as they are mistaken – Peel is Evidently Setting him on to make himself of consequence for his own purposes & poor Lincoln is weak & vain Enough to think that this Jesuit is doing it for his advantage & to shew what he can do –

I forgot to notice that Lord Besborough [*sic*] Lord Lieutenant of Ireland died about the 15th or 17th of last month – Lord Clarendon has been appointed in his place =

*7 June 1847.*[426] I have for some time been looking out for a Seat for [my son] Charles – it has been at last decided that he Should go to Sandwich – accordingly on Friday morning last (4th) he Started for that place all on the spur of the moment, as an active attorney of Sandwich, Mr Mororylyan [John Mourilyan], came up to London Expressly to return with a Candidate – Mr Mororylyan went off to Windsor after having had a long conference with me & tore poor Charles from his ascot & party – he is laying Close Siege to a lady [Elizabeth Grant] who he hopes to marry, & brought him to London in a state of great unhappiness & nervousness – we cheered him up [,] made all arrangements [&] obtained leave from Mr Mororylyan that he might rest the night here, & off he went on Friday morning accompanied by Mr Mororylyan & Mr Stuarts younger Son – I heard from him on Saturday, announcing his favorable reception & Success on his canvas & tracing his future course of proceedings [.] Today I have a long letter from him – He had attended a meeting at Deal, where a large party was collected to meet him, to whom he was introduced by two Superior [men] Captain [Andrew Atkins] Vincent Royal Navy & Mr [George Payne Rainsford] James, who I Know, the celebrated author –

Here Charles made his first Speech = & on this occasion I rejoice to note, he did not fail & break down as he anticipated but got through very well, & hereafter I am quite Sure will not only do well but be an Efficient person, if called upon Either to defend himself or attack his opponents – I have learnt today with the greatest pleasure, through Mr Stuarts Son writing to his Father – that he Spoke very well – He Seems to be Sure of Success which is most fortunate, as I Shall have to pay a large Sum of money for him, Which though Very poor I do not in the least grudge, as I am well assured of the benefit to him which will result from thus drawing him out – which nothing but force & necessity Could do[427] –

[425] The intervention was designed to prevent the imposition of an absolutist government during the Patuleia civil war.

[426] Parliamentary Archives, London, LGC/5/4/37h: Newcastle to the lord great chamberlain, 7 June 1847, recommending Mrs E. Browne for the position of housekeeper of the Lords; also see LGC/5/4/37g, Mrs E. Browne to the lord great chamberlain, [July] 1847. On the death of Frances Brandish, the old royal office of housekeeper was abolished, and a new post of housekeeper came into being to which Jane Julia Bennett was appointed.

[427] For Lord Charles' speech, see *Kentish Gazette*, 8 June 1847. One wit observed, 'The Sandwich people intend, it is said, to elect a son of the Duke of Newcastle as their representative. If all is true that we have heard of the independent electors, there is no doubt that Sandwich knows very well on which side its bread is buttered': *Punch*, xii (1847), 255.

I have been most busily occupied all day in all sorts of business – lodging money Secretly for him &c & finishing in the House of Lords – & returning home Excessively fatigued & [with a] very bad brow & Eye ache – which tortures me Sometimes & is partly nervous, partly stomach, acted upon by the Weather –

Lord Stanley told me this afternoon that Parliament will be dissolved on the 10th [of] July – I think this is a fair & good decision, as a longer postponement would Entail great Expences upon numerous persons, who are now canvassing all over the Kingdom =

*8 June 1847.* Mr Mourilyan who look [*sic* – took] Charles to Sandwich called here today having come to London on law business – he Says that Charles is getting on very well, works well & is a favorite with the people – he believes him to be certain of Success – Captain [Swynfen] Carnegie the Peelite who had been invited to Sandwich has been Stopped –

*9 June 1847.* Engaged much of the morning in arranging & Squaring my money Concerns & after having paid Every thing of bills up to Xmas last both in town & country & all taxes & Every other payment up to this time – then reckoning all my means & my Expences up to November next [,] I bring out a balance of about £1000 – in my favor – my Expences have been more than I Expected & Several are unexpected & heavy – those connected with Charles's Election wholly So – So that in fact I have reason to be well pleased – In the Evening dined at Combermere's a large political & pleasant party[428] –

*10 June 1847.* Charles is going on well at Sandwich – He is getting through the Speaking part far beyond his Expectations & as I am informed Extremely well = They like him much for his plain dealing & Kind bearing, in short I believe he is a decided favorite & considered a <u>Champion</u>.[429]

I was called before a Commons Committee today to give Evidence respecting the Great Northern deviation by Tuxford [–] the Company is Endeavouring to give me the Slip, but I was Strong among the parties in the Committee room & I think that they will now See the propriety & necessity of adhering to their Engagements[430] –

*11 June 1847.* I learn this morning that the Committee through [*sic* – threw] out the Sheffield & Lincolnshire clause, & that in Consequence – the Great Northern deviation will proceed in their Tuxford deviation line – this will be an advantage to the town & neighborhood of Tuxford I believe & am assured[431] –

a grand Court Ball this night. The Queen as before Kind in her manner to us = She danced Several times & looked well, but Seemed tired & not in good Spirits[432] – The grand duke Constantine 2nd Son of the Emperor [of] Russia Was present – He is short & not distinguished looking, but his countenance is good & intelligent, & his manners unobjectionable, which is not usually the case with Russian Princes – He appears to be a

---

[428] K.D. 10 [*sic*] June 1847 'Dined Lord Combermere's [–] Presented to King of Spain Count Montemolin [Count of Montemolín] Met Duke of Newcastle [,] 2 Ladies Clinton [,] Dinorbens, Hudsons [,] Rothschilds'.

[429] See *Kentish Gazette*, 15 June 1847.

[430] The meeting, chaired by Henry Lowry-Corry, was in committee room 34: *Sun*, 10 June 1847.

[431] *Sun*, 11 June 1847.

[432] There were about 1,750 people present: QVJ, 11 June 1847.

greedy & Keen Enquirer – he is very young – another very different character was there a Prince of Lucca wild & free & Easy & almost always drunk = He smacks Prince albert on the back &c &c to the great annoyance of his German dignity – The royal scape grace goes by the name of "filthy lucre" = not a bad cognomer[433] – This ball was Considered to be dull & flat. People certainly are not in Spirits –

In the morning we had a meeting at Lord Stanley's to consider what part we Should take regarding the lately proclaimed armed interference in Portugese [*sic*] affairs by England, France & Spain. This interference is unquestionably one of the most Exceptionable & unfortunate in which this country has Ever been Engaged – It was Settled that Lord Stanley Should open the debate on the 15th by a motion to resolve that there is nothing to warrant our interference in the internal affairs of the Kingdom of Portugal – Lord Stanley made an admirable Statement on opening the business – Lords Brougham, Lyndhurst & Ellenborough were present – all as many of us thought interlopers – Brougham as usual was loquacious & troublesome & injudicious = & Evidently wished to introduce the resolution to the House, but this was adroitly avoided by Lord Ellenborough = We Shall have a hard fight & stirring debate [&] on the 15th we shall take our final division of this Session upon it –

*12 June 1847.* This Evening about 11 o'clock Charles arrived from Sandwich – he is looking very well after his active & fatiguing operations & is Evidently well satisfied with what has been done for him & what has been done by himself. I am confident that not only that the benefit to himself will be very great, but that it will introduce to public life as honest & as good a man as this Country can produce – He is so unpretending & retiring in his nature that nothing but obligation could draw him forth from the Shade which obscured his high & real merits – He seems to be Sure that his Success is certain =

*14 June 1847.* The Commons have their adjourned debate upon the Portugese affairs – I hear of no particular news – The Duke of Wellington gives a large dinner & afterwards a concert to the Queen on the occasion of the Christening of one of his grand children [Lady Victoria Alexandrina Wellesley], to whom the Queen Stands Sponsor =

*15 June 1847.* This Evening Lord Stanley moved his resolution relative to non interference in Portugese affairs, in an admirable speech which occupied $2\frac{1}{2}$ hours – He was followed by Lord Lansdowne in a very poor & dull reply – about this time a report reached the house that the House of Commons, which was Engaged in the Same debate, adjourned, & Either whilst Peel was Speaking or afterwards, the house was counted out & as there were not 40 members in the house, they broke up – & thus Ended in Smoke this grand debate – but we were doomed to pretty nearly the Same result: at about $\frac{1}{4}$[434] past 10 [p.m.] – Lord Granville after a Short good Speech Sat down – & nobody rising [the] question was called & the house cleared for division – The benches were almost Empty but peers from without came into the house & we divided – we 46 – Ministers 66 [majority 20] – Lord Stanley & a great many peers were not in the house – without our leader nobody took upon himself to act &

---

[433] A cognomen is a surname or nickname by which one is well known.
[434] ~~at~~ precedes this in the original.

the consequence was that nothing was done, we were disgraced & made a miserable figure, people [were] Seriously & greatly displeased = I learnt that the arrangement made was for Lord Ellenborough to Speak after Stanley & Brougham to Close the debate – Ellenborough it Seems for Some reason would not Speak – ran Sulky or restive, & Brougham would not Speak but after him, probably lest Ellenborough Should have the honour of winding up the debate – but thus were we Sacrificed – & here at the onset has been proved the truth of my invariable opinion [,] namely that we Should trust to none but true men purely of our own party & not gathered from the Peel party or strolling politicians as Brougham – these men were at Lord Stanleys meeting the other day to my Surprise & regret, & thus on the very first occasion have they proved how worthless they are & how destructive of any party of good men with whom they may feign to ally themselves, Surely as I believe to betray them. Our party is I fear broken up, & at a very critical period on the Eve of a dissolution – Our cause is not prosperous – but we must not be discouraged – I much apprehend that some of our people are too much Engaged in intrigue & Crooked ways = It will not do. Honesty alone will prosper –

*16 June 1847*. I have had a very busy day: after Seeing many people at home, I Went out & found Lords Stanley & Eglinton at home & learned from them the history of yester-day's transactions – In the House of Commons the counting [of] the house was moved by our own friends, Mr [Charles] Newdegate the mover who was <u>the only one</u> Sitting on the opposition benches [,] the whole Seemed very like Concert & collusion = The Same in the House of Lords – Lord Ellenborough was to have Spoken after Lord Lans-downe but he gave no signs of rising & the Duke of Wellington made his unintelligible Speech = which when finished still Lord Ellenborough Kept his Seat – & Lord Stanley told me that he had taken fright, was nervous & was quite lost hardly Knowing what he was about = Lord Stanley had left the house to dine & Engaged to return in less than $\frac{3}{4}$ of an hour which he did Just as the house broke up = When the critical time arrived all were mute none would speak. Brougham Said he would not for the emergency but only at the Settled time [–] two others were prepared to Speak: Lord ashburton who had been closetted [*sic*] for two hours with the Duke de Palmella [*sic*] on the previous day & Lord Hardwicke – but all were dumb when they might have been of use: now all this looks very much like concert & legur de main[435] – how Should the other Side Know all about our affairs, how Should they Know how to Strike in the nick of time [?] – Lord Stanley tells me that there was no trick & I must believe <u>him</u> = but I am in wonder that two Events Should occur in the Same night upon the Same Subject & in both houses of Parliament –

   I then went to the House of Lord's [*sic*] & afterwards to Mr [Robert] Baxter's office to puzzle out all that is doing about Several railway bills in which I am interested – afterwards to [Mr] Hendersons, where I went over & arranged Some rather Complicated business = dined out & afterwards went to the Duchess of Sutherland's Ball to the Queen at Stafford House, a brilliant & magnificent affair & an Excellent assembly = Every body Seemed to

---

[435]legerdemain, a skilful fooling of others.

be there: we did not, as we could not get away, return home untill between 3 & 4 o'clock [in the morning] = & this I call a Sufficiently busy day[436] –

*18 June 1847.* Went today to the British Museum – the collection of natural history is magnificent & I Should think Superior to the Paris collection – Especially in Shells & Minerals – but the Sculpture is poor indeed with the Exception of the Elgin Marbles – not above half a dozen Statues & a few fragments – it is a national disgrace – The Etruscan collection is fine – the Egyptian also, but art does not shine here – The building is mean, unsuitable, execrable – for the money that has been Expended upon it we might have had one of the finest buildings in Europe – I Sigh & blush when I See how inferior our national Structures are to those of any foreign country[437] –

*19 June 1847.* No particular news today – when I dined, at Lord Eglinton's [,] I was informed that in all probability Parliament would be prorogued about the 15th of July – in the Course of the month of august or October [,] probably the latter, it will be dissolved – This will be an Extreme injury & inconvenience to very many[438] –

*20 June 1847.* There is a Story about that the Duke of Wellington with his foot in the grave is to marry Miss [Angela Burdett] Coutts – I can not believe it. He is avaricious & might be glad to get her money, but what woman could bear to marry the Duke in his present State [?] –

I had the pleasure today of making the acquaintance of Sir Henry Smith, So distinguished lately in the Indian War of the Punjaub [Punjab] – He does not appear to be at all Spoiled by the fuss which has been made with him, & the various public manifestations in his favor – He is very prepossing [*sic* – prepossessing] in his manner, appearance & Conversation – & Evidently from what he Said incidentally a man of Sound principle as well as a great Soldier –

*21 June 1847.* […] I was at the Horse guards today & hope & am pretty Sure that proper consideration will be Shewn to poor Thomas if an opportunity occurs – Lord Fitzroy Somerset was very Kind about him –

*6 July 1847.*[439] […] Our triple armed intervention has settled the Portugese Civil War – The Oporto Surrendered the other day to the Spanish General [Manuel de la] Concha – The prisoners of the Queen's party were liberated, & to shew the vile Spirit of these creatures, many of them got into a house & fired upon the troops of the Junta = The business is now at an End & the rights & liberties of the people which had been outrageously violated have

[436]See QVJ, 16 June 1847.

[437]BL, Add. MS 70843, ff. 62–3: Newcastle to Sir Henry Ellis, 25 Aug. 1847: 'I did go to see the Museum on a public day, but more to See the new buildings & arrangements, than to inspect the contents closely. I was Sadly disappointed in the buildings & greatly Mortified at the poverty of the collection of marbles. The Natural history appears to be very fine'.

[438]D.P., 147/14: Newcastle to Stanley, 24 June 1847, telling him that his proxy was being sent to Eglinton for use in favour of any measure except political, religious, or educational concessions to Catholics.

[439]R.P., 1700, f. 362: Newcastle to Richmond, 4 July 1847, declining an invitation to dine on 7 July 1847.

been Sacrificed by our means, to favor the Coburgs – The less is now Said about it, the better –

*15 July 1847.* […] Parliament is to be prorogued on the 22nd & dissolved on the 23rd [–] we Shall then be put out of our present misery – & if we may be blessed with a good harvest & a good Parliament we may indeed have reason for overflowing thankfulness –

*20 July 1847.* To my infinite astonishment I learn today that [my son] Thomas has Started for Canterbury – where he is to oppose Mr [George] Smythe & in Company with another man of the name of [John] Vance, who I presume is to pay the piper; are to Endeavour to carry the place for the Protectionists & Churchmen – I have not heard from Charles, but I fear that his prospects are not So bright as they were[440] –

*21 July 1847.* It is certain that Parliament will be prorogued on the 23rd and dissolved immediately afterwards = The Proclamation will appear in the night's Gazette[441] – & the writs will be issued instantly they are all ready prepared –

*22 July 1847.* I have heard from Charles today – he writes in very bad Spirits – he tells me that he thinks he is perfectly Safe at Sandwich – they have all worked Excessively hard in the last week & have gained a great many votes – I shall be rejoiced to See him in Parliament [.] He tells me that he made another Speech of Some length the day before he came away [–] he is now in London – His friend Mr James told him that it was a very good one, but ill delivered – Mr James had closely observed, & found that his defect was want of confidence in himself & he owns, in his modesty & Singleness of heart, dear fellow, that Such is the Case, & always has been through life, which has So often Kept him back from attempting to do anything. This certainly is not the defect of the age where assurance & Empty impudence carry all before them –

*23 July 1847.* I had a letter from Thomas today from Canterbury, in high spirits [,] his canvass going on most prosperously, & he himself pleased with his oratorical Success. I have this day read the Speech & it is really Surprising how with So little advantage he has Spoken So remarkably well – the text, the composition & the matter, are worthy of a practised & reputed man[442] – They have been received with Enthusiasm [,] he & his Colleague [John Vance], I Shall not be Surprised if both Brothers Come in – I could draw a painful parallel between them & another [Lincoln] whose course has been far different from theirs –

*24 July 1847.* The Queen made her Speech yesterday & finally closed the Parliament & in the Evening it is Supposed in [*sic* – it] would be dissolved: a wretched parliament it has Shewn itself to have been, & a disgrace to this generally wise & noble Country – but alas prisca fides, pietas, nudaq veritas[443] – are nearly Extinguished – May God grant that they

[440] *Kentish Gazette*, 20 July 1847.

[441] *The London Gazette*, 23 July 1847, supplement.

[442] See the *Kentish Gazette*, 27 July 1847, for reports of the speeches of Lords Charles and Thomas Clinton.

[443] 'prisca fides, pietas, nudaque veritas' – a conjunction of different sources. The first part comes from Virgil's *Aeneid*, vi, verse 878: 'Heu pietas! Heu prisca fides!' – 'Alas, that piety! Alas that ancient faith'. The second part

may revive again in a new Parliament & that the honor of God & the good of the Country may be considered before the worship of Gold, of Self, & of bad men who may happen for our Curse to be Endowed with a Sufficiency of cleverness to do infinite mischief –

*25 July 1847.* My letters are Satisfactory today – Charles had not left London & had received all my letters – I have been able to procure the money for him, & he is gone to Sandwich with it – on Thursday next, I have little doubt that he will be returned one of the Members for the borough – an honester [*sic*] & more Worthy will not be found in the Parliament or out of it –

Thomas is going on well at Canterbury – it appears to [be] most likely that he will be Successful, although thus thrown in after the 11th hour –

among Several others put up for Marylebone, Mr Daniel Whittle Harvey was one on [the] ballot [–] he stood first on the poll & Lord Dudley Stuart next – notwithstanding this, Mr Harvey has Suddenly retreated & resigned – &, it is Said, has thereby pocketted [*sic*] £1000[444] =

*29 July 1847.* My letters today tell me that Charles is quite safe – & a letter from him gives me the Same intelligence = & more over Expresses an Elevated desire to serve his country [with a] real goodness & nobleness of heart which truly delights me – Thomas Entertains high hopes of Success – he has worked most laboriously & indefatigably –

*31 July 1847.* Poor Thomas has lost his Election for Canterbury,[445] I am truly Sorry for him, it vexes me much that he Should fail after all his labors, which have been unremitting & his Expectation which I fear had become great – I observe that we are considerably disappointed in many of our hopes – I anxiously hope that Charles may be Successful = His fate will appear in tomorrows paper – as information is now So instantly Conveyed by telegraph –

Mr [George] Spencer, Roman Catholic priest & brother to Earl Spencer is dead – he died of fever caught in attending the feverish Irish in his neighbourhood –

*3 August 1847.* To my infinite disappointment & Sorrow, I learn by this morning's post that Charles has been defeated at Sandwich.[446] This Event was wholly unexpected. I grieve to think that So much time [,] labor & anxiety have been thrown away upon that miscreant Borough – but we are amply repaid notwithstanding by what it must have done for Charles

[443] *(continued)* comes from a lament addressed to Virgil in Horace's *Odes*, i, 24, line 7: 'incorrupta fides nudaque veritas' – 'uncorrupted faith and naked truth'.

[444] The Whigs Dudley Stuart and Benjamin Hall were returned with 5,367 and 5,343 votes respectively.

[445] *Kentish Gazette*, 3 Aug. 1847. Albert Denison (Whig) polled 808 and George Smythe (Peelite) 782. Vance polled 643 and Thomas Pelham-Clinton 641.

[446] *Kentish Gazette*, 3, 10 Aug. 1847. The Whigs Clarence Paget and Charles Grenfell were returned with 459 and 437 votes. Charles Pelham-Clinton polled 392 votes. Major William Beresford told Stanley that the result was 'the thing … which annoys me most … I have been decidedly deceived there. I think that Lord Charles ought to have given us some hint if it was not going right. I am vexed at this because of the Duke's spending his money there': D.P., 149/1: Beresford to Stanley, [n.d.] 'Monday'.

by putting him forward & making him acquainted with himself – & a better acquaintance
he will not Easily fall in with –

*5 August 1847.* Gladstone is returned for Oxford – I grieve at it most Sincerely, no return
has given me more pain, a Jesuit & Specious declaimer, he is Just the man that Should not
represent Oxford University, it is a fatal blow – although I consider the man himself to be
of no weight & not likely to be an authority in any thing [,] yet he is a man of indefatigable
application, gifted with the power of Stringing words together to any Extent, & possessed
of a certain degree of talent, although pretty nearly unintelligible, So involved & mystified
is the Style of his Speaking or writing[447] –

Hitherto the Elections have gone greatly against us & much more in favor of Peel that
[*sic* – than] I Expected [–] it is not unlikely that he may count Some 50 followers or more
upon the whole return –

*6 August 1847.* Elections are Every thing just now & occupy the papers. Lincoln is Elected
for Falkirk by a very small Majority[448] – I grieve to think that he does not demur the Seat –
although to represent the Falkirk boroughs is no very Exalted honor = Charles writes that
there are ample grounds for a petition against the Sandwich return & Thomas the Same as
regards Canterbury –

*9 August 1847.* The news has arrived this Evening that [Richard] Cobden who Was Set
up at the last moment for the West Riding of Yorkshire, has been Elected [unopposed]
& thrown out Mr [Edmund] Becket Dennison – This Demagogue has been roaming all
over Europe, lecturing on free trade, followed as a lion & in most places received & feted
as Something great & wonderful – He is now in Prussia, where he is made much of = It is
truly hateful to See how Scoundrels & quacks make their way [,] Succeed & prosper – but
their Success Cannot be Envied by good & upright men – the reward of the mischievous
is in this bad world only[449] –

*10 August 1847.* The Elections are now $\frac{3}{4}$ over, & taking all things into consideration they
are not So unfavorable to us when counted up – This Evening we counted 217 [,] & by
the time the Elections are over, we shall probably be about 230 – If our leaders do their
duty, & our people Keep together, we Shall be a formidable body, & Shall be able to Keep
in check any administration –

Failures are commencing in the City & it is much feared that it is only the commencement of a fearful derangement of money matters – 500 Vessels are reported to be now in
the river loaded with corn & no End of more Expected – if this be true, corn will be down
to nothing, & the farmers, not one quarter of whom can be Said to be really Solvent [,]
Will be ruined, & the landlords with them – It is a fearful prospect, however plenty is better

---

[447]Robert Inglis (Conservative) and Gladstone (Peelite) were returned with 1,700 and 997 votes. Charles Gray
Round (Conservative) came third with 824 votes.

[448]Lincoln polled 522 votes against William Sprott Boyd (Whig) who polled 491: majority 31.

[449]See *The European Diaries of Richard Cobden, 1846–1849*, ed. Miles Taylor (Andover, 1994).

than deficiency & famine – & our anxious Study must be to make the blow fall as lightly as we can –

*12 August 1847.* I have Seen with my own Eyes that the potatoes are a good deal affected with disease – & I am told that the wheat & barley are much injured by being prematurely dried up – the yield is not Expected to be good.

*13 August 1847.* The archduke Constantine, [Konstantin Nikolayevich] has left England & Sailed With the Russian Squadron from Portsmouth a few days ago on his return to Russia – he openly inquisitive & intelligent – & having Seen all that is to be Seen in England he will no doubt have profitted [*sic*] considerably by his Visit to this country –

*14 August 1847.* No particular news = By Some means or other Lord Granville Somerset has beaten his brother [Edward Arthur Somerset] the Duke of Beauforts' Candidate & has come in for Monmouthshire. I am Sorry for it: he does not deserve his Success[450] –

*18 August 1847.* [...] Mr Spencer, the Roman Catholic priest [,] is not dead he is recovering.

*20 August 1847.* The Elections are now concluded & it Seems to me that our number, protectionists who may be relied upon, will be as nearly 250 as can be – & in all probability, out of the 80 or 90 who are called Peelites not less than 30 more probably 40 or 50 will rarely fail to vote with us – the liberals including Every Sort are reckoned at[451] 323 – So that we Shall run them pretty hard when we put forth our Strength –

*26 August 1847.* [...] My letter to the Editor of the Times [John Thadeus Delane] in consequence of Some mention of me which was connected with his frequent & Systematic attack of Dukes in general, & which made me Endeavour to stop his mischievous attempts to decry the nobility – appeared in the Standard this Evening[452] –

*29 August 1847.* No particular circumstances or news – The press has not been able to refute my letter nor to abuse me in any way = & Secretly they Shew their respect by Saying as little as possible – it is Just what I wish for, & I hope that I Shall have done good & Shall impose a better tone upon the Journals calling themselves liberal[453] –

*4 September 1847.* [...] Sir Robert Peel was invited to stop at Darlington on his way to Wynyard [,] Lord Londonderry's, in order that the Darlingtonians might present an address to them – Sir Robert complied & the address was presented by the radical Quaker Mr

[450]Octavius Morgan and Granville Somerset were returned with 2,334 and 2,230 votes against Edward Somerset on 2,187.

[451]reckoned at precedes this in the original.

[452]See Appendix A. Duke University, Rare Book, Manuscript and Special Collections Library, Newcastle MS: Lord George Bentinck to Newcastle, 26 Aug. 1847, expressing admiration for 'the gallant spirit and generous tone of your letter to the Times'.

[453]'I think the System so dangerous that if possible it ought to be Stopped. 9-10ths of the people will Suffer themselves to think as the Times writes': BL, Add. MS 56368, f. 178: Newcastle to Giffard, 24 Aug. 1847.

[Joseph] Pease – Sir Robert replied in cautious terms – but what an indignity to be so addressed by persons whom he ought not to have Countenanced –

*9 September 1847.* The failures of houses concerned in the Corn trade Still Continue, to a considerable amount – & In France an Eminent French house concerned with many English Commercial houses has failed for £940,000 –

*10 September 1847.* The Queen continues in Scotland & has had bad weather to confine the whole party to the house –

*17 September 1847.* […] The Dukes of Beaufort & Buckingham, are Said to be ruined for their lives – The Duke of Beaufort is gone abroad with his family – an Execution is [in hand] both at Badmington [Badminton] & Stowe – = at Badmington the Creditors are Selling Every thing – hounds, horses, down to the Smallest articles – the Duke's uncontrolable [*sic*] Extravagance is remarkable – It is very lamentable that Such things Should happen in these times, & both of them would be Very useful men, politically –

*22 September 1847.* It has been stated that Messrs Cobden & [Charles Pelham] Villiers have made their Elections, one to Keep his Seat at Stockport the other at Wolverhampton – & consequently that [for] Yorkshire & Lancashire[454] – if proper Exertion be made no doubt two Protectionists may be returned for these Counties –

*26 September 1847.* Trade & business, is really in an awful State – people of Stability & old firms failing all around – & people of business calling in their debts – those who have money fearing to lend it –

*1 October 1847.* The State of Europe is becoming very formidable [,] the people, (plebs) are taking the matter into their own hands & are demanding popular rights – abolition of all privileges, equal distribution of lands – in Short a democracy – & Equality – forgetting that as long as the world lasts there will always be rich & poor, Strong & weak – as we are told in Scripture – we are arriving at awful times, & God's grace & assistance can alone guide us with any Safety through the trials & difficulties which we Shall have to Encounter –

*2 October 1847.* […] The accounts from all quarters Still Shew the uneasy feeling Which prevails Every where – the desire for chance [*sic* – change] – & a Scheme for upsetting Every thing – "Progress" is the word Used, & the men who go fastest "ahead" as it is termed are considered the wisest & most Enlightened – a Wretched delusion, alas! – but Still one which gains ground & will Soon throw the world into the most fatal State of confusion – These are all Signs of the times – & fore shadow Events which are coming – another sign is the Money,[455] trade & commercial panic, another the bloody tendency of

---

[454] Cobden was returned for both Stockport and the West Riding of Yorkshire, Villiers for both Wolverhampton, and Lancashire South. Cobden continued to sit for the West Riding and Villiers for Wolverhampton.

[455] ~~pa~~ precedes this in the original.

men's minds & another pestilence & famine – If we do not wilfully blind ourselves, we may read the fate of nations –

*4 October 1847*. In our ride out today I Enquired of a farmer who was gathering them in, if [the potatoes] were diseased, he Said ["] yes, but not with the disease of last year, these potatoes are infected with the Scale or Scab ["] – & he shewed them to me, & I perceived that they [are] covered with Scaly Spots like Small pox or any irruption – this disease does not penetrate beyond the Skin, & as far as I could learn from him did not make them unfit to Eat – the disease injured their appearance as a Sample, Crippled their growth & reduced their abundance –

*5 October 1847*. The news from India is good & peaceful, & improvements are taking the place of war – The Suttee & infanticide have been abolished by conviction on the minds of the Natives. No business is done & of a Sunday – nor labor Either – at home Every thing connected with money is in a most alarming State = abroad ferment Seems general & not likely to decrease = Russia is Said to be thriving in her finances =

*7 October 1847*. It is reported that Some new peers are to be created, of which Sir John Hobhouse is one – if this be the case it is a great misfortune & much to be regretted – The House of Lords is already too numerous & considerably degraded by late additions –

The monetary State of the Country is Exciting general attention & meetings are taking place in the large towns, which possibly may lead to a revision of the laws & a better System – Peel has ruined us by his theories, which he has the influence to make law –

*12 October 1847*. The account of the Quarter's Revenue is Just published: it is, as might be Expected most unfavorable, a deficiency of [£] 1,500,000 – at the least, both on the quarter & on the year – What we are to do I Know not – with incompetent men to manage our affairs, a failing revenue, & the means of improving it destroyed, monied men of all Kinds bankrupted all around us – & nothing that I can See now left to us, but Either to Encrease the Income tax, or raise a loan – the first utter destruction by its Effects, the last less objectionable but fatal to our character & credit – In my opinion the only ray of hope for us, is that on the Meeting of Parliament we Should be able to turn out the Ministers, crush Peel & Shear him of all power, & then bring in the Protectionists, who if they are worth any thing, for honesty, plain Sense, devoted patriotism & determination, may, if Supported by the Country – in a great measure, restore what is lost – but that must be by returning to the old System –

[…] The Queen Dowager [Adelaide] Embarked on board the Howe 120 [gun three-decked ship] to take her passage to Madeira – where she means to winter – The Saxe Weimar family, many in family, accompany & are to remain with her –

*13 October 1847*. The vile Cobden is returned to England 2 or 3 days ago after a long & mischievous touring all over Europe of 14 Months. In parliament I think he will be matched by Several honest & plainly Spoken men, & if So his poison may be neutralised.

*14 October 1847*. […] some other nations are nearly as bad as they can be – we ought to look at home & see if we are So worthy as we ought to be – for one thing See the state of Ireland, for another See the State of our Government: untill the rulers & the ruled act upon a different principle based on truth, Equity & Christianity [,] we shall never Either deserve or Enjoy the prosperity which we perfect merely because we obstinately persist in doing what is wrong, instead of what is right –

*17 October 1847.* Sir Robert Peel has honored Liverpool – with a visit – no doubt to make his cause good & Keep up an interest in himself, assisted by his friend [Edward] Cardwell who has been chosen Member [of Parliament] for the town – From Some cause or other the adventure Seems to have been a failure – The reception was none at all, & it Seems that Sir Robert did not appear on the Exchange, nor were reporters permitted to be present at the dinner given to him by the Mayor Mr [G.H.] Lawrence, Son of the gentleman [Charles Lawrence] at whose Villa [Carnatic Hall] Sir Robert is a guest –

*18 October 1847.* Yesterday was the day fixed for the general Thanksgiving for God's peculiar mercies in granting us a most abundant & favorable harvest – an act of grace & mercy which Cannot be too greatly estimated as it is not fully deserved by us but unfortunately, two things were done to marr the Effect of this becoming & required duty = one that it was fixed to be made on a Sunday & not on a week day – the other that a collection was ordered to be made by a Queen's letter in all Churches for the Suffering Irish – thus in one Case not Setting apart a day for this Special purpose, the other mixing up Extraneous matter with what Should have been select & Especial – This however is, most unfortunately, the View which our rulers, nowadays, take of Such matters –

*20 October 1847.* Consols are at 79 – 80 – The Mercantile & monied World is Evidently in Extreme perplexity & alarm – & is now beginning to Stir –

*24 October 1847.* The papers today mention the Sudden arrival in London of Sir Robert Peel, he arrived says the account at 8 o'clock at his own house [4 Whitehall Gardens] & almost immediately after, the Chancellor of the Exchequer [Charles Wood] called upon him & remained for 4 hours: the next morning Lord John Russel came to London & had a long conference with the Chancellor of [the] Exchequer & Sir Robert & Lady Peel were invited by the Queen to Windsor Castle where they will remain from Saturday / yesterday / to Tuesday – Of course it is thought that all this relates to a coalition or something of the Kind.

*25 October 1847.* Specie is returning a little from america – two vessels from thence have brought one £40,000 – Sovereigns, the other above £200,000 – but the money market is in a deplorable condition & the state of the country, is I believe unexampled –

In an account of comparison of periods of years, the last 5 years forming one period out of three – the Exports from Hence to america / United States / amount to £30,458,573 – the Imports to £66,136,454 – balance against England £35,677,941 – this change has taken place during Peel's administration, & the growth & Extension of free trade principles – to shew the Change I Should append the result in the first of the 3 periods of five years. Exports £43,710,101 – Imports, £15,822,686 – balance in favor of England – £27,837,415 – This period is from 1815 to 1819 – the other from 1842, to 1846 – the result is as formidable as it is Significative –

I wrote to Lord Palmerston to Enquire whether he had given leave of absence to [my son] William & if not to grant it – in answer he tells me that he has granted it but that he does not Know when he / William / may avail himself of it, as that will depend upon the state of work doing & to be done, at present they were very full of work[456] –

*26 October 1847.* at last the Government has been forced into doing something to relieve the pressure which weighs upon trade & all money transactions but whether it will be productive of public benefit, I cannot pretend to pronounce – as far as I can Judge, I think it will do good – the measure simply is that the Bank of England under Government authority Shall discount all bills of not less than £2000 with 95 days to run, at a rate of 8 per Cent discount – this no doubt will counteract one immense present Evil – namely that foreigners will not now accept our bills, because, they Know that the Bank of England will not discount them – I have no doubt that the interview with Sir Robert Peel, was to ascertain whether he would Sanction this measure, as all would depend upon that whether or not they would have a majority when the question came before Parliament –

*27 October 1847.* The papers Seem to think that the measure taken by Lord John Russell will do good, but that it comes too late to do all the good which it would have done Some time ago =

*3 November 1847.* The proclamation is out & the new Parliament is to be called together on the 18th & the Queen will open the Session in person on the 23rd [.] I Suspect that it will be an Enigma & very possibly may upset the Government [–] at all Events it will Clearly Show that it cannot Stand alone –

*4 November 1847.* I have received notice today that after Christmas the interest on my mortgages will be Encreased to 5 per Cent a circumstance which will be ruinous to me, as it may make a difference to me of between [£] 3 & 4000, a year [,] & if to that shall be added as I Expect it certainly will, another $2\frac{1}{2}$ or 3 per Cent to the Income tax, I shall then be unable to go on at my present reduced rate of Expenditure & Shall be obliged to discharge all Extra laborers & Servants & live in the humblest way, so as to live within my means & Keep clear of debt[457] –

*6 November 1847.* a letter from William – he was Expecting to receive his leave & Start immediately = but my notion is that Lord Palmerston would have neglected to give it, if I had not written to him, & if I am right, I am as Sure that he only Sent the leave about

---

[456] Southampton University Library, Palmerston MS, PP/GC/NE/69: Newcastle to Palmerston, 7 Oct. 1847. Newcastle also recalled their conversation about European affairs the year before: see above, 26 Oct. 1846.

[457] N.U.M.D., Ne C 7234: Coutts bank to Newcastle, 3 Nov. 1847. Bentinck told Disraeli that Newcastle and Richmond, 'My two Ducal friends are making a terrible outcry … at having their mortgages raised to 5 per cent: they ought to glorify themselves that they are not foreclosed': Dep Hughenden, B/XX/Be/42: Bentinck to Disraeli, 14 Nov. 1847.

10 days or a fortnight ago – we shall, by God's goodness, See dear William here before Christmas –

*7 November 1847.* The State of Ireland is dreadful, no one's life is safe, murders committed Every day, the law useless, & force the only rule = The distress amongst all classes Extreme, rents not paid, the rates cannot be collected, & now numerous Meetings declare, that the state of the country is Such that[458] disease, & pestilence & famine are likely to be much Worse than last year – & they demand more assistance from England – The beginning & Ending of all this is popery – the Scourge is what they are now Suffering, poor wretches ! –

*8 November 1847.* The archbishop of York is dead: archbishop [Edward Venables] Vernon or as he has lately been called (Harcourt) was a very old man 90 years old, but So green in his old age, So lively, active & intellectual that he was a wonder – the very day that We arrived in York, he had been in the morning to See the new Chapter house – he probably caught cold there – he was suddenly taken ill, continued to get worse & worse & died in three days – He had been archbishop above 40 years – He was a clever & very agreeable, but not a Shining man – as a Church man he lent to all classes of dissenters, & really Sound Churchmen complained of him much – He leaves a very large family behind him & must be rich – he has already provided well for his family & they have taken good care of themselves – his death will be a great blow to them & their consequence = I fear that it is too much to hope that a good man will be appointed to Succeed him –

*9 November 1847.* Birmingham has led the way & invites all other great towns to join them in petitioning the Queen & Parliament to alter the money laws, & the present bad System of finance –

*10 November 1847.* No particular news – a Coalition of Peel with Russel & a dissention in the Cabinet, are mentioned, neither are out of probability –

*11 November 1847.* Lord John Russell at the Lord Mayor's [John Kinnersley Hooper] dinner, observed, "We Shall not hesitate to administer, &, if need be, to Exceed the law, if we think it necessary for the public welfare" – let us hope then that he will take proper & decisive Steps to conquer Ireland &, when really conquered, then to Endeavour to civilise & convert them from brutes into humanised beings –

*13 November 1847.* Lord Henry Bentinck who came this Evening tells me that his brother Lord George had Just arrived at Welbeck as he came away & brings the report that Parliament will Sit till Christmas – adjourn merely for 3 weeks holidays, & then resume business: also that Peel would be in office, by coalition, very Shortly –

*14 November 1847.* To Judge by appearances, Ministers have resolved upon adopting Some very Strong measures with regard to Ireland – If so, they are right – but no parliamentary

---

[458] that precedes this in the original.

Enactment will Establish peace & protection, nothing can Effect this in Ireland but military law – Lord Yarborough & Lord Besborough [*sic*] are to move & Second the address in the House of Lords – on the 23rd [.]

*15 November 1847.* It was told me today that [Thomas] Musgrave Bishop of Hereford is to be the archbishop of York –

*16 November 1847.* Lord George Bentinck was here today – we had a talk of two hours, in the Course of which I Endeavoured to persuade him from favouring or advocating the Cause of the Romanists [,] but he Entertains the notion that paying the Priests & giving the people the full Enjoyment of their religion is the only way to obtain quiet, & I could not prevail – I fear that whenever the question is mooted that he will as before take a part against his party & thereby destroy the public good opinion of him – I much regret this, for I take great interest in his career, & Should rejoice in Seeing him Successful in a right Cause[459] –

*18 November 1847.* Parliament meets this day – Members will be Sworn in & a Speaker chosen & on the 23rd the Session will [be] opened by the Queen's Speech = It will be a great curiosity to See what Members will do –

*19 November 1847.* The Parliament assembled yesterday & the House of Commons has chosen its Speaker = Mr [Charles Shaw] Lefevre is rechosen – Nothing has transpired respecting the contents of the Speech & the measures which Ministers will adopt – We learn that Lord Stanley is ill with the gout at Knowsley, if this be true we Shall have no dinner & meeting at his house on Monday 22nd & if these are postponed I shall not go to London, otherwise I Shall fulfill my intention of being there on the 22nd –

Our party here has broken up today [–] the Combermeres go Early tomorrow morning –

*21 November 1847.* I am informed that it is the intention to Encrease the Income tax to 5 per Cent [.] I am not Surprised at it, I always foresaw that this would be the use made of this tax & I predicted the precise Sum to which the tax would be Encreased on this occasion = I deplore it [–] it will ruin the country & induce a national bankruptcy – I have no time to add more – I am preparing to go Early tomorrow or rather this morning –

*22 November 1847.* Left Clumber at 8 [a.m.] only & unfortunately was 20 Minutes too late for the $10\frac{1}{2}$ train = I changed train at Rugby & was in Portman Square at $6\frac{1}{2}$ – dressed & was in time for Lord Stanley's dinner = after dinner he gave us his views at considerable length, & they were So much in unison with those of the company present that they met with warm & general approbation – it is delightful to find a person of Lord Stanley's talent & Standing advocating Just & high principles upon all occasions [–] all that he Said today was noble & high–minded, a perfect contrast to the peddling, mean & hypocritical views & Selfish Schemes of Peel –

---

[459] Newcastle invited Stanley, but he was unable to attend: D.P., 177/2, p. 165: Stanley to Newcastle, 1 Nov. 1847.

We are to oppose Jews sitting in Parliament – to require the adoption of Strong & Effectual means for the preservation of life & property in Ireland – to oppose determinedly the Encrease of the Property tax – to censure the foreign policy with regard to Spain & Portugal, Switzerland & Italy – & to reprove the monetary measures, at the Same time Setting forth the rightness of our views in all their bearings upon free trade & the new system – Ministers propose to alter the Navigation laws, but we are Stoutly to uphold them –

*23 November 1847.* I took the oaths & my Seat today, & afterwards was present at the debate on the Speech, which is an usually wretched performance, untrue & in Some respects ridiculous. In his answer Lord Stanley handled it [in] a most masterly manner – his Speech Could not be Excelled by any one ancient or modern – it was full of argument, high feeling, right Sentiments, & the highest order of Eloquence – His picture of Ireland & the state of things there, was as touching as it was magnificently Eloquent – & I could not wish one word to be altered, omitted, or added [,] it touched upon Every thing, & Stated all that was required without a Single loose or idle word – Lord Lansdowne attempted to answer but was more than usually feeble & ineffective – Lord Stanley's Speech has strangled the Ministers & the Peelites – The Queen did not attend, She is pregnant & heavy & it is Said that she did not like to mix herself up with the Contents of the Speech –

*24 November 1847.* a large Meeting of Peers at Lord Stanley's today to consider what we Should do in the Ensuing Session – Subject to what should pass in the House of Commons tonight, it was the general opinion that we Should give notice tomorrow of our intention to move for a Committee in the House of Lords upon the Bank Charter question to sit contemporaneously with that to be moved for tonight in the House of Commons. If the Minister refuses it then a debate & division will be taken upon the motion – It was Said that all business of this nature will be postponed untill after [the] Christmas holidays.

*25 November 1847.* The Jew bill, it is now Settled, will Commence in the House of Commons which is only right – Lord Lansdown is not well & was not in the House of Lords tonight. Lord Grey put off Lord Stanley's questions, & it was Subsequently announced to us that we need not remain in London to our inconvenience – I shall therefore return to Clumber the day after tomorrow –

*30 November 1847.* […] I had a letter this morning from William dated Constantinople November 3 – it [*sic* – in] which[460] he States that he has again been very ill with fever, a bad return of the former attack, but the Convalescent now, yet very weak – he was most anxious to move but had heard nothing of his leave – I wrote yesterday to enquire of Lord Palmerston, the <u>date</u> of[461] his Sending out the leave to him =

*3 December 1847.* The ministerial plan for tranquilising Ireland & for Securing life & property is worth nothing at all – The Same may be Said of the Chancellor of the Exchequer's

---

[460]will precedes this in the original.
[461]of precedes this in the original.

Scheme for the removal of distress & restoration of public credit – We are in a woefull [*sic*] plight –

*4 December 1847*. Nothing particularly worth notice – I received <u>no</u> answer from Lord Palmerston. Strange Enough, but Stranger Still when I told him that William had been Seriously ill again, that I was very anxious about him & greatly desired change of air & place for him –

*5 December 1847*. There has been a good deal of talking & 3 nights' debate upon the Government motion for a Committee to Enquire into the Effects of the Banking act of 1844 – Lord George Bentinck is very unwell with influenza, & not fit for any business although he attends the house, consequently he has not attempted to Speak – but it has been remarked what a damp his illness has given to the party & how completely he is the life & Soul of it, & that without him it would not have been what it is & deprived of him, that it will be nothing.

*7 December 1847*. another letter from William date 19th November [–] he does not mention his health So I trust that he is pretty well again. He has heard nothing whatever of his leave, nor any answer to his repeated letters to Lord Palmerston – This is my case also. I wrote to Lord Palmerston above a week or ten days ago, but have had no reply – There must be Some reason for not noticing William's letters, or mine – & Lady Cowley Enquired of these of the foreign office people & could obtain nothing but a mysterious answer – I have requested Lord Palmerston to give me the date of William's leave – I have written again today – I Expect no Satisfactory answer –

   William tells me that Lord Cowley is appointed to Switzerland, a pleasant appointment I should think – & a Very good thing to rout out young Peel, wild & half crazy [,] a mere boy only 4 or 5 & twenty, nor more than 3 or 4 years in the profession – having remained nowhere, & having passed his time in roaming about Europe & playing the fool wherever he was – & otherwise wholly unfitted for a responsible Situation = His Slipping into an official post in Switzerland was a gross case of nepotism –

*8 December 1847*. Ireland is the uppermost theme of debate, & is necessarily mixed up in almost all discussions in both Houses – the State of the Country is not blinked by the Government but it is averse to any Strong measure – My belief is that nothing Short of martial law, can Effect any good = & I am of opinion that if martial [law] Were proclaimed, that murders & outrages of all Kinds would immediately cease, from the fear of its Exercise –

*9 December 1847*. When I wrote to Lord Palmerston, I also wrote to Mr [George Lenox] Conyngham of the Foreign Office & from him I have an answer today, but none from Lord Palmerston – Mr Conyngham tells me that in consequence of being So "undermanned" at Constantinople, he does not think that William will get away for Some time longer = & he Expects that I shall hear from Lord Palmerston upon the Subject – This is not only an extraordinary disappointment to us, but to William himself it will be almost intollerable, [*sic*] as the climate disagrees with him & almost incapacitates him for business, & he has most anxiously reckoned upon Seeing & passing the Christmas with us this winter –

*10 December 1847.* No notice from Lord Palmerston – this is a queer way of proceeding –
In the debate on Mr [Thomas Chisholm] anstey's motion for doing away with all dis-abilities to Roman Catholics William Ewart Gladstone M.P. [for] Oxford University, voted in favour of it. I wish I could think that they would require him to resign in Consequence – but alas those days are gone by – & woe alone will happen to us, for our national Sin – We Shall be Severely punished for it – The bill was carried on[462] division by 32[463] – !!!

*11 December 1847.* Today, I have a cool answer from Lord Palmerston making no apology for not answering my letter, & merely informing me that he had that day Sent off the leave of absence to William – This man is false, dishonest, uncourteous & Slippery but clever –
[…] The Mortality in London is very great, above 2000 more in a fortnight, than the usual ratio – The Cholera only took a total of above 5000, whilst it lasted here […] influenza which has Seized almost Every one [,] although thank God as yet we have been Spared, has carried [a]way a vast many more – Let us hope that this is about the last pouring out of [the] last Vial[464] – for our Whole State is very fearful & terrible –

*15 December 1847.* […] The appointment of Dr [Renn] Hampden to the See of Hereford, is meeting with the most Strenuous remonstrance & resistance: a declaration from the Laity has been Sent to Lord John Russell & another from 13 or 15 of the Bishops. Lord John's answer to the Bishops has drawn down upon him an instant reply at great length from the Bishop of Exeter [Henry Phillpotts], which taking into consideration also the Shortness of time is one of the most masterly productions Ever produced in controversy. Lord John is now obstinate & determined, he will not give way – but the Bishops letter will force him to think many times over, & he may think it the wiser Course not unnecessarily to meet the rising tempest[465] –

*16 December 1847.* To Settle the matter, I See by this day's paper that Dr Hampden is gazetted as future Bishop of Hereford –
Lord Stanley has made an Enquiry in the House of Lords relative to what the Privy Seal / Lord Minto / is doing in Italy & at Rome –

*17 December 1847.* Reform, popular clamour & meetings to obtain popular rights & ame-liorated government, are gaining Strength & becoming general all over the continent – I Knew that it would be So [,] by what I observed last year, when on my tour[466] – In Italy the reformers have the rule, & in France the progress is really alarming, as it is assuming a very determined aspect – the proceedings are bold & open = & no military force will put it down, it is of a nature to have its own way –

[462] by precedes this in the original.

[463] The vote was 168–135: majority 33.

[464] Revelation 16.

[465] The documents to which Newcastle refers, regarding the 'Hampden Controversy', were published in *The British Magazine*, xxxiii (1848), 63–178; also see *Unrepentant Tory*, 293.

[466] Newcastle and his daughters had visited northern France a year earlier: N.U.M.D., NPC/2/22: passport, 19 Sept. 1845.

*18 December 1847.* The debate upon the admission of Jews to Sit in Parliament has commenced – Baron [Lionel] Rothschild was Elected one of the M.Ps for London – Lord John Russell the Prime Minister, brings forward the bill, it is understood to be an open question, but in the wretched state of liberalism (as it is called) in which we are now placed I much fear that the bill may pass the House of Commons – I own to taking the deepest interest in the Jews – but admission to political power, & legislation on Church matters I would delegate to none but Christians, & I wish I could hope, of a pure faith = It is miserable to See how rapidly the connection of Church & State is diminishing – it must lead to Events of a dangerous & desperate nature –

*19 December 1847.* The first Step is taken by the House of Commons. Lord John Russell's motion for a resolution of the House to go in to Committee on his Jew bill was carried by a majority of 67 [–] the numbers were 253 & 186 – On Monday (tomorrow) it was fixed to read the Bill a first time – Sir Robert Inglis gave notice that he Should not oppose it, but begged for time before the 2nd reading – Lord John Russell answered that he Should not bring forward the 2nd reading before the 7th [of] February — So that there will be plenty of time to consider of resistance if Such be the disposition of people in general[467] –

*20 December 1847.* Parliament will be prorogued or adjourned today to the 3rd [of] February – what it has now met for nobody can comprehend – my notion is, that it has been to ascertain the state of parties – & During the Recess that Several changes & appointments will be made =

In the debate on the Jews, Mr Gladstone's was a very clever but very villainous Speech & I trust that the Member for Oxford University will be made to account for his vote & opinions upon this & the Papists disabilities bill = He is a thorough Jesuit & unfit to hold any trust – Lord George Bentinck most unwisely took upon himself not only to vote in favor of the bill, but to make a long Speech, one of considerable ability & Eloquence, in favor of the measure, not only arguing in its favor but using all his ingenuity to upset the preceding arguments of his own friends = It is very bad & most unfortunate –

*21 December 1847.* The Dean [John Merewether] for himself & the Chapter of Hereford has Sent a long & Strong Memorial to the Queen, full of loyalty & attachment & courteous Expressions, but informing H.M. that Dr Hampden is not a proper person to Select & praying her Majesty Either to Send them another or to relieve them from Electing him untill the whole Case has been rigidly investigated & Sifted by able Divines & others fitted for the undertaking – The affair Will make a great noise – the proceedings in it have Excited great & general indignation & I doubt much whether this [,] the Jew business & the Popish disabilities bill, will not haul Lord John from his Seat & include all Peelites & others who have Sided with him in a general Exclusion from Office – The feeling is Certainly Strong – We Shall Soon See if it be Strong & Sincere Enough to be lasting –

[467] This possibility was also recognised by the Bill's supporters: N.U.M.D., Ne C 11943: Lincoln to Sidney Herbert, 19 Dec. 1847.

*23 December 1847.* Parliament was prorogued on the 20th [–] it is difficult to discover why it was called together – Except to do a great deal of mischief which is [*sic* – in] a Short time has been done –

*24 December 1847.* There is not much novelty in what is passing [–] the Same Events are pursuing their course, apparently to Evil & disaster, but let us <u>hope</u> Eventually for good = Sir George Grey has given an answer to the Dean of Hereford, informing him that he had laid his Memorial before the Queen = & that Her Majesty had given no farther directions – as much as to Say [" ] refuse to assent & Elect at your peril ["] –

*27 December 1847.* The arch duchess Maria Louisa is dead at 56. Once occupying the <u>post</u> of Empress of the French as wife of Napoleon Bonaparte – She was afterwards Duchess of Parma – It was remarkable that from the period when from ambition he repudiated his faithful wife Josephine & married the remarriable Maria Louisa [,] his happiness & good fortune began to wane, until at last disaster upon disaster overwhelmed him, up to the battle of Waterloo which terminated his Extraordinary Career & Sent him Captive to end his days in St Helena =

*28 December 1847.* Received a letter from dear William today dated Constantinople December 3[rd]: he had at last received my letter from Filey communicating Lord Palmerston's letter to me, informing me that he had Sent William his leave – which has proved to have been a lie. William Was quite well again, but did not anticipate an Early period when he might be able to leave Constantinople as the work, continued to be & was likely So to remain, as heavy as Ever –

*29 December 1847.* a letter from his Brother Rodney Mundy announces the unexpected & lamented death of Frederick [Clinton Mundy] the 3rd Son of General [Godfrey Basil] Mundy – He was ill only 2 days & died on Christmas day – Frederick was a Clerk in the Colonial Office & the only one absent of the Godfrey Mundy family who was not present at a large family party collected at Tredegar, Sir Charles Morgave's [Morgan's] who married the General's daughter [Rosamund], & when assembled on Christmas Evening an Express arrived announcing the Sudden & dangerous illness of Frederick, Mrs [Sarah Brydges] Mundy immediately left with her Son Rodney, but arrived too late to find him alive [–] he had been dead two days – He was a very useful, clever & good young man & leaves a family.

*30 December 1847.* The Election of Dr Hampden is concluded – at the Chapter; only one Canon voted with the Dean, Mereweather [,] against Dr Hampden [–] that was Dr Huntingford – Both made Speeches at the Chapter – What will be done with them now remains to be Seen – Lord John Russell's answer to the[468] Dean was very brief – that he had received his letter & perceived that he (the Dean) was determined to Violate the law – Lord

John throughout has behaved in a most overbearing & reckless manner – The Exhibition is not a pleasing one, but I think that the Stir & agitation will be productive of good –

*31 December 1847.* […] Trade is reported to be giving Some Slight Symptoms of revival – it is needed for it is in an abject State – Of 170,000 people who work in the Manufactures of Lancashire, it is computed that not more than 48,000 are now Employed – The prospect all around is Most gloomy, & here we close the old year, which has been one of Signal disaster [,] misery & wretchedness to this Country – Parliament & public men have done all in their power to contribute to the moral & political downfall of the State = The prostitution of character of public men, is one of the most deplorable & mischievous features of the present day – Confidence is lost & despair Seems to make[469] all listless & powerless – we want someone in whom we may thoroughly rely & Such a being is not forthcoming –

*1 January 1848.* I cannot do better than follow my usual Custom of Earnestly & heartily & gratefully thanking God for having preserved me in health & vigour, although depressed in Spirit up to this day, let us hope that this year may be less disastrous than the last, I wish I could think that it will be, but alas I fear that it may be Even worse – Our principle is So undermined that we have nothing to Support us – we quarrel with & cease to regard our Religion & our Church as supereminent – we can fraternise with Sects & denominations whether Jews [,] Turks or Infidels [,] it matters not to us, modern liberality levels all distinctions & we are now plunging into a republic of religion of politics, & of all private as well as public Considerations, & what can be Expected from Such Sources [?] – Surely neither the favor of God or man – and consequently we are being punished & Shall be more awfully for our abominable delinquencies –

*5 January 1848.* a letter from the Duke of Wellington to Major General [John] Burgoyne written, in January of last year, has just now been published[470] why one cannot see – Nothing can be more injudicious & mischievous than the publication of Such a letter from Such a person – What his motive can be, it is difficult to divine – He must have been doting when he wrote it, to allow him to publish the letter is the Extreme of folly – it is an invitation to the Enemy, information to him of our weakness, & detailed description of how he Should avail himself of our indefensible position –

all nations now Kick at England in her fallen State: america is not backward in doing So – She boasts of her prosperity & of her greatness, tells us that English Credit is gone, and that the period is near at hand when New York will be the Emporium of the World – Who has caused all this? Sir Robert Peel is the miscreant – & if in our mad folly we Still adhere to his accursed policy, English greatness is at an End, & ruin & anarchy will hurry on the dreadful catastrophe – Which may God in his Mercy avert –

*6 January 1848.* The accounts of the Revenue are made up but not yet published – it is understood that they will show a very material decrease in the Revenue, for Which we

---

[469] ~~render~~ precedes this in the original.

[470] *Life and Correspondence of Field Marshal Sir John Burgoyne*, ed. George Wrottesley (2 vols, 1873), i, 444–51. The letter, dated 9 Jan. 1847, commented on the state of British defences, esp. in the event of an invasion from the continent.

were prepared, & which could not reasonably be Expected to be otherwise as the result of the measures of the last few years –

*7 January 1848.* The accounts of the Revenue are published – & it appears that there is a deficiency of above £2,000,000 – on the Whole year – if this does not open the Eyes of the Nation & show them the direful Evils of free trade & our present (Peel) System, the national Skull must be impenetrable – and it is at this time that Several boobies[471] think themselves wise in following the Duke of Wellington's dream, & proclaim the country in danger from foreign invasion whilst we are at peace, & utterly defenceless against an invading army, the Success of which is proclaimed to be certain = People are frightened out of their wits & can hardly Sleep in their beds from fear of the bug bear – Every body Knows not only now but Ever Since they Knew that England was an island that an invasion is possible & has often been Successfully made = but former times are not present times & unquestionably invasion never was less possible than in the present day = Some Encrease of the army, I have long thought to be not only desirable but necessary as long as Ireland is in a[472] state of feverish rebellion, & our colonies as Extensive as they are, I have been & am desirous of Seeing the Militia Kept up, & in a State of Efficiency, but beyond that I would do nothing – more, I am convinced, is not required =

*9 January 1848.* [...] The Irish agitators are outrageous against Lords Shrewsbury & arundel & Surrey, for having written to their Bishops reflecting upon the infamy of priests denouncing from the altar & other matters which Stamp them to be devils rather than men – There is now a complete feud between the loyal & well disposed Papists & the rebellious & disaffected of the Same faith – this may Eventually lead to good – at all Events, nothing can be Worse than the present state of things in Ireland[473] –

*11 January 1848.* [...] There is an account in the news paper of the Confirmation of the new Bishop of Manchester (first) Reverend [James Prince] Lee: objections were made to him by a Mr [Thomas] Gutteridge, but he was not attended to –

*13 January 1848.* The Bishops of Manchester & Hereford have been confirmed but neither without objections – The latter has been formally objected to by Counsel with long & able Speeches – & it is understood that the whole case is to be tried in the Ecclesiastical Court =

The discussion respecting the <u>defence</u> of the Country is Still Carried on – occasioned by the Duke of Wellington's foolish & most indiscreet letter – it is mischievous as well as indiscreet. The new Lord Ellesmere who has the reputation of a clever man & has filled

[471]precedes this in the original.

[472]its precedes this in the original.

[473]Shrewsbury's correspondence with George Joseph Plunket Browne, bishop of Elphin, and John MacHale, archbishop of Tuam, was published in *The Times*, 5 Jan. 1848. John O'Connell's response was published in *The Times*, 8 Jan. 1848.

high offices, has also written upon the Subject & has shewn how very ill & unintelligibly he writes, & what nonsense Such a clever man, So writing, can put to paper[474] –

*14 January 1848.* The Irish Romans of the worst description are furious against Lords Shrewsbury & Surrey, for having written letters, censoring denunciations from the altars by the priests, & their consequences, murder, Spoliation, & revenge – instead of inducing them to be more Christianlike [–] these appeals to the Romish hierachy [sic] has only tended to make them more fiendish –

*17 January 1848.* [My son] Charles arrived this Evening from London – He brings a report which I anxiously trust may not be true, that Lord Powis is Either dead or dying –

*19 January 1848.* To my infinite dismay & grief I learn today that Lord Powis is dead – He was one of my oldest & most valued friends – & a valuable man publicly & privately – His death arises from this frightful cause [–] he was out shooting with Several of his Sons, & one of them (Robert [Charles Herbert]) by a miserable accident Shot him in the legs – The accident was lightly treated & it was Said that he was doing well & fast recovering – I never thought of writing to Enquire, believing the accident to have been free from all danger whatever – However it now appears that the wounds mortified & his valuable life has fallen a Sacrifice to this most melancholy & truly shocking accident: the feelings of the poor young man must be beyond idea: bitter & intolerable – It is a most Excellent family & I grieve for their affliction & Situation –

*23 January 1848.* No very particular occurrence = Events of portentous magnitude are pursuing their prescribed course –

*27 January 1848.* […] The Birmingham men will not accept the low wages offered to them & are parading about in a very disorganised State – this is the case Elsewhere – & in London it is said that distress prevails to a very Serious Extent, & that Suffering is Endured by the distressed – The clouds are gathering around us fearfully –

*29 January 1848.* a letter from [my son] William today dated the 3rd of this month from Constantinople – he had at last received his leave – but he [did] not anticipate that he would be likely to avail himself of it for many weeks –

*1 February 1848.* […] I wished to take Some notice of two Sons of Ibrahim Pacha who [are] at School at Worksop & they accompanied me & remained close to me all day to see the Sport – They are fine boys & now speak English very well, they Conducted themselves in the best possible manner, are quite civilised, remarkably civil & obliging, quick [,] alive,

---

[474]Ellesmere's original letter in *The Times*, 25 Dec. 1847, led to two further letters on the subject: *The Times*, 1, 12 Jan. 1848.

active & intelligent, the name of the Eldest Hassan, the youngest Mustapha [Mustafa]: they dine[475] & Slept here, & will go home tomorrow about 1 o'clock –

*3 February 1848.* Parliament meets today. Lord George Bentinck will bring forward his motion on West Indian affairs & no doubt will make a most brilliant Speech [.] He has resigned the leadership, & wishes it to be bestowed upon Lord Granby, after himself, he is the best man that can be Selected. His age & inexperience may seem to disqualify, but his right Judgement, good sense, steady application, & his being right upon all points make him an Eligible man, & my opinion is that before the year is out, he will Shew that he is peculiarly fitted for the Situation – & Some day will be a great Man –

*5 February 1848.* Parliament opened on the 3rd [.] Lord George Bentinck made a very long & able Speech comprehending Every point, introductory to his motion for a Committee to Enquire into the State of West Indian affairs & Especially into the Sugar question. The motion will not be opposed but the debate is adjourned – […] 3 per Cent Consols are 89 – The deficiency on the year [£] 4,000,000.

*6 February 1848.* The archbishop of Canterbury [William Howley] is very ill, his strength has failed him So much & he is in Such a State of exhaustion that [,] at his age & previously bad health, recovery is next to impossible & probably in a few days his Existence will be terminated – & who will these mischievous men appoint? probably the most unfit of all men to be placed in this most important & responsible Situation. It is grievous to think how the interests of the Church are now periled For good purposes, doubtless it is the will of God that it Should be So – but appearances are awful & perplexing –

*8 February 1848.* […] Lord Lansdowne has brought in a bill to legalise inter-Communication with the Church of Rome = & that we Should Send a minister to Rome & the Pope a nuncio to us – It is a villainous procedure & a flagrant violation of our national policy & may be called a breach of the Constitution Seriously criminal towards the Nation – & nationally culpable in the Sight of God – it is another of those free thinking measures which have so abounded of late & which must bring a curse upon us –

*9 February 1848.* The debate on the Jew bill is adjourned. I do not hear how it is likely to terminate, but I fear that there [is] no probability that it will not pass the Commons –
  a meeting took place at Lord Stanley's when Lord George Bentinck's resignation of the leadership in the House of Commons was formally announced, but another was not chosen [–] this will be done today at a Meeting at Mr [George] Bankes' [–] Lord Granby will probably be the man, & probably a fitter cannot be chosen – I believe that he is right on Every point. His ability will I am convinced be Shewn after a little trial, his great good Sense [,] temper, & Excellent Judgment will Soon distinguish him as the fittest man that

---

[475] dined in the original.

Could be chosen – He is modest & retiring, but these he will feel obliged to cast away, & then he will Shew himself worthy of the Selection, & confidence placed in him.

*10 February 1848.* I have had a very private & confidential letter today from Lord Stanley[476] – I wrote to him yesterday on the Subjects on which he has written to me = & I grieve to find that we Shall differ & that I must act in open opposition to him – he is in favour of the bill for renewing diplomatic relations with Rome, & I not only am totally opposed to it, but for the Sake of the Country I Shall feel it to be my duty to Speak upon it & moreover Shall be forced up to London next week Sorely against my will – Lord Stanley frankly imparts his views to me & wishes for mine, knowing how deeply I feel upon Such Subjects = I shall answer him Equally frankly & I much fear that all these disagreements & dissentions must break up our party: but of this [I] am convinced that in as much as the Public naturally Expects from us "protection" in "Every["] thing, if we fail to protect & follow the wicked & revolutionary course of the Country's Cursers, all confidence in us will cease [–] we Shall be ranked among the faithless traitors of their Country's Cause –

*11 February 1848.* The great procession of above 10,000 – Ship owners & Sailors to present a memorial to the Queen against the Ministerial intention of abolishing or attenuating the Navigation laws, So as to destroy their Efficiency – took place the day before yesterday = they all went in Steamers to Hungerford or Whitehall Stairs, assembled in Trafalgar Square, & then marched in procession to the Home Office, where they deposited their Memorial to be laid before the Queen – I am in great hope, that this determined manifestation may avert the ruthless mischief =

[…] I have answered Lord Stanley's letter today, & have told him decidedly that I cannot agree with him, & that I shall feel absolutely obliged to be in my place on the 17th to oppose the popish diplomatic intercourse bill – We want no Nuncios or Legates here, & God grant that the bill may not pass =

*12 February 1848.* This day's post brings us the news of the death of the archbishop of Canterbury. He has passed off tranquilly to his End, mildly & meekly as he lived – a pious and Excellent man [–] doubtless he will meet with his reward. His faults were constitutional = He was not formed for times of trouble & difficulty & contention – It Seems that he was Just Entering on his 84th year [–] a much greater age by many years than I Should have given him = It will be a point of Extreme difficulty to Select his Successor – I dread the Selection of our present Rulers =

*13 February 1848.* The Jew bill has passed the 2nd reading in the House of Commons by a majority of 73 [–] the numbers being 277 & 204 – we Shall probably have the bill in our house in the course of the next week – Sir Robert Peel's Speech was the richest Specimen of himself I Ever read = made up of <u>fustian</u> declamation, hypocrisy, Scripture quotation, largely, professions of deep attachment to the Church & Christianity, & assuming

---

[476] On the Diplomatic Relations Bill, recommending that they should 'not object to the 2nd Reading of the Bill; but to propose in Committee a Clause prohibiting the reception of any Roman Catholic Ecclesiastic in the capacity of Minister': D.P., 177/2, p. 270: Stanley to Newcastle, 8 Feb. 1848. Also see R.P., 1712, f. 1248: Newcastle to Richmond, 9 Feb. 1848.

to himself, profanely, the attributes of the Deity, & almost impugning the Justice of God, yet as a Christian professing the duty incumbent upon him to make reparation to the Jews to Soothe their Sorrows, to palliate their offences, & [as] a Christian to indemnify them for the miseries & punishment Suffered by Gods' high decree to avenge the Shedding of the blood of His Son attended with all the cruelty, revilings [*sic*] & torture which were Used by His murderers, who themselves challenged the punishment by crying out, "His blood be upon us & our Children["][477] –

*16 February 1848*. [John Bird] Sumner, Bishop of Chester is made archbishop of Canterbury – Lord Granby has refused the leadership in the House of Commons – Winchilsea writes that the illness of Lady Winchilsea about whom he is very uneasy retains him at Haverholme [Priory, Lincolnshire] to his great annoyance in Every way –

*17 February 1848*. I communicated with Lord Stanley & he very Kindly arranged for me to Speak Early, & I ventured up after Lord Lansdowne – as I had written nothing but what I thought would best Suit the opening, I was Sure to make a Confused & most imperfect Speech – but nevertheless, although I Said nothing but what chanced to come upper most I hobbled & went through my task better than I Expected – but I omitted many things which were important & which I ought to have mentioned: But I ought to be, and am, truly thankful that I was Enabled to Enounce [*sic*] without disgrace, the few remarks which I made upon & against this most dangerous wanton, & perfidious bill[478] – The Bishop of Exeter [Henry Phillpotts] had intended to move the rejection of the bill, but on my Speaking to him he most handsomely waived his intention & gave up to me – Lord Stanley made an admirable, & convincing Speech, & used Every [argument] that Could be used against the bill, So much So that I Expressed to him my utter Surprise that he Should vote for a measure, which he made out to be a[s] monstrous as it was Useless – I was plagued to death not to divide the house, but I persisted to the last, being really of opinion that for the Effect on the Country it was best to have no Sham fighting – I resisted all Solicitation for a long while, but at the End of the debate, seeing how numbers had fallen off – & that I Could not divide with so many as a dozen Supporters, I consulted those who were about me & finally determined that it would be the better course to abandon division: at this announcement Lord Stanley was greatly gratified, & although I myself was not at all Satisfied at giving way – yet I am convinced that this proceeding amongst ourselves will be productive of the best Effects – anxiously do I hope that So it may be[479] –

*18 February 1848*. In committee on the Popish intercourse bill. I wished that Some resolutions which I Submitted Should be adopted instead of Lord Eglintons which I think will be productive of little or no good – but they have been rejected = Lord Eglinton's Were

[477] Matthew, 27: 24–25.

[478] Newcastle told Giffard, 'I Shall do my best of course, but under Every possible disadvantage, for You Know that I am a wretched Speaker, unpractised [,] hating the thing, inaudible & Confused in thought & delivery – but it must be, & shall be though a forlorn hope – Could you Select a reporter with wonderful Ears & an acute mind, Such a man May be able to interpret My meaning': BL, Add. MS 56368, ff. 183–4: Newcastle to Giffard, 16 [Feb.] 1848. Regrettably, they could not: *The Standard*, 18 Feb. 1848.

[479] Hansard, *Lords Debates*, 3rd ser., xcvi, cols 770–1: 17 Feb. 1848; K.D., 17 Feb. 1848, 'House of Lords Diplomacy with Rome – Duke of Newcastle'.

put [to] the vote in Committee & we beat the Ministers by 3 only = they 64 we 67 – occasioned by [the] Duke of Wellington voting with us & of course bringing his shadow Lord Clanwilliam – untill a few minutes before, he / the Duke [/], did not Know what he was about & mistook one thing for another & was speaking very Energetically but Very incoherently, but Seeing his Error Lord Ellenborough rose & Settled him, by Speaking in a very loud voice which he Could hear, & Explaining to him the true State of the case, he Stared about him & Enquired & at last perceived his Error – The bill is made Something better by this amendment, but it must always be a noxious, wanton & most objectionable bill. I at first thought of not voting for this amendment but on consideration I resolved to do So giving my reasons for So doing, one of them being because the Ministers made So much objection to them[480] =

*19 February 1848.* I hear nothing very particular today. I have been told that the Queen was very angry that Lord John Russell did or rather would not appoint [Samuel] Wilberforce Bishop of Oxford to Either York or Canterbury = He would be as bad a Man as could be appointed, but those who are Selected are very ill fitted for the Situations –

*20 February 1848.* I fear that it is not a very proper way of passing the Sunday, but I have been walking myself off my legs from 2 to 7, o'clock Seeking political people, in order to learn what we are about & what is likely to Ensue – as regards our own party we are all to pieces & in a Most Unfortunate way – Lord George Bentinck has resigned the leadership in the House of Commons [–] it was proposed to Elect Lord Granby, but the offer being made he declined it [,] & now they have no leader at all & are not likely to find one – I tried to find Lord Stanley today that I might See [him] in private & have a full conversation with him – but he was gone to Church – I do not make out what he is at, & Should like to dive into his Sentiments & views & intentions – which will not be very Easy = Lord George Bentinck Says that if he (Lord Stanley) turns his coat on the Jew bill, that he will be a renegade, like Peel, & that he will never Enter his house again = & he will be as good as his word – Whereas if Lord Stanley does not oppose the Jew bill, we shall all be against him, & Shall find that he does [not] represent the views & opinion of the party – In Short all is division & danger – Ministers will have there [*sic*] wicked way – Every thing most injurious to the Country will be perpetuated & our noble Country will be ruined.

Lord John Russell has "opened his budget" & [a] pretty thing it is – his language in my opinion was most indiscreet [,] talking of invasion in detail, & Stating the Encrease in the army & navy which he proposed to make – disclosing to our Enemies all our Weakest points & much over stating what may be truths – He proposes to add 2 per Cent to the Income tax for 2 years & to continue the now Standing 3 per Cent Income tax for five years longer, & no one who Knows any thing of Such matters can doubt that the full intention is to Establish both in perpetuity as a fixed tax – I am told that the Statement was very ill received by the whole house [–] & I think it very likely that he will not Carry his measure –

*21 February 1848.* The feeling & sentiments of Condemnation of Lord John Russell's Speech & financial Scheme is general & unequivocal – I do not think it will pass = but, if the Minister is beaten, where is another to be found [?] –

---

[480] Hansard, *Lords Debates*, 3rd ser., xcvi, col. 894: 18 Feb. 1848.

I was told tonight in the House of Lords that the Chancellor of the Exchequer [Charles Wood] had just moved for a Secret Committee to Enquire into the State of the army [,] navy, ordnance [,] national defences &c — So that this humbug is to have its run —

*22 February 1848.* Very busy all day & now thoroughly tired out by walking & thinking — I have nearly but not quite finished all I have to do — two days of this Kind of incessant fatigue of mind & body is very harassing — I have been with Lord Stanley this Evening: he & Lady Stanley Were tete a tete [–] & it is delightful to see them together So confidently depending on Each other — We talked over all present & Some future matters, & I found him determined to act without considering whether it would turn out the Ministers or not — This is quite to my taste.

*27 February 1848.* The post of today, including the two posts, brings us news with a vengeance — France is in revolution again, by some unaccountable occurrences, the people have had their way, Scarcely any resistance has been made to the multitude, the people have over come Every obstacle & they are triumphant — The King [Louis Philippe] tried to conciliate by a change of Ministers, first he Sent to Count Mole [Louis–Mathieu Molé] to form an administration but that would not do, & then to [Adolphe] Thiers to whom was Joined Odillon Barrot, but that would not do = various Scenes too long to describe Succeeded Each other in rapid Succession, & finally a republic was proclaimed & a provisional government formed[481] […]

*4 March 1848.* […] The Ministers have given up the additional Income tax, the public voice against it was universal[482] —

*5 March 1848.* It is quite true that Louis Philippe & his Queen [Maria Amalia] are arrived in England: he landed from an English Steamer at Newhaven the day before yesterday & Was heartily welcomed by the Kind & noble English — Who Ever Sympathise with the Suffering & pity Misfortune & fallen greatness —

*6 March 1848.* […] I am told that [my son] Robert is gone to Ireland to Stand for Kinsale!! on what interest I Know not, or who is to pay for him, or how it can Serve him to be in Parliament unless he Knows or fancies that he can Speak well = after being plucked four times for a common pass [at Oxford], he must be much altered if he Shines in Parliament [.] Still I think it not unlikely that he may do pretty well if he takes a liking to the thing — as

[481] N.U.M.D., Ne2F8/8: diary enclosure, John Evelyn Denison to Newcastle, 25 Feb. 1848: 'The Report here [in the Commons] just arrived is, That the King of France is deposed. All the Royal Family rejected — All Expelled from Paris, The Palace Sacked, a Republic Established … I fear much of this is true'; Ne2F8/7/1: diary enclosure, Denison to Newcastle, 28 Feb. 1848: 'As I Sent you Such very bad news a day or two ago, it is but fair I Should have the Satisfaction of Sending you the Somewhat better news of today. The Report is that the National Guard are disposed for a Monarchy, & will not have the Republic, and that Some of the great Towns are of the Same mind. This is the first glimmer of Light … The King is Said to have Shown no courage or determination'.

[482] D.P., 147/14: Newcastle to Stanley, 29 Feb. 1848, recommending non-interference in French affairs. Stanley replied 'I do not know which cuts the worst figure — Louis Philippe & Co. in their abandonment of the cause without a struggle, or our Ministers in their proposition & sudden abandonment of their additional Income Tax. They would have been infallibly beaten had they not succumbed': 177/2, p. 317: Stanley to Newcastle, 2 Mar. 1848.

a Son he is behaving Shockingly ill, God forgive him – in other things I hope he may do better, but under the Wicked Weight of undutifulness, I have little idea of his prospering in any way –

*7 March 1848.* It Seems to be too true that Louis Philippe from Some unaccountable deficiency has totally destroyed not only his own cause but that of royalty in France, with all its consequences to Europe […] If the Smallest Effort had been made to rally the Troops out of Paris [,] it is pretty well ascertained that Louis Philippe might now have been at the head of his army dictating terms to his Parisian rebels – The whole affair appears to be one of the most ill Judged & disgraceful cessions that Ever as by magic hurled a Kingdom from monarchy to Republicanism –

*8 March 1848.* Louis Philippe takes the name of Compte de Neuilly: he wrote to our Queen from Newhaven: on receiving her answer he left for Claremont, which place it Seems has been allotted to him for his residence = He told the people at Newhaven, that he Should never leave England again –

*9 March 1848.* It appears that Mr [Charles] Cochrane, who Stood for Westminster, invited the people to an open air meeting in Trafalgar Square but this he abandoned on learning that it would be illegal, the Subject being the abolition of the Income Tax, to meet any where for public debate any where within one mile of the Houses of Parliament when the Parliament is Sitting – although Mr Cochrane did not appear [,] the people came & then began to riot & use Seditious language – The mob has paraded about the Town for two days [,] breaking windows & lamps, & breaking open & Stealing from the Shops – There were Several affrays with the Police, who have always been Victors. The Soldiers were not required – This business is nearly if not quite at an End now [,] but a very large meeting is announced for Monday 13th on Kennington Common – when it is Supposed that the rabble will Endeavour under Some paltry leaders, a Mr [G.W.M.] Reynolds & Some others, to make a great demonstration = Doubtless they will give a good deal of trouble, but the well disposed are So numerous & So active that the rabble can Effect nothing but temporary mischief.

*10 March 1848.* The riots at Glasgow have been very Serious, there has been a great destruction of property [–] as the object of the rioters has been pillage, attacking the Jewellers [,] watchmakers & other valuable Shops – it is Said that robbery to the amount of upwards of £15000 – has been Committed by these vagabonds – They were fired upon & Several lives have been lost – at Edinburgh, Manchester &c riots have been raised by the Scum of the Towns & I have no doubt that this will run as a fashion, through all the populous & large manufacturing towns in the Kingdom –

*11 March 1848.* all is quiet now in London. Glasgow & Edinborough [*sic*] are Settled & Manchester nearly So – Symptoms of outbreaks Elsewhere –

Germany is very uneasy, the people are determined to have free & representative governments [–] with this perhaps in the first instance they may be Satisfied – but when they have tasted the Sweets of popular power & freedom, more will be required & must be ceded – they are on a Volcano – Prince Metternich has resigned. The Emperor of Russia [Nicholas I] is Said to be very ill –

I omitted to mention yesterday that I received the Melancholy intelligence of the death of my old friend & brother in law General [Godfrey Basil Meynell] Mundy. When I Saw him in London he looked remarkably well & as young as he did 20 years ago – he was taken Suddenly with a Shivering fit, Succeeded by violent vomiting – on the third day he was dead –

*12 March 1848.* Much uneasiness & a strong tendency to rioting from Manchester northwards – but disturbance has been put down & all is pretty quiet at present –

*14 March 1848.* The meeting at Kennington Common yesterday, from Which So much was Expected went off without any tumult up to the time of the post leaving – The reports say that there [were] not above 4000 people present – Mr Reynolds as before harrangued the people, but did not make much impression = In Ireland however the language used at meetings is most Shameful = & it is Said that Cobden is Establishing a new League [the Financial Reform Association], for all Sorts of revolutionary purposes – among the most mischievous to abolish the law of Entail, & of primogeniture [.]

*15 March 1848.* […] Robert it Seems has failed at Kinsale – it is best So – Mr [Benjamin] Hawes – under Secretary to the Colonies, has been chosen.[483]

*16 March 1848.* The words, "liberte, Egalite, fraternite" are perpetually in the mouths of Frenchmen now – but when it comes to apply these words towards the English Workmen in France, they are immediately an Exception – one of the first impulses of these tigro–monkies,[484] was to maltreat & Expel all the men who had been & who were then working on the railways, there was no fraternite for them, they drove them out without compunction & Without mercy – & more they would not pay them their Wages – & the poor wretches came over here by hundreds in the most miserable plight – but for the bodily aid & Skill of these men they Could not have made their railroad's & Executed the great works which have been completed of late = but gratitude & mercy they have not: at Paris, now, the war against the labouring English, & artisans [,] is very fierce – they are about to Expel & Eradicate them from Paris if they can, & So great is their prejudice & hostility, that they have declared that no English Servants Shall be permitted in Paris or France, & that if an English man is Seen driving he Shall be pulled off his box – it is a Known fact that English artisans & mechanics have taught Frenchmen what they Knew not before, & what they Know & do now as well as Englishmen – Spinning [,] Engineering, machine making, Steam apparatus, all the larger & most important branches of arts & manufactures.

*17 March 1848.* Great preparations were making in Ireland to meet whatever violation of the law may result from the celebration of St Patrick's day (this day) in Ireland = The demagogues are become most inveterate, & the language Spoken & written is most atrocious

---

[483] The Whig Hawes won by 97 votes to Robert Pelham-Clinton's 94 votes: majority three.

[484] The story of the tiger and the monkey was the origin of the Chinese saying 'the monkey reigns in the mountains when the tiger is not there'.

– Lord John Russel openly admits in the House of Commons that treason is publicly spoken at Dublin = a rising or outrages are confidently Expected on this day throughout Ireland, but Especially in Dublin –

*19 March 1848.* a few lines by telegraphic dispatch are published in the Standard [&] announce, that all went off peaceably on St Patrick's day as far as Dublin was concerned –

*20 March 1848.* To my great surprise I was awakened this morning but a little after 7 [a.m.] by a Knocking at my door, & found that it was [my son] Charles who had Just come from London – his Errand that he had been requested to Stand Bewdley – in the room of Mr [Thomas James] Ireland who had been voted out on petition – on talking the matter over, we concluded that it might be better to decline the honor as it might look as if a Clinton was to be first turn for any vacancy that might occur = He was to return an answer immediately by telegraph to London which he did by 9 o'clock = I Should think the place tolerably certain but if he were to fail, it might Seem as if a Clinton were always to [be] unsuccessful, besides which we have no more money to throw away upon Elections = Notwithstanding I am most anxious to see him in Parliament = He brings no news from London – The Queen was yesterday delivered of a Princess – the 4th [Princess Louise] She & the child are doing well –

*22 March 1848.* […] Vienna is now under mob, or popular law. Prince Metternich has now finally retired – & with the Exception of the Royal family running away [,] the austrian revolution appears to have been a counterpart of the French or Parisian – Questionless these are all Signs of the times & of the latter days = the Events of the present days have the finger of God upon them – they are not otherwise within human occurrence = The like has never been before & must prelude Something wonderful.

*24 March 1848.* […] In Ireland 3 of the leading people who have Spoken & written the most traiterous & Seditious language have been arrested & are to take their trials in the beginning of april – these men are Messrs [William Smith] O'brien – [Thomas Francis] Meagher & [John] Mitchell Editor of the new paper, "United Irishman" –

*26 March 1848.* […] The Signs of the times are truly wonderful – if I recollect rightly many "Kings of the Earth" are to be destroyed & here we may observe the fulfilling of prophetic declaration & as it were without a cause[485] – But unless God intends to use the people to accomplish good [,] how fearful & terrible may be the anarchy & outrage of the people – for the people of themselves & by themselves have accomplished those wonders – & it Seems to [be] authentically Stated that the Germans when the French Revolution broke out were determinedly loyal & faithful to their Sovereigns – but that now having found their own Strength & what their power can Effect, they Even are fast becoming Republicans, & I confess that I, (in the Common course of Events) & unless God wills it otherwise, See nothing but heaps of Republics, where formerly were Kingdoms & States.

---

[485]See Isaiah, 24; Revelation, 11: 18.

*28 March 1848.* [...] The language used at the last meeting of the Irish Confederation, was audacious & treasonable beyond all belief – I am confident that such Sentiments & Expressions were never before used in any public assembly, in a Country where there is a Semblance of Law – why are they not Seised & Shut up instantly [?] –

*3 April 1848.* Wrote to Lord John Russell today Entreating him to do three things [–] to Smother the Jew bill, & Popish intercourse bill, & to Suffer no consideration whatever to draw us into a Continental War – The doing the two first; I conceive will be So well pleasing to God, that we may hope for His more favorable Consideration in permitting us to maintain peace & to Spare us the horrors & miseries which will So awfully afflict other Countries through war & revolutionary frenzy – The result to us would be; that we Should manufacture & do the Commerce of the Whole World, & at the last when others were utterly Exhausted, we might Step in as moderators and arbiters of the World[486] –

*7 April 1848.* Ministers are acting well & vigorously, they have made Extensive & well devised plans & preparations to meet any thing which may happen on the 10th at the great Chartist Meeting [on Kennington Common] = They have also brought in "a bill for the better protection of the Crown & Government of the United Kingdom" = & are Shewing the most praise worthy determination to arrest republicanism & disorganisation, & to Secure order & tranquillity –

*8 April 1848.* [...] all the troops that are any where near to London have been ordered up in case of accident, although after all there will not be above 10,000 men = But the great reliance will be on the Police & Constabulary force which will be made to act in the first instance & if required: aided by the military force – This is quite the right mode, & Meets with the most Strenuous Support from all classes & has brought out the best & noblest feelings from all well thinking men – all have Stepped forward & have been Sworn Special Constables – Nobles, gentlemen, the middle classes, professional men of all Kinds [,] Shopkeepers, working men, Every body – a most admirable Spirit prevails, & by Gods' will we Shall be Secure –

*9 April 1848.* The last weeks have made one think deeply & reflect upon the past & the future – For myself, reasoning upon what has passed Elsewhere, & being Convinced that God is acting in a Special manner towards Nations & in fulfilment of what has been prophecied of these times concerning them – I have come to the Conclusion that tomorrow may decide the future fate of England; & be indicative of God's will towards us – as other Nations & Kings have been Sacrificed to the first burst of popular action almost without a Struggle so may we, if Such be God's decree, So that if we are respited that may be

---

[486] TNA, PRO/30/22/7b, ff. 278–81: Newcastle to Russell, 12 Apr. 1848; PRO30/22/7c, f. 10: Newcastle to Russell, 6 May 1848. In offering this advice, Newcastle stressed that he was acting independently of anyone else.

a warning to us & a token that we are not to be afflicted to the Same degree as other Nations[487] =

*10 April 1848*. This is Monday & no post from London – I had made arrangements to receive advices from all quarters if any thing were happening to day within a circle of 30 miles round this place – but I am informed this Evening that all is quiet up to 2 o'clock, a traveller brought an account to Worksop that at Some Station which he passed [,] news had been received from London by telegraph that all was quiet at 12 o'clock – I Shall most anxiously open the newspapers tomorrow morning –

*11 April 1848*. The boasted meeting which was to carry all before it has vanished, not into thin air perhaps, but into the Smoky air of London – The Standard States that not above 10,000 at the utmost could have been present. Some inflammatory Speeches Were made by the leaders, when a Police constable went up to O'Connor & spoke to him [–] when O'Connor informed the people that he had been desired to desist, & advised the meeting to disperse quietly as resistance would be in vain as they Were unarmed – at another time if they wished to resist the government they must come armed: the crowd then dispersed & the petition which Mr Feargus O'Connor Said was Signed by more than 5,000,000 – was rather unceremoniously taken from the Stately van & 8 horses, & bundled into 3 Cabs & Sent thus to the House of Commons – Where Shortly after the Knavish O'Connor presented it to the house – & there was an End of this grand bravado – Every thing was quiet afterwards – O'Connor & the leaders are accused by the Chartists of treachery & I believe that they were not very far wrong – In this county all went off quietly [,] the Same at Liverpool & Manchester & probably Elsewhere, but they talk of all meeting again in a few days – I hope that this will not be permitted & the absolute repression of these nuisances is called for by all, Even by the Manchester people, who Entertain a Strange dislike to being robbed & plundered themselves although they have no feeling for others – and now I thank God that He has deigned to avert mischief from our land, & may we be Sensible of the inestimable blessing; & may we as a Nation So order ourselves that we may become an acceptable people in His Sight, & a glorious Example of a righteous Nation – Eschewing Evil, & cleaving to what is good –

*12 April 1848*. Lord Lansdowne has brought in an alien bill to Enable the Government to deal with the vast number of mischievous foreigners who have come over here in large numbers & who are busily Employed wherever they can do Mischief – in Ireland they are hard at work [.]

*14 April 1848*. […] The Chartist petition to the House of Commons has been discovered to be a gross & insulting fraud upon the House – There are hundreds & thousands of pretended Signatures [,] in the names of Various persons, Such as The Queen, Prince albert

---

[487] Newcastle wrote in a similar vein to Stanley, assuring him, 'You know that I am not a fanatic although I Certainly do attribute to God, His workings Whether great or Small & in all that is passing': D.P., 147/14: Newcastle to Stanley, 10 Apr. 1848. Newcastle later told Disraeli 'I am not a fanatic or Enthusiast but one whose Very Existence is involved in the well being of his Country & I must add of the whole human race': Dep Hughenden, 137/3, ff. 136–8: Newcastle to Disraeli, 27 Feb. 1849. For Newcastle 'in a hermitage, with a flowing beard and long tails, in mourning for the destruction of his unhappy country', see *Punch*, xi (1847), 188.

&c &c & there [are] all sorts of low [,] filthy & obscure words, & low cant terms – in short this famed petition of 5 millions, does not Contain, Such as there are [,] more than about $1\frac{1}{2}$ millions & very many of them Such as above described – By this all Self respect has been forfeited, & I trust that on this account the petition will be indignantly rejected by the House –

*15 April 1848.* The English news of the 10th has caused the most Severe disappointment to the French republicans – They had already reported London to be a prey to anarchy & contest = How Surprised foreigners must be at the Strength of our government & [the] vigour & right mindedness of our people – They must be [the] Wonder & Envy of all well thinking foreigners –
   […] a ludicrous Scene has occurred in the House of Commons [,] on the report on the Chartist petition – which the house thought would End in a duel between Messrs O'Connor & [William] Cripps = O'Connor was called before the house [,] Explanations were made by the parties, & the affair Ended =

*17 April 1848.* O'Connor has announced publicly & it has long been Said that On Good Friday, there will be general & Simultaneous rising & meeting of the Chartists all over the Country = if this be true, we Shall yet have Something to do – but what a day for any but Roman Catholics to Select for Such a vile & unlawful purpose! –

*19 April 1848.* I learn today that mischief is not Expected from Chartist Meetings Even although [*sic*] they may all Simultaneously meet on Good Friday – It is Even thought that there will be no outbreak in Ireland. There as here the agitators perceive that public opinion is not with them, & moreover that all due preparation is made to put them down, if they attempted to rise —

*20 April 1848.* I see with the very greatest Satisfaction that the archbishop of Canterbury [John Bird Sumner] has been called upon by the Queen to frame a thanksgiving Service to be read in all Churches & Chapels of this Kingdom on Good Friday (tomorrow) & for the 4 Succeeding Sunday, to return our humble & dutiful thanks to almighty God for preserving us in peace & the observance of Our laws, whilst all other Countries are Scourged & devoured by the rage & ruin of fierce & furious anarchy & revolution – The Singular blessing cannot be too highly prized & it is right & our bounden duty to humble ourselves before God & offer the heartful tribute of our thanksgiving for the wonderful preservation from the direst Evil that can befall a Nation = This is quite as it Should be & I believe is almost unanimously felt throughout the Nation – for many of us had already proposed to do that Separately which is now more properly & reverently to be performed by National thanksgiving – & now too much Stress cannot be laid upon a national Endeavour to make ourselves more & more worthy to merit & to receive the Divine favour –

*23 April 1848.* The Chartists are Still Stirring & use the most Seditious & infamous language = in my opinion the Government ought not to permit them to meet, or if they meet not to be allowed to collect in larger numbers than 50[488] – at the very most – a larger meeting could not be for discussion – but for intimidation –

*29 April 1848.* […] There have been two melancholy deaths lately – one of Lady Mary Fitzroy, Sister to the Duke of Richmond & wife of Sir Charles Fitzroy – Governor of australia – She was Killed by the horses running away & throwing her out of the carriage, when She pitched upon her head, & was Killed instantly – The other Lady Catherine [Katherine Isabella] Jermyn, daughter of the Duke of Rutland, who caught measles from attending upon her husband Lord Jermyn & died in a few days, being pregnant at the time – Both ladies, with reason, are greatly regretted –

*1 May 1848.* […] The Queen by the Lord Chamberlain [Earl Spencer] has issued a notice Expressing a desire that all Ladies coming to Her Drawing rooms, or who may be invited to Buckingham Palace Shall be dressed in articles of British manufacture only – a very Seasonable & proper notice, truly, which is followed up by the remark, "of the distressed Condition of trade" – now what can be more humiliating than this remark to the free traders, with Sir Robert Peel at their head [?] – it is a complete upset of their System, & a proof that distress has been occasioned by this insane & ruinous System –

*9–11 May 1848.* I have set political Events quite aside indeed I have hardly looked at the papers –

*13 May 1848.* I find the Ministry Extremely weak, but no organisation of any consequence against it – We are much & fatally divided – & Every party Seems to be cut into bits – Changes are taking place in the Ministry & more are talked of – they wish to get rid of Lord Palmerston – but if he goes, they take Lord Clarendon from Ireland & put him in his place – & they have no one for Ireland – We require a strong & vigorous Set of men at this time [,] but these are not Easily found when most wanted –

*14 May 1848.* This being Sunday = by way of Combining Exercise with amusement I went to lionise the new buildings in the Parks = […] to Lord Ellesmere's new house in Cleveland court[489] – With three decorative fronts & [a] garden in front of that which faces the Park – In my opinion this is the finest & handsomest house in London, & as it strikes me [,] possesses more beauties & fewer defects than any Elevation I have Seen of modern date […] I then went to the new point of Buckingham Palace – but what a thing! One felt quite humbled & down hearted to See anything So wretched & contemptible by way of Palatial architecture in Seeing, our Sovereign's Palace after leaving that of her [subject] one cannot Endure the Comparison, it is quite provoking & one laments to see money which has been freely voted by the Nation devoted to a purpose So very unworthily Executed, when all would be proud to See their Sovereign housed in a Stately Palace instead of a

---

[488] This was the same limit on meetings that was set in the so-called 'Two Acts' of 1795 and the 'Six Acts' of 1819.

[489] Bridgewater House, which was completed to the designs of Sir Charles Barry.

mean House = It is indeed a most miserable performance & disgraceful to any architect who gave the design – I believe this architect to be [Edward] Blore[490] –

*15 May 1848.* […] The Chartist conventional assembly is dissolved & is totally defunct – in Ireland Mr [John] Mitchell is Seised & incarcerated under the new act for traiterous & Seditious publications in his villainous paper "The United Irishman" – This will do – & if Such measures are closely & vigilantly followed up, we Shall Soon hear no more of, rebellion &ca =

Ld ashburton is dead – when I Entered the House of Lords this Evening [,] Lord Stanley was Eulogising his memory & was followed by Lord Lansdowne & other Lords = it is Singular that of three Brothers all Eminent in their way – Sir Thomas [Baring] died first then Mr Henry Baring, & now Ld ashburton & all within a fortnight of Each other =

Lord Stanley's bill to regulate Parliamentary proceedings & to provide the power to postpone to a Succeeding Session bills which come So late from the Commons that they Cannot be reasonably considered in a confused & hasty manner at the very tail of the Session – met with much opposition this Evening – indeed it appears Evident that although well intentioned it is open to many objections – it will be very much modified at all Events –

*19 May 1848.* We went to a State Ball at Buckingham Palace this night – a very great assemblage = The Queen is a good deal altered in appearance, looking more matronly, though not out of health – but thoughtful & Serious – & it must be admitted that there is Sufficient cause for this – The Prince [William] of Prussia was there, a tall, unaffected military looking man – The Prince [Leopold Count] of Syracuse, the Duke of Mecklenburg Shelitz [George, Grand Duke of Mecklenburg-Strelitz] & various other royal personages – The Queen was Kind & gracious to us & rose to receive us when we went towards her – It is Evident to me that most people have a thoughtfulness about them which clouds the hilarity of a Ball[491] –

*21 May 1848.* I was told today by a friend that the Danish Minister [Count Reventlow] had informed him at the Queen's Ball that Russia had declared in favor of Denmark – & consequently would declare War against Prussia & the Germans – Sweden has already declared for Denmark & is assisting with men & ships to defend that Country = The alliance therefore will be Russia & Sweden for Denmark & against the German Confederation if that wild scheme can Ever be matured = There is little doubt of the issue – The Germans will be beaten = but it is to be feared that Russian friendship will be the hug of the bear – The part which Russia may play in the great coming war of nations may be Stupendous – our part will be to look on, & to Keep at peace – If we pursue this course & improve ourselves as a Nation in virtue & goodness great & happy shall we be – I had a good deal of conversation upon this Subject, at the Queen's Ball, with Lord Palmerston & he

[490]Edward Blore completed the plans for Buckingham Palace which had been drawn up by John Nash but executed them in a plainer style. He designed the great facade facing The Mall which enclosed the central quadrangle.
[491]QVJ, 19 May 1848.

assured me most unequivocally, if he be to be believed – that to Keep at peace was his firm intention[492] –

From this day I must be Seriously engaged in looking into the whole question of the Jew bill which we are to debate on the 25th & if I can put any thing together satisfactorily to myself So as to be able to Say any thing which may be of use, I Shall Speak upon it –

*22 May 1848.* It was told me in the house of Lords this Evening that nothing could Equal the Exertions making by the Jews to induce The Lords to pass the Shameful bill to give them Seats in Parliament [–] it is positively asserted that money & promises of many good things are held in Expectation to effect the purpose – my informant told me that he heard Mr Henry Fitzroy Say this at a dinner at Lord Lyndhurst's – Mr Fitzroy married a Jewess – a [Hannah] Rothschild.

*23 May 1848.* I heard this Evening that Mr [Henry] Buller [*sic*] our Minister at Madrid had been Expelled from thence by the Spanish Government – his correspondence of late has been So impertinent & offensive that no independent Government Could tolerate it [,] & although this happens to [be] our ambassador I think the Spaniards have only acted with proper Spirit & dignity in Sending him away –

I made the acquaintance of Prince Louis Bonaparte this Evening – He appears to be a quiet gentlemanlike Man, & not[493] the Sort of person I Expected to find him: he is middle Sized, thick Set, not good looking, but disguised with very Strong & large mustaches [*sic*][494] –

*24 May 1848.* Mr Bulwer is actually arrived = The Duc de Sotomayor was so incensed against him from his insulting conduct, that he Sent Mr Bulwer his passport & desired him to quit Madrid & [leave within] 48 hours = It is much to be lamented that Lord Palmerston Should act in this manner – I cannot See the object of it. Moreover I believe that he acts without concert with his Colleagues – for when first questioned Lord Lansdowne certainly was ignorant of what had passed, & applied to Lord Palmerston for Explanation, which led to a very Serious misunderstanding, & Lord Palmerston was on the point of resigning, but the matter was Subsequently made up – Lord Palmerston is a very clever man – but nobody respects him or follows him as a politician, he would Carry one vote with him – it can only be from the fear he would go over to the Enemy that can induce them to Keep him in his place[495] –

*24 May 1848.* [...] Our Queen, I am told, is awfully impressed by the State of things around – I plainly perceived her Sadness the other night – & although in the performance of a duty she opened her Palace for the festivity of a Ball, She herself for the first time did not partake

[492]The First Schleswig War (1848–51) ended in a Danish victory over the Schleswig-Holstein rebels and resulted in the signing of the London Protocol in 1852.

[493]the precedes this in the original.

[494]K.D., 23 May 1848, 'Dined Lord Combermere [–] Duke of Newcastle [,] 2 Ladies [Clinton]' were among those present.

[495]Bulwer was accused of interfering in Spain's domestic affairs, at the behest of Palmerston, by encouraging the Progresistas, who wished to restore the liberal constitution of 1812.

of it – She did not dance neither did Prince albert – & I have heard that She feels that She ought not Even to Seem frivolously happy when So many Sovereigns are dejected & herded from their Thrones, with the attendant outrageous results.

*25 May 1848.* Debate this night in the House of Lords on the Jew Bill – I thought to have spoken upon it – & had prepared for it, but had not perfectly completed my Enquiries or arrangements – However I started with the full intention of Speaking, but I found that my ground was taken up by all the first Speakers, & So much better than I could have given it, that I continually held back & Eventually did not Say a word – There were only two or three points left imperfectly touched – & that was all that was left me unless I chose to bore the house by travelling over worn out ground – besides I found that all the Speakers on our Side were impressed with & gave utterance to the very best doctrine; political & religious = & perceiving this I was satisfied & considered that non interference, if I could add nothing new [,] was the best course that I could take – I was highly Satisfied with the tone of the debate – & I will venture to assert that Such a debate, So peculiarly distinguished by the finest views of Christian matters, & of principles of Government founded Solely upon a Sound religious faith, was never before carried on within the walls of Parliament – The debate will be productive of the very best Effects throughout the Country & will not only confirm the usefulness of the House of Lords but also raise it highly in the Estimation of the Country – & raise our party in particular – for us alone belonged the merit of proclaiming the true view of things – Lord Lansdowne Spoke weakly & Could Say nothing in favour of the bill – Lord Ellenborough moved the rejection of the bill in an animated [*sic* – animated] & Excellent Speech – The Bishop of Oxford – Wilberforce – made One of the finest Speeches that was Ever heard in our House & Lord Stanley also – the result was a majority of 35 [–] i.e. in the house for 96 – against the bill 125 – proxies for 32 – against 38 [128–163: majority 35] – a larger majority than was Expected – The Peelite party alone disgraced themselves –

*26 May 1848.* an Enquiry is to be made into Mr Bulwers' correspondence with the Spanish Government – I was told yesterday that Lord Palmerston means to throw him over & lay all the blame upon him, but he (Mr Bulwer) swears that if he does so he will turn the tables upon Lord Palmerston & divulge Every thing =

*27 May 1848.* The [Prime] Minister has Signified his intention to push the [Bill] to alter & destroy the Navigation laws through the House of Commons & it is our duty to do our utmost to defeat the Suicidal bill – I have been Speaking about it to Lord Stanley today & I had the pleasure to find him all in arms about it – a grand fight is to be made in the House of Commons but by the intervention of the Peelites we Shall be beaten there, but in the House of Lords, he thinks that we may beat them well – & this is a real comfort, for it would be absolute perdition to England if through the infatuated folly & blind vanity of our wretched modern Statesmen Peel & Co. other measures were to [be] adopted, following upon the heels of free trade & other abominations, by which this noble Country would be rendered nerveless & impotent – God grant that we may never See the day when the English Navy & her mercantile marine may be unable to maintain her Superiority on the Seas, all over the world = but we must deserve Divine Support & having that we may be strong to invincibility –

I heard this Evening that a telegraphic despatch had been received that [John] Mitchell the vile & audacious Editor of the "United Irishman" has been convicted under the new [Treason Felony] act – & that so prompt were the measures following upon conviction that he was instantly conveyed from his prison to Ship board & packed off for transportation to Botany Bay[496] – It is a Sad thing thus to tear[497] a man away from his family – but the decision & punishment in this case is as admirable as it is well deserved –

*28 May 1848.* The Princess Sophia died yesterday Evening – She has been ill for Some time & almost Entirely blind = Latterly She has been So reduced, that she was only Kept alive by artificial means – Turtle & brandy – The King of Hanover, Duke of Cambridge [,] & Duchess of Gloucester are now the only remains of George 3rd's family –

*29 May 1848.* The Bulwer affair in Spain & his dismissal by the Spanish government will occupy attention for Some days & a full Enquiry will be made into it – it is thought that Lord Palmerston must be Expelled from the administration. No better act can be done by the Ministers than his Expulsion – he is totally unfit to Conduct our foreign affairs with dignity & advantage to our interests – He lies too So Excessively that one Knows [not] what to believe which falls from him – as for instance, he asserted in Parliament the other day, that negociations were in forwardness for terminating the Danish war – where as it would rather appear, that Sweden has already Entered into the war by alliance & common cause with Denmark, & that Russia is upon the point of doing so – & if So a war must be general in Europe –

*31 May 1848.* […] Some rows here in London with Chartists, but Settled by the Police –

*1 June 1848.* The Chartist meetings are becoming very troublesome not that we Know any thing of them in this part of the Town! for they meet in Clerkenwell to the amount of Some thousands – but they require much watching both by police & Soldiers – at Bradford there has been a very Serious affair, & the rioters were very difficult to beat =

*2 June 1848.* […] In the House of Lords notice was taken of the tumultuous assemblies holden Every night in the Eastern parts of this metropolis – destructive of the peace, good order, & mercantile transactions of the inhabitants = The Police, Special Constables & Soldiers have been out Every night of the week – amongst only Peers the Duke of Wellington called upon Ministers to put down this nuisance, & Suggested two modes [,] Either to prevent assemblage by dispersion before meeting, or Else to make the ring leaders personally responsible for all damage done; & for all delinquency Either by word or deed. Lord Lansdowne promised that the Evil Should be put down – It is time that it Should, the citizens Complain of it bitterly –

*4 June 1848.* The Chartists have been out Every night this week & today / being Sunday / they were out by ten o'clock & continued to hold meetings throughout the day in various

[496]Mitchel went by way of the hulks in Bermuda and only reached Hobart Town in Apr. 1850.

[497]~~Snatch~~ precedes this in the original.

parts of the town – The Police had to be on the alert throughout the day & had Some Very sharp affrays with them – on one occasion they broke all the windows of a Church – Their conduct has been very scandalous & they give out that they Shall go on untill they have worn out the authoritie[s], & Shall have carried their point – The desecration of the Sabbath is a new feature in English outrage – They say openly that in Whitsun week they Shall make Such a demonstration throughout the Kingdom as the like has never been Seen before –

*5 June 1848.* Sat for a Small portrait to Mr [Henry Nelson] O'Neil[498] –
    There was a large meeting of the Country party today where it was determined to fight & oppose Lord John Russells' bill to alter the parliament oath tooth & nail =

*7 June 1848.* a man of the name of [Ernest] Jones, a Chartist orator & firebrand, & another have been arrested[499] – Their language has been So outrageous that there can be but little doubt that they will Soon follow Michell [*sic*] to the penal Colonies – Yesterday & the day before these miscreants have not Shewn themselves as they announced: possibly they may think it adviseable not to meet the police untill they may be better organised & prepared –

*8 June 1848.* Several more of these miscreant Chartist leaders & orators have been arrested – they are all upon their guard just now, & Since the beginning of this week have been very quiet – but I Suspect that they are now waiting for an opportunity, it is Expected that on the 12th they will shew themselves in many places – Great preparations are making to meet them wherever they may appear – For the first time they are Secret as to their intentions – which appears the more like Earnest = The Queen is gone to the Isle of Wight –

*10 June 1848.* It is intimated to us that the Government & the Vestry are very desirous that Special Constables Should be made & sworn in – & that we Should Send our Servants for that purpose, also go ourselves if we do not object to it – I Sent many of my Servants & they went With great good will & alacrity = I myself went to the office & Enquired of the Magistrate whether if I were to be Sworn in I could be Excused from ordinary work, & might only be called upon when danger threatened & there was a foe to meet: he told me that he thought no Exceptions could be made & that I could not be Excused if others were called out. He mentioned a report that tomorrow (Sunday) [,] the Specials would be called upon to do the duty of the Police who were to have rest to better able to undergo the probable fatigues of Whit Monday – This seared me & I retired telling [him] that if on Monday (12) I found that there was really likely to be a great Stir, [that] I should probably call after him to be Sworn a Special Constable – I will do so if occasion requires [,] but I have no taste for acting Police watchman in the Streets –

*11 June 1848.* There is a terrible rumour of the arrival of advices by telegraphic Express from Marseilles, that the Sicks [*sic*] have risen upon [us] at Lahore, have murdered two Com-

---

[498] See cover image. The painting was exhibited at the Royal Academy in 1850 (item no. 480).
[499] Alexander Sharp, John Fussell and Joseph Williams were also arrested on the morning of 7 June 1848.

missaries & destroyed all the British troops in the place[500] – Notwithstanding its French origin – I much fear that the account is too true – I think it very likely – I always considered it to be a fatal Error of Lord Hardinge to imagine himself in Security & to End by reducing our force to Numbers far too weak to repress this Subtle, fierce & warlike people – I fear that this fatal truth will be confirmed tomorrow –

The navigation laws are tottering, the villainous Ministerial measure to cut them up by roots, is greatly carried by a large majority for going into Committee. The protectionists, or Country party [,] divided 177. Peel took only 36 or 7 with him over to the Russell Camp & the total majority was 117 [294–177] –

*12 June 1848.* I am now writing at past 7 o'clock [.] I have heard of no disturbance any where, & I was told today that telegraphic accounts had been received from all the great Northern [towns that] there had been meetings, but all had gone off quietly & the mobs had dispersed = a meeting Was camping near Mr O'Neils' by Westbourne Grove – – but Since 1 o'clock it has so absolutely poured with rain that no mob would like to be washed by it –

*13 June 1848.* Not the Slightest disturbance or appearance of disturbance occurred yesterday = & today Every where all has been Equally quiet – The Chartists have taken us in most completely – & if they Ever intend to do any thing, it will now not be attempted Except when we may be Entirely off our guard –

*15 June 1848.* It was disclosed this Evening that as if in retaliation for what the Spanish Government did by our Minister at Madrid, So are we to do here – & Lord Palmerston has intimated to Monsieur Setwritz [Don Xavier Isturiz] that he has nothing more to do here – & that he is at liberty to return to Spain as[501] his diplomatic Services are not required here – Such proceedings are quite unintelligible – & none[502] Can be more objectionable or in worse Style – The question now is – is this tantamount to a declaration of war?

*16 June 1848.* […] Lord Stanley made a proposal in the House tonight that the duty on corn imported of 7 or 8s Should be continued on its Expiring at the next meeting of Parliament – it brings in a revenue of [£] 8 or 900,000 –

*22 June 1848.* […] At the opera tonight – God Save the Queen was Suddenly called for at the conclusion of the Opera – the Band had retired & it was not immediately given – The audience became impatient & called upon the band to play – The Queen was in the house & must have been truly gratified by the ardor & loyalty displayed[503] –

[500] On 19 Apr. 1848, Patrick Vans Agnew of the civil service and lieutenant William Anderson of the Bombay European regiment were murdered at Multan, and Sikh troops subsequently joined in open rebellion.

[501] as precedes this in the original.

[502] nothing precedes this in the original.

[503] QVJ, 22 June 1848, 'we saw "Roberto Diavolo", compressed into 3 acts, thereby entirely leaving out the principal parts'.

*23 June 1848.* […] I am informed today that Government will be very Strongly pushed by the opposition to their Sugar measure for their idea of relief to the Colonies – Lord John Russell is represented as being Sick of the whole thing & wishes to get out of it, & this is the Case with most public Men who are worth anything –

I hear Sad things of the State of the Country, the deplorable prostration of trade, & the Expected fearful Crisis in trading, commercial, & mercantile affairs – & all may be traced to Peels' Suicidal & most mischievous measures –

*24 June 1848.* Confined to the house all day seeing people on business – doing paper work, arranging writing &c – at Lord George Bentinck's suggestion [I] composed a letter to Lord John Russell[504] – but I Shall not Send it without more consideration =

*25 June 1848.* Sunday – The air was very delightful today after having been confined to the house for 2 days – Saw Many people & gathered much information – amongst other things, I make out an under Current which I have long Suspected – & it is clear to me that our people meditate a Junction With the Peelites – Peel only being accepted [*sic* – excepted] – This will not do. I for one never will accede to it = It would ruin us in public Estimation & be a last fatal blow to the consistency & character of public men –

*29 June 1848.* […] Here there has been much Said about the Statement & charge by Lord George Bentinck that important despatches & information had been Suppressed by the Colonial office & not laid as required before the Committee on the State of the Colonies & the Sugar question – It is now terminated by an Explanation in the House of Lords by Lord Grey & Some Strong remarks by Lord Stanley –

*1 July 1848.* […] The Debate upon the Sugar Duties has ended – Division for the Government measure 260 – against 245. Majority 15 – The trick has been that Sirs Robert Peel & James Graham, Shall Vote with the Ministers & the Peel Satellites Shall feign to leave him – this is in hopes of being included in the new administration – Lord Eglinton, one of our Whippers in, told me, ["] What we Say is nothing Shall induce us to Suffer Peel as first Minister – that is all we Say – we make no objection to his followers ["] – thence this base & Shabby Scheme deserting their idol leader, deserting their new – but basely adopted [–] doctrines[505] – but grasping at office, not from love of country & generous devotion to high principles, but merely to gain place & power & Self – it is a wretched contemplation – & deserves to be defeated & Shall not Succeed if I can aid in preventing it[506] = Such Examples in public men are So dangerous & demoralising, that they ought to be Execrated & annihilated –

---

[504] Newcastle wrote to Bentinck on 25 June 1848 seeking advice: Benjamin Disraeli, *Lord George Bentinck: A Political Biography* (4th edn, 1852), 569.

[505] ~~principles~~ precedes this in the original.

[506] BL, Add. MS 56368, ff. 179–80: Newcastle to Giffard, 3 July 1848: 'our underlings have been running about at the Carlton [Club] & Elsewhere, Endeavouring to bring about an union – they drop "protection" & resume "conservatism" – So at the Carlton, with <u>whippers in</u> &c, … I am nothing, but I never will agree to it […] do not name me, but from time to time, let them Know that they are discovered & warn us'.

*4 July 1848.* […] Lady De Grey I see is dead – It grieves me to read it – She & Lord De Grey were formerly our very intimate friends –

*5 July 1848.* The Divisions in the House of Commons are remarkably near & this happens very Constantly, So much So as to make it appear like a balance of parties, but this is not the Case – The near parity arises from accident more than any design – The number of Protectionists is probably about 170 – Peelites from 30 to 50 – but scarcely So many at the very most – Radicals, Chartists & other vagabonds at the head of whom is Joseph Hume – from 30 to 50 – The Government, I think, is losing Every day – Peelites Ditto in a Still greater degree –

*6 July 1848.* […] a very pompous & magnificent Shew has been attempted & by all accounts achieved [*sic*] by the Papists at the opening of what they call their new Cathedral in Lambeth, close by the archbishop's Palace – 6 Foreign Bishops attended & no End of other dignitaries, priests, monks & the like – Such an Event Say the News papers has not occurred Since the days of Queen Mary [I] – These people will not be quiet untill popular clamour is raised against them –

*7 July 1848.* The celebrated [François-René de] Chateaubriand is dead, & much lamented Even now, in France [–]
[…] The revenue Shews a falling off in the Quarter of [£] 327,741 – nothing very alarming, but Still by no means Satisfactory – The Decrease on the year, is 2,587,709 £ – which is a Serious Matter & will not Easily be provided for –

*9 July 1848.* The Protectionists are going on well in the House of Commons – they are obstructing the Minister[ial] measure for the West Indian Colonies So that he can hardly move, this is quite right – the Measure ought not to pass – The Colonies require & could have given to them Efficient relief –

*12 July 1848.* Lord George Bentinck in a pamphlet of a Speech has laid before the House of Commons his view of the Sugar question, Embracing Every part of it, & in Such a manner as no other man in the House Could do = a division took place [–] the majority was Small[507] –

*13 July 1848.* […] I See that Lady Winchilsea [Emily Georgiana Bagot] is dead – this I Know will be a great grief & affliction to my Excellent friend but it Should & will be hereafter a great relief to him – She was a terrible Woman, & the only Excuse was that she was insane, poor creature – & on this account a heavy load of anxiety will be removed from him – He was Sadly altered when I Saw him in London –

*14 July 1848.* […] Stratford Canning is at last arrived at Constantinople & we may now Soon hope to hear of William being on his return, & once more have him a most agreeable member of our now too restricted family Circle =

---

[507] The vote was 180–124: majority 56.

*19 July 1848.* The Queen has abandoned her intention of going to Ireland this year = it is most wise to do So – there is no Saying What might have been the Extreme Embarrassments in Which Her Majesty Might be placed were She to visit Ireland – =

Lord John Russell has announced his intention not to press the Navigation Laws question this Session – he also abandons many other measures – He & his Party make a very Sorry figure – it is pitiable & moreover Contemptible –

*21 July 1848.* The King of Hanover has declared his determination not to Surrender his independence as a Sovereign to any person who may be chosen Chief of the German Empire, he will not object to form a part of the Confederation but he will not Consent to be a vassal to any other [–] this Example will probably be followed by other Smaller heads of German States & principalities =

*23 July 1848.* The State of Ireland is Such that Ministers have at last determined to adopt Strong measures – The habeas Corpus act is to be Suspended in Ireland untill March of next year & the bill is to be hurried through Parliament with all possible Expedition = It is impossible to get a verdict in Ireland, So that this is the only measure that can check the Seditious & treasonable proceedings of the rebellious Villains who are now agitating Ireland with a ferocity & audacity, quite beyond example in these countries = Even in Ireland = In a debate on the Subject in [the] House of Lords Lord Glengall make [*sic* – made] a clear, forcible, & very Excellent Speech upon the Subject – Exposing the present State of Ireland in all its dangers & horrors –

*25 July 1848.* […] Parliament has passed the Habeas Corpus suspension bill with railroad Speed – it will have been passed in a few hours, & now is law in Ireland –

*26 July 1848.* […] Nothing particular from Ireland – Several regiments with artillery from hence are sent over to Ireland.

*27 July 1848.* If the leading notice in the Standard is to be believed "the South of Ireland has broken out into open rebellion & there has been Some fearful fighting in which the troops have been over powered – & some of these latter have been found disaffected" – The Standard believes that its news is greatly exaggerated – In parliament questions were asked but the Government Knew nothing of Such Events – although despatches had been received dated So late as 7 o'clock of the previous day – We will hope that this Electric telegraph news may not be true –

*28 July 1848.* Mr [William] Henderson came here today from London, & brings a Times newspaper of this morning with him – He Says that the Whole is a vile hoax, for stock Jobbing or Some other bad purpose – Sir George Grey announced in his place that he Should do all he could to discover the authors of this diabolical deception, & punish the guilty parties –

*29 July 1848.* all quiet in Ireland, although Evidently collecting their Strength & preparing for mischief – I think it not unlikely that when they begin in Ireland – the many Irish here with the Chartists will Endeavour to operate a diversion here –

*30 July 1848.* No Encounter has taken place in Ireland – but it appears that Mr [William Smith] O'brien is in the field with an armed force of Some 2000 men, he himself strutting about in a flashy rebel uniform = We shall Soon here [*sic* – hear] more about him if this is the Case –

*2 August 1848.* a letter from William today [–] he rejoices me by telling me that at last he has Sir Stratford Canning's promise that he Shall go without fail on the 19th of this Month – So that by Gods' blessing we may hope to See him before the 10th of September – it will indeed be a day of rejoicing to have him with me again once More –

Mr O'Brien & his people have been put to route by 50 or 60 determined police men under Mr [Thomas] Trant – He fired upon them & Killed Some ten of them – when they all took to their heels & dispersed in Every direction – a contemptible termination truly to ferocious threats & boastful insult – Lord Hardinge is Said to be appointed to the Command in Ireland in Some peculiar way, not yet Explained – but if this is all, he may be Spared the trouble of Crossing[508] the Channel – –

*3 August 1848.* Nothing new from Ireland – what is called the rebellion is the [most] pitiful thing in that Shape that Ever transpired – nobody Engaged in it from the leader downwards Seems to possess the Slightest capability for such an undertaking, & if no one of mind & Energy turns up – this I conclude Will be the last Scene of bug bear farce which has been[509] the phantom or Moloch to which Every thing valuable has been Sacrificed for the last thirty years & more –

*11 August 1848.* […] I went to O'Neil to have my figure drawn in –

*14 August 1848.* In Ireland, the Jury, has returned a verdict of not guilty to one of the worst of the Irish Sedition Mongers [Kevin O'Doherty] – & it appears, likely that no verdict will be had against any traitor or rebel[510] – It is Said that provisions are running very Short & that in the Course of a short time many districts will be actually Starved out – The English will no longer Submit to being taxed to Support traitors & rebels – & it is very difficult to Know how to act –

*20 August 1848.* The Ministers are going on in a most Extraordinary manner – hurrying through measures of the greatest importance, that have been Suspended during the whole of this tedious & protracted Session, in their houses of not 100 Members & at the very fag End of the Session, when Scarcely any one can be inclined to stay in London – it is really Scandalous & most indecent – as Colonel [Charles] Sibthorp tells, want of decency is want of Sense = "The Diplomatic relations with Rome bill" is one of these So hurried through at the last moment, when there is no one to discuss it & probably no Pope to have relations with = Bills are Even now originating which are to be Smuggled through the

---

[508] ~~going over to Ireland~~ precedes this in the original.

[509] which has been precedes this in the original.

[510] O'Doherty, one of the proprietors and editors of *The Tribune* newspaper, was tried for seditious libel under the Felony Act but the jury was unable to reach a verdict: *The Times*, 14 Aug. 1848.

houses & made law before the 24th on which day Parliament is to be prorogued – & this is the barefaced & scandalous way in which business is now done –

*31 August 1848.* Nothing new. Parliament is to be prorogued on the 5th if the business is completed –

*1 September 1848.* […] I was told yesterday by a young man now at Oxford, that democratical & the worst principles are gaining ground among the young men – Especially those who were pupils under the late Dr [Thomas] arnold, & Some of these openly declare that they hope to see the day "when the last priest will bury the last King" –

*6 September 1848.* Parliament was prorogued yesterday by the Queen in person. The renewal of our diplomatic relations with France & the uninterruption of good understanding with that Country are prominently brought forward, as if it were a boast worthy of the Sovereign of England to be in close alliance & the bosom friend of a Country, which in fact has no regular Government, no Constitution, is a wild Republic, & if it were not for military rule, would be in a State of the most horrible anarchy – But thus terminates a Session, which has done many bad things, fewer good things & has lasted longer & done less than any Session I Ever remember –

*7 September 1848.* To my infinite Surprise & joy I this morning received a letter from [my son] William himself dated London & telling me that he should be with us today[511] […] it may be Supposed that our Salutations were not very Cool = He is to my great Surprise, very much as he last left us – & I thought looking very well, though rather thin [–]

*11 September 1848.* One of the worst features of the times is, that people are So turbulent & unruly = at the Same time So Capricious & vindictive that those capable of Conducting affairs are Either tired of remaining in thankless office, or Else are afraid of undertaking it. this is the Case to Such an Extent on the Continent that it becomes Scarcely possible to persuade good men to Engage in the attempt –

*15 September 1848.* I am buying Some things at the Stowe Sale by Commission = Portraits are what I Shall most probably obtain as the good pictures will be too high for my purse[512]

*20 September 1848.* Portraits only have been bought for me at the Stowe Sale = Lord Clinton by Sir a. More, is one of them.[513] I do not think that my Commissioner [Joseph

---

[511] N.U.M.D., Ne C 5650: Lord William Clinton to Newcastle, 6 Sept. 1848.

[512] N.U.M.D., Ne C 8306: Thomas W. Corbett to Newcastle, 29 Aug. 1848.

[513] For £7 7s.: Henry Rumsey Forster, *Stowe Catalogue, Priced and Annotated* (1848), lot 323. Also see lots 217, 226, 312, 313.

Browne] has done his duty fairly by me – Many Valuable pictures have gone at a very low price – & within my range[514] –

*21 September 1848.* The Queen Seems to be Enjoying herself in Scotland in rural retirement giving loose to her Simple & amiable propensities [,] & no doubt laying up a Store [of] health & happiness –

*22 September 1848.* This morning I have been Shocked beyond all description by an account of the death of Lord George Bentinck – My Valet told me that it was reported that Lord George had dropped down dead yesterday Evening – I immediately Sent over to Welbeck & found to my Sorrow & dismay that this was but too true […] Thus has his Country lost the most Valuable public man in it. The only honest, fearless & unconquerable politician in public life = Whose career has been like a meteor, full of fire & transcendent brightness & like fire purifying all it touched – Whilst he lived political treachery & rascality were impossible, he would bear them[515] to the bone & With a power & ability that no Sophistry Could Withstand & no mean artifice could cover. Such a man will not be found again, few Such men have been Seen before him – He was a patriot in public & a real friend in private life –

*25 September 1848.* […] I hear today that nothing has occurred in the post mortem Examination of Lord George which can guide them to any conclusion as to the cause of his deeply lamented death – His Excessive & incessant labors were a Sufficient cause – they Would have Killed any other man in much less time[516] –

*2 October 1848.* William has been urged by Lord Cowley, who is now at Francfurt [*sic*] to apply for the Secretary Ship to the Embassy which will be vacant, as Mr Molineux [Francis George Molyneux] does not mean to return – If he will have to go out immediately, I Shall Scarcely be in favor of the application, for I Should wish him to be at rest a little & make acquaintances here, & attend a little to public affairs here, & if possible to find Some amiable & Suitable woman for a wife – he may then renew his professional career with my ready assent[517] –

*3 October 1848.* The Queen has left Scotland, the weather would not permit her to go by Sea – She went by rail & has arrived in London –

---

[514]'I can only now say many of those that sold at the prices you name were not worth taking away – those that were good for anything and genuine fetched much higher prices – but taking the collection as a whole with the exception of about fifty paintings they were of very inferior class [,] the subjects were good enough, but few of them original Paintings': N.U.M.D., Ne C 7599: Joseph Browne to Newcastle, 19 Sept. 1848.

[515]it precedes this in the original.

[516]D.P., 147/14: Newcastle to Stanley, 23 Sept. 1848; N.U.M.D., Ne C 5178: Stanley to Newcastle, 24 Sept. 1848: 'They suppose it to have been a spasm of the heart, but there was nothing in that, nor in any other organ, to indicate the presence of disease, though the lungs had been formerly affected'.

[517]N.U.M.D., Ne C 5651: Lord William Clinton to Newcastle, 4 Oct. 1848. Newcastle sought the assistance of Stanley: Ne C 5179, Stanley to Newcastle, 18 Oct. 1848.

*4 October 1848.* I have written both to London & to Nottingham about promoting Seriously a testification of the public Sense of Lord George Bentinck's merits by Such means as will most lastingly Serve to honor the dead & Stimulate the living to do likewise – It has already been hinted to raise a monument in Westminster abbey, this idea I adopt, with an appropriate inscription to be written by Mr D'Israeli[518] – The County Memorial I propose to be a Statute within an open Circular Temple Supporting a dome with a figure of Fame on the top – to have a general Meeting of County "friends & admirers" to Effect this by Subscription = These ideas hitherto are approved, but there is yet much to do to atchieve [*sic*] a truly Satisfactory result[519] –

*7 October 1848.* Lord Carlisle is dead, he has long been in a miserable State of health, Eaten up with gout & its attendant diseases = a vacancy is thus Created for the West Riding of Yorkshire by the Elevation of Lord Morpeth to the Peerage –

*10 October 1848.* […] The Cholera has appeared at Edinburgh, Hull, Sunderland & London –

*11 October 1848.* O'Brien has been found Guilty, & has been Condemned to be hanged as a Traitor, but it is thought that his life will be Spared. He ought to Suffer, he plays with treason to the last moment, an[d] the Example alone is dangerous –

*22 October 1848.* It is believed that Smith O'Brien & his followers, will Escape Capital punishment, to what it will be commuted is not Known. Lord Clarendon was leaving Dublin for England for two purposes – one to be made a K[night of the] G[arter] the other to confer with the Government here, what Shall be done with the Traitors –

*17 November 1848.* […] Lord Henry Bentinck called here this morning & Sat with me a long while – he is very Keen about Keeping our Country party together = I was rather Surprised but most highly gratified to find how strict he is in his political principles – how tenacious he is of a most unsullied & unsuspectable honor & how Extremely anxious he is that our Existence as a party Should depend upon our maintenance of the purest principles upon which alone we can hope to benefit our Country – He is right too upon all Christian & Protestant points – He is most anxious that Mr Disraeli Should be our Leader in the House of Commons & if it can be Effected he Expects from it the most auspicious results – He is certainly the Man of the most powerful mind & highest intellect

---

[518] Newcastle took up this hint from *The Standard*: BL, Add. MS 56368, ff. 181–2: Newcastle to Giffard, 2 Oct. 1848; Dep Hughenden, 89/2, ff. 216–19: Newcastle to Disraeli, 22 Oct. 1848; N.U.M.D., Ne C 5475: Disraeli to Newcastle, 24 Oct. 1848; Ne C 8365, Coutts bank to Newcastle, 17 Nov. 1848; K.D., 21 Nov. 1848, '£10 10s to Lord George Bentinck Memorial'.

[519] N.U.M.D., Ne C 8341: 'To the Friends & Admirers of the late lamented & patriotic Lord George Bentinck' appealing for subscribers to a memorial, [4 Oct. 1848]. Also see Ne C 8776: Portland to Newcastle, 23 Oct. 1848, enclosing (Ne C 8777–8) sketches of proposed memorials; BL, Add. MS 56368, ff. 185–6: Newcastle to Giffard, 20 Oct. 1848.

in the Country & Could destroy any man or body of men by his Eloquence & raise any Cause by his commanding abilities[520] –

*26 November 1848*. Lord Melbourne is dead – Soon after he resigned Office he was taken ill & paralysis Ensued from which he never recovered, although he was able to go about, & often to attend in the House of Lords – He was Captain of the house / Dr [William] Langford's / when I first went to Eton, & was then & Ever after Exceedingly Kind to me[521] — He was a clever man but not much of a Statesman – as a very old acquaintance & a pleasant, popular man I am sorry to lose him – His only brother Lord Beauvale succeeds him – he has no family & [,] at his death, the title will be Extinct –

*30 November 1848*. The flight of the Pope is positively confirmed: he is gone to take refuge in France, & there I hope he will remain & not come here – where I do not wish him to be well received – he could do no good & might possibly do much harm in conjunction with the vile Irish priesthood – The Cardinals it Seems have also quitted Rome in all haste – the Revolution is prefect [*sic* – perfect], & the Whole concern is now in the hands of some democratic Clubs –

*5 December 1848*. The accounts from India, do not represent matters as in a pleasant State – The Natives are adopting a very awkward trick of resisting us whenever they can – & now too often with considerable success = Lord Hardinge has done more harm, in my opinion, than any preceding governor of late years – Neither his civil nor his military rule have added to his fame or our advantage [.]

*8 December 1848*. […] an Excellent letter in the papers from Lord Stanhope on the duties of a Conservative, & the disgraceful betrayal of the friends of the Constitution by Judas Peel.[522]

*9 December 1848*. another Event that at other times would astonish & dismay has just occurred = The Emperor of austria [Ferdinand I] has abdicated in favor of his nephew "Francis Joseph", son of Francis Charles, his Brother, who himself declines his hereditary right; – & makes it over to his Son – Francis Joseph is only 18 years old – but a very fine youth & of great promise. This [my son] William tells me – In one week the Pope & the Emperor

---

[520]Newcastle admired Bentinck's 'able, honest & correct view of our condition & future prospects', his 'unsuspectable rectitude', and his belief that Disraeli was 'the man to be the Leader': N.R.A.(S), GD205/46/16: Newcastle to R.A. Christopher, [25] Nov. 1848.

[521]'Lord Melbourne was at school with [Newcastle] in the same house; 12 of them all together; and he said Dr Langford used to say to the Duke of Newcastle: "Remember when you are a man, and a great blockhead, for that you will be, that it is not my fault; remember it's your inattention, and that you must exonerate me, from that". "I have heard him say that a hundred times", Lord Melbourne said laughing; and he was so funny about it. He don't think he's so stupid as "wrong-headed"': QVJ, 1 Nov. 1838.

[522]The letter, dated 5 Dec. 1848, appeared in *The Standard*, 7 Dec. 1848.

have ceased to be Sovereigns, one representing the Holy Roman Church, the other the Holy Roman Empire – a wonderful development this of Sacred prophecy !!!

*10 December 1848.* Lord Melbourne by his Will constitutes Lord Brougham & Mr Edward Ellice his Executors – of Course all his Papers fall into their hands, & no doubt the former will give them in Some Shape to the Public[523] –

*13 December 1848.* [Stoke Edith] is really a very fine place with a Capital house & Lady Emily [Foley] has done much lately to improve it – opening views, planting, thinning &c. which have been very Successful – Herefordshire is a beautiful county. Soil good & Well wooded – but ill formed & drowned in Water – with dry land & improved farming the produce would be boundless – at present I am told that the average rate of produce in wheat is taken at 18 bushels an acre – which appears to me incredible –

*15 December 1848.* […] went to See Some Hereford's cattle which are feeding here, they are very much Smaller than I Expected, but make & quality Equal to any thing – they will weigh when fatted about 80 Stones of 8lb [–] here the Stone is 12lb & the farmer Expects to get only 18£ for them – meat is now only 5s 6d – a pound – markets low – & much behind other places owing to the absence of railways & facility of transport =

*17 December 1848.* Louis Bonaparte is Elected President of France by an immense majority, at present his numbers are nearly 3 millions but all the returns are not come in [–] [Louis–Eugène] Cavaignac has not reached a Million[524] –

The West Riding Election has terminated in favour of Mr Beckett Denison by an Enormous majority of nearly 3000.[525]

*21 December 1848.* […] Parliament is prorogued to the 1st February but it does not Say then to meet for despatch of business –

Lord aberdeen, who is staying at Ossington came over here this afternoon with Mr [John Evelyn] Denison to See the place [–] he Seemed to be very much taken with it, & Evidently was Surprised & greatly pleased with what he Saw in & out of doors –

*31 December 1848.* […] Here Ends the most Extraordinary & Eventful year that has occurred since the coming of our Saviour [.] The rapid fulfilment of prophecy is most marked & indubitable – & is but a Small beginning of more immense Events yet to come – For these may God in his infinite mercy prepare us individually & nationally –

*1 January 1849.* […] I am most wretched today & feel as if the world is a blank to me – all flat & uninteresting, mournful [,] uninspiring & woefully inauspicious – I feel as if I could never be tranquil again or Survive the calamity – However I Know that as heretofore after having Suffered awhile, the Holy Spirit will Stablish [*sic* – Stabilise], Strengthen [,] Settle

---

[523] *Lord Melbourne's Papers*, ed. L.C. Sanders (1889).

[524] The final result was 5,434,226 votes for Louis Bonaparte; Cavaignac came second with 1,448,107 votes.

[525] Edmund Beckett-Denison (Conservative) polled 14,743 votes to Culling Eardley (Whig) 11,795: majority 2,948.

me – I am resolved to do my best & utmost to gain Gods favor & do my duty by correcting what may be wrong & Strenuously following after what is right –

*3 January 1849.* Lord auckland has died Suddenly – He was out Shooting at Lord ashburton's place [The Grange, near Northington] in Hampshire – When he mentioned to the Keeper that he felt rather unwell & Should go home, he had not proceeded far before he staggered & fell down – Supposed to be a paralytic attack he could not Speak & died very shortly after – He was 1st Lord of the admiralty & greatly esteemed & loved in that Office –

*6 January 1849.* Returned to Clumber today to receive Several persons who are come to us – among them Lord Henry Bentinck who is warm & able in his advocacy of Mr Disraeli [–] to be our Leader in the House of Commons – His reasons & arguments are So conclusive that I yield to them Entirely & Shall write to Lord Stanley tomorrow Signifying that I consider Mr Disraeli as the fittest & only man to fill that Situation.[526]

*8 January 1849.* Left Clumber at a little after 2 o'clock & arrived here Bloreholme [Bloxholm, Lincolnshire], Mr Christopher's at a little after 6 [p.m.,] having been 4 hours doing the 40 miles – We found that the dinner was ordered for $\frac{1}{4}$ to 8 – as the guests were not all arrived. The road from Leadenham to this place is very bad & jolting –

*9 January 1849.* as Mr Christopher Seemed to wish it, I let him mount me & we went to the meet of the hounds this morning not far from hence = There were not many gentlemen in the field = The hounds Duke of Rutlands' are very handsome & I believe, very good – in the Evening we all went to Sir Thomas & Lady Whichcote's Ball at aswarby [Park] about 10 miles off – We staid [*sic*] there to a very late hour; perhaps $\frac{1}{4}$ to five – of Course we were late home & not in bed very much before 7. – The Ball was a very good one; & Very prettily arranged – We Knew So few people, that to us it was not So interesting as to others – Lord Granby, Lord John Manners were there & I tried to pump out of the former what his wish & opinion was of Disraeli as leader of the House of Commons, but he was too Cautious to give me any direct answer –

*12 January 1849.* Trade is said to be reviving a little, & the reports rather tend to confirm the Statement =

*13 January 1849.* No news of any Consequence: a new Commission consisting of 5 Members has been appointed to investigate & consider how Church property can be managed = I ask this question – – What right have we to Enquire how Church property is managed [?], we have nothing to do with it. Such an Enquiry is an arbitrary & unwarrantable assumption.

*14 January 1849.* The news of the day is, that there is about to be a change in the administration – after a Cabinet Council held a few days ago, a letter was sent to Sir James Graham, who left immediately; at 2 or 3 hours notice, with Lady Graham, & on arriving in London

---

[526]D.P., 147/14: Newcastle to Stanley, 7 Jan. 1849; *DL*, V, 123–6, 130–1.

remained at the railway Hotel as no preparation had been made at his own house – this being Sunday we shall have no more accounts untill Tuesday –

*15 January 1849.* My letter from Lord Stanley today tells me that negociations had been going on lately & now through Sir James Graham to coalesce with the Peelites[527] = & I think I see how this will be done = Lord John Russell will resign – Lord Clarendon will give up the Lord Lieutenancy of Ireland, & will be 1st Lord [of the] Treasury – Lord Carlisle will give up Woods & Forests & will take Lord Clarendon's place in Ireland – Lord Grey will move from the Colonies to the admiralty vacant by Lord aucklands' death – Sir James Graham will be Chancellor of the Exchequer & certain other Peelites will have places [,] Lincoln I fear amongst them [,] as I am pretty Sure that I have Seen him laying himself out for it for Some time past & very possibly he aims at the Colonies[528] for which he must be Even less fitted than those who have preceded him – Sidney Herbert [,] Cardwell & a few others will have places [,] but of this I am certain that none of them will hold them long [–] the coalition will be ruin to themselves & the making of their opponents –

*16 January 1849.* The negociation with the Peelites through Sir James Graham has failed as stated in the News Papers = Why does not appear & it Seemed to be So probable as to amount almost to a certainty – with Sir James's name were also given those of Lincoln & Mr Cardwell, which is most unfortunate for them = the circumstance must ruin their names & reputations = I still can hardly believe that the negociation has failed –

*18 January 1849.* I was told today that the reason why Sir James Graham failed in his negociation with Lord John Russell was because Lord John would not go far Enough in reform – & also that he required that Lord aberdeen Should be received with him into the administration – I was also informed that Lord Clarendon had declared that he will not Stay in Ireland unless[529] a bill is passed to pay the priests there –

*20 January 1849.* I am informed that Lord John Russell proposed to his Cabinet to continue the duties on Corn but was outvoted in the Cabinet – I have learned lately that the Duke of Bedford is become quite a Conservative – he has a great influence not only over his Brother, but also over a large portion of his Party –

Lord Henry Bentinck is quite alive & roused to action & has been & now is very busily Employed in going to Various houses to make the different proprietors & others Sensible of the absolute necessity of Selecting & installing a leader of the House of Commons & determining upon a plan of Conduct & policy which may Ensure our credit & Strength = His object is that Disraeli Shall be that leader, & that honor & principle & patriotism shall invariably determine our purposes & actions –

*21 January 1849.* another of those murderous Skirmishes has taken place with Some of [the] Sickhs [*sic*] in which there has been a great loss of life on our parts [–] two Cavalry

---

[527] D.P., 178/1, pp. 218–20: Stanley to Newcastle, 14 Jan. 1849. Newcastle quoted the letter to R. A. Christopher: N.R.S., GD205/46/16: Newcastle to Christopher, 15 Jan. 1849.

[528] at the Colonies precedes this in the original.

[529] ~~if~~ precedes this in the original.

Colonels are Killed, both of tried ability & several Subalterns Killed & wounded – finally the Enemy was forced back & dispersed but only to form again & renew the Combat[530] – The warlike spirit of the natives is roused & they find that they can make So good head against us, that they will never rest untill they have Expelled us from India – This may not be for many years to come – but it seems as if it were an Event not altogether impossible unless our policy be more decisive & unwavering –

*24 January 1849.* Lord Henry Bentinck was here today & came from London last night where he has been very busy, & I should think very tolerably Successful – He states that all of our best & principal people are in favor of Disraeli for Leader [– John Charles] Herries has signified that he would not accept the post if it were offered to him & Lord Granby has refused, therefore Disraeli is the only man & this all must admit = Lord Henry wishes me to write to Several Members to be in London on the day of the meeting – & I do it –

Lord Henry tells me that all Peel's followers including Lincoln profess to be in favor of the Extension of the Suffrage & reform of all Kinds – & that Sydney Herbert is the loudest of all = Who could have Supposed that my debauched Son Could Ever have permitted himself to be drawn into the advocacy of principles, the very opposite of all that he formerly professed & in which he was Carefully & anxiously Educated [?] — Peel has done this, & has ruined him & disgraced his family – it is one of the very bitter afflictions which I have had to Endure, & which I lament more than I can Express –

*28 January 1849.* My letter to Lord John Russell in July last, on the Navigation laws, has been published in the Standard of yesterday – I wish it may be of use in causing the people of the <u>interior</u> of England to take more interest in this vital question.[531]

*31 January 1849.* Left Nottingham by the $10\frac{1}{2}$ train & arrived here in London at $4\frac{1}{2}$ – & was in good time for Lord Stanley's dinner[532] – We Were in all 26 including Lord Stanley: after dinner the Speech was read & discussed – for a long while Lord Stanley parried all attempts to induce him to move an amendment, although he admitted that the Speech was the most audacious he had Ever read = However So many remarks Were made urging him to a plain & Straight forward Course, that at last he Said that he would consider the matter between this & tomorrow Evening, when he would Endeavour to frame an amendment which he hoped Would Suit us – We afterwards more privately discussed the immense advantage of opening the Session with a distinct Statement of our views & a determination to abide by them – & to resolve to do what is purely right Without any view of catching Peelite or other votes –

*1 February 1849.* I was so Sleepy & dull yesterday Evening that I Could not think & could propose nothing to meet the very difficult case before us – This morning I felt more

---

[530] General Charles Robert Cureton and Colonel William Havelock of the 14th light dragoons were killed in the battle of Ramnagar on the banks of the river Chenab on 22 Nov. 1848. In the battle of Chillianwallah on 13 Jan. 1849, Brigadier John Pennycuick, commander of the 5th brigade, and Brigadier Alexander Pope, commander of the 2nd brigade of cavalry, were killed.

[531] See Appendix A.

[532] D.P., 147/14: Newcastle to Stanley, 30 Jan. 1849, recommending 'a full, fair & open declaration … of our faith & principles & of our determination to support them with all our Energies through good & Evil Report'.

Capable & I wrote down Some heads of remarks which I thought calculated to make a good amendment & I Sent it to Lord Stanley with an accompanying letter – read & Saw many people this Morning, but was unable to go out & refresh myself With outward air & Exercise which I have not had for 5 days – dined & went to the House of Lords where I was at 5 o'clock – Lords Bruce & [Bateman] were the Mover & Seconder, & did their work very respectably [,] Lord Bruce in a dull gotten by heart tone but Still a very good Speech which took him $\frac{1}{2}$ an hour. Evidently gotten by heart – but Still never failing for a moment, which proves that he has Self possession & a Strong memory – When I came into the house Lord Stanley Shewed me his amendment which to my infinite Satisfaction I could approve of – & inwardly rejoiced at the Steps which were taking, & which are Sure if maintained to lead to the best results = The Superlatively impudent Brougham opened the debate [,] Winchilsea Spoke, & then finding that no Minister Would rise Stanley Spoke, & though Evidently labouring under disadvantages of weakness of voice & convalescence from the worst attack of gout he has Ever had [,] he made an admirable Speech & in the highest tone that I have yet heard from him – his declarations Were distinct & unmistakable & the result must be Such as I have many times lately most anxiously urged to him – The deed is now done, he is pledged [,] his party & the Country will be delighted – & the banner of high principle & patriotism is hoisted, & will be rallied to by the Country.

Old Wellington tried to do all the mischief in his power, but people are now up to him, & disregard his petulant twaddle – he carries very few with him – we divided, & notwithstanding that the ministers were joined by the Peelites – we divided So closely that we were within 2 of them – their numbers being 52, ours 50: a great many peers had left the house = at one time there must have been at least 50 or 60 more than divided =

This Exploit has been Consummated with much difficulty – but his mind being made up Stanley Stood as firmly as a rock – & the result while it has cheered our friends, has I plainly perceived Surprised & [,] I am in hopes, Confirmed Stanley – On leaving the house I Saw Some House of Commons men who told me that Disraeli in that house had moved the Same amendment – as ours & in an Extraordinarily brilliant Speech – I look for the brightest & most favorable results from all this – & may God grant it to be So & to guide us to the purest & loftiest aspirations –

*2 February 1849.* The House of Commons did not divide upon, the principal amendment that [was] moved by Mr Disraeli – the debate is to be resumed tonight & most probably they will divide – I am informed today that it was yesterday Settled that the leadership in the House of Commons Shall be in commission as it were consisting of 3, Lord Granby, Disraeli, & Herries – None of the Peelites Spoke last night – I Suspect that they are looking after Office, & hope to Join the ministry – if it Were not for Lincoln who will be for Ever damaged by it [,] I Should wish that Such might be the case –

*3 February 1849.* In the House of Commons last night (an adjourned debate on the address) they Suffered the debate to Expire without a division – this I think a very great & decided fault [,] & so I told them at the Carlton [Club] today = they were afraid of a Weak division = but what does that Signify [?] – it is of importance [to] open the campaign manfully, & valiantly to Stand to our guns – besides, as we divided in the Lords at all hazards, So Should they have done in the Commons, & this those who I Spoke to admitted – I was very much disappointed at this result –

*5 February 1849.* I have learnt today with infinite regret, that our political affairs are by no means prospering – The triumvirate [of] Lord Granby, Disraeli & Herries does not prove a good arrangement & Every thing is at sixes & sevens – I have been told that in the divisions upon adjournment there were about 33 Peelites & of those it is Supposed 20 Would come to us if we were Strong Enough –

*6 February 1849.* […] Mr Disraeli called upon me & remained a long time with me, it is the first confidential interview that I have had With him – & my impression, indeed Conviction, is that he is most anxious to do Every thing that is right, & that he is faithful, in Earnest & will do his best to make our great cause triumph. I am Sure that he is to be relied upon – He is perfectly teachable, possesses high & aspiring feelings, very quickly sensitive, but I think generous & free from meannesses & pettinesses. He is too theatrical [,] has Evidently not been hitherto in the best school, but is most truly anxious to give himself up to habits of thinking & to mould himself for a destiny which he sees may await him, if he identifies himself with all that is good & great, So as to Serve his God & his Country in the most Essential & Efficient manner – able & clever as he is, he has much to learn, but I am convinced that he will acquire whatever it is needful that he Should Know & practice[533] – Called upon Lord Stanley, saw him, & had a most Satisfactory interview –

*9 February 1849.* […] By the public accounts it appears – that our Minister at Berlin – Lord Westmorland has been instructed to protest against the assumption of the Imperial dignity by the King of Prussia [Frederick William IV] – & it was Signified at the Same time, that if persisted in the Courts of Russia & austria would withdraw their representatives –

*11 February 1849.* In parliament Lord Stanley in the House of Lords has done Service on the Irish poor law question – & in the House of Commons Disraeli has done particularly well on the Irish habeas corpus Suspension bill –

*13 February 1849.* The Countess of Bridgewater [Charlotte Catherine Anne Haynes] is dead at 86. The immense property which She possessed for life, will go to Lord Brownlow's Sons, to the Eldest Lord alford "if his father Can obtain a higher title["], otherwise to the Second Son Should this condition of Lord Bridgewater's will not be fulfilled[534] =

*18 February 1849.* The mines in California, are Exciting the avidity of the world, one may Say. It Seems that the gold continues to be found in great quantities & pure quality = in another direction branching from Where it has already been found, veins have been discovered Equally good & abundant – So that the Mines give promise of being inexhaustible – These

[533]Newcastle followed up the interview with a gift of game: Dep Hughenden, 195/4, f. 159: 13 Feb. 1849.

[534]Under the seventh earl of Bridgewater's will, his estates were left to John Hume Egerton, Viscount Alford, provided he became duke or marquess with a suitable remainder. Egerton failed to fulfil this requirement and died in 1851. John Egerton-Cust, 2nd Earl Brownlow, brought a lengthy lawsuit which resulted in him inheriting the Bridgewater estates in 1853.

Mines together with those So productive in Russia will probably occasion a revolution in Money Matters.

*19 February 1849*. It is understood that the Pope [Pius IX] has been formally dethroned & a Republic regularly proclaimed – In England at this time there are many royal refugees. Louis Philippe late King of France & all his family Except the Duc d'angouleme with the Duchess in Spain, the [Infante Carlos], Count [of] Montemolin, really rightful King of Spain = The Prince of Parma who is married to the Sister of the Duc de Bordeaux rightful King of France – besides the Prince of Orange, on a visit – the deposed Duke of Brunswick & Several others of minor note –

*23 February 1849*. Lord John Russell has brought in a new Jew Bill in the Shape of an alteration of the oaths to be taken – the Whole affair is very distasteful – it will be carried in the House of Commons – but is Expected to be lost in the House of Lords = Disraeli wishes it was in the Red Sea[535] –

*24 February 1849*. The Farmers are at last roused, roused by the Effects of free trade upon them, & their bad circumstances, & in their despair & blindness they are disposed to Side with Cobden & obtain the repeal of the Malt Tax & any other taxes that oppress them = Under these circumstances it has been thought adviseable to take the matter up, in Parliament [,] & Disraeli with the Concurrence of the heads of the Country party, has given notice of a motion for considering the taxes that press upon the Land & to devise means of Equalising the taxation which is to be borne by all Classes – This is a prodigious question – & I hope will be well Weighed & considered before it is announced to the Public[536] –

*27 February 1849*. […] The Expected repeal of the Navigation Laws, has caused a panic & an immense depreciation of Native timber – I have fortunately Sold my wood / 2 years clip / Just in good time, it was Sold at 30s a tod[537] – The State of the Country is very alarming = & ruin & confusion will come upon us, unless the vile Measures which are resorted to can be checked & a better System Established which Shall restore that confidence which is utterly lost –

*1 March 1849*. People in the interior of the Country Such as the Spital fields weavers & others are moving Strenuously in favor of preserving the Navigation laws Seeing well <u>now</u>, that their loss would, be the ruin of the Country – the public is beginning to perceive that all that has been doing lately & is proposed to be done, tends to [their] destruction – if <u>we</u>

[535] N.U.M.D., Ne C 5476: Disraeli to Newcastle, 23 Feb. 1849.

[536] Newcastle counselled Disraeli against repealing the malt tax: Dep Hughenden, 137/3, ff. 136–8: Newcastle to Disraeli, 27 Feb. 1849.

[537] N.U.M.D., Ne C 8381: Henry Heming to Newcastle, 27 Feb. 1849. Newcastle told Disraeli that he could only sell £900 of an estimated £5,000 worth of wood: Dep Hughenden, 137/3, f. 131: Newcastle to Disraeli, 6 Mar. 1849.

are active, bold & honest we may yet Save the Country (with Gods' help) from impending ruin[538] –

*3 March 1849.* a very large meeting at Liverpool against a repeal or alteration of the Navigation laws – & resolutions almost unanimously Voted against the Ministerial Measure – The Country protectionist party is proceeding So well & the others So very ill, that confidence is fast growing in our favor & fast diminishing from the Ministers – the Peelites have fallen below the dust –

I received a letter today from Miss Wilmot who was directed by her Mother Lady Wilmot [Maria Mundy] to inform me that her Brother Edward [Miller] Mundy had died at Barbados on the 29th January – although he had gone to the West Indies for the benefit of climate & care of Consumption by Which he was attacked, he did not die of that Complaint but by dysentery which carried him of[f] in 3 days – He was an Excellent man, & will be greatly missed in his family – I have heard it Supposed the [*sic* – that] William Mundy of Markeaton will probably Succeed him in the representation of [South] Derbyshire[539] –

*5 March 1849.* The news from India has frightened our ruling people at home – orders have been hastily Sent to all the Colonels of regiments not to discharge any more men: a great many, though, have already been discharged, to their great discontent & dissatisfaction = One of them was heard the other day to curse the Duke of Wellington for discharging him – he complained of his destitute State & being able Just now to do nothing but beg to Sustain himself & family. He Said, "it is all along of that damned old Duke of Wellington, that I am obliged to beg my bread = he cares nothing what becomes of the poor Soldier but he takes precious good care not to do any thing to hurt himself" [–] he went on in this Strain for Some time, & then added, "but it won't be long before we are Wanted again, & then He will be Sorry that he has treated us in this Manner" – I Suspect the man is right, & that much is going on Secretly, which a chance opportunity may cause to Explode in a most unpleasant manner –

*6 March 1849.* The dispatches from India appear in yesterday's papers: there is a very long one from Lord Gough = which is very guardedly worded, & which if private accounts be true, must be disingenuous – but we must not hastily condemn a man who has So often Exposed his life to Serve the cause of his Country, & who if he is in Error, as in a military point of view he certainly is, has Erred in Judgment & not by design –

*7 March 1849.* The newspapers & the public have taken up the Indian disasters with So much Earnestness, that the Government has been obliged to alter its course & Endeavour to repair the Evils which have been permitted – The command of the Indian army has been offered to & declined by Several officers = [at] last it was Settled that Sir William Gomon [Gomm] Governor of the Mauritius Should be the man, & orders were Sent out to him to replace Lord Gough = but the public discovered that Sir William Gomon had never been distinguished for any thing & was no better in all probability than Lord Gough,

[538] N.U.M.D., Ne C 6479: Henry Horton Marriott to Newcastle, 28 Feb. 1849.
[539] He did and was unopposed.

& Such a <u>row</u> has been made about all this that at last they have thought fit to yield to public opinion & have appointed the only man who has given proof that he is qualified to retrieve our tarnished arms – Sir Charles Napier – is appointed & has accepted, & is to go out Without delay – able as he is, my belief is that our rule in India is drawing to a Close, & that not Even he will be permitted to restore our rule – If it be God's will [,] we cannot Succeed –

*8 March 1849.* I was so busy writing last night that I was not in bed untill 4 o'clock this morning – my principal object was to finish a long letter to Mr Disraeli, to Endeavour to Secure him in advocating a line of policy which by being based on our duty to God & man may Enlighten the Nation & induce God's blessing upon us[540] –

*9 March 1849.* The farmers are now greatly on the alert, & now that they have Stirred themselves they will doubtless gain their End & regain protection for British industry –

*10 March 1849.* Todays' papers bring us Disraeli's Speech announcing his views of Equal taxation & justice in taxing the land – It is one of the most masterly Statements that Ever was Made, it is one of consummate ability, & the tone & Style So admirable, the arrangement So Simple, & yet So Explicit that no one of modern days, I doubt if any one before him [,] Ever made Such a Speech – It is a paternal Speech – it cares for all, it inculcates goodness, Justice & Christanity [*sic*], & is a model of goodness & greatness – it is an Example fit to be followed & worthy of imitation by a great Christian Country – & it will produce an Effect not Easily forgotten – I heartily thank God that Such a Speech has been made, & I trust, & others Seem to think So too, that a new era, by the blessing of God [,] may be breaking in upon & will be followed up with Zeal, courage, & perseverance[541] =

*11 March 1849.* The debate upon the navigation Laws is opened – Lord Granby Spoke upon it, & Seems to have made an Excellent Speech & in the best tone & frame of mind – Mr Herries too, one of our triumvirate [,] Spoke well – the debate is adjourned, the next day will probably finish it = We Shall have to Stop this nefarious bill in the House of Lords =

*13 March 1849.* The foreign news are So confused that one is able to make very little out of them – Russia, who intended to force the Dardanelles & march troops towards Italy, has been checked, principally by the Serious & Strong remonstrances of Sir Stratford Canning at Constantinople – The Turks are bestirring themselves actively, both by land & Sea –

*14 March 1849.* [At Worksop] I saw a Sample of wheat, (rather indifferent) for which the man asked 17[s] 6[d] a load of 3 bushels: – 5s 10d a bushel: that is only 46s 8d a

[540]Newcastle offered detailed suggestions for financial policy, including repealing the hop duty, removing the taxes on windows, inhabited houses, legacies, and transfer of property. He went on to quote liberally from a book which explained the prophecies 'which I am Convinced intimately Concerns us of the present day': Dep Hughenden, 137/3, ff. 122–31: Newcastle to Disraeli, 6 Mar. 1849.

[541]Dep Hughenden, 137/3, ff. 132–5: Newcastle to Disraeli, 14 Mar. 1849, congratulating him on the speech and outlining proposals for the cultivation of land in Ireland.

quarter – a man Standing near Stepped forward & told me that Corn in the Northern foreign ports was Selling at 45s a quarter [&] with 6s freight would be altogether landed in England [for] 51s a quarter [–] This person was a Mr Pettinger, or Pettifar [,] a corn dealer at Gainsbrough [*sic*] –

In the division on the repeal of the Navigation Laws, the ministerial majority was only <u>56</u> [266–210] last year it was 115[542] an ominous reduction –

*15 March 1849.* The debate on Mr Disraeli's motion is Still going on [–] it will probably terminate tomorrow –

*16 March 1849.* The debate on Disraeli's motion did End last night. Division against – 280 – for 189 – Majority 91 – which following the division on the navigation Laws – was Equal of a triumph – Disraeli made an admirable reply – Neither Sirs [Robert] Peel or [James] Graham dared to Speak –: they Know what would have been their fate in Disraeli's reply – We are going on well, as I understand – a good understanding & more unanimity prevails amongst us –

*20 March 1849.* The King of the Netherlands, or rather of Holland [William II] has died Suddenly of inflammation of the bowels = he is Succeeded by his Son Prince William [as King William III] who is now in this Country & has Just gone on a visit to the Duke of Cleveland at Raby Castle – He has not a very good reputation & is not popular –

*23 March 1849.* There is no news from the Continent – From the East there are despatches from the army – Lord Gough has thrown up Entrenchments for the protection of the British army – against the Seikhs [*sic*] encamped about 4 miles off – Lord Gough awaits reinforcement's & will then attack the Enemy = It is Said that this is the first time that our army in India has Ever Sought Safety behind Entrenchments –

*24 March 1849.* […] The Ministers have announced that they Shall resign if they fail in carrying the repeal of the Navigation Laws.

*25 March 1849.* The Navigation laws bill is gone into Committee. Disraeli made a grand attack towards the close of the debate – as So much difference of opinion Exists generally [,] & Even it is Said among Ministers themselves, the idea is the bill must be abandoned = The report is that Lord John Russell is ill –

*27 March 1849.* […] Lord John Russell is ill & his ministry in a most tottering condition = It is looked upon as certain that the Peelites will join him, & that Some partial changes will be made in the administration during the recess –

*29 March 1849.* It is a curious, but Sure fact that at this moment there is a great & Simultaneous movement amongst the Jews on the continent of Europe – It is a popular movement in which they are Engaged & are Every where putting themselves forward as leaders of the

[542] Hansard, *Commons Debates*, 3rd ser., lxxxix, cols 275–80: 22 Jan. 1847; the second reading passed by 50–188: majority 138.

people & are likely to be followed by them: another "sign of the Times", & cause for deep reflection –

*3 April 1849.* News from India of a great victory for our arms = but no particulars have arrived = I rejoice at this on account of Lord Gough, whose age & gallant, though not able, Services Entitle him to respect & Sympathy =

*4 April 1849.* The rate in aid bill, for Ireland [,] is vigorously opposed & is very much on the wane [.]

*9 April 1849.* attended the last meeting of the Committee for the Bentinck Memorial [in Mansfield] when the Sub Committee for making the building arrangements reported their proceedings[543] = Unfortunately I was late, & the Inscription which was the first point considered, was passed & approved – it Was by Colonel [Thomas] Wildman = a very good inscription for an ordinary man, but not for a man So Extraordinary as Lord George Bentinck.[544]

*13 April 1849.* […] Young [Edward Henry] Stanley, Lord Stanleys Son, who was Elected to Succeed Lord George Bentinck at [King's] Lynn, whilst he was in america – has been to see his Constituents, & made them a Speech of no pretension, but as is very Evident, of high promise[545] –

*14 April 1849.* It is asserted that Lord Melbourne towards the latter End of his life became a Roman Catholic & that he had a Jesuit Confessor.

*20 April 1849.* […] Lord Gough's victory at Goojerat [Gujarat] turns out to be a great affair in its results, our loss very small, that of the Enemy great, all their guns, ammunition, Camp Equipage Every thing in Short taken from them, the army dispersed, & driven as far as we could follow them, a large force under General [Sir Walter] Gilbert[546] Sent after the flying Enemy under Shere Sing [Sher Singh], who is Said to have been wounded. This battle has been won in true military Style, & not a fault committed & the consequence has been that

---

[543] For preceding events, see *Unhappy Reactionary*, 150–7; *Morning Post*, 28 Oct. 1848; N.U.M.D., Ne C 5637: Lord Thomas Clinton to Newcastle, 28 Oct. 1848; Ne C 5616: Lord Charles Clinton to Newcastle, 31 Oct. 1848; Ne C 8376: Charles Lindley to Newcastle, 7 Dec. 1848.

[544] 'To the memory of Lord George Frederick Cavendish Bentinck, second surviving son of William Henry Cavendish-Scott, fourth Duke of Portland. He died the 21st day of September, An. Dom. MDCCCXLVIII, in the forty-seventh year of his age. His ardent patriotism and uncompromising honesty were only equalled by the persevering zeal and extraordinary talents which called forth the grateful homage of those who, in erecting this memorial, pay a heartfelt tribute to exertions which prematurely brought to the grave one who might long have lived the pride of this his native county'.

[545] D.P., 178/1, pp. 262–5: Stanley to Newcastle, 4 Apr. 1849, discussing Edward Stanley and Gough's victories in India, and discouraging Newcastle from accepting the presidency of the colonial association, which had been offered to him; N.U.M.D., Ne C 6483: H.P. Huntley to Newcastle, 28 Mar. 1849.

[546] ~~Bernard~~ precedes this in the original.

the Enemy has been <u>Knocked</u> to <u>Shivers</u> – It has been a glorious feat of arms & has totally restored the British reputation[547] –

*21 April 1849.* […] To a question put to Lord Lansdown he replied that he was aware of the French Expedition to Italy, but that we had no Share in it, & neither Suggested nor incited it – we were taking no part to restore the Pope –

*22 April 1849.* No fresh accounts of any importance = From Rome it is Stated that Every thing whatever belonging to the Romish Churches & Convents, all the fine things [,] chalices, relics, Every thing of gold & Silver belonging to religious Establishments [,] has been melted down by the Republicans, & Even the inlaid metal on monuments &c [–] does not all this betoken the fall of Popery & the fulfilment of Prophecy [?] –

*23 April 1849.* […] The fall of Popery is truly miraculous, & the announcement of it to the very year by [the Reverend Robert] Fleming is most Extraordinary[548] – The Pope is a refugee at [the Castle of] Gaeta – His power is taken from him by republicans, who have Established a republic in his Dominions, & there people are removing all the Symbols of Popery & Exposing all its iniquities [–] all the documents are made public, the archives & correspondence & intrigues of the Popes &c – the whole Secrets of the Inquisition are laid bare, the dungeons are being Explored & opened to the public to behold & to be Eye witnesses of the horrors that have been perpetrated therein, & thus by Simple means God is vindicating His Majesty, & purifying & Chastising the profane impiety of antichrist – – The facts are truly amazing –

*24 April 1849.* […] I observe a Statement made that 14,000 of our Seamen deserted last year from our mercantile marine, 8000 of these went into the american Service = Things look very ill in Canada – The rightly thinking English party in Canada are outrageous at the Vote of liberation of the rebels – We Shall lose the Colony[549] –

*26 April 1849.* The Navigation laws repeal bill, or nearly tantamount to it, has passed the Commons by a majority of about 60 [275–214: majority 61] =

*30 April 1849.* Lord Stanley has declared in the noblest & most uniquivocal [sic] manner that he will oppose the Navigation Laws bill by Every means in his power & no doubt he will be as good as his word[550] –

*1 May 1849.* […] The King of Hanover has dissolved his diet many Members of which had Signed a bond to compel the Government to assent to the German Constitution to

[547]On 13 Feb. 1849, Gough attacked the Sikh army at the battle of Gujarat. On 12 Mar. 1849, the Sikhs surrendered near Rawalpindi.

[548]Robert Fleming, *The Rise and Fall of the Papacy* (1701), argued for the prophetic value of the Revelation. Newcastle owned the 1848 edition, *The Rise and Fall of Rome Papal*: N.A., DD/271/1.

[549]The Act to provide for the indemnification of parties in Lower Canada whose property was destroyed during the Rebellion in the years 1837 and 1838 received the royal assent on 25 Apr. 1849.

[550]D.P., 147/14: Newcastle to Stanley, 30 Apr. 1849, expressing his admiration for the speech.

which the King is opposed – [...] If foreign reports are to be believed our ambassador at Vienna [Viscount Ponsonby] is recalled, whether on account of his insufficiency or from differences with austria is not Stated –

*3 May 1849.* Most prosperous news from India – The Sickhs have Entirely given in = Their Chief Sheer Sing has Surrendered with all his army, his ally Goolab Sing [Gulab Singh] also – & our army under General Gilbert is close upon the heels of the affghans, who are flying home with all rapidity – This last fight has terrified them all [–] it was so complete & triumphant that the consequences are more positive than any I Ever remember in India – The fact is that no one but Lord Ellenborough has for years done anything but mismanage your [sic] concerns most grossly – It is Said to be the intention of Lord Dalhousie to annex the Punjaub [sic] to our Indian possessions – & to have no free power Existing between the Ganges & the Indus – This is the right & the only proper view – but we must Keep up our immense army to Keep down aggressors & Secure so vast a territory[551] –

There is to be a meeting of the Country party tomorrow at Lord Stanley's [–] I am very sorry that I cannot be there –

*5 May 1849.* Up at 7 – & hard at work throughout the day – at 5 o'clock to my great relief I found that I had Completed all my Work; & I resolved to try my fortune on the railway – Tomorrow is Sunday, & not a travelling day – & on Monday our debate on the Navigation comes on in the House of Lords – besides, Lord Winchilsea had fixed to dine with me tomorrow [–] these with other things induced me to venture on the Experiment – accordingly at $5\frac{1}{2}$ we left Clumber for Nottingham [–] there we found, (after being properly refused) a Special train, that a train for Rugby would Start at $8\frac{1}{2}$ = We took it & reached Rugby by $11\frac{1}{2}$ – we there found that we Must Stay there 2 hours & take the main train to London & they very obligingly allowed my carriages to go with us – at $1\frac{1}{2}$ we left Rugby & arrived in Portman Square at 5 o'clock = My Daughters were much amused with the change = & I hope will not be the worse for this Scrambling about in the night – It is a great comfort to have reached London – & Without the Slightest Mischief –

*6 May 1849.* We were Soon in bed, but did not rise till late, & could only attend Evening Church = Winchilsea Came to dine with us = From him & others I learn that we are to be beaten tomorrow = The Ministers as they Say are to win [–] Some[552] Say by 6 – others by as many as 20 – Our Exertions must be Extreme & I do not despair of Success [–] Whilst they [sic – there] is life there is hope –

*7 May 1849.* [...] I have had no time for looking into the Subject of the Navigation Laws, Engaged looking into the question as much as the Short time Will allow but there is so much to do that I could accomplish So little as to amount to almost nothing – So much to do Since my arrival, that I have had little time for reading & research[553] – had my dinner [&]

[551] On 30 Mar. 1849, Maharaja Duleep Singh signed away all claims to the rule of the Punjab.

[552] by precedes this in the original.

[553] For example, Newcastle had requested a copy of Joseph Allen's *The Navigation Laws of Great Britain: Historically and Practically Considered, with Reference to Commerce and National Defence* (1849): N.U.M.D., Ne C 6493: Joseph Allen to Newcastle, 2 May 1849.

went Early to the House of Lords – The Debate was long & dull – Lord Lansdown opened with a fair speech – Lord Brougham, good but as usual too wandering to please me = Lord Granville – Duke of argyll – a clever but quaint young Man = Lord Colchester, who moved the amendment – Lord Ellenborough who made the best Speech of the Evening – Lord Carlisle Moved the adjournment of the house at Somewhere about $12\frac{1}{4}$. The interest was very great – the house crowded with Strangers.[554]

*8 May 1849.* Lord Carlisle opened the adjourned debate – Lord Nelson followed in a Maiden Speech, which promises well = his allusions to his ancestor [Horatio Nelson] were in good taste & appropriate = Lord Bruce in a gotten by heart Speech which I Could not hear – Then Lord Talbot – Lord Harrowby, Lord Londonderry who was against the bill – Then Lord Wharncliffe & after him Lord Grey, the Ministerial great gun of the Evening, he made a long Speech & as I thought by no means a good on[e –] when he Sat down Lord Stanley rose to utter one of the Very finest orations that Ever was heard within the walls of Parliament it really was mighty = a complete refutation of the measure – able beyond measure, Clear, convincing & true = His appeal to the Duke of Wellington towards the close was a[s] beautiful as any thing Ever uttered in the English language & his wind up invocation upon almighty God to continue blessings upon the Country & to rule & guide the hearts, & understandings of Senators to wisdom was as fine as Could be imagined, it was a triumphant Speech = The Duke of Wellington Said nothing but went with the Contents below the bar, looking like a traitor cut down – In the house our numbers were 119. Ministers, Peelites & others 105 – Proxies added the total numbers [were] 173 for the bill 163 against – Majority 10 – & with this Scanty numbers [*sic*] they Still hope to pass the bill – the proceeding is truly Scandalous – – the house broke up at $\frac{1}{4}$ to 5. I was at home at $5\frac{1}{4}$[555] –

*11 May 1849.* I See that there were 21 decided Peelites & Wellingtonians who voted against the Navigation Laws on Tuesday night – not including any Bishops =

*13 May 1849.* I hear today that a partial change in the Ministry is about to take place = Sir Francis Baring to be made a Peer & Sir James Graham to have the admiralty, Sydney Herbert & it is also Said Lincoln to go with him, & I presume also Mr Cardwell & a few others – This is the old Story revived: it may be true of Sir James Graham – I disbelieve the rest –

*15 May 1849.* News today of an outbreak in Canada – The English party can Endure no longer the domination of the French party & have risen Either to put down the French party or to fight it out with them = They have driven out the Parliament [,] have burned down the Parliament House, With all the archives, valuable library &c – They have assaulted the Governor [Lord Elgin] with hisses & Execrations [,] with Stones & Eggs & other missiles & were committing other outrages when the accounts came away – If the accounts are to be believed, there will be a general rising of the English party which is determined to

[554] K.D., 7 May 1849, 'Debate Navigation Laws [–] brought home by Duke of Newcastle'.

[555] K.D., 8 May 1849, 'We lost by 10 Proxies [–] Stanley admirable [–] brought home by Duke of Newcastle'.

Contend for the ascendancy – Their fury is great against the indemnity bill for the French traitors & they are determined to repudiate the measure = The accounts are at present only forwarded or rather anticipated by telegraph –

*18 May 1849.* In the House this Evening Lord aberdeen was particularly Severe upon Lord Lansdowne who pretended to be very open & communicative about Italian affairs –

Lord Stanley annoyed the Ministers, by telling them that his amendments in the Committee on Navigation Laws would go to the Extent of repealing all the Clauses of the bill after the first word – & that he Should take for his groundwork the old law & merely introduce as amendments Some modifications – I Shall not be Surprised if he carries his amendments – if So of course the whole bill drops to the ground –

*19 May 1849.* It is announced this afternoon that a great change is to take place in the Ministerial Camp. Lord Lansdowne to be made a Duke – 4 Peers made – Messrs Sydney Herbert & [Henry] Labouchere, Sir John Hobhouse & Sir Francis Baring – & Lord John Russell = Lord Lansdown – resigns the Presidency to him – Lord Clarendon to be Premier – Sydney Herbert to Succeed him in Ireland – Sir James Graham 1st Lord of [the] admiralty – Mr Cardwell for his Secretary – Gladstone President [of the] board of Trade & Lincoln [*unclear*] pudor[556] !!! President [of the] board of Control – if this be So it is the most disgraceful business on record = but I cannot believe it – Some of these would certainly not find Seats again –

The Queen was Shot at this afternoon, but too late for the circumstances to transpire – Her Majesty had holden a Drawing room in the morning, & this day is Kept as her birth day = To refresh herself after the heat & fatigue she drove out with her children & returned through this [Portman] Square about 6 in the Evening, & returning to the Palace was Shot at –

*20 May 1849.* This is Sunday, but the Event of Yesterday has, now transpired – The Queen was Shot at as She was passing, along Constitution Hill – the man was an Irish bricklayer [William Hamilton] out of work – he Stood near one of the Small gates [–] as the Queen passed he fired his pistol, ran through the gate which he Slammed to behind him & instantly ran away across the Park, he was pursued & taken = at present no more is Known =

*21 May 1849.* The account circulated yesterday was not correct [–] the man is an Irish bricklayer but he did not run away & was taken instantly = He gives or we hear of no reason why the man Shot at the Queen – probably merely to be Shut up & taken care of as the man is out of work – nobody Seems to be much interested about the affair which is treated with contempt [–] the fact is people are in Such a State of apathy & inanition that nothing stirs or interests them –

We went into committee upon the Navigation tonight & Lord Stanley moved his amendments, which to Say truth I do not like at all – they are principally founded upon reciprocity & our Navigation laws properly Speaking have nothing to do with reciprocity = Either we Should have vigorously maintained the old law, or we Should propose nothing which

---

[556]Possibly 'for shame', as in 'Pudor' – 'Shame'.

Seemed in any way of the new System – which is utterly to be deprecated = I though[t] Lord Stanley less great than I Ever heard him – We Made a bad division, we were only 103 in the house whereas in our division – upon the 2nd reading; we were 112 in the house[557] = Where were the 9? our division was 116 for [–] 103 against the bill [majority 13] = I went away quite Sick & disheartened –

*22 May 1849.* The Committee [on the] navigation laws was postponed tonight [.] So much time was occupied to a late hour in discussing a question relative to the Scotch Episcopal Church –

*23 May 1849.* all the town is agog today – a fine day & Epsom races – I might have mentioned a very significant Expression of feeling which took place on the river among the shipping, although on the Queen's birthday [,] not a flag was hoisted on board of any one of the Ships – So I have been informed –

*24 May 1849.* In committee again on the navigation laws – We were Surprised by a Speech from the Duke of Northumberland, who is a captain in the Navy = He is a very accomplished man in information, (general) [*sic*] in arts & sciences, & has been in all parts of the world, an observer & well acquainted with most Countries – He Spoke admirably & made a great impression upon the house = He proved himself to be a great acquisition & in my opinion well fitted for any Situation. We were beaten in two divisions & Stanley then withdrew from the Contest & discharged Some galling vollies against the Peelites, whom he denounced & renounced unsparingly[558] =

*27 May 1849.* No particular news today. The House of Lords is in recess untill the 5th [of] June –

*31 May 1849.* I am told today that it is in contemplation within the Cabinet to bring forward Some measure to Strip the English Church in Ireland of their revenues & benefices & to hand them over to the Popish Clergy – It is incredible but yet I believe that there is Something in it, & I see no reason Why they Should not as well Carry Such a Measure as well as the new Navigation Law, or any other measure of a Kindred nature –

It has been decided today that a motion on the State of the Nation Shall be made on or about the 14th [of] June –

*12 June 1849.* This Evening the Navigation bill passed the 3rd reading in the House of Lords = I was not in the House at the time but I was told that Lord Ellenborough made a Striking Speech & other Lords made short speeches all protesting against the bill in the

---

[557] The vote on 8 May was 173 (105 present and 68 proxies) against 163 (119 present and 44 proxies): majority ten.

[558] In two divisions on the Navigation Bill, the numbers were 44–57: majority 13, and 49–37: majority 12.

Strongest terms[559] – The Jew bill came into the house from the Commons where it passed by a diminished majority of 66 [272–206] –

*13 June 1849.* a great ball at the Queen's Which we attended[560] –

*20 June 1849.* I was obliged to leave Clumber Very Early this morning in order to be in London in good time as I was Engaged [.] I arrived in time, but was very unwell & very unfit for a dinner[561] =

*22 June 1849.* […] The "affirmation Bill" most fortunately has been thrown out of the House of Lords[562] =

*23 June 1849.* although much better but not well, I dined today with the Lord Mayor at the Mansion House – & was much gratified that I did so = The Lord Mayor, [Sir James Duke] being a Whig or Something of that Kind invited Lord Stanley & all his party of protectionists to dine with him they & their Ladies = there were about 200 – The Lord Mayor played his part admirably & managed the political part most dexterously [.] Lord Stanley Spoke for the Lords, Disraeli for the Commons. It was a very agreeable Sight to me to see Every male guest Seated by his Wife, if he had one, which alas I have not, the whole was remarkably done, & as pleasant a dinner as I Ever was at – Politics were talked very freely & openly & the Lord Mayor Evidently was well disposed to us – a Mr [Duncan] Dunbar Chairman of the Shipping Company was called by the Suggestion of the Lord Mayor & he told us plainly, that a most vigorous & determined reaction was taking place, & that England was determined no longer to be overridden by Cobbett [*sic* – Cobden] & Co. [.] I believe him to be perfectly right –

*25 June 1849.* […] I was at the House of Lords this afternoon [–] nothing particular passing – Tomorrow we Shall have a hard tussle on the Jew Bill, which I trust in God we shall throw out –

*26 June 1849.* Once more we have Saved ourselves from perdition – The Debates upon the "Parliamentary oaths bill", was long but thank God we finished by again throwing out the bill.[563] The numbers on division were for the bill 70 – against it 95 – Majority against 25[564] –

*28 June 1849.* Mr Lionel Rothschild has accepted the Chiltern 100s & has resigned his Seat in order that there may be a fresh Election & starts again to make mischief – in his address to the City [of London] Electors, he tells them that the fight is between them & the House

[559] *L.J.,* lxxxi, 285; *Protests,* iii, 362–4.

[560] There were about 1,700 people present: QVJ, 13 June 1849.

[561] K.D., 20 June 1849, 'Had to dine Duke of Newcastle [,] Lady Georgiana Clinton'.

[562] The division was 10–34: majority 24.

[563] bills in the original.

[564] K.D., 26 June 1849, 'Jew Bill Thrown out 95 to 70 [–] Very able Speech Bishop Wilberforce [–] Brought home by Duke of Newcastle'.

of Lords & that the House of Lords is the last hold of bigotry & intolerance – I trust that he will hurt his own cause by his intemperance & mischievous insolence –

*30 June 1849.* I am informed this Evening that it is determined to start a candidate to oppose the Jew Rothschild for the City – Lord John Manners is to be that man – He is late as the Election comes on in 3 days – but he may win [–] he will be powerfully & actively assisted –

*1 July 1849.* I learn today that they have Some Scheme by Which they hope to win the Election, [William] Beresford did not tell me what it was, but I was not to mention that there was a Scheme untill after the Nomination for the City.

*3 July 1849.* […] I learn this Evening that at 3 o'clock today, the Jew Rothschild was a head [*sic*] of Lord John Manners by 3000 –

*4 July 1849.* The total numbers polled yesterday were Rothschild 6619, Lord John Manners – 3104 – This is certainly more than could be Expected in only 24 hours for preparation = I See but little prospect of unseating the Jew = The Protest appears to me but a feeble production[565] –

*15 July 1849.* […] I have the great pleasure to record that Peace has been concluded & preliminaries Signed between the Germans & Danes on most honorable terms to the latter – at this I truly rejoice, & I trust we shall now hear no more of this Shameful War – the able & unwearied mediation of our Minister at Berlin, Lord Westmoreland, is Said to have Effected this –

*20 July 1849.* I believed that Combermere had left London yesterday but today I learned that he had been taken very ill with English Cholera which is diarhaea [*sic*] yesterday or the day before & wished to see me, as soon as I Could I went to him & was rejoiced to find him much better & quite Easy & I trust going on perfectly well – Lady Combermere had also been ill – in fact the Town is very unhealthy now & many people are ill with these Complaints & what is called Cholera –

*21 July 1849.* Combermere is better & doing well – More of the Servants have been taken ill – Numbers of people are ill, but I believe the cause may be traced to defective drainage – It is Said that this is the Case in what is called Belgravia on the neighbourhood of Belgrave Square –
   I was Sent to at 12 last night to go to the House of Lords to assist in the Division on Brougham's motion on Foreign affairs – I was just going to bed, fatigued & Sleepy, & did not attend to the Summons –

[565] Lionel de Rothschild (Whig) won the election with 6,017 votes to 2,814 for Lord John Manners: majority 3,203.

*23 July 1849*. [...] Went to the House of Lords this afternoon, & presented the Petition from Nottinghamshire lately holden at Newark – I gave the <u>Noble Lords opposite</u>, a little bit of my mind on the occasion[566] –

*2 August 1849.* The Queen has prorogued Parliament & now will be at liberty to Commence her progresses, She will go first to Ireland where we all Expect that She will do much More harm than good – The Speech is a meagre matter & is a fit conclusion to one of the most meagre but Still most mischievous Sessions that Ever passed –

*3 August 1849.* The Queen has Sailed or rather Steamed for Ireland. There are Various rumours of how She intends to act [–] one positively asserts that Her Majesty has by her Secretary announced that She will not receive any purely – Protestant address or petition = We shall see, but if this really be So it may Cost her her Throne – Such Errors as these are Sure to be Committed by Sovereigns visiting Ireland, with bad & dangerous advisers –

*8 August 1849.* The propitious weather which had made Every thing fruitful has brought forward the harvest & in a few days they will begin to Cut, the generality of the corn crops is magnificent = all live Stock also is in the most thriving & Extraordinary Condition altogether I never Saw Such a prosperous state of rural affairs = if the markets shall be as favorable as the produce of the land – the farmer will do well this year = but prices I much fear will be too low for him –

*10 August 1849.* The Queen landed & was Joyously greeted by the people of Cork – nothing untoward has hitherto occurred –

*11 August 1849.* Her Majesty has been most enthusiastically Welcomed at Dublin – She Seems to have committed a gross violation of the law by admitting the Roman Catholic Prelates as Such & by name & title to her Levees & granting them the Entree by title as Catholic "Primate of Ireland, Catholic Bishop of Dublin" & so forth – a vast & Singular indiscretion –

*12 August 1849.* Her Majesty in the warmth of her heart has declared to her peaceable & loyal people of Ireland that She is delighted with Ireland, with Dublin [,] with her warm hearted Subjects, & if She has health & Strength will Certainly go to Ireland next year, remain among them for Some time, & hold her Courts there.

*13 August 1849.* [...] The Queen has left Ireland & is gone to Glasgow where great preparations are making to receive her – She & the royal family are going to Balmoral –

[566] The petition, from the Nottinghamshire branch of the Agricultural Protection Society, was for the restoration of protective duties on foreign produce: Hansard, *Lords Debates*, 3rd ser., cvii, col. 817: 23 July 1849; N.U.M.D., Ne C 6490: J.H. Stenton to Newcastle, 28 Apr. 1849.

*14 August 1849*. I have been very much grieved to hear of the death of Lady Dartmouth = He is an old School fellow & friend of mine & is left with 15 Children by the deceased who are all under age, the youngest infants – Lord Dartmouth himself is apparently aging very fast & may not live long – one laments that Such good people Should leave us –

*18 August 1849*. The Queen is making her way to Balmoral, & was to Sleep at Perth on her road there –

*26 August 1849*. We learn by this day's post, that Lincoln's Yatch [*sic* – Yacht] the Gitana has been <u>wrecked</u> at Ryde on her passage from Portsmouth to Cowes – if She were So ill appointed that the man in charge could not Sail her in Safety from Portsmouth to Cowes – may it not be considered a most Providential & merciful dispensation, that Lincoln had not Sailed in her, on this most ill considered & perilous Expedition = May God grant him wisdom to[567] discover the right Course, & learn what he ought to do under this & all other Circumstances = for his present welfare & Eternal happiness – Lincolns' loss will be Considerable – he gave £1700 for the Yatch [*sic*] – William tells me = all their things & Stores were on board = & they were to Sail from Cowes in a few days – these are most of them lost or damaged to a considerable amount[568] –

*30 August 1849*. a letter from Mr [William] Henderson, this morning, informs me that Mr [John] Parkinson had called upon him, thinking it right that I Should be made acquainted with Lady Lincolns' present State. She left England for Ems, in the very beginning of august of last[569] year – She then became acquainted with Lord Walpole – From Ems She went to Rome, & Lord Walpole followed her there by a different route = Lady Lincoln afterwards took a villa on the Lake of Como – There Lord Walpole was always in her Society – He passed under a feigned name – She became pregnant, & it is understood that She is to lie in at the End of this month of august = I have written at Some length to Henderson, with particulars of how he Should advise Mr Parkinson to proceed, So that Lady Lincoln's infancy Shall be completely proved & Exposed & that this little bastard Shall not be palmed upon my family as a legitimate child & a Clinton. It is a[570] most Scandalous & horrible affair, but it is no more than I Expected, & foretold of Lady Lincoln when Lincoln So Weakly & So inconceivably took her back, when She took him by Storm at Ryde in the Isle of Wight Some years ago[571] –

---

[567] to precedes this in the original.

[568] Lincoln was departing on a yacht cruise to the Mediterranean: N.U.M.D., Ne C 5909: Lincoln to F.R. Bonham, 23 Aug. 1849. For attempts to affect a reconciliation between Lincoln and Newcastle, see N.U.M.D., Denison MS, Os C 602: Gladstone to John Evelyn Denison, 12 Aug. 1849; Ne C 5908: Countess Manvers to Newcastle, 19 Aug. 1849.

[569] ~~that~~ precedes this in the original.

[570] a precedes this in the original.

[571] 'She is now at liberty to do as she pleases, She may run off with a Man tomorrow & you cannot touch her': N.U.M.D., Ne C 5854: Newcastle to Lincoln, 22 Sept. 1844. For Lincoln's troubled marriage, see Virginia Surtees, *A Beckford Inheritance: The Lady Lincoln Scandal* (Wilton, 1977).

*2 September 1849*. No very particular news – Except that Every thing has been done to bring Lady Lincoln's filthy wickedness to light = & possibly a divorce may follow as well as illegitimatising [*sic*] the bastard.[572]

*5 September 1849*. Lord Elgin has been made an English Peer – ["] what for? ["], we may ask – The only answer can be, ["] for Miserably Mismanaging Canadian affairs – & fearing the Storm which he has raised ["] – It Seems that the British party is Still dissatisfied with the ascendancy of the French party & is determined to over come it – Some rioting has recommenced –

*6 September 1849*. […] The Effects of the Queens visit to Ireland are beginning to come out in a manner by no means auspicious = Nothing could be more injudicious than giving the Popish prelates rank at Court & other partial & improper acts –

*9 September 1849*. at last an order is published in the Gazette for public prayer "on account of the great mortality by Cholera"[573] – with no More Solemnity or Seriousness than those words, but I trust that the minds of the Nation are better disposed than those of Her Majesty's Ministers –

*11 September 1849*. The Queen is still in Scotland at Balmoral – The Prince of Wales has Just been made Earl of Dublin =

*12 September 1849*. [Edward] Stanley Bishop of Norwich a very Eccentric & bad Bishop has died rather Suddenly – whoever may be approached to Succeed him, there is this advantage [,] that a worse choice can not be made = another Bishop in Ireland (Fernes) [James Keating, Bishop of Ferns] is announced as having died –

*13 September 1849*. No news, Except an account of disturbances in our own colonial island of Cephalonia, on which occasion Mr [Henry George] Ward, late M.P. for Sheffield, the Governor, has conducted affairs in a very different manner from Lord Elgin, & no doubt that the results will be very different –

*14 September 1849*. The prayer to avert the wrath of God, to confess our Sins, & pray for Mercy & that He may Stay His hand & remove from us this pestilence, appears in yesterday Evening's Standard & is good as far as it goes, but no order for reading it throughout the Nation & on a day Set apart Specially for the purpose, & for general & National humiliation, is Even Mentioned by authority, & the Nation is left to its own guidance. We are in the hands of a Scandalous & almost impious Set, who will doubtless be made to feel the Effects of their own vile doings[574] –

[572] N.U.M.D., Ne C 5910: William Henderson to Newcastle, 1 Sept. 1849.

[573] *The London Gazette*, 7 Sept. 1849, supplement.

[574] *The Standard*, 13 Sept. 1849.

*15 September 1849.* […] Lord Grey, by his obstinacy, folly & Langour [,] has raised another Storm at the Cape of good Hope, the Colonists there are resolutely determined to resist its being made a penal Colony, & will not permit the Convicts to remain there –

*18 September 1849.* Their [*sic*] Seems to be no news – By the later accounts it appears that the Cholera is abating in London = Prayer & Humiliation have been heartily resorted to in London, the people are most anxious upon the point, & I doubt [not] that God in his Mercy will hear their prayers, will pity, & mitigate their Sufferings, & allay the pestilence. We shall soon Know, but I have a hope & firm reliance that God will graciously hear a humbled & Supplicant people.

*20 September 1849.* The Queen is about to leave her Scotch residence & return to the Isle of Wight = Her life is[575] a very restless one =

*24 September 1849.* Outrages in Ireland are again Commencing, Secret Societies are forming upon an Extensive Scale –

*25 September 1849.* Today we had Service here, & the neighbouring villages the Same, to confess our Sins & to humble ourselves before God & to beseech Him to avert from us the dire disease of Cholera with which in his wrath & as a Just chastisement he has inflicted upon us – May our prayers be heard & may we as a Nation So conduct ourselves as more Worthily to merit His blessings & favors –

*27 September 1849.* The mortality by Cholera in London has very Much decreased. In the last day[576] it was 102, instead of 4000 a week which it was about a month ago –

*3 October 1849.* Soon after going to bed last night, I had a Siesiure [*sic*] of a most alarming Kind – I have had indications of it lately, but wheesing [*sic*] & impediment of breathing Came on & Encreased to such a degree that, I could Scarcely inspire or Expire, & I thought that death Was coming on – it was I Suppose an asthmatic affection of the most distressing Kind, & for Some time it became worse & worse until we hit upon a remedy, in Salvolatile & hot water[577] – Our Doctor ([John] Dethick) was Sent for, but God in his Mercy had relieved me from all the worst of the attack, & I think he has put me upon a System which may tend to relieve me in future from attacks of Such a Serious nature –

*8 October 1849.* Nothing new Except a good Speech of Disraeli's at Hedingham Castle at an Essex agricultural meeting [.][578]

*11 October 1849.* […] The Government [,] Lord Clarendon in particular, has thought fit to dismiss Lord Roden from the Magistracy in Ireland, an affront & an injustice that will

---

[575] is precedes this in the original.

[576] ~~week~~ precedes this in the original.

[577] Sal volatile is a solution of ammonium carbonate in alcohol or ammonia water, used in smelling salts.

[578] *An Account of the Meeting of the Hinckford Agricultural and Conservative Club in the Baronial Hall, Hedingham Castle, Together with a Corrected Report of the Speeches of Benjamin Disraeli, etc* (1849).

be resented by all Ireland.[579] There is not a better & more Eminent man in the Country than he – & to dismiss Such a Man merely because he Suffered the Protestants to assemble in his Park on their annual Holiday is an indignity which will neither be unnoticed nor unresented – The object of the Government is to pamper & cajol[e] the Papists & to degrade the Protestants but they will not Succeed – the reverse will be the Consequence – The Protestants will not Suffer themselves to be treaden [sic] upon any longer –

Mr [Isaac] Butt has offered himself a Candidate for Cork, his address is a manifesto, purposely, it is of the right Sort, he Speaks out manfully, he Cannot be mistaken[580] – he is as courageous as he is able. He defended the Irish Corporations at the bar of the House of Lords When a very young advocate – as his ability was of a most remarkable Kind – He & Mr [T.W.] Booker will be insuperable in the Next Session –

*13 October 1849.* Lord Roden's reply to the Chancellor of Ireland [Maziere Brady] appears today, I do not like it: it is mild, temperate & polite, all which is very right [,] but this is too much humility & not Enough out Speaking [–] the times & circumstances forbid the one & require the other[581] –

*16 October 1849.*[582] The Irish accounts are full of the dismissal of Lord Roden and of the insults to Protestantism So Shamefully Exhibited by the Lord Lieutenant [Clarendon] = He & his fellows will be Signally punished Ere long –

*17 October 1849.* Mr Butt has resigned his pretensions at Cork – he has done well – his address was long & betrayed many failings & Errors – The Protestants & Steady Irish do not approve of his advocating the Cause of the rebels in the late trials – He would not have answered in Parliament & it is well that he Should be out of the way –

*18 October 1849.* Winchilsea was married yesterday, may Every happiness & good fortune attend him – he deserves them – I much fear that the bad health of his new wife [Fanny Margaretta Rice] = may renew his troubles & anxieties –

*25 October 1849.* Today was the dinner of the "Labourer's Friend Society" of which I am President & they wished me to take the Chair – at Worksop – as I am So much better I determined to fulfill the duty & did So – There was a good meeting & all went off very

---

[579] The Dolly's Brae conflict in County Down took place on 12 July 1849 when a contested procession led to a disturbance resulting in fatalities. Orangemen had gathered at Tollymore Park, Lord Roden's estate, earlier in the day. Roden, a deputy grandmaster of the Orange Order, and two other Orange magistrates, Francis Beers and William Beers, were dismissed following a report by Walter Berwick QC which criticised their actions. The affair led to the Party Processions Act of 1850, which prohibited all political processions in Ireland.

[580] See *The Times*, 10 Oct. 1849.

[581] The letter, dated 8 Oct. 1849, was published in *The Freeman's Journal*, 12 Oct. 1849.

[582] N.U.M.D., Ne C 5477: Disraeli to Newcastle, 16 Oct. 1849, expressing a wish 'to build up the Country party on two great popular principles – the dimunition [sic] of public burthens & the Maintenance of public credit, & thus to associate the interests of the land with the general Sympathies of the Country'. Newcastle replied, 'Equalising the public burdens would no doubt be Just & beneficial, but it will not raise prices although it would lighten the payment of taxes now falling unfairly upon land, the Sinking fund too would be an Excellent Expedient': Dep Hughenden, 30/6, ff. 84–91: Newcastle to Disraeli, 21 Oct. 1849, enclosing a letter from John Parkinson to Newcastle, 16 Oct. 1849.

pleasantly – When the business of the day was over we went into politics. – I gave them my Mind & they gave Me theirs[583] –

*13 December 1849.* On the 28th of October illness came on rapidly & I was obliged to take to my bed to which I was closely Confined for above a month – Doctors from London Came down to me & others from the country, but I Was Very ill indeed [–] my disease was pluerisy [*sic*] from which I suffered much & at length became so weak & reduced that I could not move in bed without assistance […] on the 25th or 26th [of] November I was forced out of my bed & in about a fortnight afterwards I was fit to leave my rooms upstairs & was carried below to my room at the bottom of the back-stairs Which I have inhabited Ever Since – I do no business, it as well as writing are forbidden[584] –

*30 December 1849.* […] The Queen Dowager adelaide has died to the deep regret of the Nation, which Sincerely Mourns her loss & rightly appreciated her great worth & remarkable goodness – –

*31 December 1849.* […] This year of 1849 – Now concluded has been a remarkable year for reaction Every where, abroad for the reestablishment of order & the overthrow of the most fearful general revolution that Ever appeared; In our own Country for an almost miraculous return to right principles, a general desire to have a new & thoroughly protectionist Parliament, to Extinguish all the loose & free trade measures which have of late been proposed & carried in Parliament & a desire to See England great [,] glorious & happy – May God grant that She may be So! but to obtain Such an End will Engage us in a Serious & formidable Struggle –

*5 January 1850.* […] Went to see the French <u>Exposition</u> as it is called, which I had heard So much Vaunted, but in my opinion it consisted of Some of the poorest rubbish I Ever Saw –

*13 January 1850.* [At St Leonard's-on-Sea] Our Search for Comfortable lodging's having failed I have determined to remain in this (Victoria) Hotel. They have consented to make us very Comfortable here & we are to have Some of the rooms Occupied by Louis Philippe & his family when he was here[585] –

*1 February 1850.* […] amendments were moved in both Houses last night [–] the debate in the House of Lords closed at 1 o'clock. 103 for the amendment 152 against – Majority for <u>Ministers</u> 49[586] – I looked forward to quite a different result, but Stanley Seemed to have

---

[583] *Nottinghamshire Guardian*, 1 Nov. 1849. This was interpreted as a sign of support for Disraeli's proposals: *Buckinghamshire Herald*, 20 Oct. 1849; *DL*, V, 240–1.

[584] 'You will have heard of the Duke of Newcastle's Serious illness – [Francis] Bonham desires Me to say the Medical men told him there was much danger at one time but it has passed and he is now convalescent': N.U.M.D., Ne C 12230: John Young to Lincoln, 6 Nov. 1849. Also see BL, Add. MS 44261, f. 115: 'The Duke of Newcastle returns his grateful thanks for Mr & Mrs Gladstone's very kind enquiries during his late protracted illness, 31 December 1849'.

[585] The Royal Victoria Hotel, situated on the seafront, was built in 1828 by the architect James Burton.

[586] The vote was 103 (69 present and 34 proxies) to 152 (86 present and 66 proxies): majority 49.

been Weak & not to have uplifted the feelings of the house nor to have given adequate Encouragement to his friends out of it – I do not like the Commencement =

*1 March 1850.* […] as if we had not Enough upon our hands, our fools of Ministers have presumed to tarnish the honor of the National name, & have to the wonder of Every human being picked a quarrel with Greece a friendly & the weakest of all powers, & the proceedings are conducted after the manner of a blustering bully or highwayman, & Scandalous to the English name = we are Eternally disgraced by what has been done & is doing[587] –

*April 1850.* […] From the unsettled State in which I have been placed Since & by my illness I have Kept no daily journal & have only recorded a few facts from memory. Ministers are daily diminishing in Strength & Character, they are Constantly out voted in the House of Commons & frequently upon tax & financial questions – they cannot remain long – if we, the Country party [–] had had any one who Could have played his Cards well, there would have been an Entire change long ago[588] –

*24 April 1850.* Went to visit ashburnham Place [in Sussex] – Lord ashburnham was there & very Kindly shewed us what there was to be seen, it is rather wet in winter, but in Summer it must be a delightful place – Lord ashburnham is Said to be a particular & Severe man, but We found him most civil, obliging [,] intelligent & gentlemanlike –

*25 April 1850.* I forgot to mention that the people of Hastings were anxious to receive the Lord Mayor of London at their festive board, the Mayor & Corporation & inhabitants assisting to do him honor – Lord Mayor [Thomas] Farncomb is a native of the place, born of farmer parent's, but now possessed of great wealth as a general Merchant. He went in procession from the Station here to Hastings, the Lord Mayor in his own State carriage & the natives in carriages & on horseback to the best of their Means, & what they called in State – – it was a very pretty Sight though humble to what a city pageant is –

*1 May 1850.* The Queen was brought to bed of a Prince [Arthur] –

*3 May 1850.* […] we were informed that towards the End of the Month the Lord Mayor of London [Farncomb] would Come to dine with the Corporation & inhabitants of Rye, as he had before done at Hastings – His Lordship Evidently has the wish to represent Rye

[587]i.e. 'The Don Pacifico affair'. Lord William Clinton was in Greece in July 1850 and charted events in his journal: N.U.M.D., Ne C 5932/13–16. He died two months later.

[588]Similar sentiments were expressed in Newcastle's correspondence at this time: 'Politics are Enough to sicken anyone. I almost despair, but I most anxiously hope that all will End well for the Safety & prosperity of the Country': H.P., Bundle 901: Newcastle to the duke of Hamilton, [18] Mar. 1850; N.U.M.D., Ne C 5919: Hamilton to Newcastle, 23 Mar. 1850. Also see N.L.S., MS 4090, ff. 201–2: Newcastle to John Blackwood, editor of *Blackwood's Magazine*, 8 Apr. 1850.

whenever an opportunity occurs – he tried it at the last general Election – as I have been told –

*4 May 1850.* The Ex King of France & all his family are Coming here to occupy this Hotel & I have to leave it on the 13 or 14th. I shall go to London –

*18 May 1850.* London is all in an uproar – The French Minister Monsieur Drouoyn de Lhuys [Édouard Drouyn de Lhuys], has left London in haste, Said [to] be recalled by his Government & it is Supposed that there Will be a war between England & France = I myself do not apprehend it. Lord Palmerston is a detestable man to be at the [head of] foreign affairs of England, he ruins our prospects & gains us a bad name with Every other Country in the world –

*19 May 1850.* The Explanations in Parliament have been disgraceful to our Ministers: they are too long to detail – The Whitsun holidays will Save them for a week –

*25 May 1850.* I go on from day to day much in the Same manner [,] living, taking my medicines, my meals & my Exercise very much by rule, – I See a good many people in my own house, but I do nothing Else, I am forbidden the House of Lords, & I go to no public places.

*27 May 1850.* The Lord Chancellor Cottenham is about to resign & it is Said that we are now to have two Separate officers instead of one Chancellor – a Measure highly objection-able in my opinion –

Lincolns Divorce bill has passed the Second reading [in] the House of Lords – His Vile & abandoned Wife offered no defence[589] –

*30 May 1850.* I went with my daughters to see the Hippopotamus [Obaysch] Just arrived at the Zoological gardens,[590] & was seating myself near[591] to one of the Houses, when one of my daughters Came up & told me that we had Just passed two of Lincolns' children, Edward the Second boy & the daughter, Susan = She Said they were close by & that the boy in the blue Jacket was Edward, I looked at him with wonder for I could [not] recognise a feature of his Countenance or See any likeness to his family [–] the girl I afterwards found, I had Even touched as I passed her on the walk & heard her Voice but did not Know her though She is less altered than the boy – I Subsequently Came up to them near Where the hippopotamus is Kept & renewed my acquaintance with them = It must be 5 or 6 Years Since I have Seen them – they were Very Civil & well behaved as to a Stranger, & Stared at me very much, but Showed no Emotion – They were with Mrs [Catherine] Gladstone –

---

[589]See C.C. Eldridge, 'The Lincoln Divorce Case: A Study in Victorian Morality', *Trivium*, xi (1976), 21–39.

[590]Obaysch was the first hippopotamus seen in Great Britain since prehistoric times. He arrived at London Zoo on 25 May 1850: John Simons, *Obaysch: A Hippopotamus in Victorian London* (2019).

[591]at precedes this in the original.

# APPENDIX A:
# NEWCASTLE'S PUBLISHED LETTERS
# TO THE PRESS

*This appendix reproduces the published letters to which Newcastle refers in his diary between 1839 and 1850.*

1. Newcastle's correspondence on his dismissal as lord lieutenant of Nottinghamshire, with a covering letter to John Hicklin, editor of the *Nottingham Journal*. Dated: London, 20 July 1839. Source: *The Times*, 7 Aug. 1839.[1]

Sir –

At the time of my dismissal from the Lieutenancy of the county of Nottingham, I sought to allay all angry feelings, not only in my own breast, but also in the minds of all those who might have been induced to espouse my cause. I abstained, therefore, from addressing one word to the inhabitants of the county over which I had presided for so many years, although it might have been expected; nor will I even now address them, lest my motive should be misconstrued. But as so much misrepresentation was resorted to, and parts of the transaction partially divulged, so as to create an idea that there remained concealed a great deal which ought not to be brought to light, I have determined to place the correspondence in your hands, that, through the medium of your excellent journal, my fellow-countrymen may be made acquainted with the facts, & thus be Enabled to judge for themselves.

I make no appeal, but I think that those amongst whom I live, and whose respect and esteem I value, ought to know the simple truth, whether it be for or against me. The dismissal of a lieutenant of a county is an event of no ordinary occurrence – the cause ought not to be buried in mystery; and in my case it appears to me that I ought not to suffer under a more severe imputation than I deserve.

It seems to me that the fit time has arrived for disclosing particulars, and I now submit the correspondence to you. Dispose of it as you think proper. You once requested to have it; if it still appears to you desirable that it should be published, you have my consent to the publication.

I remain, Sir, yours very truly,
NEWCASTLE

[1]In addition to Newcastle's letters, the published correspondence consists of Lord Cottenham's letters to Newcastle of 18 and 28 Apr. 1839 regarding the disputed nominations to the county magistracy and Lord John Russell's letter to Newcastle of 30 Apr. 1839, informing him of his dismissal as lord lieutenant: N.U.M.D., Ne C 5075, 5077, 5079. Russell acknowledged Newcastle's apology in an unpublished letter; Ne C 5085: Russell to Newcastle, 3 May 1839.

Clumber, April 20, 1839

My Lord [Chancellor], I have received your lordship's letter informing me that you have given directions for the insertion of the names of the gentlemen recommended by me in the commission of the peace.

You also inform me that you intend to insert the names of other gentlemen not recommended by me in the commission; as you have the power to do so if you think fit, I cannot prevent you. The responsibility rests with your lordship; I have done my duty, you may enjoy the unenviable satisfaction of doing what you ought not do. Most certainly I will not condescend to renew my objections to the appointment in question, or to have any confidential communication whatever with an official who has proved his unfitness for the high dignity which has been imposed upon him.

With the very sincere hope that for the good of the country your lordship and colleagues may be speedily eased of the burdens of office, I have the honour to remain, my lord, your lordship's very obedient servant,
NEWCASTLE

Portman Square, April 28, 1839

In reply to the Lord Chancellor's note, received last night, the Duke of Newcastle begs to assure his lordship that he will readily withdraw his letter when his lordship withdraws his appointments.

Portman Square, May 2, 1839

My Lord [John Russell], – I have the honour to acknowledge the receipt of your lordship's letter of the 30th of April, communicating to me that you had received the Queen's commands to acquaint me that Her Majesty has no further occasion for my services as Lord-Lieutenant and Custos Rotulorum of the county of Nottingham. My successor [the Earl of Scarbrough], I am informed, is already appointed, and I may now admit what antecedently [*sic*] I was [not][2] disposed to acknowledge.

Distrustful of my own judgment, I have thought it to be incumbent upon me to lay the correspondence and the whole case before my friends, previously to replying to your lordship's letter. Their calmer judgment and regulated opinion have convinced me that my zeal may have outstepped my discretion, and that it would have been much better if I had abstained from the use of some expressions contained in my letter of the 20th. To their opinion I yield my assent, and I now express to your lordship my regret that, under feelings of irritation, expressions should have escaped from me which I will not attempt to vindicate.

Having thus admitted the error, I must, at the same time, be permitted to guard myself against being supposed to acquiesce in the justice of your lordship's recommendation to the Queen to dismiss from her service, on the mere ground of his having indulged in intemperate expressions, one who, for somewhere about 30 years, has loyally,[3] faithfully, and,

[2]This word appears in the manuscript draft: Ne C 5082, 1 May 1839.
[3]'honestly' in the draft.

I hope I may add, beneficially discharged his duty to Her Majesty and her royal predecessors, with a zeal which might command consideration, and a devotion which friends & enemies will equally attest.

During the period that I have held the appointment, I have scrupulously endeavoured to fulfil my duty to my Sovereigns, to their ministers, and to my country. I have lived under many changes; with some administrations I have agreed, with others I have differed, but under all alike I have been uninfluenced by party considerations, I have had but one motive, but one line of action, the single determination to execute my duty honestly and without favour or affection.

On receiving from your lordship the intimation of my having incurred this mark of her Majesty's displeasure, accompanied by my dismissal from the honourable office which I have occupied for so many years, I could not refrain from thus briefly calling your lordship's attention to the past.[4]

I have the honour to remain, my lord,
Your lordship's very obedient servant,
NEWCASTLE

2. Newcastle's letter to Sir Robert Heron on the Newark by-election of 1839. Dated: Clumber, 3 Dec. 1839. Source: *The Times*, 17 Dec. 1839.

Sir –

A placard or handbill addressed to the electors of Newark, dated Stubton Hall, November 30, and signed 'Robert Heron', has been put into my hands.[5] Statements and assertions are therein made, which no one is authorised to make for me. I am quite sure that, on reflection, you will perceive that very unwarrantable use has been made of my name; nor can I doubt that, upon the receipt of this letter, you will see the propriety of giving immediate and public contradiction to the statements contained in the handbill alluded to, coupled with a declaration that, really and in fact, you know nothing of my sentiments or intentions.

I remain, Sir, your very obedient servant,
NEWCASTLE

3. Newcastle's letter to the editor of *The Statesman and Dublin Christian Record* on the reform of Irish Corporations. Dated: Clumber, 17 Feb. 1840. Source: *The Statesman and Record*, 25 Feb. 1840.

---

[4] 'I could not refrain from calling your Lordships attention thus briefly to the past' in the draft.

[5] In his handbill, Heron suggested that 'the Duke, whom I believe to be an honest and straightforward man' would not allow his agents to 'exercise any vengeance' upon his tenants for their vote; consequently, they 'may safely make use of the free disposal of their votes, which he leaves to be decided by their principles and wishes': *The Times*, 5 Dec. 1839. Heron subsequently issued a retraction (dated 9 Dec. 1839) in which he acknowledged his mistake but pointed out that Frederick Thesiger had disavowed being anyone's nominee: *The Times*, 17 Dec. 1839.

Sir –

A copy of your Paper, 'THE STATESMAN and RECORD', has been sent to me, for which, I presume, I have to thank you. So many newspapers are sent to me, unrecommended by any remarks, that I am frequently under the necessity of allowing them to remain unnoticed.

Fortunately for myself I have read your paper of the 4th, which you sent to me, and am truly rejoiced to perceive that you are alive to the necessity as well as the importance of opposing the Irish Corporations' Bill. I never could account for the indifference which pervaded the public, and the Irish Corporators in particular, on such a vile[6] question as that of altering or depriving them of their Corporations.

To me, from the first, it appeared to be an intolerable act of arbitrary, tyrannical, and revolutionary spoliation, to think of even, much more to attempt, such a measure as the English Corporations' Bill. But how, after having had full experience of the working of the English Corporations' Act, any one who wishes well to his country can desire to impart to Ireland all the evils and perpetuated turmoil which attend, and ever will attend, its operation here, is what I am wholly at a loss to comprehend.

However, judging from your remarks, as well as from the admirable address to the Protestants of Ireland, signed THOMAS JAMES QUINTON, I trust that the eyes of all are now opened to our true interests, and that from henceforth it will be the fixed determination of the Protestants and Protestant Corporators of Ireland to preserve their Corporations (if possible) from the ruthless and revolutionary destruction which has extinguished those useful and ancient establishments in Great Britain.

In acknowledging your kindness I could not refrain from the expression of these brief observations.

I remain, Sir, your obliged and obedient servant,
NEWCASTLE

4. Newcastle's letter on the adoption of the Rural Constabulary Act (1839) in Nottinghamshire. Dated: Clumber, 19 Mar. 1840. Source: *Nottingham Journal*, 27 Mar. 1840.

## TO THE MAGISTRATES OF THE COUNTY OF NOTTINGHAM

Circumstances concurred to prevent any attendance either at the Quarter Sessions at Nottingham on the 9th, or at the subsequent Assizes, when I might have had the pleasure of meeting, and of conferring with my brother Magistrates assembled upon those occasions.

I had not anticipated that any change would have taken place in the arrangements which were made for the election of a Chief Constable at an adjourned Sessions, to be holden at Southwell, on the 21st of next April.

Anxiously desiring to impart my sentiments to you for your attentive consideration, I adopt the only mode now available for the purpose, that of a public address.

---

[6]BL, Add. MS 56368, f. 168: Newcastle to Stanley Lees Giffard, editor of *The Standard*, 29 Feb. 1840, regretting the misprint 'Vile' for 'Vital', '*Which Makes all the difference both in Sense & Style*'. *The Statesman and Record* subsequently published a correction.

In the account of what occurred at the Quarter Sessions on the 9th, as reported in the last Nottingham Journal, I most sincerely rejoice to observe that the Chairman, Colonel Rolleston, announced that the Sessions for the 21st, were adjourned sine die.

I am rejoiced because I hope that the postponement is a prelude to an abandonment altogether of the plan for establishing a Rural Police in this county.

It was a matter of deep regret to me, that I was unavoidably absent when the first meeting took place for considering the propriety of establishing a Rural Police in Nottinghamshire. If I had been present at the meeting, I should have opposed most strenuously, and to the utmost of my power, a measure which I conceive to be fraught with so many of the objections which but too generally characterise modern legislation.

Those gentlemen who were present at the Quarter Sessions, in December last, will remember that I availed myself of the opportunity then afforded me, of expressing my opinion of a measure at once unnational and impolitic. As it had already been discussed, and the system to a certain degree acknowledged, I forbore stating much more than an open declaration of my decided dissent, adding, that however much I was opposed to the measure, I still would endeavour to conform to what might be the deliberate decision of the gentlemen of the county. Up to this period I have observed the rule which I then laid down for my guidance.

The adjournment of the Sessions sine die, appears to me to afford a fair opening for the presumption that the public mind now perceives the vicious tendency and glaring evils of the measure, and of my own knowledge I am aware that it is not a favourite with many Magistrates, and possibly they would not lament its rejection.

Believing that I am acting in unison with the feelings and opinions of others, I absolve myself from restraint, and I resume the course which duty inwardly dictates.

Allow me then to call your most serious attention to the eventful nature of the steps which you are about to take.

If you adopt the new police measure, you will be proceeding to overthrow our ancient scheme of local jurisdiction, as established by the wise [King] Alfred, and transmitted to us by our Saxon forefathers, under which we have long flourished prosperously, and enjoyed greater freedom and security than any nation upon the earth.

Now, what are you to substitute in the place of this tried and admirable system? Surely you will not deliberately adopt the Frenchified [*sic*] system of centralization. If you do, you sacrifice your free institution, and you establish a rule of force and intrigue, instead of a popular control exercising a great and salutary moral influence.

The principle of the measure ought to be steadily opposed. Grant but the principle, and though the first step may appear harmless, yet what is to prevent the establishment of a regular gendarmerie, when the organization is once formed, men appointed, uniforms worn, and communication confirmed with a Minister of State? Where will then be the necessity for an unpaid Magistracy – where the deep and national interests which the country gentleman now so laudably and usefully takes in the laws, rights, liberties, privileges, and valued institutions of his country? Not here! Their departed spirits may shelter amid the centralizing depositaries of Whitehall, from hence they must, of necessity, be banished.

Besides, though quite a minor consideration, look at the enormous expense of a Police establishment – if few in number, it will be inefficient; if numerous, burthensome and oppressive.

Possibly, and I admit it, the ordinary constables may not in all cases be so efficient as could be desired in troubled times, but what can be more practicable than to make the existing constabulary as efficient as any circumstances or any emergency can demand. If you are satisfied "that", in the words of the Act, "the ordinary officers appointed for preserving the peace", &c why not revivify and re-arrange your ordinary constabulary force, adhering steadily to the old system, under suitable regulations. The laws are strong enough, if properly enforced. "Nolumus leges Angliae mutari".[7]

Allow me then most earnestly to entreat you to reject this wily project of our unwearied enemy, which, be assured, has not the welfare of the nation at heart, but seeks by subtlety and Jesuitical cunning to deprive us successively of every valued institution – to change the face of all, so that we shall no longer recognise a single feature – to bewilder, by reckless and unceasing innovations – and when all is chaos and confusion, to make us an easy and defenceless prey for tyranny and spoliation.

Our cause is common and identical, may we do nothing which can compromise the public welfare.

Confidently relying upon my brother Magistrates for the faithful discharge of their duty, and requesting their favourable consideration of this appeal,

I remain their very sincere friend,
NEWCASTLE

5. Newcastle's letter to John Walter on the Nottingham election writ. Dated: Clumber, 25 Mar. 1843. Source: *The Times*, 29 Mar. 1843.

Sir

You are well aware of the interest I took in your success at Nottingham, and when you succeeded I was really gratified, feeling that the town had done itself honour in electing you. It is, therefore, with the deepest regret that I have this morning learned that you have been unseated for Nottingham.

I lament this event less for your own sake than for the public, which will lose the service of a faithful, zealous, and able advocate. You have been most unfortunate; to what is that owing? Have you been ill used? Have you been run down? Have you been persecuted? If so, why? Is your advocacy thorny, inconvenient, or troublesome? Have you outraged the laws of your country, or have you corrupted by wholesale, and inflicted a grievous injury, by debasing those who, but for you, would have been pure and spotless?

I have not lived within 26 miles of Nottingham and yet have known nothing of the town, its proceedings, and its character; and I will take upon me to aver, that far, very far, from its reputation having been injured by you, it is to you that it justly owes a debt of gratitude for amended proceedings, a better tone and feeling, and, consequently, a much improved character.

I happen to have a great stake in this county, and not a small one in and near to Nottingham itself: and this I think I may in truth venture to assert, that if Nottingham

---

[7]'Nolumus leges mutari' – 'we do not want the laws [of England] to be changed'.

Castle were now as it was 12 years ago, it would not now, as then, be made a prey to the flames.[8]

I have the honour to have been enrolled an honorary freeman of Nottingham; and though I have never sought to exercise the right, yet I cannot, without extraordinary alarm and very heartfelt sorrow, see myself and others deprived of our privileges for a single unnecessary hour. It is in contemplation, as I understand, to suspend the issue of a new writ, and thus a great and very important manufacturing and commercial borough town, containing 70,000 inhabitants, and 6,000 voters, is to be temporarily deprived of one of its representatives, solely, it is presumed, because 27 men have been proved to have taken each a few shillings from unaccredited agents, and entirely, as admitted, without your knowledge or sanction.

As one of your late constituents, as one deeply interested in the honour and welfare of the capital of this county in which he is resident, I hesitate not to complain of the contemplation even of such a sweeping measure of harshness and injustice.

If there should subsequently be any design of disfranchising the borough, I shall oppose it by every means in my power.

My feelings are so warmly excited, that I give myself no time for deliberate consideration, and at once tender to you my regret and my brief structures upon the temper of the times. I remain, Sir,

Your very obedient servant,

NEWCASTLE[9]

6. Newcastle's letter to Stanley Lees Giffard, editor of *The Standard*, defending his honesty and integrity. Dated: Clumber, 12 Mar. 1845. Source: N.U.M.D., Ne C 8212.

Sir –

When so few are to be found who will venture to speak favorably of me, I ought to be, & I am particularly obliged to you, for the chivalrous audacity with which you dared to print the favorable view which you are good Enough to Entertain of me & My doings – I very sincerely thank you for Your prompt interposition & ready Self Sacrifice –

It has always been my strange fatality to have my motives & actions misunderstood – & probably few men living, not being public men, have been more reviled & injured than I have been – I long Endured this perversity with patience & resolution, but at last, I became disheartened & disgusted – I found myself standing alone in the maintenance of opinions which I believed to be right, Every thing fell away from me, one Event after another tended to depress my Spirits & my Energy, & to remove those inducements which Stimulated me to Exertion – My health, my peace of mind, my circumstances, as I am not ashamed to avow, arising from no discreditable cause, required my retirement for a season; – unseen & forgotten, you may well imagine that I was astonished at seeing, "The Hafod Estate" Leading a division in the columns of the Standard, appropriated to the report of the debates in Parliament –

---

[8]Newcastle's property, Nottingham Castle, was set on fire during the Reform Bill riots on 10 Oct. 1831: *Unhappy Reactionary*, 83–7.

[9]In a reply (dated 27 Mar. 1843) published below Newcastle's letter, Walter defended his record as MP for Nottingham and assured him that there was no 'contemplated disfranchisement of Nottingham' in anticipation.

I of Course read on with deep interest, & soon perceived the old leaven & the ungenerous motive for introducing my name upon the Scene, finally observing that the malignants [*sic*] professed to be perfectly Satisfied with Lord Lincoln's Statement, as well they might for its plain truth deprived malignity of its power to cavil on –

Pray observe that I by no means object to the watchfulness & untiring Scrutiny of Messrs Hume & Williams & Co. I applaud their Searching Enquiries, but I disapprove of a malign & Prejudicial influence which urges to suppose that Every transaction connected with me & my family must of necessity be Suspicious corrupt & improper –

When fairly Exercised, I should be Exceedingly Sorry to see that the vigilance of these gentlemen was in the Slightest degree relaxed – it gives health & life to them, & is constitutionally wholesome for us – Such refining & scouring is a National benefit, & Although I do not desire to follow the newest fashion, & to overwhelm these Gentlemen with fulsome compliments & eloquent laudations, yet I must confess that it would be really a public misfortune, if the nation were deprived of the now very necessary Services of such lynx-Eyed & indefatigable Scavengers of abuses, such unwearied cleansers of Augean Stables – only, may I caution them not to fall foul of me too hastily or so readily, for I can assure them that their Efforts to prove me a Scoundrel will only serve to make them appear spiteful & ridiculous – I perceive with infinite regret symptoms, on the part of one of these gentlemen, of a semi offensive character which looks too much like that of which he is apt to accuse others –

But, more than Enough of this – Sir, my principal cause for addressing you is not to censure or applaud Mr Hume, but to supply a deficiency – because Lord Lincoln in his natural Earnestness to acquit himself of all blame or dishonesty in the transaction, appears to me to have omitted to state that I also am Justly clear of all blame – I may be too sensitive, but I fancy that I perceive what may be construed by the public into a supposition that I had been requiring something which it would be improper to grant – Such was not the fact – I resisted the Claims of the Crown over my property, which I conscientiously believed not to Exist; & still think were unfounded – but that was all – I neither Expected nor Sought that favor should be shewn to me – I would not for any Consideration of paltry advantage to myself tamper with any Official Man & least of all when that man was my Son, whose honor, virtue & reputation would be dearer to me than my own –

Still, however, my own honor & reputation for unquestionable integrity are most dear to me, & I cannot Endure that Even by implication I should be suspected by my Countrymen & as my vindication, save by yourself, has not been attempted in terms, I must undertake to be my own herald, and once more proclaim my innocence; my negation of dishonesty in any shape, & call upon those who would rob me of my best possession to remember that I am the same man yesterday & today, & that whilst reason maintains her Sway I am not likely to change my nature – "Who Steals my purse steals trash, but he who filches my Good name, steals from me that which naught Enriches him Yet leaves me poor indeed"[10] –

I distinctly declare then that Lord Lincoln has Spoken the truth, the whole truth, & that pure & clear as he is of a Shadow of imputation in this transaction – I am Equally So – & in

---

[10] William Shakespeare, *Othello* (1603), act 3, scene 3, lines 155–61.

fact I only most unwillingly submitted to what by the Condition of the original purchase contract I was compelled to do, to Effect a good & perfectly valid title to the Estate – although I believed that the Vendors to me had for Expediency Engaged to Yield to the Crown a right, to which it was not Entitled – This is my case, & if I were to write volumes I could add nothing to its simple strength –

My Statement, I perceive has already run to a greater length than I intended – but whilst I am on the Subject I have undertaken to be my own herald, & most anxious as I am, more anxious possibly than I may be given Credit for, to stand well with my Countrymen whose Good opinion I value beyond all purse, I must beg to detain Your attention for a few moments whilst I allude to the past & bring you to the present, that you & they may be perfectly aware of what have hitherto been my dishonest gains –

When I began life, I had the fairest prospects before me – in a political point of view I possessed great power – Though in the Eyes of reformers I was regarded as an obnoxious boroughmonger, Still my power & influence were indubitable – I ask – Did I avail myself of my Position to do wrong – Did I sell the Seats for gain, or dishonestly traffick [*sic*] with them, Either privately or politically – Did I Ever act unconstitutionally, as regarded them, or as concerned the State [?] – I avow that to my Knowledge I never did; nor do I Conceive it to be possible that I could; as such proceedings would have been utterly repugnant to my feelings & principles – My Boroughs, then, on the one hand were not productive of profit, whilst on the other they Entailed prodigious losses & Sacrifices, by feeding the interest, by contests, petitions & finally by their parliamentary confiscation, when I was robbed without compensation of a Valuable consideration, probably not Short of £200,000 –

It is true, honorary & honorable distinctions had been conferred upon me when a very Young man – From the Excellent & revered George III I received the Lieutenancy of the County & the Rangership of Sherwood Forest – neither of these Offices Yielding one sixpence of Emolument – These appointments I solicited of the King himself, & they were bestowed without hesitation & with that paternal benignity which from my Earliest youth I invariably Experienced from His Majesty[11] – I Entered upon the Lieutenancy in times of considerable difficulty & much anxiety – I exerted myself to the utmost & I hope not unsuccessfully through many anxious years, when at length tranquillity was restored – I Spared neither my person nor my purse, it was my duty So to do, & I rendered it with alacrity & diligence – perhaps I may have fairly Earned an Expression of thanks from the proper quarter, it would have amply rewarded me, but it was forgotten. Having had the honor of Serving four Sovereigns – I may be permitted to remark that the fee costed in pounds Shillings & pence, was, the payment for the Patents on Every Accession – No great profit here –

The Garter I never would ask for, though frequently wished to solicit the honor – when offered to me I declined it, & suggested that it should be given to the Duke of Wellington, as I had no claim to distinction – I was commanded to accept it & was invested – The honor is great & I hope that I am not insensible of its value – but as my present object is

---

[11]On the recommendation of Spencer Perceval, after Newcastle's solicitation: Spencer Perceval Papers (privately owned by D.C.L. Holland), Bundle xxiii, f. 86: Newcastle to Perceval, 28 Oct. 1809; *The Later Correspondence of George III: Vol. 5*, ed. Arthur Aspinall (Cambridge, 1970), 448–9. For the rangership, see N.U.M.D., Ne C 6124: Perceval to Newcastle, 20 Mar. 1812.

to shew that I cannot be charged with dishonest Gain, I may be permitted to mention that the fees are on a Scale Commensurate with the honor[12] –

As none of these distinctions confer Emolument or patronage, it will be seen that with the Single Exception of pay when on duty with the Yeomanry Corps which I commanded, I have never drawn to the amount of one penny from the public purse – nor have I as yet obtained for my family any Situation of Emolument, though I honestly own that I will not abstain from fair & legitimate Solicitation, if I may see a prospect of Success –

It will be Seen then that the public has no great Cause to complain of my grasping or dishonest gains – It may not have approved of my acts or my opinions, the Ministers of the day may have been of the Same mind, but at least it will be admitted that I have acted from a pure & conscientious conviction, & with an utter disregard of selfish consequences –

So in all measures of which I highly disapproved whether Roman Catholic Emancipation – Reform – Ecclesiastical Commissions – Old Corporations – Irish Policy – Corn Laws – Free trade – with many others – & more recently the Income tax & Tariff, Canada corn & National Education &c in which I may not have had the good fortune to concur with the Minister of the day – on all occasions I have not scrupled to disagree & oppose whether as a Candid friend or a Candid Enemy – nor can I do my duty & abstain from dissent when I see such bills as the Jews disabilities bill, introduced into a Christian Parliament, & look forward to the promised measures which are to give a heavy blow & great discouragement to the Protestant Church whilst Popery is to be elevated & encouraged, & enemies to our Faith are to legislate for that Church which they abhor. Such measures must demand the stern opposition of Every Christian & Every conscientious Protestant – Thus, when I have differed I have never done so from waywardness or faction, but as a painful performance of a duty, from an inward persuasion that though interest & Ease forbad it, principle & conviction dictated & required it – These have been & I trust will continue to be my motives, my incentives & my Guides; & although I will not pretend to assert that I have been right, I can safely declare that I believed myself not to have been wrong –

Many, perhaps, may remark; more fool he for his pains, why does he not follow the way of the world? I can only reply that Such ways are not my ways, & that I could derive no satisfaction from exchanging principle for expediency – So like a wounded deer I am discountenanced by the whole herd –

My present position seems to be this – Though a determined upholder of the Church of England, & of the State of Protestantism & of Protestant ascendancy, an undisguised Conservative of the ancient & once admired British Constitution & the Institutions of our Country – I am disclaimed by those who I am compelled to think should be what I am – The Post which I held for many years as the Sovereign's Lieutenant in this County, my Sovereign was advised to deprive me of, & I was unceremoniously discarded, merely because I disdainfully resisted the molestations of one of Her Majesty's high officers – & this after having Served four Sovereigns loyally, faithfully, zealously & I hope efficiently.

You & others may think that I have written bitterly, it may be so, neither my recollections, nor my present situation are very pleasing or flattering – However, I may say with the

---

[12]BL, Add. MS 38328, f. 3: Liverpool to Newcastle, 12 June 1812. The fees payable are outlined in Ne C 6123/1: Sir Isaac Heard to Newcastle, 25 June 1812. Wellington was the next appointment to the Garter after Newcastle.

Frenchman – "J'ai tout perdu que mon honneur"[13] – & that I thank God is preserved to me, & it is a true & lasting consolation –

I care for, I want nothing for myself, that my Sovereign or a Minister can confer upon me – Fortunately for myself I am unambitious of power, & best pleased in the Endeavour to be a good subject and a good Citizen – & it is well that I am so, for I may liken myself as it were to an infected Plague man – Who dares to come in contact with me? To do any thing for my benefit or advantage would be to render himself suspected, he would immediately be clapped into quarantine & subjected to potent fumigations & the Severest Scrutiny –

I will add no more, though I might yet add much. Your patience must be severely tested – I have Selected a few leading points by which to illustrate the Exposition of my case, to vindicate myself from unworthy & unmerited Suspicion, & to prove to my Countrymen that if I may possess their good opinion, & the blessing of a clear conscience, I shall have attained a summit of self gratulation & self Esteem, invaluable only as I may Know that it may not be wholly undeserved –

I remain, Sir,

Yours' very Sincerely

NEWCASTLE

P.S. I have delayed writing for some days, that I might not give vent to my feelings when I was strongly nettled, & somewhat disturbed.[14]

7. *Two letters, in opposition to any increased grant or endowment of Maynooth College in Ireland, From His Grace the Duke of Newcastle, K.G. Addressed to the People of England.* Dated: Clumber, 13, 19–23 Apr., 13 May 1845. Source: N.U.M.D., Ne C 5379.[15]

MY DEAR FELLOW-COUNTRYMEN,

In the sincerity of my heart, and under an anxiety which overwhelms me, may I address to you a few hurried lines, which are intended to exhort you to adopt the most decisive measures ere the fit time for action be passed. It is now late in the afternoon, and I have only just looked cursorily over the contents of this day's post; my observations must, therefore, be very brief indeed. I would have addressed you at an earlier period, had I not wished to see what course Mr Gladstone would take. I now perceive that it is an adverse though not an intelligible course. I had hoped that he might have been found true to the great cause of Protestantism, and that in him might be supplied another among the too few and able champions of the neglected and almost persecuted Established Church of England. Alas! you have only to choose between submitting to be tramped upon, or making a loud demand by your Public voice.[16]

[13] 'I lost everything but my honour'.

[14] The manuscript version includes three amendments, the last of which was used as the postscript in the published version. The others were: 'Has not Mr Hume been appointed a Member of Some Commission for the promotion of Harbours & Fortifications' and 'Labour without pay or patronage'.

[15] This pamphlet includes a short preface and, as an appendix, a 'Recapitulation of Advice to Constituents as to their choice of Members to represent them in Parliament, in the event of a General Election'.

[16] Having read Newcastle's letter, Gladstone composed a draft response 'for consideration' which he later cancelled: *Gladstone Diaries*, iii, 447; BL, Add. MS 44261, f. 100: Gladstone to Newcastle, unsent draft, [15] Apr.

You must rouse yourselves as one man. Those who are attached to the Protestant Faith – those who wish to preserve the predominance of the English Established Church as the protection and safeguard of these realms – those who will not submit to the imposition of the Income Tax, by which means a surplus is extracted from your pockets, that is, to pay a sinful endowment of a rebellious Popish seminary, Maynooth, in Ireland, and this too, when the smallest portion of a pound is denied to your own pure and truly Christian Church. Look well into this perfidious proceeding; see with your own eyes, judge with your own good understandings, act from the stoutness of your own noble British hearts. But be quick! Lose not an instant; call county meetings, town meetings, village meetings; require your representatives to represent you in reality, and call upon them to support your petitions. You are betrayed, you are sacrificed in more instances than one, you are the victims of some deep scheme which is not yet sufficiently developed – but be beforehand with the schemers, although they may think themselves safe in their Parliamentary potency. If you hate and disapprove of this awful beginning of future awful intentions, speak out and act determinedly, insist on attention being paid to your national feelings, to your love of God, and love of country.

Petition! Petition! Petition![17] do this with zeal, peacefulness, and order, but with a per-severance and determination, that nothing shall overcome – do this, if it accords with your religious feelings, and national sentiments; if you do it, you may save our cherished land from the wrath of God, and perfidy of Man; pause even, and the same Rule which will revolu-tionise your Church, will doom your fields to be uncultivated, and your whole agricultural system to a ruthless destruction and starving desolation.

I pray you, my dear fellow-countrymen, to receive this brief and crude address written in the instant, as a proof of my deep interest in our national welfare. I make this call upon your attention, that you may be forewarned of what may happen, not by a factious demagogue, but by an unflinching Conservative of all our most loved and approved national rights, privileges, laws, and valued institutions of Church and State.

Allow me to sign myself,

Your ever faithful Friend,

NEWCASTLE

Clumber, April 19 to 23, 1845

MY DEAR COUNTRYMEN

When I last addressed you time pressed, and I was compelled to write hastily and briefly. I then had no opportunity for apology or explanation; but now that I have more leisure, and that I again venture to intrude myself upon your notice, I feel that it is incumbent upon me both to apologise and to explain – to apologise, because it may seem arrogant and presumptuous that I should assume to myself any title to address you in such a fashion

---

16 (*continued*) 1845. Gladstone told Newcastle, 'I do not feel warranted to offer to my constituents an unconditional surrender of my seat. But if it be their opinion, or if it be the opinion of Your Grace, that the course I am pursuing has falsified any expectations that I have caused them to entertain, I shall be at once prepared to retrieve into their hands the trust they have committed to me'. See 30 Apr. 1845.

[17] For the impact of this phrase, see Thelwall, *Proceedings of the Anti-Maynooth Conference*, lii–liii.

– to explain, because you may naturally desire to know why I, of all men, should attempt to place myself in a position of so much difficulty and responsibility – this position, I am well aware, is as unusual as it is hazardous; but, having fallen into it, I cannot now abandon, whilst you permit or rather do not oppose, my usurpation of it.

Pardon, then, this transgression in whosesoever eyes it may appear to be one, and generously receive the following explanation; – I will candidly acknowledge that when I wrote the letter to the editor, dated the 12th, and which was published in the *Standard* of the 25th of March, my object was vindication, perhaps not unaccompanied with complaint, thereon founding, as I hoped, and should it be necessary, my complete justification in the view of every fair and impartial judge. Of the result from that publication, I never could have entertained the most remote idea – I never could have dreamed of the consequences which have followed it. I was perfectly unconscious of the existence of any good will towards or even of any favorable thought about me, for although my constant aspiration has been to effect all the good in my power for what I consider to be the real benefit and welfare of my country – I may add of mankind in general – yet I believed myself to be so little worthy of public notice, and so inefficient for any useful purpose, that my wonder was unbounded, my astonishment overpowering, but my gratitude inexpressible, when from all quarters of this great and glorious country I received the kindest, indeed almost affectionate, expressions of good will, attachment, and much more, but which I may not repeat – giving me every encouragement, and assuring me of confidence in my good intentions, consistency, constancy, and so forth. Until then, I believed that I was working alone, unheeded, unobserved, and unsupported, pursuing in privacy my usually undeviating course. Truly a sorry, unenviable, and uninspiring state! Yet one which, as I had happened to avow it, has been made the subject of jest and derision by some; though, as I can forgive, as I shall very readily forget their jeers or their derisions, so, if I may win and retain your continued confidence and regard, the mirth and exultation will be mine, the lamentation their's [*sic*].

Thus, most unexpectedly, though not equivocally encouraged, I felt that I had a new being – that my existence was not a matter of indifference to my countrymen; that, by the peculiarity of my situation, a responsibility was thrown upon me; that I evidently had a duty to perform which had been allotted to me, and, if my perception were correct, that the question was – How can I do the most good with the smallest possibility of doing harm? – how can I, by any feeble effort of mine, contribute most largely towards the solid and lasting benefit of my country?

I should apprize you that hitherto, as now, I have had no adviser; I have purposely abstained from communicating politically with any individuals who are connected with the political world. Whatever I might do I wished to do purely, openly, and without bias, – not by combination, not by faction, not by subtlety; I was resolved to be clear of the charge of being a political intriguer – a character in my mind essentially mischievous and shunnable [*sic*].

I was thus driven to commune with myself, and constrained to act upon my own judgment and responsibility; should I have erred the fault is all my own.

Strongly, perhaps overduly [*sic*], incited, however, by a warm sense of your goodness and generosity, I owned an irresistible impulse to rest my whole confidence upon you, and to make one with you to accomplish the reclamation of our misgoverned country.

Reviewing the past, and looking to the future, I considered that we were living under the perfection of executive rule – a free monarchy – but, that we were idly squandering our immense advantages, and perhaps inadvertently, though not the less insanely, forging our own bonds and shackles. If a remedy were to be applied to the growing evil, and to an enormous public wrong, the task of inviting public attention to it must fall upon some one; no other person seemed disposed to put himself forward; I resolved to lead a forlorn hope, and to throw myself into the breach. I decided to address myself to the whole nation, and from the kindness and consideration already received I was persuaded that you would not think me presumptuous in so doing, seeing that my motive was distinctly one of a grateful return, which I owe, not of self-exultation or aggrandisement, which I absolutely repudiate.

I have not scrupled thus to unbosom myself to you, that we may perfectly understand each other.

My address of the 13th, though brief and hurried, has been rightly understood, and received in the kindliest manner. Accident has embarked me with you in a great cause. I now look, and so I hope do you, to the regeneration and redemption of our country. I shall not hang back, if you will persevere and encourage. Meriting your approbation, and meeting with your acquiescence in my views, I shall cheerfully and fearlessly proceed, in conjunction with you, to rescue our religion, our state, and our national and individual interests from the intolerable oppression and thraldom of parliamentary intrigue and machinations, with all the innumerable evils attendant thereon.

Having written so much in extenuation of what I have taken upon myself to do, I must now proceed to the performance of the painful part of my presumed duty, in thus addressing you a second time, intending to supply evident deficiencies in my former brief address.

I must deal critically and severely with measures and political delinquencies, frequently emanating from one [Sir Robert Peel] whose friendship and intimacy I have rejoiced in, from whom it pains me to differ widely, but from whom, if conscientiously differing, I should be ashamed of myself if I did not openly and publicly avow my dissent from his doctrines, his measures, and his contrivances.

It must then appear to you that the present struggle is made to be a contest between the Parliament and the people. The national opinion is one way, the majority in Parliament is in another. Why is this? Ought not the representation to reflect the opinions of its constituents – especially so, it may be supposed, since its imagined purification by the Reform Bill? The fact, however, is otherwise. I would not object, neither I am convinced would you, that a man should vote according to his conscience; but if he knows that he is so doing in opposition to the declared sentiments of his constituents he is bound to resign the trust into their hands. This would be honourable. If he failed to do so, you, no doubt, would take good care that he should never again be chosen to represent you. I will hereafter refer to what should be done in this case.

But it is hinted, "Oh, if the Minister finds himself in a minority he will resign, or else compel the majority to regorge [*sic*] their votes". You probably will reply, "Well, let him do so, and we shall be quit of a very dangerous Minister; as to the other, it is an event of such rare and hitherto unparalleled occurrence, that we hope never again to witness an exhibition equally disgraceful to the forcer and the forced, and so derogatory to the dignity and use-fulness of Parliament". The example, however, furnishes a proof of the unmitigated power and straight-waistcoat control which is exercised over the well-meaning and independent portion of the House of Commons.

'Then', they observe, 'what are we to do? If the Minister is beaten and resigns, where are we to find a successor, and who can supply his place with a chance of carrying on the Government?". I admit the full pertinence of this observation. I have observed with fearful anxiety this growing mischief, I have not been blind to the strategetical [*sic*] manner in which the Government has entrenched itself in the parliamentary camp; nor have I witnessed without great personal inquietude [*sic*], and continued alarm and jealousy, the successful modes and inducements by which the Minister has drawn around himself almost all those who could be troublesome in opposition. It has been frequently remarked that all who have any pretension to the name of Statesman are on the Government side, and how can any other administration be formed, since all pretension to statesmanship is engrossed by the existing Government? It should be recollected that many requisites are necessary to form a Statesman, besides some degree of cleverness and being able to recite a smart or passable speech; or being a very praiseworthy office man, very drudging, diligent, and attentive to business; or an eager and supple Ministerial partisan; or an assiduous parliamentary tactician, and perhaps not very squeamish purveyor of votes. Such men, though they may be useful in their way, are not consequently or necessarily statesmen. A real Statesman need not be a Machiavel – he should benefit the State not perplex and embroil it. A high range of intellect, a great mind, a great soul, should be his, with ample experience, a sufficiency of practical knowledge of home and foreign concerns; a capacity for viewing affairs solidly and extensively, embracing the future as well as comprehending the present; possessed of prudence, sagacity, judgment, unquestioned integrity, and irreproachable public virtue. To such a man may be awarded his rightful claim to the name of Statesman. Surely we may hope and believe that there can be no lack of equally good statesmen in this kingdom of England, if opportunity should call them forth.

Of the Prime Minister's talent in debate, his dexterity in parliamentary management, his knowledge of his audience, his extensive information, his long experience in public affairs, and of his parliamentary omnipotence there can be no question; but of his right use of these mighty advantages there may be, and is, very great question indeed. I have elsewhere stated, some time ago, how that by loosening one stone in the building we have engendered the whole fabric – so, repealing the Combination-laws brought about the repeal of the Corporation and Test Act – as a consequence the emancipation of the Roman Catholics followed – then reform in parliament; from thence arose a cry against the Church; to appease this cry the Ecclesiastical commission was devised – the revenues or resources of the Church establishment were to be drained, and exhausted, Bishoprics and various other dignities abolished – everything done to abuse, humiliate, and impoverish the Church which an improvident meddling could devise, and only stopping where shame forbade to proceed further; next, the old Corporations were destroyed – the Education Bill passed; and these acts followed one upon the other; one in consequence of another, and one after the other, were recommended to the Legislature, and the reason why was, apparently, because the preceding acts had become law.[18] I will not enumerate many other bad measures, such as the new Poor-law, Rural Police Act, &c., enacted, no doubt, to restrain that very poverty and crime which confusion and uncertainty had created. My object is to show that one bad precedent begot another, and that this stratagem has been systematically pursued, as a sure though unperceived mode of stealing a march, of sapping our morality, undermining our civil and religious institutions, and, in fact, of revolutionising the state.

[18]Newcastle outlined this argument in *Thoughts in Times Past*, xviii–xxvi.

As far as my recollection serves me, not one good measure has passed since the entrance into office of the present Administration; the *amor patriae* [love of country] appears to me to have been lamentably disregarded, and the *amor sui* [love of self] cherished as a more expedient and more suitable substitute, Whatever misdeeds were committed by the former Government – and they were many and glaring – they were forced out of office by the expectation that the new Government would set all to rights; but, to our astonishment, we soon perceived that the very measures the enforcement of which unseated the former, were adopted by the new Administration with an utter disregard of its own credit, and of our private feelings and national interests.

I ask you, whether your expectations have been fulfilled? – whether you are satisfied with the honesty, good faith, and gratitude of our rulers? – or whether bitter disappointment and unalterable distrust do not more generally prevail?

The cultivator of the soil is in utter despondency and alarm; he has been the most ill-used and most neglected of our fellow-subjects; he knows not how to act. He feels from sad experience that he who is the mainstay of the country is buffeted about in bewildering uncertainty, knowing that he is not protected or encouraged, but milked like his own cows, or shorn like his own sheep, to pay, mayhap, for some Popish endowment or other misapplication of his contributions. When he complains, he is derided, and told, if you are not satisfied with the corn-law, the tariff, the Canada [corn] law, or other depressive measures, you must take them as we give them to you, and make the best of them. We know that you will be put to it, and, without hard labour and industry, you will scarcely be able to stand your ground and compete with the foreigner, but still there is a road to wealth open to you; seek for – and you will find it by a spirited expenditure in application of the latent secrets of science and chemistry.

What is the consequence of all this? Prices fall. The farmer is obliged to economise, fewer labourers are employed, many are thrown out of work, and necessitated to seek shelter and subsistence in the [workhouse] unions. Of what consequence can it be to the poor labourer that prices should be low if he has not the means wherewith to purchase food and raiment? The landlord must suffer with his tenants and his poor labourers, and it is impossible to foresee how far the mischief of the present system may extend.

But you must be already weary of following me through this (from memory) imperfect enumeration of bad and, as I think, dangerous measures, because uncalled for and empirical, and tending to alter the very nature of minds and things.

I will merely touch upon the late Jew's Bill and the Maynooth endowment, and then proceed to remedies.

The bill to remove the disabilities of the Jews is one of the most remarkable features of the day, exhibiting the laxity of principle which has crept in, and the mawkish sentimentality and liberalism, as it is called, which distinguish too many of our public men, and lead to the very verge of indifference as to the prevalence of any particular religion, too often to the forgetfulness of any religion as a necessary ingredient in all Christian legislation. Towards the Jews, individually, I profess to entertain a very strong and deep interest, and it may be that I am impressed with a persuasion approaching to conviction that their redemption is nigh at hand. I should glory in their conversion, and gladly behold their exaltation to the first rank of nations; but is any Christian legislator justified in raising to political honour or authority one who, whilst he continues a Jew, must continue to deny our Saviour, and must, *de facto*, be incompetent to exercise any political authority over a Christian community?

Show him every kindness and consideration – extend to him the fullest toleration; but, without grave offence, you cannot confer upon him any administrative functions. Here, again, is exemplified the danger of the new doctrine of legislation – so and so has been done for the Moravians and others, it will be injustice not to do the same for the Jews, as if it were possible to palliate the commission of one crime by alleging that another had passed unpunished.

We are now arrived at the Maynooth Bill, and a more daring attempt to take a nation by storm, and force upon it a measure repugnant to all faithful Protestants, conscientiously regarded by them as a criminal deed, an artful decoy to a feared apostasy, a jesuitical entrapment of a deluded few, to attain by small incipient means, the accomplishment of a most formidable and most guilty end, never was perpetrated by any rulers of a free country.

Many conjectures may be hazarded to account for this extraordinary attempt – surmise alone can account for it; but this we know, that, although might may be applied to overpower right, the exercise of such power is intolerable and odious, and submission to it is rendered as impossible as it would be culpable; and here I arrive at our remedy. It is short and simple.

I mentioned in a former part that I would refer to what should be done in the case of constituents and representatives. I ventured to recommend you to petition; but, if petitioning should fail, you may follow it up by calling upon your representatives to resign their trusts.[19] Suppose that they decline; follow this up by strong declaratory resolutions; persist in this course, and try its effect; if unavailing, which I can hardly believe to be possible – still continue a steady and resolute determination – so situated, the Minister may resign; he will calculate that no other Administration can be formed, and that he must be recalled and reinstated, but in this calculation, if it should be your pleasure to defeat it, you will do well to act thus:– Whenever the time arrives, be unanimously resolved to elect such members only as you know to be well affected to the preservation and maintenance of our purely protestant constitution in Church and State, to the exclusion of all noxious measures. If you cannot find them among those who have usually represented you, search for others – look for worth wherever and in whomsoever it lie – look for devotion to his country's cause, for sound sense, for a loyal subject, a faithful citizen, a good man, and a good Churchman. The highest talents, unless combined with these, are more than worthless. Care not for wealth if you can find integrity – refrain from all sordid considerations – banish the very idea of bribery, or payment of votes, or spending of money. Such proceedings would do you unfading honour, and it would immortalize you; success must await it, and you will be invincible, whilst you act wisely and well. I confidently call upon all good men to act thus, and show themselves to be true patriots of a new school. To Dissenters, I would say, what form of religious faith can equal or surpass the pure, the simple, yet sublime and earnest doctrine of the Established Church of England? Join her if you can, and make one of an united brotherhood; but, if you cannot, still give all your support to a Church and State which tolerate you and tolerate all. To those who entertain party views, I will say, throw aside party, and act upon principle. You are Britons, you love your country and your Queen – let us all unite for their welfare; they pressingly require your manful aid and

---

[19] For the use of Newcastle's name and influence with Arthur Duncombe, MP for East Retford, see Thelwall, *Proceedings of the Anti-Maynooth Conference*, 145.

pious defence; they are in difficulty and danger, and demand your honest and strenuous support.

Party has done but little for you of late years. When has it promoted any good end, or anything but a competition in change and destruction? – one side, when in power, scarcely differing in a shade from the other. Reform has proved to be a delusion – political economy a mischievous conceit. But, of all the subtle contrivances for misgovernment planned by the great corrupter of souls, political expediency has been the bane of modern times. Rejoicing in crookedness and deformity, it miscalls good, evil, and transposes vice for virtue; itself generated in a total abandonment of all principle, it corrupts, demoralises, and degrades all who give in to its practices, engendering perfidy, deceit, treacherous dereliction, and every nameable political wickedness, most unworthy of every great, of every noble mind. Let it be shunned, disgraced, and relinquished.

Lay the foundation of a new school, and henceforth let the school of political virtue be the basis of England's grandeur as it would be of her settled happiness.

It may be said, this is an Utopian vision. But I reply, why so? Is it impossible for a nation to be good and great? If we may be nationally good, if we habituate ourselves to the practice of virtue, assuredly our virtue will bind us together by ties of mutual respect and mutual confidence; suspicion and discord will cease, and something more approaching to one mind will appease our contentions, curb our evil passions, "idem velle atque idem nolle, vera est amicitia";[20] united thus, and acting in faithful union for our country's welfare, must we not be as powerfully great as we shall have proved ourselves nationally good?

I will allow that little short of a miracle may of a sudden constitute us such a nation as this; but let us make a beginning – the British constitution was not built up in a day, although it may be destroyed in an incredibly short space of time. Form yourselves into a fit state of heart and mind for the practice of political virtue, and on this occasion let your conversion be as sudden as it may be sure – no relapse is to be apprehended from such suddenness of exalted and virtuous purposes – and procrastination, or irresolution, should your minds be willing but your spirits weak, would only give advantage to those whose evil influences so sorely oppress us.

Heresies and false doctrines have had their sway; duped thousands have been followers and worshippers and disciples, whether in religion or politics. Error, I am aware, has its blandishments and its alluring attractions, while truth has been compelled to halt along with a far scantier following, and, with chastened diffidence, rarely adventuring to contend with its more popular rival.

But, my dear countrymen, let it not be thus for ever. The time, I believe, is favourable; events, I believe, are ripening, if not ripe. Cast off the dynasty of error, imposture, and impurity; cause it to cease by inanition, and let that of healing and healthy truth prevail; enthrone it with your free and generous sympathy, your united acclamation, your calm, moderate, but settled and determined resolve.

May I venture to add a few words of caution? Should it be your disposition of mind to think well of these remarks, and to adopt them into your practice, carefully study to repel all fanciful theories and experiments. We should have but one object in view – the steady

---

[20]'Idem velle atque idem nolle, ea demum firma amicitia est' – 'Agreement in likes and dislikes – this, and this only, is what constitutes true friendship'. A quotation from Lucius Sergius Catilina [Catiline] (108–62 BC).

maintenance of our Protestant constitution. This maintenance has been threatened. We must oppose and overcome the menacing danger which besets us. We, as a nation, are now so strangely situated, that no ordinary appliance will avail; we have wandered into the maxes of error; and are entangled in the perplexities of a false, tainted, and unprincipled system; purification is our only remedy, political regeneration the consequence; the prevalence of truth and honesty will effect this, and render us politically virtuous. Obedient to the laws, walking firmly in the steps of the Constitution, we may zealously rally for their secure protection, and to the succour of our gracious and beloved queen, whose painful position we must all lament, as much as we are well aware that it is now one of extreme difficulty and danger.

With this caution I conclude. Grateful, indeed, shall I be if this address be well received and rightfully understood. I have endeavoured to collect my thoughts and opinions, and to convey them to you in plain and intelligible language. If I have failed, it is not for want of anxious care and study; still you will give me credit for good intentions, of that I am well assured – actuated by no ill-will against any individual, by no hatred or malice in my heart, I would not personally offend even my greatest enemy; I entertain no unkindly feelings towards any human being; but when I see danger, I would avert it. I can only hope to succeed by warning, by exposing error which involves the conduct of individuals, and by espousing truth which is to counteract that error.

It is our inherent right to canvass political errors, political measures, and political government. I have ventured to do this in a political sense only. I could have no right, nor have I dared, to make allusion or to cast the slightest reflection upon private motives or private character; and I beg that this may be distinctly understood.

It is the political system which I have fairly attacked and have endeavoured to expose; and if by this appeal to you, and by the constitutional expression of your sentiments, imminent evil may be averted from the State, the Queen and Parliament be relieved from the intrusion of bad measures – and if, instead of beautifying and endowing Popish colleges, our surplus millions may be worthily spent in erecting Protestant Temples for the worship of the God who blesses and defends us – then, indeed, shall I rejoice, and behold with admiring thankfulness the prosperity of the British empire.

Allow me to sign myself,

Your grateful and ever faithful Friend,

NEWCASTLE

P.S. Contrary to my first expectation, I have found the task which I had imposed upon myself to be one of extreme delicacy. I commenced and wrote this address between the 19th and 23d [*sic*] of April, and to ensure a due consideration of the whole matter of it, instead of issuing it in print, I have read and re-read it whilst it has remained with me – most anxiously desiring that nothing exceptionable should proceed from my pen, nothing, that is, which by indiscretion or imprudence should injure the great public cause which I desire to serve. I wish I may have succeeded, and that you may not have to blame me for having again addressed you. I find that this letter has run to very much greater length than I think advisable, or than I had anticipated. I tried to condense, but I do not possess the art, and found greater condensation, to me, impossible.

I now take my leave with every fervent wish for your welfare.

N.

May 13, 1845[21]

8. Newcastle's letter to William C. Espy, Secretary, Dublin Protestant Operative Association and Reformation Society. Dated: Clumber, Apr. 28, 1845. Source: *The Statesman and Dublin Christian Record*, 6 May 1845.

Sir –

I have had the pleasure of receiving your letter of the 19th transmitting a copy of a resolution passed at a meeting of the Dublin Protestant Operative Society, expressive of their thanks for, and approbation of, my appeal to the people of Great Britain. I am very sensible of the kindness with which my endeavours to be useful have been viewed. When Great Britain was mentioned in the resolution, I hope it was intended to include Ireland as an integral part of Great Britain. Whatever may be the geographical distinctions, I know none; and save the intervention of the Channel, I trust we may always consider ourselves, and ever remain, one and indivisible.

I am, sir, your obliged and obedient servant
NEWCASTLE

9. Newcastle's letter to the Electors of South Nottinghamshire on the by–election. Dated: Clumber, 17 Feb. 1846. Source: *The Illustrated London News*, 28 Feb. 1846.

Gentlemen –

In addressing you on the present occasion, I am quite aware of the unusualness of the proceeding. For the last ten days I have noticed what has been passing in our county with indescribable pain and annoyance. It seems to me that the time has more than arrived when a period ought to be put to the discord which now agitates us. I deeply lament that any member of my family should be the cause of this most unnecessary agitation. I have most deeply to lament it for still more serious reasons than because it creates odious quarrels, feverish convulsions, expense, and extreme inconvenience among yourselves.

Lord Lincoln has been the deluded victim of bad counsel, and in no instance more conspicuously than in the course which he has pursued upon the present occasion.

Under this influence has he been induced to accept an inferior office, that his seat may be vacated, and a desperate experiment attempted. He suddenly appeared among you before you could be aware of the transaction. He does this, as he tells you, that he may make an appeal from the Protection meeting to the whole constituency. By this surprise he has been enabled to ascertain the undisguised and almost universal feelings and opinions of this important county.

---

[21] See BL, Add. MS 56368, ff. 172–3: Newcastle to Stanley Lees Giffard, 13 May 1845, explaining the delayed response.

Doubtless it was expected that the constituency would be found to possess easy consciences, and that the public voice would be raised in favour of Free Trade, and the other newly disclosed enormities of Sir Robert Peel's Government, although we have neither asked for nor desire Free Trade nor any other vicious and revolutionary system. But why should any one from authority be sent as a Government emissary to force upon us opinions which we hate, and the country hates and deprecates with indignant hostility – and why should anyone fortified with Government means, presume to operate the disgraceful seductions which are said to be used upon this lamentable occasion – and why are you to be drilled into the adoption of the ruinous principles and fatal doctrines at which you now naturally shudder and recoil? Our worthy farmers are sturdy and clear-sighted, and your phalanx is not to be broken by bold axioms, artful assertions, or any other evil appliances.

Still, however, the move has been made; and although we may justly condemn it as a very great mistake, there may be some shadow of pretence for it, if it were intended by the experiment to test the public opinion. Now, however, that it has been in a course of most diligent trial for ten days, that the fullest proof has been elicited, and the result known to be totally adverse to the new doctrines, and unsuccessful to the deceived advocate of them, in the sincerity of my heart, and as a member of the constituency, I suggest to Lord Lincoln the propriety of withdrawing from an useless, and, to all, most painful struggle against a long-tried and approved principle and policy, and at once to restore tranquillity to the country, and the undisturbed possession of its unquestionable convictions.

In the anxious hope that this address may meet with your approval, and that the appeal may not be made in vain,
I remain, Gentlemen, your sincere and faithful servant
NEWCASTLE

10. Newcastle's letter to his countrymen on the repeal of the corn laws. Dated: London, Mar. 1846. Source: *The Times*, 14 Mar. 1846.

To my Countrymen –

Encouraged by your former kindness and consideration, I trust that I may not be mistimed nor unacceptable that I now again venture to intrude upon your attention.

About this time last year I presumed to address you upon a subject of intense national interest then in progress. I then hazarded an opinion that the same ruthless hand which planned the elevation of Popery would not scruple to work the downfall of our agricultural system. You have now too much cause to lament with me that my words have not proved untrue. You have witnessed with astonishment and detestation the hideous treachery and tergiversation of public men, which burst forth suddenly upon your incredulous view in the full blaze of its triumphant deformity, supported by a shameless effrontery unexampled in the annals of well-regulated states.

As virtue is proverbially said to be its own reward, so treachery may be said to be its own perdition – and thus it is in this case. The Prime Minister expected that he had so contrived and so securely plotted his arrangements that success was certain, failure impossible. No man was ever more mistaken in his calculations, no minister ever more deceived in an estimate of his own controlling (if not despotic) power, and individual essentiality. Instead of dismay from the fear of losing him, he finds that no one desires to retain his services, and where he thought to raise entreaty, he has only raised a pitiless storm of scoffs and indignation. Faith and confidence in him have ceased, and his political sun is set.

Under protective laws we have flourished; under them and by them – observe well, not in spite of them – Great Britain has grown into an empire of the first rank for wealth and power in the universe. Who, in truth, can deny this fact? Not the merchant, the manufacturer, the tradesman, the shopkeeper, the artisan, or that humbler but most deserving class upon whose industry and labour the wealthiest merchants and producers depend, as in turn the workman depends upon his employer for ample remuneration in the shape of liberal wages; all of these must perceive that without protection their prosperity will decline into abject poverty, and that a full protection is as indispensably necessary to them as to the British farmers and labourers in husbandry.

Now, then, gentlemen of England, stand forward. The clergy, bold yeomen, trusty farmers, worthy labourers – all those interested in the cultivation of the soil – stand forward. Must I stop here? No, general protection is a question of vital interest to you also, and you cannot, must not, shall not, be excluded from the appeal. Without the grossest injustice to your high national feelings, and an unpardonable insult to your patriotism, to your acknowledged intellect, and comprehensive understanding, I cannot omit you. I call upon you, merchants, manufacturers, and traders of England, to come forth frankly, boldly, nobly, as an essentially component part of our great English brotherhood – stand forward, join us freely, without any mental reservation whatsoever and unite with us, your British brothers, with all your heart and all your soul, in defence and preservation of our Church and State, for involved in and most intimately connected with them is the all absorbing question of general protection to British industry.

I confidently call upon you, all and each, for your assistance. By your timely aid and determined support you may bring into power men who, I trust, think like yourselves, and will act as yourselves – men who have no party but their country, no aspirations but for its solid and permanent welfare – who are identified with you and your interests, and who, by their plan dealing, honesty, and English uprightness, will scorn all crooked ways and will undeviatingly [*sic*] pursue those of equity and truth.

You must be prompt and energetic, A general election may be near at hand. I have just witnessed in my own county a most extraordinary result of British virtue and moral courage, emanating from and conducted by the agricultural interest alone, which may well be a model of action and an example to the whole country.

Believing, as I confidently believe, that we all most earnestly desire the peace, welfare, order, and prosperity of our loved native soil, allow me to entreat you to adopt the measures so successfully employed in Nottinghamshire.

Then lose not a day or an hour; instantly and busily set to work to form and organise protection societies in every county in England, specially make choice of a good and influential chairman and a working committee – associate with you, all the friends of protection to British industry, whether farmers or others – make yourselves acquainted with all your brother electors – pay the closest and most minute attention to the registers – and select and communicate with fit, and none but the fittest men, to represent you in Parliament. Leave nothing undone; let your preparations be complete at the earliest period; and, this done, calmly, but most determinedly, await the hour of trial, and, whenever it does arrive, take into your own hands what is your own business: regulate, execute everything for yourselves, with the energy, the intelligence, the just and fair, but unbending determination of

Englishmen, and you may reasonably hope that by God's blessing you may be enabled to save your insulted and injured country from the most fearful perils which the machinations or infatuation of false men and treacherous statesmen ever devised for the degradation and ruin of the land of their birth – a land whose natives are worthy of all protection, and deserving the most ardent exercise of your purest and most exalted patriotism.

Believe me to be your ever faithful friend
NEWCASTLE

P.S. I can scarcely anticipate that this revolutionary measure, now under discussion, can ever become the law of the land; but if, most unfortunately, it should be so, assuredly a future national majority will at once decide that an enactment so atrocious shall no longer continue on the statute book.

11. Newcastle's letter to John Thadeus Delane, editor of *The Times*, defending the aristocracy. Dated: Clumber, 20 Aug. 1847. Source: *The Times*, 26 Aug. 1847.

TO THE EDITOR OF THE TIMES

Sir –

After several days' reflection I have concluded upon sending you the enclosed letter, which I was averse to forward yesterday, and on the preceding day there was no post from hence to London.

Possibly I ought not to notice articles in any newspaper of such a nature as that referred to in *The Times* of the 13th,[22] and I should entirely disregard them elsewhere; but the editor (or editors) of *The Times* is not an ordinary man; he has great power and influence, and he should feel himself to be a responsible man, and accountable for the mischief which he may create.

I am aware of the hazard to which I expose myself, and that there are writers in *The Times* who, if they think fit, can lampoon me most severely; let them write nothing but what is true, and I shall be surprized indeed if they can make anything out of a bad case. I have waited to see if the sentiments and the article referred to would be noticed by others. The *Morning Post* alone has referred to it partially in a very good article. Seeing this, I have entered the lists on behalf of the calumniated body to which I belong; and although the least worthy of being their champion, I trust that I do not injure their cause, nor misrepresent what must be the feeling of the nobility and that of the mass of the honest people of this fair-play loving nation.

I trust that you will do me the favour to insert this note as well as the letter in your next number.[23]

[22]On 13 Aug. 1847, *The Times* considered 'the tyrannical influence of great landed proprietors' over the house of commons. It suggested that 'Lord John Manners does not stand inspection at Newark, and has been cashiered. He is now looking for a more generous and a more modern patron than the Lord of Clumber'.

[23]In addition to publishing Newcastle's letter, the newspaper defended itself against the 'Jupiter Tonans [Thundering Jove] of Clumber': *The Times*, 26 Aug. 1847.

I write in earnest, but not in anger, and remain, Sir, your very obedient servant,
NEWCASTLE
Clumber, August 23.

Sir —

In your blind and unworthy crusade against Dukes, as you are pleased to call them, as if
Dukes were a peculiar genus devoid of every quality estimable in man, and merely intended
as game to be hunted down by envious and overbearing levellers, I observe in your paper
of the 13th you have mentioned me in connexion with Lord John Manners, and for the
sake of a point you venture to deceive the public by telling it that Lord John did not stand
inspection at Newark, has been cashiered, and that he is now looking for a more generous
and a more modern patron than the Lord of Clumber.

In justice to Lord John Manners and myself, I will not suffer this dishonest assertion to
go forth without notice and contradiction.

The assertion may be very well suited to excite indignation, and extract the round de-
nunciation of some fancied political friends, as well as of, I hope, but a very few malignants
[*sic*].

Allow me to inform you that, unfortunately for your anti-ducal argument, the assertion
respecting me is not fact. Lord John Manners never owed his seat at Newark to my patronage. He solicited and gained the goodwill of the electors, and, as I hope, received the
full benefit of any influence that I may possess in the borough. His cashiering, as you term
it, arose from his own delicate and high sense of honour, or believing that he owed his
seat to the uncle of the present member, he resolved not to be in his way, and signified his
intention to retire.

No one can more sincerely lament the bias towards Romanism professed by Lord John
than I do; but as to having had any hand in cashiering him, I disclaim it utterly. It is not
true. What is true is, that I wished him to remain.

With the exception of this error, as I think it, Lord John appears to me to be free of
all others; a more promising young man, one of more exalted views and high principle, of
more inflexible integrity, with perfect amiability and all the best qualities of head and heart
that can adorn the Christian and the patriot senator, would with difficulty be found in Her
Majesty's dominions. Any constituency might justly be proud of him. His country may be
proud to own him as one of her sons, worthy of their race, who will be conspicuous in the
annals of their country. Their characters and abilities insure that.

Having dispelled your cashiering story, I must now notice your reprehensible calumny,
that Lord John is now looking for a more generous and a more modern patron than the
Lord of Clumber. Why not call me plainly by my usual name, unless you have a sinister
motive in doing otherwise, which it may not be very difficult to discover?

As to generosity, first, I never introduced and seated Lord John Manners; it could not,
as affecting him, therefore, be called in question. Next, I should be glad to know in what
instance I have ever shown a want of generosity. If I did my utmost to oppose the return
of Mr Gladstone, there were good reasons for it, but no want of generosity. I detest a mean
and dirty trick as much as you can, or any man living; but until you can fasten upon me the
perpetration of a mean or ungenerous act, do not accuse me of a want of generosity. The
more "modern patron" only remains. I must presume that the word "modern" is intended to

be applied to my views, and not to my age. If to my views. I thank you for the compliment, although unintended. I will not express myself pharisaically,[24] and say I thank God that I am not as some other men are, or even as this editor, but I will say that I am shocked, distressed, and humiliated by the tergiversation, the duplicity, the ingratitude, the utter want of principle, the sordid selfishness, the wavering view, the pliant conscience, the perverted mind, the hardened unfeeling heart, which too miserably betoken the tone and temper and false philosophy of so many of this modern but degenerate age. Far from approving modern sophistries, I like good old plain dealing. I loved the good old constitution in church and State. I venerated the *pietas et prisca fides*[25] of bygone days. What have we gained by modern innovations, by modern destruction, by turning almost everything inside out, by displacing, for mere change's sake, whatever was not new and speculative? Alas! Nothing but confusion, discord, and unhappiness, which, if unheeded, must result in our ultimate ruin. As this is my firm opinion, and I know the sentiments to be true, I declare it openly, and I defy you, or any man of your force and ability, to prove me in the wrong. You dare not to argue upon fallacies, your reputation must hold you to the truth; if you assert falsehoods, your reputation dies, your defamations will be unheeded, your attempts to traduce will be condemned, and your envenomed arrows will fall harmless to the ground, – and here I terminate your out-of-place and uncalled-for remarks upon myself. Now, Sir, is it not a shame, is it not most discreditable that a newspaper like *The Times*, which claims for itself the title of the leading journal of Europe, should so soil its paper and lose its dignity and caste, as to stoop to mislead, defame, or traduce, and that the nobility should be the principal butt, and Dukes in particular be selected as an especial object of detraction? Where is the wit, the wisdom, or the justice of such systematic and malevolent proceedings? Does it raise the character of your daily work, does it benefit your country? If it does neither, what can induce it but the indulgence of a bad and mischievous spirit? You know that such sweeping assertions are not true; you know well that if you were to select other 26 men to set against the 26 Dukes, which I believe is the number of those who own that rank – you know very well that in essential and sterling qualities, in patriotic and worthy deeds, the Dukes would lose nothing by the comparison. After scanning their own worth do not forget that of their offspring, as nothing degenerating from their sires. The same I may assert of the nobility generally. It is a foul libel to decry the nobility as a class, and if the leading journal were believed and followed, let it reflect what extensive mischief it might create. Then let it cease to traduce, and let it turn its great influence and high talents to a better account; let it uphold the character of the press; let it diffuse everything able, elevated, patriotic, and soundly useful to the minds of its readers, instead of instilling deadly poison to afflict, to deaden, and destroy.

I remain, Sir,
Your very obedient servant,
NEWCASTLE

12. Newcastle's letter to Lord John Russell on the Navigation Acts. Dated: London, 24 June 1848. Source: TNA, PRO/30/22/7c, ff. 34–7.

---

[24]i.e. in a self-righteous, sanctimonious, or hypocritical fashion.
[25]See 24 July 1847.

My Lord

It has been with the utmost concern, Mortification & alarm for the future, that I have observed the course pursued in parliament with a view to an Extensive alteration or Entire abolition of the Navigation Laws –

In such a question I can have no other interest than the welfare of my Country which I confess to be an all engrossing & paramount Consideration with me – & that no mere party view should be Suffered to abstract a particle of consistency from that consideration – In that Spirit I Should certainly not feel myself impelled to say "no", merely because the Minister Said "yes" – & I Should unfeignedly rejoice, if I could approve of Ministerial doings which to the best of my belief were calculated for general benefits.

When I write thus I write Sincerely – May I hope that your Lordship will forgive me, if I address a few lines to you on the Subject of the Navigation Laws –

To me it appears that this is a subject of such vital & paramount importance that to maintain & foster the Navigation laws is a matter absolutely Essential to the Existence of the Empire, if it be intended that England should continue to preserve her Maritime Superiority all over the World –

All that promotes the formation of Sailors & a Sea faring life, Especially by long voyages, is of Course attained by frequency & Exercise – This is now attained by us by our Extensive commerce & our distant Colonies, as well as by the genius of the people – But cripple & discourage the Extent of our Commerce with the Employment of our Ships & Seamen & how changed May be our position – How will it not affect the Shipowner, the Builder, the artisan, & the Seaman & all connected with Shipping – & if, as must follow, the great nursery for Seamen Should be diminished, What a lamentable alteration Would be needlessly Effected in our situation & how deeply Would it be to be deplored, when a necessity might occur for manning our War fleets, for the protection of our Commerce & the defence of our own home shores –

Our natural cheapest, Surest & most practicable home defence, is by our Navy – If our Ships be Sufficiently numerous & well manned, I am fully possessed with the belief, that by God's aid we may Justly consider the Island to be impregnable, for we Know the stuff of which our Sailors are made & the invincible Spirit which inspires them –

Looking then at the state of Empire & of the World, & at what may be coming upon all of us, if we ourselves as a Nation or by our Rulers be heedless of our duties & unmindful of consequences, daring, tempting, & Experimentalising, when we ought to be contented with, & Grateful for, the Known blessings which we possess, I write to Entreat & beseech your Lordship to stay all farther proceedings in this fearful measure & save us from the awful consequences which may attend its adoption –

These are not times in which we may hazard lightly the loyalty & devotedness of any portion of our People. Sooner let us unite all classes in one Sentiment of attachment to our public men & national Institutions, giving them cause to feel as well as to Know, that they are paternally watched over, that although for good but inscrutable reasons Nations as well as Individuals May be subjected to afflictions & Severe trials, yet that a manly Submission, & a noble determination will in good time Extricate them from the heaviest Evils – & here Comes the consideration Whether the Land we live in, is worthy of our love, & affection & devoted attachment – No good Englishman can or does think otherwise – but then it must be to him the Same land of his birth, not a disfigured chaos, the Same land of generous, rational & Well tempered freedom & Constitutional Security – Not a counterfeit Substitute, under the tyrannising rule of the Sordid & Selfish, a land of confidence & stability, not the baseless fabric of a vision, where Empyrical [*sic*] politicians, money worshippers, with heartless & greedy demagogues, Sap its foundations, tear down its walls & leave not a wreck behind.

The good Englishman desires to be peaceful & happy, not the agitated puppet of Experiment, he is, as your Lordship Knows, quite willing to labour, but he naturally Expects to enjoy the fruits of his industry. Every Man alike looks for this protection whether he be high or low, rich or poor – but withdraw the protective arm of the State, cease to Enforce the protection of wise & good Laws – & Security is gone, Confidence is lost, prosperity vanishes as a passing cloud – So, remove protection from the Shipowner, the Builder, the Merchant Seaman, throw open the traffick [*sic*] of the Seas, let in a host of foreigners to Swarm along our coasts, carry our goods, & Eat the very bread out of our honest sailors Mouths, and a wanton injury is inflicted upon men whose livelihood depends upon their Employment, whose labor is their capital, who must Starve if an unnatural State forcibly robs them of their Capital & Confiscates their property for the benefit of the foreigner as our landed properties have been Confiscated to the Income tax by act of Parliament, for the benefit of the foreigner & a one Sided & irreciprocal [*sic*] free trade –

With a plain, but most Earnest, & I trust not a rude & offensive freedom, I thus venture to address your Lordship before it be too late – I call upon you, I implore, I beseech You to retract the fatal Measure which I am led to believe is no favorite of Yours – I have been induced & urged on to Write this in behalf of our Maritime interests by the receipt of the letter from Captain Martin which I herewith Enclose – & which I conceive to be worthy of your Lordship's gravest attention. May I request that it may be returned to me when duly considered –

My desire is to render service to avert Evil & rouse to the Sane & Safe, the unadventurous though the most courageous course of letting well alone –

With all due apology & with all possible respect – I have the honor to remain, My Lord, Your Lordship's Very Sincere & obedient Servant, Newcastle.[26]

[26]The manuscript includes two unpublished postscripts, the first apologising for its legibility, the other for its lateness: 'May I request your Lordship to excuse the blotted state of my letter Which owing to the hurry of departure I have been unable to copy with My own hand & which has been more hastily Written than I Could have Wished in transmitting to You any Communication on a Subject of Such Varied & Supreme importance – N'; 'July 15. I left London & put this letter into my writing box; I had forgotten it untill [*sic*] by accident it came under my observation, I now send it that it may accompany Captain Martin's letter which ought not to have been withholden [*sic*] from your Knowledge, & I am Sorry that I have omitted to Send it Sooner'.

# APPENDIX B: NEWCASTLE'S MOVEMENTS

The following itinerary shows where Newcastle was each night; he continued at each place named until he moved to the next. Clumber, in Nottinghamshire, was Newcastle's principal residence and his London home was in Portman Square. He also owned Worksop Manor in Nottinghamshire (from 1839) and Hafod in Cardiganshire (until 1846). Ranby Hall near East Retford was the Nottinghamshire home of the earl and countess of Lincoln. Newcastle usually specified his departures and arrivals, but, where he does not, dates are estimated within brackets.

## 1839

| | | | |
|---|---|---|---|
| 1 Jan. | Clumber | 3 Sept. | Aberystwyth, |
| 9 Jan. | Stoke Hall, Newark, | | Cardiganshire |
| | Nottinghamshire | 18 Sept. | Tan y Bwlch, |
| 12 Jan. | Clumber | | Maentwrog |
| 14 Jan. | Drayton Manor, | 19 Sept. | Beddgelert, Gwynedd |
| | Staffordshire | 20 Sept. | Aberystwyth, |
| 19 Jan. | Clumber | | Cardiganshire |
| 4 Feb. | Wansford, | 21 Sept. | Hafod |
| | Cambridgeshire | 1 Oct. | Rhayader, |
| 5 Feb. | Portman Square | | Radnorshire |
| 9 Feb. | Worthing, Sussex | 3 Oct. | Hafod |
| 11 Feb. | Portman Square | 8 Oct. | Aberystwyth, |
| 13 Feb. | Stevenage, | | Cardiganshire |
| | Hertfordshire | 9 Oct. | Hafod |
| 14 Feb. | Clumber | 20 Nov. | Drayton Manor, |
| 23 Apr. | Grantham, | | Staffordshire |
| | Lincolnshire | 23 Nov. | Clumber |
| 24 Apr. | Portman Square | 10 Dec. | Portman Square |
| 8 May | Nottingham | 24 Dec. | Clumber |
| 9 May | Newark, | | |
| | Nottinghamshire | **1840** | |
| 11 May | Clumber | 10 Jan. | Newark, |
| 22 May | Nottingham | | Nottinghamshire |
| 23 May | Portman Square | 11 Jan. | Clumber |
| 12 Aug. | Birmingham, Warks | 13 Jan. | Watnall Hall, |
| 13 Aug. | Clumber | | Nottinghamshire |
| 23 Aug. | Shrewsbury, | 15 Jan. | Portman Square |
| | Shropshire | 20 Jan. | Clumber |
| 24 Aug. | Hafod | 25 Mar. | Nottingham |

| | | | |
|---|---|---|---|
| [27 Mar.] | Portman Square | 12 Nov. | Derby |
| 20 Apr. | Nottingham | 13 Nov. | Clumber |
| 21 Apr. | Clumber | 12 Dec. | Nottingham |
| 24 Apr. | Portman Square | 13 Dec. | Portman Square |
| 14 July | Birmingham, Warks | 20 Dec. | Clumber |
| 15 July | Shrewsbury, | 27 Dec. | Firbeck Hall, |
| | Shropshire | | Yorkshire |
| 16 July | Hafod | 29 Dec. | Clumber |
| 5 Aug. | Aberystwyth, | 31 Dec. | Thoresby Hall, |
| | Cardiganshire | | Nottinghamshire |
| 7 Aug. | Hafod | | |
| 28 Aug. | Aberystwyth, | **1842** | |
| | Cardiganshire | [1 Jan.] | Clumber |
| 29 Aug. | Hafod | 22 Jan. | Portman Square |
| 19 Oct. | Shrewsbury, | 25 Jan. | Windsor Castle, |
| | Shropshire | | Berkshire |
| 20 Oct. | Clumber | 26 Jan. | Portman Square |
| 23 Oct. | Ranby Hall | 28 Jan. | Clumber |
| 24 Oct. | Clumber | 15 Feb. | Kirkby Rectory, |
| 19 Nov. | Ranby Hall | | Nottinghamshire |
| 21 Nov. | Clumber | 17 Feb. | Clumber |
| 14 Dec. | Thoresby Hall, | 8 Apr. | Portman Square |
| | Nottinghamshire | 4 June | Clumber |
| 15 Dec. | Clumber | 9 June | Portman Square |
| | | 24 June | Clumber |
| **1841** | | 1 Aug. | Derby |
| 7 Jan. | Stoke Hall, Newark, | 2 Aug. | Newtown, |
| | Nottinghamshire | | Montgomeryshire |
| 9 Jan. | Clumber | 3 Aug. | Hafod |
| 12 Jan. | Thoresby Hall, | 26 Aug. | Kington, |
| | Nottinghamshire | | Herefordshire |
| 14 Jan. | Clumber | 27 Aug. | Portman Square |
| 25 Mar. | Ranby Hall | 1 Sept. | Clumber |
| 27 Mar. | Clumber | 13 Sept. | Ranby Hall |
| 30 Mar. | Ranby Hall | 14 Sept. | Clumber |
| 1 Apr. | Clumber | 20 Sept. | Langold, |
| 1 May | Markham Clinton, | | Nottinghamshire |
| | Nottinghamshire | 22 Sept. | Clumber |
| [3 May] | Clumber | 30 Sept. | Markham Clinton, |
| 19 July | Lichfield, Staffordshire | | Nottinghamshire |
| 20 July | Shrewsbury, | [1 Oct.] | Clumber |
| | Shropshire | 11 Oct. | Portman Square |
| 21 July | Hafod | 18 Oct. | Clumber |
| 24 Sept. | Aberystwyth, | 14 Dec. | Portman Square |
| | Cardiganshire | 23 Dec. | Clumber |
| 13 Oct. | Hafod | | |
| 11 Nov. | Welshpool, | **1843** | |
| | Montgomeryshire | 10 Jan. | Portman Square |

23 Jan. Clumber

25 Jan. Worksop Manor

[26 Jan.] Clumber

2 Feb. Worksop Manor,

5 Feb. Clumber

10 Feb. Worksop Manor

15 Feb. Clumber

1 Mar. Portman Square

11 Mar. Clumber

13 June Portman Square

4 July Hereford, Herefordshire

5 July Hafod

26 Aug. Aberystwyth

28 Aug. Dolgellau, Merioneth

29 Aug. Tan y Bwlch, Maentwrog

30 Aug. Llanberis, Gwynedd

31 Aug. Conwy, Gwynedd

1 Sept. Llangollen, Denbighshire

2 Sept. Liverpool, Lancashire

4 Sept. Combermere Abbey, Cheshire

7 Sept. Clumber

15 Nov. Ossington Hall, Nottinghamshire

[19 Nov.] Clumber

30 Nov. Thoresby Hall, Nottinghamshire

2 Dec. Clumber

**1844**

8 Jan. Ranby Hall

11 Jan. Clumber

29 Feb. Portman Square

8 Mar. Clumber

11 Apr. Nottingham

12 Apr. Clumber

24 June Portman Square

26 June Clumber

1 July Portman Square

4 July Clumber

25 July Nottingham

26 July Clumber

4 Sept. Markham Clinton, Nottinghamshire

5 Sept. Clumber

14 Sept. Liverpool, Lancashire

15 Sept. Llangollen, Denbighshire

16 Sept. Aberystwyth, Cardiganshire

[17 Sept.] Hafod

25 Sept. Lichfield, Staffordshire

26 Sept. Bridlington, Yorkshire

11 Nov. Hull, Yorkshire

13 Nov. Clumber

[13 Dec.] Firbeck Hall, Yorkshire

[18 Dec.] Clumber

**1845**

31 May Portman Square

6 June Clumber

16 June Portman Square

25 July Ramsgate, Kent

19 Sept. Calais, Hauts-de-France

20 Sept. St Omer, Hauts-de-France

22 Sept. Amiens, Hauts-de-France

23 Sept. Abbeville, Hauts-de-France

24 Sept. Montreuil, Hauts-de-France

25 Sept. Boulogne, Hauts-de-France

26 Sept. Calais, Hauts-de-France

27 Sept. Portman Square

1 Oct. Clumber

25 Oct. Combermere Abbey, Cheshire

3 Nov. Manchester, Lancashire

[6 Nov.] Clumber

**1846**

5 Jan. Ossington, Nottinghamshire

7 Jan. Clumber

21 Jan. Nottingham

22 Jan. Portman Square

27 Jan. Clumber

| | | | |
|---|---|---|---|
| 29 Jan. | Thoresby Hall, Nottinghamshire | 1 Apr. | Clumber |
| 30 Jan. | Clumber | 26 Apr. | Markham Clinton, Nottinghamshire |
| 9 Mar. | Portman Square | 27 Apr. | Clumber |
| 13 Mar. | Clumber | 12 May | Portman Square |
| 20 May | Portman Square | 26 June | Clumber |
| 10 July | Clumber | 9 Aug. | Portman Square |
| 15 July | Portman Square | 18 Aug. | Clumber |
| 27 July | Ramsgate, Kent | 16 Oct. | Nottingham |
| 1 Sept. | Dover, Kent | 17 Oct. | Clumber |
| 3 Sept. | Northern France | 1 Nov. | Watnall Hall, Nottinghamshire |
| 25 Oct. | Portman Square | | |
| 26 Oct. | Clumber | 3 Nov. | Clumber |
| 19 Dec. | Portman Square | 11 Dec. | Derby |
| 24 Dec. | Clumber | 12 Dec. | Stoke Edith Manor, Herefordshire |
| | | 18 Dec. | Clumber |
| **1847** | | | |
| 14 Jan. | Newark, Nottinghamshire | **1849** | |
| 15 Jan. | Clumber | 5 Jan. | Newark |
| 18 Jan. | Portman Square | 6 Jan. | Clumber |
| 25 Jan. | Clumber | 8 Jan. | Bloxholm Hall, Lincolnshire |
| 22 Apr. | Nottingham | | |
| 23 Apr. | Portman Square | 10 Jan. | Clumber |
| 23 June | Nottingham | 30 Jan. | Nottingham |
| 24 June | Clumber | 31 Jan. | Clumber |
| 2 July | Nottingham | 6 Feb. | Watnall Hall, Nottinghamshire |
| 3 July | Portman Square | | |
| 12 July | Clumber | 8 Feb. | Clumber |
| 25 Aug. | Combermere Abbey, Cheshire | 5 May | Portman Square |
| | | 16 June | Clumber |
| 30 Aug. | Clumber | 20 June | Portman Square |
| 28 Sept. | Filey, Yorkshire | 2 July | Ramsgate, Kent |
| 28 Oct. | Scarborough, Yorkshire | 24 July | Clumber |
| 1 Nov. | York | **1850** | |
| 2 Nov. | Clumber | 4 Jan. | Portman Square |
| 22 Nov. | Portman Square | 8 Jan. | St Leonards, Sussex |
| 27 Nov. | Clumber | 26 Feb. | Portman Square |
| | | 1 Mar. | St Leonards, Sussex |
| **1848** | | 13 May | Portman Square |
| 16 Feb. | Portman Square | 26 June | Clumber |
| 23 Feb. | Clumber | | |
| 29 Mar. | Thoresby Hall, Nottinghamshire | **1851** | |
| | | 12 Jan. | died at Clumber |

# BIOGRAPHICAL APPENDIX

*This appendix contains the names of all those persons mentioned by Newcastle in his diaries for 1839–50. Principally, it consists of the MPs, peers and bishops who were sitting in parliament at the time they are mentioned in the diaries, or, in the case of MPs, were about to be elected. The biographical and constituency information given only relates to the time covered by the text (except in the case of peerages, where relevant titles granted or succeeded to precede the period). For peerages [G.B.] = British (post-1707 Union), [I] = Irish, [S] = Scottish (pre-1707 union) and [U.K.] = United Kingdom (post-1800 Union).*

**Abercromby**, James (1776–1858). MP for Edinburgh 1832–9. Speaker of the house of commons 1835–9.

**Aberdeen**, George Hamilton-Gordon (1784–1860); succ. as 4th earl of [S] 1801 and cr. Viscount Gordon of Aberdeen [U.K.] 1814. Foreign secretary 1841–6.

**Abingdon**, Frederika (née Ker); m. Montagu Bertie, 5th earl of 1841.

**Abingdon**, Montagu Bertie (1784–1854); succ. as 5th earl of 1799.

**Abinger**, James Scarlett (1769–1844); cr. 1st baron 1835. Chief baron of the exchequer 1834–44.

**Adams**, John Quincy (1767–1848). Former president of the U.S.A.

Amelia **Adelaide** Louisa Theresa Caroline (1792–1849); m. William, duke of Clarence (afterwards King William IV) 1818–37; queen consort 1830–7.

**Albert** (1819–61); prince of Saxe-Coburg-Gotha; consort of Queen Victoria 1840–61.

**Alexander** (1818–81). Heir to Nicholas I, emperor of Russia.

**Alford**, John Hume Egerton (1812–51), viscount. MP Bedfordshire 1835–47.

**Alfred** Ernest (1844–1900); 2nd son of Queen Victoria.

**Alice** (1843–78); 2nd daughter of Queen Victoria.

**Alvanley**, William Arden (1789–1849); succ. as 2nd baron 1804.

**Amherst**, William Pitt (1773–1857); cr. 1st earl 1826.

**Anglesey**, Henry William Paget (1768–1854); succ. as 2nd earl of Uxbridge 1812 and cr. 1st marquess of 1815. Master-general of the ordnance 1846–52.

**Angoulême**, Marie-Thérèse Charlotte (1778–1851), duchess de, widow of Louis Antoine duke d'Angoulême (1775–1844).

**Anstey**, Thomas Chisholm (1816–73). MP for Youghal 1847–52.

**Argyll**, George William Campbell (1768–1839); succ. as 6th duke of [S] 1806. Lord keeper of the great seal of Scotland 1830–9; lord steward of the royal household 1835–9.

**Argyll**, John Douglas Edward Henry Campbell (1777–1847); known as Lord John Campbell until succ. as 7th duke of [S] 1839. Lord keeper of the great seal of Scotland 1841–6.

**Armistead**, Elizabeth (1750–1842); widow of Charles James Fox.

**Arnold**, Dr Thomas (1795–1842). Master of Rugby school 1828–42.

**Arthur** (1850–1942); 3rd son of Queen Victoria.

**Ashburnham**, Bertram (1797–1878); succ. as 4th earl of 1830.

**Ashburton**, Alexander Baring (1774–1848); cr. 1st baron 1835.

**Astell**, John Harvey (1806–87). MP for Cambridge 1852–3.

**Attwood**, John (*d.* 1865). MP for Harwich 1841–8.

**Auckland**, George Eden (1784–1849); succ. as 2nd baron 1814 and cr. 1st earl of 1839. Governor-general of India 1836–42; first lord of the admiralty 1846–9.

**Augusta** (1822–1916); granddaughter of King George III; m. Frederick William, grand duke of Mecklenburg-Strelitz 1843–1904.

**Augusta**, Sophia (1768–1840); daughter of King George III and Queen Charlotte.


**Baden**, Stéphanie de Beauharnais (1789–1860); grand duchess of.

**Bagot**, Sir Charles (1781–1843). Governor-general of Canada 1841–3.

**Bagot**, Richard (1782–1854). Bishop of Oxford 1829–45; bishop of Bath 1845–54.

**Baines**, Edward (1774–1848). MP for Leeds 1834–41. Editor and proprietor of *The Leeds Mercury* 1801–48.

**Baird**, William (1796–1864). MP for Falkirk Burghs 1841–6.

**Baker**, Thomas (*fl.* 1845), of Hammersmith, former Metropolitan Police superintendent, C division.

**Balmaceda**, Captain Juan Martin de (*fl.* 1840), Carlist general in Spain.

**Bankes**, George (1787–1856). MP for Dorset 1841–56.

**Baring**, Sir Francis Thornhill (1796–1866); 3rd bt. MP for Portsmouth 1826–65. Financial secretary to the treasury 1835–9; chancellor of the exchequer 1839–41; first lord of the admiralty 1849–52.

**Baring**, Henry (1777–1848); brother of Lord Ashburton.

**Baring**, Sir Thomas (1772–1848); 2nd bt. Elder brother of Lord Ashburton.

**Barnard**, Captain Edward (*fl.* 1797–1857). Captain of HMS Cambridge from 1840.

**Barrot**, Odillon (1791–1843). French minister.

**Barry**, Charles (1795–1860). Architect principally famous for the post-1834 houses of parliament.

**Bateman**, William Hanbury (1780–1845); cr. 1st baron 1837.

**Baxter**, Robert (1802–89), of Doncaster. Solicitor to the Great Northern Railway Company.

**Bean**, John William (1824–82). Attempted to assassinate Queen Victoria.

**Beaufort**, Henry Somerset (1792–1853); succ. as 7th duke of 1835.

**Beaumont**, Miles Stapleton (1805–54); recognised as 8th baron 1840.

**Beauvale**, Frederick James Lamb (*d.* 1853), baron; succ. his brother as 3rd Viscount Melbourne 1848.

**Bedford**, Francis Russell (1788–1861); styled marquess of Tavistock until succ. as 7th duke of 1839.

**Bedford**, John Russell (1766–1839); succ. as 6th duke of 1802.

**Bedford**, *also see* Tavistock.

**Behnes**, William (1795–1864). Sculptor.

**Bentinck**, Lord George Frederick Cavendish-Scott (1802–48). MP for King's Lynn 1828–48.

**Bentinck**, Lord Henry Cavendish (1804–70). MP for North Nottinghamshire 1846–57.

**Beresford**, John George (1773–1862). Archbishop of Armagh 1822–62.

**Beresford**, Reverend Marcus Gervais (1801–85). Held the vicarages of Drung and Larah in the diocese of Kilmore, Ireland, 1828–54.

**Beresford**, Major William (1797–1883). MP for Harwich 1841–7, North Essex 1847–65. Secretary at war 1852.

**Bexley**, Nicholas Vansittart (1766–1851); cr. 1st baron 1823.

**Blomfield**, Charles James (1786–1857). Bishop of London 1828–56.

**Blore**, Edward (1787–1879). Architect of Buckingham Palace.

**Bonaparte**, Joseph (1768–1844). Brother of Napoleon and former king of Naples and Spain.

**Bonaparte**, Josephine de Beauharnais, wife of Napoleon 1796–1810.

**Bonaparte**, Louis (1778–1846). Brother of Napoleon and former king of Holland.

**Bonaparte**, Louis (1808–73). Nephew of Napoleon; first president of France 1848–52.

**Bonaparte**, Marie Louise, archduchess of Austria, wife of Napoleon 1810–21.

**Bonaparte**, Napoleon (1769–1821). Emperor of the French 1804–15.

**Booker**, Thomas William (1801–58). Leading Protectionist politician. Potential candidate for Cork City, 1849; elected MP for Herefordshire Sept. 1850.

**Bordeaux**, Henri (1820–83), duc de. Pretender to the throne of France.

**Brady**, Sir Maziere (1796–1871). Solicitor-general for Ireland 1837–9; attorney-general for Ireland 1839–40; chief baron of the Irish exchequer 1840–6; lord chancellor of Ireland 1846–52.

**Brady**, Sir Nicholas (1791–1843). Lord mayor of Dublin 1839–40.

**Bremer**, Sir Gordon (1786–1850). Commander-in-chief of British forces during the Anglo-Chinese war.

**Bridge**, John Gawler (*fl.* 1834–43). Partner in Rundell, Bridge and Company, Jewellers and Goldsmiths; Royal Goldsmith, 1834–43; Prime warden from 1839.

**Bridgewater**, Charlotte Catherine Anne Haynes (1763–1849); widow of the 7th earl of.

**Bright**, John (1811–89). Quaker; co-founder of the Anti-Corn Law League. MP for Durham 1843–7, Manchester 1847–57.

**Broadfoot**, Major George (1807–45). Died from injuries sustained at the battle of Ferozeshah, 21 Dec. 1845.

**Brougham**, Henry Peter (1778–1868); cr. 1st Baron Brougham and Vaux 1830.

**Browne**, Mrs E. (*fl.* 1847), daughter of Mrs Ward, keeper of 'The George IV Hotel', Nottingham.

**Browne**, George Joseph Plunket (1795– 1858). Bishop of Elphin.

**Browne**, Joseph (*fl.* 1836–48). Partner in Messrs Browne and Company, London.

**Brownlow**, John Cust (1779–1853); cr. 1st earl 1815.

**Bruce**, Charles Brudenell- (1773–1856), 1st marquess of Ailesbury.

**Bruce**, Ernest Brudenell- (1811–86). MP for Marlborough, 1832–78; vice-chamberlain of the household, 1841–6.

**Brunnow**, Ernst Philipp von (1797–1875). Russian ambassador to the United Kingdom, 1840–54.

**Brunswick**, Charles, duke of (1804–73). Ruled the duchy of Brunswick, 1815–30.

**Buccleuch**, Lady Charlotte Anne Montagu-Douglas (*née* Thynne) (1811–95), duchess of; m. Walter Francis Scott, 5th duke of 1829–84.

**Buccleuch**, Walter Francis Scott (1806–84); succ. as 5th duke of 1819. Lord privy seal 1842–6; lord president of the council 1846.

**Buckingham and Chandos**, Richard Temple-Nugent-Brydges-Chandos-Grenville (1776–1839); cr. 1st duke of 1822.

**Buckingham and Chandos**, Richard Plantagenet Temple-Nugent-Brydges-Chandos-Grenville (1797–1861); succ. as 2nd duke of 1839. Lord privy seal 1841–2.

**Buller**, Edward Manningham (1800–82). MP for North Staffordshire 1833–41, Stafford 1841–7.

**Buller**, Sir John (afterwards Yarde-Buller) (1799–1871); 3rd bt. MP for South Devon 1835–58.

**Bullock**, Captain Frederick (1788–1874). Commanded HMS Porcupine, 1844–8.

**Bulwer**, Henry Lytton (1801–72). Ambassador to Spain 1844–8, to the U.S.A. 1849–52.

**Burdett**, Sir Francis (1770–1844); succ. as 5th bt, 1797. MP for North Wiltshire 1837–44.

**Burdett**, Sophia Coutts (*d.* 1844). m. Sir Francis 1793–1844.

**Burgoyne**, Major-general John Fox (1782–1871). Appointed inspector-general of fortifications in 1845.

**Burnes**, Sir Alexander (1805–41). Scottish explorer and diplomat.

**Burton**, Charles (1760–1847). Judge of queen's bench, Ireland.

**Bute**, John Crichton-Stuart (1793–1848); succ. as 2nd marquess of 1814.

**Butler**, Pierce Somerset (1801–65). MP for Kilkenny County 1843–52.

**Butt**, Isaac (1813–79). Irish barrister.

**Bygrave**, Captain Bulstrode (1802–1873). Paymaster general in Afghanistan, 1838–42.

**Cabbell**, Benjamin Bond (1781–1874). MP for St Albans 1846–7, Boston 1847–57.

**Cabrera**, **Ramón** (1806–77); 1st duke of Maestrazgo.

**Calthorpe**, George Gough (1787–1851); succ. as 3rd baron 1807.

**Cambridge**, Adolphus Frederick (1774–1850); cr. duke of 1801; 7th son of King George III and Queen Charlotte.

**Cambridge**, Augusta of Hesse-Kassell (1797–1889); duchess of. m. Adolphus Frederick, duke of, 1818–50.

**Cambridge**, George William Frederick Charles (1819–1904); succ. as duke of 1850.

**Camden**, John Jeffreys Pratt (1759–1840); succ. as 2nd earl 1794 and cr. 1st marquess 1812. Chancellor of the University of Cambridge 1834–40.

**Camoys**, Thomas Stonor (1797–1881); succ. as 3rd baron 1839.

**Campbell**, Sir John (1779–1861); cr. 1st baron 1841. MP for Edinburgh 1834–41. Attorney-general 1835–41; lord high chancellor of Ireland 1841; chancellor of the duchy of Lancaster 1846–50; chief justice of queen's bench 1850–9.

**Campbell**, John Henry (1798–1868). MP for Salisbury 1843–7.

**Canning**, Charlotte Stewart (1817–61); countess of. m. Charles, 1st Earl Canning 1835–61.

**Canning**, George (1770–1827). Prime minister 1827.

**Canning**, Sir Stratford (1786–1880). MP for King's Lynn 1835–42. Ambassador to the Ottoman Empire 1841–58.

**Canterbury**, Charles Manners-Sutton (1780–1845); cr. 1st viscount 1835. Former speaker of the house of commons.

**Cardigan**, James Brudenell (1797–1868); succ. as Lord Brudenell 1811 and as 7th earl of 1837.

**Cardwell**, Edward (1813–86). MP for Clitheroe 1842–7, Liverpool 1847–52. Financial secretary to the treasury 1845–6.

**Carlisle**, George Howard (1773–1848); succ. as 6th earl of 1825.

**Carlile**, Richard (1790–1843). Writer and publicist for freedom of the press. Noted Deist.

**Carlisle**, *also see* Morpeth.

**Carlos**, Don (1788–1855). Pretender to the Spanish throne.

**Carnarvon**, Henry John George Herbert (1800–49); succ. as 3rd earl of 1833.

**Carnegie**, Captain Swynfen Thomas (1813–79). MP for Stafford, 1841–7; lord of the treasury, 1846.

**Carrington**, Robert (1796–1868); succ. as 2nd baron 1838.

**Castlereagh**, Frederick William Robert Stewart (1805–72); styled viscount; heir to the 3rd marquess of Londonderry. MP for County Down 1826–52.

**Cavaignac**, Louis-Eugène (1802–57). Prime minister of France 1840–8.

**Cavendish**, Mrs. R. (*fl.* 1845). Society hostess.

**Chalmers**, Dr Thomas (1780–1847). Theologian, preacher, and philanthropist.

**Charlotte** Augusta (1796–1817); princess of Wales, granddaughter of King George III.

**Chateaubriand**, François-René (1768–1848); vicomte de. French author and diplomat.

**Christie**, William Dougal (1816–74). MP for Weymouth 1842–7.

**Christopher**, Robert Adam (1804–77). MP for North Lincolnshire 1837–57.

**Clanricarde**, Ulick John de Burgh (1802–74); cr. 1st marquess of [I] 1825 and Baron Somerhill [U.K.] 1826. Ambassador to Russia 1838–40; postmaster general 1846–52.

**Clanwilliam**, Richard Charles Francis Meade (1795–1879); succ. as 3rd earl of 1805.

**Clarendon**, George Villiers (1800–70); succ. as 4th earl of 1838. Lord privy seal and chancellor of the duchy of Lancaster 1840–1; president of the board of trade 1846–7; lord lieutenant of Ireland 1847–52.

**Clark**, Sir James (1788–1870), 1st bt. Physician to Queen Victoria 1837–60.

**Clay**, Henry (1777–1852). American senator and presidential candidate.

**Cleveland**, Henry Vane (1788–64); succ. as Viscount Barnard 1792, earl of Darlington 1833 and 2nd duke of 1842. MP for South Shropshire 1832–42.

**Cleveland**, William Harry Vane (1766–1842); succ. as 3rd earl of Darlington 1792, cr. marquess 1827 and 1st duke of 1833.

**Clinton**, Charles Rudolph Trefusis (1791–1886); succ. as 19th baron 1832.

**Clinton**, Colonel Frederick (1804–70), 2nd son of Sir William.

**Clinton**, Sir Henry (1771–1829). Cousin of the 4th duke of Newcastle.

**Clinton**, Mary Margaret (née Montagu-Scott) (1807–85). Daughter of Henry James Montagu-Scott, 2nd Baron Montagu of Boughton (1776–1845). Married Colonel Frederick Clinton in 1840.

**Clinton**, Sir William Henry (1769–1846). Cousin of the 4th duke of Newcastle; governor of Chelsea Hospital, 1842–6.

**Clive**, Edward (*d.* 1845). MP for Hereford 1826–45.

**Cobden**, Richard (1804–65). Co-founder of the Anti-Corn Law League. MP for Stockport 1841–7, the West Riding of Yorkshire 1847–8.

**Cochrane**, Charles (1807–55). Founder of the National Philanthropic Association 1842.

**Cockburn**, Sir William (1773–1858); 11th bt. Dean of York 1823–58.

**Codrington**, Caroline Georgiana Harriet Foley (*d.* 1843). m. Sir Christopher.

**Codrington**, Sir Christopher Bethell (1764–1843).

**Colborne**, Sir John (1778–1863); cr. G.C.B. 1815, 1st Baron Seaton 1839. Commander-in-chief North America 1836–9.

**Colchester**, Charles Abbot (1798–1867); succ. as 2nd baron 1829.

**Combermere**, Stapleton Cotton (1773–1865); cr. 1st baron 1814 and 1st viscount 1827. Former brother-in-law of the 4th duke of Newcastle.

**Concha**, General Manuel Gutiérrez de la Concha e Irigoyen (1808–74); led expedition to Portugal to uphold the rule of Queen Maria II.

**Conroy**, Sir John Ponsonby (1786–1854); cr. 1st bt, 1837. Comptroller of the duchess of Kent's household 1820–39.

**Conyngham**, Francis Nathaniel (1797–1876); succ. as 2nd marquess 1832. Lord chamberlain of the royal household 1835–9.

**Conyngham**, George Lenox (c.1796–1866). Chief clerk at the foreign office.

**Cooper**, Anthony Ashley (1801–85); styled Lord Ashley; heir to the 6th earl of Shaftesbury. MP for Dorset 1831–46, Bath 1847–51.

**Cottenham**, Charles Christopher Pepys (1781–1851); cr. baron 1836, Viscount Crowhurst 1850, earl of 1850. Lord chancellor 1836–41, 1846–50.

**Courvoisier**, François Benjamin (1816–40). Swiss valet who murdered Lord William Russell.

**Coutts**, Angela Burdett (1841–1906). Philanthropist.

**Cowley**, Henry Wellesley (1804–84); succ. as 2nd baron 1847. Minister plenipotentiary to the Swiss Cantons 1848–51, to the German confederation 1848–52.

**Cowley**, Olivia Cecilia Fitzgerald (*d.* 1885). m. Henry Wellesley, baron 1833–84.

**Cowper**, George (1806–56), 6th earl. Nephew of 2nd Viscount Melbourne.

**Cripps**, William (*d.* 1848). MP for Cirencester 1841–8. Junior lord of the treasury 1845–6.

**Croker**, John Wilson (1780–1857). Irish statesman and author.

**Croly**, George (1780–1860). Author and divine.

**Cumberland**, Ernest Augustus (1771–1851); cr. duke of 1799; 5th son of King George III and Queen Charlotte. King of Hanover 1837–51.

**Cumberland**, George Frederick Alexander Charles Ernest Augustus (1819–78); son and heir of Ernest Augustus, duke of Cumberland and king of Hanover.

**Cumberland**, Marie (1818–1907); princess of Saxe-Altenburg. m. George, crown prince of Hanover 1843–78.

**Dalhousie**, James Broun-Ramsay (1812–60); succ. as 10th earl of [S] 1838, cr. 1st marquess of [U.K.] 1849. President of the board of trade 1845–6; governor-general of India 1848–56.

**Dartmouth**, Frances Barrington (*d.* 1849). m. William Legge, earl of 1828–49.

**Dartmouth**, William Legge (1784–1853); succ. as 4th earl of 1810.

**Davys**, Mary Anne (*fl.* 1837–88). Daughter of George Davys, dean of Chester. Lacking the qualifications for a lady of the bedchamber, Queen Victoria retained her as Resident Woman of the Bedchamber.

**Dawkins**, Clinton George Augustus (*fl.* 1841–60). Private secretary to Lord Aberdeen.

**De Grey**, Thomas Philip (1781–1859); succ. as 2nd earl 1833. Lord lieutenant of Ireland 1841–4.

**De Grey**, Henrietta Cole (1784–1848); countess of. m. Thomas, Earl De Grey 1805–48.

**De la Warr**, George John Sackville-West (1791–1869); succ. as 5th earl 1795. Lord chamberlain 1841–6.

**Dedel**, Salomon (1776–1846); baron. Dutch minister in London.

**Delane**, John Thadeus (1817–79). Editor of *The Times* 1841–77.

**Denison**, Edmund Beckett (1787–1874). MP for the West Riding of Yorkshire 1841–7, 1848–59.

**Denison**, Edward (1801–54). Bishop of Salisbury 1837–54.

**Denison**, John Evelyn (1800–73). MP for Malton 1841–51.

**Denman**, Sir Thomas (1779–1854); cr. 1st baron 1834. Chief justice of king's bench 1832–7, queen's bench 1837–50.

**Derby**, Edward Smith Stanley (1775–1851); succ. as 13th earl of 1834.

**D'Este**, Augustus Frederick (1794–1848). Illegitimate son of Augustus Frederick, duke of Sussex.

**Dethick**, John (*fl.* 1812–50). Trained in medicine at the University of Edinburgh; after serving in the army during the Napoleonic Wars, went into private practice. Attended the Newcastle family from c.1849.

**Dillon**, John (*fl.* 1843), of 157 Strand, London. Formerly served in the navy; sent threatening letters to the chancellor of the exchequer, Henry Goulburn.

**Dinorben**, William Lewis Hughes (1767–1852); cr. 1st baron 1832.

**Disraeli**, Benjamin (1804–81). MP for Maidstone 1837–41, Shrewsbury 1841–7, Buckinghamshire 1847–76.

**Disraeli**, Issac (1766–1848). Writer and scholar.

**Dorset**, Charles Sackville Germain (1767–1843); succ. as 5th duke of 1815.

**Douglas**, Charles (1775–1848); succ. as 3rd baron 1844.

**D'Oultremont**, Countess Henrietta (1792–1864); 2nd morganatic wife of William I of Holland.

**Downshire**, Arthur Blundell Sandys Trumbull (1788–1845); succ. as 3rd marquess of 1801.

**Drouyn de Lhuys**, Édouard (1805–81). French diplomat.

**Drummond**, Edward (1792–1843). Private secretary to Sir Robert Peel.

**Duke**, Sir James (1792–1873); 1st bt. MP for Boston 1837–49, City of London 1849–65. Lord mayor of London 1848–9.

**Dunbar**, Duncan (1803–62). London-based shipowner of Duncan Dunbar & Company.

**Duncannon**, John William Ponsonby (1781–1847); cr. 1st baron 1834; succ. as 4th earl of Bessborough [I] 1844. First commissioner of woods, forests and land revenues 1835–9; lord privy seal 1835–40; lord lieutenant of Ireland 1846–7.

**Duncombe**, Hon. Captain Arthur (1806–89). MP for East Retford 1835–51.

**Duncombe**, Thomas Slingsby (1796–1861). MP for Finsbury 1834–61.

**Dundas**, Colonel Henry (1804–76); heir of the 2nd Viscount Melville.

**Dungannon**, Arthur Hill-Trevor (1798–1862); succ. as 3rd viscount [I] 1837. MP for Durham 1835–41, 1843.

**Durham**, John George Lambton (1792–1840); cr. baron 1828 and 1st earl of 1833. Governor-general of Canada 1838–9.

**Dysart**, Louisa Manners Tollemache (1745–1840); 7th countess of.

**Ebrington**, Hugh Fortescue (1783–1861); styled viscount; succ. as 2nd Earl Fortescue 1841. MP for North Devon 1832–9. Lord lieutenant of Ireland 1839–41; lord steward of the royal household 1846–50.

[Albert] **Edward** (1841–1910); prince of Wales, 1st son of Queen Victoria.

**Egerton**, Lord Francis (1800–57); cr. 1st earl of Ellesmere 1846. MP for South Lancashire 1835–46.

**Eglinton**, Archibald Montgomerie (1812–61); succ. as 13th earl of 1819.

**Eldon**, John Scott (1751–1838); cr. baron 1799 and 1st earl of 1821.

**Elgin**, James Bruce (1811–63); succ. as 8th earl of [S] 1841. MP for Southampton 1841–2. Governor of Jamaica 1842–6; governor-general of Canada 1847–54.

**Elizabeth** (1770–1840); princess, 3rd daughter of King George III and Queen Charlotte, m. Frederick VI, landgrave of Hesse-Homburg 1818–29.

**Ellenborough**, Edward Law (1790–1871); succ. as 2nd baron 1818; cr. earl of 1844. President of the board of control 1841; governor-general of India 1842–4; first lord of the admiralty 1846.

**Ellesmere**, *see* Egerton.

**Ellice**, Edward (1781–1863). MP for Coventry 1830–63.

**Elliot**, Captain Charles (1801–75). Chief superintendent of British trade in China 1836–41; administrator of Hong Kong 1841; governor of Bermuda 1846–54.

**Elliot**, Charles Gilbert John Brydone (1818–95). As a junior naval officer, was involved in the bombardment of Acre (3 Nov. 1840) during the Egyptian–Ottoman War.

**Elliot**, Edward Granville (1798–1871); styled Lord Elliot until succ. as 3rd earl of St Germans 1845. MP for East Cornwall 1837–45. Chief secretary for Ireland 1841–5; postmaster-general 1845–6.

**Elphinstone**, Major-general William (1782–1842). Commander of British garrison in Kabul.

**Ely**, John Loftus (1770–1845); succ. as 2nd marquess of [I] and Baron Loftus [U.K.] 1806.

**Espartero**, Baldomero (1793–1879). Spanish marshal and statesman.

**Evans,** Colonel George de Lacy (1787–1870); cr. K.C.B. 1837. MP for Westminster 1833–41.

**Evans**, William (*d.* 1856). Sheriff of London and Middlesex 1839–40.

**Exeter**, Brownlow Cecil (1795–1867); succ. as 3rd marquess 1804. Groom of the stole to Prince Albert 1841–6.

**Faber**, Frederick William (1814–63). Hymn writer and theologian.

**Falmouth**, Edward Boscawen (1787–1841); succ. as 4th viscount 1808 and cr. 1st earl of 1821.

**Farncomb**, Thomas (1779–1865). Lord mayor of London 1849.

**Ferdinand I** (1793–1875). Emperor of Austria 1835–48.

**Ferdinand II** (1816–85). King of Portugal.

**Ferrand**, William (1809–89). MP for Knaresborough 1841–7.

**Feversham**, Charles Duncombe (1764–1841); cr. 1st baron 1826.

**Feversham**, William Duncombe (1798–1867); succ. as 2nd baron 1841. MP for the North Riding of Yorkshire 1832–41.

**Ffrench**, Charles Austin, 3rd baron (1786–1860). Dismissed from the magistracy of Galway, Ireland for attending a pro-Repeal meeting.

**Fitzgerald**, *see* Vesey-Fitzgerald.

**Fitzgibbon**, Gerald (1793–1882). Irish lawyer and author.

**Fitzroy**, Charles Augustus (1796–1858). Governor of Prince Edward Island 1837–41, of Antigua 1842–6, of New South Wales 1846–55.

**Fitzroy**, Henry (1807–59). MP for Lewes 1837–41, 1842–59.

**Fitzroy**, James Henry Somerset (1788–1855); styled Lord Fitzroy Somerset. Military secretary at the war office 1827–52.

**Fitzroy**, Mary (*née* Lennox) (1820–48). m. Charles Augustus Fitzroy 1820–48.

**Fitzwilliam**, Charles William Wentworth-Fitzwilliam (1786–1857); succ. as 5th earl [I] and 3rd earl [U.K.] 1833.

**Fleetwood**, Sir Peter Hesketh-Fleetwood (1801–66). MP for Preston 1832–47.

**Fleming**, Reverend Robert (c.1660–1716). Presbyterian minister and religious writer.

**Foley**, Lady Emily (1805–1900). Widow of Sir Thomas Foley, bt, of Stoke Edith, Herefordshire (*d.* 1846). Newcastle unsuccessfully proposed marriage to her.

**Follett**, Sir William Webb (1796–1845). MP for Exeter 1835–45. Solicitor-general 1841–4; attorney-general 1844–5.

**Forbes**, James Ochoncar, 17th baron (1765–1843). Colonel of the 21st (Royal North British) Fusiliers from 1816.

**Fortescue**, *see* Ebrington.

**Fox**, Charles James (1749–1806). Whig statesman.

**Francia**, Francesco (Francesco Raibolini) (1447–1517). Italian painter.

**Francis Joseph I** (1830–1916); emperor of Austria.

**Frederick Augustus II** (1797–1854); king of Saxony.

**Frederick William III** (1770–1840); king of Prussia.

**Frederick William IV** (1795–1861); king of Prussia.

**Fremantle**, Sir Thomas (1798–1890); 1st bt. MP for Buckingham 1826–46. Parliamentary secretary to the treasury 1841–4; secretary at war 1844–5; chief secretary for Ireland 1845–6.

**Frost**, John (1784–1877). Chartist leader of the Newport Rising.

**Gage**, Henry Hall (1791–1877); succ. as 4th viscount [I] 1808.

**Garbett**, James (1802–79). Professor of poetry at the University of Oxford.

**Giffard**, Stanley Lees (1788–1858). Founding editor of *The Standard* 1827–57.

**Gilbert**, Ashurst Turner (1786–1870). Bishop of Chichester 1842–70.

**Gilbert**, General Sir Walter (1785–1853), 1st bt. Army officer in East India Company.

**Gilmour**, Allan (1775–1849). Merchant and shipowner. Purchased the Eaglesham estates from the earls of Eglinton and Winton in 1844.

**Gilmour**, James (1782–1858). Co-founded Gilmour, Rankin & Company. With his brother Allan, purchased the Eaglesham estates from the earls of Eglinton and Winton in 1844.

**Gladstone**, Helen Jane (1814–80); younger sister of William Ewart Gladstone.

**Gladstone**, John (1764–1851); cr. 1st bt of Fasque 1846. Father of William Ewart Gladstone.

**Gladstone**, William Ewart (1809–98). MP for Newark 1832–45, the University of Oxford 1847–65. President of the board of trade 1843–5; secretary of state for war and the colonies 1845–6.

**Glenelg**, Charles Grant (1778–1866); cr. 1st baron 1835. Secretary of state for war and the colonies 1835–9.

**Glengall**, Richard Butler (1794–1858); succ. as 2nd earl of [I] 1818.

**Glenlyon**, George Murray (1814–64); succ. as 2nd baron 1837.

**Gloucester**, Mary (1776–1857); 4th daughter of King George III and Queen Charlotte; m. William Frederick 2nd duke of Gloucester 1816–34.

**Golightly**, Charles Pourtales (1807–85). Anglican clergyman and religious writer.

**Gomm**, Sir William Maynard (1784–1875). Governor of Mauritius 1842–9.

**Gordon**, Sir Robert (1791–1847). Ambassador to the Austrian Empire 1841–6.

**Gosset**, Major-general Sir William (1782–1848). Serjeant-at-arms at the house of commons 1835–48.

**Gough**, Sir Hugh (1779–1869); G.C.B. 1841, bt, 1842, cr. 1st viscount 1849. Commander-in-chief in India 1843–9.

**Goulburn**, Henry (1784–1856). MP for the University of Cambridge 1831–56. Chancellor of the exchequer 1831–56.

**Grafton**, George Fitzroy (1760–1844); succ. as 4th duke of 1811.

**Graham**, Sir James Robert George (1792–1861); succ. as 2nd bt, 1824. MP for Pembroke 1838–41, Dorchester 1841–7, Ripon 1847–52. Home secretary 1841–6.

**Granby**, Charles Cecil John Manners, marquess of (1815–88). MP for Stamford 1837–52, North Leicestershire 1852–7. Lord of the bedchamber to Prince Albert, 1843–6.

**Grant**, Elizabeth (*d.*1899). Married Lord Charles Pelham-Clinton, 10 Aug. 1848.

**Grant**, James (1802–79). Parliamentary sketch writer.

**Granville**, Charles Henry Somerset (1792–1848). MP for Monmouthshire 1816–48. Chancellor of the duchy of Lancaster 1841–6.

**Granville**, George Leveson-Gower (1815–91); succ. as 2nd earl 1846. MP for Morpeth 1837–40, Lichfield 1841–6. Paymaster-general 1848–52; vice president of the board of trade 1848–52.

**Grattan**, Henry (1789–1859). MP for Meath 1831–52.

**Gray**, Dr John (1815–75). Indicted on a charge of conspiracy and sedition against the British establishment.

**Gregg**, Reverend Tresham Dames (1800–81). Irish clergyman.

**Grey**, Charles (1764–1845); succ. as 2nd earl 1807.

**Grey**, Sir George (1799–1882); 2nd bt. MP for Devonport 1832–47, North Northumberland 1847–52. Chancellor of the duchy of Lancaster 1841; home secretary 1846–52.

**Grey**, *also see* Howick.

**Grimstone**, James Walter (1809–95); styled viscount [I] until succ. as 2nd earl of Verulam [U.K.] 1845. MP for Hertfordshire 1832–45.

**Grissell**, Thomas (1801–74). Of Grissell and Peto, builders.

**Guilford**, Francis North (1772–1861); succ. as 6th earl of 1827.

**Gurney**, Sir John (1768–1845). Baron of the Exchequer 1832–45.

**Gurwood**, Colonel John (1790–45). Editor of the duke of Wellington's *Dispatches*.

**Gutteridge**, Thomas (*fl.* 1847–8). Author of *Three pamphlets, containing the charges of immorality publicly brought against James Price Lee, the lately nominated Bishop of Manchester* (1847).

**Haddington**, Thomas Hamilton (1780–1858); styled Viscount Binning until succ. as 9th earl of [S] 1828. First lord of the admiralty 1841–6; lord privy seal 1846.

**Hall**, George Webb (1765–1824). Lawyer; chairman of the Agricultural Association.

**Hamilton**, Alexander Hamilton Douglas (1767–1852); succ. as 10th duke of [S] and 7th duke of Brandon [G.B.] 1819.

**Hamilton**, William (b. 1827). Unemployed Irish bricklayer; attempted to assassinate Queen Victoria in 1849.

**Hampden**, Dr Renn Dickson (1793–1868). Regius professor of divinity at the University of Oxford 1836–47; bishop of Hereford 1848–68.

**Hardinge**, Henry (1785–1856); cr. viscount 1846. MP for Launceston 1834–44. Secretary at war 1841–4; governor-general of India 1844–8.

**Hardwicke**, Charles Yorke (1799–1873); succ. as 4th earl of 1834.

**Harewood**, Henry Lascelles (1767–1841); succ. as 2nd earl of 1820.

**Harford**, John Scandrett (1785–1866). Banker and abolitionist.

**Harlow**, John (*fl.* 1845), of 9 Leicester Square, London. Brought a case of privilege against Thomas Baker.

**Harmer**, James (1777–1853). Alderman of London; proprietor of the *Weekly Dispatch*.

**Harrison**, William Henry (1773–1841). President of the U.S.A. 1841.

**Harrowby**, *see* Sandon

**Harvey**, Daniel Whittle (1786–1863). MP for Southwark 1835–40. Commissioner of the city of London police 1839–63.

**Hastings**, Barbara Yelverton (*d.* 1858); Baroness Grey de Ruthyn; widow of Francis George Augustus, 2nd marquess of.

**Hastings**, Lady Flora Elizabeth Rawdon (1806–39), lady-in-waiting to the duchess of Kent.

**Hastings**, Francis George Augustus (1808–44); succ. as 2nd marquess of 1826.

**Hastings**, George Fowler (1814–76). Naval commander.

**Hawes**, Benjamin (1797–1862). MP for Lambeth 1832–47, Kinsale 1848–51.

**Helena** Augusta Victoria (1846–1923); 3rd daughter of Queen Victoria.

**Henderson**, William (*fl.* 1827–51). Attorney of 11 Lancaster Place, London. Legal adviser to the 4th duke of Newcastle.

**Herbert**, Sidney (1810–61). MP for South Wiltshire 1832–61. First secretary of the admiralty 1841–5; secretary at war 1845–6.

**Herries**, John Charles (1778–1855). MP for Harwich 1823–41, Stamford 1847–53.

**Hertford**, Francis Charles Seymour-Conway (1777–1842); succ. as 3rd marquess of 1822. Lord warden of the stannaries 1812–42.

**Hertford**, Richard Seymour-Conway (1800–70); succ. as 4th marquess of 1842.

**Heytesbury**, William A'Court (1779–1860); cr. 1st baron 1828. Lord lieutenant of Ireland 1844–6.

**Hicklin**, John (1805–77). Co-owner and editor of the *Nottingham Journal* from 1832.

**Hildyard**, Thomas Thoroton (1821–88). MP for South Nottinghamshire 1846–52.

**Hill**, Rowland (1772–1842); cr. baron 1814 and 1816, viscount 1842. Commander-in-chief of the army 1828–42.

**Hobhouse**, Sir John Cam (1786–1869); succ. as 2nd bt, 1831. MP for Nottingham 1834–47, Harwich 1848–51. President of the board of control 1835–41, 1846–52.

**Hogg**, Sir James Weir (1790–1876); bt. MP for Beverley 1835–47, Honiton 1847–51.

**Holland**, Henry Richard Vassall Fox (1773–1840); succ. as 3rd baron 1774. Chancellor of the duchy of Lancaster 1835–40.

**Holmes**, William 'Billy' (1779–1851). MP for Berwick-upon-Tweed, 1837–41.

**Hooper**, John Kinnersley (1791–1854). Lord mayor of London 1847.

**Hope**, Charles (1808–93). MP for Linlithgowshire 1838–45; whip and secretary to the treasury 1844–5.

**Hopetoun**, John (1803–43); succ. as 5th earl of 1825.

**Howard**, Edward Granville George (1809–80). MP for Morpeth 1833–7, 1840–53.

**Howard de Walden**, Charles Ellis (1799–1868); 6th baron; succ. as Baron Seaford 1845.

**Howick**, Henry George Grey (1802–94); styled viscount; succ. as 3rd Earl Grey 1845. MP for North Northumberland 1832–41, Sunderland 1841–5. Secretary at war 1835–9; secretary of state for war and the colonies 1846–52.

**Howley**, William (1766–1848). Archbishop of Canterbury 1828–48.

**Hudson**, George (1800–71). Lord mayor of York 1837–9, 1846–7. MP for Sunderland 1845–59.

**Hughes**, John (1819–1905). Farmer and ploughman, transported to Van Diemen's land for his part in the Rebecca riots.

**Hume**, Joseph (1777–1855). MP for Kilkenny 1837–41, Montrose Burghs 1842–55.

**Humphry**, John (*d.* 1863). MP for Southwark 1832–52. Lord mayor of London 1842–3.

**Ibbetson**, Charles Parke (1820–98). Colonel in the 11th (Prince Albert's Own) Hussars; eloped to Gretna Green with Lady Adela Child Villiers (1828–60). The couple were legitimately married at Old Church, St Pancras, London, on 17 Nov. 1845.

**Ingestre**, *see* Talbot

**Inglis**, Sir Robert (1786–1855); 2nd bt. MP for the University of Oxford 1829–54.

**Inverness**, Cecilia Buggins (*née* Gore) (c. 1785–1873); cr. duchess of 1840. Widow of Sir George Buggins and of Augustus Frederick, duke of Sussex.

**Ireland**, Thomas James (1792–1863). MP for Bewdley 1847–8.

**Isabella II**, queen of Spain 1833–68.

**Isturiz**, Xavier (1790–1871). Prime minister of Spain 1846–7.

**Jackson**, Sir Richard Downes (1777–1845). Commander-in-chief, north America 1839–45.

**James**, George Payne Rainsford (1799–1860). Novelist.

**Jermyn**, Frederick William Hervey (1800–64); styled earl; heir to the 1st marquess of Bristol. Treasurer of the royal household 1841–6.

**Jermyn**, Lady Katherine Isabella (*née* Manners) (1809–48); m. Frederick William Hervey 1830–48.

**Jersey**, George Child-Villiers (1773–1859); succ. as 5th earl of 1805. Master of the horse 1841–6.

**Jocelyn**, Robert (1816–54); viscount, heir apparent to the 3rd earl of Roden. MP for King's Lynn 1842–54. Joint secretary to the board of control 1845–6.

**John** (1801–73), prince of Saxony; heir to his brother Frederick Augustus II, king of Saxony.

**Joinville**, Francois Ferdinand Philippe Louis Marie d'Orléans (1818–1900); prince of.

**Jones**, Edward (1824–93). Frequent intruder at Buckingham Palace. Removed to Brazil and later Australia.

**Jones**, Ernest (1819–69). Poet, novelist, and Chartist.

**Junot**, Jean-Andoche, general (1771–1813). Had a relationship with the 3rd marchioness of Hertford in Paris.

**Keane**, John (1781–1844); cr. baron 1839. Commander-in-chief of the Bombay army 1834–40.

**Keating**, James (1783–1849). Bishop of Ferns 1819–49.

**Kelly**, Fitzroy Edward (1796–1880). MP for Ipswich 1838–41, Cambridge 1843–7. Solicitor-general 1846.

**Kent**, Victoria Mary Louisa Antony (1786–1861); widow of Prince Emich Charles of Leiningen-Dachsburg-Hardenburg; m. Edward Augustus, duke of Kent 1818–20.

**Kenyon**, George (1776–1855); succ. as 2nd baron 1802.

**Kinnaird**, George William Fox (1807–78); succ. as 9th baron [S] 1826 and cr. baron Rossie [U.K.] 1831. Master of the buckhounds 1839–41.

**Khan**, Akbar (1816–45). Emir of Afghanistan 1842–5.

**Khan**, Dost Mohammad (1793–1863). Emir of Afghanistan 1823–39, 1843–63.

**Knatchbull**, Sir Edward (1781–1849); succ. as 9th bt, 1819. MP for East Kent 1832–45. Paymaster general 1841–5.

**Knight**, Henry Gally (1786–1846). MP for North Nottinghamshire 1835–46.

**Konstantin** Nikolayevich, grand duke of Russia (1827–92); son of Nicholas I.

**Labouchere**, Henry (1798–1869). MP for Taunton 1830–59. President of the board of trade 1838–41; chief secretary for Ireland 1847–52.

**Lafontaine**, Louis-Hippolyte (1807–64). First premier of the United Province of Canada 1848–51.

**Lal**, Mohan (1812–77). Commercial agent for the British and political assistant in Kabul during the first Anglo-Afghan war, 1838–42. Helped to secure the release of British prisoners held hostage in Afghanistan.

**Lambruschini**, Luigi (1776–1854). Cardinal; secretary of state to the Pope.

**Lane-Fox**, George (1793–1848). MP for Beverley 1837–40.

**Lane-Fox**, Sackville (1797–1874). MP for Beverley 1840–1, Ipswich 1842–7, Beverley 1847–52.

**Lansdowne**, Henry Petty-Fitzmaurice (1780–1863); succ. as 3rd marquess of 1809. Lord president of the council 1835–41, 1846–52; leader of the house of lords 1846–52.

**Law**, Charles Ewan (1792–1850). MP for the University of Cambridge 1835–50.

**Lawrence**, George Hall (1802–69). Mayor of Liverpool 1846–7.

**Leader**, John Temple (1810–1903). MP for Westminster 1837–47.

**Ledru-Rollin**, Alexandre Auguste (1807–74). Political champion of the working classes; a key figure in the French Revolution of 1848.

**Lee**, Henry (*fl.* 1840). Builder and contractor of Chiswell Street, Finsbury, London.

**Lee**, James Prince (1804–69). Bishop of Manchester 1848–69.

**Lee**, John (*fl.* 1840). Builder and contractor of Chiswell Street, Finsbury, London.

**Lefevre**, Charles Shaw (1794–1888). MP for North Hampshire 1832–57; speaker of the house of commons 1839–57.

**Leicester**, claimant as earl of, *see* Townshend.

**Leicester**, Thomas Coke (1822–1909); styled viscount until succ. as 2nd earl of 1842.

**Leith**, James (*fl.* 1833–49); accountant, of London.

**Leopold**, count of Syracuse (1813–60).

**Leopold**, prince of Saxe-Coburg (1790–1865). King of the Belgians 1831–65.

**L'Estrange**, Reverend (*fl.* 1845). Possible familial relationship with Henry L'Estrange of Moystown, King's County, Ireland.

**Lewis,** Thomas Frankland (1780–1855). Created bt, 1846. MP for New Radnor Boroughs, 1847–55.

**Liddell**, Henry (1797–1878). MP for North Durham 1837–47.

**Limerick**, Edmund Henry Pery (1758–1844); cr. 1st earl of [I] 1803 and 1st Baron Foxford [U.K.] 1815. Irish representative peer for Ireland 1800–44.

**Lincoln**, Henry Pelham (1811–64); styled earl of; heir of the 4th duke of Newcastle. MP for South Nottinghamshire 1832–46, Falkirk Burghs 1846–51. First commissioner of woods and forests 1841–6; chief secretary for Ireland 1846.

**Lincoln**, Susan Douglas-Hamilton (1814–89). m. Henry Pelham, earl of 1832, div. 1850.

**Listowel**, William Hare (1801–65); succ. as 2nd earl of [I] 1837. MP for St Albans 1841–6.

**Litchfield**, Thomas Anson (1795–1854); succ. as Viscount Anson 1818, cr. earl of 1831. Postmaster-general 1835–41.

**Littler**, General John Hunter (1783–1856). Officer in East India Company's Bengal army.

**Liverpool**, Charles Cecil Cope Jenkinson (1784–1851); succ. as 3rd earl of 1828. Lord steward of the royal household 1841–6.

**Lockhart**, William (1820–92). First of the Tractarian movement to convert to Roman Catholicism.

**Locock**, Dr Charles (1799–1875). Obstetrician to Queen Victoria.

**Londonderry**, Charles William Vane (formerly Stewart) (1778–1854); succ. as 3rd marquess of [I] 1822 and cr. 1st Earl Vane [U.K.] 1823.

**Londonderry**, Frances Anne Emily Vane-Tempest (1800–65); m. Charles William Stewart, afterwards 3rd marquess of 1819–54.

**Lonsdale**, William Lowther (1757–1844); cr. 1st earl of 1807.

**Louis-Philippe** (1773–1850). King of the French 1830–48.

**Louise** (1848–1939); 4th daughter of Queen Victoria.

**Lowther**, Elizabeth Fane (*d.* 1844); m. Sir John 1790–1844.

**Lowther**, Sir John (1759–1844); 1st bt.

**Ludlow**, George (1758–1842); succ. as earl [I] 1811, cr. baron [U.K.] 1831.

**Lyndhurst**, John Singleton Copley (1772–1863); cr. 1st baron 1827. Lord chancellor 1841–6.

**Lynedoch**, Thomas Graham (1748–1843); cr. baron 1814.

**Lyttelton**, George William (1817–76); succ. as 4th baron 1837. Under-secretary of state for war and the colonies 1846.

**Macaulay**, Thomas Babington (1800–59). MP for Edinburgh 1839–47. Secretary at war 1839–41; paymaster-general 1846–8.

**MacKenzie**, Captain Colin (1806–81). Army officer in East India Company.

**Macnaghten**, Sir William (1793–1841). British envoy in India.

**Maitland**, Thomas (1803–78). Admiral.

**Malcolm**, George Alexander (1810–88). Colonial secretary of Hong Kong 1843.

**Malmesbury**, James Edward Harris (*d.* 1841); succ. as 2nd earl of 1820.

**Malmesbury**, James Harris (1807–89); styled Viscount Fitzharris until succ. as 3rd earl of 1841. MP for Wilton 1841.

**Maltby**, Edward (1770–1859). Bishop of Durham 1836–56.

**Manners**, Charles Henry Somerset (1780–1855). Second son of the 4th duke of Rutland. MP for North Leicestershire 1835–52.

**Manners**, Lord John (1818–1906). MP for Newark 1841–7, Colchester 1850–7.

**Manners–Sutton**, John Henry (1822–98). MP for Newark 1847–57.

**Mansfield**, David William Murray (1777–1840); succ. as 3rd earl of 1796.

**Mansfield**, William David Murray (1806–98); styled Viscount Stormont until succ. as 4th earl of 1840. MP for Perthshire 1837–40.

**Manvers**, Charles Herbert Pierrepont (1778–1860); succ. as 2nd earl 1816.

**Maria II** (1819–53). Queen of Portugal 1834–53.

**Maria Amalia** of Naples and Sicily (1782–1866). Queen-consort of Louis Philippe, king of the French.

**Marlborough**, George Spencer-Churchill (1766–1840); succ. as 5th duke of 1817.

**Marshall**, Sir Chapman (1786–1862). Lord mayor of London 1839.

**Mary I** (1516–58); succ. as queen of England 1553.

**McCaskill**, Major-general Sir John (*d.* 1845).

**McLane**, Louis (1786–1857). American minister to the United Kingdom, 1845–6.

**McLeod**, Alexander (1796–1871). Canadian tried for murder in U.S.A. 1841.

**McNaughton**, Daniel (1813–65). Glasgow woodturner who shot Edward Drummond on 20 Jan. 1843. He was acquitted on the ground of insanity; the basis of this judgment became the 'McNaghten rules'.

**Meagher**, Thomas Francis (1823–67). Irish nationalist.

**Mecklenburg-Strelitz,** George, grand duke of (1779–1860).

**Melbourne**, William Lamb (1779–1848); succ. as 2nd viscount [I] and 2nd baron [U.K.] 1828. Prime minister 1835–41.

**Melville**, Robert Saunders Dundas (1771–1851); succ. as 2nd viscount 1811. Succ. his father as lord privy seal of Scotland 1811–51; chancellor of the University of St Andrews 1814–51.

**Merewether**, John (1797–1850). Dean of Hereford 1832–50.

**Metcalfe**, Charles Theophilus (1785–1846); bt. cr. 1st baron 1845. Governor of Jamaica 1839–42; governor-general of Canada 1843–5.

**Metternich**, prince Klemens von (1773–1859), Austrian diplomat.

**Mexborough**, John Savile (1783–1860); succ. as 3rd earl of [I] 1830.

**M'Ghee**, Robert James (1789–1872). Church of Ireland clergyman and anti-Catholic polemicist. Appointed minister of the proprietary chapel of Harold's Cross, Dublin, in 1838.

**Michele**, Charles Eastland de (1810–98). Editor of *The Morning Post*.

**Miles**, Philip William Skinner (1816–81). MP for Bristol 1837–52.

**Miles**, William (1797–1878). MP for East Somerset 1834–65.

**Milton**, William Wentworth-Fitzwilliam (1815–1902); styled viscount; heir to the 5th Earl Fitzwilliam. MP for Malton 1837–41, 1846–7, Wicklow 1847–57.

**Minto**, Gilbert Elliot Murray Kynynmound (1782–1859); succ. as 2nd earl of 1814. First lord of the admiralty 1835–41; lord privy seal 1846–52.

**Mitchell**, John (1815–75). Irish nationalist.

**Molé**, Louis-Mathieu (1781–1855); 1st count. French statesman and friend of Louis Philippe.

**Molesworth**, John Edward Nassau (1790–1877). Vicar of Rochdale 1840–77.

**Molyneux**, Francis George (1805–84).

**Montagu**, Henry Scott (1776–1845); succ. as 2nd Baron Montagu of Boughton 1790.

**Monteagle**, Thomas Spring-Rice (1790–1866); cr. 1st Lord Monteagle of Brandon 1839. MP for Cambridge 1832–9. Chancellor of the exchequer 1835–9.

**Montemolin**, Carlos Luis de Borbón (1818–61); count of.

**Montrose**, James Graham (1799–1874); succ. as 4th duke of [S] 1836.

**Morgan**, Sir Charles (1760–1846); 2nd bt.

**Morgan**, Octavius (1803–88). MP for Monmouthshire 1841–74.

**Morgan**, William (*fl.* 1841). Implicated in the exchequer bill fraud relating to fraudulent treasury bills.

**Mornington**, William Wellesley-Pole (1763–1845); succ. as 3rd earl of [I] 1842.

**Morpeth**, George William Frederick Howard (1802–64); styled viscount; succ. as 7th earl of Carlisle 1848. MP for the West Riding of Yorkshire 1832–41, 1846–8. Chief secretary to the lord lieutenant of Ireland 1835–41; first commissioner of woods and forests 1846–50; chancellor of the duchy of Lancaster 1850–2.

**Morris**, Henry Gage, naval officer (b. 1811). First-lieutenant on HMS Harlequin during operations on the coast of China in 1842.

**Morrison**, General Edward (*d.* 1843). Colonel of 13th regiment of foot (1st Somerset-shire) 1813–43.

**Mourilyan**, John (*fl.* 1847). Attorney of Sandwich, Kent.

**Mousley**, William Eaton. Solicitor to the 4th duke of Newcastle.

**Muñagorri**, José Antonio (1794–1841). Spanish politician.

**Mundy**, Edward Miller (1800–49). MP for South Derbyshire 1841–9.

**Mundy**, Frederick Clinton (*d.* 1847). Assistant clerk, colonial office, 1840–7.

**Mundy**, George Rodney (1805–84). Educated at the Royal Naval College, Portsmouth; pursued a successful naval career, culminating in becoming admiral of the fleet in 1877.

**Mundy**, General Godfrey Basil (1776–1848). Brother-in-law of the duke of Newcastle.

**Mundy**, Major-general Godfrey Charles (1804–60); eldest son of Godfrey Basil. Soldier and author.

**Mundy**, Rosamund (*d.* 1883). Married Charles Morgan Robinson Morgan, 6 Oct. 1827.

**Mundy**, Sarah Brydges (c. 1780–1871). Daughter of Admiral George Brydges Rodney. Married General Godfrey Basil Meynell Mundy, 26 Nov. 1801.

**Mundy**, William (1801–77). MP for South Derbyshire 1849–57.

**Munster**, George Augustus Frederick Fitzclarence (1794–1842); cr. 1st earl of 1831; eldest child of William, duke of Clarence (afterwards King William IV) by the actress Mrs Jordan (1761–1816).

**Murray**, Alexander (1789–1845). MP for Kirkcudbright Stewartry 1838–45.

**Murray**, Sir George (1772–1846); cr. K.C.B. 1813. Master-general of the ordnance 1841–6.

**Musgrave**, Thomas (1788–1860). Bishop of Hereford 1837–47; archbishop of York 1847–60.

**Napier**, Sir Charles James (1782–1853). Commander of Northern District 1839–40; governor of Sindh 1843–7; commander-in-chief of India 1849–51.

**Nelson**, Horatio (1823–1913), 3rd earl. Protectionist Tory, served as a whip in the house of lords before 1852.

**Nemours**, Louis Charles Philippe Raphael d'Orleans (1814–96); duc de; second son of Louis-Philippe, king of the French.

**Newdegate**, Charles (1816–87). MP for North Warwickshire 1843–85.

**Newman**, John Henry (1801–90). Theologian; renounced the Anglican church to join the Catholic church 1845.

**Newport**, Sir Simon John (1756–1843); cr. 1st bt, 1789. Comptroller-general of the exchequer 1834–9.

**Nicholas I** (1796–1855); emperor of Russia.

**Norbury**, Hector John Graham-Toler (1781–1839); succ. as 2nd earl of [I] 1831.

**Norfolk**, Bernard Edward Howard (1765–1842); succ. as 12th duke of 1815. Earl marshal 1824–42.

**Normanby**, Constantine Henry Phipps (1797–1863); styled viscount until succ. as 2nd earl of Mulgrave 1831 and cr. 1st marquess of Normanby 1838. Lord lieutenant of Ireland 1835–9; secretary of state for war and the colonies 1839; home secretary 1839–41.

**Normanby**, Maria Liddell (1798–1882); m. Constantine Henry Phipps, afterwards 1st marquess of 1818–63.

**Norreys**, Montagu Bertie (1808–84); styled lord; heir to the 5th earl of Abingdon. MP for Oxfordshire 1832–52.

**Northumberland**, Algernon Percy (1792–1865); cr. Baron Prudhoe 1816, succ. as 4th duke of 1847.

**Northumberland**, Lady Charlotte Florentia Clive (*d.* 1866); m. Hugh Percy, Baron Percy and afterwards 3rd duke of Northumberland 1817–47.

**Northumberland**, Hugh Percy (1785–1847); succ. as 3rd duke of 1817. Lord of the bedchamber 1821–47; chancellor of the University of Cambridge 1840–7.

**Nott**, General Sir William (1782–1845). Military leader in India.

**Nugent**, Admiral Sir Charles Edmund (1759–1844). Naval officer.

**Nugent**, General Sir George (1757–1849). Held the distinction of being the oldest general officer in the army at the same time as his brother, Admiral of the Fleet Sir Charles Edmund Nugent, held the equivalent distinction in the navy.

**O'Brien**, Augustus Stafford (1811–57). MP for North Northamptonshire 1841–57.

**O'Brien**, Elizabeth Rebecca (née Trotter), marchioness of Thomond (1775–1852). Her husband was William O'Brien, 2nd marquess of Thomond [I], 6th earl of Inchiquin [I] and Baron Tadcaster [G.B.] (1765–1846).

**O'Brien**, Timothy (1787–1862); 1st bt. Lord mayor of Dublin, 1844, 1849. MP for Cashel 1846–59.

**O'Brien**, William Smith (1803–64). MP for County Limerick 1835–49.

**O'Connell**, Daniel (1775–1847). MP for Dublin City 1837–41; Cork County 1841–7. Lord mayor of Dublin 1841–2.

**O'Connell**, John (1810–58). Irish MP and political campaigner. MP for Athlone 1837–41, Kilkenny 1841–7, and Limerick, 1847–51. Held in Richmond prison during the State Trials of 1843–4.

**O'Connor**, Feargus (1796–1855). Irish Chartist leader.

**O'Ferral**, Richard More (1797–1880). MP for Kildare 1830–47. First secretary of the admiralty 1839–41; governor of Malta 1847–51.

**O'Higgins**, William (1829–53). Bishop of Ardagh 1829–53.

**O'Neil**, Henry Nelson (1817–80). Artist.

**Orange**, William, prince of (1840–79); heir apparent to the Dutch throne.

**Oranmore**, Dominick (1787–1860); cr. 1st Baron Oranmore and Browne [I] 1836.

**Orléans**, Ferdinand Louis Philippe (1810–42); succ. as duc of 1830. Son of Louis-Philippe, king of the French.

**Otho** or **Otto** (1815–67); king of Greece 1832–62.

**Owen**, Robert (1771–1858). Welsh philanthropist and social reformer.

**Palmerston**, Henry John Temple (1784–1865); succ. as 3rd viscount [I] 1802. MP for Tiverton 1835–65. Foreign secretary 1835–41, 1846–51.

**Parker**, Admiral Sir William (1781–1866).

**Parkinson**, John (*fl.* 1821–49). Of Leyfields, Newark, Nottinghamshire. Agent to the 4th duke of Newcastle.

**Parma**, Carlo III di Borbone, Duca di Parma e Piacenza (1823–54). Duke of Parma from 1849. Married Louise Marie Thérèse d'Artois, 10 Nov. 1845. His brother-in-law was Prince Henri, count of Chambord and duke of Bordeaux (1820–83).

**Pasha**, Ibrahim (1789–1848). Wāli of Egypt and Sudan 1848.

**Pasha**, Muhammad Ali (1769–1849). Wāli of Egypt and Sudan 1805–48.

**Pattison**, James (1786–1849). MP for London 1835–41, 1843–9.

**Pease**, Joseph (1799–1872). MP for South Durham 1832–41; the first quaker MP.

**Peel**, Eliza (1832–83). Youngest of the seven children of Sir Robert Peel.

**Peel**, Julia (1821–93). Eldest daughter of Sir Robert Peel, 2nd bt.

**Peel**, Julia (née Floyd) (1795–1859); m. Sir Robert Peel, afterwards 2nd bt, 1820–50.

**Peel**, Robert (1822–95), eldest son of Sir Robert. MP for Tamworth 1850–80.

**Peel**, Sir Robert (1788–1850); succ. as 2nd bt, 1830. MP for Tamworth 1830–50. Prime minister 1841–6.

**Peel**, William (1824–58), 3rd son of Sir Robert.

**Pelham-Clinton**, Lord Charles (1813–94). Son of the 4th duke of Newcastle.

**Pelham-Clinton**, Lord Edward (1816–42). Son of the 4th duke of Newcastle.

**Pelham-Clinton**, Lord Robert Renebald (1820–67). Youngest surviving child of the 4th duke of Newcastle.

**Pelham-Clinton**, Lord Thomas (1813–82). Son of the 4th duke of Newcastle.

**Pelham-Clinton**, Lord William (1815–50). Son of the 4th duke of Newcastle.

**Pennefather**, Edward (1774–1847). Solicitor-general for Ireland 1841; lord chief justice of Ireland 1841–6.

**Pepys, Henry** (1783–1860). Bishop of Sodor and Man 1840–1; bishop of Worcester 1841–60.

**Peto**, Samuel Morton (1809–89). Civil engineer. MP for Norwich 1847–54.

**Phillpotts**, Dr Henry (1778–1869). Bishop of Exeter 1830–69.

**Pirie**, Sir John (1781–1851); 1st bt. Lord mayor of London 1841–2.

**Pitt**, William 'the younger' (1759–1806). Prime minister 1783–1801, 1804–6.

**Plymouth**, Henry Windsor (1768–1843); succ. as 8th earl of 1837.

**Plymouth**, Mary (*née* Sackville) (1792–1864); widow of Other Windsor, 6th earl of (1789–1833); m. Earl Amherst 1839–57.

**Polk**, James Knox (1795–1849). President of U.S.A. 1845–9.

**Pollington**, John Charles Savile (1810–99); styled viscount, heir to the 3rd earl of Mexborough. MP for Pontefract 1841–7.

**Pollock**, Sir Frederick (1783–1870). MP for Huntingdon 1831–44. Attorney-general 1841–4; lord chief baron of the exchequer 1844–66.

**Pollock**, General George (1786–1872). British Indian army officer.

**Ponsonby**, John (1770–1855); succ. as 2nd baron 1806; cr. 1st viscount 1839. Ambassador at Constantinople 1832–41; to the Austrian Empire 1846–50.

**Portarlington**, John Dawson (1781–1845); succ. as 2nd earl of 1798.

**Portland**, William Henry Cavendish Scott-Bentinck (1768–1854); succ. as 4th duke of 1809.

**Portman**, Emma (*née* Lascelles) (1809–65); baroness. Lady of the bedchamber to Queen Victoria 1837–51.

**Pottinger**, Sir Henry (1789–1856). Governor of Hong Kong 1843–4, of the Cape Colony 1847, of Madras 1848–54.

**Powell**, William Edward (1788–1854). MP for Cardiganshire 1816–54.

**Powis**, Edward Herbert (1785–1848); styled Viscount Clive until succ. as 2nd earl of 1839. MP for Ludlow 1806–39.

**Powis**, Robert Charles Herbert (1827–1902), son of the 2nd earl of. Accidentally shot (and killed) his father during a pheasant hunt at Powis Castle.

**Prince**, John (1796–1870). Colonel in the Canadian militia; fought border incursions by those seeking a republican government in Upper Canada.

**Pryse**, Loveden Pryse (1774–1849). MP for Cardigan Boroughs 1818–49.

**Purvis**, Thomas (*fl.* 1843). Unsuccessful Conservative candidate for Durham in 1843.

**Pusey**, Dr Edward Bouverie (1800–82). Regius professor of Hebrew at the University of Oxford 1828–82.

**Radnor**, William Pleydell-Bouverie (1779–1869); succ. as 3rd earl of 1828.

**Ravensworth**, Maria Susannah (*née* Simpson) (*d.* 1845). m. Thomas Henry Liddell afterwards 1st baron, 1796–45.

**Ravensworth**, Thomas Henry Liddell (1775–1855); cr. 1st baron 1821.

**Reventlow**, Ludvig Christian Detlev Frederik, Graf zu Reventlow (1824–93). Danish nobleman and diplomat.

**Reynolds**, George W.M. (1814–79). British writer and journalist from Sandwich, Kent. He founded *Reynolds' Miscellany* and *The London Journal* in 1846 and *Reynolds' Weekly Newspaper* in May 1850.

**Reynolds**, John William (1817–75). Captain in the 11th royal lancers.

**Reynolds**, Sir Joshua (1723–92). Artist.

**Richmond**, Charles Lennox (afterwards Gordon-Lennox) (1791–1860); succ. as 5th duke of 1819.

**Ripon**, Frederick John Robinson (1782–1859); cr. 1st Viscount Goderich 1827 and 1st earl of 1833. President of the board of trade 1841–3; of the board of control 1843–6.

**Robins**, George Henry (1777–1847). Auctioneer.

**Roden**, Robert Jocelyn (1788–1870); succ. as 3rd earl of [I] 1820 and cr. 1st baron Clanbrassill [U.K.] 1821.

**Roebuck**, John Arthur (1801–79). MP for Bath 1841–7, Sheffield 1849–68.

**Rolfe**, Robert (1790–1868); cr. 1st Baron Cranworth 1850. MP Penryn and Falmouth 1832–40. Solicitor-general 1835–9; vice-chancellor 1850.

**Rolle**, John (1756–1842); cr. baron 1796.

**Ronge**, Johannes (1813–87). Principal founder of the New Catholic movement.

**Ross**, David Robert (1797–1851). MP for Belfast 1842–7.

**Rothschild**, Hannah (1815–64). Daughter of Nathan Mayer Rothschild. In 1839, she married Henry FitzRoy (1807–59).

**Rothschild**, Lionel Nathan de (1808–79); succ. as Baron de Rothschild of the Austrian Empire 1836. MP for London 1847–68.

**Rous**, Henry John (1795–1877). Younger brother of John Rous, 2nd earl of Stradbroke (1794–1886). MP for Westminster 1841–6.

**Roxburghe**, James Innes-Ker (1816–79); succ. as 6th duke of [S] 1823, cr. Earl Innes [U.K.] 1837.

**Russell**, Lord George (1790–1846). 2nd son of the 6th duke of Bedford and brother of Lord John. British minister to Prussia 1835–41.

**Russell**, Lord John (1792–1878). MP for Stroud 1835–41, London 1841–61. Home secretary 1835–9; secretary of state for war and the colonies 1839–41; leader of the house of commons 1835–41; prime minister 1846–52.

**Russell**, Lord William (1767–1840), brother of the 5th and 6th dukes of Bedford.

**Rutland**, John Henry Manners (1778–1857); succ. as 5th duke of 1787.

**Sale**, Florentia (*née* Wynch) (1796–1853). m. Sir Robert Sale 1809–45.

**Sale**, Major-general Sir Robert Henry (1782–1845). British army officer.

**Salisbury**, James Brownlow William Gascoyne-Cecil (1791–1868); succ. as 2nd marquess of 1823.

**Saltoun**, Alexander George Fraser (1785–1853); succ. as 17th baron [S] 1793.

**Sandon**, Dudley Ryder (1798–1882); styled viscount until succ. as 2nd earl of Harrowby 1847. MP for Liverpool 1831–47.

**Scarbrough**, Frederica Mary Adeliza Drummond, countess of (*d.* 1907). In Oct. 1846, she married lieutenant-colonel Richard George Lumley, 9th earl of Scarbrough (1813–84).

**Seaford**, Charles Rose Ellis (1771–1845); cr. 1st baron 1826.

**Seaford**, *also see* Howard de Walden.

**Seager**, Charles (1808–78). Orientalist, converted to Catholicism.

**Sebastiani de la Porta**, Horace (1772–1851). French diplomat.

**Sheil**, Richard Lalor (1791–1851). MP for County Tipperary 1832–41, for Dungarvan 1841–51. Vice president of the board of trade 1839–41; master of the mint 1846–50.

**Shore,** Reverend James (1805–74). Curate at Berry Pomeroy, Devon. In 1843, he fought for the right of a clergyman to secede from the established church; subsequently founded the Free Church of England.

**Shrewsbury**, John Talbot (1791–1852); succ. as 16th earl of, and earl of Waterford [I] 1827.

**Sibthorp**, Colonel Charles de Laet Waldo (1783–1855). MP for Lincoln 1835–55.

**Sibthorp**, Richard Waldo (1792–1879). Fellow of Magdalen college, converted to Catholicism.

**Sidmouth**, Henry Addington (1757–1844); cr. 1st viscount 1805.

**Smith**, Edward Beaumont (1797–1877). Chief clerk in the controller of the exchequer's office.

**Smith**, Sir Henry George Wakelyn Smith (1787–1860), 1st bt; commanded forces at Battle of Aliwal.

**Smith**, Robert Vernon (1800–73). MP for Northampton 1839–41.

**Smith**, Thomas Cusack (1795–1866). MP for Ripon 1843–6. Solicitor-general for Ireland 1842; attorney-general for Ireland 1842–6; master of the rolls in Ireland 1846–66.

**Smythe**, George (1818–57); heir to the 6th Viscount Strangford. MP for Canterbury 1841–52. Under-secretary of state for foreign affairs 1846.

**Somerset**, Edward Arthur (1817–86). MP for Monmouthshire 1848–59.

**Somerset**, Edward St Maur (1775–1855); succ. as 11th duke of 1793.

**Somerton**, James Agar (1818–96); styled viscount, heir to the 2nd earl of Normanton. MP Wilton 1841–52.

**Sondes**, George John Milles (previously Watson) (1794–1874); succ. as 4th baron 1836.

**Sophia** (1777–1848); 5th daughter of King George III and Queen Charlotte.

**Sotomayor,** Don Carlos Martínez de Irujo y McKean, duc de (1802–55). Spanish noble and politician; in 1844 he married Gabriela del Alcázar, 7th duchess of Sotomayor (1826–89) and gained the courtesy title of duke. He was Spain's minister of state, 1847–8.

**Southampton**, Charles Fitzroy (1804–72); succ. as 3rd baron 1810.

**Southey**, Robert (1774–1843). Poet laureate 1813–43.

**Soyer**, Alexis (1810–58). Celebrated French chef.

**Spencer**, Frederick (1798–1857); succ. as 4th earl 1845; K.G. 1849. MP for Midhurst 1837–41. Lord chamberlain of the royal household 1846–8.

**Spencer**, George (1799–1864). Roman Catholic priest; brother to Earl Spencer.

**Spencer,** John Charles (1782–1845); styled Viscount Althorp until succ. as 3rd earl 1834.

**Spring-Rice**, *see* Monteagle.

**St Germans**, William Elliot (1767–1845); succ. as 2nd earl of 1823.

**St Germans**, *also see* Elliot.

**St John**, Ambrose (1815–75). Classical scholar who converted to Catholicism.

**Stanhope**, Philip Henry (1781–1855); succ. as 4th earl 1816.

**Stanley**, Edward (1779–1849). Bishop of Norwich 1837–49.

**Stanley**, Edward George Geoffrey Smith (1799–1869); cr. baron 1832; heir to the 13th earl of Derby. MP for North Lancashire 1832–44. Secretary of state for war and the colonies 1841–5.

**Stanley**, Edward Henry (1826–93); heir to the 14th earl of Derby. MP for King's Lynn 1848–69.

**Stanley**, William Owen (1802–84), younger twin brother of Edward Stanley, 2nd Baron Stanley of Alderley. MP for Anglesey 1837–47, Chester 1850–7.

**Steele**, Thomas (1788–1848). Irish political activist; known as 'Honest Tom Steele'.

**Stephens**, Lady Frances Augusta Pierrepont (1781–1847). She married Henry William Stephens on 30 July 1821.

**Stewart** *or* **Stuart**, Charles (1779–1845); cr. 1st Baron Stuart de Rothesay 1828. Ambassador to Russia 1841–4.

**Stockdale**, John Joseph (1770–1847). Printer and publisher.

**Stopford**, Edward Adderly (*d.* 1850). Bishop of Meath 1842–50.

**Stopford**, Sir Robert (1768–1847). Commander-in-chief of the Mediterranean fleet 1837–41; governor of Greenwich Hospital 1841–7; rear-admiral of United Kingdom, 1834–47; vice-admiral 1847.

**Stopford**, William Bruce (1806–72). On 20 June 1837, he married Caroline Harriet Sackville (1815–1908), daughter of Hon. George Sackville (1770–1836).

**Stowell**, Hugh (1799–1865). Clergyman and preacher.

**Strachan**, Lady Louisa (*née* Dillon) (*d.* 1868). m. Sir Richard Strachan 1812.

**Stradbrooke**, John Edward Cornwallis Rous (1794–1886); succ. as 2nd earl of 1827.

**Strangford**, Percy Clinton Sydney Smythe (1780–1855); succ. as 6th viscount [I] 1801 and cr. 1st Baron Penshurst [U.K.] 1825.

**Stuart**, Lord Dudley Coutts (1803–54). MP for Marylebone 1847–54.

**Stuart**, John (1793–1876). MP for Newark 1846–52.

**Sturge**, Joseph (1793–1859). Chartist.

**Suffolk**, Thomas Howard (1776–1851); succ. as 16th earl of 1820.

**Sugden**, Sir Edward Burtenshaw (1781–1875). MP for Ripon 1837–41. Lord high chancellor of Ireland 1837–41.

**Sumner**, Charles Richard (1790–1874). Bishop of Winchester 1827–69.

**Sumner**, John Bird (1780–1862). Bishop of Chester 1828–48; archbishop of Canterbury 1848–62.

**Surrey**, Henry Granville Fitzalan-Howard (1815–60); earl of; heir to the 13th duke of Norfolk. MP for Arundel 1837–51.

**Sussex**, Augustus Frederick (1773–1843); cr. duke of 1801; 6th son of King George III and Queen Charlotte.

**Sutherland**, Elizabeth Leveson-Gower (*d.* 1839); *suo jure* 19th countess of. m. George Leveson-Gower (1758–1833), 1st duke of 1785–1832.

**Sutherland**, George Granville Leveson-Gower (1786–1861); succ. as 2nd duke of 1833.

**Sutherland**, Harriet Elizabeth Georgiana Howard (1806–68); duchess of. m. George Granville Leveson-Gower, 2nd duke of 1823–61.

**Sydenham**, *see* Thomson.

**Sydney**, John Robert Townshend (1805–90); succ. as 3rd viscount 1831.

**Symons**, Dr Benjamin Parsons (1785–1878). Warden of Wadham College, Oxford 1831–71; vice chancellor of the University of Oxford 1844–8.

**Tagore**, Dwarkanath (1794–1846). Indian industrialist.

**Talbot**, Henry John Chetwynd-Talbot (1803–68); Viscount Ingestre; succ. as 3rd earl 1849. MP for South Staffordshire 1837–49.

**Tavistock**, Anna Maria Russell (1808–57); marchioness of. m. Francis Russell, marquess of Tavistock and 7th duke of Bedford 1808–57.

**Temple**, William (1788–1856). Brother of Viscount Palmerston.

**Thesiger**, Frederick (1794–1878); cr. 1st Baron Chelmsford 1834. MP for Woodstock 1840–4, Abingdon 1844–52. Solicitor-general 1844–5; attorney-general 1845–6.

**Thiers**, Adolphe (1797–1877). French statesman.

**Thirlwall**, Connop (1797–1875). Bishop of St David's 1840–74.

**Thomond**, *see* O'Brien.

**Thomson**, Charles Edward Poulett (1799–1841); cr. Baron Sydenham 1840. MP for Manchester 1832–9. President of the board of trade 1835–9; governor-general of Canada 1839–41.

**Thorn**, Nathaniel (*d.* 1857). Colonel commanding the Midland District during Chartism.

**Tindal**, Sir Nicholas Conyngham (1776–1846). Chief justice of the common pleas 1829–46.

**Townshend**, Charles Vere Ferrers (1785–1853). Brother of Marquess Townshend.

**Townshend**, George (1778–1855); succ. as 3rd marquess 1811.

**Townshend**, John (1811–1903). Claimant as earl of Leicester; elected Conservative MP for Bodmin in 1841. His claims were rejected at law in 1843, after which he changed his name to John Dunn Gardner.

**Tracy**, W.H. (*fl.* 1841). Resigned candidacy for Monmouthshire during by-election in Feb. 1841.

**Trant**, Thomas (*fl.* 1848). Sub inspector of police, Ireland. Defeated the 'Young Ireland' rebellion at the 'Battle of Ballingarry', 29 July 1848.

**Troubridge**, Sir Edward Thomas (c.1790–1852), 2nd bt. MP for Sandwich, 1831–47; Lord of the admiralty, 1835–41.

**Tuckett**, Captain Harvey Garnett Phipps (*fl.* 1841). Officer in the 11th Hussars; fought a duel with James Thomas Brudenell, 7th earl of Cardigan (1797–1868), on Wimbledon Common, London, 12 Sept. 1840.

**Tupper**, Martin (*d.* 1844). Apothecary and physician.

**Turner**, General Sir Tomkyns Hilgrove (1764–1843).

**Tyler**, John (1790–1862). Vice-president of U.S.A. 1841; president 1841–5.

**Van Buren**, Martin (1782–1862). President of the U.S.A. 1837–41.

**Vance**, John (1808–75). Unsuccessful candidate as MP for Canterbury 1847.

**Velde**, Willem van de, 'the younger' (1633–1707). Dutch marine painter.

**Vernon**, Edward Venables (1757–1847). Archbishop of York 1808–47.

**Vernon** (afterwards Harcourt Vernon), Granville Venables (1792–1879). MP for East Retford 1831–47.

**Vesey-Fitzgerald**, William (?1782–1843); succ. to his mother's title as 2nd baron [I] 1832 and cr. baron [U.K.] 1835.

Alexandrina **Victoria** (1819–1901); succ. as queen of Great Britain and Ireland 1837.

**Victoria** (1840–1901); princess royal, eldest child of Queen Victoria.

**Villiers**, Adela Corisande (1828–60); daughter of George, 5th earl of Jersey, eloped with Capt. Charles Ibbetson 1845.

**Villiers**, Charles Pelham (1802–98). MP for Wolverhampton 1835–98.

**Vincent**, Andrew Atkins (*fl.* 1796–1849); entered the royal navy 1796; captain 1832. In 1849, was gentleman usher to Queen Adelaide and captain of Sandown Castle, Kent.

**Vyvyan**, Sir Richard Rawlinson (1800–79); succ. as 8th bt, 1820. MP for Helston 1841–57.

**Walker**, Baldwin Wake (1802–76). Admiral.

**Walker**, George Townshend (1764–1842); 1st bt. Army officer.

**Walpole**, Horatio (1813–94); styled lord, heir to the 3rd earl of Orford.

**Walsh**, Sir John Benn (1798–1881), 2nd bt. MP for Sudbury 1838–40, Radnorshire 1840–68; lord lieutenant of Radnorshire 1842–75.

**Walter**, John (1776–1847). MP for Nottingham 1841–3. Second editor of *The Times*.

**Warburton**, Henry (1784–1858). MP for Bridport 1826–41, Kendal 1843–7.

**Ward**, Henry George (*d.* 1860). MP for Sheffield 1837–49.

**Ward**, William George (1812–82). Theologian expelled from the University of Oxford for converting to Roman Catholicism.

**Waterford**, Louisa Anne (née Stuart) (1818–91), marchioness of. In 1842, she married Henry de La Poer Beresford, 3rd marquis of Waterford (1811–59).

**Watson**, James; removed as magistrate and deputy-lieutenant of county Antrim, Ireland, 1845.

**Watson**, William Henry (1796–1860). MP for Kinsale 1841–7.

**Wellesley**, Richard Colley (1760–1842); cr. 1st baron [G.B.] 1797 and 1st marquess [I] 1799.

**Wellesley**, Victoria Alexandrina (1847–1933); granddaughter of the duke of Wellington and god-daughter of Queen Victoria.

**Wellington**, Arthur Wellesley (1769–1852); cr. viscount 1809, earl of 1812, marquess of 1812 and 1st duke of 1814.

**West**, John Beattie (1790–1841). MP for Dublin 1841.

**Westmeath**, George Nugent (1785–1871); succ. as earl of 1814, cr. marquess [I] 1822.

**Westminster**, Robert Grosvenor (1767–1845), succ. as 2nd Earl Grosvenor 1802 and cr. 1st marquess of 1831.

**Westmorland**, John Fane (1759–1841); succ. as 10th earl of 1774.

**Westmorland**, John Fane (1784–1859); styled Lord Burghersh until succ. as 11th earl of 1841. Envoy extraordinary and minister plenipotentiary to Prussia 1841–51.

**Wetherell**, Sir Charles (1770–1846). Recorder of Bristol 1827–46.

**Wharncliffe**, James Archibald Stuart-Wortley-Mackenzie (1776–1845); cr. 1st baron 1826. Lord president of the council 1841–5.

**Wharncliffe**, John Stuart-Wortley-Mackenzie (1801–55); succ. as 2nd baron 1845. MP for the West Riding of Yorkshire 1841–5.

**Whichcote**, Sir Thomas (1813–92), 7th bt.

**White**, Sir Thomas Woollaston (1801–82), 2nd bt of Tuxford and Wallingwells (Notts).

**Whiteside**, James (1804–76), Irish politician and judge. Noted for his defence of Daniel O'Connell in 1843 and William Smith O'Brien in 1848.

**Wicklow**, William Howard (1788–1869); succ. as 4th earl of [I] 1818.

**Wilberforce**, Samuel (1805–73). Bishop of Oxford 1845–69.

**Wilde**, Thomas (1782–1855); cr. 1st Baron Truro 1850. MP for Worcester 1841–7. Solicitor-general 1839–41; attorney-general 1841, 1846; chief justice of the common pleas 1846–50; lord high chancellor 1850–2.

**Wildman**, Colonel Thomas (1787–1859).

**Wilkie**, David (1785–1841). Scottish painter.

**William**, prince of Prussia (1783–1851); son of Frederick William II.

**William I** (1772–1843); king of Holland 1815–40.

**William II** (1792–1849); king of Holland 1840–9.

**William III** (1817–90); king of Holland 1849–90.

**William IV** (1765–1837); cr. duke of Clarence 1789 and succ. as king of Great Britain and Ireland 1830; third son of King George III and Queen Charlotte.

**Williams**, William (1788–1865). MP for Coventry 1835–47, Lambeth 1850–65.

**Wilmot**, Maria Mundy (1805–65). m. Henry Sacheverel Wilmot.

**Wilson,** Cauas (*fl.* 1843). London attorney rumoured to be leader of the 'Rebecca' riots in Wales.

**Wilson,** John (1789–1851), of Dundyvan, North Lanarkshire, Scotland. Iron master operating the Dundyvan iron works; unsuccessful candidate for Falkirk Burghs in 1846.

**Wilton**, Thomas Egerton (formerly Grosvenor) (1799–1882); succ. as 2nd earl of 1814.

**Winchester**, John Paulet (1801–87); succ. as 14th marquess of 1843.

**Winchilsea**, Emily Georgiana Bagot (*d.* 1848). m. to the 10th earl of 1837–48.

**Winchilsea**, Fanny Margaretta Rice (*d.* 1909). m. to the 10th earl of 1849–58.

**Winchilsea**, George William Finch-Hatton (1791–1858); succ. as 10th earl of and 5th earl of Nottingham 1826.

**Wood**, Sir Charles (1800–85); succ. as 3rd bt 1846. MP for Halifax 1832–65. Secretary to the admiralty 1835–9; chancellor of the exchequer 1846–52.

**Wyndham**, Wadham (1773–1843). MP for Salisbury 1835–43.

**Wynford**, William Draper Best (1767–1845); cr. 1st baron 1829.

**Wynn**, Charles Watkin Williams (1775–1850). MP for Montgomeryshire 1799–1850.

**Wynter**, Philip (1793–1871). President of St John's College, Oxford, 1828–71; vice chancellor of the University of Oxford 1840–4.

**Yarborough**, Charles Anderson-Pelham Worsley (1809–62); styled Lord Worsley until succ. as 2nd earl of 1846. MP for North Lincolnshire 1832–47.

**Young**, John (1807–76); 2nd bt. MP for Cavan 1831–55. Junior lord of the treasury 1841–4; financial secretary to the treasury 1844–5; parliamentary secretary to the treasury 1845–6.

**Zetland**, Thomas Dundas (1795–1873); succ. as 2nd earl of 1839. MP for Richmond 1835–9.

**Zichy-Ferraris**, Charlotte Leopoldina de (née Strachan), countess (1815–51). Inherited Hertford villa in 1842.

# Index